Cyber Security, Forensics and National Security

The book serves two very important purposes. Firstly, the concept of vulnerabilities due to cyberattacks in all walks of lives are explained along with how to detect and reduce the risk through digital forensics. Secondly, the book describes how such threats at a larger scale can threaten national security. This book discusses for the first time various dimensions of national security, the risks involved due to cyber threats, and ultimately the detection and prevention of cyber threats through cyber forensics and cybersecurity architectures. This book empowers readers with a deep comprehension of the various cyber threats targeting nations, businesses, and individuals, allowing them to recognize and respond to these threats effectively. It provides a comprehensive guide to digital investigation techniques, including evidence collection, analysis, and presentation in a legal context, addressing a vital need for cybersecurity professionals and law enforcement. The book navigates the complex legal and policy considerations surrounding cybercrime and national security, ensuring readers are well-versed in compliance and ethical aspects.

The primary purpose of *Cybersecurity, Forensics and National Security* is to fill a critical gap in the realm of literature on cybersecurity, digital forensics, and their nexus with national security. The need for this resource arises from the escalating threats posed by cyberattacks, espionage, and other digital crimes, which demand a comprehensive understanding of how to investigate, respond to, and prevent such incidents.

Features:

1. This book consists of content dedicated to national security to assist law enforcement and investigation agencies.
2. The book will act as a compendium for undertaking the initiatives for research in securing digital data at the level of national security with the involvement of intelligence agencies.
3. The book focuses on real-world cases and national security from government agencies, law enforcement, and digital security firms, offering readers valuable insights into practical applications and lessons learned in digital forensics, as well as innovative methodologies aimed at enhancing the availability of digital forensics and national security tools and techniques.
4. The book explores cutting-edge technologies in the field of digital forensics and national security, leveraging computational intelligence for enhanced reliability engineering, sustainable practices, and more.

Cyber Security, Forensics and National Security

Edited by
Vinay Aseri, Sumit Kumar Choudhary,
and Adarsh Kumar

CRC Press
Taylor & Francis Group
Boca Raton London New York

CRC Press is an imprint of the
Taylor & Francis Group, an **informa** business

Designed cover image: Shutterstock Image ID 2434972683

First edition published 2026
by CRC Press
2385 NW Executive Center Drive, Suite 320, Boca Raton FL 33431

and by CRC Press
4 Park Square, Milton Park, Abingdon, Oxon, OX14 4RN

CRC Press is an imprint of Taylor & Francis Group, LLC

ISBN: 978-1-032-80237-4 (hbk)
ISBN: 978-1-032-80642-6 (pbk)
ISBN: 978-1-003-49786-8 (ebk)

DOI: 10.1201/9781003497868

Typeset in Times
by KnowledgeWorks Global Ltd.

Contents

About the Editors

Mr. Vinay Aseri is a postgraduate scholar at the School of Behavioral Sciences & Forensic Investigations, Rashtriya Raksha University, Gandhinagar, Gujarat, under the Ministry of Home Affairs, Government of India. He holds postgraduate degree in Forensic Science, Information Technology, and Security, along with a diploma in Forensic Science and Techniques (Photography), in addition to his Bachelor's degree in Forensic Science. His primary research interests include digital forensics, cyber forensics, and national security.

An accomplished researcher, he has published over 44 papers in Scopus-indexed journals and contributed more than 20 book chapters with national and international publishers. He has presented his research at over 20 national and international conferences. His innovations include a German Patent for Banana Peel Nano Bio-char and an Indian Copyright for Sugarcane Bagasse Nano Bio-char, both with applications in forensic science.

He has received several honors, including the InSig Fellowship 2022 from the Hyderabad Chapter and the Junior Researcher Award 2023 by Legal Desire at the International Forensic Science Conference in Jaipur. His technical expertise encompasses cybersecurity tools and bug detection, and he has contributed to the Internet Society Consolidation. He is an active member of ACM chapters, ISOC Delhi, and serves as a member of the UN-IGF in Riyadh, Saudi Arabia. Additionally, he is a youth ambassador for the International Telecommunication Union (ITU).

As the Managing Director of CiphersSecurity, a non-profit cybersecurity education organization, he is dedicated to advancing cybersecurity research and education. In 2022, he successfully completed a Ministry of Home Affairs-sponsored CDFS project. Furthermore, he serves as a reviewer for multiple prestigious journals, including MDPI, Springer, Elsevier, IntechOpen, River Publisher, and the International Journal of Biosciences and Pharmacy Sciences (IJBPS).

Dr. Sumit Kumar Choudhary is an established academician, researcher, author, editor, consultant, and influential thought leader in forensic science. He is a Gold Medalist in Forensic Science from the National Institute of Criminology and Forensic Science, Ministry of Home Affairs, New Delhi. Dr. Chaudhary holds a Ph.D. degree in Forensic & Behavioural Science and has a highly decorated academic profile. His professional experience of more than a decade involves his association with the first forensic science university in the world as a UGC Research Fellow which was followed by his appointment as the first faculty member in the first police university of India, Raksha Shakti University (RSU). He went on to become one of the youngest officiating registrars of the university at the age of twenty-nine years and held the office for more than three years.

Dr. Choudhary is also the longest serving Dean/HOD of School of Forensics, Risk Management & National Security. He has also served as the founding Dean of Executive Development Centre at RSU. He is actively involved in teaching, training, research, and forensic case consultancy. He is a sought-after speaker and faculty on a range of forensic subjects. He has been delivering lectures to serving police officers, judges, private security officers, and students of Indian and renowned foreign universities. He has trained police officers of more than ten foreign countries under ITEC programmes of the Ministry of External Affairs.

He has organized, attended, chaired, and convened a number of conferences, seminars, and workshops of national and international level and has presented a number of research papers and addressed scientific and technical sessions in such conferences and seminars. He is Managing Editor of *International Research Journal on Police Science, Scilla Journal of Forensic Science, International Journal of Forensic Science & Legal Medicine*, and *'Kavach' Magazine*. He is founder and chair of FIRST Dialogue, a forensic ideation forum, and he is Principal Investigator of more than three research projects at present. He is life member of the Indian Science Congress Association, the Forensic Science Development Society, the Indian Society of Criminology, and the Indian Criminology and Forensic Science Association. He has to his credit more than 30 high impact research publications, 4 invited book chapters and is currently advising many research scholars for their doctorate, M.Phil. and master's degrees. His area of research interest touches emerging forensic areas, primarily encompassing but not limited to crime investigation and national security.

Dr. Adarsh Kumar is a Professor at the School of Computer Science, University of Petroleum & Energy Studies, Dehradun, India. He received his Master's degree (M. Tech) in Software Engineering from Thapar University, Patiala, Punjab, India, and earned his Ph.D. degree from Jaypee Institute of Information Technology University, Noida, India, followed by Post-Doc from Software Research Institute, Athlone Institute of Technology, Ireland. From 2005 to 2016, he was associated with the Department of Computer Science Engineering & Information Technology, Jaypee Institute of Information Technology, Noida, Uttar Pradesh, India, where he worked as Assistant Professor. His main research interests are cybersecurity, cryptography, network security, and ad-hoc networks. He has many research papers in reputed journals, conferences, and workshops. He participated in one European Union H2020 sponsored research project and he is currently executing two research projects: one sponsored from UPES SEED division and the other from Lancaster University.

Foreword

It is with immense pleasure and deep respect that I pen the foreword in my personal capacity and from purely academic point of view for this seminal work, 'Cybersecurity, Forensics and National Security' edited by the distinguished editors Mr. Vinay Aseri, Dr. Sumit Kumar Choudhary, and Dr. Adarsh Kumar. This book represents a monumental contribution to the interdisciplinary domains of cybersecurity, digital forensics, and national security, offering a rich tapestry of insights into the pressing challenges and innovative solutions in these fields.

The editors of this volume are not only leading experts in their respective areas but also passionate advocates for fostering academic rigor and practical innovation. Mr. Vinay Aseri brings unparalleled expertise in digital forensics, evidenced by his groundbreaking research and numerous publications. Dr. Sumit Kumar Choudhary, with his illustrious academic career and leadership in forensic science, has continually set new benchmarks in research and pedagogy. Dr. Adarsh Kumar, renowned for his profound contributions to cybersecurity, blockchain and cryptography, has consistently pushed the boundaries of technological advancement.

This book is a timely and comprehensive endeavor, encompassing a wide array of topics ranging from cutting-edge cybersecurity frameworks to advanced digital forensic techniques. It meticulously addresses the complexities of securing critical infrastructures, safeguarding sensitive data and ensuring national resilience in the face of evolving cyber threats. Each chapter has been meticulously curated to provide readers with both theoretical foundations and practical applications, making it an indispensable resource for academics, practitioners, policymakers, and students alike.

The collaborative efforts of the editors and contributing authors underscore a shared vision of enhancing the understanding and implementation of cybersecurity and forensics in a rapidly digitilizing world. This book not only equips readers with the tools and knowledge to tackle current challenges but also inspires them to envision and create future solutions.

As you embark on this intellectual journey through the pages of this book, I am confident that you will find it both enlightening and empowering. It is a testament to the dedication, intellect, and collaborative spirit of its editors and contributors.

I wholeheartedly commend the efforts of Mr. Vinay Aseri, Dr. Sumit Kumar Choudhary, and Dr. Adarsh Kumar, and I hope that this work contributes to academic knowledge and provides the much needed reference material for all readers without exception. I found it rich and invaluable for the curious and those with interest in the subject. The material does not serve to dictate or pronounce any policy direction for the reader.

On a personal level, I am truly honored to contribute this foreword and to support a work that so powerfully advances the fields of cybersecurity, forensics, and national security.

Dr. Cosmas Zavazava
Director Telecommunication Development
Bureau of International Telecommunication Union

Contributors

Manimaran A.
VIT-AP University
Amaravati, India

Nitin Agarwala
Centre for Joint Warfare Studies
New Delhi, India

Tabrej Ahamad
Department of Computer Science & Engineering
Jamia Hamdard
New Delhi, India

Mohammed I. Alghamdi
Computer Science Department
Faculty of Computing and Information
Al-Baha University
Al-Baha, Saudi Arabia

Mazen AlWadi
Department of Cybersecurity
Faculty of Computer & Information Technology
Jordan University of Science and Technology
Irbid, Jordan

Qasem Abu Al-Haija
Department of Cybersecurity
Faculty of Computer & Information Technology
Jordan University of Science and Technology
Irbid, Jordan

Shahad AL-Tamimi
Department of Cybersecurity
King Hussein School of Computing Sciences
Princess Sumaya University for Technology (PSUT)
Amman, Jordan

Vinay Aseri
School of Behavioural Sciences & Forensic Investigations
Rashtriya Raksha University
Ministry of Home Affairs, Govt. of India
Gandhinagar, Gujarat, India

Shantanu Bindewari
IILM University
Greater Noida, Uttar Pradesh, India

Sumit Kumar Choudhary
School of Behavioural Sciences & Forensic Investigations
Rashtriya Raksha University
Ministry of Home Affairs, Govt. of India
Gandhinagar, Gujarat, India

Paul Joseph D.
Department of Computer Science and Systems Engineering
Andhra University
Visakhapatnam, India

Arnav Dua
Department of Information Technology
Tecnia Institute of Advanced Studies
Guru Gobind Singh Indraprastha University
Delhi, India

Mohammad Gouse Galety
Samarkand International University of Technology
Samarkand, Uzbekistan

Aayush Gupta
Department of Computer Science Engineering
Manav Rachna University
Haryana, India

Shashi Kant Gupta
Department of Computer Science and Engineering
Eudoxia Research University
New Castle, Delaware

Vinayak Gupta
Department of Forensic Sciences
School of Bioengineering and Biosciences
Lovely Professional University
Phagwara, Punjab, India

Mohammad Israr
Maryam Abacha American University of Nigeria
Hotoro GRA, Kano State, Federal Republic of Nigeria

Muhammad Adnan Kaim Khani
Department of Information Systems
Kulliyyah of Information & Communication Technology
International Islamic University (IIUM)
Gssombak Campus, Kuala Lumpur, Malaysia

Saydulu Kolasani
Fisker Automotive
Manhattan Beach, California

Adarsh Kumar
School of Computer Science
University of Petroleum and Energy Studies
Dehradun, India

College of Computing
Mohammed VI Polytechnic University
Benguerir, Morocco

V. Suresh Kumar
Department of Information Technology
Vel Tech Multi Tech Dr. Rangarajan Dr. Sakunthala Engineering College
Avadi, Chennai, India

Asif Ali Laghari
Software College
Shenyang Normal University
Shenyang, China

Adidah Lajis
Department of Computer Engineering
University of Kuala Lumpur (UniKL-MIIT)
Kuala Lumpur, Malaysia

Renuka Lenka
GITAM (Deemed to be University)
Visakhapatnam, India

Neeraj M.
Department of Computer Science and Systems Engineering
Andhra University
Vishakhapatnam, Andhra Pradesh, India

Prabu M.
Amrita Vishwa Vidyapeetham
Erachakulam, Andhra Pradesh, India

Amena Mahmoud
Department of Computer Science
Faculty of Computers and Information
Kafrelsheikh University
Kafr El Sheikh, Nile Delta, Egypt

Akhil John Mampilly
Centre of Postgraduate Studies
Lincoln University College
Petaling Jaya, Malaysia

Vijaya Kittu Manda
PBMEIT
Visakhapatnam, India

Surbhi Mathur
School of Forensic Science
National Forensic Sciences University
Gandhinagar, Gujarat, India

Ali Mehndi
Department of Computer Science & Engineering
Jamia Hamdard
New Delhi, India

Nilamadhab Mishra
VIT Bhopal University
Bhopal, India

Haidawati Nasir
Department of Computer Engineering
University of Kuala Lumpur (UniKL-MIIT)
Kuala Lumpur, Malaysia

Arul Kumar Natarajan
Samarkand International University of Technology
Samarkand, Uzbekistan

Roopali Pahwa
Cyber Forensic Laboratory
Panchkula, Haryana, India

Gobi Ramasamy
Christ University
Bengaluru, India

Morad Rawashdeh
Department of Cybersecurity
School of Computing Sciences
Prince Sumaya University for Technology
Amman, Jordan

Amal Saif
Department of Computer Science
School of Computing Sciences
Prince Sumaya University for Technology
Amman, Jordan

Abdul Salam Shah
Department of Information Systems
Kulliyyah of Information & Communication Technology
International Islamic University (IIUM)
Gssombak Campus, Kuala Lumpur, Malaysia

Asadullah Shah
Department of Information Systems
Kulliyyah of Information & Communication Technology
International Islamic University (IIUM)
Gssombak Campus, Kuala Lumpur, Malaysia

Anubhav Singh
School of Forensic Science
National Forensic Sciences University
Gandhinagar, Gujarat, India

Khadija Slimani
LDR Laboratory
Higher School of Computer Science Electronics and Automation (ESIEA)
Paris, France

Mansi Trivedi
Amity University
Gwalior, Madhya Pradesh, India

Gopichand Vemulapalli
Principal Data Architect
Agero Inc.
Phoenix, Arizona

Anumaan Whig
Department of Computer Science
Delhi Technology University
New Delhi, India

Pawan Whig
Threws
Vivekananda Institute of Professional Studies-TC
New Delhi, India

Nikhitha Yathiraju
University of the Cumberlands
Williamsburg, Kentucky

Justyna Żywiołek
Czestochowa University of Technology
Czestochowa, Poland

1 Intertwined Concept of Cybersecurity, Digital Forensics, and National Security

Vinay Aseri, Sumit Kumar Choudhary, and Adarsh Kumar

1.1 INTRODUCTION

The internet has been an essential part of global communication for over 20 years and has been more ingrained in people's lives all around the world. The availability, use, and performance of the internet have been greatly increased by innovations and low costs in this field, and as a result, there are presently around 3 billion internet users worldwide [1].

The internet has created a vast global network that generates billions of dollars for the world economy each year [2]. Currently, the majority of international connections and activities, including those between individuals, non-governmental organizations, and government agencies, as well as commercial, cultural, social, and economic activities, take place online [3]. Important and sensitive systems and infrastructures are either integrated into cyberspace or are controlled, managed, and exploited via it. A significant amount of sensitive and important data is either moved to or, more fundamentally, created in cyberspace [4]. A significant portion of residents' time and activities are spent in this region, which also houses the majority of media activities and financial transactions [5].

Threats like cyberwarfare, cybercrime, cyberterrorism, and cyberespionage have been brought about by both strong and weak actors, including governments, organized and terrorist groups, and even individuals, as well as by the low cost of entry, secrecy, unpredictable nature of the threatening geographic area, dramatic impact, and lack of public transparency in cyberspace [6]. This sets cyber threats apart from traditional national security threats, which are primarily transparent in nature and whose actors are identifiable governments and nations in a particular geographic area. As a result, traditional national security has become ineffective and challenged in this area [7]. Experts have been considering the potential consequences of cyberattacks for over ten years [8].

DOI: 10.1201/9781003497868-1

Digital forensics (DF) is the newest and popularity gaining innovation of all time in the field of computer investigation. The technology can examine and analyze illegal criminal activities of state and federal government law enforcement departments [9]. The concept of data storage on forensics was coined in the early 1970s to 1980s, the area gained more attention at the era because the agent had long worked to seize, retain, and analyze suspects documentation, manual documentation takes a longer time as compared to computer systems. In 1984, the Federal Bureau of Investigation (FBI) launched the 'magnet media program'; this was the first official DF program at a federal agency, mainly used to tackle suspicious activities on the cyber environment.

Over half of the world's population now lives in cities, and this figure is expected to climb as the population grows [10]. Modern civilizations rely on cutting-edge information technology, which includes communication networks, cloud services, cybersecurity, the internet of things (IoT), and ubiquitous and mobile appliances. It aids commercial and governmental growth efforts, conducts corporate transactions, and alters individual lives [11]. No doubt, the mentioned technology provides lots of benefits, however, at the same time the impact of cybercrime on the peak, several new threats evolve in the past few years namely, spoofing, identity theft, cyberbullying, malicious attacker, malware, distributed denial of service (DDoS), zombie, and data leakage exploitation. The consequences of cyberattacks have major brunt on both governmental and individual levels. Therefore, DF becomes essential for protecting evidence by attacks or securing evidence by forgery and makes it possible to present in the courtroom.

In a few decades, the DF framework evolved daily, diversity in crime investigation emerged, and sophisticated improvements were required to improve the analysis of digital investigations. The framework structure was manipulated based on the various crimes committed, such as the transition from early computer systems to mobile devices and storage devices, and it was modified over time based on the crimes committed [12, 13]. The first formal framework, which was developed in 1995, is primarily divided into four steps: admittance, assessment, identification, and acquisition [14]. The proposed framework did not fit for the generalized form of evidence investigation, only allowed for the physical, logical, and legal contexts [15].

Unquestionably, cybersecurity and DF are the norm in today's society. Law uses the constitution and laws to make decisions when assessing people. There are lots of factors that go into making a good choice, and the law is one of those factors [16]. Forensic medicine, forensic microbiology, forensic audio, and computer forensics are examples of these auxiliary components, which are often referred to as forensic science. Incomplete or faulty data or evidence in the report will do harm to the legal system and social justice in our nation at any point throughout the legal procedure that the forensic science court authorities give [17]. As a result, forensic science professionals must exercise caution while doing forensic analysis and observe the present research in order to challenge the forensic science notion.

Because of the legal process, our topic, cybersecurity and DF, and its specialists should constantly be aware that there may be opposing forensic investigations throughout their studies and should not provide an interpretation of their unfavorable findings. Numerous bad reflections may follow from these unfavorable outcomes that begin with people and extend to the business and governmental sectors [18].

As part of the National Security Agency's endeavor to create a curriculum that would meet India's security requirements, the author had the advantage of collaborating closely with the country's information security educators. As part of an information security curriculum, the author created courses in cybersecurity and DF. The author learned that faculty from other universities were interested in launching a comparable course at their own schools after presentations about these initiatives were given at regional conferences [19–21]. National security, a cornerstone of sovereignty and stability, extends its purview to encompass the protection of a nation's critical infrastructure, economy, and citizenry against both traditional and emerging threats, including those emanating from the cyber realm. The increasing digitization of critical infrastructures, government services, and defense systems has heightened the importance of cybersecurity and DF in safeguarding national interests and preserving strategic advantage [22–24].

1.2 FUNDAMENTAL CONCEPTS OF CYBERSECURITY AND DIGITAL FORENSICS

For people, businesses, and governments alike, the interconnected ideas of cybersecurity, DF, and national security are becoming more and more important and urgent issues that are difficult to overlook. The main elements that make cybersecurity important but difficult to attain are examined in this chapter. Analyses start with a look at the changing digital landscape, where the spread of linked systems and devices increases the attack surface and the possible effect of cyberthreats [25–28]. The discussion then delves into the dynamics that compound the complexity of cybersecurity, including the sophistication of threat actors, the rapid pace of technological innovation, and the global nature of cyber threats. Furthermore, the chapter considers the role of DF in the aftermath of cyber incidents, highlighting its pivotal role in gathering, analyzing, and interpreting digital evidence to attribute attacks and inform proactive cybersecurity measures [21, 29]. Finally, the chapter underscores the intersectionality of cybersecurity with national security, emphasizing the imperative of protecting critical infrastructure, sensitive data, and national interests in the face of evolving cyber threats.

This research aims to dispel the myths surrounding cybersecurity and provide the reader a clear, but nuanced, understanding of what matters and why. This is difficult in situations where basic ideas are often misunderstood and when there are strong political and financial incentives to inflate perceived risks.

Cyberspace can be divided into a multi-layer model comprising:

1. **Physical Foundation:** Satellites, data storage systems, land and undersea cables, and routers that route information to its destination are a few examples of communication channels.
2. **Logical Building Block:** For instance, including web browsers, operating systems, and apps for smartphones that enable the physical foundations to operate and interact.

3. **Information:** That travels across the internet, including text messages, social media postings, money transactions, or movie downloads. This data is often saved on (and altered by) PCs, mobile devices, and public or private cloud storage services both before and after transportation.
4. **People:** That communicate, alter data, and provide the logical and physical framework of cyberspace.
5. **National Information Security Frameworks:** This layer is additionally added by the authors according to fulfill this book framework standards for delves to the society. NIST is an authority to set the standards for the global information technology innovations. They gave the global authorization for serving the technical terminology.

> Collectively these concrete and ethereal layers compose cyberspace, which we are increasingly depending on for fundamental components of everyday life. A robust and stable cyberspace is important for the seamless running of vital infrastructure sectors such as energy, transport, food, health and finance. As dependency develops, so do the consequences of disruption—whether unintentional or intentional—as well as potential for exploitation and abuse.
>
> **[30–33]**

1.3 EVOLUTION OF CYBERSECURITY IN 2023 AND 2024

Driven by the always rising complexity of cyberattacks, the growth of geopolitical tensions, and the increasing dependence on digital infrastructure, cybersecurity in 2023 and 2024 featured amazing breakthroughs. To offset the swiftly shifting threat landscape, these years have brought novel concepts, technology, and regulatory structures. Following is a closer look at important themes and case studies defining the cybersecurity development throughout this period of time [34].

1.4 EMERGENCE OF ZERO TRUST ARCHITECTURE AS THE GOLD STANDARD

Adoption of Zero Trust Architecture (ZTA) has been one of the most important changes in cybersecurity within the last two years. This perspective holds that no network—internal or outside—can be trusted. Minimizing the risks connected with insider threats, credential theft, and lateral movement within networks, ZTA focuses on ongoing validation of both people and devices. Major companies like Google, Microsoft, and Amazon adopted ZTA as part of its security architecture in 2023, therefore indicating a change from perimeter-based security models to more exact access limits [35].

Following the 2023 National Cybersecurity Strategy, CISA (Cybersecurity and Infrastructure Security Agency) ordered in the public sector the implementation of ZTA across US federal agencies stressing the necessity of strong defenses in view of recent supply-chain breaches. ZTA became critical for reducing risks as hackers progressively took advantage of supply-chain weaknesses—best seen by the SolarWinds and Log4j events [36, 37].

1.5 RANSOMWARE AS A MAJOR THREAT VECTOR

Ransomware attacks dominated the cybersecurity environment in 2023 and 2024, as operations got more sophisticated and economically damaging. Ransomware-as-a-Service (RaaS) is developing as a viable business model, with unskilled attackers paying a fraction of the price for ransomware kits obtained from criminal groups. Targeting vital institutions such as healthcare and education, the Clop ransomware group is evolving by utilizing MOVE it's file transfer system weaknesses to achieve huge operations [38, 39].

Ransomware attacks started targeting cloud service providers in 2023, requiring organizations to modify their cloud security protocols. In December 2023, Rackspace was the target of a widely reported breach that briefly disrupted their hosted exchange services, causing multiple organizations to suffer. In response to the growth in remote work, this incident called attention to the rising inclination of attackers targeting cloud infrastructure [39].

1.6 AI-POWERED ATTACKS AND DEFENSE

In cybersecurity today artificial intelligence (AI) is a two-edged blade. On the one hand, AI-driven tools have enhanced businesses ability to detect anomalies, automate responses, and strengthen defenses. Tools like Darktrace and Vectra AI help fast identification of suspicious activity by using machine learning to review massive amounts of network traffic in real-time. AI has made it possible to detect zero-day vulnerabilities, which are security flaws that hackers exploit before a patch is developed [40–42].

However, by 2023 and 2024, the employment of AI with malevolent purpose has skyrocketed. Malware powered by AI is becoming a serious concern since it may change on its own to avoid detection. For example, the polymorphic virus BlackMamba has shown its ability to use AI to generate new attack signatures on demand, therefore evaluating the efficacy of current detection techniques [43, 44].

Dealing with these such challenges relies on increasingly more vital security solutions bolstered by AI. By 2024, many businesses will have used AI and predictive analytics-based threat intelligence systems to identify risks dependent on prior data and patterns. This proactive strategy represents a major progress over conventional reactive security tactics [44].

1.7 SUPPLY-CHAIN ATTACKS AND THEIR IMPACT

Supply-chain attacks attracted great attention in 2023 as the SolarWinds hack affects US government organizations as well as corporations. Attackers target third-party suppliers or service providers in early steps toward gaining access to more vast networks. Previously unprecedented focus on software supply-chain security was given by the 2023 National Cybersecurity Strategy [36].

The approach promoted cooperation between government departments and businesses to raise knowledge of software components and guarantee that software vendors take responsibility for safety concerns.

Following SolarWinds and similar events, businesses-embraced solutions like Software Bill of Materials (SBOM) to provide visibility into the components of software they depend on. When security problems like the Log4j vulnerability found in late 2021 surface, an SBOM offers a comprehensive list of all software libraries and components utilized, therefore enabling speedier discovery of vulnerabilities [45].

Reflecting Europe's focus on software responsibility in view of supply-chain concerns, the Cyber Resilience Act, which demands security certificates for software providers and enforces fines for non-compliance, was adopted by the continent by 2024 [46].

1.8 GEOPOLITICAL CYBER THREATS

Given Russia's geopolitical posture—constant conflict with Ukraine—cyberattacks seem very likely. Russian cyber activities in 2023 comprised wiper malware as well as DDoS assaults against Ukrainian government networks and critical infrastructure. Ukraine followed up on damaging Russia's command and control framework, therefore improving its cyber capacity in a form of return-oriented pay-back. The conflict set a new standard for cyber warfare used in combination with traditional military operations [47].

Beyond the conflict between Russia and Ukraine, China remained a top target for cybercrime concerns. Thought to be linked to the Chinese government, the APT41 group—also known as Winnti—was engaged in a cyberespionage operation targeted at government organizations and healthcare systems all across several countries in 2023. Emphasizing data exfiltration and intellectual property theft, they underscored the continuous exploitation of cyberspace to support national objectives [48].

1.9 PRIVACY AND DATA SECURITY: A GLOBAL REGULATORY PUSH

In 2023 and 2024, data privacy became a worldwide issue as high-profile hacks revealed the personal data of millions. In response, countries worldwide developed stringent data protection rules and regulations. For example, the California Privacy Rights Act (CPRA), which went into effect in January 2023, built on the California Consumer Privacy Act (CCPA), allowing customers more choice over how their data is gathered and used. Through increasingly complex client permission procedures and regular audits, the CPRA expects businesses to exhibit compliance with data privacy regulations [49–51].

In accordance with this, Europe approved the Digital Services Act (DSA) in 2024, therefore increasing the accountability of internet behemoths like Meta and Google for the content and data submitted on their platforms. Apart from safeguarding of user privacy, these guidelines provide algorithmic openness and content management [52].

1.10 THE EXPANDING ROLE OF DIGITAL FORENSICS

DF has transcended its role as a post-incident investigation tool. In 2023 and 2024, it plays a proactive role in detecting advanced threats. Real-time forensics, where forensic analysis happens concurrently with security monitoring, is increasingly being used to stop breaches in progress. This is critical in Zero-Day Attacks and Advanced Persistent Threats (APTs), where attackers stay hidden for extended periods [53].

Automation and AI in Forensics: Using AI and machine learning techniques has automated evidence collecting and processing in extensive enquiries. With digital attribution tools, AI aids in identifying attack patterns from millions of logs, putting together attack paths, and assigning the assaults to particular threat actors. By offering insights into fresh malware strains that avoid conventional detection techniques, tools like AI-driven malware analysis have transformed the field of research [54].

Forensics and Ransomware: Many cases using double extortion—where attackers not only encrypt data but also threaten to reveal significant information—showcased in 2023 ransomware occurrences, much more than in previous years. DF is very crucial for tracking ransom payments utilizing blockchain technology and spotting attacks to nation-state actors or organized cybercrime groups [54, 55].

Collaboration with Law Enforcement: National and international law enforcement operations are becoming to revolve on DF. Spending much on DF labs, Interpol and Europol have promoted cross-border cooperation in fighting cybercrime. By extending its purview in 2024, the Joint Cybercrime Action Taskforce (J-CAT) will help to destroy cybercrime networks including those enabling RaaS operations [56].

1.11 NATIONAL SECURITY AND CYBER THREATS

In recent years, cybersecurity has become a cornerstone of national security strategy. Governments increasingly acknowledge that cybersecurity failures may directly influence national defense, economic stability, and public safety. The Ukraine-Russia crisis in 2023 revealed how cyberattacks are becoming employed in warfare, with Russian cyber operations attacking Ukrainian key infrastructure and armament systems. This merging of conventional and cyber warfare has led to several governments stepping up their cyber defense forces, creating cyberwar capabilities alongside traditional military divisions. Cyberespionage and Political Interference: A key issue for national security in 2023 and 2024 has been the growth in state-sponsored cyber espionage. The SolarWinds attack and subsequent cyber breaches related to nation-state actors have proved that even sophisticated networks may be compromised. Nations are establishing strategies to resist misinformation efforts, notably during elections, by increasing cybersecurity surrounding voting systems and public databases [57, 58].

1.12 CYBER-PHYSICAL SYSTEMS AND NATIONAL INFRASTRUCTURE

Cyber-physical systems (CPS) stand as the crucial infrastructure of the modern national landscape, blending computational elements with physical processes. Providing power to necessities like energy grids, transportation networks, water treatment plants, and telecommunications. On one hand, CPS has brought unparalleled efficiency with real-time controls to the infrastructure; on the other hand, it also introduces important vulnerabilities which makes them prime and primary target for cyberattack. The more nations depend on these systems, which are interconnected worldwide, the greater risk there is to malicious actors shutting them down [58, 59].

In recent years, CPS have become the subject of increasingly pervasive threats such as ransomware and state-sponsored hacking. The most famous is the Colonial Pipeline attack of 2021, which was a crippling ransomware breach that led some eastern US states to suffer through fuel shortages. It served as an example of how a CPS system can have cascading impacts, resulting in significant disruptions from even a relatively small attack on one of its components. As a result of the breach, several governments launched highly repressive cybersecurity regulations and the US-signed executive orders targeting better cyber defenses by critical infrastructure sectors [60].

1.13 KEY THREATS TO CYBER-PHYSICAL SYSTEMS

Ransomware Attacks on Infrastructure: Ransomware is no longer just a threat to corporate networks—increasingly, it now represents a direct hit against CPS in the critical infrastructure sector, which has been shown to almost eliminate OWASP with industry ransomware payment demands on average 15% their previous revenue. And the breach of Colonial Pipeline, an incident where ransomware knocked out gas distribution in multiple US states, was a tipping point. The attack showed that even relatively minor cyber intrusions could do great harm to the economy and society. The US government issued executive orders after the attack requiring pipeline operators and other critical infrastructure sectors to shore up cybersecurity defenses [61].

APT: CPS have been increasingly targeted by state-sponsored cyberattack operations, usually executed as APTs. In 2022, it was determined that the China-linked group APT41 is actively targeting CPS in sectors like energy and manufacturing with plans to steal IPR and overtime disrupt operations. A year later, amidst reports of European power grids simultaneously being targeted by advanced threat groups allegedly linked to Russia–spurred concerns that cyberattacks could serve as instruments for geopolitical influence and coercion [62, 63].

Supply-Chain Vulnerabilities: This emphasis on supply-chain attacks is well-placed because the operations of CPS rely heavily upon third-party software and hardware. When US government departments and private firms were compromised by the 2020 SolarWinds attack—taking place through a software update—it highlighted vulnerabilities in supply chains as being a feasible method for penetrating critical infrastructure. In reaction, governments are implementing SBOM regulations that mandate CPS operators to publicly disclose components and software in use on their platforms [64, 65].

1.14 EMERGING TECHNOLOGIES AND CPS SECURITY CHALLENGES

5G and IoT Integration: The emergence of 5G networks and the IoT had been a major catalyst in the use of CPS in national infrastructure. 5G—low latency and high bandwidth: Enables real-time control of physical systems

IoT devices—facilitates better automation, monitoring. On the other hand, this growing interconnection leads to a larger attack surface. Similarly, in IoT-based CPS for power distribution in Spain using Smart Meters, a cyber-attack controlled all the meters and affected large consumers with service disruption across the country during 2023. This pointed to the requirement of secure security measures for IoT devices in CPS networks [66].

AI and Machine Learning: CPS security is strengthened by utilization of AI as well as machine learning. A predictive algorithm allows detecting anomalies and preventing real-time failures, ensuring proactive maintenance revolves around threat detection. But AI is also being weaponized. In 2024, security researchers had unveiled a new AI malware that altered CPS processes by using its ability to learn normal system behavior over time and thus behave in a way not causing any alarm. Stressing the importance of ongoing innovation in AI powered by security to evolve with emerging threats.

Quantum Computing: The advancement of quantum computing, although in its nascent phase, is the key driving factor threatening the security of CPS. Excluding deprecated CPS security methods quantum computers will be able to crack, there are numerous encryption algorithms in use for securing networks which allow transmission of the data. Pioneering governments, including the United States and some EU member states, have appropriated funds to develop quantum-resistant encryption as well as new quantum-proof algorithms that NIST established in 2024 to be used for securing CPS in a post-quantum world [67, 68].

1.15 NATIONAL POLICIES AND INTERNATIONAL COOPERATION

US Executive Orders on Critical Infrastructure: To the Colonial Pipeline attack and other major cybersecurity breaches, the US government reacted decisively in 2023/2024 by issuing a number of executive orders to fortify the security of critical infrastructure, particularly CPS. The orders underscore that the Department of Homeland Security (DHS) needs to work more closely with owners and operators in the private sector representing essential critical infrastructure to address risks that could lead to similar types of attacks again in the future. Further, the CISA has broadened its mandate to provide a range of guidance, resources, and assistance to help organizations more effectively defend CPS, strengthening national resiliency against increasingly sophisticated cyberattacks [69].

EU Cybersecurity Act: The growing amount of cybersecurity threats have caught the attention of the European Union (EU), which has reviewed its Cybersecurity Act including upgraded demands with regard to cybersecurity for relevant infrastructure operators. One of such event even dates back in 2024 where the European Cybersecurity Certification Framework has been updated to encompass CPS—the type of systems which if did not met some minimum security requirements should be forbidden for use, for example, in critical sectors like energy, healthcare or transportation. It can be used as a benchmark to ensure security and resilience of the economy's most important systems and it can reduce general cyber-threats throughout the EU infrastructure, while simultaneously securing businesses/entities more, resulting in further protection for individuals [70, 71].

International Cooperation: With attacks on critical infrastructure having worldwide implications, the rest of the world should especially help to secure CPS. In response to this need, the Global Forum on Cyber-Physical Security was formed in 2024, bringing together governments, industry leaders and cybersecurity experts from across the globe. The forum enables the sharing of information, tactics, and best practices for securing CPS against new cyber threats. It is now a pivotal tool in the collaboration of North America, Europe, and Asia Pacific nation cooperation to tackle the increasing threats to national infrastructure and provides a stronger global resilience to cyber defense [72].

1.16 THE ROLE OF QUANTUM COMPUTING IN CYBERSECURITY

Quantum computing is the major game-changer for the cybersecurity industry, as it comes with both opportunities (in threat detection and breach mitigation) and threats. Quantum machines perform computations with the help of quantum bits (qubits) which are able to leverage the principles of quantum mechanics to solve problems exponentially faster than traditional systems. Quantum computers can solve difficult problems, for example, efficiently factoring the large composite numbers that are at the heart of contemporary cryptographic systems such as RSA and Elliptic Curve Cryptography (ECC). The most well-known example is Shor's factorization algorithm, which showed that one day quantum computers would be able to crack many encryption systems vital for secure communication, such as those used in commercial and financial transactions over the internet, or to secure classified government communications. Thanks to this rapid advancement, it has become clear that industries and governments must increase their research and deployment of quantum-resistant cryptography in an effort to contain the potential fallout from these newfound shortcomings [72–75].

1.17 GOVERNMENTS AND CORPORATIONS PREPARING FOR THE QUANTUM THREAT

Knowing that quantum computing represents a very serious threat to classical cryptography, governments and companies are not just standing still; they are even working on post-quantum cryptography which is nothing else than those specific algorithms designed to withstand future attacks powered by quantum computers. The National Institute of Standards and Technology (NIST) has been coordinating efforts to standardize these next-generation cryptographic protocols in the United States, with a completed selection process anticipated by 2024. At the same time, fields such as finance and defense already incorporate hybrid encryption models together with classical and post-quantum cryptography mechanisms to pave the way toward a change from classic crypto to quantum-safe requirements. For a concrete example, financial institutions are deploying quantum-resistant cryptographic pilots to future-proof the security of their most sensitive information as new capabilities develop. These kinds of investments are vital for ensuring that we never confront another quantum-powered breach in civilian or military infrastructures [75–79].

1.18 QUANTUM KEY DISTRIBUTION AND ITS APPLICATIONS

In addition to post-quantum cryptography, Quantum Key Distribution (QKD) provides one of the most convincing avenues for secure communication in a world dominated by quantum technologies. This is possible only because QKD relies on the properties of quantum mechanics and allows for an exchange of encryption keys that would betray any eavesdropping, since even a passive listener trying to intercept them, changes their state. From large-scale quantum networks realized in 2023 based on the QKD technology refunding China to inaugurate secure communication with global separation, it is clear again that this new race related to quantum between countries continues with the leading position of China. European and Japanese quantum communication networks protecting government and military communications are expected to also be in place by 2024. As the world gets ready for the new age, should quantum computers come with a bit of chaos through secure communication channels into national security frameworks; these efforts underscore a broader global trend toward quantum-secured communication channels [77].

1.19 QUANTUM COMPUTING AND CYBER DEFENSE

Quantum computing's potential for cyber defense is viewed as a potentially game-changer, offering superior skills in threat detection and cybersecurity analytics. The ability of quantum algorithms to handle and analyze vast amounts of data in real-time could transform the speed and precision with which cyberattacks are recognized and neutralized. For example, quantum-enhanced machine learning algorithms could recognize abnormalities in network traffic, indicating prospective intrusions before they grow. This technology's future usage in national defense plans, particularly for essential infrastructure such as electrical grids and communication networks, is anticipated to increase a country's cyber resilience. By 2024, pilot programs researching these quantum-based defensive systems are being built in nations with large cybersecurity stakes, such as the United States and China, giving a proactive strategy to guard against future quantum-empowered cyber assaults [71, 72].

1.20 GEOPOLITICAL IMPLICATIONS OF QUANTUM COMPUTING

The advent of quantum computing is poised to dramatically alter geopolitical power dynamics, since states that achieve quantum domination may dominate both offensive and defensive cyber operations. Nations such as the United States, Europe, and China are at the forefront of the quantum research race; Europe's Quantum Flagship Program and China's breakthroughs in quantum satellite communications suggest that quantum domination may be achieved soon. The ability to decrypt encrypted communications on a large scale would provide nations with unprecedented intelligence-gathering capabilities, raising concerns about global espionage and cyber warfare. As a result, governments throughout the globe are putting more focus on the development of quantum technologies, both to avoid falling behind in the quantum arms race and to protect their own national interests against quantum-enabled foes.

1.21 PREPARING FOR A QUANTUM-RESILIENT FUTURE

The emergence of quantum computing has made it vital for the public and commercial sectors to act together to construct quantum-resilient infrastructures. Tech giants like Google, IBM, and Microsoft are pushing research into quantum-safe security measures, while concurrently boosting quantum computer development. In the United States, government programs such as the Department of Energy's Quantum Computing Roadmap have created the basis for strong links between academics, business, and government, all striving to future-proof the nation's essential systems. Concurrently, efforts are being done to establish offensive and defensive quantum capabilities under the EU's Quantum Flagship Program. As quantum developments emerge, the emphasis will continue on creating quantum-resistant cryptographic standards to safeguard the digital world's security against the future problems of the quantum age.

1.22 CONCLUSION

The integration of cybersecurity, forensics, and national security have become important for society as a whole, linked by networks and cyber dangers. Although they are separate and vary substantially in their methodologies, they each constitute a vital element of the other for the aim of preserving key infrastructure, protecting sensitive data, and highlighting the national resilience of the country.

Cybersecurity provides proactive defenses to overcome attacks and manage risks that result while DF acts as a tool for examining the performance of cyber incident trace analysis. The two aims at protecting the wide paradigm of national security against developing dangers that can interrupt the smooth circuitry operations of social, economic, and governmental activities. The integrated fields are found to increase and empower country's abilities to identify, prevent, and react natural assault by hackers to diabolic threats by state-sponsored aggressors.

They strive to integrate worlds in as a technique that relies on the beneficial qualities of all disciplines. To drum up the defenses that an agile guard may become against such dangers, culture promotes multi-sectorial cooperation, good technology solutions, and ongoing research to embrace the ever-evolving threats. By additionally adopting this global alignment, governments may boost readiness and resilience as well as establish a digital ecosystem that will promote sustainability and security. Such a condition is not a theoretical idea, however; it is a real requirement in a society where the stakes created by cyberspace are at the greatest level ever.

REFERENCES

1. Krause, T., Ernst, R., Klaer, B., Hacker, I., & Henze, M. (2021). Cybersecurity in power grids: Challenges and opportunities. *Sensors, 21*(18), 6225.
2. He, X., Qiu, R. C., Ai, Q., Chu, L., Xu, X., & Ling, Z. (2016). Designing for situation awareness of future power grids: An indicator system based on linear eigenvalue statistics of large random matrices. *IEEE Access, 4*, 3557–3568.
3. Suciu, G., Sachian, M. A., Vulpe, A., Vochin, M., Farao, A., Koutroumpouchos, N., & Xenakis, C. (2021). Sealedgrid: Secure and interoperable platform for smart grid applications. *Sensors, 21*(16), 5448.
4. Klaer, B., Sen, O., van der Velde, D., Hacker, I., Andres, M., & Henze, M. (2020, September). Graph-based model of smart grid architectures. In *2020 international conference on smart energy systems and technologies (SEST)* (pp. 1–6). IEEE.
5. Wang, T., Long, Q., Gu, X., & Chai, W. (2020). Information flow modeling and performance evaluation of communication networks serving power grids. *IEEE Access, 8*, 13735–13747.
6. Javaid, N., Hafeez, G., Iqbal, S., Alrajeh, N., Alabed, M. S., & Guizani, M. (2018). Energy efficient integration of renewable energy sources in the smart grid for demand side management. *IEEE Access, 6*, 77077–77096.
7. Figueroa-Acevedo, A. L., Tsai, C. H., Gruchalla, K., Claes, Z., Foley, S., Bakke, J., Okullo, J., & Prabhakar, A. J. (2020). Visualizing the impacts of renewable energy growth in the US Midcontinent. *IEEE Open Access Journal of Power and Energy, 7*, 91–99.
8. Phuangpornpitak, N., & Tia, S. (2013). Opportunities and challenges of integrating renewable energy in smart grid system. *Energy Procedia, 34*, 282–290.
9. Ahmed, S. D., Al-Ismail, F. S., Shafiullah, M., Al-Sulaiman, F. A., & El-Amin, I. M. (2020). Grid integration challenges of wind energy: A review. *IEEE Access, 8*, 10857–10878.
10. Henze, M., Hiller, J., Hummen, R., Matzutt, R., Wehrle, K., & Ziegeldorf, J. H. (2017). Network security and privacy for cyber-physical systems. *Security and Privacy in Cyber-Physical Systems: Foundations, Principles and Applications*, 25–56.
11. Hiller, J., Komanns, K., Dahlmanns, M., & Wehrle, K. (2019, September). Regaining insight and control on SMGW-based secure communication in smart grids. In *2019 AEIT international annual conference (AEIT)* (pp. 1–6). IEEE.
12. Pennekamp, J., Henze, M., Schmidt, S., Niemietz, P., Fey, M., Trauth, D., & Wehrle, K. (2019, November). Dataflow challenges in an internet of production: a security & privacy perspective. In *Proceedings of the ACM workshop on cyber-physical systems security & privacy* (pp. 27–38).
13. Khurana, H., Hadley, M., Lu, N., & Frincke, D. A. (2010). Smart-grid security issues. *IEEE Security & Privacy, 8*(1), 81–85.
14. van der Velde, D., Henze, M., Kathmann, P., Wassermann, E., Andres, M., Bracht, D., & Sethmann, R. (2020, September). Methods for actors in the electric power system to prevent, detect and react to ICT attacks and failures. In *2020 6th IEEE international energy conference (ENERGYCon)* (pp. 17–22). IEEE.
15. Zhang, H., Jin, X., Li, Y., Jiang, Z., Liang, Y., Jin, Z., & Wen, Q. (2019). A multi-step attack detection model based on alerts of smart grid monitoring system. *IEEE Access, 8*, 1031–1047.
16. Karimipour, H., Dehghantanha, A., Parizi, R. M., Choo, K. K. R., & Leung, H. (2019). A deep and scalable unsupervised machine learning system for cyber-attack detection in large-scale smart grids. *IEEE Access, 7*, 80778–80788.
17. Serror, M., Hack, S., Henze, M., Schuba, M., & Wehrle, K. (2020). Challenges and opportunities in securing the industrial internet of things. *IEEE Transactions on Industrial Informatics, 17*(5), 2985–2996.

18. Lee, R. M., Assante, M. J., & Conway, T. (2017). *CRASHOVERRIDE: Analysis of the threat to electric grid operations.* Dragos Inc.
19. Petermann, T., Bradke, H., Lüllmann, A., Poetzsch, M., & Riehm, U. (2014). What happens during a blackout: Consequences of a prolonged and wide-ranging power outage. Office of Technology Assessment at the German Bundestag (TAB), Berlin, Germany.
20. Segall, A. (1983). Distributed network protocols. *IEEE Transactions on Information Theory, 29*(1), 23–35.
21. E-ISAC. (2016). Analysis of the cyber-attack on the Ukrainian power grid. *Electricity Information Sharing and Analysis Center (E-ISAC), 388*(1–29), 3.
22. Chapman, J. P., Ofner, S., & Pauksztelo, P. (2016, November). Key factors in industrial control system security. In *2016 IEEE 41st conference on local computer networks (LCN)* (pp. 551–554). IEEE.
23. Istiaque Ahmed, K., Tahir, M., Hadi Habaebi, M., Lun Lau, S., & Ahad, A. (2021). Machine learning for authentication and authorization in IoT: Taxonomy, challenges and future research direction. *Sensors, 21*(15), 5122.
24. Maynard, P., McLaughlin, K., & Haberler, B. (2014, September). Towards understanding man-in-the-middle attacks on IEC 60870-5-104 SCADA networks. In *2nd international symposium for ICS & SCADA cybersecurity research 2014 (ICS-CSR 2014).* BCS Learning & Development.
25. Radoglou-Grammatikis, P., Sarigiannidis, P., Giannoulakis, I., Kafetzakis, E., & Panaousis, E. (2019, July). Attacking IEC-60870-5-104 SCADA systems. In *2019 IEEE world congress on services (SERVICES)* (Vol. 2642, pp. 41–46). IEEE.
26. Robinson, M. (2013, September). The SCADA threat landscape. In *1st International Symposium for ICS & SCADA Cybersecurity Research 2013 (ICS-CSR 2013).* BCS Learning & Development.
27. Darwish, I., Igbe, O., Celebi, O., Saadawi, T., & Soryal, J. (2015, November). Smart grid DNP3 vulnerability analysis and experimentation. In *2015 IEEE 2nd international conference on cybersecurity and cloud computing* (pp. 141–147). IEEE.
28. Xu, Y., Yang, Y., Li, T., Ju, J., & Wang, Q. (2017, November). Review on cyber vulnerabilities of communication protocols in industrial control systems. In *2017 IEEE conference on energy internet and energy system integration (EI2)* (pp. 1–6). IEEE.
29. Henze, M. (2020, June). The quest for secure and privacy-preserving cloud-based industrial cooperation. In *2020 IEEE conference on communications and network security (CNS)* (pp. 1–5). IEEE.
30. International Electrotechnical Commission. IEC 61850 Standard. Available online: https://webstore.iec.ch/publication/20082
31. Hummen, R., Hiller, J., Henze, M., & Wehrle, K. (2013a). Slimfit—A HIP DEX compression layer for the IP-based internet of things. In *2013 IEEE 9th international conference on wireless and mobile computing, networking and communications (WiMob)* (pp. 259–266). IEEE.
32. Hummen, R., Hiller, J., Wirtz, H., Henze, M., Shafagh, H., & Wehrle, K. (2013b). 6LoWPAN fragmentation attacks and mitigation mechanisms. In *Proceedings of the sixth ACM conference on Security and privacy in wireless and mobile networks* (pp. 55–66).
33. Ackerman, P. (2017). *Industrial cybersecurity: Efficiently secure critical infrastructure systems.* Packt Publishing Ltd.
34. Parfomak, P. W. (2014). *Physical security of the US power grid: High-voltage transformer substations.* Congressional Research Service.
35. Lee, R. M., Assante, M. J., & Conway, T. (2016). Analysis of the recent reports of attacks on US infrastructure by Iranian actors. *SANS Industrial Control Systems, 4,* 9.
36. Xie, J., Stefanov, A., & Liu, C. C. (2019). Physical and cybersecurity in a smart grid environment. *Advances in Energy Systems: The Large-Scale Renewable Energy Integration Challenge,* 85–109.

37. Brdiczka, O. (2014). Insider Attacks Pose a Serious Threat to Critical U.S. Infrastructure. *Vectra.ai*. Available online: https://www.vectra.ai/blog/insider-attacks-pose-a-serious-threat-to-critical-u-s-infrastructure.
38. Falliere, N., Murchu, L. O., & Chien, E. (2011). *W32. Stuxnet dossier.* White Paper, Symantec Corp., Security Response, White Pape 5(6), 29.
39. Farwell, J. P., & Rohozinski, R. (2011). Stuxnet and the future of cyber war. *Survival*, *53*(1), 23–40.
40. Amini, S., Pasqualetti, F., & Mohsenian-Rad, H. (2016). Dynamic load altering attacks against power system stability: Attack models and protection schemes. *IEEE Transactions on Smart Grid*, *9*(4), 2862–2872.
41. Dabrowski, A., Ullrich, J., & Weippl, E. (2017). *Grid Shock: Coordinated Load-Change Attacks on Power Grids.* In *Proceedings of the 33rd annual computer security applications conference (ACSAC)*, Orlando, FL, USA.
42. Symantec Security Response (2014). Dragonfly: Cyberespionage attacks against energy suppliers. *Rapp TEC*, *7*.
43. Ligh, M., Adair, S., Hartstein, B., & Richard, M. (2010). *Malware analyst's cookbook and DVD: Tools and techniques for fighting malicious code.* Wiley Publishing.
44. Andress, J. (2014). *The basics of information security: Understanding the fundamentals of InfoSec in theory and practice.* Syngress.
45. Petermann, T., Bradke, H., Lüllmann, A., Poetzsch, M., & Riehm, U. (2014). *What happens during a blackout: Consequences of a prolonged and wide-ranging power outage.* BoD.
46. Knight, U. G. (2001). *Power systems in emergencies: From contingency planning to crisis management.* Wiley
47. Google (n.d.). Reliability. Available online: https://support.google.com/googlecloud/answer/6056635.
48. Wang, J., Wang, X., & Wu, Y. (2005). Operating reserve model in the power market. *IEEE Transactions on Power Systems*, *20*(1), 223–229.
49. ENTSO-E. Operation Handbook. Available online: https://www.ucte.org/resources/publications/ophandbook/.
50. Kenyon, R., Maguire, J., Present, E., Christensen, D., & Hodge, B. M. (2021). Bulk electric power system risks from coordinated edge devices. *IEEE Open Access Journal of Power and Energy*, *8*, 35–44.
51. Dahlmanns, M., Lohmöller, J., Fink, I. B., Pennekamp, J., Wehrle, K., & Henze, M. (2020, October). Easing the conscience with OPC UA: An internet-wide study on insecure deployments. In *Proceedings of the ACM internet measurement conference* (pp. 101–110).
52. U.S. Department of Energy. (2007). An Assessment of Copper Wire Thefts from Electric Utilities. Office of Electricity Delivery and Energy Reliability. Available online: https://www.oe.netl.doe.gov/docs/copper042707.pdf.
53. ICS-CERT (2012). Malware Infections in the Control Environment. ICS-CERT Monitor Newsletter ICS-MM201212. https://us-cert.cisa.gov/ics/monitors/ICS-MM201212
54. Henze, M., Matzutt, R., Hiller, J., Mühmer, E., Ziegeldorf, J. H., Van Der Giet, J., & Wehrle, K. (2017, April). Practical data compliance for cloud storage. In *2017 IEEE international conference on cloud engineering (IC2E)* (pp. 252–258). IEEE.
55. Henze, M., Matzutt, R., Hiller, J., Mühmer, E., Ziegeldorf, J. H., van der Giet, J., & Wehrle, K. (2020). Complying with data handling requirements in cloud storage systems. *IEEE Transactions on Cloud Computing*, *10*(3), 1661–1674.
56. Kruglov, K., & Goncharov, E. (2018). Threats posed by using RATs in ICS. Available online: https://securelist.com/threats-posed-by-using-rats-in-ics/88011/.
57. ICS-CERT (2014). Internet Accessible Control Systems at Risk. ICS-CERT Monitor Newsletter ICS-MM201404. Available online: https://www.cisa.gov/sites/default/files/publications/ICS-CERT_Monitor_April-2014_S508C.pdf

58. Lynn, W. F. III (2010). Defending a new domain-the Pentagon's cyberstrategy. *Foreign Affairs*, *89*, 97.
59. Hannan, N. (2018). An assessment of supply-chain cyber resilience for the international space station. *The RUSI Journal*, *163*(2), 28–32.
60. Cardenas, D. J. S., Hahn, A., & Liu, C. C. (2020). Assessing cyber-physical risks of IoT-based energy devices in grid operations. *IEEE Access*, *8*, 61161–61173.
61. Pudjianto, D., Ramsay, C., & Strbac, G. (2007). Virtual power plant and system integration of distributed energy resources. *IET Renewable Power Generation*, *1*(1), 10–16.
62. Rossow, C., Andriesse, D., Werner, T., Stone-Gross, B., Plohmann, D., Dietrich, C. J., & Bos, H. (2013, May). SoK: P2PWNED-modeling and evaluating the resilience of peer-to-peer botnets. In *2013 IEEE symposium on security and privacy* (pp. 97–111). IEEE.
63. Asghari, H., Ciere, M., & Van Eeten, M. J. (2015). Post-mortem of a Zombie: Conficker cleanup after six years. In *24th USENIX security symposium (USENIX Security 15)* (pp. 1–16).
64. Herwig, S., Harvey, K., Hughey, G., Roberts, R., & Levin, D. (2019, January). Measurement and analysis of Hajime, a peer-to-peer IoT botnet. In *Network and distributed systems security (NDSS) symposium*.
65. Falk, R., & Fries, S. (2012). Electric vehicle charging infrastructure security considerations and approaches. *Proceedings of INTERNET*, 58–64.
66. Yahya, O., Alrikabi, H., & Aljazaery, I. (2020). Reducing the data rate in internet of things applications by using wireless sensor network.
67. Irons, A., & Lallie, H. S. (2014). Digital forensics to intelligent forensics. *Future Internet*, *6*(3), 584–596.
68. Muda, A. K., Choo, Y. H., Abraham, A., & Srihari, S. N. (Eds.). ((2014). *Computational intelligence in digital forensics: Forensic investigation and applications*. Springer International Publishing.
69. Adedayo, O. M. (2016, June). Big data and digital forensics. In *2016 IEEE international conference on cybercrime and computer forensic (ICCCF)* (pp. 1–7). IEEE.
70. Agrawal, S., & Agrawal, J. (2015). Survey on anomaly detection using data mining techniques. *Procedia Computer Science*, *60*, 708–713.
71. Ahmed, M., Mahmood, A. N., & Hu, J. (2016). A survey of network anomaly detection techniques. *Journal of Network and Computer Applications*, *60*, 19–31.
72. Al-Barazanchi, I., Abdulshaheed, H. R., & Sidek, M. S. B. (2019). Innovative technologies of wireless sensor network: The applications of WBAN system and environment. *Sustainable Engineering and Innovation*, *1*(2), 98–105.
73. Dezfouli, F., & Dehghantanha, A. (2014). Digital forensics trends and future. *International Journal of Cybersecurity and Digital Forensics (IJCSDF)*, *3*(4).
74. Lewis, J. A. (2002). *Assessing the risks of cyber terrorism, cyber war, and other cyber threats*. Center for Strategic and International Studies.
75. Lidén, G. (2020). Cybersecurity and data protection in the European Union: A critical perspective. *International Journal of Law and Information Technology*, *28*(3), 215–233.
76. McDougal, M. S., Lasswell, H. D., & Reisman, W. M. (1980). The world constitutive process of authoritative decision. In *International law essays* (pp. 191–226). Brill.
77. Mitnick, K. D., & Simon, W. L. (2011). *The art of deception: Controlling the human element of security*. Wiley.
78. NIST. (2020). Framework for improving critical infrastructure cybersecurity (Version 1.1). National Institute of Standards and Technology. Available online: https://www.nist.gov/
79. Pérez, R. E., & Zeadally, S. (2021). Cybersecurity and critical infrastructure: Security, resilience, and defense. *International Journal of Critical Infrastructure Protection*, *33*, 100425.

2 Cybersecurity, Forensic Tools, and Risk Mitigation Techniques

Morad Rawashdeh and Qasem Abu Al-Haija

2.1 INTRODUCTION

Cybersecurity is essential in today's world. While Information and Communication Technology (ICT) provides tremendous opportunities for innovation and progress, it also exposes individuals, organizations, and societies to risks such as cyberattacks, cybercrimes, and cyber-warfare [1, 2]. Strong cybersecurity practices are vital to building trust in the digital world and protecting the systems, services, and data we increasingly depend on.

2.1.1 Cybersecurity as a Strategic Imperative for Modern Organizations

Cybersecurity has become integral to modern organizational strategy, supporting digital transformation and innovation efforts. Strong cybersecurity practices allow organizations to achieve their business goals and protect the interests of customers, stakeholders, and society. It provides a structured framework for managing cyber risks and ensuring compliance with ever-evolving regulatory requirements.

Cybersecurity should be viewed as a strategic imperative rather than a purely technical concern. Planning and decision-making must include cybersecurity considerations and confirming alliance with the organization's vision, mission, and core values. Prioritizing business initiatives such as digital transformation, improved customer experience, or innovative new product development requires implementing parallel cybersecurity measures to protect assets and capabilities and support desired business outcomes.

2.1.2 Historical Evolution of Cybersecurity

We can broadly classify the evolution of cybersecurity into four distinct phases, each characterized by major shifts in ICT development and the corresponding transformation of the cyber environment:

2.1.2.1 Phase One (1940s and 1950s): The Dawn of the Digital Age

The invention of large-scale electronic computers, such as the ENIAC (illustrated in Figure 2.1) and EDVAC were built on vacuum tube technologies and used primarily

DOI: 10.1201/9781003497868-2

FIGURE 2.1 ENIAC computer.

for scientific and military calculations [2]. These systems represent an emerging and relatively isolated electronic environment. Concerns have mostly centered around physical security and preventing unauthorized access to computing systems. Early hacking cases were often driven by curiosity within academia rather than malicious intent [3].

2.1.2.2 Phase Two (1960s and 1970s): Expansion and Interconnection

The development of transistor-based computers [4], such as the IBM System/360 series [5], shifted toward smaller, more powerful, and commercially viable systems (illustrated in Figure 2.2). Computing has expanded to include industrial and commercial applications, resulting in a growth in the size and interconnectedness of the cyber environment. Concerns have shifted toward data security and protecting sensitive information stored within these systems. AC mechanisms and basic encryption techniques are beginning to emerge. During this period, cybersecurity begins to consolidate as a distinct discipline.

2.1.2.3 Phase Three (1980s and 1990s): Personal Computing and the Internet

The advent of integrated circuits and microprocessors ushered in the era of personal computers and desktop computing [6]. Significantly, the birth of the internet fundamentally reshaped the cyber landscape, enabling widespread communication and exchange of information globally.

FIGURE 2.2 IBM System360 series.

During this period, we have witnessed an explosion in the number and complexity of cyber threats. Malware, viruses, and network-based attacks have become increasingly prevalent, increasing public awareness of cybersecurity risks. In response, innovative defense technologies, such as antivirus software and firewalls, have been developed.

2.1.2.4 Phase Four (21st Century to Present): Excessive Communication

The cyber environment has become defined by ubiquitous computing and the widespread adoption of mobile devices, IoT, cloud computing, and AI [7]. Cybersecurity becomes deeply intertwined with national security, economic competitiveness, and personal privacy issues.

The history of cybersecurity has been one of constant adaptation in the face of relentless technological innovation and a changing threat landscape. New technologies will inevitably create unique vulnerabilities and expand the attack surface, requiring continuous evolution in cybersecurity practices and solutions.

2.1.3 Overview of the Current Cyber Threat Landscape

Contemporary cyber threats represent a dynamic and multifaceted challenge. The rapid pace of technological innovation and threat actors' increasing sophistication and resources create a constantly evolving environment where organizations must remain vigilant to protect their systems, data, and operations. This section overviews the prevailing cyberattack types, origins, and emerging trends shaping the current threat landscape.

Dominant Attack Types

1. **Ransomware:** This malware encrypts the victim's files or systems, making them inaccessible until the ransom is paid. Ransomware has become a highly profitable and destructive threat, with attackers using advanced methods such as "double extortion" (where data is encrypted and exfiltrated, increasing stress on the victim). A 2023 PwC report indicated that 64% of CIOs and IT managers surveyed expect a rise in reportable ransomware incidents [8]. Expanding the targets to include critical infrastructure sectors, such as healthcare and education, is particularly worrying.
2. **Software Supply-Chain Attacks:** Exploit software development and distribution vulnerabilities, putting widely used applications or services at risk. Its ability to have a far-reaching impact across many organizations makes it particularly malicious. CrowdStrike's 2021 Global Threat Report noted a 430% increase in supply-chain attacks in 2020 [9], highlighting the increasing severity of this threat.
3. **Cloud Breaches:** Widespread adoption of cloud services offers many advantages and exposes organizations to risks associated with misconfigurations or vulnerabilities within cloud environments. Tenable's 2021 Threat Landscape Retrospective reported a 78% increase in cloud data breaches during 2020 [10]. Attackers leverage various techniques, including brute force attacks, phishing campaigns, and exploiting vulnerabilities in cloud APIs to access cloud-based systems and data.
4. **Threat Actor Profiles:** The term "cyber adversary" includes a wide range of actors with different motivations, capabilities, and resources:
   - **Nation States:** Government-supported or affiliated actors that engage in cyber operations to achieve political, military, or economic goals. These groups often have advanced capabilities and significant resources, enabling them to carry out complex and ongoing campaigns. Some researchers stated an increase in cyberattacks due to nation-state actors [11], focusing on targets within government, critical infrastructure, and strategic industries such as healthcare.
   - **Cybercrime Actors:** Financially motivated cybercriminals engaging in various attacks, including extortion, data theft, and fraud. This category is particularly prolific due to its relatively low barriers to entry and the potential for significant profits. CrowdStrike's 2021 Global Threat Report indicates that cybercrime actors targeted retail, banking, and education industries [12].
   - **Hackers:** individuals or groups motivated by ideological or social reasons who conduct cyberattacks to disrupt operations, make statements, or draw attention to their targets. Although generally less sophisticated than other threat actors, hacking attacks can cause significant disruption.

The Main Trends Shaping the Landscape

1. **The Role of AI:** Cyber attackers and defenders increasingly use AI techniques.[13]. Adversaries leverage AI to automate tasks, enhance attack effectiveness, and evade detection [14]. Conversely, AI-powered tools are

integrated into defensive strategies to strengthen threat detection, response capabilities, and risk analysis.

2. **Focus on Cloud Environments:** The accelerating move to cloud services and infrastructure creates new attack vectors and potential vulnerabilities [15]. Organizations must consider security implications when adopting cloud technologies, ensuring proper configuration, ACs, and ongoing monitoring.
3. **Collaboration Between Adversaries:** Increased cooperation and resource sharing between threat actors [16], including nation-states and cybercriminal groups, amplifies the potential impact of attacks and fuels the rapid evolution of their tactics and tools.

The cyber threat landscape is a dynamic and complex environment that poses significant risks to individuals, organizations, and society.

2.1.4 Emerging Technologies and Cybersecurity Challenges

Cloud Computing: While cloud providers invest heavily in security, adopting cloud services inevitably expands an organization's attack surface. Threat actors can exploit misconfigurations, inadequate ACs, and vulnerabilities within the shared infrastructure of cloud environments. The shared responsibility model for security in the cloud can also lead to ambiguity regarding the precise roles and responsibilities of the cloud provider and the organization using its services.

Big Data (BD): Collecting, storing, and analyzing large data sets provide powerful insights for cybersecurity operations. BD analytics can reveal patterns, anomalies, and potential threats, enabling proactive defense strategies [17]. However, BD's sheer volume and complexity create challenges for data protection, privacy compliance, and secure management of sensitive information throughout its lifecycle.

Blockchain: Thanks to its decentralized architecture and cryptographic mechanisms, blockchain technology promises to enhance data integrity, transparency, and trust in digital transactions. While blockchain technology is designed to be highly tamper-resistant, its implementation in real-world applications can introduce new vulnerabilities. Smart contracts, the self-executing programs that govern transactions on blockchain networks, are vulnerable to coding errors or logic flaws that attackers can exploit [18]. Additionally, blockchain systems may face scalability limitations and be susceptible to consensus-based attacks, such as "51% attacks," where a malicious actor gains control of most of a network's computing power [19–21].

2.2 THE ROLE OF FORENSICS IN CYBERSECURITY

Digital forensics faces many challenges unique to the nature of digital evidence [22]:

- **Data Volatility:** Digital evidence can easily be modified, overwritten, or deleted, making it essential to preserve potential evidence promptly and using established forensic methodologies.

- **Complexity of Systems:** The increasing complexity of computer systems and networks and the increasing use of encryption and obfuscation techniques can hinder forensic analysis.
- **Legal and Regulatory Considerations:** Digital forensics practitioners must be familiar with relevant laws, regulations, and privacy considerations to ensure evidence is collected and handled legally and ethically. Cross-border investigations or involving cloud-based systems can create additional legal complexities.

2.2.1 Definition, Purpose, and Evolution of Forensic Tools

Forensic tools include specialized software and hardware solutions to facilitate digital evidence identification, collection, preservation, analysis, and reporting. Digital evidence refers to any information stored or transmitted in a digital format that has the potential to support or refute a hypothesis during legal or investigative proceedings. Forensic tools play a critical role in DIs, helping forensic professionals maintain the integrity of evidence, extract insights from complex systems, and reconstruct events for IR and legal purposes.

Purpose of Forensic Tools: Digital forensic tools serve several key purposes in the context of cybersecurity and broader investigations:

- **Data Acquisition:** Capture potential evidence from a wide range of sources, including computer hard drives, mobile devices, network logs, and cloud storage, in a forensically sound manner that maintains integrity.
- **Data Recovery:** Recover deleted files, extract data from damaged or corrupted storage devices, and decrypt encrypted information to reveal potential evidence.
- **Analysis:** Using various techniques to examine digital evidence and identify patterns, anomalies, and potential indicators of compromise (IoC).
- **Reporting:** Create comprehensive reports that document the findings of a criminal investigation in a clear, concise, and legally defensible manner.

Development of Forensic Tools: Forensic tools have been closely linked to the development of information and communications technology (ICT). We can broadly classify this development into four phases, corresponding to major shifts in the ICT landscape:

- **Phase One (From the 1940s to the 1950s): The dawn of digital computing**
  - Limited digital evidence, primarily limited to early large-scale computing systems.
  - Rudimentary or non-existent forensic tools dedicated to digital evidence.
- **Phase Two (1960s and 1970s): Growth and interconnection**
  - The advent of transistor-based computers expanded the cyber environment.
  - Digital evidence has become more widespread, resulting in forensic tools emerging as a distinct discipline.

- **Phase Three (1980s and 1990s): Personal computing and the internet**
  - The widespread adoption of personal computers and the advent of the internet has greatly increased the volume and complexity of digital evidence.
  - This period saw rapid innovation and development of specialized forensic tools.
- **Phase Four (from the 21st century to the present): Advanced technologies**
  - Ubiquitous computing, cloud technologies, the IoT, and the widespread use of AI define the cyber environment.
  - Forensic tools continue to evolve, becoming increasingly sophisticated and specialized to meet the challenges of this complex digital landscape.

While the widespread application of forensic tools occurred in later stages, the crucial theoretical foundation was laid during the early stages of computing. Key historical examples include:

- **1949:** John von Neumann developed a theory of self-replicating computer programs [23], which provided a basis for understanding and analyzing computer viruses.
- **1978:** Parkerian Hexade identifies six key aspects of computer crime that remain relevant to modern digital forensics [24].

2.2.2 Types of Forensic Tools

Digital forensic tools are categorized according to the types of digital evidence designed to collect, process, and analyze. These tools equip investigators with specialized capabilities to support various investigative functions. This section provides an overview of common tool categories, including network forensics, disk forensics, and memory forensics, highlighting their unique contributions to cybercrime investigations.

A. **Network Forensic Tools:** Network forensic tools capture, monitor, and analyze network traffic data. They are invaluable for investigating cyber incidents such as network intrusions, denial-of-service (DoS/DDoS) attacks, and other malicious activity. Network forensic tools generally fall into two subcategories:
   - **Passive Tools:** These tools observe and record network traffic without introducing any modifications to the data flow. Examples include protocol analyzers, network IDS, and network event logging systems.
   - **Active Tools:** These tools interact directly with network traffic, potentially altering or injecting data packets. Examples include network vulnerability scanners, port scanners, and traffic generators.

B. **Disk Forensic Tools:** Disk forensic tools focus on acquiring, preserving, and analyzing data stored on physical storage devices such as hard disk drives (HDDs), solid-state drives (SSDs), and other non-volatile storage media. These tools are essential for recovering deleted or damaged files, examining file system metadata, and analyzing user activity. There are two main subcategories of disk forensic tools:

- **Physical Tools:** These tools interface directly with storage devices at the hardware level. Examples include disk imaging tools, write blockers (which prevent accidental modification of evidence), and hardware-based data recovery solutions.
- **Logical Tools:** These tools interact with storage devices through software interfaces, operating at the file system level. Examples include file viewers, data carving tools, and file recovery software.

C. **Memory Forensic Tools:** Memory forensic tools analyze volatile data stored in random access memory (RAM), system caches, and other temporary storage areas. This data is crucial for investigating malware infections, rootkits, and other attacks that may not leave persistent traces on non-volatile storage [25]. Memory forensic tools generally fall into two subcategories:

- **Live Acquisition Tools:** These tools analyze the memory contents while running the system. Examples include memory dump utilities, process analysis tools, and malware scanners.
- **Postmortem Acquisition Tools:** These tools capture the contents of memory after a system has been shut down or powered off. Examples include memory imagers and offline memory analysis frameworks.

D. **Additional Forensic Tool Categories:** Beyond the core categories discussed above, a wide range of specialized digital forensic tools exist to support investigations involving specific types of digital evidence. These include:

- **Mobile Device Forensics Tools:** Designed to extract and analyze data from smartphones, tablets, and other mobile devices.
- **Database Forensics Tools:** Specialized tools for examining relational databases, recovering deleted records, and analyzing database activity logs.
- **Cloud Forensics Tools:** Tools and methodologies adapted to the unique challenges of investigating incidents in cloud computing environments.
- **Malware Analysis Tools:** These are tools for reverse engineering malware executables, analyzing code, and identifying behavioral patterns.

2.2.3 Real-World Applications of Digital Forensic Tools

Digital forensic tools play a critical role in addressing the challenges of the modern cybersecurity landscape. They provide the means to investigate cyber incidents, protect sensitive assets, and support legal proceedings. Forensic tools have diverse applications across law enforcement, corporate environments, and individual use cases.

1. **Law Enforcement and Criminal Investigations:** Digital forensics is essential to modern law enforcement and criminal justice [26]. Forensic tools and

methodologies empower investigators to collect, preserve, and analyze digital evidence on a wide range of cybercrimes, including:

- **Fraud and Identity Theft:** Forensic tools assist in investigating fraudulent financial transactions, misusing personally identifiable information (PII), and creating counterfeit identities.
- **Intellectual Property Theft:** Protecting intellectual property frequently necessitates forensic analysis of compromised systems and networks to identify unauthorized access, exfiltration of trade secrets, and distribution of copyrighted or patented materials.
- **Cyberstalking and Harassment:** Forensic techniques can aid in tracing the source of online harassment, collecting evidence from social media platforms, emails, and messaging services, and analyzing data from the victim's and perpetrator's devices.
- **Child Exploitation:** Specialized forensic tools and investigative protocols are crucial for combating online child exploitation, recovering deleted or hidden evidence from digital devices, and tracking the activities of perpetrators within online networks.

  Law enforcement agencies and forensic practitioners utilize a variety of tools, including:

- **Comprehensive Forensic Suites:** Solutions such as ***OpenText EnCase Forensic*** [27], ***FTK (Forensic Toolkit)*** [28], and ***Axiom*** [29] provide various capabilities, including disk and memory imaging, data recovery, timeline analysis, and mobile device forensics.
- **Specialized Tools:** Tools like ***Cellebrite*** (mobile device forensics) [30], ***Wireshark*** (network packet analysis) [31], ***Volatility*** (memory forensics) [32], and ***Oxygen Forensic Detective*** (multi-platform data extraction) [33] are tailored to specific investigative needs.

2. **Corporate Cybersecurity Applications:** Within the corporate sector, digital forensic tools play a vital role in safeguarding sensitive data, maintaining operational continuity, and complying with regulatory requirements. Key applications include:
   - **IR:** In the aftermath of a cyberattack or data breach, forensic tools and techniques are crucial for determining the scope of the incident, identifying the root cause, understanding attacker methodologies, and gathering evidence to inform remediation strategies.
   - **Network Monitoring and Intrusion Detection:** Network forensic tools facilitate the analysis of network traffic patterns and protocols. They enable the detection of anomalies, potential attack signatures, and IoC that may signal malicious activity. Tools like ***Wireshark***, ***Snort*** [34], and ***Security Onion*** [35] are widely used.
   - **Data Recovery and Restoration:** In the event of data loss, corruption, or ransomware attacks, forensic tools can be instrumental in recovering deleted files, extracting data from damaged or inaccessible storage devices, and decrypting data held for ransom.
   - **Regulatory Compliance:** Many industries are subject to stringent data privacy and security regulations, such as ***HIPAA*** (healthcare), ***PCI DSS***

(payment card industry), and ***GDPR*** (European Union). Forensic tools and methodologies assist organizations in demonstrating compliance by providing detailed logs of security events, user activity, and system configuration changes.

2.2.4 Forensic Tool Evaluation and Selection

The selection of appropriate digital forensic tools is critical in determining the success of investigations and the quality of the evidence obtained. A systematic approach to tool evaluation and selection is essential to ensure that chosen tools align with the specific requirements of the investigative scenario. This process generally involves the following key steps:

1. Define Investigative Objectives and Requirements

- **Scope of the Investigation:** Clearly articulate the goals of the investigation, specifying the types of cyber incidents, potential perpetrators, and the legal or regulatory context within which the investigation is conducted.
- **Types of Digital Evidence:** Identify the anticipated types of evidence that will need to be collected, preserved, and analyzed. Consider potential sources of evidence, such as computers, mobile devices, cloud storage, network infrastructure, and IoT devices.
- **Technical and Legal Constraints:** Consider any technical limitations (e.g., available hardware, file system compatibility, network protocols) and legal or ethical considerations relevant to the acquisition and analysis of digital evidence.

2.3 KEY ELEMENTS OF IR PLANNING (IRP)

The IBM Cost of a Data Breach 2022 report highlights that organizations with routinely exercised IR schemes experienced an average data breach cost reduction of USD 4.45 million. This represents a 2.3% increase from the 2022 cost of USD 4.35 million. Taking a long-term view, the average cost has increased by 15.3% from USD 3.86 million in the 2020 report [36].

Key Elements of IR Planning

- **Scope and Objectives:** Clearly define the types of cyber incidents covered by the plan (e.g., malware infections, data breaches, DoS attacks), the overarching goals of IR efforts, and any applicable legal or regulatory requirements.
- **Roles and Responsibilities:** Specify the roles and responsibilities of the IR team and other involved individuals, such as the IR coordinator, cybersecurity analyst, information technology specialist, legal advisor, communications officer, and executive leadership. Include contact information for each role and establish communication protocols and escalation procedures.

2.3.1 IR Frameworks

- **NIST:** CSF and its associated publications, such as NIST Special Publication 800-61 Revision 2 [37], provide comprehensive guidance on IR.
- **ISO:** ISO/IEC 27000 series standards, including ISO/IEC 27035 [38], offer detailed guidance on information security incident management, covering principles, processes, and specific incident handling procedures.
- **SANS Institute:** The SANS Institute, a leading provider of cybersecurity training and resources, has developed a widely respected IR framework [39].

Key Differences: While these frameworks share many core concepts, there are subtle differences in their structure, emphasis, and level of detail (Table 2.1 contrasts the major IR frameworks):

- **Scope:** Both NIST and SANS frameworks focus primarily on technical aspects of IR. ISO/IEC 27035 takes a broader view, encompassing organizational, procedural, and human factors in incident management.
- **Process Detail:** ISO/IEC 27035 offers the most granular guidance on specific incident handling processes and techniques.

TABLE 2.1
Comparison of IR Frameworks

Feature	NIST (SP 800-61 Rev. 2)	SANS	ISO/IEC 27035
Scope	Technical focus on IR	Specialized focus on IR	Broader scope, including organizational and procedural aspects
Phases	Preparation Detection and Analysis Containment, Eradication, and Recovery Post-Incident Activity	Preparation Identification Containment Eradication Recovery Lessons learned	Principles Processes Techniques
Process Detail	Moderate	Moderate	High-granular guidance on specific processes and techniques
Evidence Handling	Emphasized in the Detection and Analysis phase	Focus on preservation in the Recovery phase	Detailed emphasis throughout the response process
Strengths	Adaptable, well-aligned with NIST CSF	Practical focus, well-known in the industry	Comprehensive, aligned with broader ISO/IEC 27000 standards
Considerations	It may require customization for specific needs	May lack detail for complex compliance requirements	It can be more prescriptive, potentially less flexible

- **Evidence Handling:** The NIST framework emphasizes evidence collection throughout the detection and analysis phase. The SANS framework incorporates evidence preservation within the recovery phase, while ISO/IEC 27035 provides detailed guidance on evidence collection and handling throughout the IR process.

2.3.2 Digital Investigations: Process and Techniques

Digital forensic investigations are essential for understanding the complexities of modern cyberattacks, attributing them to their perpetrators, and supporting legal or disciplinary actions. These investigations involve the systematic identification, collection, preservation, analysis, and interpretation of digital evidence to reconstruct the events surrounding a cyber incident. Digital evidence can be gleaned from many sources, including traditional computers, mobile devices, embedded systems, cloud environments, and the ever-expanding network of IoT devices.

Key Phases of a Digital Forensic Investigation: The digital forensic investigative process generally adheres to the core phases in Figure 2.3.

Identification and Collection: The initial phase focuses on identifying potential sources of digital evidence and acquiring that evidence forensically soundly. This may involve:

- **Seizure of Physical Devices:** Securing computers, servers, smartphones, external storage media, embedded systems, or other devices containing relevant data.
- **Network Data Capture:** Intercepting and recording network traffic that may contain evidence of malicious activity, potentially utilizing network taps or specialized network monitoring tools.
- **Cloud Forensics:** Employing specialized methods to collect and analyze data from cloud environments, navigating the complexities of remote access, multi-tenant architectures, and diverse cloud service models (IaaS, PaaS, SaaS).

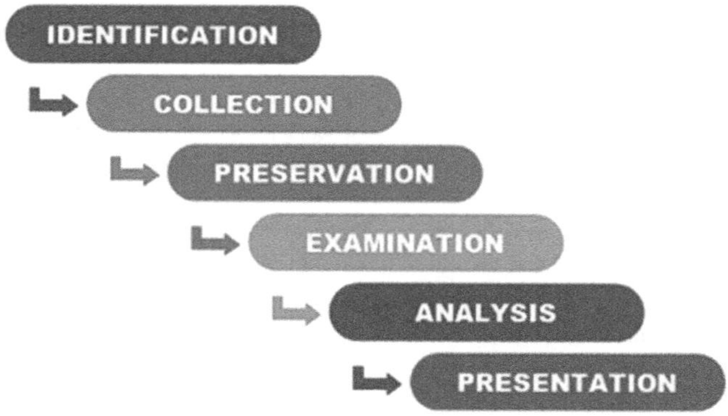

FIGURE 2.3 Digital forensic investigation phases.

Analysis: Techniques may include:

- **Log File Analysis**: Inspection of system logs, application logs, and network security logs for IoCs.
- **Network Traffic Analysis**: Employing tools like Wireshark and NetworkMiner to identify malicious patterns, command-and-control (C2C) communications, and data exfiltration.
- **Memory Forensics**: Analyzing volatile memory (RAM) using tools like Volatility for evidence of malware infections, rootkits, and other attacks that may leave few traces on non-volatile storage.
- **Malware Reverse Engineering**: Disassembling and analyzing malicious code (within legal and ethical bounds) to understand its functionality, potential targets, and authorship clues.

Reporting: Findings are compiled into a comprehensive report documenting the investigative process, analyzed evidence, and the conclusions drawn. The report should be written in a manner understandable to both technical and non-technical audiences and admissible as evidence in court.

Tools and Techniques: Digital forensic investigators rely on a variety of specialized tools and techniques, including:

- **Forensic Software Suites:** Integrated tools like ***EnCase***, ***Forensic Toolkit (FTK)***, and ***Axiom*** provide a range of capabilities for disk imaging, data recovery, memory analysis, and mobile device forensics.
- **Network Forensic Tools:** Tools like ***Wireshark***, ***NetworkMiner*** [40], and ***Snort*** are used for packet analysis, intrusion detection, and the investigation of network-based attacks.
- **Memory Analysis Tools:** Frameworks like ***Volatility*** and ***Rekall*** [41] allow investigators to examine volatile memory (RAM) for evidence of malware infections, rootkits, and other malicious activity that may not leave traces on persistent storage.

2.3.3 Evidence Management, Analysis, and Presentation

a. **Evidence Management**

- **Chain of Custody:** This involves documenting the following for each interaction with the evidence:
  - The individual who handled the evidence.
  - Date and time of transfer.
  - Location where the evidence was handled.
  - Reason for handling the evidence.
  - Any changes made to the evidence, along with justification.
- **Secure Storage:** Digital evidence must be stored in a secure environment that prevents unauthorized access, modification, or damage. This may involve:
  - **Physical Security:** Controlled access to evidence storage facilities, locked cabinets or safes, and security cameras.
  - **Technical Controls:** Encryption of sensitive data (both at rest and in transit), robust AC mechanisms, and logging of access attempts.

- **Evidence Tracking:** A comprehensive evidence tracking system should be in place to maintain a clear audit trail. This system should record:
  - Unique identifiers for each item of evidence.
  - The movement and handling of evidence throughout its lifecycle.
  - Details of any analyses performed on the evidence.

b. **Analysis**
- **Forensic Examination:** Forensic analysts employ specialized tools and techniques to examine digital evidence in a non-destructive manner that preserves its integrity. Key goals include:
  - Recovering deleted or hidden files.
  - Extracting metadata (e.g., timestamps, geolocation data)
  - Analyzing system logs and network traffic.
  - Reverse engineering malware to understand its capabilities.
- **Cross-Validation:** Forensic analysts should seek to corroborate evidence from multiple sources whenever possible to increase confidence in findings. This may involve comparing data from different devices, analyzing network traffic patterns, or correlating digital evidence with physical evidence collected from the crime scene.
- **Documentation:** Thorough documentation of all analytical procedures is essential. This documentation should include:
  - The specific tools and techniques used.
  - A detailed description of the analysis process.
  - The results obtained and the rationale behind the analyst's conclusions.

c. **Presentation:** Forensic findings must be presented in a well-organized, understandable report to technical and non-technical audiences.

2.4 ANTI-FORENSIC COUNTERMEASURES

The field of digital forensics is engaged in an ongoing arms race against anti-forensics. Researchers and practitioners constantly develop new techniques and tools to detect and counteract anti-forensic measures. Key countermeasures include:

- **Live System Forensics:** Analyzing volatile data (e.g., running processes, network connections) that may offer clues about anti-forensic tools or hidden data.
- **Advanced File Carving:** Developing techniques to recover deleted files or fragments of data, even when overwritten or partially damaged.
- **Anti-Anti-Forensics:** Creating tools specifically designed to detect and neutralize the effects of common anti-forensic techniques.

2.4.1 Data Destruction and Overwriting

Data destruction and overwriting are fundamental anti-forensic techniques designed to prevent the recovery of deleted data [42]. These techniques make information permanently inaccessible, hindering forensic investigations and potentially allowing cybercriminals to cover their tracks. This section explores these techniques' methods, tools, and limitations.

Common Data Destruction Techniques

- **Physical Destruction:** The most definitive data destruction method is the physical destruction of the storage medium itself. This includes:
  - **Shredding:** Reducing hard drives, SSDs, tapes, or other media into small fragments.
  - **Incineration:** Destroying storage devices through burning.
  - **Pulverizing:** Grinding storage media into fine particles.
- **Degaussing:** Degaussing involves exposing magnetic storage media (e.g., HDDs, tapes) to a powerful magnetic field. This disrupts the magnetic patterns that represent data, rendering it unreadable. It's important to note that degaussing is generally ineffective on SSDs due to their non-magnetic storage mechanisms.
- **Overwriting:** Overwriting involves replacing existing data with new data, typically patterns of random characters or zeros. This can be achieved using:
  - **Specialized Software:** Tools like DBAN (Darik's Boot and Nuke) [43] erasers are designed to overwrite entire disks or partitions, often using multiple passes to increase the thoroughness of erasure.
  - **Built-in Secure Erase Commands:** Many modern hard drives and SSDs support firmware-level commands that trigger a comprehensive internal overwrite process. These commands can be more effective than software-based overwriting, as they can access areas of the device that are not normally accessible to the operating system (e.g., bad sectors, wear-leveling blocks).
  - **File Shredders:** These tools target individual files, overwriting their contents and often renaming them to obscure the original filename.

Challenges and Limitations

- **Incomplete Physical Destruction:** If physical destruction is not performed thoroughly, it may be possible to recover data from fragments of storage media. Specialized forensic techniques can sometimes reassemble shredded documents or extract data from partially damaged devices.
- **Degaussing Limitations:** The effectiveness of degaussing can vary depending on the strength of the degausser and the type of storage media. Degaussing may not be fully effective on modern high-density hard drives or SSDs.

2.4.2 Minimizing Digital Footprint

A central tenet of anti-forensics is the proactive reduction of the volume and discoverability of digital evidence. This can be achieved through various techniques that limit data persistence or obscure its existence, hindering forensic analysis and making it more difficult to trace an individual's actions within the cyber domain.

Techniques for Minimizing Digital Traces

- **In-Memory Execution:** Modern malware increasingly employs "***fileless***" techniques [44]. This involves injecting malicious code directly into the memory of a running process (e.g., through reflective DLL injection or process hollowing). This tactic allows malware to operate without creating artifacts on the file system that might be detected by traditional antivirus software.
- **Exploiting Volatile Storage:** Volatile memory (RAM) loses its contents when a device is powered off. By executing code and storing data primarily within RAM, adversaries can limit the amount of recoverable evidence that persists on hard drives or SSDs. However, forensic investigators can often extract valuable evidence from memory dumps or page files.
- **Cleaning Utilities:** Specialized tools exist to securely erase browser history, temporary files, system logs, and other potentially incriminating artifacts. Some of these tools support automation to reduce the risk of human error in performing cleanup tasks.
- **Anti-Forensic File Systems:** Certain file systems incorporate specific features that impede forensic analysis. These features may include:
  - **Default Encryption:** Encrypting files automatically, making recovery more difficult if the encryption key is not obtained.
  - **Limited Metadata:** Storing minimal file metadata (e.g., creation times, access times, file owners), obscuring potential clues about file usage.
  - **Self-Destruction Triggers:** Configuring data to be automatically deleted or overwritten upon meeting specific conditions (e.g., after a set number of accesses or a predefined time).
- **Obfuscation:** The use of packers, crypts, and other techniques to disguise the true nature of executable files. Obfuscation aims to hinder reverse engineering efforts, requiring investigators to invest additional time and specialized tools to analyze the malware.
- **The Importance of Live Analysis:** In-memory execution and the use of volatile storage emphasize the need for live system forensics, focusing on analyzing running processes, network connections, and other temporary data that may not be preserved on persistent storage.
- **Advanced-Data Recovery:** Erased files, overwritten data, and encrypted volumes may require specialized data carving tools, file system analysis, and cryptographic techniques to recover evidence.

2.4.3 Artifact Wiping

- **Protecting Sensitive Data:** Ensuring that confidential information or PII cannot be recovered after deletion, safeguarding privacy, and preventing data breaches.
- **Thwarting Forensic Investigations:** Obscuring evidence of illegal or unauthorized activities.
- **Secure Decommissioning of Storage Devices:** Ensuring no residual data can be recovered from storage media before disposal, resale, or repurposing.

2.5 RA AND THREAT MODELING

RA is the cornerstone of effective risk management. Key components include:

- **Asset Identification:** Generating a thorough portfolio of the organization's critical information assets, including:
  - **Systems:** Servers, workstations, network devices, cloud-based infrastructure.
  - **Data:** Customer data, intellectual property, trade secrets, financial records, etc.
  - **Software:** Operating systems, applications, custom-developed software.
- **Threat Identification:** Building profiles of potential adversaries and their motivations, including:
  - **External Threats:** Cybercriminals, nation-state actors, hacktivists, and competitors.
  - **Internal Threats:** Disgruntled employees, careless users, malicious insiders.
- **Vulnerability Assessment:** Proactively identifying weaknesses that could be exploited, including:
  - **Technical Vulnerabilities:** Unpatched software, misconfigurations, inadequate ACs.
  - **Operational Vulnerabilities:** Poor security policies, user awareness, and inadequate IR processes.
- **Risk Analysis:** Evaluating the impact of potential threats exploiting known vulnerabilities. Risk scoring may use qualitative (e.g., high, medium, low) or quantitative (e.g., estimated financial loss) methods.

RA is iterative, ensuring the security posture aligns with the evolving threat landscape.

Threat Modeling: Threat modeling complements RA by taking a proactive, attacker-centric approach. Key activities include:

- **System Modeling:** Developing models (e.g., data flow diagrams, attack trees) to represent systems, applications, data flows, trust boundaries, and potential attack surfaces.
- **Identifying Security Objectives:** Defining the CIA requirements for the assets in scope.
- **Attacker Profiling:** Analyzing the motivations, capabilities, and likely tactics, techniques, and procedures (TTPs) of potential adversaries.
- **Attack Vector Enumeration:** Identifying the methods attackers might use to compromise the system (e.g., malware, phishing, social engineering, supply-chain attacks).

Integrating RA and Threat Modeling: By combining RA and threat modeling, organizations gain a deeper understanding of their security posture, enabling:

- **Prioritization of Risks:** Focus mitigation efforts on the most critical threats.

- **Resource Allocation:** Informed decision-making about investments in security controls.
- **Cloud Security:** Specialized security measures tailored to protect cloud-based environments.

2.6 VULNERABILITY MANAGEMENT

Identifying Vulnerabilities: The vulnerability management process begins with comprehensively discovering potential weaknesses. Key tools and techniques include:

- **Vulnerability Scanners:** Automated software solutions designed to identify known vulnerabilities. Common types include:
  - **Network-Based Scanners:** Scan networks to identify misconfigured devices, open ports, and vulnerable services (e.g., ***Nessus***, ***OpenVAS***, ***Qualys***).
  - **Host-based Scanners:** Examine operating systems, applications, and configuration settings of individual systems for known vulnerabilities (e.g., ***Microsoft Baseline Security Analyzer***, ***Nikto***).
  - **Web Application Scanners:** Specialized tools that analyze the security of web applications, detecting common web vulnerabilities like SQL injection, cross-site scripting (XSS), and other OWASP Top 10 risks [45] (e.g., ***Acunetix***, ***Netsparker***).
  - **Container Security Scanners:** Tools designed to scan container images and registries for vulnerabilities (e.g., ***Clair***, ***Anchore***).
- **Penetration Testing:** Ethical hacking simulations that go beyond automated scanning to uncover exploitable weaknesses and regulate the security postures. Penetration testing often includes both external and internal network assessments, as well as targeted application testing.

Evaluating and Prioritizing Vulnerabilities: A risk-based approach is essential for prioritizing vulnerability remediation efforts. Factors influencing RA include:

- **Severity:** The potential impact of a successful exploit, typically using standardized metrics like the Common Vulnerability Scoring System (CVSS).
- **Ease of Exploitation:** The technical difficulty of exploiting the vulnerability and the availability of public exploits.
- **Prevalence:** The number of affected systems within the organization's environment.
- **Exposure:** The accessibility of the vulnerability from external networks or by internal users.
- **Remediation Complexity:** The effort and potential disruption in fixing the vulnerability.

Remediation Strategies: Remediation involves taking corrective actions to mitigate or eliminate vulnerabilities. Common strategies include:

- **Patch Management:** The process of applying software updates (patches) from vendors to address security vulnerabilities. Effective patch management requires a centralized inventory of software assets and a structured process for testing and deploying patches.
- **Configuration Changes:** Modifying system or application settings to harden them against attacks (e.g., turning off unnecessary services, implementing least privilege ACs).
- **Compensating Controls:** Implementing additional security measures (e.g., IDS/IPS, web application firewalls) to reduce risk when patching or configuration changes are not immediately feasible.
- **Vulnerability Mitigation:** Taking temporary or partial steps to decrease the impact of exploitation until a permanent fix can be implemented.
- **Risk Acceptance:** In some cases, an organization may formally accept the risk associated with a vulnerability after carefully considering the costs and benefits.

2.7 PATCH MANAGEMENT

- **Enhanced Security:** Applying patches promptly closes known vulnerabilities, significantly reducing an organization's attack surface and making it more difficult for attackers to compromise systems.
- **Improved Stability:** Software patches often address bugs, performance issues, and compatibility problems, leading to a more reliable and predictable computing environment.
- **Regulatory Compliance:** Many industry standards and regulations (e.g., PCI DSS, HIPAA, CSF) mandate timely patching systems that process sensitive data.

Challenges in Patch Management

- **Complexity:** Large organizations with diverse IT environments often face challenges managing and tracking patches across numerous systems and software versions.
- **Downtime:** Certain patches may necessitate system reboots or temporary service disruptions, potentially impacting business operations.

2.8 BUSINESS CONTINUITY (BC) AND DISASTER RECOVERY (DR)

A systematic process to identify the organization's most critical business processes, assess the potential financial, operational, and reputational consequences of disruption, and determine the maximum tolerable downtime (MTD) for each process.

- **Alternate Work Sites:** Pre-designated locations where operations can be resumed if the primary work site becomes inaccessible (e.g., hot sites, warm sites, cold sites).
- **Remote Work Policies:** Plans and technology infrastructure to enable employees to work remotely in the event of a disruption.

- **Crisis Management:** Protocols for decision-making, communication, and coordination with internal and external stakeholders during and after a crisis event.

The Role of Disaster Recovery: After a disruptive incident, DR focuses on restoring IT infrastructure, applications, and data. A robust DR plan includes:

- **Recovery Time Objective (RTO):** The target time within which critical IT systems and applications must be restored to support essential business functions.
- **Recovery Point Objective (RPO):** The maximum acceptable amount of data loss (measured in time) during a disruption. The RPO determines the frequency of backups.
- **Data Backup and Replication:** Implementing a data protection strategy based on the RTO and RPO. This includes selecting backup methods (full, incremental, differential), storage media (on-premise, off-site, cloud), and potentially real-time data replication.
- **Failover and Failback:** Detailed procedures for switching to redundant systems during a disaster and reverting to primary systems once the crisis has subsided.
- **Recovery Sites:** Provisioning alternate locations for restoring IT operations. Options include:
    - **Hot Site:** A fully equipped data center ready for immediate failover.
    - **Warm Site:** A partially equipped site that can be operational quickly.
    - **Cold Site:** A basic facility requiring hardware provisioning and setup before operations can resume.

Developing and Implementing a BC/DR Plan

- **Planning Committee:** Establish a cross-departmental team representing IT, business units, legal, risk management, and senior leadership.
- **Scope and Objectives:** Define the plan's parameters according to risk appetite and regulatory requirements.
- **Plan Development:** Involve subject matter experts to develop detailed strategies, procedures, and timelines for recovery, ensuring they align with the BIA and RA.
- **Implementation:** Deploy necessary technology solutions, establish recovery sites, and procure required resources by the plan.

Challenges in Business Continuity and Disaster Recovery

- **Complexity:** Developing and maintaining comprehensive BC/DR plans remarkably for big organizations with distinct functions.
- **Cost:** Implementing technologies like redundant systems, data replication, and alternate work sites can be costly.
- **Lack of Awareness:** Organizations may underestimate the importance of BC/DR or lack sufficient awareness of potential threats.
- **Change Management:** Ensuring BC/DR plans remain up-to-date and aligned with the evolving business environment presents an ongoing challenge.

2.9 CLOUD SECURITY

Cloud security is a specialized cybersecurity domain that safeguards data, applications, and the underlying infrastructure within cloud-based environments. This section investigates the complexities of securing cloud deployments, emphasizing the shared responsibility model, specific risk vectors, countermeasures, and future trajectories within cloud security.

Understanding Cloud Security: The distribution of security responsibilities varies based on the service model:

- **Infrastructure-as-a-Service (IaaS):** Provides the basic building blocks of IT infrastructure (compute, storage, network). Customers have the greatest control and, therefore, the most security responsibility.
- **Platform-as-a-Service (PaaS):** Offers a platform for application development and deployment. The CSP manages the underlying infrastructure and middleware while customers focus on securing their applications and data.
- **Software-as-a-Service (SaaS):** Delivers fully managed applications over the internet. While the CSP handles most security aspects, customers retain some responsibilities, particularly data security and user ACs.

Cloud Security Controls

- **Identity and Access Management (IAM):** Enforcing strict authentication for managing permissions in complex cloud environments.
- **Encryption:** Using robust techniques to protect data at rest (e.g., volume-level or file-level encryption) and in transit (e.g., with TLS).
- **Network Security:** Implementing virtual firewalls, segmentation, and IDS/IPS to protect cloud-based workloads and filter anomaly traffic.
- **Monitoring and Logging:** Continuous monitoring of cloud resources, applications, and user activity.
- **Vulnerability Management:** Proactive vulnerability scanning, penetration testing, and timely remediation of vulnerabilities in cloud infrastructure, operating systems, and applications.
- **IR:** Developing cloud-specific IR plans that include procedures for notifying the CSP, isolating affected resources, and conducting forensic investigations.

REFERENCES

1. N. Goyal and D. Goyal, "Cybercrime in the society: Security issues, preventions and challenges," Research Journal of Engineering and Technology, vol. 8, no. 2, pp. 73–80, 2017.
2. R. Prasad and V. Rohokale, Cybersecurity: The lifeline of information and communication technology, Springer, 2020.
3. B. J. Shelburne, "The ENIAC at 70," Math Horizons, vol. 24, no. 3, pp. 26–29, 2017.
4. A. Nathan, S. K. Saha and R. M. Todi, 75th anniversary of the transistor, John Wiley & Sons, 2023.

5. G. O'Regan, "The IBM System/360," in A brief history of computing, Springer, 2021, pp. 97–102.
6. M. F. Collen and C. A. Kulikowski, "The development of digital computers," The History of Medical Informatics in the United States, pp. 3–73, 2015.
7. G. Mastorakis, C. X. Mavromoustakis, J. M. Batalla and E. Pallis, Convergence of artificial intelligence and the internet of things, Springer, 2020.
8. S. Joyce and J. Nocera, The cyber-threat landscape: The digital rush left many exposed, PwC, 2021.
9. T.-M. Georgescu, "A study on how the pandemic changed the cybersecurity landscape," Informatica Economica, vol. 25, no. 1, 2021.
10. Tenable, "Tenable Research Reveals Over 40 Billion Records Were Exposed in 2021," January 2022. [Online]. Available: https://www.tenable.com/press-releases/tenable-research-reveals-over-40-billion-records-were-exposed-in-2021.
11. J. Kose, "Cyber warfare: An era of nation-state actors and global corporate espionage," ISSA Journal, vol. 19, no. 4, 2021.
12. K. D. Strang and N. R. Vajjhala, "Why cyberattacks disrupt society and how to mitigate risk," in Cybersecurity for decision makers, CRC Press, 2023, pp. 1–28.
13. K. Shaukat, S. Luo, V. Varadharajan, I. A. Hameed and M. Xu, "A survey on machine learning techniques for cybersecurity in the last decade," IEEE Access, vol. 8, pp. 222310–222354, 2020.
14. N. Kaloudi and J. Li, "The AI-based cyber threat landscape: A survey," ACM Computing Surveys (CSUR), vol. 53, no. 1, pp. 1–34, 2020.
15. D. A. Fernandes, L. F. Soares, J. V. Gomes, M. M. Freire and P. R. Inácio, "Security issues in cloud environments: A survey," International Journal of Information Security, vol. 13, pp. 113–170, 2014.
16. W. Tounsi and H. Rais, "A survey on technical threat intelligence in the age of sophisticated cyber attacks," Computers & Security, vol. 72, pp. 212–233, 2018.
17. R. A. A. Habeeb, F. Nasaruddin, A. Gani, E. AhmedEjaz, M. Ahmed and Imran, "Real-time big data processing for anomaly detection: A survey," International Journal of Information Management, vol. 45, pp. 289–307, 2019.
18. H. Zhou, A. Milani Fard and A. Makanju, "The state of ethereum smart contracts security: Vulnerabilities, countermeasures, and tool support," Journal of Cybersecurity and Privacy, vol. 2, no. 2, pp. 358–378, 2022.
19. S. Sayeed and H. Marco-Gisbert, "Assessing blockchain consensus and security mechanisms against the 51% attack," Applied Sciences, vol. 9, no. 9, p. 1788, 2019.
20. V. Zimmermann and K. Renaud, "Moving from a 'human-as-problem" to a 'human-as-solution" cybersecurity mindset," International Journal of Human-Computer Studies, vol. 131, pp. 169–187, 2019.
21. F. Salahdine and N. Kaabouch, "Social engineering attacks: A survey," Future Internet, vol. 11, no. 4, p. 89, 2019.
22. E. A. Vincze, "Challenges in digital forensics," Police Practice and Research, vol. 17, no. 2, pp. 183–194, 2016.
23. A. Brazma, Living computers: Replicators, information processing, and the evolution of life, Oxford University Press, 2023.
24. D. B. Parker, Fighting computer crime: A new framework for protecting information, John Wiley & Sons, Inc, 1998.
25. N. R. Mistry and M. Dahiya, "Signature-based volatile memory forensics: A detection-based approach for analyzing sophisticated cyber attacks," International Journal of Information Technology, vol. 11, pp. 583–589, 2019.
26. M. M. Losavio, K.-P. Chow, A. Koltay and J. James, "The internet of things and the smart city: Legal challenges with digital forensics, privacy, and security," Security and Privacy, vol. 1, no. 3, p. e23, 2018.

27. "OpenText EnCase Forensic," OpenText, [Online]. Available: https://www.opentext.com/products/encase-forensic#features. [Accessed March 2024].
28. "FTK Forensic Toolkit," exterro, [Online]. Available: https://www.exterro.com/digital-forensics-software/forensic-toolkit. [Accessed March 2024].
29. "Recover & Analyze Your Evidence in One Case," MAGNET Forensics, [Online]. Available: https://www.magnetforensics.com/products/magnet-axiom/. [Accessed March 2024].
30. "Accelerate justice with Cellebrite," Cellebrite, [Online]. Available: https://cellebrite.com/en/home/. [Accessed March 2024].
31. "The world's most popular network protocol analyzer," WIRESHARK, [Online]. Available: https://www.wireshark.org/. [Accessed March 2024].
32. "The Volatility Framework," The Volatility Foundation, [Online]. Available: https://volatilityfoundation.org/the-volatility-framework/. [Accessed March 2024].
33. "Oxygen Forensic Detective," OXYGEN Forensics, [Online]. Available: https://oxygenforensics.com/en/products/oxygen-forensic-detective/. [Accessed March 2024].
34. "Snort - Network Intrusion Detection & Prevention System," Snort, [Online]. Available: https://www.snort.org/. [Accessed March 2024].
35. "Security Onion Solutions," Security Onion Solutions, [Online]. Available: https://securityonionsolutions.com/. [Accessed March 2024].
36. IBM, "Cost of a Data Breach Report 2023," IBM Security, 2023.
37. P. Cichonski, T. Millar, T. Grance and K. Scarfone, "Computer Security Incident Handling Guide, NIST Special Publication 800-61, Revision 2," NIST, 2012.
38. V. A. Aleksandar, H. Venter and R. Petrović, "ISO/IEC 27043: 2015—Role and application," in 2016 24th telecommunications forum (TELFOR), IEEE, 2016, pp. 1–4.
39. P. Kral, Incident handler's handbook, SANS Institute, 2011.
40. "NetworkMiner - The NSM and Network Forensics Analysis Tool," NETRESEC, [Online]. Available: https://www.netresec.com/?page=NetworkMiner. [Accessed March 2024].
41. "Rekall," Rekall Forensic, [Online]. Available: https://github.com/google/rekall?tab=readme-ov-file#readme.
42. "Data Removal: Darik's Boot and Nuke - DBAN," DBAN, [Online]. Available: https://dban.org/. [Accessed March 2024].
43. A. Afreen, M. Aslam and S. Ahmed, "Analysis of Fileless Malware and Its Evasive Behavior," in 2020 International Conference on Cyber Warfare and Security (ICCWS), IEEE, 2020, pp. 1–8.
44. D. Pandya and N. Patel, "OWASP top 10 vulnerability analyses in government websites," International Journal of Enterprise Computing and Business Systems, vol. 6, no. 1, 2016.
45. S. M. Mohammad and L. Surya, "Security automation in information technology," International Journal of Creative Research Thoughts (IJCRT)–Volume, vol. 6, 2018.

3 Securing Digital Documents

Advanced Cybersecurity and Forensics Techniques for Data Protection

Akhil John Mampilly and Vijaya Kittu Manda

3.1 INTRODUCTION

3.1.1 Definition and Scope of Cybersecurity and Digital Forensics

The Merriam-Webster Dictionary defines Cybersecurity as 'measures taken to protect a computer or computer system against unauthorized access or attack' [1]. The rise of Cyberattacks due to digitalization presents a grave global challenge for organizations and institutions. The challenge lies in protecting data from cybersecurity threats. The motive behind cyberattacks could be monetary, political, and military gains [2]. Cybersecurity follows the triad fundamentals of confidentiality, integrity, and availability (CIA) (Figure 3.1) [3].

Confidentiality involves safeguarding assets by providing access to authorized users only. Integrity grants authority to add, modify, or delete sensitive information only to authorized users. Lastly, availability ensures that data is always accessible on demand within the Service Level Agreements (SLA) [2].

Malicious software and programs innovated and implanted daily severely threaten all networks and organizations by extracting their sensitive information. Digital forensics plays a significant role in countering this grave threat [4]. Digital forensics scientifically identifies, collects, validates, interprets, documents, and presents digital evidence. Courts accept digital evidence without further validation [5]. The combination of Cybersecurity and digital forensics plays a vital role in safeguarding data in today's digital world. This comprehensive approach secures digital information and supports investigations related to cybercrimes.

3.1.2 Overview of Cybersecurity and Its Importance

Threats continue to evolve in the digital world, which is alarming and has become a prominent task for all organizations and institutions worldwide. Every cyberattack

DOI: 10.1201/9781003497868-3

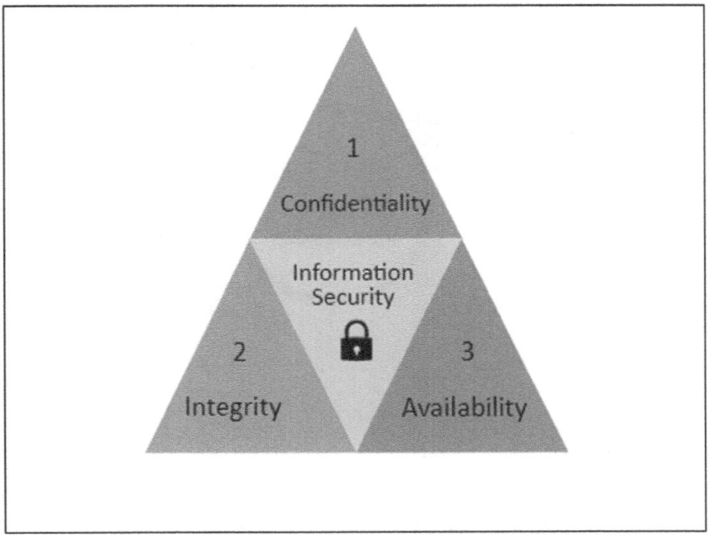

FIGURE 3.1 CIA triad of cybersecurity.

aims to penetrate and exfiltrate sensitive information from the organization or wipe off the data for monetary gains and derail the competitor [6]. Cybersecurity must be injected into every organization's DNA to stay abreast of cyberattacks and protect their business [2]. Artificial intelligence (AI) and machine learning (ML) detect threats in advance to enable us to take preventive measures and mitigate them timely [7].

3.1.3 Role of Digital Forensics in Investigating Cyber Incidents

Due to the rapid digitalization and exponential increase in data production, the multilayered and sophisticated cyber threats, including advanced persistent threats (APTs), necessitate advanced forensic methods [8]. Judicial authorities require digital forensic information as evidence to substantiate cyber-related crimes. As shown in Figure 3.2, digital forensics aims to answer the 5WH questions (Who, What, When, Where, Why, and How) to confirm or contradict the allegations in a case [9].

3.1.4 Importance of E-documents and Data Protection

Securing data stored and transmitted is crucial as data breaches can inadvertently destroy the trust and reputation of an organization, in addition to causing financial loss. Data encryption is essential, and adherence to regulatory standards is mandatory to ensure the security and integrity of sensitive information [10]. There are various institutions, like Health Insurance Portability and Accountability Act (HIPAA), to regulate the procedures for securing data in the healthcare industry [11]. Therefore, all organizations should adopt proactive measures and strategies to safeguard critical information and avoid data breaches.

FIGURE 3.2 Digital forensics—5WH.

3.1.5 Legal and Regulatory Framework for E-document and Data Protection

The advent of digitalization necessitated the formulation of legal and regulatory frameworks to protect the storage and transmission of data, ensuring transparency accepted by judiciary systems everywhere. The launch of GDPR by the European Union (EU) in early 2018, replacing the Data Protection Directive (DPD) in 1995, and fulfilling the objective of personal data protection accountability and meeting with compliance [12]. Similar to the GDPR, India enacted the DPDP Act in 2023. DPDP stands for the Digital Personal Data Protection Act, which safeguards personal data. This Act envisages measures to protect digital data from breaches [13].

3.1.6 Challenges in Cybersecurity and Forensics of E-documents

The relevance of digital forensics is exponentially increasing with the large volumes of data stored in the cloud. Multiple data centers across the globe distribute the data, making retrieval challenging. Physical verification to pinpoint the compromised stored device is a daunting task compared to traditional data storage. Since different regions store the data, varying rules and regulations make it difficult to retrieve and investigate the data as needed [14]. The non-availability of standard reporting procedures hinders the regular auditing process [15].

3.1.7 Objectives and Scope of the Chapter

This chapter emphasizes the importance of Cybersecurity and forensics data protection. It highlights the CIA triad, which lays down the principles of CIA. The chapter highlights the importance of digital forensics in detecting and countering cyber threats. To stay abreast and mitigate threat actors, the usage of advanced tools such as AI ML is also discussed. Digital forensics scientifically retrieves digital data as evidence acceptable to judiciary systems by answering the 5WH questions. It explores how to highlight the need for regulatory standards and procedures such as GDPR, HIPAA, and the DPDP Act. Finally, the chapter details the challenges in retrieving the relevant data stored in the cloud scattered across the globe.

3.2 CYBERSECURITY THREATS AND VULNERABILITIES IN E-DOCUMENTS

3.2.1 Understanding Different Types of Electronic Documents

PDF Documents: Adobe invented the Portable Document Format (PDF) is widely accepted as a standard format for transferring and exchanging electronic information in document form. It is often considered a secure document transfer form compared to other formats and is compatible with many applications. However, PDFs are still prone to vulnerabilities [16].

As shown in the attached images, one notable example is an HTML Document named 'index.html' (Figure 3.3), which checks the viewer version and redirects to a safe (or) malicious website classified as 'malicious' by 11 out of 91 security vendors by Virus Total (Figure 3.4). Threat actors can use this redirection script to embed malicious JavaScript code into a PDF document, thereby projecting it as a security risk.

Text Documents: Text documents represented as .txt are unstructured but are easy to use and convey information. Descriptions on text documents could be more precise but challenging to render [17].

Spreadsheets: Users use spreadsheet software tools to calculate and store data. They can enter, analyze, and visualize the data in the spreadsheet. Microsoft Excel (.xls) is the most common example of a spreadsheet [18].

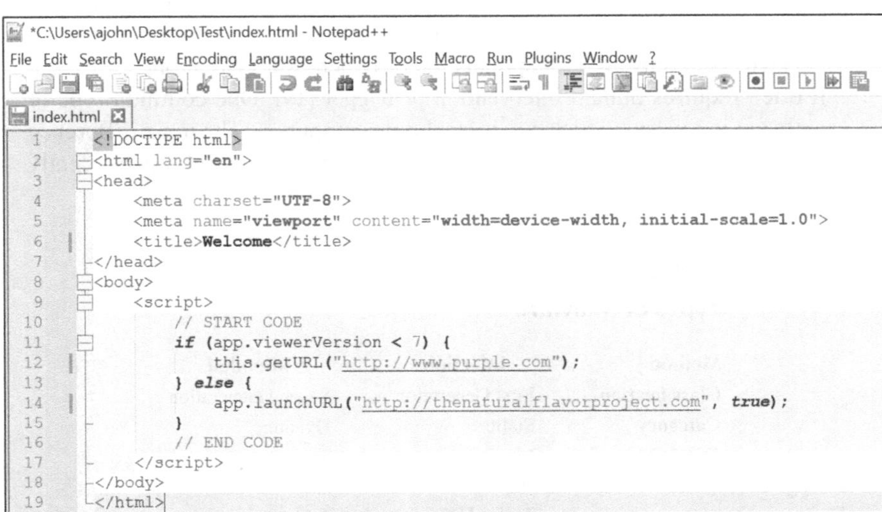

FIGURE 3.3 Authors' compilation of an example of HTML document which checks the viewer version.

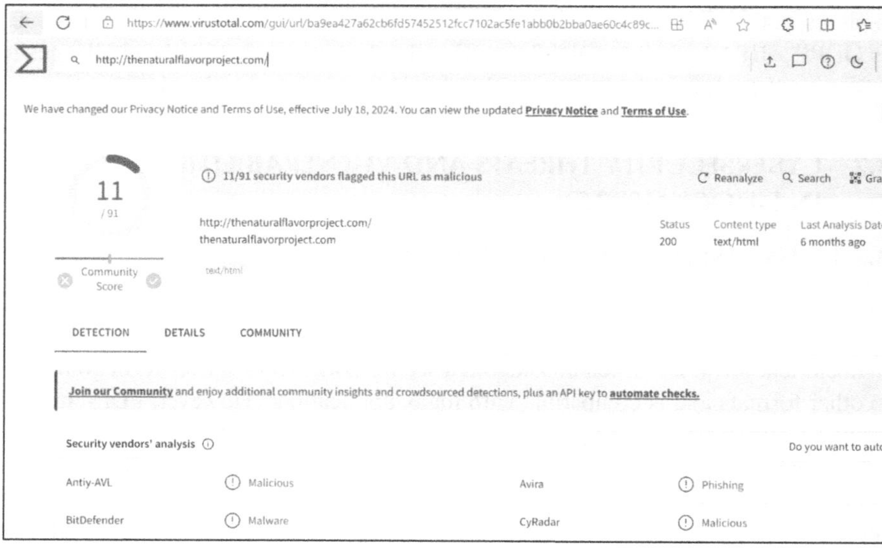

FIGURE 3.4 The natural flavor project's analysis on malicious redirection.

3.2.2 Cyber Threats to E-documents

Malware and Viruses: Malware is malicious software that threat actors use to intrude into organizational systems, evade access controls, and exfiltrate data. There are two categories of malware: static malware, which remains unchanged after infection, and dynamic malware, which changes its structure after infection (Table 3.1). Malware can cause severe damage to systems, leading to breaches of e-documents [19].

Virus is a malware that spreads laterally across a system once infected. It often requires human intervention or trigger [19]. One common type of malware is a worm, which can infect home computers. The main difference between worms and other viruses is that worms can spread independently

TABLE 3.1
Types of Malware

Method	**Infection**	**Intended**
Classification	First Generation	Second Generation
Category	Static	Dynamic
Examples	Viruses	Spyware
	Worm	Ransomware
	Trojan Horse	Adware
	Spam	Keylogger
	Rootkit	

without needing a host program or code. In contrast, other viruses must write and execute a host program to spread [20].

Ransomware is a malware that encrypts data after infection. Traditional antivirus solutions generally cannot detect it. Threat actors demand a ransom, often in cryptocurrencies, to decrypt the encrypted data. One notable example is the WannaCry ransomware that caused chaos in 2017 by exploiting a vulnerability in the SMB protocol of the Windows Operating System [20]. Keylogger is a malware that logs each keystroke on the affected system. It enables threat actors to access and use sensitive information for financial and identity theft [21].

Unauthorized Access and Data Breaches: In system intrusion form, threat actors commit data breaches to gain control of the system. They get access to the system because of weak passwords and software vulnerabilities without the knowledge or consent of users. Threat actors commonly conduct phishing attacks via email and trick the end user into clicking and downloading a malicious link. The link allows them to access the system, including electronic documents and stored credentials [22]. A brute force attack is when the threat actor repeatedly uses different combinations of passwords to find the correct one. For example, if a threat actor wants to brute force a Gmail account, they must make several attempts with multiple combinations of passwords to succeed and gain access. Weak passwords make the process quicker [23].

Threat actors can also exploit software vulnerabilities to gain access to systems. One example is the Equifax data breach in 2017, where data from 144.5 million users was exposed and compromised [24].

Insider Threats: Organizations spend enormous amounts of money to counter external cyberattacks but often fail to consider or give equal importance to insider threats, which can be devastating. Insiders may abuse their authorized access to gain control of sensitive information for monetary purposes. It poses severe damage to both private and government organizations. For example, a user trying to gain access to the system during unusual working hours could be an insider threat. Different Insider threats are malicious insiders, compromised insiders, and careless insiders.

Malicious insiders use their credentials to abuse the system for monetary gains.

Compromised insiders have their credentials exposed by threat actors, who then gain access to the system to exfiltrate confidential information, resulting in the theft of the company's intellectual property.

Careless insiders unintentionally expose their credentials to threat actors due to a lack of security awareness [25].

3.2.3 Vulnerabilities in E-document Management Systems

Software Vulnerabilities: Software vulnerabilities can lead to security breaches. Hence, proactive detection and fixing is essential. These vulnerabilities can occur during the software design phase, including common issues like buffer overflow and SQL injection (SQLi).

Buffer overflow is an inefficient software management in which memory space outside its allocated area is allowed. For example, the strcpy function in C programming language copies a string from one location to another without checking the capacity of the destination buffer. This leads to a buffer overflow if the destination buffer is not large enough to hold the copied string [26].

SQLi is a security attack in which the threat actor (attacker) executes arbitrary SQL statements on a database server. It is among the top ten security risks listed in the Open Web Application Security Project (OWASP). It is a common form of web application security vulnerability where threat actors bypass security measures to penetrate the database of a system. Some examples of SQLi are Blind SQLi and Error-Based SQLi [27].

Static code analysis is a great tool to improve the quality of the code. These tools detect bugs and vulnerabilities in the application without running the program to understand its behavior [28]. They help in multiple ways: detect issues early, improve code quality, reduce debugging time, and improve security. They can detect a wide range of issues:

1. Syntax errors
2. Potential runtime errors (such as null pointer dereferences)
3. Security vulnerabilities (such as SQLi buffer overflows)
4. Code style and maintainability issues
5. Performance inefficiencies

Some popular static code analysis tools are SonarQube, CodeSonar, Klocwork, Coverity, and CodePro AnalytiX.

Human Factors and Social Engineering: Humans stand in the lowest layer of the security chain. Threat actors can exploit humans through social engineering. Humans often trust each other and share sensitive information through social networking sites and other online services. These websites generally need more security features to protect this information. Threat actors exploit this vulnerability to gain information and victimize individuals through cyberattacks [29].

Governments and institutions should impart training and awareness to protect themselves from cyberattacks. Creating awareness of cyber threats and staying up to date to protect against cyberattacks is paramount. Respective organizations should offer proper training and awareness programs. Users often develop passwords without paying attention to their strength, which increases the risk of cyberattacks [30].

Secure and efficient electronic document management systems (e-DMS) are essential for every organization in this digital era. Even though organizations adopt paperless documentation, they also store hard copies due to the vulnerability of digital documents to cyberattacks. Accessibility and security are two cornerstones of Cybersecurity, with technologies like near field communication (NFC) and biometric systems playing key roles [31].

3.2.4 Techniques for Preventing and Mitigating Cyber Threats

Cybersecurity plays a significant role in mitigating risks and securing organizations in the dynamic landscape of threat actors. Safeguarding e-documents from data breaches is essential to maintain data CIA. The section discusses the importance of spreading awareness among users and the techniques to combat and protect sensitive information.

Encryption: Encryption is a coding method used to secure the confidentiality and integrity of data. In this, messages are converted into cryptic/hidden text. The reverse process of encryption is called decryption. Encryption is to secure data. However, it is not a foolproof solution. It is vulnerable to specific threats. Organizations use Digital Signatures with Public Key Infrastructure (PKI) to ensure the authenticity of documents, such as emails and other e-documents. The process confirms that no one has altered the records after the signature. The Advanced Encryption Standard (AES) is a flexible and highly trusted algorithm for encryption [32].

Multi-Factor Authentication (MFA): Legacy authentication relied on single-factor authentication and hence needed to be more secure against threats. MFA increases security by providing a double layer of authentication. This process combines a username and password with other factors, such as biometrics or one-time passwords (OTP) [33].

Intrusion Detection Systems (IDS): IDS monitor abnormal behaviors and threats in the network. Organizations collect data from various sources for analysis, such as network traffic, application logs, and security logs. Host-based IDS (HIDS) detect anomalies from individual hosts, while network-based IDS (NIDS) detect threats across the entire network. These are the two main categories of IDS [34].

Secure Payment Gateway: A payment gateway securely facilitates the three-tier payment process between the consumer, merchant, and bank over the Internet. The sensitive information regarding the payment is encrypted and protected from threat actors. This information is passed securely between the parties [35].

Periodic Software Updates: Organizations must perform periodic software updates due to the rise of threat actors using sophisticated technology to infiltrate systems by exploiting vulnerabilities. To counter these threats, organizations must regularly update software and apply patches to fortify defenses [36].

Proactive Measures to Safeguard Data: Organizations must safeguard sensitive corporate data to prevent security breaches. Falling prey to threat actors could cause severe financial, reputational, and operational damage. Organizations should take proactive measures to safeguard classified information and prevent it from being exfiltrated [37].

Security Awareness Training: Organizations should create awareness among their employees by adequately training them on cybersecurity threats and mitigations [38].

IRP and CSIRT Measures: No matter how strong the defense mechanisms are to counter threats, threat actors find new ways to penetrate systems. Organizations should necessitate an Incident Response Plan (IRP) and appropriate measures. All organizations, including government departments, should constitute a Cybersecurity Incident Response Team (CSIRT) to respond swiftly to an incident [39].

3.2.5 Common Vulnerabilities and Risks Associated with E-documents

E-documents are gaining popularity in organizations and have become indispensable to the modern digital environment. Due to its popularity threat actors continue to evolve, causing significant risks. The section draws the common vulnerabilities and risks associated with it.

Crafting Malicious Code nto PDF: Threat actors commonly use PDFs for cyberattacks. They can craft malicious JavaScript code into a PDF and email it to users' inboxes. Upon opening the PDF document, the script executes, potentially compromising the victim's system. For example, a malicious PDF document was sent to a user's email in January 2014, pretending to be from the Israeli Ministry of Defence [40].

Security Risks in E-documents: E-documents are commonly used and pose significant security risks. Government agencies often use email as a mode of communication, which is at risk. The increase in malware, phishing emails, and other techniques threatens personal data [41].

Vulnerabilities in network-connected devices: Before selling network-connected devices such as printers and photocopy machines at the end of their life, wipe off the data to prevent them from being utilized for malicious activities [42].

Cross-Site Scripting (XSS) in Web Application: Threat actors can exploit a vulnerability in a web application using Cross-Site Scripting (XSS). It is one of the greatest threats, where they exploit a vulnerable web application to carry code to other users' browsers [43].

3.3 DIGITAL FORENSICS OF E-DOCUMENTS AND DATA

Digital forensics experts analyze data from digital devices, preserve the originality of the data, and conduct a structured investigation to reconstruct historical events (Figure 3.5).

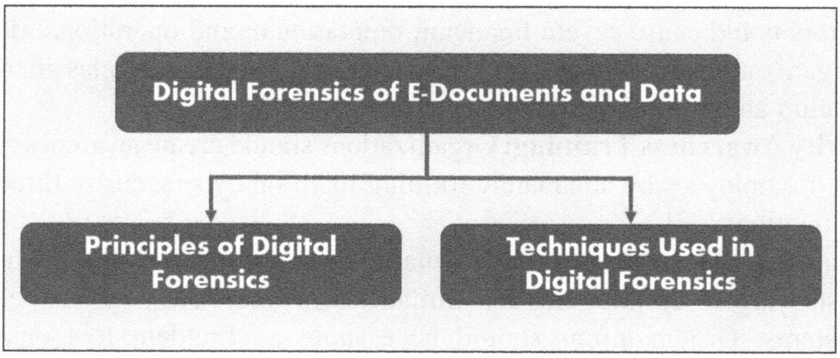

FIGURE 3.5 Classification of digital forensics of e-documents and data.

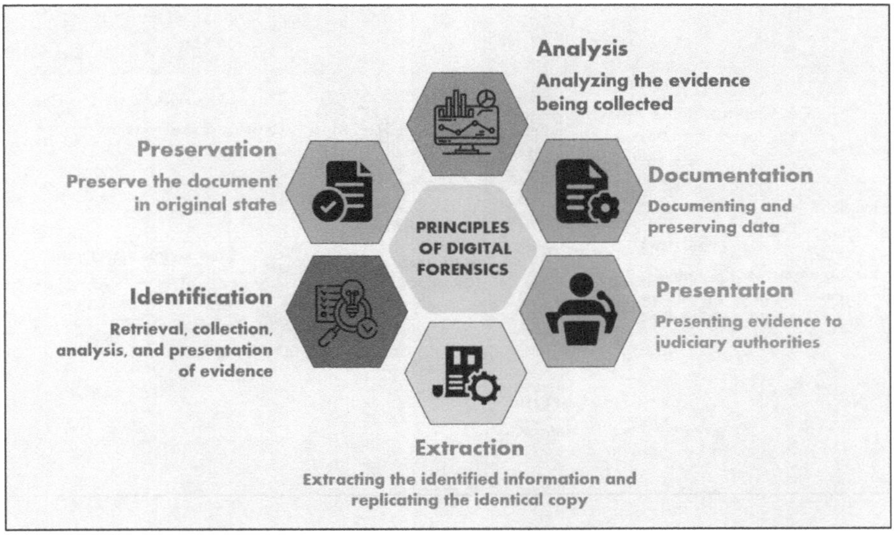

FIGURE 3.6 Six fundamental principles of digital forensics.

3.3.1 Principles of Digital Forensics

Preservation: Digital forensics is crucial in incident response against cyberattacks. It is essential to preserve the document in its original state using reliable tools and techniques. Six fundamental principles of digital forensics are discussed (Figure 3.6).

Identification: This is the most pivotal part of an investigation involving the retrieval, collection, analysis, and presentation of evidence [44].

Extraction: This process involves extracting the identified information and replicating the identical physical media copy digitally, such as the hard disk. It is also called bitwise imaging [45].

Analysis: The acquired evidence can be analyzed using various tools, including Kali Linux [46].

Documentation: This is a fundamental principle of digital forensics. Documenting and preserving data for traceability, ownership, and records is paramount [47].

Presentation: The evidence collected is analyzed and presented to the respective judiciary authorities [45].

3.3.2 Techniques Used in Digital Forensics

Imaging: Developing an identical copy of a storage device. Memory storage and estimation require more effort and time as disk sizes increase. Five popular digital forensic techniques are discussed (Figure 3.7).

Hashing: Using algorithmic techniques to ensure the sovereignty and integrity of the data [48].

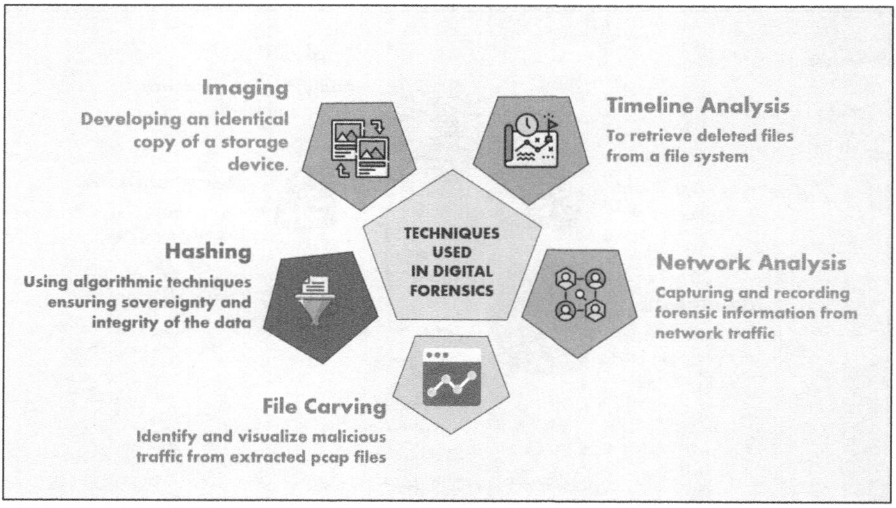

FIGURE 3.7 Five popular digital forensic techniques.

File Carving: To retrieve deleted files from a file system [49].

Timeline Analysis: Analysis tools such as PcapXray identify and visualize malicious traffic from the pcap files extracted [50].

Network Forensics: Capturing and recording forensic information from a series of network events that can be used as substantial evidence to understand cyberattack events [51].

3.3.2.1 Techniques for Digital Evidence Collection and Preservation From Various Sources

Computers: Forensic analysts take the total hard disk or a portion of it for analysis and use forensic tools like MDD and FTK Imager to retrieve digital evidence. They preserve the integrity and authenticity of the digital data for judicial requirements [52].

Mobile Devices: Threat actors are gaining an advantage due to the exponential rise of mobile users. However, inventing a comprehensive tool for all smart device OSs takes time and effort. Digital evidence in mobile phones is prone to deletion but can be retrieved anytime for forensics. Tools such as MicroSystemation's XRY help with mobile forensics analysis [53].

Cloud Storage: Retrieving digital evidence stored in a cloud environment is challenging as cloud services are available online to the public, facilitating criminal activities by threat actors. Several technological advancements in forensics are required to address the issue [54].

3.3.3 Digital Forensics Techniques for E-documents

Digital forensics is a scientific discipline that retrieves evidence of unlawful activities, particularly e-crimes. It involves systematically applying scientific methods and techniques to trace and analyze data stored in digital devices, such as computers, and presenting it as genuine evidence to judicial authorities. Digital forensics is crucial in uncovering financial fraud, identity theft, and other digital crimes. The severity of such crimes is substantial. There will be implications for financial institutions and other organizations. Therefore, digital forensics is invaluable to judicial authorities in combating cybercrime [55].

3.3.3.1 Data Acquisition and Preservation

Reversible Data Hiding (RDH): Steganography is a security technique for hiding data within an image or video. This poses a severe threat because criminals can exfiltrate data without detection [56]. RDH is a technique within the broad digital steganography and information security umbrella. It allows hidden data insertion within digital media, such as images or videos, with minimal alterations. The RDH method also allows restoring the original data without any changes after extracting the hidden secret data [57]. It is commonly used in Medical imaging, Military communication, Law enforcement, and Cloud storage. Figure 3.8 shows the four steps involved in RDH.

Cross-drive Analysis: It is common in forensic investigation to confiscate digital storage devices like USBs, Hard Disk Drives, and other storage devices. They contain sensitive information that needs to be retrieved promptly. Careful steps are to be taken to retrieve data from such devices. To simplify the process, correlating data across multiple disks can address this difficulty using statistical techniques [58].

Live Analysis: The volatile data in RAM requires special care, as the chances of losing the data are higher when switching the system off. Since data is crucial, organizations should adopt methods such as memory forensics

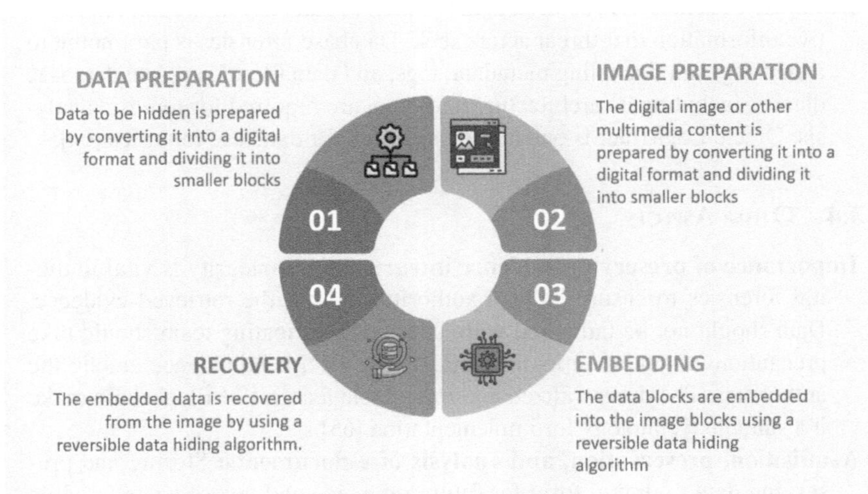

FIGURE 3.8 Steps involved in reversible data hiding (RDH).

to safeguard the volatile data and ensure data integrity. Classify memory forensics into traditional forensics, which involves shutting down the compromised system to prevent threat actors from deleting sensitive information, and live forensics, an enhanced form conducted live and further subdivided into internal and external analyses [59].

Deleted File Recovery: Files are recovered and reinstated from the directories of the targeted disk [60].

3.3.3.2 Data Analysis and Examination

Stochastic Forensics: This method can examine all the data stored in a system and determine whether files have been copied, even after several months. This new technique enhances and sharpens the ability of digital forensics to recover evidence [61].

File Forensics: System files are an essential source of information for recreating crime events by threat actors. Reconstructing events related to a crime requires identifying the affected system files [55].

Memory Forensics: RAM imaging and technical examination are crucial steps in forensic investigations. Since malware often resides in RAM, analyzing this volatile data is essential for retrieving evidence of cybercrimes. Traditional forensics cannot detect malware in RAM because it leaves no trace on the hard drive. Stuxnet, one of the first known computer worms, primarily operated in RAM, leaving minimal traces on the computer system. Its objective was to disrupt Iran's nuclear centrifuges [62].

Network Forensics: It helps investigators identify malicious threats within the network. It is data-centric and assists network administrators in enhancing the detection and prevention mechanisms against cyber threats. Some essential tools for analyzing network traffic include Wireshark, tcpdump, and Burp Suite [63].

Database Forensics: Structured data is stored in databases and contains sensitive information that threat actors seek. Database forensics is paramount to analyzing data, including metadata, logs, and data files. Complete database details, including its architecture and type, are required for forensic analysis. Oracle LogMiner is one of the tools used for database forensics [64].

3.3.4 Other Aspects

Importance of preserving evidence integrity: Data integrity is vital in digital forensics to ensure judicial authorities accept the retrieved evidence. Data should not be tampered with, and the investigating team should take precautions to maintain its integrity, as this instills confidence among the authorities. The decentralized and immutable features of Blockchain make it a suitable technology for implementation [65].

Acquisition, preservation, and analysis of e-documents: Storing and preserving data in digital form for future reference and record-keeping while maintaining its integrity and durability is ideal. It involves protecting the files without losing any data, extending their lifespan [66].

3.3.5 Challenges in E-documents Forensics

Electronic document forensics faces significant challenges in maintaining the integrity and authenticity of collected data. Threat actors use anti-forensics tools to evade detection mechanisms and tamper with or delete data.

Authenticity and Integrity Verification: Maintaining the integrity and authenticity of data is crucial, but managing digital forensics presents serious challenges, including inefficient incident management, the absence of standard procedures, and ineffective forensic readiness.

Inefficient Incident Management: Forensic investigators cannot detect and act in time. Also, there are no proper tools to promptly detect and respond to incidents, nor provisions to prevent future occurrences. This makes incident management inefficient.

Absence of Standard Procedures: Standard procedures enable investigators to act swiftly and appropriately when an incident occurs. However, such standard procedures rarely exist.

Ineffective Forensic Readiness: Forensic investigators often cannot act appropriately during incidents due to a lack of standard procedures and the necessary knowledge to manage incidents [67]. Further, their readiness levels are relatively low.

Anti-Forensics Techniques: Despite the benefits of anti-forensics techniques to find evidence for several crimes, criminals have turned them into tools for tampering with and permanently destroying proof, leaving no trace and hampering the investigation process. They can tamper with the data and even permanently destroy the evidence, leading to no sign of a trace, thus obstructing the investigation [68].

Data Hiding: It is a tool used by threat actors, who apply several techniques, including steganography. For instance, threat actors hide data in volatile RAMs. Switching off the power supply will wipe out data stored in RAM.

Data Wiping: The investigation of data by forensics investigators became tedious as threat actors used every available means to delete and wipe out the data.

Encrypting Data: IT professionals secure the data by encrypting it. But at the same time, threat actors misuse encryption to slow the digital forensics investigation. The decryption of the data encrypted by the threat actors is challenging and time-consuming.

Hashing: IT professionals use several techniques for hashing, including SHA-1 and MD5, which can alter data integrity. Any changes to a file result in modification of the hash value, making it difficult to retrieve the original file.

Trail Obfuscation: It diverts and slows down digital forensics investigation. P2P protocols mitigate biometrics by threat actors for concealing the evidence and hiding their criminal activities.

Anti-Forensic Tools: They obstruct digital forensics investigations with sophisticated and automated tools for destroying and hiding data. It paves the way for the easy escape of cyber criminals.

Insufficient Training and Awareness: A forensic tool would not wholly safeguard the data. Adequate training is essential to capture the knowledge needed to operate the advanced forensics tool. Proper training and conducting technical workshops to create awareness and improve the skills [67].

3.4 DATA PROTECTION AND PRIVACY IN THE ELECTRONIC ENVIRONMENT

3.4.1 Laws and Regulations Governing Data Protection and Privacy

Handling users' data is often complex and risky. Several data protection laws address these challenges. However, determining what constitutes private data is the real difficulty. Technical data is usually not considered private or personal. However, using such data to infringe on an individual's fundamental rights constitutes a privacy breach and a law violation [69].

Among the numerous data protection and privacy laws, the General Data Protection Regulation (GDPR) was formalized by the EU in May 2018, replacing the traditional 'DPD' 95/46/EC. The GDPR envisages a state-of-the-art framework to protect the privacy and freedom of individuals and their data. It ensures no restrictions on the transfer or mutual exchange of personal data within the EU [70].

3.4.2 Encryption Methods for Securing E-documents

The internet is an open network system that allows instant global message exchange, accessible to anyone anytime. However, it has several shortcomings that threat actors exploit to perform unauthorized activities [71].

Cryptography techniques can mitigate cyberattacks and ensure the integrity and authenticity of documents. It involves encryption methods that can be decrypted only by the sender or the receiver. This chapter explores the art of encryption, focusing on symmetric and asymmetric encryption techniques [72].

3.4.2.1 Symmetric Encryption

The system uses a single key for encryption and decryption. There are three types of symmetric encryption.

Advanced Encryption Standard (AES): It is a robust global cryptographic method to generate efficient and vital keys of 128, 192, and 256 bits.

Data Encryption Standard (DES): Previously used to protect financial and classified records in the United States, it became an authenticated standard encryption technique used by ANSI.

Triple DES (3DES): An advanced technique that applies DES three times: first for encryption, then for decryption, and finally for encryption again. The drawback of 3DES is that it takes three times longer to encrypt data [73].

3.4.2.2 Asymmetric Encryption

There are two keys used in this type of encryption. The key used for encryption is public, and a private key for decryption. The private key also signs documents, and the public key verifies the signature. Asymmetric encryption is of two types:

Rivest-Shamir-Adleman (RSA): RSA is a widely used form of asymmetric encryption. It is considered a standard in many applications, but its decryption could be more efficient than encryption.

Elliptic Curve Cryptography (ECC): ECC provides the same level of security as RSA but with shorter key lengths, making it more efficient in data processing power. This efficiency makes ECC suitable for devices with limited memory, such as smartcards and smartphones [72]. However, ECC is more complex than traditional public-key encryption techniques. Also, implementation is a little complex because it requires specialized software and hardware components.

3.4.2.3 Access Control Models and Policies

Access Control Models are designed to ensure that only the right users can access the data. Thus, they safeguard the data from unauthorized access and prevent breaches or incursions. Table 3.2 shows three components of Access control models.

Some common access control models in practice are:

1. Discretionary Access Control (DAC)
2. Mandatory Access Control (MAC)
3. Role-Based Access Control (RBAC)
4. Attribute-Based Access Control (ABAC)

DAC: In DAC, access to documents is controlled based on the identity of authorized users. Users have complete control over their documents and can allow others to access their systems to make changes. Examples include Windows and Unix operating systems.

MAC: In MAC, Users' authority levels characterize this model by preserving the integrity and confidentiality of data. Classification labels often include Public, Internal, Confidential, and Restricted (or Secret). For example, the

TABLE 3.2
Three Components of Access Control Models

Name of the ACM Component	Constituents of the Component
Subjects	Users, applications, or systems that need access to resources.
Objects	Data, applications, or systems that require protection.
Access-control decisions	Determines whether a subject's request to access an object is granted or denied.

user cannot downgrade a document classified as Top Secret to a lower classification labeled as Internal, Confidential, or Public to share outside.

RBAC: In RBAC, user roles determine access, and identical roles receive similar access. For example, a user from the Information Security Team can access data based on their role (Auditor) with read-only permissions.

ABAC: In ABAC, access control model, grants or denies access to resources based on a user's attributes, such as their role, department, job function, or clearance level.

Access control policies ensure that users have the minimum access levels required to perform their assignments. All organizations should allot separate duties and responsibilities to users according to their respective roles.

When a user's role changes, assign a new entitlement according to the new role and take precautions to remove previous entitlements. Doing so will avoid authorization creep. Conduct regular audits to ensure that entitlements stay intact, as this can increase the risk of compromising accounts and undermining the principles of least privileged access [74].

3.4.3 Data Loss Prevention, Techniques, Tools, and Protection

Data breaches always pose a significant risk to organizations, prompting a continuous search for methods to prevent the leakage of sensitive information. Data Loss Prevention (DLP) involves using tools, techniques, and procedures to protect sensitive information from being exfiltrated outside the organization's boundaries. Organizations must protect data at all times and at any cost, whether at rest, in motion, or in use.

3.4.3.1 Tools and Techniques Used

Content Inspection and Contextual Analysis: The tool performs content inspection and contextual analysis to determine the sensitive nature of the data. The actions are analyzed to check whether they conform to the predefined policies. Once a policy is triggered, actions such as blocking, encrypting, alerting, or notifying security administrators for investigation. For example, by setting a policy to block a confidential keyword in Microsoft Office applications (Word, Excel, PowerPoint) using the conditional operator 'AND,' and prevent the data from being exfiltrated through email, web, LAN, and removable media.

Policy Enforcement: The tool operates based on predefined or custom policies. The policies contain sensitive information and suitable actions to be triggered, as defined by the organization when a violation is triggered.

Data Labeling: Organizations label data based on their requirements to restrict content sharing according to defined controls. Documents would be classified and labeled manually or automatically. For example, 'Internal' documents are classified and cannot be shared outside the organization.

Endpoint DLP: Organizations usually install an agent on their employee workstations or laptops as a security measure. These tools help monitor and prevent the leakage of sensitive information due to data breaches. Endpoint DLP offers a broad spectrum of controls. These controls include:

1. Data discovery and preventing actions like printing or transferring sensitive information
2. Dealing with removable media (such as USB drives)
3. Endpoint applications by controlling cut, copy, and paste operations.

Network DLP: Network DLP protects sensitive data by passing through the network and preventing unauthorized access. For example, Network DLP can detect and block the transfer if a user tries to upload sensitive data via network email or web applications. They help in:

1. Real-time monitoring
2. Pattern-based detection
3. Policy-based controls
4. Alerts and reporting

Cloud DLP: Organizations are increasingly using cloud-based solutions. Owing to this, they need Cloud DLP solutions. These solutions enable the discovery and control of data stored in cloud environments. They provide visibility and protection for sensitive information. Some use cases for Cloud DLP include Cloud storage control, Cloud application control, Cloud email control, and Cloud collaboration control.

Secure Email Gateways (SEGs): Organizations use SEGs integrated with DLP functionalities to monitor sensitive data via email channels. SEGs are architected internally within the organization's ecosystem. They help inspect mail traffic and prevent data from entering or leaving the network without authorization. For example, if an external sender receives an encrypted attachment, the organization can block the attachment based on its policy.

3.4.3.2 Protecting Data

DLP solutions help protect sensitive data from leaving the organization's network. These are done in four steps:

1. Safeguarding from Unauthorized Access
2. Monitoring Data Transfers
3. Encrypting Sensitive Data
4. Audit Trails

Blocking Unauthorized Actions: DLP tools are programmed to take appropriate action when detecting a violation. These actions can include stopping the transfer of sensitive data to removable media, preventing sensitive documents from being printed on the network or local printers, blocking the upload of sensitive information to web channels, and controlling cut/copy/paste operations on endpoint applications [75].

3.4.4 Features of Rights Management—IRM and DRM

The objective of Information Rights Management (IRM) and Digital Rights Management (DRM) is to safeguard the contents of digital information.

IRM: IRM allows organizations to track and secure sensitive data regardless of location, preventing unauthorized access. Organizations can monitor the storage locations of their files, whether on removable media (USB), in a file share, or a cloud repository. IRM can trace all users who access the files, whether within or outside the network and detect unauthorized access attempts. Additionally, IRM can revoke permissions granted to a user at any time. For example, suppose a user in an organization accidentally shares a confidential Word document with the wrong email address. In that case, the external recipient cannot open it, thus protecting data privacy and preventing leakage [76].

DRM: A DRM solution protects digital media from unauthorized access. The data is encrypted and transferred to authorized users, with decryption controlled by the DRM system. Copyright holders use DRM technologies to enforce copyright laws, and the law prohibits and punishes the unauthorized use of copyrighted materials. For example, Netflix is a cloud-based application that provides unlimited access to movies and series for a subscription fee. It uses DRM to protect its content from unauthorized copying and distribution [77].

3.4.5 Challenges, Best Practices for Data Protection and Privacy

Organizations should visualize the comprehensive structure of their infrastructure and data environment to safeguard sensitive information from insider threats and external interferences from threat actors. As threat actors rise, organizations must remain vigilant and continuously monitor their infrastructure by taking preventive measures within the SLA to counter incidents and safeguard data integrity. The challenges faced by most DSPM vendors include its limited integration with third-party security products, which hinders data analysis. Organizations often fail to address the issue of shadow data, which refers to sensitive data existing outside the security boundaries of the organization. It can lead to various security implications and expose the organization to privacy risks. Due to inadequate control and negligence, information security departments often need to pay more attention to shadow data. Shadow data keeps the door open for external entities like vendors, suppliers, and contractors to access the data without adequate authorization, posing security risks. Organizations should implement a Data Security Posture Management (DSPM) framework to mitigate these security and privacy risks. Organizations scatter data across geographical locations and cloud providers. DSPM helps to identify, categorize, and prioritize risks associated with the data and to locate data repositories that are idle and hidden. The identified sensitive information, including the organization's structured and unstructured data, is mapped and checked for indicators of compromise. The organization performs risk management to meet compliance and mitigate any possible ransomware attack [78].

3.5 CHALLENGES, EMERGING TRENDS, AND FUTURE DIRECTIONS

3.5.1 Emerging Technologies and Their Impact

New and Emerging Technologies bring opportunities and challenges regarding cybersecurity and data protection. The large-scale adoption of technologies will only increase the importance of cybersecurity and data protection. In some cases, the new technologies force the development of new techniques and strategies to deal with digital forensics. Overall, it requires organizations and individuals to continue to invest in security hardware and software, directly or indirectly.

3.5.2 Cloud Computing and E-document Security: Its Implications for Data Protection

Cloud computing has gained popularity due to the convenience of data storage and computing services it offers organizations. Cloud services are available anytime over the network. They are flexible, scalable, and cost-effective. However, the technology brings challenges such as data protection, access control, and compliance.

Cloud Service Providers (CSPs) generally take the primary steps required to protect customer data stored. They implement RBAC mechanisms for the resources stored on their servers. CSPs insist on Multi-Factor Authentication (MFA) [79]. It is used to authenticate the identity of users accessing cloud resources. MFA becomes a supplementary layer of security that prevents illegal access.

Organizations also should take their safety steps. They must ensure their data is encrypted before being put on the cloud. They must also conform to various regulations under various jurisdictions. The GDPR and the HIPAA are popular regulations. Organizations can avoid any potential liabilities by staying compliant, especially when customer data is being stored.

3.5.3 Blockchain and Distributed Ledger Technologies and Their Impact on E-document Security

Blockchain is a distributed ledger technology that offers several use cases in management case studies and technical use cases [80, p. 3]. Data is stored on multiple nodes of the network, which is called the decentralized network. The technology has several built-in features that provide secure and transparent data storage. It is a groundbreaking technology that protects data. To do so, it uses tamper-proof record-keeping mechanisms to preserve data integrity and security. Blockchain uses cryptographic hashing. It is a process in which mathematical functions are used to convert data into a fixed-size hash value. The hash value is distinctive to the input data. It changes if the data is changed (such as when data is tampered with). This simple yet powerful feature ensures that data stored on the Blockchain is tamper-proof.

Blockchain uses consensus mechanisms. The consensus mechanism ensures that all network nodes agree on the ledger state. A process called validation and verification will take care of this. Nodes compete to crack complicated mathematical problems to get the authority to validate transactions. Smart Contracts are used to automate tasks and enforce business rules. Data access control and protection policies are some areas where these features can be used.

Privacy is an important consideration on Blockchain. By default, a copy of all transactions on the Blockchain is available on all nodes. This visibility can be problematic for applications requiring privacy. Applications such as financial transactions or medical records might not be like this. New Blockchain platforms have proposed several workarounds to address this challenge, thanks to recent developments. They implemented privacy features, such as zero-knowledge proofs allowing private transactions.

Regulatory compliance is also a challenge. Blockchain, a decentralized network, operates outside of traditional regulatory frameworks. Of course, several exciting and secure know-your-customer (KYC) and anti-money laundering (AML) checks have been introduced. It is yet to be seen how regulators worldwide will respond.

3.5.4 Artificial Intelligence and Machine Learning in Cybersecurity and Forensics

AI and ML are increasingly used to identify and react to cyber threats. ML-powered systems can examine vast amounts of data in real-time. They can identify patterns and anomalies that may indicate a potential threat. Cyber threats, if they follow a pattern, can be quickly identified. ML algorithms can be trained to recognize and respond to specific types of attacks. Certain cybersecurity tasks and response mechanisms can be automated. AI is perceived to fuel future cybersecurity threats. Such threats will also be counter-attacked with AI. One issue with AI-related technologies is that they increasingly lead to concerns about privacy, bias, and potential misuse. This makes them an essential tool in the fight against cybercrime.

3.5.5 Quantum Computing

Quantum computing is considered the next 'prominent research frontier.' Considerable research interest is pouring into the field. 'Quantum cryptography and information security' is one of the five most promising themes within quantum computing reviews [81]. The development of quantum computing rose because of significant advancements in computing power and speed. The technology has implications for scientific research and various industries.

Quantum computers are evolving to perform calculations much faster than classical computers. Consider a quantum computer that can potentially break the RSA encryption algorithm. RSA is the most extensively used to safeguard data in transit and at rest. If quantum computers succeed in breaking widely used encryption algorithms, it would significantly impact Cybersecurity.

However, it raises concerns about the potential impact on encryption algorithms and cybersecurity measures. Considering the challenge, organizations have already started working on mechanisms such as:

1. Adopting quantum-resistant encryption algorithms [82]
2. Using post-quantum cryptography (PQC) [83]

3. Using secure communication protocols such as global-scale Quantum Key Distribution (QKD) networks [84]
4. Implementing other cybersecurity measures (such as MFA, among others) [79]

3.5.6 Emerging Threats

1. **Ransomware** is a type of malicious software (malware). It encrypts the victim's files or locks their device and demands a ransom for the decryption key or unlock code. This results in significant financial losses and damage to an organization's reputation and customer trust. Studies show that ransomware is only a distraction and that the attackers will make other attacks, such as data theft or lateral movement within a network. There are several types of ransomware: Encrypting Ransomware, Locker Ransomware, and DoS Ransomware. There are three ways ransomware enters into a computer (or network):
   a. Ransomware spreads through phishing emails that trick victims into opening malicious attachments or clicking on links.
   b. Malware gets installed through software downloaded from a compromised website through which the.
   c. Malware exploits vulnerabilities in the operating system or software installed on the victim's computer.

   Individuals and organizations have to maintain regular backups of critical data. They need to keep software and systems updated with the latest security patches. Installing a good antivirus and anti-malware software helps.
2. **Internet of Things (IoT)** allows devices and networks to connect physical objects to the Internet, enabling data collection and remote control. Some popular IoT applications include smart home devices, industrial control systems, and medical devices. While IoT offers numerous benefits, it also expands the attack surface and creates vulnerabilities that threat actors can exploit. Some common IoT vulnerabilities are using weak passwords, insecure communication protocols, and outdated software. Organizations and individuals should implement strong access controls, use secure communication protocols, and keep software updated with the latest security patches to prevent this.
3. **Other similar threats** are now possible. The list includes Phishing attacks, Data breaches, Cryptojacking, Remote Access Trojans (RATs), Wiper malware, Banking Trojans, Fileless malware, Botnets, and Social Engineering Attacks. Forensic investigators use data carving, log analysis, and network traffic analysis to recover and analyze electronic evidence.

3.5.7 Advancements in Forensic Tools and Techniques

There are five popular digital forensic tools (Figure 3.9). A list of popular software in each category is presented (Table 3.3).

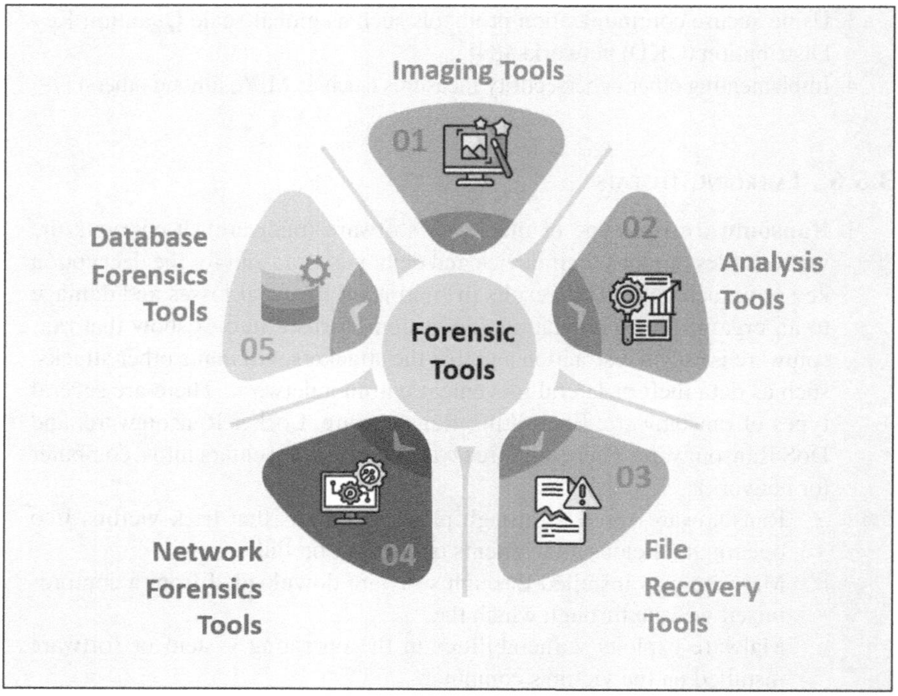

FIGURE 3.9 Five popular digital forensic tools.

TABLE 3.3
List of Popular Digital Forensic Software

Digital Forensic Tool Category	Examples of Some Famous Software
Imaging Tools	FTK Imager, EnCase Forensic, and Helix Forensic
Analysis Tools	Autopsy, Volatility, and X-Ways Forensics
File Recovery Tools	Puran File Recovery, Glary Undelete, Recuva Data Recovery, PhotoRec, and Scalpel
Network Forensic Tools	Wireshark, tcpdump, and SolarWinds Network Forensics
Database Forensic Tools	Autopsy, EnCase Forensic, and Helix Forensic

3.5.7.1 Imaging Tools

Imaging tools create a replica of a storage device, such as a hard drive or a USB flash drive. These tools are essential for digital forensics because they allow investigators to analyze the original device without altering it [85].

3.5.7.2 Analysis Tools

Analysis tools are used to examine the data collected during an investigation. These tools can help investigators in three ways:

1. Identify patterns
2. Correlate data
3. Visualize results

3.5.7.3 File Recovery Tools

File Recovery and Data Carving Tools recover deleted or lost files from various storage devices. These tools can be helpful in cases where data has been intentionally or accidentally deleted [86]. The efficiency and effectiveness of such tools have been examined in studies comparing their performance in data recovery scenarios. These tools can prove invaluable in digital investigation and computer forensics by enabling critical data and evidence recovery.

3.5.7.4 Network Forensics Tools

Network forensics tools capture and analyze network traffic. These tools can help investigators identify malicious activity, detect intrusions, and investigate cybercrimes. Such a tool box includes a variety of tools for traffic capture, protocol analysis, packet inspection, intrusion detection, malware identification, data reconstruction, timeline analysis, and legal evidence gathering.

3.5.7.5 Database Forensics Tools

Database forensics tools examine and analyze database records. These tools can help investigators identify patterns, correlate data, and visualize the results.

3.5.8 Future Research Directions and Open Challenges

The subject of security and forensics is ever evolving. Hence, it raises several research directions and open challenges. Some of these include:

1. Developing new methods for detecting and preventing ransomware attacks.
2. Improving the security of IoT devices using secure communication protocols, device hardening, and data encryption.
3. Bringing standardization in IoT devices can help develop effective countermeasures.
4. Developing new forensic techniques for e-documents and data.
5. Addressing the legal and ethical challenges of Cybersecurity and forensics.
6. Integrating AI and ML techniques to improve the detection and prevention.
7. Using human-centered design principles to develop more effective and user-friendly cybersecurity solutions.

3.6 CONCLUSION

This chapter focuses on Cybersecurity and data protection for e-documents. Emphasis is drawn toward threats, vulnerabilities, and mitigation strategies. It highlighted digital forensics techniques for investigating cyber incidents and preserving evidence. Legal frameworks and emerging technologies like Cloud computing, Blockchain, AI, and Quantum computing are discussed. The chapter stressed the importance of adopting comprehensive strategies to safeguard e-documents and sensitive information. It emphasized that Cybersecurity is an ongoing process requiring continuous monitoring and adaptation. Future research directions include developing new threat detection methods, improving security for emerging technologies, and addressing legal and ethical implications. Ongoing research, innovation, and education investment are crucial for advancing Cybersecurity and creating a more secure digital environment.

REFERENCES

1. H. Taherdoost, "Cybersecurity vs. information security," *Elsevier*, vol. 215, pp. 483–487, 2022. https://doi.org/10.1016/j.procs.2022.12.050.
2. Y. Li and Q. Liu, "A comprehensive review study of cyber-attacks and cybersecurity: Emerging trends and recent developments," *Elsevier*, vol. 7, pp. 8176–8186, 2021. https://doi.org/10.1016/j.egyr.2021.08.126.
3. J. Kaur and K. Ramkumar, "The recent trends in cybersecurity: A review," *Journal of King Saud University - Computer and Information Sciences*, vol. 34, no. 8, pp. 5766–5781, 2022. https://doi.org/10.1016/j.jksuci.2021.01.018.
4. M. Alghamdi, Digital forensics in cybersecurity: Recent trends, threats, and opportunities. In: *Cybersecurity threats with new perspectives*, M. Sarfraz, Ed., IntechOpen, 2021.
5. R. Stoykova, "Digital evidence: Unaddressed threats to fairness and the presumption of innocence," *Elsevier*, vol. 42, 2021. https://doi.org/10.1016/j.clsr.2021.105575.
6. A. Haider and W. Bhatti, "Importance of cybersecurity in software quality assurance," *IEEE*, pp. 6–11, 2022. https://doi.org/10.1109/ICET56601.2022.10004656.
7. W. Admass, Y. Munaye and A. Diro, "Cybersecurity: State of the art, challenges, and future directions, cybersecurity and applications," *KeAi*, vol. 2, 2024. https://doi.org/10.1016/j.csa.2023.100031.
8. A. Nisioti, G. Loukas, A. Mylonas and E. Panaousis, "Forensics for multi-stage cyber incidents: Survey and future directions," *Elsevier*, vol. 44, 2023. https://doi.org/10.1016/j.fsidi.2022.301480.
9. A. Dimitriadis, N. Ivezic, B. Kulvatunyou and I. Mavridis, "D4I - digital forensics framework for reviewing and investigating cyber attacks," *Elsevier*, vol. 5, 2020. https://doi.org/10.1016/j.array.2019.100015.
10. I. Gupta, A. Singh, C.-N. Lee and R. Buyya, "Secure data storage and sharing techniques for data protection in cloud environments: A systematic review, analysis, and future directions," *IEEE*, vol. 10, pp. 71247–71277, 2022. https://doi.org/10.1109/ACCESS.2022.3188110.
11. N. Shingari and B. Mago, "The importance of data encryption in ensuring the confidentiality and security of financial records of medical health," *IEEE*, pp. 1–6, 2024. https://doi.org/10.1109/IATMSI60426.2024.10503174.
12. T. Katulić and N. Protrka, "Information security in principles and provisions of the EU data protection law," *IEEE*, pp. 1219–1225, 2019. https://doi.org/10.23919/MIPRO.2019.8757153.
13. D. Korff, "The Indian digital personal data protection act, 2023, viewed from a European perspective," *SSRN*, p. 58, 2023. http://dx.doi.org/10.2139/ssrn.4614984.
14. X. Feng and Y. Zhao, "Digital forensics challenges to big data in the cloud," *IEEE*, pp. 858–862, 2017. https://doi.org/10.1109/iThings-GreenCom-CPSCom-SmartData.2017.132.
15. F. Casino *et al.*, "Research trends, challenges, and emerging topics in digital forensics: A review of reviews," *IEEE*, vol. 10, pp. 25464–25493, 2022. https://doi.org/10.1109/ACCESS.2022.3154059.

16. A. Castiglione, A. Santis and C. Soriente, "Security and privacy issues in the portable document format," *Elsevier*, vol. 83, no. 10, pp. 1813–1822, 2010. https://doi.org/10.1016/j.jss.2010.04.062.
17. K. Raja, V.R. Kanagavalli, P.K. Nizar Banu and K. Kannan "An efficient methodology for resolving uncertain spatial references in text documents," *IGI Global*, vol. 11, no. 3, pp. 1–17, 2020. https://doi.org/10.4018/IJSSMET.2020070101.
18. K. Broman and K. Woo, "Data organization in spreadsheets," *Taylor & Francis*, vol. 7, no. 1, pp. 2–10, 2018. https://doi.org/10.1080/00031305.2017.1375989.
19. M. Alenezi, H. Alabdulrazzaq, A. Alshaher and M. Alkharang, "Evolution of malware threats and techniques: A review," *IJCNIS*, vol. 12, no. 3, pp. 326–337, 2020.
20. G. Tsochev, R. Trifonov, O. Nakov, S. Manolov and G. Pavlova, "Cybersecurity: Threats and challenges," *IEEE*, pp. 1–6, 2021. https://doi.org/10.1109/ICAI50593.2020.9311369.
21. A. B. Ruhani and M. F. Zolkipl, "Keylogger: The unsung hacking weapon," *Majmuah Enterprise*, vol. 6, no. 1, pp. 33–43, 2023.
22. D. Tai, P. Gallus and P. Františ, "Macro malware development issues," *IEEE*, pp. 1–6, 2023. https://doi.org/10.1109/ICMT58149.2023.10171257.
23. T. Gautam and A. Jain, "Analysis of brute force attack using TG—Dataset," *IEEE*, 2015. https://doi.org/10.1109/IntelliSys.2015.7361263.
24. A. Novak and M. Vilceanu, "The internet is not pleased": Twitter and the 2017 Equifax data breach," *Taylor & Francis*, vol. 22, no. 3, pp. 196–221, 2019. https://doi.org/10.1080/10714421.2019.1651595.
25. N. Saxena, E. Hayes, E. Bertino, P. Ojo, K.-K. Choo and P. Burnap, "Impact and key challenges of insider threats on organizations and critical businesses," *Electronics, Vol.* 9, no. 9, p. 1460, 2020. https://doi.org/10.3390/electronics9091460.
26. J. Pereira, N. Ivaki and M. Vieira, "Characterizing buffer overflow vulnerabilities in large C/C++ projects," *IEEE*, vol. 9, 2021. https://doi.org/10.1109/ACCESS.2021.3120349.
27. O. Ojagbule, H. Wimmer, and R. Haddad, "Vulnerability Analysis of Content Management Systems to SQL Injection Using SQLMAP.," *IEEE*, pp. 1–7, 2018. https://doi.org/10.1109/SECON.2018.8479130.
28. D. Stefanović, D. Nikolić, D. Dakić, I. Spasojević and S. Ristić, "Static code analysis tools: A systematic literature review," *DAAAM International*, vol. 31, no. 1, pp. 565–573, 2020. https://doi.org/10.2507/31st.daaam.proceedings.078.
29. F. Salahdine and N. Kaabouch, "Social engineering attacks: A survey," *MDPI*, vol. 11, no. 4, pp. 1–17, 2019. https://doi.org/10.3390/fi11040089.
30. S. Tirumala, M. Valluri and G. Babu, "A survey on cybersecurity awareness concerns, practices, and conceptual measures," *IEEE*, pp. 1–6, 2019. https://doi.org/10.1109/ICCCI.2019.8821951.
31. S. S. Zainal Abidin and M. Husin, "Improving accessibility and security on document management system: A Malaysian case study," *Emerald Publishing Limited*, vol. 16, pp. 137–154, 2018. https://doi.org/10.1016/j.aci.2018.04.002.
32. M. Alenezi, H. Alabdulrazzaq and N. Mohammad, "Symmetric encryption algorithms: Review and evaluation study," *IJCNIS*, vol. 12, no. 2, pp. 256–272, 2020.
33. A. Ometov, S. Bezzateev, N. Makitalo, S. Andreev, T. Mikkonen and Y. Koucheryavy, "Multi-factor authentication: A survey," *MDPI*, vol. 2, no. 1, 2018. https://doi.org/10.3390/cryptography2010001.
34. A. Ocaka, D. Briain, S. Davy and K. Barrett, "Cybersecurity threats, vulnerabilities, mitigation measures in industrial control and automation systems: A technical review," *IEEE*, pp. 1–8, 2022. https://doi.org/10.1109/Cyber-RCI55324.2022.10032665.
35. K. Oo, "Design and implementation of electronic payment gateway for secure online payment system," *IJTSRD*, vol. 3, no. 5, pp. 1329–1334, 2019. https://www.ijtsrd.com/papers/ijtsrd26635.pdf.
36. Ö Aslan and R. Samet, "Mitigating cybersecurity attacks by being aware of vulnerabilities and bugs," *IEEE*, pp. 222–225, 2017. https://doi.org/10.1109/CW.2017.22.

37. S. Liu and R. Kuhn, "Data loss prevention," *IEEE*, vol. 12, no. 2, pp. 10–13, 2010. https://doi.org/10.1109/MITP.2010.52.
38. Z. Zhang, W. He, W. Li and M. Abdous, "Cybersecurity awareness training programs: A cost–benefit analysis framework," *Emerald Publishing Limited*, vol. 121, no. 3, pp. 613–636, 2021.
39. A. Fernandes, A. Oliveira, L. Santos and C. Rabadão, "A strategy for implementing an incident response plan," *ProQuest*, 2021. https://doi.org/10.34190/EWS.21.080.
40. X. Lu, F. Wang, C. Jiang and P. Lio, "A universal malicious documents static detection framework based on feature generalization," *Applied Sciences*, vol. 11, no. 24, 2021. https://doi.org/10.3390/app112412134.
41. C.-M. Chiu, F.-M. Hsu, M.-H. Shen and C.-M. Lin, "An architecture for electronic exchange of official documents based on email and blockchain," *JIT*, vol. 24, no. 2, 2023. https://doi.org/10.53106/160792642023032402012.
42. N. Al-Dmour *et al.*, "Cybersecurity threats on multifunctional devices and mitigation techniques," *IEEE*, pp. 1–6, 2023. https://doi.org/10.1109/ICBATS57792.2023.10111138.
43. A. Nunan, E. Souto, E. Santos and E. Feitosa, "Automatic classification of cross-site scripting in web pages using document-based and URL-based features," *IEEE*, 2012. [Online]. Available: https://ieeexplore.ieee.org/stamp/stamp.jsp?tp=&arnumber=6249380
44. C. Neale, I. Kennedy, B. Price, Y. Yu and B. Nuseibeh, "The case for zero trust digital forensics," *Elsevier*, vol. 40, 2022. https://doi.org/10.1016/j.fsidi.2022.301352.
45. M. Yip, "Signature Analysis and Computer Forensics," pp. 1–11, 2008.
46. S. Parasram, "Digital Forensics with Kali Linux," 2017. [Online]. Available: https://api.semanticscholar.org/CorpusID:231157986
47. A. Nieto, R. Rios and J. Lopez, "IoT-forensics meets privacy: Towards cooperative digital investigations," *MDPI*, vol. 18, no. 2, 2018. https://doi.org/10.3390/s18020492.
48. M. Rafique and M. N. A. Khan, "Exploring static and live digital forensics: Methods, practices, and tools," *IJSER*, vol. 4, no. 10, pp. 1048–1056, 2013.
49. K. Mohamad, A. Patel and M. Deris, "Carving JPEG images and thumbnails using image pattern matching," *IEEE*, pp. 78–83, 2011. https://doi.org/10.1109/ISCI.2011.5958888.
50. N. Koroniotis, N. Moustafa and J. Slay, "A new intelligent satellite deep learning network forensic framework for smart satellite networks," *Elsevier*, vol. 99, 2022. https://doi.org/10.1016/j.compeleceng.2022.107745.
51. N. Meghanathan, S. Allam and L. Moore, "Tools and techniques for network forensics," *IJNSA*, vol. 1, no. 1, pp. 14–25, Apr. 2009. https://doi.org/10.48550/arXiv.1004.0570.
52. S. Soltani and S. Seno, "A survey on digital evidence collection and analysis," *IEEE*, pp. 247–253, 2017. https://doi.org/10.1109/ICCKE.2017.8167885.
53. E. Casey and B. Turnbull, "Digital evidence on Mobile devices," *Elsevier*, vol. 3, pp. 1–44.
54. C. Karagiannis and K. Vergidis, "Digital evidence and cloud forensics: Contemporary legal challenges and the power of disposal," *MDPI*, vol. 12, no. 5, 2021. https://doi.org/10.3390/info12050181.
55. R. Mohammad and M. Alqahtani, "A comparison of machine learning techniques for file system forensics analysis," *Elsevier*, vol. 46, pp. 53–61, 2019. https://doi.org/10.1016/j.jisa.2019.02.009.
56. Z. Jianfeng, Z. Wensheng and X. Jingdong, "StegEraser: Defending cybersecurity against malicious covert communications," *IOS Press*, vol. 32, no. 2, 2023. https://doi.org/10.3233/JCS-220094.
57. T. Li, H. Li, L. Hu and H. Li, "A reversible steganography method with statistical features maintained based on the difference value," *IEEE*, vol. 8, pp. 12845–12855, 2020. https://doi.org/10.1109/ACCESS.2020.2964830.
58. S. Garfinkel, "Forensic feature extraction and cross-drive analysis," *Elsevier*, vol. 3, pp. 71–81, 2006. https://doi.org/10.1016/j.diin.2006.06.007.

59. G. Mutiara, R. Wijaya and Periyadi, "Digital forensics random access memory using live technique based on network attacked," *IEEE*, pp. 1–6, 2017. https://doi.org/10.1109/ICoICT.2017.8074695.
60. X. Zha and S. Sahni, "Fast in-place file carving for digital forensics," *Springer*, vol. 56, pp. 141–158, 2011.
61. J. Grier, "Detecting data theft using stochastic forensics," *Elsevier*, vol. 8, pp. S71–S77, 2011. https://doi.org/10.1016/j.diin.2011.05.009.
62. K. Hausknecht, D. Foit and J. Burić, "RAM data significance in digital forensics," *IEEE*, pp. 1372–1375, 2015. https://doi.org/10.1109/MIPRO.2015.7160488.
63. S. Qureshi, S. Tunio, F. Akhtar, A. Wajahat, A. Nazir and F. Ullah, "Network forensics: A comprehensive review of tools and techniques," *Science and Information Organization (SAI)*, vol. 12, no. 5, pp. 879–887, 2021. https://doi.org/10.14569/IJACSA.2021.01205103.
64. R. Chopade and V. K. Pachghare, "Ten years of critical review on database forensics research," *Elsevier*, vol. 29, pp. 180–197, 2019. https://doi.org/10.1016/j.diin.2019.04.001.
65. S. Al-E'mari, Y. Sanjalawe, S. Makhadmeh and H. Alqudah, "Digital forensics meets blockchain: Enhancing evidence authenticity and traceability," *IEEE*, pp. 1–6, 2024. https://doi.org/10.1109/ICCR61006.2024.10532961.
66. E. Nwankwo and Prisca, "Use of information technology by the libraries in digitally preserving of information resources in the 21st century," *Nigerian Journal of African Studies (NJAS)*, vol. 5, no. 1, 2023. [Online]. Available: https://www.nigerianjournalsonline.com/index.php/NJAS/article/view/3909/3805
67. J.-P. Yaacoub, H. Noura, O. Salman and A. Chehab, "Digital Forensics vs. Anti-Digital Forensics: Techniques, Limitations, and Recommendations," *arXiv*, 2021. https://doi.org/10.48550/arXiv.2103.17028.
68. K. Conlan, I. Baggili and F. Breitinger, "Anti-forensics: Furthering digital forensic science through a new extended, granular taxonomy," *Elsevier*, vol. 18, pp. S66–S75, 2016. https://doi.org/10.1016/j.diin.2016.04.006.
69. V. Rupp and M. Grafenstein, "Clarifying 'personal data' and the role of anonymisation in data protection law: Including and excluding data from the scope of the GDPR (more clearly) through refining the concept of data protection," *Elsevier*, vol. 52, 2024. https://doi.org/10.1016/j.clsr.2023.105932.
70. R. Becker *et al.*, "Purpose definition as a crucial step for determining the legal basis under the GDPR: Implications for scientific research," *Oxford*, vol. 11, no. 1, 2024. https://doi.org/10.1093/jlb/lsae001.
71. D. Mahto and D. Yadav, "RSA and ECC: A Comparative Analysis," *Research India Publications*, vol. 12, no. 9, pp. 9053–9061, 2017.
72. F. Lalem, A. Laouid, M. Kara, M. Al-Khalidi and A. Eleyan, "A novel digital signature scheme for advanced asymmetric encryption techniques," *MDPI*, vol. 13, no. 8, pp. 1–15, 2023. https://doi.org/10.3390/app13085172.
73. M. Smid, "Development of the Advanced Encryption Standard," *National Institute of Standards and Technology (NIST)*, vol. 126, pp. 1–18, 2021, doi: 10.6028/jres.126.024.
74. E. Conrad, S. Misenar and J. Feldman, *Eleventh hour CISSP*, 2nd ed. ScienceDirect, 2014. [Online]. Available: https://www.sciencedirect.com/book/9780124171428/eleventh-hour-cissp
75. A. Carpino, "Choosing the Right Data Loss Prevention Architecture," Gartner, G00780385, 2023. [Online]. Available: https://www.gartner.com/document/4237199?ref=solrAll&refval=418011753&
76. S. Ahmad, S. Mehfuz and J. Beg, "Cloud security framework and key management services collectively for implementing DLP and IRM," *Elsevier*, vol. 66, no. 7, pp. 4828–4836, 2022. https://doi.org/10.1016/j.matpr.2022.03.420.

77. A. Rafi, C. Shepherd and K. Markantonakis, "A first look at digital rights management systems for secure Mobile content delivery," *IEEE*, pp. 549–558, 2023. https://doi.org/10.1109/TrustCom60117.2023.00087.
78. B. Lowans, J. Fritsch and A. Bales, "Innovation Insight: Data Security Posture Management," Gartner, G00784502, 2023. [Online]. Available: https://www.gartner.com/en/documents/4405499
79. M. Syahreen, N. Hafizah, N. Maarop and M. Maslinan, "A systematic review on multi-factor authentication framework," *International Journal of Advanced Computer Science and Applications*, vol. 15, no. 5, 2024. https://dx.doi.org/10.14569/IJACSA.2024.01505105.
80. A. Yadav and S. Sagi, "Management cases studies and technical use cases on web 3." In: *Advances in web technologies and engineering*, D. Darwish, Ed., IGI Global, 2024, pp. 267–287. https://doi.org/10.4018/979-8-3693-1532-3.ch013.
81. S. K. Sood and Pooja, "Quantum computing review: A decade of research," *IEEE Trans. Eng. Manage*, vol. 71, pp. 6662–6676, 2024. https://doi.org/10.1109/TEM.2023.3284689.
82. O. A. Ajala, "Exploring and reviewing the potential of quantum computing in enhancing cybersecurity encryption methods," *Magna Scientia Advanced Research and Reviews*, vol. 10, no. 1, pp. 321–329, 2024. https://doi.org/10.30574/msarr.2024.10.1.0038.
83. B. S. Rawal and A. Biswas, "A comprehensive survey of post-quantum cryptography and its implications," *Engineering Science & Technology*, vol. 5, no. 2, pp. 256–269, 2024. https://doi.org/10.37256/est.5220244169.
84. E. Dervisevic *et al.*, "Quantum Key Distribution Networks – Key Management: A Survey," 2024, *arXiv*: arXiv:2408.04580. Accessed: August 21, 2024. [Online]. Available: http://arxiv.org/abs/2408.04580
85. A. Al-Sabaawi, "Digital Forensics for Infected Computer Disk and Memory: Acquire, Analyse, and Report," in *2020 IEEE Asia-Pacific Conference on Computer Science and Data Engineering (CSDE)*, Gold Coast, Australia: IEEE, 2020, pp. 1–7. https://doi.org/10.1109/CSDE50874.2020.9411614.
86. P. S. Priya, N. S. Rokade, D. M. More, M. K. Adsure, R. T. Mayur and P. T. Purushottam, "Analytical forensic investigation with data carving tools," *International Journal of Innovative Science and Research Technology*, vol. 8, no. 3, pp. 1685–1696, 2023. https://doi.org/10.5281/ZENODO.7797118.

4 Cybersecurity and Forensic Facet of Border Security

Nitin Agarwala

4.1 INTRODUCTION

With the advancements in digital technology the world has become smaller. With a click of a button, messages and information can be shared between two people or organisations sitting in two opposite corners of the world, almost instantaneously. With time, digitalisation has even permitted movement of money to encourage e-commerce resulting in obliterating physical geographic boundaries that define a nation. Even though physical boundaries continue to exist with boots on the ground to ensure physical security, in reality these boundaries have become only notional since information and finances can cross these traditional borders instantaneously, seamlessly and without control. Since money transfers are possible, the digital world has attracted criminals who aim to exploit vulnerabilities of the existing system to threaten finances, privacy and security of the users [1]. This necessitates the need of looking at cybersecurity and cyber forensics to ensure security, both traditional and non-traditional, in this digitalised environment.

Border threats have been an area of concern for humankind since the advent of civilisation. When we were nomadic, the threat on camp boundaries or borders was from wild animals for the safety and security of vulnerable members of the group. As settlements came about, the threat increased to attacks from other clans and tribes along with those of wild animals. With time, the threat evolved to be from neighbouring/regional/global powers and the domain of concern increased from land to the sea and the air and now space at the national level. When looked from the point of view of an individual, such threats exist for every individual wherein the border is set to be defined as the area of influence they control [2].

While the definition of 'border' may be debated, the threat remains consistent to be from the cyber domain as a result of the percolation of digital technologies into our lives. This digitalisation has automated biometrics, banking, travel, access, entertainment, services and other numerous aspects that define the present life of an individual. This has made security of cyber systems a critical element of our daily lives. Threats such as data breach, disruption and degradation of systems, espionage and physical attacks need to be addressed. A malicious hacker can attack as nation by targeting critical infrastructure to disrupt their functioning [3]. Yet another

DOI: 10.1201/9781003497868-4

security concern from this digital world is the operation of drug syndicates on the 'dark web' that allow easy access to various narcotic substances. These dark webs allow hiding the identity and location of the user from law enforcement agencies making them hard to catch.

From security viewpoint of a nation, four critical targets exist. These include the physical infrastructure, human resource, technology and information and data [4]. These could be protected by either unilateral border security or through cooperative border security. A unilateral border security is required when there is state of conflict or confrontation on the border. On the other hand, the cooperative arrangement is feasible when both nations have a mutual understanding and a common security goal. This protection is provisioning physical barriers which unfortunately have lost relevance in this evolving digital age. Technologies like drones with Global Positioning System (GPS) can cause *physical* damage while gaming platforms can act as a messaging medium. When tracking of these technologies is originally difficult, it is made trickier when Virtual Private Networks (VPNs) are used. The *human resource* can be targeted through social media and honey trapping that can lead to sharing of sensitive information. Similarly, attacks on *technology* and *data* can occur by exploiting the vulnerabilities of the operating systems or phishing through the internet. This can result in financial, security or functional degradation of the country attacked. Of these, humankind is the weakest link as they are not adequately trained and are natural victims to money and sex. The cyber thus provides an opportunity to threaten the security of a nation and perpetrate crime without physically resolving to aggression. This has allowed cyber threat to converge with traditional threats to either complement them or provide fresh opportunities thereby making numerous older security threats obsolete.

Cyber threat in the recent past has become a reality and has been encountered by all those who are connected to the digital world. To ensure that the known vulnerabilities of this cyber world are avoided, cybersecurity is exercised. However, to get better insights to the growing cyber threats, use of cyber forensics is considered important. This chapter thus will aim to bridge the gap of what needs to be done in cybersecurity and cyber forensics to counter crimes and maintain security of the border by studying the recent trends in digital forensics. This would allow improved awareness and greater resilience to cyber-attacks to ensure that own data is not compromised. Accordingly, the chapter will first discuss the basic terminologies to dispel confusion created by incorrect use of terms before the various types of cybersecurity and digital forensics including recent trends are discussed. The challenges and way ahead are discussed next before the chapter is concluded.

4.2 TERMINOLOGIES

A number of terms and jargons are used to address issues in the cyber space. Many of these terms are confusing and tend to even confuse the computer professionals. To ensure that such confusion is avoided here, we begin by discussing the terminologies associated with the topic of discussion.

4.2.1 Cyber-Crime

When an electronic communication device is used to commit a crime, it is called as a cyber-crime. In this act, the criminal may access information of the victim that may be personal or economic in nature. To achieve this end, the criminal may introduce a malicious code for progressive theft of information or may undertake outright theft of the desired information. Such crimes can be committed either against individuals or nations. To undertake these attacks, the criminals may use private networks of the like of VPNs or The Onion Router (TOR), or any other means to establish communication that is anonymous to surveillance and investigation. This crime may be committed by any of the following means [5].

a. *Crime-as-a-Service (C-aa-S)* is a toolkit that is provided by professionals to the less experienced to carry out the crime. Such toolkits allow even the inexperienced to undertake sophisticated cyber-attacks. Such services are provisioned by using crypto currencies.
b. *Ransomware* is a subset of malware which locks the data on a victim's computer by encryption. The motive is usually monetary.
c. *Misuse of data* by criminals is done to harass the privacy of individuals and to impact business. Over the years, numerous data breaches have been reported while numerous others have gone unreported. Some big names that have experienced such breaches include Yahoo. Aadhaar, Alibaba, LinkedIn, Sina Weibo, Facebook, Marriott International, Adult Friend Finder, MySpace, NetEase, Adobe and many other [6].
d. *Online payment frauds* is yet another major cyber-crime that is committed on individuals across the globe. The crime may be committed with bank cards or internet banking and are said to be on the rise both in numbers and value.
e. *Cyber-attack on core banking system* has also been on the rise. This crime occurs on the core banking system, and may be conducted from across the border or within the country.
f. *Pornography* has continued as a crime due to the Dark Net. Use and custody of pornography is not a punishable crime in most countries. However, child pornography is punishable.
g. *Dark net crime* is affected on the dark net by using private networks to allow anonymous trading of drugs, pirated items, arms and ammunition. These are a serious threat to the law enforcing agency.
h. *Social engineering crimes* trick users into making security mistakes or sharing sensitive information. The crime uses phishing attacks.

4.2.2 Cybersecurity

Cybersecurity is predicting cyber threats and cyber-crimes, and developing, implementing and auditing processes by means of which individuals and organisations protect their information from cyber threats. The protection could be of physical electronic systems such as computers, servers, mobile devices, networks or against malicious attacks initiated by hackers. This security is developed using programmes, encryptions, security tools, policies and educating users. The other terms used for cybersecurity are information technology security and electronic information security [1].

Cybersecurity is applied to a number of categories [7]. *Network security* addresses weaknesses that exist in the operating system, network servers, network hosts, system firewalls, wireless access points and protocols used for network configuration. *Application security* ensures that software and devices remain free from threats and do not provide vulnerabilities in design, code, publishing or on the website. *Information or data security* aims to provide integrity and privacy to the data, when it is either stored or is in transit. *Operational security* is to ensure that sensitive data does not reach the wrong hands by appropriately handling and protecting data assets. Permissions of users determine data storage and sharing. *Disaster recovery security* provides an organisation to restore its functionality to the original after it has been cyber attacked. By having a business continuity plan, the organization can continue to function even when their digital systems are being restored after a cyber-attack. *End-user education* is an essential part of cybersecurity as people operating digital systems can accidentally introduce a vulnerability by following unsafe practices such as opening suspicious attachments, unknown links, unidentified flash drives, and installing freeware, to name a few.

Cybersecurity is a pre-emptive and proactive activity that looks to ensure that the digital infrastructure is resilient to the cyber-attacks likely to be inflicted on them [8]. To achieve their requirement, cybersecurity professionals use tools like Web Application Firewall, Website Malware Detector, Penetration Testing Tools, Network Mapping and Security Tools, and others as shown in Figure 4.1.

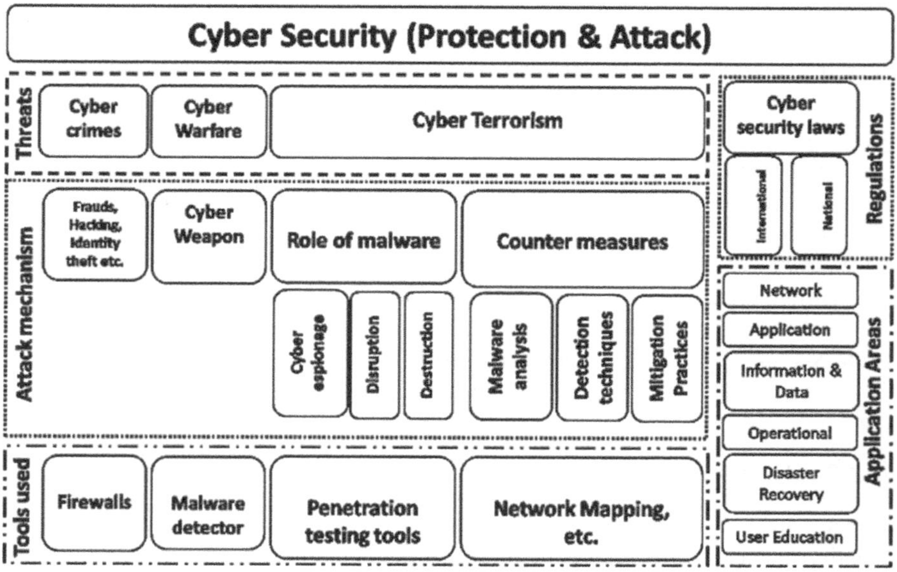

FIGURE 4.1 Cybersecurity.

Source: Author.

4.2.3 Border

The outer edge of a system is defined as its border. For a nation, the concept of border as a boundary between two sovereign states is essentially a Westphalia concept. This concept provided a clear demarcation of where the rights and duties of jurisdiction of a government applied and where it did not. These borders are intimately connected to the security of the nation as governments are elected by the people with a view that they would provide security, prosperity and wellbeing to the people [9]. While borders are known to evolve across history through a dynamic process, the international law considers borders as static [10]. This is based on the understanding that globalisation and information revolution have modified the original assumption on which the understanding of border is established.

This concept can be applied to land, oceans, air and space. Accordingly, the land border is defined by treaties made by countries; the maritime borders are defined by the Law of the Sea Treaty [11], the air borders by the Chicago Convention [12] and that of the space by the Outer Space Treaty [13]. These laws and treaties define the land order by a line while the maritime and air border is governed by the land boundary. But for space, the borders have not been drawn and have been declared the Common Heritage of Mankind (CHM) [14]. However, these borders have been challenged by globalisation and ingress of the digital world. The globalisation has ensured that one country is dependent upon the other for some essential item or the other for its sustenance and economic growth. Similarly, the spread of digitalisation has ensured that information and knowledge sharing is not confined to a territory. These two have thus blurred the concept of physical lines of border.

If one was to extrapolate the concept of borders to activities within a country such as businesses and even simple households, each one of them can be said to have a border which eventually need to be protected and like the border-line of the nation, the border-line of these smaller entities also is being blurred due to the spread of digitalisation to every facet of our lives.

4.2.4 Threats

Since borders are created to provide security, the understanding of threats within these borders is essential to look at the nature of the security to be provided. As discussed, as the borders can be in various domains, the associated threat too would vary as per the domain. This notwithstanding, the broad demarcation of these threats is *traditional* and *non-traditional.*

Of these, the *traditional* threats are those that challenge the political sovereignty and territorial integrity of a nation. Such threats require weapons, military and diplomatic means to be handled. On the other hand, *non-traditional* threats challenge the survival and wellbeing of the state and its citizens. They arise from non-military activities. Climate change, natural disasters, food shortage, irregular human migration, pollution, human trafficking, drug trafficking are some non-traditional threats that are on the rise [15]. These threats could be natural, man-made or interplay of both, as is the case of threat arising from climate change due to global warming and environmental degradation. These threats are valid for the land and the maritime domain, however, that for the air domain they are slightly different and include insider threat, civilian unrest, operating near conflict zone, terrorist attacks, human trafficking, drug smuggling, inadequately documented passengers and use of aircraft for bombing, or suicide attacks [16]. Similarly, vulnerabilities to space infrastructure can be on any of the ground, communication (link) or space segments. The ground segment consists of the fixed or mobile equipment that may be land based, sea based or airborne and is used to interact with the space segment. This segment is threatened by physical and virtual attacks. The link segment is the data transmitted between the ground and space segments and is threatened by manipulation of radio signals transmitted by satellite to ground station or by altering the signal for use for some other purpose (also called broadcast signal intrusion). The space segment consists of satellites, space stations and transportation systems for astronauts. This segment is threatened by debris collision, radiations, physical kinetic or non-kinetic attack either in space or from the ground or from cyber-attacks due to weakness in the ground station, network components or receivers receiving data from satellites [17].

With technological changes, political evolution and new ideas, these threats are evolving [18]. Of these, technological changes and innovations are considered drivers of social and economic development. In the recent past, the speed of these changes has been stupendous that has been driven by a digital revolution based on gathering, processing and analysing the data collected. While these technologies can be beneficial, they can also be misused or abused [19]. In most cases, these technological advances are occurring beyond the realms of the government and at a rate that is far more than what the state can keep abreast with [20]. With digital revolution the threat of an attack on the data collected has evolved. This has adversely affected the privacy and security of users and is termed as 'cyber threat'. Even though the Human Rights Council upholds the right to privacy, the efforts to address crime in the cyber domain are slow in this digital age as states refuse to agree on an international framework to counter cybercrimes [21].

4.2.5 Border Security

Border security is said to be achieved when desired border control policies are enforced and cross-border movement of unrequired items is disallowed. As the concept of border can be extrapolated to the smallest component of the society, the need for border security too can be extrapolated to these smallest components thereby requiring that the security of each component in the system called 'nation' has a border and needs border security. Since handling the security of an individual is more of a subset of the security of the nation and can be subsumed in the rules and regulations provided by the government of the people, the discussion in this chapter will be limited to the border security of the nation. The discussion with respect to the individual on the other hand will be discussed explicitly when and where required. Need and nature of security on the border will be defined by the type of the border. The border may be either an open border (as the Schengen) or a controlled border (India-Pakistan). The former may require just an outpost for surprise checks while the latter would require much more elaborate arrangements on the border of both human resource and material leading to need for extensive surveillance and checking.

4.2.6 Need for Cybersecurity as Part of Border Security

With increasing ingress of digital technologies, criminals, terrorists, nation states and perpetrators have been using cyber methods to circumvent physical borders and take advantage of its asymmetry. In doing so they can attack critical infrastructure, steal sensitive government information, steal trade secrets, import hazardous material, siphon funds from banks and individuals and deliver ammunition using drones without physically moving their personnel across the border. With this new form of threat converging with the traditional border security the threat environment has been enhanced and in some cases was made traditional border security efforts obsolete.

This necessitates that healthy cybersecurity practices are adhered to and followed by every citizen at all times to ensure that the security of the individual and hence the nation is not compromised. The problem at hand becomes even more complex as the response of governments towards cyber-attacks is usually responsive and not preventive. The defence from such attacks has been defined as the responsibility of the individual or that of the organisation and mostly handled by private agencies that have knowledge of technology. Since a compromised device can act as an additional source of attack, subsequent attacks would be easier making defence difficult.

Since cyber threats are relevant to daily lives of the common citizen through smart cities, shipping sector, banking sector, gaming, e-commerce, automobiles, connectivity, transportation, power grids and many more, cybersecurity has emerged as a critical threat in this digital world where individuals are required to protect their own borders when interacting in this world. However, while physical boundaries exist for data transmission lines, there are no boundaries in the cyber world and the attack may be initiated from any direction and on anyone. Hence, there is a need for an adaptive and evolutionary approach for creating a cyber border as has been done for air travel by creating a border control for foreign travellers [22].

4.2.7 Need for Cyber Forensics as Part of Border Security

A tight coupling between the physical and digital world has provided both benefits and issues of cybersecurity. Since cyber-attacks can impact individuals and businesses socioeconomically, they need to be promptly identified and prosecuted which requires evidence. Cyber forensics aims to provide such evidences by analysing the data that has been stored and the existing file system. This is done by carrying out forensics of the network, or by reverse engineering the attack by inspecting the malware, log files, network traffic etc. on the compromised device. Since the required information may be scattered at various physical and virtual locations and can deteriorate with time, a large human resource, equipment and time is required. To improve speed, automation may need to be resorted to. Issues like privacy concerns, lack of standards for forensics, rise of antiforensic techniques such as encryption, obfuscation and cloaking, and different jurisdictions and legal systems for systems across borders are some challenges that the digital forensics will need to face [23]. This requires that the forensic investigators should handle multidisciplinary processes that may include law, criminal justice, finance, computer science, data mining and networking.

Since governments have so far preferred to be reactive towards cyber-attacks, it is imperative on the security agencies to ensure that acts of cyber-attacks are analysed adequately. This would ensure that such events are not repeated and necessary mechanisms towards cybersecurity are developed and positioned to make the cyber domain safer for the user. As such activities remain a cat and mouse game, cyber-attacks and cyber forensics are an ever evolving threat and response.

4.2.8 Areas Where Cybersecurity Is a Matter of Concern

With digitalisation becoming the back bone of smart equipment and connected devices through Internet of Things (IoT), cyber threat has become a part of our day-to-day living. High-profile incidents such as cryptocurrency thefts, banking system malware, cyber-attacks on national defence networks, and disruptions to critical infrastructure continue to emphasize the global scope of cyber threats [36–46]. As smart cities aim to look at transportation, community, living and environment with an aim to improve the lives of the people, cyber-attacks can cause serious damage to both life and property [47]. Cyber-attacks in various other sectors such as aviation, banking, defence, energy, industries, water and power and other areas have been reported as shown in Table 4.1. With space infrastructure slowly becoming an essential element for everyday services like communication, air transportation, maritime trade, weather monitoring and forecasting, remote sensing, financial services, television, they too are exposed to the risk of cyber threats and have been discussed in detail elsewhere [17]. Recent cyber-attacks in the aviation sector, including large-scale data breaches and system shutdowns, have highlighted the vulnerability of this critical infrastructure [48–51].

The Triton malware represents a sophisticated attack that specifically disabled safety systems at energy facilities, raising significant concerns for industrial cyber defence [52]. Industrial Control Systems (ICS) have been repeatedly targeted by attackers leveraging vulnerabilities in communication protocols and system operations [53].

The events discussed here are not considered exhaustive as they get reported much later than the occurrence of the event. A more extensive list which is regularly updated can be found in a publication of the Center for Strategic and International Studies (CSIS) for cyber-attacks events after 2006 to date [54].

4.2.9 Cyber Forensics/Digital Forensics

Cyber forensics or digital forensics includes forensics of computers, network, mobiles, and cloud with an aim to find the attacker, mechanism used, source of security breach and evaluate impact of attack by gauging loss of information. It provides a means to improve cybersecurity and helps prosecute perpetrators responsible for the attack [55] and to inform the customer of a breach if it were to occur. To undertake cyber forensics, electronic data needs to be retrieved, gathered and analysed from the impacted assets. When doing so, the legal protocols and regulations must be adhered. It is reactive as it is employed once the attack has been completed. Even though the cybersecurity and cyber forensics complement each

TABLE 4.1
Cyber-Attacks 2008–2020

Sectors	Year	Type	Nature	Description of Target	Reference
Aviation	2016	Attack	Shamoon no. 2	Civil aviation of Saudi Arabia	[24]
Banking	2011	Botnet Malware	Gameover Zeus	Steal information	[25]
	2013	Attack	Target Stores	To exploit information of bank cards	[25]
Defence	2010	Malware	Stuxnet	To modify centrifugal speed of Iranian nuclear facility	[26]
	2011	Malware	Duqu/Flame/Gauss	Developed on basis of Stuxnet Malware	[26]
Energy	2008	Attack	Vulnerability in network	Turkish Pipeline Explosion	[26]
	2010	Malware	Night Dragon	Possible through command-and-control servers of energy sector companies	[27]
	2012	Campaign	Spear-phishing email	Gas Pipeline Cyber Incident	[28]
	2012	Malware	Shamoon no. 1	Attacked Aramco network (Oil company) of Saudi Arabia	[29]
	2014	Campaign	Dragonfly/Energetic Bear	Energy sectors	[30]
Iron & Steel	2014	Attack	Spear-phishing and social engineering technique	German Steel mill	[31]
	2019	Attack	Ransomware	Norsk Hydro company	[32]
Water & Power	2015	Attack	Email phishing and black energy malware	Ukraine power grid no. 1	[33]
	2016	Attack	Vulnerabilities in old SCADA system	Kemuri Water Company	[33]
	2016	Attack	CRASH OVERRIDE malware	Power supply cut to Ukraine power grid no. 2	[33]
Others	2013	Malware	Crypto Locker	New family of ransomware	[34]
	2017	Group	APT33 Group	A Hacktivist group of Iran	[34]
	2017	Attack	NotPetya malware	Encrypts data but unable to decrypt it	[34]
	2017	Malware	TRITON/Trisis HatMan	Industrial safety systems	[34]
	2017	Attack	TSMC WannaCry	Affected TSMC	[34]
	2018	Malware	SamSam-like attack	Installed through Windows server	[34]
	2018	Malware	Kovter	A file-less malware	[34]
	2020	Malware	EKANS	New family of ransomware	[34]
	2021	Ransomware Attack	Colonial Pipeline	Pipelines managed by computers impacted. Stopped all pipeline operations	[35]
	2013	Attack	New York Dam	Possible due to vulnerable internet connection	[34]
	2013	Malware	Crypto Locker	New family of ransomware	[34]

Source: Author.

other, there can be a conflict when cyber forensics finds lapses in cybersecurity responsible for an attack. The forensics undertaken may be on two types of digital data. One that is gathered from the internet and the other retrieved from electronic, optical or magnetic media.

To collect evidence, a number of computer forensics tools are used. Some common ones include *database forensics* (to retrieve and analyse data from databases); *email forensics* (to retrieve and analyse information on platform); *mobile forensics* (to retrieve and analyse data from mobile devices); *memory forensics* (to retrieve and analyse data on RAM and/or cache); *network forensics* (to monitor intrusion detection systems and firewalls on network); and *malware forensics* (to identify malicious programs using code). The evidence collected may be done by recovering deleted files, reverse-steganography (recover hidden data inside a digital message or file), cross-drive analysis (cross-referencing computers to detect anomalies) and live analysis (analysing the RAM of a running computer to identify abnormal traffic).

As digital technology evolves, the associated cyber-threats too are evolving on a near daily basis. Accordingly, the research associated with data security is ongoing and ever evolving as attackers are experimenting with new techniques to steal or delete data of users. Since attackers in this industry are always a few steps ahead, digital forensics is considered essential as it allows an insight to the new techniques being employed by the attacker that helps evolve new and refined protocols for cybersecurity. When investigating computers, the investigator must have a brief idea of the nature of the evidence expected. Based on this understanding, the tools to use are to be selected. Since there is a high probability that the required files may have been either deleted, damaged or encrypted, the investigator needs to use an array of tools, methods or software to prevent further damage and permit early recovery of the desired information. The data that can be collected may be persistent data (which remains resident on a drive even when the computer is turned off) or volatile data (which is resident in the memory and is lost on turning off the computer). Since volatile data is short lived, the investigator should know the means to capture such information. Some tools that can be used by the investigator are shown in Tables 4.2 and 4.3 while the approach followed as shown in Table 4.4.

This requires forensic tools for different environments. Accordingly, research has been conducted to undertake digital forensics for web environment [57, 58], cloud environment [59], email environment [60], UNIX file system [61], from an android mobile phone [62], from MySQL database file system [63], from SQLite used mostly for mobile phones [64], from database triggers [65], file metadata [66], from the dump of a volatile memory [67], from unsealed encrypted drives [68] and many more. Similarly, substantial research has been conducted on tools available for undertaking digital forensics such as TrueCrypt [69], use of different forensic tools on a USB or DVD for live analysis and Automated Image and Restore software for static analysis [70], Cafegrid [71] and many others [72].

The tools used by digital forensic professionals include Redline (to collect and analyse data from network activity logs), Helix3 (an intuitive investigative tool), COFEE (Computer Online Forensic Evidence Extractor for extracting evidence from computers using Window OS), Autopsy (to undertake timeline analysis, hash filtering and deleted file recovery), CelleBrite Physical Analyzer (to detect and examine

TABLE 4.2
Some Powerful Tools to Gather Digital Evidence

Tool Name	Description	Usage	Purpose
X-Ways WinHex	Tool	For low-level data processing, inspecting files, recovering digital camera card	Recovering original file from corrupt files systems
First On Scene (FOS)	Visual Basic script code	With other tools (PSTools, LogonSessions, FPort, NTLast, PromiscDetect, FileHasher, etc.)	Creating log report of evidence which can be analysed by experts
Rifiuti	Tool	Recover files from Recycle Bin	Helps in collecting deleted and undeleted files
Pasco/browse	Tool	Analyse browsing data of a computer	Gathering records of internet activities
Galleta/Cookie	Tool		Examining contents of cookies on a computer
Forensic Acquisition Utilities (FAU)	Set of tools	Checker; file wiper, etc	Assorting research and investigation
NMap	Port scanner tool	Finds open ports on a remote machine Works without activating Intrusion Detection System (IDS) alarms	Network security systems
Ethereal	Network packet sniffer	Can be used only if strong encryption algorithms not present	Provides incoming - outgoing data over network
BinText	Tool	Filtering and pattern matching of evidence log files	To browse evidence files generated by other forensic tools.
PyFlag Tools	Tool		Log analysis
Encrypted disk detector (EDD)	Tool	Command-line	Checks local physical drives for encrypted volumes
MemGator	Memory file interrogation tool	Automates extraction of memory details, processes, network connections, malware detection, and passwords and encryption keys	Automates compilation of report for investigator
Encase	Tool	Running hash (#) functioning will identify file headers and mark them as incorrect if data is hidden	To decipher if data is hidden in an image/ music/video file

Source: After [56].

TABLE 4.3
Tools Commonly Used for Live Digital Forensic Analysis

Name of Tool	Platform	Description	Availability
AIR (Automated Image and Restore)	Windows	A GUI Creates live image dump of memory	Freeware/ Commercial
Autopsy	Window/Linux	For disk analysis	Freeware
PDUMP	Windows	To take live memory dump	Freeware
WFT (Windows Forensic Toolchest)	Windows	To automate incident response Perform live digital analysis	Freeware
SMART	Linux	Performs live digital forensic analysis	Commercial
DEFT (Digital Evidence & Forensic Toolkit)	Linux	For live computer forensic systems	Commercial
BinDiff	Windows	Extension of Interactive Disassembler (IDA) pro Identifies and highlights changes Compares code before and after running	Commercial
SIFT (SAN Investigation Forensics Toolkit)	Ubuntu	For live digital forensic in operating system	Commercial
IEF (Internet Evidence Finder)	Windows	To collect evidence from Internet	Freeware
FTK (Forensic Toolkit)	Windows	To index digital evidence	Commercial
DFF (Digital Forensic Framework)	Windows/ Linux/Mac	To collect and analyse digital evidence	Commercial
OS Forensics	Windows	To perform forensic analysis on web browsers, emails, Files, & images	Freeware/ Commercial
CAINE (Computer Aided Investigative Environment)	Linux	Toolkit for live computer forensics	Freeware/ Commercial
COFEE (Computer Online Forensic Evidence Extractor)	Windows	For live digital forensic analysis	Commercial
CMAT (Compile Memory Analysis Tool)	Windows	To analyse memory	Freeware
Wire Shark	Windows/Mac/ Linux	To capture and analyse packets on network	Open source
Network Miner	Windows/ Linux	Extracts files, images and other metadata from PCAP files on the network	Freeware
Hash Keeper	Windows	Database application for storing file hash signatures	Freeware

Source: After [74].

TABLE 4.4
Different Approaches Used for Live Digital Forensic Analysis

Focused Area	Technique Used	Merits	Limitations/Caveats
Win system	"Niglant32" and pattern matching tools	Detects applications and events by users and groups relevant events	Collected information is incoherent and usually less relevant for forensics
Linux system	Command line tool "Grep" used	Classification and training of evidence data in live and static conditions possible	Reduces data by selecting relevant evidence Specific to Linux Requires client server architecture
	LECT (Linux Evidence Collection Tool) framework	Automatic identification of targeted system Maintains integrity of evidence	Report generation based on hash values and timestamps Works for specific Linux versions – Ubuntu, Debian and Fedora (Red Hat)
On USB/DVD	Autopsy, FDumper, Scalpel, Fundl and AIR (Automated Image and Restore)	Used for live and static analyses Collects volatile information automatically	For Chinese language only
Encrypted drives	TrueCrypt	Recovers decryption keys from live image of a volatile memory	Decryption keys cannot be extracted if data on disk degrades
BitLocker encrypted drives – Live forensics	Step by step procedure Use AES and Brute force	Find password and ".BEK" file for BitLocker Then decrypt by using brute force	Works for Win 7 or NTFS drives
Data structure analysis – Live and static forensics	Cafegrid	Works on Win and Linux Works only on shared libraries and binaries where compilation done with debugging	Does not work properly if compiler stores pointers in registers and not in stack.
Mobiles	Triaging and self-knowledge	Uses self-knowledge and triaging concept for identification, acquisition and reporting Reduces amount of data for analysis by classifying relevant and similar data	Used for cold or dead analysis Lacks analysis reports and relevant data considered essential for forensic analysis
Android mobiles	Logcat and PCAP (Packet Capture) analysis	Identifies malware in mobiles Decrypts code	Demands manual steps Hence, time consuming Requires expertise
Automatic data collection	XOVAL framework	Data collected automatically from compromised system Data presented by defining data primitives	Limited to objects defined in XOVAL framework Ignores user login information

(*Continued*)

TABLE 4.4 (*Continued*)
Different Approaches Used for Live Digital Forensic Analysis

Focused Area	Technique Used	Merits	Limitations/Caveats
As a Service	HDFS (Hadoop Distributed File System) ETL (Extract Transform, and Load)	Live analysis technique Supports remote services Reduces hardware required Supports wired and wireless connections Quick index matching reduces data required	ETL process necessary for large data
Monitoring policy violation on network	Live monitoring of system behaviour	Identifies violation of security policies, monitors hidden processes and network connections automatically on standalone and network systems	Complexity in monitoring of network nodes and collaboration among them
Protection of data for digital investigation	Cryptographic model	Gathered data for forensic analysis is in encrypted form, and index file search is performed	Process slow due to encrypted data and hence large file size May cause loss of information

Source: After [74].

digital evidence), DumpZilla (to inspect browsers) and others. The international standards [73] that are considered relevant for forensics investigations are:

a. ISO/IEC 27037:2012 regarding guidelines for identification, collection, acquisition and preservation of the digital evidence
b. ISO/IEC 27042:2015 regarding guidelines for analysis and interpretation of digital evidence
c. ISO/IEC 27041:2015 regarding guidelines for assuring suitability and adequacy of incident investigative method
d. ISO/IEC 27017:2015 regarding code of practice for information security controls specifically cloud services
e. ISO/IEC 27050-1:2019 regarding requirements and guidance on activities in electronic discovery

4.3 TECHNOLOGIES TO AID BORDER SECURITY

In earlier days, border agencies relied upon physical numbers, and good observation to perform their duty of border security. With advancement and increased use of technology, the security personnel are required to operate advanced digital equipment for imaging and identification. In addition, information collected from other sensors and sensing devices need to be used to get a complete picture. At times, additional information provided by other law enforcement agencies needs to be superimposed on the available information while at times, the information collected needs to be shared with other law enforcement agencies. In the public domain, these agencies need to ensure that there is effective communication to ensure that the public is aware of the procedures and the privacy policy and is not unduly alarmed by the procedures being followed to avoid possible conflict.

4.3.1 Methods Employed for Border Security

Though the discussion on border security has slowly moved from conventional human patrolling to smart and virtual barriers using technological advancements, the procedures used are not limited to only physical or technology driven solution but a mix of both. Accordingly, these methods can be organised in four categories. These include (a) physical barriers, (b) contraband detection technologies, (c) technologies to track people in remote areas and (d) identification technologies. Technologies such as sonar equipped robotic dogs have been developed for use in inherently dangerous situations without risking human life [75]. However, use of such technology requires trained human resource. The advantages and disadvantages of the other methods are discussed in Table 4.5.

4.3.2 Averting a Single Point of Failure

Even while the technologies being employed are sophisticated, the effort is to ensure that multiple layers of border checks are employed so that a single point failure does not allow the infiltrator to cross the border. Accordingly, multiple points of intervention are created wherein both physical and digital examination is undertaken and evaluated.

4.3.3 Use of Artificial Intelligence

Though artificial intelligence has made inroads in nearly every aspect of our living including border control and border security, there are concerns regarding the reliability of AI in facial recognition [76]. These concerns include those over inconsistent accuracy obtained by existing algorithms [77]. Accordingly, fundamental concerns over discrimination, human rights [78], privacy risks and unlawful profiling have been raised. These need to be managed, studied and regulated according to the needs of the user.

4.3.4 Future Border Surveillance

The speed at which technology is advancing including autonomous and robotic systems, it is possible to imagine that in the years to come the borders will be completely manned by autonomous vehicles on ground and in the air. These vehicles will be continuously monitoring movement on the border and providing necessary alarms and input to the operator siting remotely. In the eventuality of a breach, the security forces will be intimated to take necessary action. While this may be a considered future, Israel has been using sensor-based high technology fences to guard

TABLE 4.5
Methods Used for Border Security

Technology Used	Pros	Cons
Physical Barriers	Useful in densely populated regions	Can be demolished and breached Costly to construct and maintain
Cargo Scanners (using air pressure change or analysing gases emitted)	New generation X-ray and gamma-ray scanners highly effective	Expensive Require trained human resource Large size Difficult to handle and install
Ground sensors - Seismic, acoustic & infra-red (To track people in remote areas)	Ground sensors allow wide range of coverage Can be used in rugged terrain	Can provide false alarms (animals) Regular maintenance required Susceptible to being vandalized
Fixed surveillance towers - with radar, high-resolution and IR cameras	Highly effective to identify people and vehicles from long distances at low-cost	Terrain can block radar Visible and can easily avoided by infiltrators
Planes and helicopters - with IR cameras and night-vision equipment	Highly effective Covers large areas	Expensive to operate and maintain Limited use in bad weather
Unmanned aerial vehicles (UAVs/drones)	Covers large areas quickly Low cost	Limited battery life and range Raise privacy concerns
Biometric Identification Devices backed by AI (digital passports, biometric data on RFID chip, fingerprint readers, IRIS scanners, facial recognition)	High reliability, High accuracy No direct contact with security personnel required	Raise privacy and data protection concerns Need trained human resource
Facial Recognition	Easier identification of personnel using available database	Low levels of trust Raises concerns of discrimination, privacy, and unlawful profiling
Drones	Enhances situational awareness Enables silent tracking of unauthorized border activities	Trained human resource essential for effective use
AI drones	Do not need human operators	Raises concerns of reliability and privacy when used with AI
Sensor-equipped robot dogs	Used in dangerous situations without risking human life	Needs qualified human resource to analyse information collected

Source: Author.

their border with Gaza. The 20-foot high fence uses multilayered wire, steel and concrete and has a network of cameras, sensors, radars and weapon systems that are monitored by towers and observation and listening posts [79]. These notwithstanding, the recent surprise attacks by Hamas across these high-technology fences raise questions on the efficacy of technology and the need of the human element behind such technologies. The vibrations created by the music carnival being conducted in the border area made the ground vibration sensors ineffective while a major Jewish holiday on the day of attack added to the surprise element and increased the ineffectiveness of the system. Since people and not machines fight wars, the focus on human resource cannot and should not be overlooked to address border security.

The case of Israel shows that borders fences are prone to physical damage and technology in such cases can be driven ineffective [79]. Yet another means of making the technology ineffective are attacks from the cyber world that are silent and at times not found till after the damage has been done. This requires the need for cybersecurity and cyber forensics to ensure border security.

4.4 CHALLENGES

Digital forensics is a powerful tool to address cybersecurity. It is still in its infancy, and knowledge about this field is limited. Since this field has a high potential in addressing the ever growing cyber challenges, the field is developing fast. However, effective use of this technology has its own challenges.

a. New devices are being developed on a near daily basis. This added with the advances in the field of software and communication makes it challenging to keep up with the diversity and complexity of digital evidence sources.
b. The growth of strong encryption techniques including end-to-end encryption hinders access and analysis of the data for digital investigation.
c. Being cross border in nature, digital forensics and the resulting outcome can face jurisdictional and logistic challenges.
d. Limitation of resources such as budget, equipment and human resource can hinder ability to conduct a thorough digital investigation.
e. Due to the amount of data generated on a daily basis, sorting out relevant data for digital forensics is time-consuming and resource-intensive.
f. Data retention by companies and organisations is yet another challenge. With no clear policy available in this regard, digital forensics can be difficult since usually the time gap between cyber-attack and acknowledgement is high due to issues such as ignorance, security and company image. This makes conduct of digital forensics difficult and even prohibitive since the data to be examined may have been deleted due to lack of the required data retention policy. This impedes realisation of justice and national security.
g. As digital evidence is feasible only after infringing privacy, it is essential that legal frameworks addressing this challenge be framed to ensure timely and effective digital forensics.
h. As digital technologies advance, cybercriminals too evolve in their means to infiltrate systems and evade detection. Keeping pace with the technological advances and advances made by cybercriminal is a challenge and requires constant vigilance and innovation.
i. Since data is spread across various devices and platforms, reconstructing a complete digital picture can be a challenge.
j. To ensure quality and reliability of evidence generated from digital forensics, requisite standards and certificates are required to be put in place which can be a complex process and a challenge.

4.5 MODELS FOR DIGITAL FORENSICS

Digital forensics is a systematic process based on scientific methodologies. A number of defined models have been proposed by researchers since 1984 since the time law enforcement agencies such as the FBI began developing procedures for undertaking digital investigation. Some of the models are generic in nature and can be applied over a wider spectrum of issues while others are specific and are relevant to a specific problem. While developing these models it is essential to remember that the framework of the model should not be too simplistic as it may not provide the necessary guidance, nor be too complicated as it would create limitations of its usage. While it may be impossible to design a universal and perfect process, an ideal framework is one that is general and can adopt new techniques with ease.

Since a number of models have been proposed over the years, they can be categorised into three:

a. *General models.* These models, proposed from 2000 to 2010, define the entire digital forensics process. In this period the exact process of digital forensics was still controversial and being developed. Most of the subsequently proposed models refine the existing model.
b. Investigation-specific models
c. Define new problems/methods

4.5.1 Computer Forensic Investigative Process

The first model given by Pollitt in 1984 [75] consists of four phases of acquisition, identification, evaluation and admission as shown in Figure 4.2.

Based on this basic computer forensic investigation model, the models have evolved over the years and can be tabulated as given in Table 4.6.

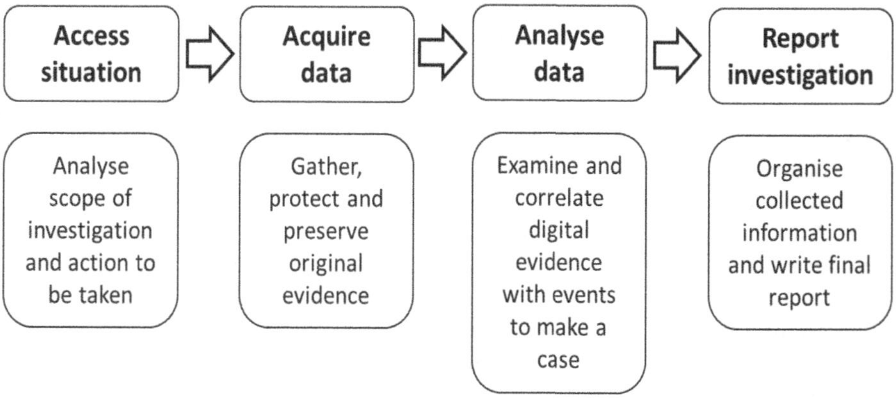

FIGURE 4.2 The process followed in computer forensics investigative process.

Source: After [75].

TABLE 4.6
Evolution of Digital Forensics Models

Initial Model	Model Given By	New Model	Model Given By
DFRWS Model	Palmer et al. [80]	**Systematic Digital Forensic Investigation Model (SRDFIM)**	Agarwal et al. [81]
		Abstract Digital Forensics Model (ADFM)	Reith et al. [82]
Integrated Digital Investigation Process (IDIP)	Carrier and Spafford [83], DCSA by Rogers [84]	**Cyber Forensic Field Triage Process Model (CFFTPM)**	Rogers et al. [84]
Carrier & Spafford Model	Carrier and Spafford [85]	**Enhanced Integrated Digital Investigation Process (EIDIP)**	Baryamureeba and Tushabe [86]
Integrated Digital Forensic Process Model (IDFPM)	Kohn et al. [87]	**Digital Forensics as a Service (DFaaS) Process Model**	van Baar et al. [88]

Source: Author.

4.5.2 DFRWS Investigative Model

A general purpose digital forensics framework proposed in 2001 by the Digital Research Workshops. It consists of six main phases as shown in Figure 4.3.

Identification	Preservation	Collection	Examination	Analysis	Presentation	Decision
Event/ Crime Detection	Case Management	Preservation	Preservation	Preservation	Documentation	
Resolve Signature	Imaging Technology	Approved Methods	Traceability	Traceability	Expert Testimony	
Profile Detection	Chain of Custody	Approved Software	Validation techniques	Statistical	Clarification	
Anomalous Detection	Time Synchronisation	Approved Hardware	Filtering techniques	Protocols	Mission Impact Statement	
Complaints		Legal Authority	Pattern Matching	Data Mining	Recommended Countermeasure	
System Monitoring		Lossless Compression	Hidden data discovery	Timeline	Statistical Interpretation	
Audit Analysis		Sampling	Hidden data extraction	Link		
Etc.		Data Reduction		Spacial		
		Recovery Techniques				

FIGURE 4.3 The DFRWS investigative model.

Source: After [80].

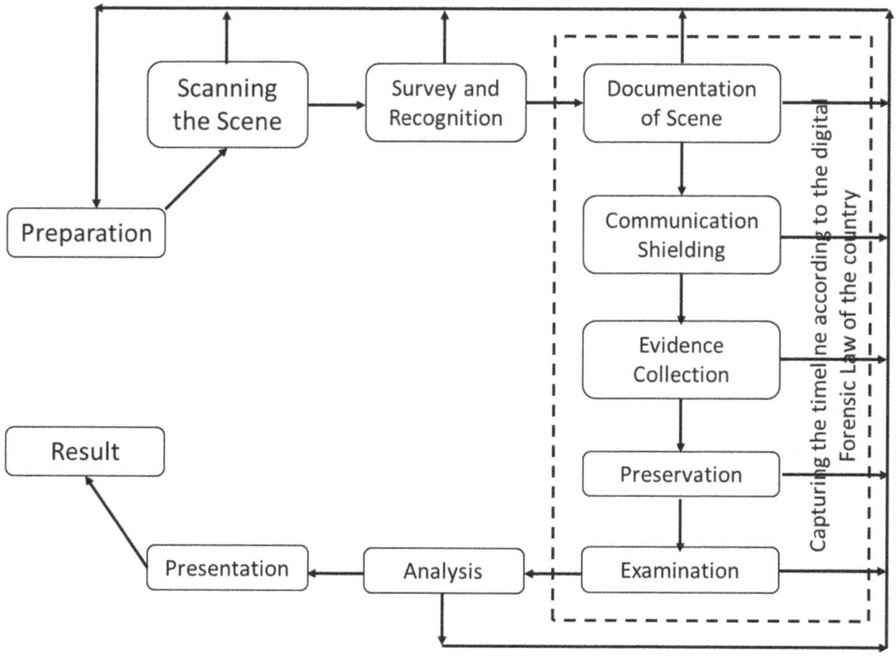

FIGURE 4.4 Phases of Systematic Digital Forensic Investigation Model (SRDFIM).

Source: After [81].

4.5.3 Systematic Digital Forensic Investigation Model (SRDFIM)

The model addresses some shortcomings of previous methods. It provides a consistent, standardized and systematic framework that works systematically according to captured evidence and provides a generalized methodology for non-technical observers. The flowchart for this model is shown in Figure 4.4.

4.5.4 Abstract Digital Forensics Model (ADFM)

Proposed in 2002, the Abstract Digital Forensic Model is inspired by the DFRWS model. This model contains nine phases as shown in Figure 4.5. Because of the additional phases, the likelihood of successfully identifying and prosecuting crimes increases.

a. **Identification** – Identify evidence.
b. **Preservation** – Perform maintenance of integrity and security of evidence.
c. **Collection** – Record evidence and make a duplicate copy of main evidence.
d. **Examination** – Examine relevant information and finding.
e. **Analysis** – Link data to recover and identify damaged and deleted files. If required, re-examine information for clarity.
f. **Reconstruction** – Reconstruct situation with obtained evidence.

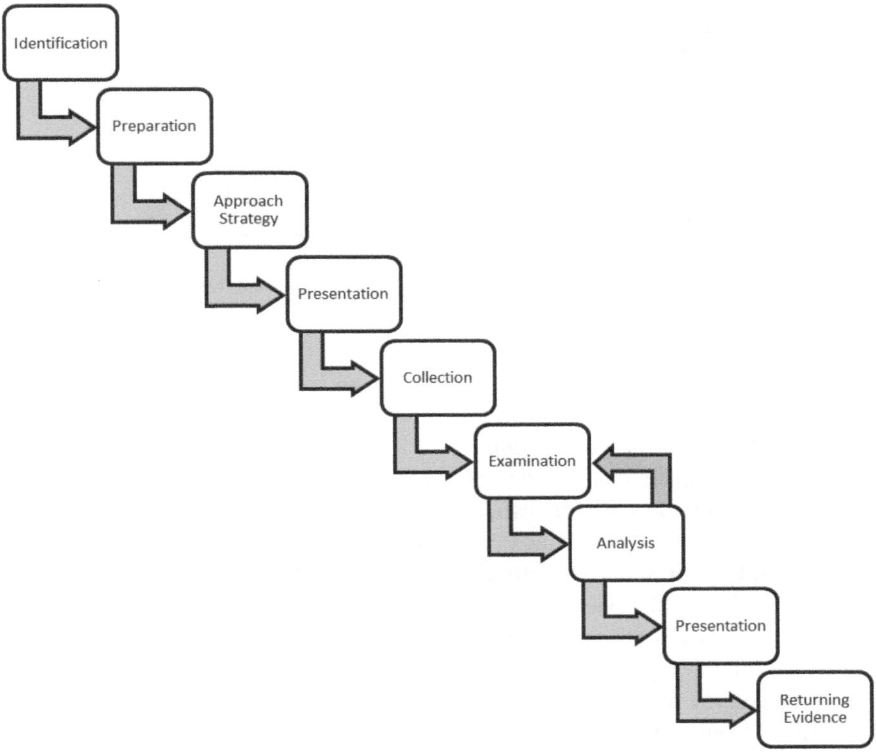

FIGURE 4.5 Phases of Abstract Digital Forensics Model (ADFM).

Source: After [78].

g. **Documentation** – Document information found and recreated till now to assist legal proceedings.
h. **Presentation** – Present findings in form of graphs, reports and visual aids to further investigation process.
i. **Returning evidence** – Return evidence to original evidence on completion of examination.

4.5.5 Integrated Digital Investigation Process (IDIP)

To integrate available models, IDIP was proposed in 2003. It aims to map digital and physical investigations. The model has five groups (Figure 4.6) and 17 phases.

a. **Readiness group** to ensure that investigation can be supported. Consists of:
   i. *Operations readiness* where training and equipment to investigators is provided.
   ii. *Infrastructure readiness* phase ensures availability of needed data.
b. **Deployment group** provides a mechanism for incidents to be detected and confirmed.

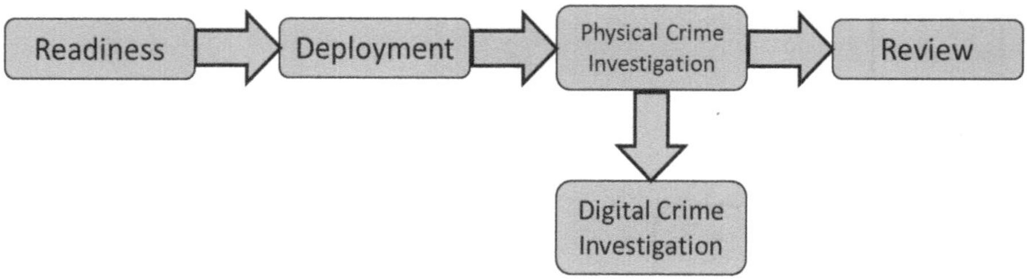

FIGURE 4.6 Phases of Integrated Digital Investigation Process (IDIP).

Source: After [79].

Consists of

i. *Detection and notification*
ii. *Confirmation and authorization*

c. **Physical crime scene investigation group** collects and analyses physical evidence to recreate the incident. It consists of six phases.
d. **Digital crime scene investigation group** undertake analysis by considering each digital device to be an independent crime scene. Collection of all electronic evidence is done here. Consists of
   i. Preservation
   ii. Survey for physical/digital evidence
   iii. Document evidence and scene
   iv. Search for physical/digital evidence
   v. Physical/digital crime scene reconstruction
   vi. Presentation of physical/digital scene theory
e. **Review group** reviews the whole process with an aim to identify new procedures, their training requirements and improve existing ones.

4.5.6 Cyber Forensic Field Triage Process Model (CFFTPM)

CFFTPM formalizes the investigative approach into a model. It believes that since some investigations are time-sensitive, a delay can allow the suspect to escape or can lead to the death of a victim. However, it is not an ultimate solution and should be used when appropriate after weighing legal and technical considerations.

It requires a field approach to identify, analyse and interpret digital evidence without taking the involved system(s)/media to the lab as shown in Figure 4.7. The model has been successfully used in various real-world cases [89].

4.5.7 Enhanced Integrated Digital Investigation Process (EIDIP)

The EIDIP was given in 2004 and is an extension of the IDIP model. In IDIP, the investigator considers the machine as the primary crime scene and the physical crime scene is considered as the secondary scene [90]. However, in EIDIP two additional phases (traceback and dynamite) are added as shown in Figure 4.8.

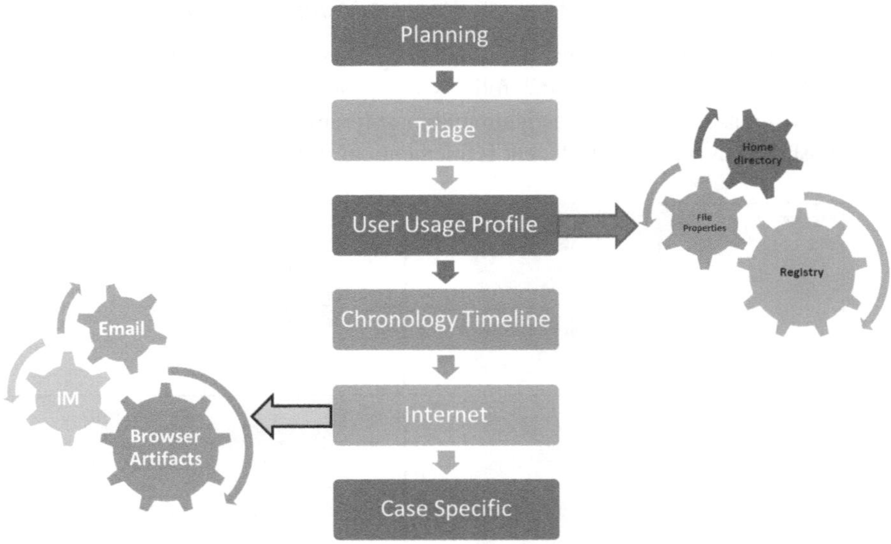

FIGURE 4.7 Cyber Forensic Field Triage Process Model (CFFTPM).

Source: After [89].

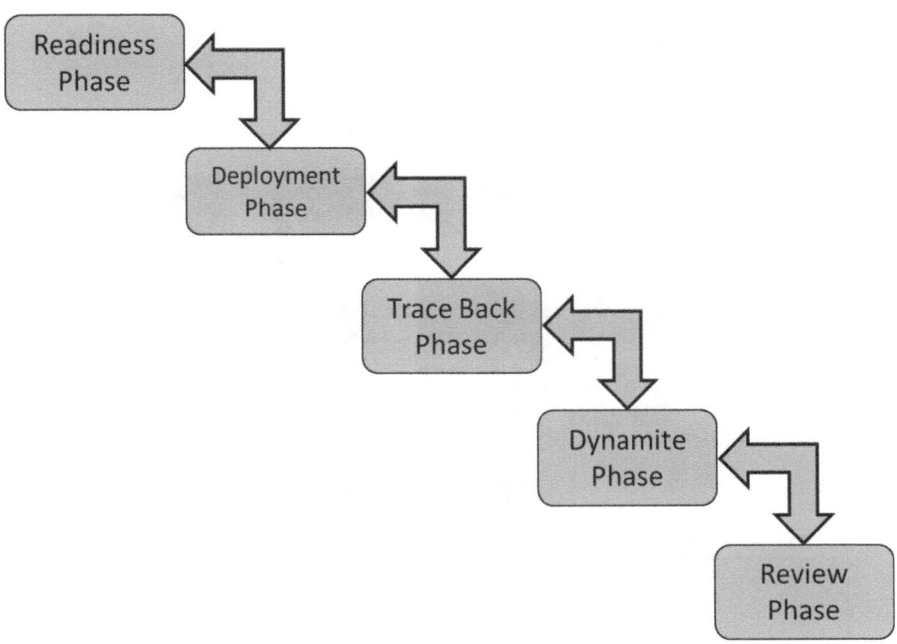

FIGURE 4.8 Enhanced Integrated Digital Investigation Process (EIDIP).

Source: After [91].

4.5.8 Integrated Digital Forensic Process Model (IDFPM)

The IDFPM was developed to follow an integrated and standardised process for digital forensics [92]. The model follows the processes of preparation, incident, incident response, physical investigation, digital forensic investigation and presentation as shown in Figure 4.9. Recent refinements of digital forensic process models

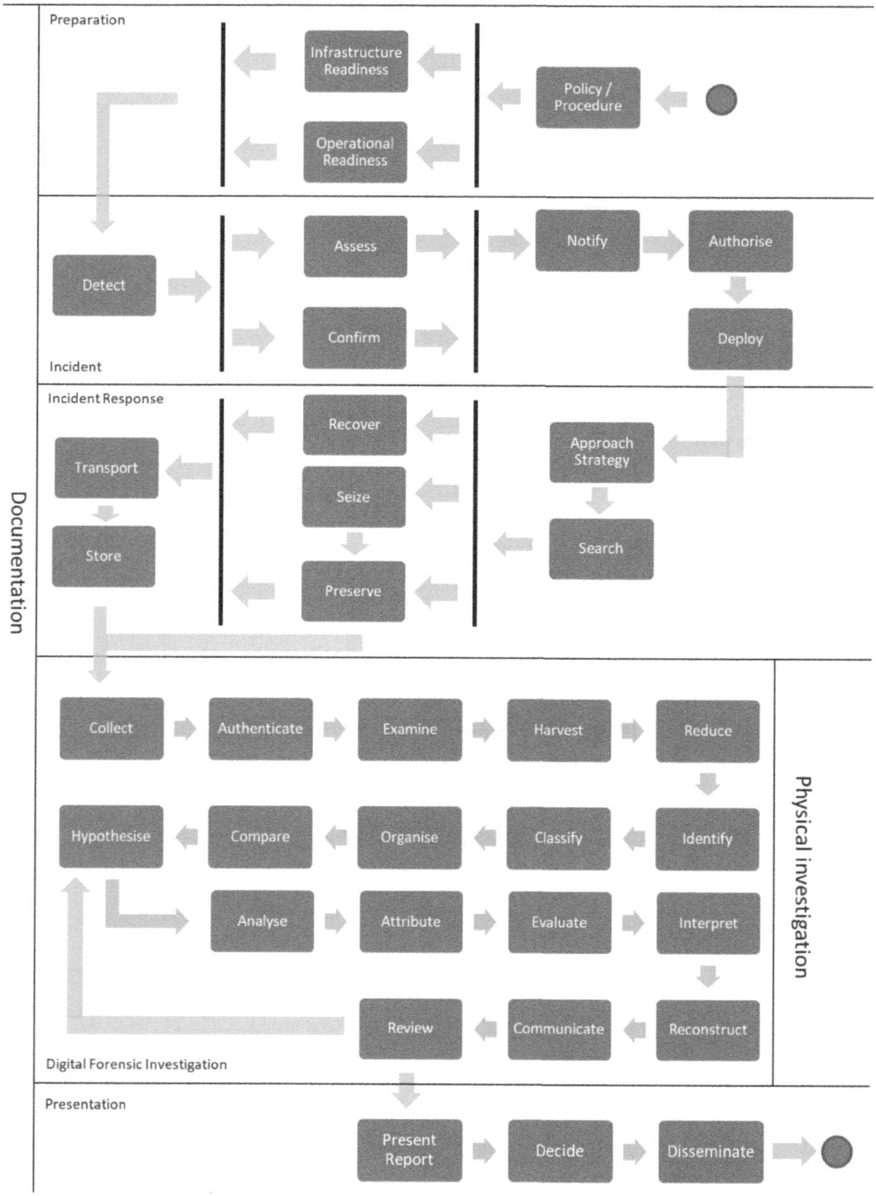

FIGURE 4.9 Integrated Digital Forensic Process Model (IDFPM).

Source: After [92].

aim to address challenges in investigating cyber incidents across interconnected systems [87].

4.5.9 Digital Forensics as a Service (DFaaS) Process Model

The Digital Forensics as a Service (DFaaS) process model [93] uses a new service-based approach for processing and investigating the high volume of seized digital material. The process allows *identification*, *classification*, *organizing* and *comparing* the traces within seconds, based on the *hypotheses* and the questions of the investigators. The process can be used at any time during the investigation.

4.5.10 Ciarhuain's Methodology

This model given in 2004 is one of the most comprehensive models. It has 12 stages and substages. The model was developed to address cyber forensics for Malaysia and specifies phases that are pertinent to a digital forensics investigation. While the model is effective, it has a number of redundant stages with no mention of preservation of acquired evidence.

4.5.11 Salemat and Perumal Methodologies

These two models are recent models and considered more comprehensive. Salemat was given in 2008 while Perumal in 2009. The models use the previously proposed frameworks and eliminate redundancies of earlier models. The new model is a five-phase model with phases of preparation, collection and preservation, examination and analysis, presentation and reporting.

4.6 DISCUSSION

With increased activities of everyday life becoming reliant on the cyber domain, the threat from cyber is increasing exponentially on a near daily basis. Since both, the cyber threat and the perpetrator (cyber attacker), have no physical face and abstract, it is usually difficult to identify them. Even if the criminals are apprehended, a successful conviction requires hard evidence for the judiciary to take action. This necessitates conduct of cyber forensics.

Since cyber forensics is not an exact science but a procedure that allows the collection of necessary information to piece together a series of activities that would eventually help identify a crime or a criminal act, cyber forensics need to be performed in a systematic manner such that the trail of events is maintained and visually appreciated by others. As the same is to be used by the judiciary, this source of information needs to be preserved and maintained to ensure that if challenged its correctness can be displayed to ensure the correctness of the evidence.

Yet another area of use of digital forensics is to understand new processes and procedures being employed by the criminals in undertaking a cyber-attack. This necessity evolves from the fact that like all criminals, cyber criminals too are one step ahead of the regulators and enforcement agencies. To ensure that the enforcement agencies and the public at large understand the modus operandi of the criminals to minimise future attacks such cyber forensics are considered critical.

As for looking at the cyber forensics for border security, the concern is much larger and serious. This is because the delivery mechanisms for attacks and suspicious material (drugs, contrabands, ammunition, etc.) have increased many folds with advances in the digital world. Today, with many national resources connected to the internet, attacks can be carried out remotely by merely disabling the functioning of these critical infrastructure or support systems. To ensure that such attacks can be avoided and managed efficiently, if conducted, cyber forensics is an essential tool. An analysis using cyber forensics allows greater understanding of the attack procedure and the vulnerability exploited by the attacker thereby ensuring that the system is hardened and future attacks of a similar nature can be avoided for all possible systems with such vulnerabilities.

Unfortunately, since cyber forensics is not an exact science, but involves collection of evidence of an event, a number of procedures exist for conduct of cyber forensics. Defining which is the best process/model to be followed would be incorrect and can be said to largely depend on the experience of the investigator and their acumen.

It is because of this that over the years a number of models for cyber forensics have been provided and new ones are being developed regularly. Each model has some limitation which the subsequent ones have tried to address. Since cyber forensics cannot be defined as an exact science, the new models continue to focus on defining phases and sequence of a typical investigation and defining the key concepts of each phase. In recent times, the focus of these models has moved to solving more specific issues or steps. The strengths and weaknesses of some of these models are tabulated in Table 4.7 while the steps that each of the models follow are shown in Figures 4.10 and 4.11.

4.7 WAY AHEAD

Since challenges exist for digital forensics, they need to be addressed adequately to extract the best out of the available resources and procedures [95]. Hence, some strategies and recommendations that can help address the known challenges to strengthen capabilities in digital forensics and enhance national security are:

4.7.1 Increased Investment

Digital forensics in the present form is not well established or well understood. This requires allocation of dedicated resources for the modernisation of digital forensics with the law enforcement agencies to increase its effectiveness and visibility. Such an investment will allow digital forensics to effectively combat cybercrimes and evolve faster to stay ahead or in sync with the criminals.

4.7.2 Centralised Services

Availability of centralised digital forensics centres that could be at the regional or national level will encourage collaboration and resource sharing. This would encourage efficient investigations, improved response to cyber threats and tackling of criminals.

TABLE 4.7
Strengths and Weaknesses of Digital Forensic Models

Model	Designer	Year	Strengths (Includes)	Weaknesses (Excludes)	Reference
—	M. Pollitt	1995	Identification	Authorization, Live acquisition	[75]
—	W. Kruse II, G. Heiser	2001	Authentication	Authorization, Live acquisition	[76]
Scientific Crime Scene Investigation (SCSI)	H. Lee	2001	Identification, Reconstruction	Preservation, Authorization, Presentation, Moving of evidence to controlled area	[77]
Abstract Digital Forensics Model (ADFM)	M. Reith, C. Carr, G. Gunsh	2002	Identification	Authorization, Live acquisition, Moving of evidence to controlled area	[82]
—	E. Casey	2004	Identification, Reconstruction	Focus is on investigation, Authorization, Moving of evidence to controlled area	[83]
—	S. O. Cuardhuain	2004	Awareness, Preservation, Cybercrime focus	Overlapping of steps, Live acquisition	[84]
—	C. Bogen, D. Dampier	2005	Includes various digital devices	Technical-oriented	[84]
FORZA	R. Ieong	2006	Legal inclusion	Focuses on legal aspects	[84]
—	Y. D. Shin	2008	Criminal profiling	Classification of crime, Legal aspects	[85]
—	S. Perumal	2009	Archiving	Classification of crime	[86]

Source: Author.

4.7.3 Capacity Building and Training

Since the effectiveness of digital forensics is person dependent, it is important that adequate human resource is developed through comprehensive training and certification. This would encourage more individuals to look at digital forensics as their future so as to eventually enhance cybersecurity. Such capacity building needs to be fostered with the assistance of academic institutions and the industry to provide the latest industry information duly supported by strong theoretical basis.

4.7.4 Legal Framework and Standards

To ensure that the criminals can be punished for their crime, legal framework needs to be updated and reviewed regularly. Such an update would strengthen the evidence collected by digital forensics, safeguard individual privacy rights and meet requirements of law enforcement. Such legal frameworks must adapt to the dynamic nature

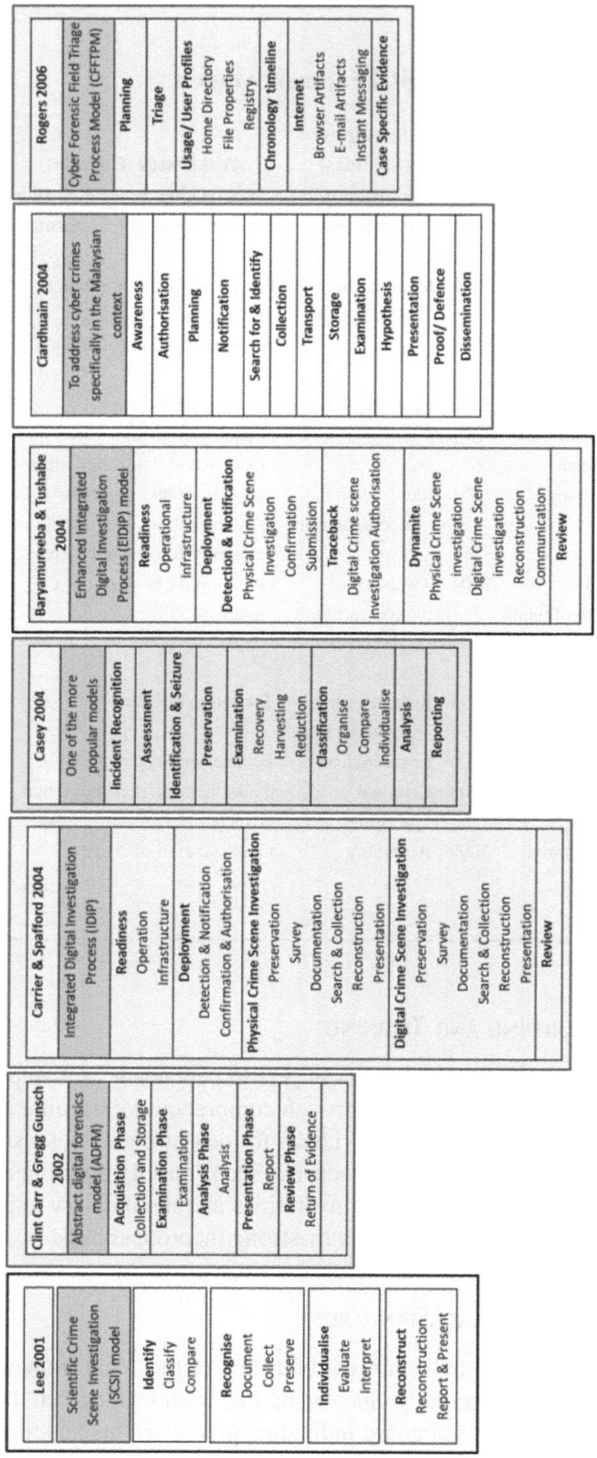

FIGURE 4.10 Proposed digital forensic framework in initial phase.

Source: After [94].

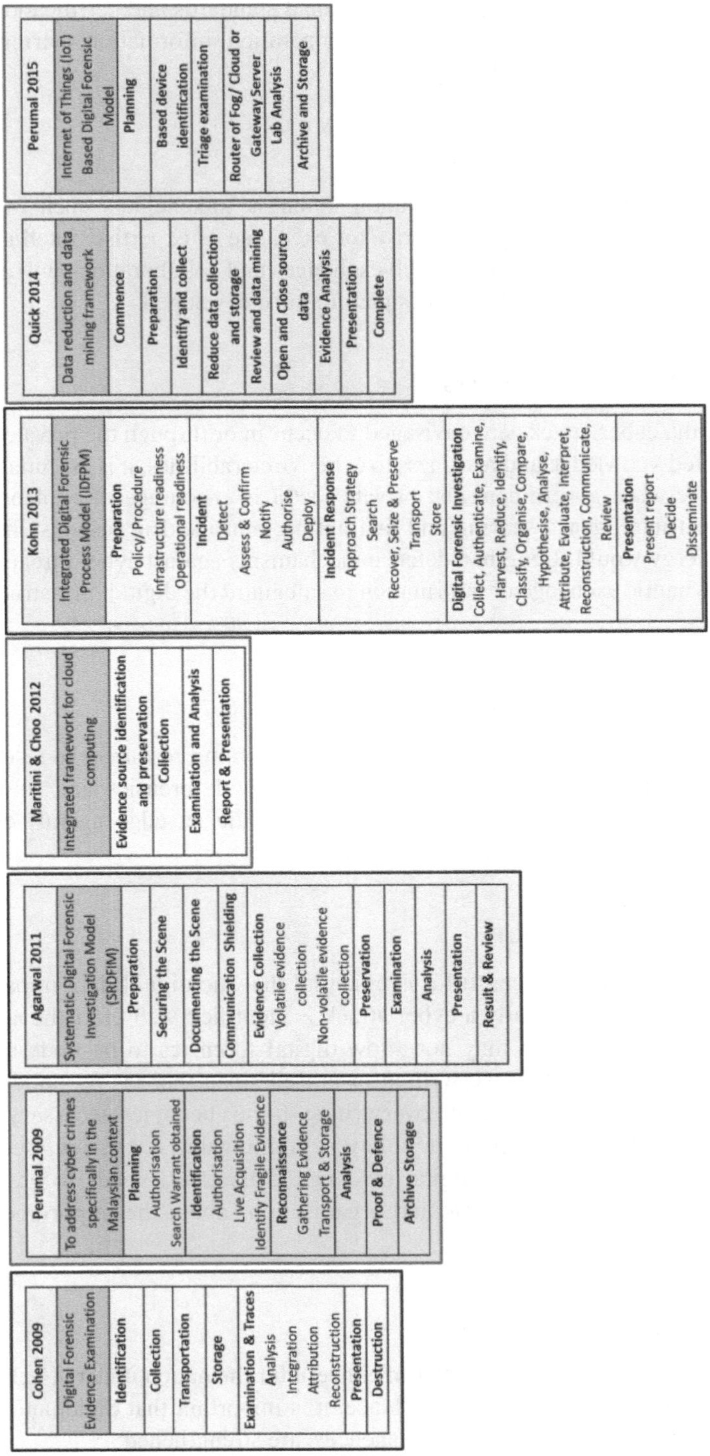

FIGURE 4.11 Digital forensics frameworks focusing on a specific use cases.

Source: After [94].

of digital technology and adhere to the international standards and certifications of digital forensics. It would allow international cooperation, information sharing and fair and effective application of digital forensics.

4.7.5 Interagency Collaboration

For effective digital forensics, collaboration amongst stakeholders such as law enforcement, intelligence and cybersecurity for exchange of expertise, intelligence and resources is considered essential. Such exchanges and collaborations will allow an effective and complete digital forensics picture to be developed.

4.7.6 Public-Private Partnerships

Since most of the cyber-attacks are envisaged to occur in or through the private sector due to limited knowledge and readiness to cyber vulnerabilities, it is essential that collaboration between government and private sector is encouraged for encouraging cyber threat intelligence sharing and facilitating joint incident response initiatives. This synergy would strengthen defence mechanisms against cyber threats and encourage a dynamic exchange of information to safeguard the digital infrastructure of the nation.

4.7.7 Research and Development

Since cyber threats are ever evolving, it is essential to commit resources to research and development for enhancing advancements in digital forensics and towards increasing cybersecurity. R&D in this field may provide an edge against cyber attackers and develop tools for improved digital forensics.

4.7.8 Data Retention Policies

For digital forensics to be successful it is essential that the digital data impacted by the attack is analysed. Usually a cyber-attack is identified well after the attack has occurred. This realisation may not allow digital forensics to be undertaken as usually the data attacked is overwritten or erased since there is no policy for retention of such magnetic media from overwriting. It thus becomes necessary that a clear and standardized data retention policy is promulgated for various sectors to ensure preservation of critical digital evidence. This effort needs to be supported with awareness among people and organisations about the importance of data preservation.

4.7.9 International Cooperation

Cyber-attacks across borders are a matter of concern for the nation under attack and from where the attack is being initiated. Hence, it is important that diplomatic ties and cooperation between law enforcement agencies are strengthened.

4.7.10 Create Public Awareness and Education

Cybersecurity can be achieved through public awareness and participation. If adequate cybersecurity mechanisms and procedures are adhered to, the possibility of cyber-attacks can be reduced. Hence, by ensuring awareness and education of the public about the concerns of cyber-attacks, need for adhering to cybersecurity protocols and need to report cyber breach immediately can help address the menace of cyber-attacks.

4.7.11 Continuous Monitoring and Adaptation

Due to the continuously changing landscape of cyber threats, there is a need to continuously monitor the threats evolving in this domain. This could be addressed better if a dedicated agency were to continuously monitor these ever-changing threats. They need to track and address the emerging threats swiftly to minimise damage. In addition, they need to periodically assess digital forensics for effectiveness, improvement and policy updating.

4.8 FUTURE TRENDS

Even though major efforts have been made by the cybersecurity community to minimise the threats to cyber connected devices and hence reduce the chances of cyber-attacks, they continue to occur due to range of vulnerabilities, ease of implanting a backdoor in the systems and inadequate means of cyber-defence mechanisms. To address these limitations advances are being made in ensuring higher level of cybersecurity. Some of these trends are:

4.8.1 Dynamic Defence Mechanisms

Dynamic defence mechanism is one such method which aims to confuse the attacker by continuously changing defence strategies and mechanisms. Moving target defence (MTD) is one such technique that is being experimented with [96].

4.8.2 Use of AI and ML

The strength of AI to predict is being used in cybersecurity to achieve early detection of cyber threats likely to impact the system. Using ML algorithms, the threats can be recognised and provisions to address the threat are being evolved. It is expected that with time AI and ML as a combine may update security protocols automatically to achieve a more secure system. This may even be supported with AI-driven bots to identify and neutralise cyber threats before they can cause damage [97].

4.8.3 Enhancing IoT Security

As IoT devices increase, they present a serious challenge to cybersecurity as these IoT devices are inherently vulnerable to attacks. Hence, efforts are being made to ensure that security of the IoT devices is enhanced to ensure that their vulnerability is reduced and existing backdoors are closed and made tight [98].

4.8.4 Securing Remote Access and Remote Work

With 'Work from Home' increasing in the recent past, primarily due to the pandemic, companies have been forced to enable remote access to their servers for their employees. Enabling this remote access to servers has become a source of major vulnerability. With remote working procedure here to stay, mechanisms need to be evolved to ensure safety remote servers against cyber-attacks and provide a safe and secure environment for the staff connected to these servers.

4.8.5 Use of Quantum Technology

Advances in quantum technology have allowed it to be used for enhancing computing, making the system robust and for being a cybersecurity threat. While the technology provides numerous options of greater cybersecurity, it also enhances the cyber threats likely to emanate from the cyber domain. Efforts to ensure that this new technology can provide the required benefits are being progressed [99].

4.8.6 Use of Zero-Trust Framework

Zero-trust framework works on the principle that the threat can exist both internal and external to the system. Hence, no request can be trusted and needs to be verified. Developing such provisions allows the systems to be continuously monitored and verified and hence reduces the chances of an attack [100].

4.8.7 Blockchain

Using blockchain as a mechanism to address the security concerns of a supply chain can reduce the cyber threats associated with supply chains. Ensuring that data tampered can be identified immediately and the process halted improves the cybersecurity of systems and disallows spread of malicious codes through cyber-attacks into the system.

4.9 CONCLUSIONS

With major activities at the border being automated to improve user experience and reduce waiting time, the need for increased cybersecurity has become a focus area. While cybersecurity can ensure resilience for these digital systems to some extent the automated systems continue to be under threat from cyber criminals who are continuously advancing their skills to attack these systems innovatively. With most of the serious attacks supported by state actors, the security vulnerability for the nation increases. Yet another area of concern is the dark net that allows easy access to drugs, arms and ammunitions at a price. Such easy access is a direct security threat to the nation and needs to be addressed in time. Autonomous systems such as drones too have become a threat as they have the ability to deliver their payload ranging from drugs, arms, explosives, etc. across the border with ease. All this added with communication strategies that use digital systems, encryption protocols and VPNs have become a serious challenge for the security agencies to monitor. At the social level, hacking of accounts for information and financial gains have also begun to emerge as serious threats for the security agencies and need to be controlled and analysed for further control. These all eventually necessitate the use of digital forensics to ensure that hackers are kept at bay, malwares, viruses and Trojans are prevented, vulnerabilities identified and information deleted by criminals is retrieved so as to ensure the integrity of digital systems and hence national security.

With increasing usage of the cyber domain for nearly every activity and facility, the threat of malicious activities is increasing which need to be tracked to protect operations in law and government enforcement, ensure public and national security and protect citizens. The need for digital forensics that aims to extract data, process it for actionable intelligence and present it for prosecution has thus become a requirement for the law enforcement and legal entities while helping improve cybersecurity by learning how systems become vulnerable to cyber-attacks through malwares or inbuilt vulnerabilities. New digital forensic frameworks have been developed to address emerging cybercrime patterns and technological complexities, focusing on flexible yet systematic investigation models [101].

As the field of digital forensics evolves and grows, there are a number of areas where more research is required including the proper mechanism to be followed to recover data from digital media. Though several tools have been designed for safe data recovery, these are not universal, suffer from limitations and cannot be used for all cases. Accordingly, the chapter has discussed cybersecurity, cyber forensics or digital forensics and their need in ensuring the safety of a border. While the term 'border' itself is multifaceted, the discussion has been kept general since cyber lacks boundaries and can be threat to any system be it personal level, the national level or international level.

DISCLAIMER

The views expressed in the paper are those of the author and do not represent the official policy of the Indian Navy or the Government of India.

REFERENCES

1. Ciarli, T., Kenney, M., Massini, S., Piscitello, L., (2021), Digital technologies, innovation, and skills: Emerging trajectories and challenges, *Research Policy*, *50*(7), 104289, https://doi.org/10.1016/j.respol.2021.104289
2. Côté-Boucher, K., Infantino, F., Salter, M. B., (2014), Border security as practice: An agenda for research. *Security Dialogue*, *45*(3), 195–208, https://doi.org/10.1177/0967010614533243
3. Humayun, M., Niazi, M., Jhanjhi, N., *et al.*, (2020), Cybersecurity threats and vulnerabilities: A systematic mapping study, *Arabian Journal for Science and Engineering*, *45*, 3171–3189, https://doi.org/10.1007/s13369-019-04319-2

4. Li, Y., Liu, Q., (2021), A comprehensive review study of cyber-attacks and cybersecurity: Emerging trends and recent developments, *Energy Reports*, *7*, 8176–8186, https://doi.org/10.1016/j.egyr.2021.08.126
5. Murugan, S., (2019), Cyber crime: Challenges to law enforcement agencies, INFOSEC depot, Cyber Investigation and Cyber Forensics, https://www.infosecawareness.in/gallery/annual-magazines/InfoSec-Depot-19/11_Cyber-investigation-forensics.pdf
6. Hill, M., Swinhoe, D., (8 November 2022), The 15 biggest data breaches of the 21st century, CSO, https://www.csoonline.com/article/534628/the-biggest-data-breaches-of-the-21st-century.html
7. Perwej, Y., Abbas, S. Q., Dixit, J. P., Akhtar, N., Jaiswal, A. K., (2021), A systematic literature review on the cybersecurity, *International Journal of Scientific Research and Management*, *9*(12), 669–710, https://dx.doi.org/10.18535/ijsrm/v9i12.ec04
8. Du, D., Zhu, M., Li, X., Fei, M., Bu, S., Wu, L., Li, K., (2023), A review on cybersecurity analysis, attack detection, and attack defense methods in cyber-physical power systems, *Journal of Modern Power Systems and Clean Energy*, *11*(3), 727–743, doi: 10.35833/MPCE.2021.000604
9. Starr, H., (2006), International borders: What they are, what they mean, and why we should care, *The SAIS Review of International Affairs*, *26*(1), 3–10, https://www.jstor.org/stable/26999290
10. Rigg, M., (2017), *The relevance of borders in the 21st century*, thesis, school of advanced air and space studies, Air University, Alabama, https://apps.dtic.mil/sti/pdfs/AD1047350.pdf
11. UNCLOS, (n.d.), United Nations Convention on the Law of the Sea, https://un.org/depts/los/convention_agreements/texts/unclos/unclos_e.pdf
12. ICAO, (n.d.), Convention on International Civil Aviation – Doc 7300, https://www.icao.int/publications/pages/doc7300.aspx
13. UNOOSA, (n.d.), Treaty on principles governing the activities of states in the exploration and use of outer space, including the moon and other celestial bodies, https://www.unoosa.org/oosa/en/ourwork/spacelaw/treaties/introouterspacetreaty.html
14. Wang, G., Huang, X., (2023), On the common heritage of mankind principle in space, *Acta Astronautica*, *211*, 926–938, https://doi.org/10.1016/j.actaastro.2023.07.002
15. Caballero-Anthony, M., (2016), Non-traditional security concept, issues, and implications on security governance, *Georgetown Journal of Asian Affairs*, 3(1), 5–13, https://hdl.handle.net/10356/145776
16. Schóber, T., Koblen, I., Szabo, S., (2012), Present and potential security threats posed to civil aviation, *INCAS Bulletin*, *4*(2), 169–175, http://dx.doi.org/10.13111/2066-8201.2012.4.2.17
17. Agarwala, N., (2024), Cyber attack against satellites, synergy, *Journal of the Centre of Joint Warfare Studies*, *3*(1), https://cenjows.in/pdf-view/?pID=23273&url=2024/05/SYNERGY_Journal_Online_CENJOWS_Feb_2024_Edition.pdf
18. Attinà, F., (2016), Traditional security issues, In: Wang, J., Song, W. (eds) *China, the European Union, and the International Politics of Global Governance*, Palgrave Macmillan, New York, https://doi.org/10.1057/9781137514004_10
19. Rolenc, J. M., (2020), Technological change and innovation as security threats, *SHS Web Conference* 74 02015, doi: 10.1051/shsconf/20207402015
20. Agarwala, N., (2022), Role of policy framework for disruptive technologies in the maritime domain, *Australian Journal of Maritime & Ocean Affairs*, *14*(1), 1–20, doi:10.1080/18366503.2021.1904602
21. Kavanagh, C., (2019), New tech, new threats, and new governance challenges: An opportunity to craft smarter responses?, Carnegie Endowment for International Peace, Working Paper, https://carnegieendowment.org/files/WP_Camino_Kavanagh___New_Tech_New_Threats1.pdf

22. Osborn, P., (2017), Cyber border security – Defining and defending a national cyber border, *Homeland Security Affairs*, 2017 UAPI Summit Special Issue, https://www.hsaj.org/articles/14093
23. Caviglione, L., Wendzel, S., Mazurczyk, W., (2017), The future of digital forensics: Challenges and the road ahead, *IEEE Security & Privacy*, *15*(06), 12–17, doi: 10.1109/MSP.2017.4251117
24. Pagliery, J., (2 December 2016), Hackers destroy computers at Saudi aviation agency, *CNN Business*, https://money.cnn.com/2016/12/01/technology/saudi-arabia-hack-shamoon/
25. Binsalleeh, H. *et al.*, (2010), On the analysis of the Zeus botnet crimeware toolkit, *2010 Eighth International Conference on Privacy, Security and Trust*, Ottawa, ON, Canada, 31–38, doi: 10.1109/PST.2010.5593240
26. Hemsley, K., Fisher, R., (2018), A history of cyber incidents and threats involving industrial control systems, In: Staggs, J., Shenoi, S. (eds) *Critical Infrastructure Protection XII*. ICCIP 2018, IFIP Advances in Information and Communication Technology, vol. 542, Springer, Cham., https://doi.org/10.1007/978-3-030-04537-1_12
27. Middleton, B., (2017), Chapter 16 – Night dragon – 2006, In: *A History of Cybersecurity Attacks: 1980 to Present* (1st ed.), Auerbach Publications, New York, https://doi.org/10.1201/9781315155852
28. CISA, (21 July 2021), Chinese gas pipeline intrusion campaign, 2011 to 2013, *Cybersecurity and Infrastructure*, https://www.cisa.gov/news-events/cybersecurity-advisories/aa21-201a
29. Alshathry, S., (2016), Cyber attack on Saudi Aramco, *International Journal of Management and Information Technology*, *11*, 3037–3039, https://doi.org/10.24297/ijmit.v11i5.5613
30. Jeffray, C., (26 September 2014), Of energetic bears and dragonflies: Espionage and the energy sector, *RUSI Defence Systems*, *16*, https://rusi.org/explore-our-research/publications/rusi-defence-systems/of-energetic-bears-and-dragonflies-espionage-and-the-energy-sector
31. Lee, R. M., Assante, M. J., Conway, T. (2014), German Steel Mill cyber attack, ICS defense use case, *SANS*, Bethesda, Maryland, https://assets.contentstack.io/v3/assets/blt36c2e63521272fdc/bltc79a41dbf7d1441e/607f235775873e466bcc539c/ICS-CPPE-case-Study-2-German-Steelworks_Facility.pdf
32. Adamov, A., Carlsson, A., Surmacz, T., (2019), An analysis of LockerGoga ransomware, *2019 IEEE East-West Design & Test Symposium (EWDTS)*, Batumi, Georgia, 1–5, doi: 10.1109/EWDTS.2019.8884472
33. Whitehead, D. E., Owens, K., Gammel, D., Smith, J., (2017), Ukraine cyber-induced power outage: Analysis and practical mitigation strategies, *2017 70th Annual Conference for Protective Relay Engineers (CPRE)*, College Station, TX, USA, 2017, pp. 1–8, doi: 10.1109/CPRE.2017.8090056
34. Alladi, T., Chamola, V., Zeadally, S., (2020), Industrial control systems: Cyber-attack trends and countermeasures, *Computer Communications*, *155*, 1–8, https://doi.org/10.1016/j.comcom.2020.03.007
35. Srinivasan, S., Li-Kuan N. (2023), Ransomware attack at Colonial Pipeline company, Harvard Business School Case 123-069, https://www.hbs.edu/faculty/Pages/item.aspx?num=63756
36. Faife, C., (2022, April 19), Beanstalk cryptocurrency project robbed after hacker votes to send themselves $182 million, *The Verge*, https://www.theverge.com/2022/4/18/23030754/beanstalk-cryptocurrency-hack-182-million-dao-voting
37. Melnykov, B., Ladutska, R., (14 March 2023), South Korean banking menace – Fakecalls, *Checkpoint*, https://research.checkpoint.com/2023/south-korean-android-banking-menace-fakecalls/

38. Coble, S., (22 February 2022), Moscow Exchange downed by cyber-attack, *Inforsecurity*, https://www.infosecurity-magazine.com/news/moscow-exchange-cyber-attack/
39. Zilbermints, R., (15 February 2022), Ukraine Defense Ministry, banks hit by cyberattack amid tensions with Russia, *The Hill*, https://thehill.com/policy/international/594330-ukraine-defense-ministry-banks-hit-by-cyberattack-amid-tensions-with/
40. CSIS, (n.d.), Significant cyber incidents, Centre for Strategic and International Studies, https://www.csis.org/programs/strategic-technologies-program/significant-cyber-incidents
41. Miller, B., Rowe, D., (2012), A survey SCADA of and critical infrastructure incidents, In: *Proceedings of the 1st Annual Conference on Research in Information Technology* (RIIT'12), Association for Computing Machinery, New York, NY, USA, 51–56, https://doi.org/10.1145/2380790.2380805
42. Lee, D., (28 May 2012), Flame: Massive cyber-attack discovered, researchers say, *BBC News*, https://www.bbc.com/news/technology-18238326
43. Satter, S., (15 March 2022), Satellite outage caused 'huge loss in communications' at war's outset – Ukrainian official, *Reuters*, https://www.reuters.com/world/satellite-outage-caused-huge-loss-communications-wars-outset-ukrainian-official-2022-03-15/
44. Park, J-m., (20 August 2023), North Korean hackers target U.S.-South Korea military drills, police say, *Reuters*, https://www.reuters.com/world/north-korean-hackers-target-us-south-korea-military-drills-police-say-2023-08-20/
45. Pearson, J., Deutsch, A., (6 February 2024), Chinese spies hacked Dutch defence network last year – intelligence agencies, *Reuters*, https://www.reuters.com/technology/cybersecurity/china-cyber-spies-hacked-computers-dutch-defence-ministry-report-2024-02-06/
46. Angle, M. G., Madnick, S., Kirtley, J. L., Khan, S., (2019), Identifying and anticipating cyberattacks that could cause physical damage to industrial control systems, *IEEE Power and Energy Technology Systems Journal*, *6*(4), 172–182, doi: 10.1109/JPETS.2019.2923970
47. Kim, K., Alshenaifi, I., Ramachandran, S., Kim, J., Zia, T., Almorjan, A., (2023), Cybersecurity and cyber forensics for smart cities: A comprehensive literature review and survey, *Sensors*, *23*, 3681, https://doi.org/10.3390/s23073681
48. BBC, (25 October 2018), Cathay Pacific data hack hits 9.4 million passengers, *BBC News*, https://www.bbc.com/news/business-45974020
49. Wakefield, J., (19 May 2020), EasyJet admits data of nine million hacked, *BBC News*, https://www.bbc.com/news/technology-52722626
50. Georgilidakis, S., (29 March 2022), Russian aviation authority suffers cyberattack, *Mentour Pilot News*, https://mentourpilot.com/breaking-russian-aviation-authority-suffers-cyberattack/
51. Antonuik, D., (28 September 2023), Russian flight booking system suffers 'massive' cyberattack, *The Record*, https://therecord.media/russia-flight-booking-system-leonardo-ddos
52. Gibbs, S., (15 December 2017), Triton: Hackers take out safety systems in watershed attack on energy plant, *The Guardian*, https://www.theguardian.com/technology/2017/dec/15/triton-hackers-malware-attack-safety-systems-energy-plant
53. Md Touhiduzzaman, Hahn, A., Lotfifard, S., (2019), An distributed cyberattack diagnosis scheme for malicious protection operation based on IEC 61850, In: *ICSS: Proceedings of the Fifth Annual Industrial Control System Security* (ICSS) Workshop, Association for Computing Machinery, New York, NY, USA, 21–29, https://doi.org/10.1145/3372318.3372326
54. CSIS, (2023), Significant cyber incidents since 2006, https://www.csis.org/programs/strategic-technologies-program/significant-cyber-incidents (accessed 18 March 2024).
55. Yusoff, Y., Ismail, R., Hassan, Z., (2011), Common phases of computer forensics investigation models, *International Journal of Computer Science and Information Technology*, *3*(3), 17–31.

56. Tomar, A. S., (2014), Cyber forensics in combating cyber crimes, *PARIPEX – Indian Journal of Research, 3*(9), https://www.worldwidejournals.com/paripex/recent_issues_pdf/2014/September/September_2014_1410775556__23.pdf
57. Guo, H., Jin, B., Huang, D., (2011), Research and review on computer forensics, In: Lai, X., Gu, D., Jin, B., Wang, Y., Li, H. (eds) *Forensics in Telecommunications, Information, and Multimedia. e-Forensics 2010.* Lecture Notes of the Institute for Computer Sciences, Social Informatics and Telecommunications Engineering, vol. 56, Springer, Berlin, Heidelberg, https://doi.org/10.1007/978-3-642-23602-0_21
58. Kaur, M., Kaur, N., Khurana, S., (2016), A literature review on cyber forensic and its analysis tools, *International Journal of Advanced Research in Computer And Communication Engineering, 5*(1), 23–28, doi: 10.17148/IJARCCE.2016.5106
59. Simou, S., Kalloniatis, C., Kavakli, E., Gritzalis, S., (2014), Cloud forensics solutions: A review, In: Iliadis, L., Papazoglou, M., Pohl, K. (eds) *Advanced Information Systems Engineering Workshops.* CAiSE 2014. Lecture Notes in Business Information Processing, vol. 178, Springer, Cham, https://doi.org/10.1007/978-3-319-07869-4_28
60. Hatole, P. P., Bawiskar, D. S. K., (2017), Literature review of email forensics, *Imperial Journal of Interdisciplinary Research, 3*(4), https://gifsa.ac.in/wp-content/uploads/2023/06/3.pdf
61. Jo, W., Chang, H., Shon, T., (2016), Digital forensic approach for file recovery in unix systems – Research of data recovery on unix file system, In: *2016 IEEE Information Technology, Networking, Electronic and Automation Control Conference*, pp. 562–565, Chongqing, China, doi: 10.1109/ITNEC.2016.7560423
62. Chang, X., Tang, X.-h., Wu, J., (2013), Forensic research on data recovery of android smartphone, In: *Proceedings of the 2nd International Conference on Computer Science and Electronics Engineering* (ICCSEE 2013), http://dx.doi.org/10.2991/iccsee.2013.299
63. Noh, W.-s., Jang, S.-m., Kang, C.-h., Lee, K.-m., Lee, Sang Jin, (2016), The method of deleted record recovery for MySQL MyISAM database, *Journal of the Korea Institute of Information Security & Cryptology, 26*(1), 125–134, https://doi.org/10.13089/JKIISC.2016.26.1.125
64. Pawlaszczyk, D., Hummert, C., (2021), Making the invisible visible – Techniques for recovering deleted SQLite data records, *International Journal of Cyber Forensics and Advanced Threat Investigations, 1*(1-3), 27–41, doi:https://doi.org/10.46386/ijcfati.v1i1-3.17
65. Hauger, W., Olivier, M., (2015), Determining trigger involvement during forensic attribution in databases, In: Peterson, G., Shenoi, S. (eds) *Advances in Digital Forensics XI. Digital Forensics, IFIP Advances in Information and Communication Technology*, vol. 462, Springer, Cham, https://doi.org/10.1007/978-3-319-24123-4_10
66. Buchholz, F., Spafford, E., (2004), On the role of file system metadata in digital forensics, *Digital Investigation, 1*(4), 298–309, https://doi.org/10.1016/j.diin.2004.10.002
67. Bolagh, S., Pondelik, M., (2011), Capturing encryption keys for digital analysis, In: *Proceedings 6th International Conference on Intelligent Data Acquisition and Advanced Computing Systems (IDAACS)*, 759–763, Prague, https://doi.org/10.1109/IDAACS.2011.6072872
68. Dija, S., Balan, C., Anoop, V., Ramani, B., (2011), Towards successful forensic recovery of BitLocked volumes, In: *Proceedings 6th International Conference on System of Systems Engineering (SoSE)*, pp. 317–322, Albuquerque, NM, 27-30 June 2011, https://doi.org/10.1109/SYSOSE.2011.5966617
69. Zhang, L., Zhou, Y., Fan, J. (2014), The forensic analysis of encrypted Truecrypt volumes, In: *2014 IEEE International Conference on Progress in Informatics and Computing*, 405–409, doi: 10.1109/PIC.2014.6972366
70. Yang, C.-H., Yen, P.-H., (2010), Fast deployment of computer forensics with USBs, In: *Proceedings of International Conference on Broadband, Wireless Computing, Communication and Applications (BWCCA)*, pp. 413–416, Fukuoka, 4–6 November 2010

71. Chan, E., Venkataraman, S., Gutierrez, A., Campbell, R. H., (2011), Characterizing data structures for volatile forensics, In: *Proceedings of 11th International Workshop on Systematic Approaches to Digital Forensic Engineering (SADFE)*, pp. 1–9, Washington, DC, USA, doi: 10.1109/SADFE.2011.5
72. Sachdeva, S., Raina, B. L., Sharma, A., (2020), Analysis of digital forensic tools, *Journal of Computational and Theoretical Nanoscience, 17*(6), 2459–2467, doi: 10.1166/jctn.2020.8916
73. ISO, (n.d.), Standards, https://www.iso.org/standards.html
74. Bashir, M. S., Khan, M. N. A., (2013), Triage in live digital forensic analysis, *The International Journal of Forensic Computer Science* http://dx.doi.org/10.5769/J201301005
75. USSNT, (2022), Feature article: Robot dogs take another step towards deployment at the border, https://www.dhs.gov/science-and-technology/news/2022/02/01/feature-article-robot-dogs-take-another-step-towards-deployment
76. Robins-Early, N., (2024, April 19), How Israel uses facial recognition systems in Gaza and beyond, *The Guardian*, https://www.theguardian.com/technology/2024/apr/19/idf-facial-recognition-surveillance-palestinians
77. Dumbrava, C., (2021), Artificial intelligence at EU borders, European Parliamentary Research Service, https://www.europarl.europa.eu/RegData/etudes/IDAN/2021/690706/EPRS_IDA(2021)690706_EN.pdf
78. Šehović, B. A., (2018), Re-bordering state responsibilities and human rights, *Reimagining State and Human Security Beyond Borders, 14*, 57–72, doi: 10.1007/978-3-319-72068-5_5
79. Saddiki, S., (2017), 1- Israel and the fencing policy, In: *World of Walls: The Structure, Roles and Effectiveness of Separation Barriers*, Open Book Publishers, Retrieved from http://books.openedition.org/obp/4560
80. James, J. I., Shosha, A. F., Gladyshev, P., (2015), Digital forensic investigation and cloud computing, In: I. Management Association (ed.) *Cloud Technology: Concepts, Methodologies, Tools, and Applications*, pp. 1231–1271, IGI Global, https://doi.org/10.4018/978-1-4666-6539-2.ch057
81. Sivaprasad, A., Jangale, S., (2012), A complete study on tools & techniques for digital forensic analysis, *2012 International Conference on Computing, Electronics and Electrical Technologies (ICCEET)*, Nagercoil, India, 881–886, doi: 10.1109/ICCEET.2012.6203877
82. Kruse II, K., Heiser, J., (2002), *Computer Forensics: Incident Response Essentials.* Addison Wesley, Boston.
83. Lee, H. C., Palmbach, T. M., Miller, M., (2001), *Henry Lee's Crime Scene Handbook*, Academic, San Diego, California; London.
84. Casey, E., (2004), *Digital Evidence and Computer Crime: Forensics Science, Computers and the Internet* (2nd ed.), Elsevier Academic Press, Amsterdam: 690 pp.
85. Cuardhuain, S. O., (2004), An extended model of cyber crime investigation, *Journal of Digital Evidence, 3*(1).
86. Bogen, C., Dampier, D., (2005), Preparing for large-scale investigations with case domain modeling, In: *Proceedings of the Digital Forensic Research Conference DFRWS 2005*, USA New Orleans, LA (August 17th-19th), https://dfrws.org/sites/default/files/session-files/2005_USA_paper-preparing_for_large-scale_investigations_with_case_domain_modeling.pdf
87. FORZA – A Zachman based digital forensics investigation framework, unpublished, 2006.
88. Shin, Y.-D., (2008), New digital forensics investigation procedure model, *2008 Fourth International Conference on Networked Computing and Advanced Information Management*, Gyeongju, Korea (South), 528–531, doi: 10.1109/NCM.2008.116
89. Rogers, M. K., Goldman, J., Mislan, R., Wedge, T., Debrota, S., (2006), Computer forensics field triage process model, *Journal of Digital Forensics, Security and Law, 1*, article 2, doi: https://doi.org/10.15394/jdfsl.2006.1004

90. Carrier, B. D., Spafford, E. H., (2004), An event-based digital forensic investigation framework, In: *Proceedings of the Digital Forensic Research Conference*, DFRWS USA 1–12.
91. Baryamureeba, V., Tushabe, F., (2004), The enhanced digital investigation process model, In: *Proceedings of the Digital Forensic Research Conference*, DFRWS USA 1–9.
92. Kohn, M. D., Eloff, M. M., Eloff, J. H. P., (2013), Integrated digital forensic process model, *Computers & Security, 38*, 103–115, doi:10.1016/j.cose.2013.05.001
93. van Baar R. B., van Beek, H. M. A., van Eijk, E. J., (2014), Digital forensics as a service: a game changer, *Digital Investigation, 11*(Supplement 1), S54–S62, https://doi.org/10.1016/j.diin.2014.03.007
94. Du, X., Le-Khac, N., Scanlon, M., (2017), Evaluation of digital forensic process models with respect to digital forensics as a service, *ArXiv, abs/1708.01730*
95. Kumar, R., Singh, I., (2023), Pointers on the increasing significance of digital forensics in national security, *DefStrat, 17*(5), https://www.defstrat.com/magazine_issues/vol-17-issue-5-nov-dec-2023/
96. Zheng, Y., Li, Z., Xu, X., Zhao, Q., (2022), Dynamic defenses in cybersecurity: Techniques, methods and challenges, *Digital Communications and Networks, 8*(4), 422–435, https://doi.org/10.1016/j.dcan.2021.07.006
97. Das, R., Sandhane, R., (2021), Artificial intelligence in cybersecurity, *Journal of Physics: Conference Series, 1964*, 042072, doi:10.1088/1742-6596/1964/4/042072
98. Lee I., (2020), Internet of Things (IoT) cybersecurity: Literature review and IoT cyber risk management, *Future Internet, 12*(9):157, https://doi.org/10.3390/fi12090157
99. Abushgra, A. A., (2023), How quantum computing impacts cybersecurity, *2023 Intelligent Methods, Systems, and Applications (IMSA)*, Giza, Egypt, pp. 74–79, doi: 10.1109/IMSA58542.2023.10217756
100. Kang, H., Liu, G., Wang, Q., Meng, L., Liu, J., (2023), Theory and application of zero trust security: A brief survey, *Entropy, 25*(12):1595, https://doi.org/10.3390/e25121595
101. Perumal S., (2009), Digital forensics model based on Malaysian investigation process, *International Journal of Computer Science and Network Security,9*(8), 38–44, http://paper.ijcsns.org/07_book/200908/20090805.pdf

5 Cybersecurity and Forensics in Banking Systems and Financial Institutions

Vinayak Gupta and Roopali Pahwa

5.1 INTRODUCTION

The swift growth of information technology has brought about significant technological advancements in various sectors, leading to substantial improvements across the finance sector. This evolution by different financial institutions has been characterised by introducing innovative platforms such as electronic banking, digital payment systems, mobile banking apps, plastic money, etc. These platforms have significantly enhanced consumer convenience, making transactions faster and more efficient. However, it is essential to note that along with these benefits, there is an increased risk of various cybercrimes associated with these technological advancements. The rise in cybercrime has caused significant financial losses for many banking systems, government agencies, and individuals. These losses have had far-reaching consequences, contributing to the proliferation of other criminal activities, funding for terrorism, and impacting the physical and mental well-being of affected individuals. Therefore, while embracing these changes, consumers and financial institutions must proactively address cybersecurity concerns, thereby empowering themselves and taking control of their digital safety [1].

Consumers from around the globe have reported a wide range of cybercrimes, such as spear phishing, cryptojacking, denial of service attacks, unauthorised backdoor entry, balance inflation, and identity theft. Every individual who utilises online banking platforms, whether for checking account balances, transferring funds, or making online payments, is at risk of falling victim to the ever-increasing prevalence of cybercrimes and cyber-related theft. The reach of cybercrimes extends beyond geographical borders, allowing them to have a far-reaching impact on individuals, organisations, and even nations. As technology advances, the magnitude and frequency of cybercrimes have grown exponentially, posing significant challenges to cybersecurity and law enforcement agencies. These criminal activities have significantly impacted individuals and organisations, leading to financial losses, privacy breaches, and other detrimental effects [2].

 DOI: 10.1201/9781003497868-5

Banks and financial institutions have agreed to implement comprehensive policies and various cybersecurity measures to safeguard their banking platforms in response to the increasing number of potential cyber threats. These policies and cybersecurity measures shall address various cyber threats to ensure the security of financial institutions and their customers [3]. To deal with the cybercrimes associated with the banking sector, a thorough analysis of the factors corresponding to the banking system must be identified, which might be used to execute cyberattacks. Some of the banks or specific sets of consumers are often targeted by financial malware due to their vulnerabilities and lack of cybersecurity measures and awareness. It is also important to understand these vulnerabilities and patterns of targeting that will help to develop effective cybersecurity measures [4]. Thus, it is crucial to implement robust cybersecurity measures and risk mitigation techniques to prevent a wide range of financial crimes in cyberspace. Additionally, promoting awareness and providing comprehensive training on cybersecurity best practices can further enhance the overall resilience against financial cybercrimes.

5.2 SPHERES INVOLVING BANKING SYSTEM AND FINANCIAL INSTITUTIONS

5.2.1 Electronic Banking

Electronic banking (e-banking) refers to the ability to conduct transactions, investments, and other banking-related activities using the Internet or other networks on gadgets like mobile phones, computers, tablets, etc. Unlike traditional banking methods, this allows consumers to access their accounts, transfer funds, pay bills, invest, take loans, and perform other financial tasks without physically visiting a bank. It typically provides 24×7 access to account information and services, offering convenience and flexibility to users. Thus, e-banking is essentially the delivery of traditional banking services through an electronic communication framework, namely the Internet, also called online banking.

There are three levels of services provided by the banks using the Internet.

5.2.1.1 Basic Level Services

At this level, the system is responsible for sharing information about a wide range of products and services offered by banks and other financial institutions to customers and the general public. It manages receiving and responding to customer inquiries through e-mail, messages, etc., ensuring that all questions and concerns are addressed promptly and effectively. This level does not require authentication.

5.2.1.2 Simple Transactional Level

At this level, customers can submit various instructions, such as applying for different products and services, raising queries regarding their account balances, etc. However, fund-based transactions, such as deposits, withdrawals, and transfers, are not permitted on their accounts at this level. This level requires authentication.

5.2.1.3 Fully Transactional Level

At this level, customers can manage their accounts by transferring funds, making payments for various bills, subscribing to additional products and services offered by the bank, and conducting transactions to purchase and sell securities. Various measures protect this level and require single or multiple layers of authentication [5–7].

5.2.2 Electronic Commerce

Electronic commerce (e-commerce) refers to the buying and selling goods and services over the Internet. It involves exchanging business information and instructions between individuals and business organisations using electronic media such as computers, telephones, and other telecommunication equipment. The emergence of the Internet has significantly transformed the landscape of e-commerce. It is no longer just an additional channel for information exchange. Rather, it has become a platform for new business strategies and models.

There are two primary types of e-commerce ventures in operation. The first type includes businesses that have integrated the electronic medium to enhance their existing products and services or to offer new ones. The second type comprises pure e-ventures, which have no visible physical presence. These businesses operate solely digitally, conducting transactions, providing services, and delivering products online. Overall, e-commerce has revolutionised the way businesses operate and interact with customers, offering unparalleled convenience and accessibility to both consumers and businesses.

E-commerce can be categorised into three broad categories based on the business's intended recipient, whether the counterpart is a consumer or another business. It's crucial to remember that some businesses are highly intricate and may fit into multiple categories. Thus, the classification includes:

5.2.2.1 Business-to-Consumer (B2C)

This involves transactions between businesses and individual consumers. It represents a rapidly expanding market that offers access to increasing potential customers across various geographical locations. The Internet is a platform through which virtually anyone, regardless of physical location, can be considered a potential customer for e-commerce businesses. Therefore, any business that targets end consumers falls into this category. Notable examples of successful e-commerce websites include Adidas, Puma, Apple, Samsung, Dominos, etc. These platforms have effectively harnessed the power of e-commerce to reach and serve customers on a global scale.

5.2.2.2 Business-to-Business (B2B)

In the context of business-to-business (B2B) transactions, it is common for the parties involved in a deal to occupy different nodes within the product supply chain. This network typically encompasses the company, its suppliers, dealers, and bankers, all collaborating to finalise and settle the various aspects of a deal through online channels. The physical movement of goods usually occurs between the supplier and the dealer at different processing stages. As the sophistication of available systems increases, this arrangement can be extended to include shippers, providers of ancillary services, IT service providers, payment system gateways, and more. Moreover, online portals function as meeting grounds for buyers and sellers of diverse products within the supply chain, resembling international trade conventions. This digital platform has facilitated the entry of relatively smaller companies into the global market, effectively levelling the playing field. Notably, banks participating in these portals offer various financial services tailored to support deals settled through the platform. Alibaba, Amazon Business, Microsoft, PayPal, Google Pay, etc. are certain examples.

5.2.2.3 Business-to-Business-to-Customer (B2B2C)

In this model, two companies collaborate to deliver products or services directly to end consumers. This relationship involves one company leveraging the capabilities of another to expand its reach and provides a service that may not be feasible to offer independently. This approach allows for a broader audience to be targeted and for more efficient and cost-effective provision of goods and services to consumers. This type of e-commerce is readily expanding because of greater customer outreach. Amazon, Flipkart, Zomato, DoorDash, Uber, Rapido, MakeMyTrip, etc., represent the dynamic B2B2C e-commerce platforms [8].

5.3 TRANSACTION SYSTEMS

Banks and financial institutions allow consumers to engage in a wide range of financial transactions through diverse transactional systems. Each method offers unique features and benefits, catering to consumer's diverse needs and preferences. These systems include but are not limited to the following.

5.3.1 Offline Transaction Systems

5.3.1.1 Cash

Physical money, including currency notes, bank notes, and coins, is used to exchange goods and services.

5.3.1.2 Cheques

A cheque is a document that orders a bank to pay a particular amount of money to the recipient and is authorised by signature.

5.3.1.3 Demand Drafts

Demand drafts are another form of financial document that transfers money from one account to the recipient's account. They are more secure than cheques.

5.3.2 Online Transaction Systems

5.3.2.1 Internet Banking

Internet banking is a medium for transferring money, paying bills, investing, applying for loans, managing accounts, etc., using the Internet through bank websites.

Money can be transacted using National Electronic Funds Transfer (NEFT), Immediate Payment Service, Real-Time Gross Settlement (RTGS), and features of Internet banking within India.

5.3.2.2 Mobile Banking

Similar to Internet banking, all types of transactions and services can be performed using a particular bank's mobile-based applications.

5.3.2.3 Proprietary Cards

Proprietary cards include debit cards, credit cards, charge cards, stored value cards, etc. and work using near-field communication technology.

5.3.2.4 Unified Payment Interface

A mobile payment system lets users transfer money between bank accounts without entering bank details or other sensitive information for each transaction.

5.3.2.5 National Electronic Toll Collection (NETC) FASTag

The system utilises Radio Frequency Identification (RFID) technology, which uses radio waves to transmit data wirelessly to pay tolls conveniently while driving on highways or through toll booths [8–9].

Please note that these transaction systems will not be covered in depth as they fall outside the scope of this chapter.

5.4 CYBERCRIMES INVOLVING BANKING SYSTEMS AND FINANCE

In a broad sense, cybercrime refers to criminal activities in cyberspace performed using computer technology and online networks. In the banking sector, cybercrimes encompass illicit activities that use online technologies to unlawfully remove or transfer funds to various accounts. These nefarious activities are commonly classified as banking frauds [2]. Banking and finance are the most exploited sectors by cybercriminals due to their tendency to easily gain money and other assets. Banks and consumers are usually targeted because of non-compliance, lack of proper training, poor risk management, lack of awareness, the tendency of greediness, ignorance among consumers, revenge, etc. More than one type of cyberattack may be associated with each other to perform a successful fraud. Some of the common cybercrimes associated with banking systems include the following [10].

5.4.1 Advance Payment Fraud

This is also known as upfront payment fraud. This deceptive scheme involves convincing individuals or businesses to make a payment or fee in advance before receiving the promised goods, services, or financial gains. This type of fraud often occurs through online transactions, where victims are led to believe that they will benefit from a lucrative opportunity such as a lottery win, inheritance, or business deal. However, after the payment is made, the promised benefits are never delivered, leaving the victim at a financial loss. Additionally, scammers may use various tactics to entice victims, such as offering fake lottery winnings or enticing investment opportunities, only to demand a transaction fee before the supposed benefits can be claimed.

5.4.2 Brute-force Attack

In a brute-force attack, the attacker systematically tries every possible encryption key that might be used on the encrypted message to determine the correct key to decipher the original message. Thus, all the potential combinations are tested one by one till the correct key is found and the encrypted message is decoded.

5.4.3 Cryptojacking

The term cryptojacking has been devised by combining two words, cryptocurrency and hijacking. When an attacker gains unauthorised access to another person's computer to excavate cryptocurrency, it is termed cryptojacking. The access may be obtained by using malware or through some malicious link sent to the victim. People are often not aware of this criminal activity or cryptojacking because these codes function in the background without the knowledge of the person.

5.4.4 Denial of Service (DoS) Attacks

This cybercrime is committed with a deliberate intent to interrupt the normal flow of traffic over a network, system, or application. This may be performed by sending illegitimate emails, messages, or requests over that network system or application. This leads to the exhaustion of the resources of the targeted system, for example memory or disk space, processing power, bandwidth, etc. Thus, DoS attacks are aimed at disrupting the service to its genuine customers by congesting or crashing the networks, which might lead to financial or reputational harm to the customers or banks.

5.4.5 DNS Cache Poisoning

It is also known as DNS spoofing. It is a cyberattack that presents false information into a DNS resolver's cache, resulting in incorrect IP addresses for domain names, which might redirect the users to unintended websites, leading to the exploitation of the DNS cache. DNS spoofing may provoke serious security threats and unauthorised access to important financial and customer-related information. DNS cache poisoning poses a noteworthy menace to the integrity and security of the DNS system. Thus, it is important to constantly check over such risks and take preventive measures to reduce the risk of DNS spoofing.

5.4.6 Hacking

Hacking is described as the unauthorised access taken over a computer or a network to manipulate these computers or networks or gain access to confidential information. Hackers exploit cybersecurity vulnerabilities to gain unauthorised access to various digital platforms or user accounts for illegal purposes, such as theft of finances, sensitive information, disruption of operations, and causing reputational damage.

5.4.7 Insider Threats

Employees of the bank or third-party vendors involved with the financial institutions that have access to sensitive data may intentionally or unintentionally destabilise the security of sensitive financial information. In the banking sector, insider threats can comprehend various activities, like illicit data acquisition, unauthorised access, and disclosure of confidential information. Thus, it jeopardises the security of sensitive data and poses a significant risk to the integrity and confidentiality of customer's banking information.

5.4.8 Internet of Things-based Attacks

Cybercriminals exploit vulnerabilities in Internet of Things (IoT) devices like Alexa, smart thermostats, security cameras, and other gadgets to gain unauthorised access and steal sensitive data and personal information. Being a relatively newer medium of cyberattacks, it poses a threat to individuals and financial organisations, highlighting the need to secure IoT devices and networks.

5.4.9 Juice Jacking

It is a type of cyberattack in which individuals unknowingly connect their phones or computer devices to a public port that has been tampered with by a cybercriminal for data transfer or charging purposes. In certain cases, the tampered peripheral devices are purposely left over in public areas so that people may take them out of curiosity. The malicious intent behind this attack is to either steal sensitive data from the connected device or to surreptitiously install malware, which can compromise the security and privacy of the user.

5.4.10 Malware Attacks

Malware stands for malicious software and is a substantial type of cyberattack. This program is implanted into a computer system without the knowledge of the owner, who has an ill intention of gaining access to the confidential data and application of the system. These breach a network and compromise sensitive financial information, personal information, passwords, etc. It encompasses a wide range of malware, which are discussed below.

5.4.10.1 Adware

While using banking websites or applications, this type of malware may be used to advertise various contents on the user's screen, preventing them from performing the desired task and redirecting them to other commercial websites or apps.

5.4.10.2 Auto-root

It is a malicious hacking tool which allows the hacker to remotely access a user's system.

5.4.10.3 Backdoor or Trapdoor

These malware are used to gain unauthorised access to the system or a program by sidestepping the security check mechanism of the system.

5.4.10.4 Downloaders

It is a program that installs other programs on the system. These are basically a means to download other malwares to the system that may ultimately compromise the confidentiality of data.

5.4.10.5 Keyloggers

Malicious software are intentionally created to intercept and record the sequence of keystrokes entered by a user. These keystrokes are then compiled into a database of information, which can be exploited by an unauthorised individual to gain access to the user's usernames and passwords. This malware can lead to unauthorised access to sensitive personal and financial information.

5.4.10.6 Logic Bomb

Certain codes are embedded into the malware that remain inactive until a predefined action occurs. When that action is performed, the code activates the illegal activity.

5.4.10.7 Spyware

It is a software designed to collect information and transmit it to another system. This information may include keystrokes, screen data, files, etc.

5.4.10.8 Virus

Viruses are malware that replicate themselves and spread within systems. It may sometimes camouflage itself as authentic software, resulting in the stealing of information by exploiting the authorisation system.

5.4.10.9 Worm

These are malware that run autonomously and can spread within a computer system by exploiting system vulnerabilities.

5.4.11 Man in the Middle Attack

This cyberattack occurs when a hacker intrudes the communication between two parties. For example, the communication might be between a user and an access point, and the hacker makes the user believe that they are communicating with another user. In reality, the hacker alters the communication between two users without their knowledge. This leads to the loss of important and confidential information and unauthorised access to the system.

5.4.12 Phishing

Customers are deceived into revealing confidential and sensitive information, like login credentials or personal details, using fraudulent practices, such as sending deceptive emails or text messages that may contain fraudulent links. These links guide users to counterfeit websites which resemble very closely the original websites of banking platforms or payment gateways. If the customers are not vigilant and provide their user credentials on these fake websites, the attackers get access to sensitive information like passwords and usernames or pin codes and allow the attacker to exploit customer's accounts for financial gain or unauthorised access to confidential information.

5.4.12.1 Quishing/QR Code Fraud

A phishing attack that is carried out using QR Codes is known as quishing or QR code fraud. Cyber attackers create fake QR codes and might replace the original ones. These, when scanned, redirect the customers to deceptive websites or payment gateways that steal their personal and financial information. This is also a relatively new method of deceiving innocent people into accessing their bank account details and gaining financial benefits.

5.4.12.2 Spear Phishing

It is a sophisticated adaptation of phishing attacks that involve targeted and personalised attacks. To perform spear-phishing, the cyber attackers carry out detailed research on individuals that can be targeted and draft personalised emails depending on their status, business, needs, etc. This makes the email appear genuine because of personal information or references that are relevant to the recipient of that email. This approach increases the likelihood of successfully deceiving the recipient and obtaining financial gains or the desired sensitive information significantly.

5.4.12.3 Smishing

A phishing attack that is performed by using text messages is known as smishing.

5.4.12.4 Vishing

A phishing attack that is performed over voice calls is known as vishing.

5.4.13 Ransomware Attacks

As the name suggests, ransomware is malware that makes data or services inaccessible by encrypting them. The cybercriminals who execute this ransomware attack demand money from the victim to recover the encrypted data. Generally, the banking sector and its customers are targeted for such attacks, in which customer's sensitive data may be encrypted. Ransomware attacks have become common and have serious consequences.

5.4.14 SIM Cloning

It is a cyber fraud in which the attackers gain unauthorised access to a victim's phone number. Using sophisticated software and hardware, the attackers gain unauthorised access to the International Mobile Subscriber Identity (IMSI) number of the victim's SIM card and encryption key. Then, a duplicate SIM card with the victim's phone number is prepared. This allows the cybercriminals to gain full control over the victim's phone number and personal information. SIM cloning enables attackers to access OTPs and other sensitive information and makes the victims susceptible to various financial frauds.

5.4.15 Skimming

It is one of the most common ways to steal information from debit cards. In this method, the attackers install a small, inconspicuous device known as a skimmer on the payment terminal, such as ATM machines. This skimming device is equipped with a swipe reader and a memory unit. When the customers swipe their card, the skimmer clandestinely captures and stores all the data, including card details and password, from the magnetic strip of the debit card. The attackers further make a duplicate debit card and use it for carrying out fraudulent transactions, money withdrawals, and online payments.

5.4.16 Spamming

Hackers use a botnet to send a large number of spontaneous emails or messages, commonly known as spam. A botnet comprises a network of compromised computers that are controlled by the attacker and numerous bots. Spamming is performed to intentionally stop the delivery of critical and time-sensitive information, such as one-time passwords (OTPs), account sign-in details, and other important communications.

5.4.17 Spoofing

It is a sophisticated cyber activity in which the data is manipulated so that it appears original. Spoofing may be performed for email IDs, IP addresses, websites, etc., so that they appear legitimate entities of businesses or financial institutions. Spoofing aims to deceive customers to disclose confidential information, or install malware into their system. Thus, the attacker gains unauthorised access to personal data, financial resources, and sensitive information.

5.4.18 System Hijacking

Unauthorised system access or system hijacking refers to a security attack where the attacker obtains unauthorised entry into someone else's system and its resources. Every individual using computers or other digital devices connected over the Internet is susceptible to system hijacking. Attackers usually hack other's systems to gain unauthorised access to sensitive information such as bank details, debit and credit card information, email credentials, and other confidential data. Additionally, attackers may manipulate or conceal files so that no discernible traces of their activities are left behind [5, 11–17].

5.5 EFFECT OF CYBERCRIMES ON BANKING SYSTEMS AND INDIVIDUALS

In today's digital age, banking systems and individuals are highly prone to cybercrimes. It poses an ever-growing threat to everyone who relies on the Internet. Internet usage has expanded the potential for cybercrimes throughout the world. Although technological advancements have empowered the banking sector to reach a larger customer base, it has also raised concerns among customers when using banking services. Fraudulent activities are carried out to access someone's bank account illegally, with the intention of drawing funds and transferring them to their account [4].

The global banking industry is struggling with a complex and multifaceted challenge arising from geopolitical and macroeconomic conditions. One of the most critical issues is the rapid progression of cybercriminal manoeuvres, which result in the theft of finances and sensitive financial information and enable corporate espionage and unauthorised access to critical data. This has substantial effects on the financial stability of banks and financial institutions. Annually, cybercrimes lead to the loss of billions of dollars globally, and the resources utilised to combat cybercrimes are twice. Moreover, the recovery process after a cyber act is time-consuming. Banking services require a lot of time to fully restore operations, thereby further inflating operative costs. Cybercrime has a profound and extensive impact on individuals, businesses, and governments worldwide. The ramifications of cybercrime are widespread and can include severe financial harm, loss of sensitive data, and disruption of essential services and business operations [18, 19].

Banks and other financial institutions are highly vulnerable to the cybercrimes and its ill-effects. For example, banks may experience reputational damage and maltreatment of the brand identity. This might reduce profitability and reduce investor confidence. As a result, the share prices may reduce, lending costs may increase, and the complexity of securing financial backing may increase after a cyberattack. Furthermore, sensitive customer data may be compromised and may result in severe penalties and legal repercussions for banks that fail to adequately protect their customer's information. The erosion of customer trust can have permanent consequences, leading to the loss of existing customers and reducing the chances of acquiring new ones. Financially, they may incur substantial losses as a result of cyberattacks, including the cost of engaging cybersecurity firms for incident response and restoration, as well as expenses related to public relations and other services. Additionally, cybercrimes in the banking sector can significantly disrupt economic growth and development, posing a threat to financial stability and security. On an individual level, cyberattacks can have a wide-ranging impact, from the theft of personal data to financial extortion and the misuse of personal information [4, 20].

5.6 VULNERABILITIES AND PATTERNS OF TARGETING IN BANKING SECTOR

With the advancement of technology and the increased usage of the Internet, daily life has been transformed into a digital world. Almost every task is conducted using the Internet, including financial transactions. This has made individuals and organisations vulnerable to finance-related cyber offences. Hackers are constantly learning new technologies to exploit the Internet for financial gain, as it is relatively easy, fast, and transcends geographical boundaries without the need for physical theft. The rapid increase in cybercrimes can be attributed to the basic structure of computers and the malfunctioning of hardware, software, and computer networks. Furthermore, advancements in technology and increasing knowledge and awareness of cyber criminals are some of the main reasons that have led to the exploitation of different sets of people by cyber criminals. Ignoring or overlooking these flaws can lead to potential cyberattacks. Although, even the most alert and aware individuals are also at risk of cybercrimes.

Hardware-based attacks raise a lot of concerns regarding cybersecurity, as traditional software-based security tools cannot determine and prevent hardware-based attacks. It is difficult to identify and address vulnerabilities in hardware because of the complex nature of integrated circuits (IC) and the interdependence of hardware components. Even a minute alteration with a single IC can lead to comprehensive consequences, which may impact multiple other components and potentially avoid detection of the alteration over a large time period. Thus, specialised approaches are required to prevent hardware-related attacks.

As the financial transactions through the Internet and investment software are increasing, they have outgrown the implementation of thorough security testing during the development and testing phases. This deficiency has been intensified by the lack of expertise in secure software development processes. This has resulted in the escalation of software-based attacks due to the introduction vulnerabilities while development and usage of banking applications and other diverse finance-related platforms and devices. Software vulnerabilities might also arise due to bugs exploited by attackers, which compromise the system. Banking websites and applications are highly vulnerable, as they can provide a direct source for financial gains by defrauding customers.

Banks, financial institutions, and individuals are often targeted by exploiting the vulnerabilities in TCP, IP, and operating systems. Data being transmitted over the Internet is at risk of unauthorised access, manipulation, or alteration by hackers. These cyberthreats arise due to the use of computer network protocols and computer devices that lack strong cybersecurity measures. Cyberattacks on computer networks usually exploit vulnerabilities in network protocols, including Transmission Control Protocol (TCP), Internet Protocol (IP), Address Resolution Protocol (ARP), Dynamic Host Configuration Protocol (DHCP), and Domain Name System (DNS) to compromise the integrity and confidentiality of transmitted data, posing significant risks to network security and the information being transferred [16].

5.7 CYBERSECURITY MEASURES TO PREVENT CYBERCRIMES IN BANKING SECTOR

Cybersecurity is an essential tool to ensure the security, privacy, and accessibility of financial data within the global banking sector. Strong cybersecurity measures are extremely crucial as they act as a primary defence measure. Cybersecurity helps to defend against various cyber threats that banks and financial institutions might encounter, including data breaches, financial fraud, ransomware attacks, etc. Cybercrimes in banking systems not only pose a threat to finance, but these cyber threats also have the potential to diminish customer trust and sabotage the overall integrity of the global financial system. Although the digital transformation of financial services has improved the accessibility and efficiency of banking services. However, it has also broadened the potential of cyber adversaries and rendered financial institutions increasingly prone to cyberattacks. The expansion of digital banking, mobile banking, and other online services demands the implementation of effective cybersecurity strategies that are adaptable and resilient in the face of the ever-evolving nature of cyber threats. This underscores the significance of regulatory frameworks and international cooperation in cybersecurity efforts, emphasising the need for collaborative and cohesive strategies to effectively combat cyber threats on a global scale. All financial institutions face unique challenges in cybersecurity, suggesting the enhancement of measures for cybersecurity. Some of the cybersecurity measures to prevent cybercrimes in the banking sector include the following.

5.7.1 Access Control

As the name suggests, access control refers to the process of giving permission for the opportunity to enter a platform or use a service. NIST defines access control as 'the process of granting or denying specific requests to obtain and use the information and related information processing services, and to enter specific physical facilities'. Further, the Internet Security Glossary (RFC 4949) refers to it as a process by which the use of system resources is regulated according to a security policy and is permitted only by authorised entities according to that policy. Access control is a fundamental security measure that specifies the entities or processes permitted to access specific system resources and the type of access granted. Thus, maintaining the integrity of the system. It works on the principles of AAA, which are authentication, authorisation, and auditing. Access control is crucial in banking systems and other financial institutions to avoid operation from unwanted personnel. It is broadly classified into four categories.

5.7.1.1 Discretionary Access Control

This method is used to control access based on the identity of the person. It follows discretionary guidelines as to what a user can do. DAC is a framework that articulates the rights of an individual or group to access any platform.

5.7.1.2 Mandatory Access Control

This method controls access of the users on the basis of the comparison of security labels. As the name suggests, it is important to take prior security clearance before the user may access the platform.

5.7.1.3 Role-Based Access Control

This method controls access of the users on the basis of the role of the individual within the organisation like a bank. It also lays down the rules for accessing data associated with each role. The roles linked with a particular job are defined and access is granted based on these roles only.

5.7.1.4 Attribute-Based Access Control

This method controls access of the users on the basis of the characteristics of the user. It is mostly used in the banking sector and defines the authorisation of the resource and the subject.

5.7.2 Cryptographic Tools

Cryptography is the process of preventing unauthorised people from accessing or reading confidential messages or sensitive information to secure communication and protect data. Cryptography involves a hierarchy of steps such as encryption, decryption, and key management to safeguard the confidentiality, integrity, and authenticity of data. Various cryptographic tools include the following.

5.7.2.1 Symmetric Encryption

It is a cryptographic method that utilises a single key to both encrypt and decrypt the data. A strong encryption algorithm is required for successful symmetric encryption. Further, the secret key should be available to both the sender and the receiver. Two types of algorithms, namely the Data Encryption Standard (DES) algorithm and the Advanced Encryption Standard (AES) algorithm, are used to perform symmetric encryptions. Both these algorithms are used by the National Institute of Standards and Technology (NIST) and use a block cypher, which operates on blocks of plaintext data of fixed size. For each plaintext block, a ciphertext of equal size is produced. If the plaintext is longer than the block size, the algorithm processes it as a series of fixed-size blocks. Hence, the input data and output data are consistent or of a fixed size. Cybercriminals may perform cryptoanalysis to decipher the encrypted data by deducing the key, and the message may be decrypted. Further, brute force attacks may be performed to decrypt the data. Thus, symmetric encryption may not be very successful in financial setups.

5.7.2.2 Authentication Code and Hash Function

Active attacks can be protected using data authentication that allows the receiver and the sender to verify the genuineness of the data being transmitted. Thus, the source and the contents of the data being transmitted must be authentic. One method to authenticate the data is through encryption. The other method is to create an authentication tag or code. While generating the authentication code, both the sender and receiver have a common secret key. Both parties use the same algorithm, and a code is generated. The code generated at the sender's end should match with the code generated at the receiver's end. NIST suggests the use of the DES algorithm to generate this code. Alternatively, a hash function does not require a secret key. It accepts the input in a variable size and generates an output of fixed size. NIST developed the Secure Hash Algorithm (SHA), which is widely used in its revised versions. This method of cybersecurity can help to prevent intrusion attacks in the banking sector.

5.7.2.3 Asymmetric Encryption or Public Key Encryption

These are based on mathematical functions instead of the simple manoeuvre of the bit pattern. As the name suggests, this cryptographic method is asymmetric, resulting in the use of two keys. Of the two keys, one key is private, and the other key is public. The public key is utilised for encryption purposes, and the private key is used for decryption. In public key systems, the sender can use either their own private key, the recipient's public key, or both to perform a cryptographic operation, depending on the specific use case. This method is also prone to cryptoanalysis to decipher the encrypted data. This method can be used to authenticate the baking system while performing transactions.

5.7.2.4 Digital Signatures

Asymmetric Encryption has multiple applications, of which one category is a digital signature. Digital signatures are used to authenticate the source and integrity of the data but not necessarily the confidentiality of the data. These can be used by the financial institutions to transmit important information to the customers.

5.7.3 Customer Awareness

Every bank or financial institution tries its best to make customers aware of cyber threats and explain the measures to prevent them. These awareness programmes are also promoted by the government and regulatory agencies. Certain easy steps to prevent cyber fraud in financial set-up include updating genuine browsers and operating systems, installing antispyware and antiviruses, enabling firewalls, using strong passwords, updating passwords regularly, not sharing the username and passwords and PINs with others, not clicking on links, not sharing OTP, use of personal computers for financial setups, not using public networks for transactions, staying updated and informed, staying vigilant while using ATMs and other financial services, etc.

5.7.4 Database and Cloud Security

It is important to secure the financial and customer information stored in banks and financial institutions because criminals may target such information for financial gain or misuse it for unauthorised access. This financial and customer information may be stored as a structured set of records (database) offline in the computer system or online over the networks. Structured query language injection (SQLi) attacks are common network-based security threats and are designed to exploit the data of web applications. Further, database access control and database encryption can be utilised, which adds a line of defence. The following defensive coding can be used to prevent SQLi attacks.

5.7.4.1 Manual Defensive Coding

Applying relevant defensive coding practices can help eliminate vulnerabilities. Attacks that are based on forcing errors in the database can be avoided. Further, pattern matching can be performed to distinguish normal input from the nonstandard input.

5.7.4.2 Parameterised Query Insertion

In this coding method, the SQL query is specified accurately so that the value parameter can be passed separately, avoiding any contaminated input by the user which may modify the query.

5.7.4.3 SQL DOM

These permit automated data validation and encapsulate the database so that it can be accessed safely and reliably. The query is built using a systematic process.

All banking services can be accessed on the Internet, and the data is stored on the Internet-based infrastructure, often known as cloud computing. NIST defines cloud computing as a model for enabling ubiquitous, convenient, on-demand network access to a shared pool of configurable computing resources that can be rapidly provisioned and released with minimal management effort or service provider interaction. Cloud computing is highly prone to cyberattacks, which might lead to losing control over data, services, resources, etc. Certain cloud-specific security threats include abuse of cloud computing, deletion of data, insecure interfaces, data alteration, service hijacking, etc. Cloud computing is a vast field that cannot be covered in this chapter.

5.7.5 Human Resource Security

NIST has issued guidelines for the awareness, training, and education of employees to improve their behaviour, ease the accountability of the organisation, and obey the regulations. It is of paramount importance to make the employees aware of the cybersecurity threats related to finance. The development of a cybersecurity incident response team is also important for banks and financial institutions to act rapidly in case of any such incident. The human resource security team should be aware of the measures that must be taken in case of a cyberattack when they are informed internally or by the customers.

5.7.6 Intrusion Detection and Prevention

Hacking by an unauthorised intruder, commonly known as a hacker or cracker, is one of the primary threats to security in the digital world. Various security measures, such as authentication, access control, and firewalls, are used to prevent these intrusions. It serves as an important line of defence against hacking and has been the subject of extensive research and development in recent years.

5.7.6.1 Host-Based Intrusion Detection System (HIDS)

HIDS is an intrusion detection and prevention measure that employs specialised software on vulnerable systems, like database servers and administrative systems. Its primary function is to monitor system activity continuously using various methods such as log analysis, file integrity checking, and real-time monitoring of system calls and network activity. Thus, HIDS aims to identify and point out any signs that may indicate a security breach or unauthorised access. When some suspicious activity has been identified, HIDS generates alerts, records relevant events, and potentially takes proactive measures to halt an attack before any damage occurs.

5.7.6.2 Network-based Intrusion Detection System (NIDS)

NIDS is used to monitor and analyse traffic at specific locations within a network or interconnected set of networks. To identify potential intrusion patterns, NIDS is used to scrutinise the traffic packet by packet in real-time or near real-time that may be directed towards potentially vulnerable computer systems within a network. This involves the examination of network-level, transport-level, or application-level protocol activities. This system is integrated within the organisation's firewall, forming part of the perimeter security infrastructure or associated with it.

5.7.6.3 Honey Pots

This is a very interesting and important intrusion detection technology that serves as a decoy system which is specially designed to divert potential attacks on critical systems to safeguard sensitive data. Honeypots are crafted strategically to collect all the information about an attacker's activities and tempt them to extend their presence on the system so that the administrators can respond to the potential cyberattack effectively. These use deceptive systems that are equipped with fabricated information which appears valuable but would not typically be accessed by legitimate users. If access is noted to this fabricated system, it will help to raise suspicion about the access to the honeypot. Thus, to enhance cybersecurity, the honeypots are tracked continuously and event loggers are used to meticulously detect and gather data on the attacker's behaviours. An illusion of successful access is created so that the administrators gain valuable time to mobilise and track the attacker and safeguard actual systems from harm.

When an intrusion is detected, intrusion prevention systems (IPS) are used to modify or block the network packets. Similar to intrusion detection systems, IPS are either host-based or network-based. To identify attacks on network traffic content, host-based intrusion prevention systems (HIPS) study the behaviour patterns or empirical techniques using anomaly detection techniques. On the other hand, a network-based intrusion prevention system (NIPS) utilises NIDS with the additional capability to detect suspicious network activity and take action by modifying or discarding packets and terminating TCP connections.

5.7.7 Security Auditing

The process of evaluating and assessing the security of an organisation's Information System (IS) is security auditing. Security auditing is very important to ensure overall computer security. It provides a wide range of assurances, including the proper computer operation in terms of security. Security auditing not only generates valuable data for analysing attacks but also serves as a means to recognise and evaluate any shortfalls in security. Moreover, it provides detailed data that can be used to define abnormal behaviour and maintains a comprehensive record that is invaluable in computer forensics. Every financial institution must undergo continuous security auditing from time to time.

5.7.8 User Authentication

In cybersecurity, user authentication serves as the critical and initial barrier against unauthorised access. It is the foundational mechanism for enforcing various forms of access control and ensuring user accountability within digital systems. According to NIST, it is the process of creating assurance in user identities that are offered electronically to the IS. This authentication is used to determine whether the individual is authorised to perform the said task, such as access to financial data. For the purpose of e-user authentication, the user must be registered with that particular system. The user authentication process follows two steps. First, the identity of the user is identified, and second, the identity of the user is verified. The identity of the user is based on the unique identifier, for example, a unique user name taken by the customer or issued by the bank to the user. Further, the verification of the identity is performed based on the password entered by the user. You must be familiar with this user identification method if you perform financial transactions routinely. However, there are various methods of user authentication. There are four user authentication methods. These methods can be used individually or in combination with other methods.

1. Something that the user knows – This includes passwords, PIN code, answer to certain pre-decided questions, etc.
2. Something the individual possesses – This includes smart cards, physical keys, electronic keys, etc. and is commonly known as a token.
3. Static biometrics of an individual – This includes fingerprints, iris recognition, face recognition, etc.
4. Dynamic biometrics of an individual – This includes voice recognition, handwriting recognition, typing rhythm, etc.

5.7.8.1 Biometric Authentication

This authentication method utilises the unique physical characteristics of an individual to verify and authenticate the user for their authorisation to access the services. Biometric authentication might use static features like fingerprints and iris, etc., or dynamic features like voice, signatures, etc. The biometric feature has to be enrolled in the system along with a username or identifier, which is used to identify whether the user is authorised to use the platform. The biometric feature is taken using a scanner or sensor specific to that biometric feature. The system digitises the biometric feature that is used for verification. Upon successful verification, user identification is performed. This kind of user identification is typically used by bank employees who deal with the sensitive data of customers. Most of these features are unique and cannot be stolen or copied.

5.7.8.2 Password-Based Authentication

The most common line of defence is password-based authentication. Every financial platform issues a unique username or identifier to the user, and that user has to choose a strong password for the verification. The system compares the input password with the username and password already stored in the platform's database. The username determines whether the user is authorised to access the given platform and what services can be used by the user. Further, the correct password associated with that username verifies the identity and gives the user access to the services. However, this method of authentication is prone to cyberattacks like offline dictionary attacks, password cracking, popular password attacks, hijacking, etc. To prevent such attacks, user awareness is required. The password must be strong and made using alphanumeric characters; it should not be easily guessable; the password must not be shared with others and must be changed frequently, and the use of public networks to access financial platforms must be avoided.

5.7.8.3 Remote User Authentication

It is the simplest type of user authentication method. When a user wants to access any platform remotely using the Internet or a network, etc., this kind of authentication is utilised. However, it is susceptible to more security threats. Thus to protect the user from cyberattacks, this kind of user authentication method is backed up with other user authentication methods.

5.7.8.4 Token-Based Authentication

Objects like smart cards, physical keys, electronic keys, dongles, etc., are used for user authentication in token-based authentication. Automatic teller machines, POS machines, swipe machines, and EDC machines are some of the platforms that require token-based authentication for users to access products and services. The token acts as the identifier, and the user has to provide a password, usually a personal identification number (PIN) code, to authenticate themselves. Payments through debit and credit cards require the user to add the card number as the identifier and PIN to perform any transaction. Further, chip-based smart cards that use radio frequency for payment are more susceptible to cybercrimes as they do not require a PIN for a limited amount of transactions. This kind of authentication has the potential for cybercrimes like loss or theft of tokens, skimming, etc. [10, 19, 21–24].

5.8 FORENSIC TOOLS FOR IDENTIFICATION, PREVENTION, AND INCIDENT RESPONSE OF CYBERSECURITY ATTACKS

There has been a noticeable surge in cybersecurity incidents over the past decade, which can be attributed to the rapid expansion of networking capabilities through the Internet. This surge has had a profound impact on various aspects of society, including social life, financial institutions, and other commercial activities. Among the sectors affected, banks and financial institutions, as well as their customers, have borne the brunt of cybercrimes. Cybersecurity in financial institutions encompasses protection against cyberattacks, the identification of such attacks, and a thorough investigation of these incidents. Investigating cyberattacks is particularly vital as it can aid in minimising losses and devising preventive measures for future occurrences.

In case of a cyber incident, the criminals leave certain critical information like time of attack, date of attack, place, tools used for the attack, etc., that might aid in the forensic investigation of such cyber incidences. While examining digital evidence, a proper chain of custody should be maintained. While investigating a cyber incident, the forensic cyber expert, in collaboration with the investigating agency, is responsible for identifying all relevant evidence, preserving it securely, conducting thorough analysis, documenting the process, and presenting the findings accurately. Forensic tools are mostly designed to address specific aspects of evidence collection and analysis, often leaving gaps in coverage for other aspects. Kali Linux is an exception, which provides a platform to analyse multiple types of evidence like mobile devices, containers, ARM, cloud providers, windows subsystem for Linux, pre-built virtual machine, etc. While a tool may excel in one area, it may lack functionality in another. Just as there is no one-size-fits-all approach to solving a crime, there are no all-encompassing forensic tools [25–29]. Thus, cybersecurity tools can be classified into three broad categories, which are as follows.

5.8.1 Computer Forensic Tools

These forensic tools play a crucial role in extracting, recovering, and analysing information from computers and hardware components such as memory drives, hard disks, pen drives, SD cards, and other peripheral devices. In the event of a cybercrime involving banks and financial institutions, computers or storage media may be primary evidence. These computer storage devices can be examined using Computer Online Forensic Evidence Extractor (COFEE), Digital Forensics Framework (DFF), EnCase, Forensic Toolkit (FTK), Recuva, SANS Investigative Forensic Toolkit (SIFT), etc. In the event of examination of volatile memory, certain forensic tools like HxD (Hex Editor), Magnet RAM Capture, Mandiant RedLine, Nigilant32, VOLATILITY, etc. can be used.

5.8.2 Mobile Forensic Tools

Mobile forensic examination can be further divided into Android forensics and iOS forensics. Various tools used for examining mobile phones include Andriller, Belkasoft Evidence, MOBILedit, Oxygen Forensic, WhatsApp Key/DB Extractor, Universal Forensic Extraction Device (UFED), etc.

5.8.3 Network Forensic Tools

Network forensics involves analysing and capturing live network packets. The primary objective of these tools is to extract digital evidence from live networks by scrutinising packet information in real-time. Some tools used for network forensics include NMAP, WinPcap, Ethereal, etc.

5.9 CONCLUSION

The advancement of information technology led to substantial improvements across the finance sector, which has been characterised by the introduction of innovative platforms such as electronic banking, digital payment systems, mobile banking apps, plastic money, etc. These platforms have significantly enhanced consumer convenience, making transactions faster and more efficient. However, there is an increased risk of various cybercrimes associated with these technological advancements. The rise in cybercrime has caused significant financial losses for many banking systems, government agencies, and individuals. Banks and financial institutions have implemented comprehensive policies and various cybersecurity measures to safeguard their banking platforms in response to the increasing number of cyber threats. In this chapter, various cyber threats associated with different banking platforms have been discussed. Effective cybersecurity measures within the banking sector can only be developed if the banks and customers understand the vulnerabilities associated with the usage of the Internet to perform banking services and patterns of targeting. Thus, it is very important to implement strong cybersecurity measures and risk-eliminating techniques so that a wide range of financial crimes in cyberspace can be avoided before they affect the masses. Further, promoting awareness among customers and providing comprehensive training on cybersecurity approaches to the employees of the banks and finance sector can enhance the overall resilience against financial cybercrimes. If a cyberattack incident has been reported, it is of paramount importance to investigate that cyberattack as this can help to minimise losses and form preventive cybersecurity measures for future occurrences of such cyberattacks. Thus, as users, we should also be highly vigilant while performing financial transactions using the Internet and follow every possible cybersecurity measure to prevent ourselves and others from cyberattacks.

REFERENCES

1. Thangamayan, E. A. (2022). Cybercrime and cyber law in India: A comprehensive study with special reference to information technology. In *2022 IEEE international conference*, 2903–2906.
2. Wall, D. (2001). Cybercrimes and the internet. In *Crime and the Internet* (p. 1).
3. Anderson, R., Barton, C., Böhme, R., Clayton, R., Van Eeten, M. J., Levi, M., Moore, T., & Savage, S. (2013). Measuring the cost of cybercrime. *The Economics of Information Security and Privacy*, 265–300.
4. Raghavan, A. R., & Parthiban, L. (2014). The effect of cybercrime on a bank's finances. *International Journal of Current Research & Academic Review*, *2*(2), 173–178.
5. More, M. M., Jadhav, M. P., & Nalawade, K. M. (2016). Online banking and cyber-attacks: The current scenario. *International Journal of Advanced Research in Computer Science and Software Engineering*, *5*(12), 743–749.
6. Reserve Bank of India. (2001). *Report on Internet Banking.*
7. Reserve Bank of India. (2019). *Report of the High-Level Committee on Deepening of Digital Payments.*
8. Agrawal, S. (2016). Cybercrime in banking sector. *Udgam Vigyati*, *3*, 1–19.
9. Reserve Bank of India. (2022). *Concept note on central bank digital currency.*
10. Stallings, W., & Brown, L. (2015). *Computer security: Principles and practice.* Pearson.
11. Goel, S. (2016). Cyber-crime: A growing threat to Indian banking sector. *International Journal of Science Technology and Management*, *5*(12), 552–559.
12. Merwe, J. R., Zubizarreta, X., Lukčin, I., Rügamer, A., & Felber, W. (2018). Classification of spoofing attack types. In *2018 European navigation conference* (pp. 91–99).
13. Rao, H. S. (2019). Cybercrime in the banking sector. *International Journal of Research-Granthaalayah*, *7*(1), 148–161.
14. Harsham, S., Joshi, S., & Mikkelsen, D. (2019, October). *Financial crime and fraud in the age of cybersecurity. McKinsey & Company.*
15. Guers, K., Chowdhury, M. M., & Rifat, N. (2022). Card skimming: A cybercrime by hackers. In *2022 IEEE international conference* (pp. 575–579).
16. Aslan, O., Aktug, S. S., Ozkan-Okay, M., Yilmaz, A. A., & Akin, E. (2023). A comprehensive review of cybersecurity vulnerabilities, threats, attacks, and solutions. *Electronics*, *12*, 1–42.

17. Bichnigauri, A., Kartvelishvili, I., Shonia, L., Bichnigauri, D., & Gudadze, O. (2023). Unveiling quishing: The dark side of QR codes in cyberattacks. *Defence and Science*, 2, 96–98.
18. Muthukumaran, B. (2008). Cybercrime scenario in India. *Criminal Investigations Department Review*, 17–23.
19. AL-ALAWI, A. I., & AL-BASSAM, S. A. (2020). The significance of cybersecurity systems in managing risks in the banking and financial sector. *Journal of Xidian University*, *14*(7), 1523–1536.
20. Shaddad, S. A. M. (2023). Effects of cybercrime in e-banking systems (Master's thesis, Eastern Mediterranean University).
21. Borghard, E. D. (2018). Protecting financial institutions against cyber threats: A national security issue. *Carnegie Endowment for International Peace*, 1–24.
22. Khan, H. U., Malik, M. Z., Nazir, S., & Khan, F. (2023). Utilizing biometric systems for enhancing cybersecurity in the banking sector: A systematic analysis. *IEEE Access*, *11*.
23. Efijemue, O. P., Kizor-Akaraiwe, S., Obunadike, C., Olisah, S., Taiwo, E., Odooh, C., & Ifunanya, E. (2023). Cybersecurity strategies for safeguarding customers' data and preventing financial fraud in the United States financial sectors. *International Journal of Soft Computing*, *14*(3).
24. Shoetan, P. O., & Familoni, B. T. (2024). Cybersecurity in the financial sector: A comparative analysis of the USA and Nigeria. *Computer Science & IT Research Journal*, *5*(4), 850–877.
25. Lagazio, M., Sherif, N., & Cushman, M. (2014). A multi-level approach to understanding the impact of cybercrime on the financial sector. *Computers & Security*, *45*, 58–74.
26. Lazzez, A., & Slimani, T. (2015). Forensic investigation of web application security attacks. *I. J. Computer Network and Information Security*, *3*, 10–17.
27. Dimitriadis, A., Ivezic, N., Kulvatunyou, B., & Mavridis, I. (2020). D4I: Digital forensics framework for reviewing and investigating cyberattacks. *Array*, *5*, 1–8.
28. Dwelkat, M., Eleyan, D., & Eleyan, A. (2021). Digital forensic tools used in analyzing cybercrime. *Journal of University of Shanghai for Science and Technology*, *23*(3), 367–379.
29. Touloumis, K., Michalitsi-Psarrou, A., Georgiadou, A., & Askounis, D. (2022). A tool for assisting in the forensic investigation of cybersecurity incidents. In *2022 IEEE international conference* (pp. 2630–2636).

6 Cybersecurity and Digital Forensics of Vital Installations and Critical Infrastructure

Qasem Abu Al-Haija and Shahad AL-Tamimi

6.1 INTRODUCTION TO VIs AND CI

In today's world, the word "Critical Infrastructure (CI)" has become associated with the fundamental systems and assets that support the operation of societies and economies worldwide. These infrastructures are vital to countries, providing necessary services, supporting economic activity, and guaranteeing human well-being. CI is the foundation of contemporary society, spanning power grids and transportation networks to hospital facilities and banking institutions [1]. Figure 6.1 depicts the key CI networks in a society.

Virtual Infrastructures (VIs) and CIs comprise various industries, each critical to everyday life's survival. Energy infrastructure, including power plants, electrical networks, and oil refineries, assures energy and fuel availability to power homes, companies, and industries. Transportation infrastructure, which includes roads, trains, airports, seaports, and transit systems, promotes the movement of goods and people, allowing business, trade, and mobility [2]. Hospitals, clinics, laboratory spaces, and pharmaceutical facilities are examples of healthcare infrastructure that provide people and communities with basic healthcare services, diagnostic tools, and medical treatments. Information sharing, teamwork, and resource access are all made possible by the communication and connection provided by telecommunications infrastructure, which includes cables, satellites, and wireless tower networks. The banks, stock exchanges, payment systems, and clearinghouses that comprise the financial infrastructure enable investments, monetary exchanges, and economic transactions, promoting stability and development [3]. Reservoirs, treatment facilities, distribution networks, and wastewater facilities are examples of the water and sanitation infrastructure that guarantees clean water supply for industrial, drinking, and sanitation purposes. Since VIs and CIs are interrelated, disruptions or failures in one area may have far-reaching ramifications and social impacts. For example, a cyberattack on a power grid might cause extensive power outages, impacting not just homes and businesses but also key institutions like hospitals, transit systems, and communication networks [4].

DOI: 10.1201/9781003497868-6

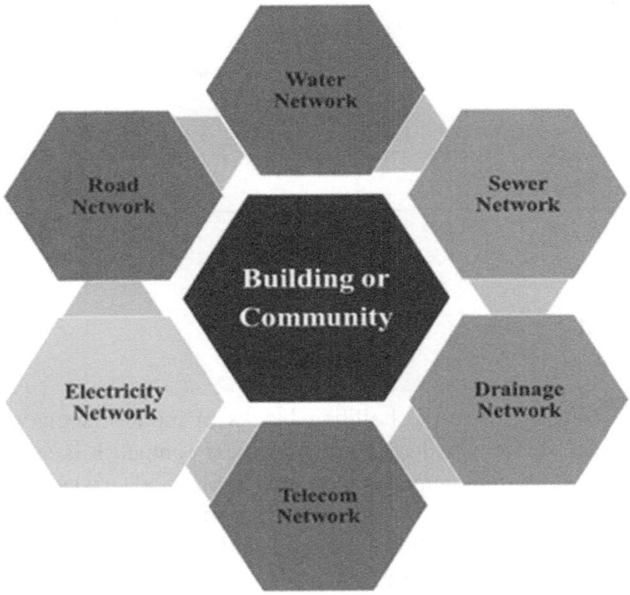

FIGURE 6.1 CI networks in the modern society.

Similarly, interruptions to transportation infrastructure, whether caused by natural disasters, accidents, or cyber events, may disrupt supply chains, stymie emergency response operations, and restrict the flow of critical commodities and persons. Cyber resilience is critical in an increasingly linked world, necessitating proactive efforts to detect vulnerabilities, minimize risks, and react effectively to attacks and disruptions. Due to the realization by governments, companies, stakeholders, and others on the need to protect VIs from natural catastrophes, physical assaults, cyberattacks, disruptions, and technology failures, CIP has, in recent years, received a fresh rebirth. As a result, it employs a comprehensive risk management strategy, which contains four primary variables: preventive, preparedness, response, and recovery measures, which will ultimately enhance the protection and resilience of CI assets and systems [5].

Key CIP participants include government agencies, law enforcement, observe categories, emergency personnel, business companies, and partners compared to other countries. They all need to work together more closely and successfully since CIP is an issue that is always growing and getting more difficult. CI is becoming a more attractive target for cyberattacks such as hacking, malware, ransomware, and standard threats comprising physical attacks and catastrophes. The digitization and connectedness of CI systems have greatly increased the potential for abuse and balancing. This has created enormous obstacles and opportunities for cybersecurity and resilience efforts. Cyberattacks within critical structures may cause various issues, such as lost services and money and threats to public safety, health, and national security. Due to this, security and being able to respond to new technologies are becoming more important for the parts of CIP.

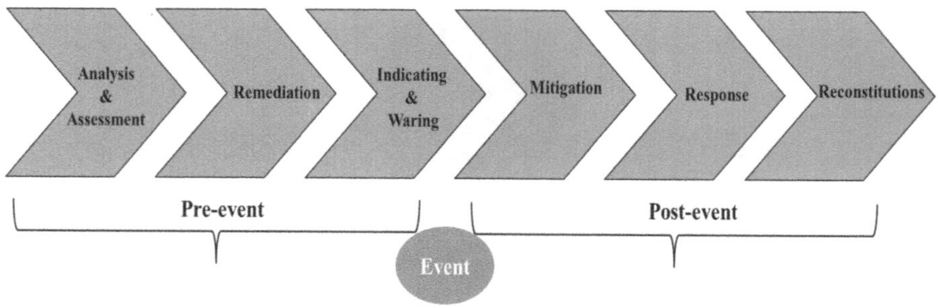

FIGURE 6.2 CIP event cycle.

In short, VIs and CI are the building blocks of modern society because they provide necessary services and encourage business contact. It is very important to keep these assets safe from many dangers, such as physical strikes, natural disasters, and cyberattacks, so they can continue providing important services and functions. Organizations, leading authorities, and stakeholders can address the dangers and boost societal continuity for future generations by adopting an innovative and collaborative approach to CIP.

Figure 6.2 and Table 6.1 illustrate the CIP event cycle, divided into Pre-Event and Post-Event phases surrounding a critical incident represented by an explosion or disruption.

6.2 CYBER THREATS AND CI

CI represents the foundation of contemporary civilization, providing vital services such as power, water, transportation, and communications. These systems become more reliant upon digital control systems, rendering them susceptible to cyberattacks. Understanding these dangers is critical to maintaining their existence [6].

TABLE 6.1
CIP Pre-Event and Post-Event Process

Pre-Event	Post-Event
1. Planning for incidents: Creating plans, processes, and resources. Training, exercises, and communication are included.	1. Response: Immediate incident management and containment. Coordinate with emergency services, deploy resources, and manage communication.
2. Prevention: Preventing incidents. This may need infrastructure upgrades, security upgrades, and risk assessments.	2. Restoring operations and fixing damage. This phase repairs infrastructure resumes services and supports impacted communities.
3. Mitigation: Reducing incident damage. Redundancies, backups, and contingencies may be needed.	3. Reviewing the event and reaction to lessons. This phase is critical for enhancing future readiness and reaction.

6.2.1 Types of Cyber Threats

- **Cybercrime:** Financial gain is a common motivator. Criminals might disrupt operations to extort ransom, steal sensitive data, or manipulate markets.
- **Cyberwarfare:** State-sponsored attacks aim to cripple or turn off CI during wartime or as a political tool. Disrupting power grids or communication networks can cause widespread chaos.
- **Cyberterrorism:** Non-state actors aim to sow fear and disruption and might target CI. These attacks are often designed to garner media attention and destabilize society.
- **Malware:** Malicious software designed to damage or gain unauthorized access to systems, including viruses, worms, trojans, and ransomware.
- **Phishing:** Fraudulent attempts to obtain sensitive information by disguising it as a trustworthy entity, often through email or fake websites.
- **Advanced Persistent Threats (APTs):** Prolonged and targeted cyberattacks where the attacker remains undetected for extended periods, often aiming for espionage.
- **Cryptojacking:** Unauthorized use of someone's computer resources to mine cryptocurrency.
- **Firmware Attacks:** Exploiting vulnerabilities in the firmware of hardware devices to gain control or disrupt functionality.

6.2.2 Attack Vectors

Cyberattack can target various components of CI [7]:

- **Information Technology (IT):** Business systems such as finance and administration are often interconnected with Operational Technology (OT) systems. Gaining access to IT can provide a stepping stone to OT systems.
- **OT:** These control systems directly manage physical processes. They may not have the same level of security as IT systems, making them more vulnerable to exploitation.
- **Supply Chain:** Attackers might target vendors or suppliers to gain indirect access to CI systems. As supply chains become more digital and global, email phishing, insider threats, and other cybersecurity hazards must be included in supply-chain security. These elements overlap in the following examples:
  1. Supply-Chain Email Phishing [8]:
     Example: An attacker sends a phishing email to a supplier employee, impersonating a valued partner. The email includes malware-installing links or attachments. This virus might access proprietary designs, order data, and shipping information in critical supply-chain systems. Hackers may modify shipping dates and product specifications to create financial or operational damage once within the network.
     Phishing prevention: Train personnel and use powerful email filters to identify dubious information.

2. Insider Threats [8]:
   Example: Within the supply chain, An unhappy employee at a vital node (e.g., warehouse, logistics firm) might misuse their access to systems and networks. They may disclose critical information, tamper with the goods, or postpone delivery. Due to partner interdependence, insider threats may cause large-scale supply-chain disruptions.
   Prevention: Monitoring employee behavior for abnormalities, stringent access rules, and frequent audits may prevent insider attacks.
3. Business Email Compromise (BEC) [8]:
   Example: A BEC fraud involves spoofing a supplier's executive or high-ranking official's email address to request immediate payment to a fake account. An assault might cause enormous financial losses in the supply chain, where large quantities of money are regularly moved between organizations.
   Prevention: Multi-factor authentication (MFA) for emails and financial transactions reduces BEC scam risk.

6.2.3 Increased Vulnerabilities

Several factors contribute to the growing vulnerability of CI to cyberattacks [9]:

- **Legacy Systems:** Many CI systems rely on outdated technology that is difficult or impossible to patch, creating exploitable vulnerabilities.
- **Interconnectedness:** The increasing use of the Industrial Internet of Things (IIoT) connects more devices to the Internet, expanding the attack surface for hackers.
- **Skilled Adversaries:** Cybercriminals and nation-states are constantly developing new attack methods, making it challenging to stay ahead of the curve.

6.2.4 Potential Impacts

A successful cyberattack on CI can have devastating consequences:

- **Physical Damage:** Tampering with control systems could damage physical equipment, leading to power outages, water contamination, or transportation disruptions [10].
  Examples:
  Power Grid Attacks: Cyber-physical threats to power systems are emerging with smart grid technologies. The area's electricity grid has been hacked for years, causing outages and equipment damage. These complex attacks often cause system failures that disrupt energy supplies, which may have major societal consequences. Preventing these attacks requires vulnerability patches and social engineering protections [10].

Manufacturing Facility Attacks: Cyberattacks halted production lines and damaged equipment at multiple factories. These assaults, frequently targeting industry 4.0 technology, may disrupt operations, lower product quality, and cost a lot [9, 10].

Transportation System Disruptions: Cyberattacks on public transport systems remain dangerous. A cyberattack on a country's train network damaged infrastructure, delaying and suspending services. These assaults may interrupt food and medical deliveries and endanger public safety [11].

- **Economic Loss:** Disruptions to CI can cause significant economic losses, impacting businesses and individuals.
- **Loss of Life:** In extreme cases, a cyberattack on CI could lead to loss of life, particularly if healthcare systems are compromised.

6.2.5 Mitigating the Risks

Several strategies can help mitigate cyber threats to CI:

- **Security Assessments:** Security assessments are conducted regularly to identify IT and OT system vulnerabilities, such as regular audits and penetration testing, compliance with industry standards (SO 27001, or IEC 62443), and continuous monitoring [11].
- **Patch Management:** Implement a robust patch management program to address vulnerabilities promptly. For instance, automated patch management, vulnerability prioritization, which assesses vulnerabilities, and testing and rollback mechanisms [12].
- **Segmentation:** Segment CI networks to limit the damage caused by a successful attack, which consists of network isolation and micro-segmentation, zero trust architecture, and firewalls and intrusion detection systems (IDS) [13].
- **Cybersecurity Awareness Training:** Educate employees about cyber threats and best practices for secure behavior. For instance, regular updates on emerging threats: cyber threats evolve rapidly, so it's important to continually update employees on new types of attacks [14, 15].
- **Information Sharing:** Encourage sharing between CI owners and operators, government agencies, and cybersecurity experts.

6.2.6 International Cooperation

Cyberattacks can transcend borders, which makes international cooperation essential. Governments and industry leaders must work together to develop and share best practices for cyber defense [12].

6.2.7 The Future of Cyber Threats

The cyber threat landscape is constantly evolving. As CI becomes even more reliant on technology, the potential for disruptive cyberattacks continues growing. Investing in cybersecurity and fostering a culture of cyber awareness is critical for ensuring the resilience of CI [16].

6.3 CYBERSECURITY MEASURES FOR VIs

VIs, the lifeblood of modern civilization, encompass many essential facilities. Services, power grids, water treatment plants, communication networks, transportation hubs, financial institutions, and hospitals. Their smooth operation is paramount for societal well-being. However, the increasing reliance on digital control systems introduces a vulnerability in cyberattacks. Understanding and implementing robust cybersecurity measures are crucial for safeguarding these VIs [17].

6.3.1 The Evolving Threat Landscape

Cyber threats to VIs come in various forms, each with distinct motivations:

- **Financial Gain:** Cybercriminals often target VIs for financial gain. They might deploy ransomware, crippling operations until a ransom is paid. Alternatively, they could steal sensitive data for sale on the black market [18].
- **State-Sponsored Attacks:** Nation-states may launch cyberattacks on VIs during wartime or as a political tool. Disrupting a nation's power grid or communication networks can cause widespread chaos and demonstrate technological prowess [19].
- **Cyberterrorism:** Non-state actors aiming to disrupt and instill fear might target VIs. These attacks are often designed to garner media attention and destabilize a nation's infrastructure [20].

6.3.2 A Multifaceted Approach to Cybersecurity

Mitigating cyber threats to VIs requires a layered approach addressing various aspects of security:

- **Network Security:** Firewalls, intrusion detection/prevention systems (IDS/IPS), and secure network segmentation form the first line of defense. These tools monitor network traffic for anomalies and prevent unauthorized access [21].
- **System Hardening:** Implementing strict system hardening practices is essential. This involves turning off unnecessary services and features, enforcing strong password policies, and promptly applying the latest security patches [22].
- **Data Security:** Sensitive data inside VIs requires extreme protection. Encryption at rest, as well as in transit, protects information even if the system is breached. This helps implement data loss prevention (DLP) technologies that could assist in avoiding sensitive data leaks [23].
- **Access Control:** The implementation of the least privilege concept is critical. Users should be granted permission to utilize the essential data and

systems to carry out their responsibilities. MFA provides additional protection for gaining control by demanding a second verification factor in addition to the login and password.

- **Physical Security:** Cybersecurity functions rely on physical protection via IDS, CCTV, and Access Control. A hacker won't be able to do it if nobody can come to the physical site and steal, tamper, install malware, etc., and thus are the digital site.
- **Cybersecurity Awareness and Training:** Workers that might be the weakest link in terms of both technological and physical security. The AI system will analyze and convert the input text into a high-quality output, employing the best-practice language processing algorithms. The ongoing training programs of employees on various cyber dangers, malware, social engineering attacks, and their vulnerable behavior in the security field for timely detection and reporting of abnormal trends is essential.
- **Incident Response Planning:** Organization of cyberattack response clearly and a plan is a key factor for early mitigation. The planner should include a component devoted to decision-making procedures, communication methods, data recovery, and resuming normal operations.
- **Vulnerability Assessment:** Therefore, it is possible to have consistent vulnerabilities and effective defense by periodic vulnerability assessment before the attackers carry out the attack. Along with evaluating the real cybersecurity attack, another approach is to do penetration tests.

6.3.3 Continuous Improvement and Collaboration

Cybersecurity improvement is not a checkmark on one's to-do list. One must constantly work on it. Organizations should constantly assess and enhance their efforts and measures to combat threats as threats evolve. In addition, they should work together. Government agencies, cybersecurity experts, and VIs may benefit from one another's best efforts and information.

6.3.4 Beyond Technology: Addressing Human Factors

Human factors can hardly be underestimated in cybersecurity, and they are as important as technology. Social engineering is key in capitalizing on vulnerabilities to gain unauthorized access to systems or data. Sensitizing the workers regarding these techniques and propagating a cyber-aware atmosphere is essential. Now, one more problem that needs to be addressed is insider threats that can be accidental or willful. Cutting the probability of such happening requires that the checks are conducted, the access records are watched, and a culture of responsible reporting is encouraged [24].

6.3.5 Emerging Technologies and New Challenges

The consequences of the development of technology of the future, in particular, the IIoT, will only make the situation worse. The need for robust security of these networked gadgets gives attackers new access possibilities. The significance of the security measures specific to IIoT devices is critical to combat this trend. The last reason is that, at the same time, special threats exist in connection with the increasing use of AI in credit risk assessment. AI systems must be safeguarded against attacks, manipulation, and guessing of their output. Verifying that the AI algorithms are safe [25].

6.3.6 A Shared Responsibility

Securing VIs requires a multi-dimensional approach involving technology, processes, and individuals. Systems with robust cybersecurity solutions, a culture of cyber awareness, and continuous collaboration are all necessary to protect the backbone of our way of living. Organizations, government bodies, and individuals are responsible for securing these installations. We can ensure security by working together to address cybersecurity and respond to new and more persistent enemies.

6.4 FORENSIC CONSIDERATIONS IN CI PROTECTION

Forensic considerations are important in CIP because they aid in identifying, managing, and responding to activities that threaten the availability and dependability of critical services and systems. In particular, DFs are used to establish the root reason for cyber events, compile evidence to back investigations, and create CIP measures that reduce CI vulnerabilities to future causes. This section investigates the importance of forensic considerations to CIP, concentrating on their value in vulnerability response, threat intelligence, and resilience-building programs [26]. As applied to CIP, DFs incorporate instruments and procedures that help collect, store, examine, and deliver digital evidence linked to cybersecurity causations. The causations described here include cyberattacks, data theft, malware, insider threats, and other harmful activities performed on, or aimed at, CI resources and organizations.

Organizations that employ forensic ideas and techniques may get helpful insights into threat actors' plans, approaches, and processes, helping them to enhance their defenses and respond more effectively to cyberattacks. One of the most significant functions of DFs in CIP is incident response. A rapid and efficient response is crucial for reducing loss and restoring activities after a cyber calamity, regardless of whether it be a ransomware attack involving a power system or a data breach that affects a financial institution. DFs enable organizations to conduct in-depth investigations into the nature and scope of cyber incidents, identify impacted data and systems, and assess the damage inflicted by attackers [27].

DFs may help identify individuals for those going through the legal system after a hacking event. Investigators who work in forensics can carefully detect and store digital evidence, which can help law enforcement purposes, regulatory bodies, and legal teams find and prosecute cybercriminals [28]. Forensic research may also help organizations to figure out these two questions: first, why do dangerous players do? Second, what do they do? These two questions can help to tell the forensic experts within organizations how to stop future attacks and make their systems more secure. Threat intelligence is another domain in which forensic concerns are critical in

CIP [29, 30]. Forensic investigators may get significant insights into cyber attackers' strategies, methods, and processes by studying digital artifacts such as malware samples, network logs, and IDS alerts. Data received from forensic experts is critical for organizations to help and support threat assessments, vulnerability assessments, and risk management strategies, which may help organizations detect and mitigate overall possible risks to CI assets and systems [31].

However, forensic analysis of previous cyber events may help organizations uncover trends and patterns within cyber threats, enabling them to forecast future attack vulnerabilities and adjust their defensive procedures appropriately [32]. Moreover, numerous organizations may need to improve their situational awareness and response capabilities by sharing threat intelligence via stakeholders, including government agencies, industry partners, and Information Sharing and Analysis Centers (ISACs), leading to an increasingly resilient and secure CI ecosystem [33]. Therefore, the CI ecosystem is secure and more robust. Thus, incident response and threat intelligence, DFs, are crucial for enhancing resilience schemes that could enhance CI systems' security and robustness by conducting forensic analyses of infrastructure components, which consist of embedded devices, Supervisory Control and Data Acquisition (SCADA) systems, and Industrial Control Systems (ICS). However, organizations may identify vulnerabilities, faults, and design flaws that hostile actors may exploit.

Furthermore, forensic analysis may assist organizations in determining the successful implementation of security controls and mitigation measures to ensure the security of CI assets and systems. By assessing the effectiveness or failure of security measures in combating cyberattacks, companies may identify areas for enhancements and prioritize investments in cybersecurity technology, training, and people to strengthen their defenses against emerging threats [19]. Forensic considerations are essential to CIP, providing firms with the tools and insights to effectively analyze, mitigate, and impact cyber risks [34].

In short, organizations must improve the security and resilience of VIs and CI systems by including DFs in incident response, threat intelligence, and resilience-building initiatives, protecting the critical services and functions on which contemporary societies rely.

6.5 INCIDENT RESPONSE AND RECOVERY FOR CI

A CIP environment with incident response and recovery policies ensures the security of VIs and systems against various threats. From cyberattacks and natural catastrophes to physical interruptions and technological failures, CI is subject to various incidents that may have far-reaching societal and economic implications [35]. This section explores the significance of incident response and recovery plans within the CIP environment, which includes basic concepts, approaches, and optimal strategies for decreasing the impacts of incidents and swiftly restoring normal operations and data with high efficiency. Incident response is recognizing, assessing, and mitigating events threatening the security and accessibility of essential infrastructure assets and systems. Moreover, it comprises an organized collection of procedures and actions to minimize the incidents' impact, prevent their replication, and accelerate the restoration to normal operations [31]. All involved parties, especially government agencies, regulators, law enforcement agencies, emergency responders, and business sector groups, must cooperate, be well-prepared, and communicate clearly. The need to stay prepared is a cornerstone of CIP event response. Strong incident response plans, including duties, responsibilities, and processes for reacting to different situations, should be developed and maintained by organizations responsible for VIs [36]. The significance of response is to identify and classify incidents, communicate and coordinate efforts, reduce the impact of incidents, and recover data affected by incidents. Consistent training, exercises, and simulations are crucial for ensuring the team has the skills and ability to cope with crises and react effectively in high-stress circumstances.

An acute recognition of the surroundings is essential for efficiently handling occurrences within CIP. Thus, organizations need real-time monitoring, detection, and analysis technologies to identify and respond to emerging risks swiftly. It is implementing State-Of-The-Art (SOTA) for monitoring and detection systems purposes, such as IDS, Security Information and Event Management (SIEM) systems, and threat intelligence platforms, which may identify and notify of questionable actions and irregularities that might lead to incidents location. Proactively identifying and detecting incident reactions within the CIP environment requires prompt, efficient communication and stakeholder cooperation.

Organizations must have clear development communication channels and escalation protocols for reporting incidents internally and externally to appropriate authorities and partners. Thus, the enhancement of creating communication channels between governments, agencies, industry partners, ISACs, and various other stakeholders for exchanging information, response coordination, and resource allocation during events scope.

CIP is based on containment and mitigation measures [37], and CIP is a successful response to incidents. For this reason, it is the responsibility of organizations to limit the effects of the incident and the escalation that was begun. When an incident occurs and is verified, it may be necessary to temporarily turn off affected services, isolate vulnerable systems and networks, and adopt mitigation stages to restrict the spread of the incident. What is required here is a quick and effective response to address this challenge, overcome it, and prevent it from spreading to other system components.

Organizations must focus on recovery and restoration after incidents. This procedure may include repairing or replacing damaged infrastructure components, restoring data and systems from backups, and implementing additional security measures to prevent catastrophes from happening again. Effective recovery and restoration require proactive planning, prioritization, and coordination of internal and external stakeholders, including suppliers, service providers, and regulatory bodies.

Last, an extensive CIP organization must encompass incident response and recovery. Therefore, enterprises may recognize, assess, and address circumstances threatening the security and reliability of VIs and systems. To protect society's crucial services and operations, companies must emphasize readiness, awareness of the situation, effective communication and coordination, containment, and reduction of risks.

6.6 CASE STUDIES AND BEST PRACTICES

In CIP case studies, actual-life incidents are investigated to highlight issues, solutions, and best practices organizations use to protect their VIs and systems from potential attacks. Case studies across various CI sectors, including banking, healthcare, energy, and transportation, are shown in this section. In each case study, there is a full review of each event. This chapter addresses the consequences of the events during the response, the lessons discovered, the optimal approaches, and suggestions for improving resilience and security.

6.7 CASE STUDY 1: CYBERATTACK ON A POWER GRID

The power grid within the provided case study focuses on highly sophisticated cyberattacks resulting in widespread outages and interruptions to vital services. Malware is employed during attempts to interfere with operations and infiltrate control systems, leaving CI open to internet threats. Which follows the incident and the affected utility, which took steps to stop the attacks, resume operations, and work to improve the cybersecurity posture. Therefore, it may employ strategies to prevent similar tragedies in the future, including system isolation, backup restoration, increased network monitoring and detection, and strengthened security measures.

Important Lessons

- Proactively monitoring and identifying online risks is essential for promptly detecting and addressing risk.
- Prompt implementing mitigation and control measures is required to reduce the impact of incidents and prevent their exacerbation.
- Regular testing and verification of backup data and systems and recovery plans are necessary to restore the continuity of processes, data, and systems.

6.8 CASE STUDY 2: PHYSICAL ATTACK ON A TRANSPORTATION NETWORK

Several attacks on bridges, tunnels, and rail lines halted train and bus services and caused widespread anxiety and traffic mayhem. Explosions near major transportation lines underlined the necessity for increased physical protection to combat terrorism. Emergency services failed to react as the assault interrupted road traffic, supply systems, and trapped goods and people. To avoid future instances and lessen the danger of similar assaults, transportation authority's immediately increased police presence, surveillance, and passenger and cargo screening. The event stressed the significance of maintaining CI for public safety and economic stability.

Important Lessons

- Certain areas can't be accessed; a fence surrounds the outside, and video cams protect CI from direct danger.
- To effectively find and respond to physical security events, all parties involved, including law enforcement, must work together and coordinate their efforts.

- Public awareness efforts and disaster recovery plans may instruct individuals how to identify unexpected behavior and actions and give them the power to do so.

6.9 CASE STUDY 3: DATA BREACH IN HEALTHCARE SYSTEM

The following case study highlights the vulnerability of patient safety, privacy, and confidentiality following a data breach that exposed sensitive medical and personal information stored within a healthcare system. The incident highlighted the significant points about protecting confidential data and adhering to applicable regulations, revealing weaknesses within the organizations, IT infrastructure, and cybersecurity protocols.

To address the breach, healthcare institutions took proactive steps, including notifying affected individuals, strengthening data encryption and access regulations, providing comprehensive employee training, and conducting a thorough forensic investigation. This includes implementing threat detection, access controls, and encryption protocols.

Important Lessons

- To safeguard confidential information and forestall intrusion, stringent cybersecurity procedures are required. These procedures must include encryption, access limits, and threat detection.
- It is essential to educate employees about cybersecurity and the best practices, raise awareness of potential threats, and promote a security culture throughout the organization.
- Ensuring compliance with data protection regulations, including HIPAA in the United States and GDPR in the EU, is crucial to preserving stakeholder trust and credibility.

6.10 BEST PRACTICES

Various suggestions discuss the enhancement of security and resilience of CIP, which have been derived from the case mentioned above studies:

1. Applying multifaceted security methods that combine human, cyber, and physical security measures to minimize the impact of possible risks and vulnerabilities.
2. It may use IPS and SIEM to build proactive monitoring and detection capabilities to detect real-time threats and react accordingly.
3. Define the roles, duties, and communication protocols for reacting to crises quickly and efficiently and set up clear plans and processes.
4. Companies should regularly conduct vulnerability scans and risk assessments to effectively deploy expenditures and resources to detect and prioritize security gaps and vulnerabilities.
5. Cooperation and data exchange among relevant parties, such as regulatory organizations, businesses, and government agencies, should be promoted to improve awareness of the environment and reaction times.

6. Apply investment within cybersecurity awareness and training programs to teach workers the ropes, foster a security culture, and encourage people to see and report danger.
7. Keep CI robust and flexible by regularly reviewing and updating security measures and processes in response to new threats and technology.

Case studies may offer valuable perspectives on challenges and remedies related to cybersecurity to secure VIs and networks from attacks. These insights underscore the importance of preparedness, collaboration, and adaptability. Historical events analysis, organizations could help to identify and detect responses to recover from security incidents. It may also help to ensure that CIP and services remain dependable and safe for the economy and society.

6.11 REGULATORY FRAMEWORKS AND INTERNATIONAL COOPERATION

Secure Worldwide requires efforts from governments, regulatory agencies, industry players, and international organizations to successfully identify threats and vulnerabilities. Implementing laws, regulations, standards, and international cooperation is crucial to improving the resilience and security of VI and systems [38]. The current section examines the role of legislative frameworks and international cooperation during CIP, focusing on the critical efforts, difficulties, and possibilities of cooperation during accelerating growth.

6.11.1 Regulatory Frameworks

In the United States, the Department of Homeland Security (DHS) is a major player in CIP through projects such as the National Infrastructure Protection Plan (NIPP) and the CI Security and Resilience (CISR) Program [39]. These programs require a framework to detect, prioritize, and mitigate CI risks while encouraging collaboration between government agencies, commercial stakeholders, and foreign partners. Furthermore, relevant guidelines, such as the EU CIP Directive and the EU Network and IT Security Directive, govern efforts to maintain CI within the Irish Republic. Uniform standards and best practices for cybersecurity are established, information exchange and cooperation are encouraged among stakeholders, and member states' flexibility and preparedness in cybersecurity are enhanced through these guidelines.

To ensure VIS and network security, the following study provides valuable perspectives on cybersecurity challenges and remedies to be safe from incidents and attacks. These ideas emphasize the importance of preparedness, cooperation, and adaptability. By analyzing historical events, companies can improve their ability to detect, respond to, and recover from security incidents.

6.11.2 International Cooperation

International collaboration is critical for tackling the global character of CI risks and providing a coordinated and coherent response to newly hired obstacles. Collaboration across nations, organizations, and stakeholders enables the exchange of knowledge, expertise, and best practices, permitting collective action to enhance the security and resilience of CI internationally [40].

CIP is where countries work together, for instance, when the International Organization for Standardization (ISO) and other relevant standard-setting bodies create global resilience, risk management, and cybersecurity standards and guidelines. Following the criteria set by ISO 27001 and ISO 22301, companies may adopt resilience and cybersecurity measures that adhere to internationally acknowledged standards. Apart from UNISDR and the Global Facility for Disaster Reduction and Recovery (GFDRR) of the World Bank, other initiatives help climate-sensitive and disaster-prone CI businesses improve their disaster preparedness and recovery efforts. The main objective of these programs is to enhance the response and preparedness capabilities in high-risk areas, focusing on fostering international cooperation, improving capacity, and facilitating the exchange of information among relevant stakeholders.

6.11.3 Challenges and Opportunities

Regarding the significance of legislative frameworks and international cooperation in protecting civilian entities, challenges remain in achieving effective cooperation and coordination between many parties. These issues consist of disparities in regulatory approaches between countries, obstacles to information sharing, resource limitations, and geopolitical conflicts, which may hinder cooperation and attempts to identify common risks. However, these issues provide an opportunity for creativity, collaboration, and partnership building in CIP. Organizations can better recognize, react to, and recover from events by adopting innovative technologies like AI, blockchain, and Machine Learning (ML). Furthermore, Public-Private Partnerships (PPPs), ISACs, joint exercises, and simulations may help stakeholders collaborate and coordinate, leading to a more robust and secure CI ecosystem [41]. Regulatory frameworks and international cooperation are essential to protect CI because they must provide global rules, standards, and methods for identifying emerging risks and vulnerabilities. Collaboration can also be undertaken between governments, regulatory bodies, industry players, and international organizations to enhance the resilience and security of VIS and its systems. This collaboration aims to ensure the continuous availability and reliability of CI services and functions to benefit society and the economy [42].

6.12 FUTURE CHALLENGES AND EMERGING TECHNOLOGIES

The CIP ecosystem faces emerging threats and challenges that result from technological advancement, and regulatory frameworks threaten firms and stakeholders. Emerging threats need proactive methods to incorporate modern technologies, promote collaboration, and adapt to changing circumstances. The current section examines future CIP issues and new technologies, focusing on key trends, opportunities, and strategies for robustness and security in a complex threat environment [35, 43].

6.12.1 Future Challenges

1. Cyber Threats: The development of networked devices, cloud computing, and the IoT may cause new attacks and vulnerabilities, which promote the risk of cyberattacks on significant assets and IT systems. Also, threat actors become progressively more sophisticated, taking advantage of weaknesses and tampering with operations via ransomware, supply-chain assaults, and zero-day vulnerabilities [18].
2. Physical Threats: CIP challenges include physical risks, such as terrorism, sabotage, and natural catastrophes. The growth of frequency and severity of severe weather events, such as hurricanes, floods, and wildfires, highlight the significance of resilience and preparation in minimizing physical disruptions' effect on VIs and systems [40].
3. Regulation Compliance: Various organizations are dependable in CIP, where challenges occur via adhering to ever-evolving rules, regulations, and standards, which include the GDPR, NIST Cybersecurity Framework, and EU NIS Directive. Securing regulatory compliance while maintaining operational effectiveness and flexibility requires consistent investment in governance, risk management, and compliance (GRC) systems [44].
4. Insider Threats: These involve malevolent insiders and careless staff and represent major dangers to CI security since they have personal knowledge of the systems and access to confidential information. Insider risks must be detected and mitigated by employing technological controls, staff training, and behavioral analysis to identify abnormal behavior and prevent illegal access or data exfiltration [45].

6.12.2 Emerging Technologies

1. AI and ML: The following innovation technologies offer businesses real-time cyber threat response via employing analysis for forecasts, anomaly detection, and automated response. Since AI-powered systems can evaluate enormous amounts of data and spot patterns and trends, they may reduce response times in CIP and improve threat detection, which provides better judgments.
2. Blockchain: Blockchain technology has an opportunity to redefine CIP by creating irreversible and accessible records of data and transaction transfers. Blockchain technology in financial and supply-chain management could improve security, integrity, and accountability by avoiding tampering, fraud, and illegal access to critical data.
3. Quantum-Safe Cryptography: Considering the recent development of quantum computing, existing cryptographic techniques are in danger of being cracked, presenting a threat to CI system security. Quantum-safe cryptography provides solutions that resist quantum assaults, maintaining the secrecy, integrity, and authenticity of communications and data transfers in the face of growing dangers.
4. Edge Computing: Edge computing solutions move the analysis and processing of data farther from the source of data collection, lowering latency and

improving reaction times in CIP. Organizations may improve adaptability, scalability, and reliability while monitoring and safeguarding VIs and systems through decentralizing computer resources and spreading workloads among edge devices [16, 44].

6.12.3 Strategies for Addressing Future Challenges

1. Employ a Risk-Based Approach: Determine which CI assets and systems are most vulnerable and what investments and resources should be prioritized based on threat information and risk assessments.
2. Promote Teamwork and the Exchange of Data: Form alliances with relevant government entities, business associations, and international organizations to pool resources and disseminate information about security threats, best practices, and CIP lessons gained.
3. Invest an Investment Within Training and Education: To educate stakeholders, workers, and contractors about cybersecurity best practices, new threats, and incident response protocols and implement cybersecurity awareness programs and training efforts.
4. Embracing Innovations and Emerging Technologies: Investigate ways to improve CIP's adaptability, security, and flexibility by using cutting-edge technologies, which include blockchain, AI, and quantum-safe encryption.

A dynamic landscape of emerging threats, technological advancements, and regulatory requirements shapes the future of CIP. Organizations and stakeholders can enhance their resilience and readiness to address evolving risks and vulnerabilities in VIs and systems by anticipating future challenges, embracing innovation, and fostering collaboration. With a proactive and adaptive approach, CIP can continue safeguarding the essential services and functions on which society and the economy depend.

6.13 CONCLUSIONS AND REMARKS

CIP is a complicated, dynamic undertaking requiring a proactive, collaborative, and adaptive strategy to handle the ever-changing risks to important global infrastructure systems. Effective protection involves resilience, the capacity to recover from interruptions and adapt to new threats and technology. Governments, regulatory authorities, industry stakeholders, and international organizations can enhance detection, response, and mitigation by working together. Innovating and improving procedures via frequent evaluations and assessments will improve CI system security and dependability, ensuring society and the economy get crucial services. Several key conclusions and remarks emerge:

- Collaboration is Key: Effective CIP requires collaboration and coordination among governments, regulatory bodies, industry stakeholders, and international organizations. By working together, sharing information, and leveraging collective expertise, stakeholders can enhance their ability to detect, respond to, and mitigate threats to VIs and systems [43].

- Resilience is Essential: Resilience is the cornerstone of CIP, enabling organizations to withstand and recover from disruptions, whether from cyberattacks, physical incidents, natural disasters, or other threats. By investing in resilience-building measures, such as redundancy, diversity, and flexibility, organizations can enhance their ability to maintain essential services and functions in the face of adversity.
- Adaptability is crucial: The danger picture changes due to technical improvements, geopolitical changes, and emergent hazards. To successfully handle potential problems, companies, and stakeholders must remain agile and adaptive, constantly reevaluating their strategies, technology, and processes to keep up with developing risks and weaknesses [44].
- Innovation Fuels Advancement: There are plenty of opportunities to improve CIP with emerging technologies like blockchain, AI, and quantum-safe cryptography. Organizations may increase their resilience, enhance their detection and response skills, and keep ahead of changing threats by welcoming innovation and investigating new approaches [45].
- Continuous enhancement is necessary: CIP is a continuous process that involves monitoring, review, and enhancement. Organizations may improve their preparedness to face future problems by performing frequent risk assessments, testing response plans, and integrating lessons gained from accidents and exercises into their strategy.

In simple terms, protecting VIs and CI is a community duty requiring a proactive, collaborative, and adaptable approach. Prioritizing resilience, embracing technological advancement, promoting cooperation, and aiming for continuous enhancement may help stakeholders optimize the security and dependability of CI systems, assuring the continuing provision of critical services and functions for society and the economy.

REFERENCES

1. I. Aljundi, M. Rawashdeh, M. Al-Fayoumi, A. Al-Badarneh and Q. A. Al-Haija (2024). Protecting critical national infrastructures: An overview of cyberattacks and countermeasures. In: Nagar, A.K., Jat, D.S., Mishra, D., Joshi, A. (eds) Intelligent sustainable systems. WorldS4 2023. Lecture notes in networks and systems, vol 803. Springer, Singapore. https://doi.org/10.1007/978-981-99-7569-3_25.
2. A. H. Kugler and J. R. Clark, "Protecting VIs: A cybersecurity perspective," IEEE Transactions on Dependable and Secure Computing, vol. 17, no. 1, pp. 124–136, 2020.
3. M. A. H. Mian and H. A. Abbasi, "Resilience assessment of CI: A review," IEEE Access, vol. 9, pp. 23733–23749, 2021.
4. S. S. Lim, "Cybersecurity Challenges in Protecting CI," in Proceedings of the IEEE International Conference on Cybersecurity and Protection of Digital Services (Cybersecurity), Dublin, Ireland, June 2019, pp. 1–6.
5. D. G. Johnson and L. K. Smith, "A review of CI protection strategies," IEEE Security & Privacy, vol. 19, no. 5, pp. 82–89, 2021.
6. A. T. Rowland and E. R. Wright, "Cyber Threats to CI: A Comprehensive Overview," in Proceedings of the IEEE International Conference on Cybersecurity and Protection of Digital Services (Cybersecurity), London, UK, June 2020, pp. 1–8.

7. S. P. Gupta and R. K. Sharma, "A survey on cyber threats and vulnerabilities in CI," IEEE Transactions on Emerging Topics in Computing, vol. 8, no. 1, pp. 162–175, 2020.
8. S. A. Al-Tamimi and Q. A. Al-Haija. (2024). Supply chain security, technological advancements, and future trends. In Smart and agile cybersecurity for IoT and IIoT environments (pp. 211–234). IGI Global.
9. K. L. Williams and J. M. Green, "An analysis of cyber threats to power grid infrastructure," IEEE Transactions on Power Systems, vol. 35, no. 4, pp. 3201–3212, 2020.
10. B. Ojo, J. C. Ogborigbo and M. O. Okafor, "Innovative solutions for critical infrastructure resilience against cyber-physical attacks," World Journal of Advanced Research and Reviews, vol. 22, no. 3, pp. 1651–1674, 2024.
11. M. Czuryk, "Cybersecurity and protection of critical infrastructure," Studia Iuridica Lublinensia, vol. 32, no. 5, pp. 43–52, 2023.
12. R. S. Patel and H. V. Patel, "Cyber threat intelligence sharing for CI protection," IEEE Access, vol. 9, pp. 104580–104592, 2021.
13. J. Henriques, F. Caldeira, T. Cruz and P. Simões, "A survey on forensics and compliance auditing for critical infrastructure protection," IEEE Access, vol. 12, pp. 2409–2444, 2024. https://doi.org/10.1109/ACCESS.2023.3348552.
14. H. Riggs, S. Tufail, I. Parvez, M. Tariq, M. A. Khan, A. Amir and A. I. Sarwat, "Impact, vulnerabilities, and mitigation strategies for cyber-secure critical infrastructure," Sensors, vol. 23, no. 8, p. 4060, 2023.
15. A. S. George, T. Baskar and P. B. Srikaanth, "Cyber threats to critical infrastructure: Assessing vulnerabilities across key sectors," Partners Universal International Innovation Journal, vol. 2, no. 1, pp. 51–75, 2024.
16. S. Altamimi, Q. A. Al-Haija and M. Al-Fayoumi, "Fog Computing Security Challenges and Open Issues: a Short Survey," 7th IET Smart Cities Symposium (SCS 2023), Hybrid Conference, Bahrain, 2023, pp. 419–425. https://doi.org/10.1049/icp.2024.0961.
17. J. D. Smith and M. R. Johnson, "Understanding the Impact of Insider Threats on CI Cybersecurity," in Proceedings of the IEEE International Conference on Cybernetics and Intelligent Systems (CIS), Bangkok, Thailand, December 2020, pp. 1–6.
18. A. J. Peterson and B. R. Smith, "Enhancing cybersecurity for VIs: A comprehensive approach," IEEE Transactions on Dependable and Secure Computing, vol. 16, no. 5, pp. 832–845, 2019.
19. H. Mouratidis, S. Islam, A. Santos-Olmo, L. E. Sanchez and U. M. Ismail, "Modeling language for cybersecurity incident handling for critical infrastructures," Computers & Security, vol. 128, p. 103139, 2023.
20. T. K. Lee and S. H. Park, "Cybersecurity measures for power grid infrastructure: A case study," IEEE Transactions on Power Systems, vol. 34, no. 6, pp. 4536–4545, 2019.
21. K. Tsantikidou and N. Sklavos, "Threats, attacks, and cryptography frameworks of cybersecurity in critical infrastructures," Cryptography, vol. 8, no. 1, p. 7, 2024.
22. Y. Jiang, M. A. Jeusfeld, J. Ding and E. Sandahl, "Model-based cybersecurity analysis: Extending Enterprise modeling to critical infrastructure cybersecurity," Business & Information Systems Engineering, vol. 65, no. 6, pp. 643–676, 2023.
23. K. Mitsarakis. (2023). Contemporary Cyber Threats to Critical Infrastructures: Management and Countermeasures. MSc thesis in Cybersecurity, International Hellenic University.
24. R. G. Martinez and J. M. Davis, " framework for evaluating cybersecurity measures in healthcare infrastructure," IEEE Journal of Biomedical and Health Informatics, vol. 24, no. 3, pp. 809–819, 2020.
25. E. W. Thompson and K. L. White, "Implementing Cybersecurity Measures for Transportation Infrastructure: Challenges and Opportunities," in Proceedings of the IEEE International Conference on Intelligent Transportation Systems (ITSC), Rhodes, Greece, September 2021, pp. 1–6.

26. A. B. Johnson and C. D. Smith, "DFs in CI protection: Challenges and opportunities," IEEE Transactions on Information Forensics and Security, vol. 14, no. 9, pp. 2345–2356, 2019.
27. S. K. Patel and R. M. Jones, "Forensic Analysis of Cyber Incidents in CI: A Case Study Approach," in Proceedings of the IEEE International Conference on Cybersecurity and Protection of Digital Services (Cybersecurity), Toronto, Canada, June 2020, pp. 1–8.
28. V. Khaustova, M. R. Tirlea, L. Dandara, N. Trushkina and I. Birca, "Development of Critical Infrastructure From the Point of View of Information Security", Strategic Universe Journal/Univers Strategic, vol. 1, no. 53, pp. 170–188., 2023
29. Y. C. Tok and S. Chattopadhyay, "Identifying threats, cybercrime, and digital forensic opportunities in smart City infrastructure via threat modeling," Forensic Science International: Digital Investigation, vol. 45, p. 301540, 2023.
30. P. Binnar and S. Bhirud, "Security analysis of the cyber-physical system using digital forensic incident response", Cybersecurity and Applications, vol. 2, p. 100034, 2023.
31. I. Yefimenko, V. Slipchenko and A Vaško, "Critical infrastructure as an object of criminal encroachment: General characteristics and features of the investigation organization," Scientific Journal of the National Academy of Internal Affairs, vol. 28, no. 2, pp. 41–51, 2023.
32. C. M. Johnson and D. L. Brown, "A Survey of Cybersecurity Measures for CI Protection," in Proceedings of the IEEE International Conference on Cybersecurity and Protection of Digital Services (Cybersecurity), Athens, Greece, June 2018, pp. 1–7.
33. R. E. Garcia and M. J. Martinez, "Digital evidence collection and preservation in CI protection: Best Practices and challenges," IEEE Security & Privacy, vol. 18, no. 6, pp. 74–82, 2020.
34. E. T. Nguyen and H. W. Kim, "Challenges and considerations in DFs for industrial control systems in CI protection," IEEE Transactions on Industrial Informatics, vol. 17, no. 2, pp. 1486–1496, 2021.
35. G. H. Lee and A. R. Gupta, "Forensic analysis of SCADA systems in CI protection: Methodologies and case studies," IEEE Transactions on Power Delivery, vol. 36, no. 3, pp. 1895–1904, 2021.
36. A. B. Smith and C. D. Johnson, "Incident response strategies for CI protection: A comprehensive overview," IEEE Transactions on Dependable and Secure Computing, vol. 18, no. 3, pp. 824–837, 2020.
37. R. E. Garcia and M. J. Martinez, "Recovery and restoration strategies for CI resilience: A case study approach," IEEE Transactions on Systems, Man, and Cybernetics: Systems, vol. 50, no. 2, pp. 412–423, 2020.
38. G. H. Lee and A. R. Gupta, "Lessons Learned from Incident Response and Recovery Efforts in CI Protection: A Retrospective Analysis," in Proceedings of the IEEE International Conference on Industrial Technology (ICIT), Cancun, Mexico, March 2021, pp. 1–6.
39. A. B. Johnson and C. D. Smith, "Regulatory frameworks for CI protection: A comparative analysis," IEEE Transactions on Systems, Man, and Cybernetics: Systems, vol. 49, no. 11, pp. 2345–2356, 2019.
40. S. K. Patel and R. M. Jones, "International Cooperation in CI Protection: Challenges and Opportunities," in Proceedings of the IEEE International Conference on Cybersecurity and Protection of Digital Services (Cybersecurity), Berlin, Germany, August 2020, pp. 1–8.
41. R. E. Garcia and M. J. Martinez, "The role of regulatory frameworks in enhancing international cooperation for CI protection," IEEE Transactions on Engineering Management, vol. 67, no. 3, pp. 456–467, 2021.
42. E. T. Nguyen and H. W. Kim, "Effective regulatory compliance strategies for CI protection: Lessons learned and best practices," IEEE Security & Privacy, vol. 20, no. 4, pp. 82–89, 2021.

43. G. H. Lee and A. R. Gupta, "Building partnerships for CI protection: The role of international organizations and regulatory bodies," in Proceedings of the IEEE International Conference on Emerging Technologies and Trends in Cybersecurity (ETTC), Virtual, December 2021, pp. 1–6.
44. A. Dabit, Q. A. Al-Haija and M. Al-Fayoumi, "Identifying Weaknesses: A Guide to Conducting an Effective Network Vulnerability Assessment," 2023 24th International Arab Conference on Information Technology (ACIT), Ajman, United Arab Emirates, 2023, pp. 1–6. https://doi.org/10.1109/ACIT58888.2023.10453877.
45. E. Aljbour, A. Dabit, M. Al-Fayoumi and Q. A. Al-Haija, "UNI-CERT: A Unified Computer Emergency Response Teams Model for Malware Information Sharing Platform," 2023 IEEE 5th International Conference on Power, Intelligent Computing and Systems (ICPICS), Shenyang, China, 2023, pp. 404–410. https://doi.org/10.1109/ICPICS58376.2023.10235378.

7 Cryptanalysis Techniques for National Security

Mazen AlWadi and Qasem Abu Al-Haija

7.1 INTRODUCTION

The desire for secrecy and the urge to protect our Message (MSGs) becomes of greater importance with the sensitivity of the information we aim to protect. Since the beginning of human society's evolution, rulers of each country have understood the importance of protecting the information used in their communications. This led to the development of certain codes and representations that can only be understood by the intended recipient. To fulfill this desire for secrecy, nations relied on the establishment of codemaking departments responsible for the invention and creation of different techniques that can be used to transform the original MSG into a form that only the envisioned recipient can recognize; this process used to be known as cyphering and currently known as Encipherion (ENC). The codemaking department created cyphering mechanisms and investigated techniques to decipher or decipher the enemies' cyphered MSGs, known as Cryptanalysis (CLSS) [1]. Before diving into the history of CLSS techniques and their details, we start by discussing the title of this chapter. While CLSS is the science of discovering the methods used to cipher MSGs and inventing a way to retrieve the original MSGs, its relation to National Security (Nsec) may still seem vague. To clarify, when discussing CLSS in the light of Nsec, we typically refer to communications intelligence spying on foreign communications to detect and prevent incidents related to the nation's security. Therefore, a country's advancement in CLSS strongly relates to the country's ability to break foreign codes, and any decline in the success of this activity will make the country less secure [2].

Before we dive into the details of CRYPTO and CLSS, let's look back at how it all started. One of the oldest known forms of secret writing to conceal MSGs dates back to Herodotus, who reported the Greece – Persia conflict in the 5th century B.C., which he classified as a conflict between the oppressive Persians and the free states of Greece. The conflict between the two reached its climax when the leader of the Persians, Xerxes, known as the king of kings, started to mobilize a force declaring that "we shall extend the empire of Persia such that its boundaries will be God's sky", which was due to what he considered as a disrespect that Sparta and Athens did not send him gifts when he started the construction of his new capital Persepolis. Xerxes devoted five years to launch a surprise attack. The techniques used to achieve secret communication relied solely on hiding the MSG, which required considerably longer than Demaratus' strategy, as he used to shave the head of his messenger and write

DOI: 10.1201/9781003497868-7

the MSG on his shaved head, then wait for the hair to grow before sending the messenger. This form of secret communication, which relies on hiding the existence of an MSG, is known as ***steganography (STGNO)***. Since then, several steganographic techniques have been used to conceal MSGs [3]. Despite the advantages of STGNO in hiding MSGs, it still suffers from fundamental weaknesses. If the messenger is caught and thoroughly searched, the MSG can be found, and the content can be easily understood. Therefore, code makers worked on developing ***CRYPTO*** in parallel with the evolution of STGNO.

The purpose of CRYPTO is different from STGNO, such that CRYPTO's goal is not to hide the MSG's existence but to hide the MSG's meaning in a process known as ENC. The ENC is done by following a predefined procedure between the sender and the receiver, which scrambles the MSG in a way that generates an incomprehensible MSG [4]. Upon receiving the enciphered MSG, the receiver can follow the reversing procedure to decipher and retrieve the unenciphered MSG. The advantage of ENC is that if the enemy intercepted the MSG, they would find it impossible or at least very difficult to understand. While CRYPTO and STGNO are independent, they still serve the same purpose: protecting the exchanged MSGs. Therefore, both can be combined to maximize the security level. One example of combining these techniques was during World War II when German spies used to write an MSG, then shrink the whole page into the size of a microdot and hide it on top of a full stop. Whenever the Americans were tipped off about this technique, the Germans started to scramble their MSGs to prevent the Americans from gaining information about their activities [5].

The ENC can be done in ***transposition*** and/or ***substitution***. In transposition, the letters of the MSG are reordered, which can be insecure for single-word MSGs due to limited possibilities. For example, if we scramble the MSG "War", there will be only six combinations, for example, war, war, war, raw, raw, rwa. However, the number of possible rearrangements increases exponentially with the increased length of the MSG. Although transposition can generate highly secure anagrams, randomly scrambling the MSG would lead to an anagram that is impossible to unscramble for the enemies and the intended recipient. For the transposition to be effective, the unscrambling should follow a straightforward procedure previously agreed on between the sender and the receiver. An example of transposition is the "rail fence" technique, which writes the MSG in two distinct lines; the letters on the first and second lines are then concatenated, and the letters of the second line are added to the end of the letters in the first line to generate the enciphered MSG. The rail fence technique is shown in the example below [6].

The MSG	THIS IS A SECRET MSG
Upper line	T I I A E R T E S G
Lower line	H S S S C E M S A E
Enciphered MSG	TIIAERTESGHSSSCEMSAE

Alternative to the transposition, substitution can be used, which works by replacing each character with another alphabet or symbol. The substitution is different from the transposition in that each character retains its position but changes the identity wherever it keeps the identity and changes the position in the transposition.

The first use of substitution ciphers is the Ceaser chipper, which used ciphers frequently in his writings; however, we have the details of one of these ciphers, which we call the Ciser shift cipher or Ciser cipher. As cryptographers, we usually use two sets of alphabets: the plain and ***cipher alphabet***. The plain alphabet is used to write the original MSG, and the cipher alphabet replaces the plain alphabet characters in the original MSG to generate the enciphered MSG [7].

Plain alphabet	**a b c d e f g h I j k l m n o p q r s t u v w x y z**
Cipher alphabet	**D E F G H I J K L M N O P Q R S T U V W X Y Z A B C**
MSG	**this is secret**
Encrypted MSG	**WKLV LV VHFUHW**

The Ceaser cipher above clearly shifts each character with the third following character in the alphabet; we could generate 25 different ciphers if we limited ourselves to shifting only. However, allowing any arrangement of the alphabet characters can generate many different ciphers as the characters can be arranged in 26! Which is over 4×10^{26}. In general, each cipher can be described by two main components: the algorithm and a key. In the case of substitution cipher, the algorithm substitutes each character in the plain alphabet with another character from the cipher alphabet, wherein the cipher alphabet can be any arrangement of characters. The key describes the exact cipher alphabet for any specific ENC. The relationship between the algorithm and the key is illustrated in Figure 7.1.

It is worth noting that the ENC algorithm is not a secret, as an attacker may know that a substitution algorithm is used to encipher the MSG. However, without knowing the exact cipher alphabet (key), he cannot decipher the MSG as trying the huge space of 4×10^{26} possible keys cannot be done within millions of years. Therefore, protecting the key is of great importance, as opposed to the ENC algorithm, which was definitively stated in what is known as Kerchoffs' principle: "The security of a cryptosystem must not depend on keeping the crypto-algorithm secret. This depends only on keeping the key secret". In addition to the secure key, the ENC algorithm

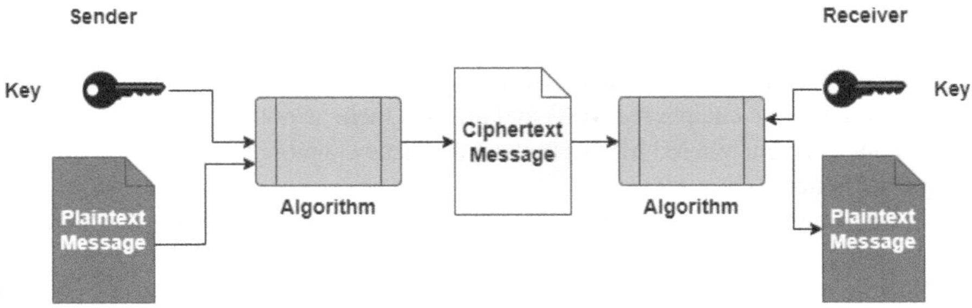

FIGURE 7.1 The relationship between the algorithm and the key in the ENC process.

Keyword	Crypto Secret
Plain alphabet	A B C D E F G H I J K L M N O P Q R S T U V W X Y Z
Cipher alphabet	C R Y P T O S E T U V W X Z A B D F G H I J K L M N

FIGURE 7.2 Cipher alphabet with a keyword/keyphrase.

should have a wide range of keys to choose from. For example, the Ceaser shift has 25 potential keys only, which makes it relatively weak, as an attacker can decipher the MSG by trying all the potential keys (25) in a process known as Brute force.

On the other hand, the general case of substitution has more than 4×10^{26} possible keys. To simplify memorizing the shared key, the sender can choose a keyword representing the start of the cipher alphabet. The generation of the cipher alphabet starts by removing spaces and repeated characters, then continuing the cipher alphabet where the keyword ends, as shown in Figure 7.2.

Due to the simplicity and the large pool of potential keys of substitution cipher, it became widespread during the first millennium A.D. The seemingly unbreakable ENC scheme led many scholars and codebreakers to believe this cipher was unbreakable. However, the breakthrough that did not require checking all the possible keys to decipher the MSG required an outstanding combination of linguistics, statistics, and religion by Muslim scholars in the East.

The Muslims have also invented ***CLSS,*** the science of deciphering an MSG without knowing the ENC key. To fulfill their religious duty of learning and spreading knowledge, they not only studied religion but also acquired, translated, and studied the knowledge of former nations. The religious scholars who aimed to establish a chronological order of the revelations in the Quran counted the frequencies of words. The theory was that some words it indicates it appeared later in chronological order. The scholars did not stop counting the words but continued to count and analyze the frequency of individual letters, leading to the CLSS breakthrough. The earliest known description of how to use the letter frequency to decipher an MSG is found in a book by "The Philosopher of the Arabs" Al-Kindi, titled "A Manuscript on Deciphering CRYPTO MSGs". Al-Kindi's technique to decipher an MSG can be described as follows.

If we want to decipher an MSG that we know its original language, start by finding a P.T. of the same language. Then, we calculate the frequency of every letter in this P.T. and arrange the letters, calling the highest frequency letter the first, the second highest frequency the second, and so on. After that, we count the frequencies of each symbol of the enciphered MSG and arrange them as done in the P.T. MSG. We then replace the enciphered MSG's highest-frequency symbol with the P.T.'s highest-frequency letter.

Taking English as an example, the most frequent letter is "e", and the second most frequent is "t", then "a", and so on, as shown in Table 7.1.

Now, to unscramble an MSG written in English, we count the frequency of each letter in the enciphered MSG and replace the letters with the corresponding letter in Table 7.1. For example, if the most frequent letter in an enciphered MSG is "K",

TABLE 7.1
English Letters and Their Frequencies

Letter	Freq.	Letter	Freq.	Letter	Freq.	Letter	Freq.
A	8.2%	H	6.1%	O	7.5%	V	1.0%
B	1.5%	I	7.0%	P	1.9%	W	2.4%
C	2.8%	J	0.2%	Q	0.1%	X	0.2%
D	4.3%	K	0.8%	R	6.0%	Y	2.0%
E	12.7%	L	4.0%	S	6.3%	Z	0.1%
F	2.2%	M	2.4%	T	9.1%		
G	2.0%	N	6.7%	U	2.8%		

then this is probably a substitute for "E", and so on. Al-Kindi's technique (***frequency analysis***) demonstrates that it's not required to examine all the keys, and it is possible to show the content of an MSG without knowing the key simply by analyzing the frequency of each letter. However, the frequency analysis technique cannot be applied unconditionally. For instance, a short MSG discussing global warming effects on Australia would yield a C.T. that deviates from the normal frequencies shown in Table 7.1. After this brief discussion about the evolution of simple ciphers and CLSS, we dive into modern CRYPTO and CLSS techniques after discussing the mathematical background required to understand these techniques [8].

7.2 MATHEMATICAL FOUNDATIONS

Current CRYPTO algorithms depend heavily on mathematical formulas devised to obscure information. Similarly, deciphering an MSG is easy if you know the algorithm and the key used for ENC. The ENC algorithms described in the introduction are called Simple ciphers, which are mechanical. The process of ENC/DEC can be done by a person or a computer using a simple algorithm. The following sections discuss recent mathematical ciphers based on recent advances in number theory and algebra. Therefore, we discuss the minimum necessary mathematics required to understand these ciphers' operation and the CLSS techniques to break them.

7.2.1 Probability

The probability (of an event) is identified as the possibility of it happening on a measure between 0 and 1, where 0 means it never happens, and 1 means it always happens. Additionally, all probabilities of the possible outcomes must sum to 1 as some event must occur. For example, if we roll a fair die once, we will get one out of six events {1, 2, 3, 4, 5, 6}, and the probability of having each number on the top side of the die is 1/6, and their sum is 1.

For another example, imagine rolling two fair dice, and we want to know the occurrences of showing 1 and 2. This can happen in two ways: (1 2) and (2 1), so there are two permutations. Notice that when we were interested in a single object, the number of occurrences was 1; when we added a second object, the number of occurrences became 2; and when we added a third object, the number of occurrences became 6. The same pattern continues; each time we add another, the pattern will multiply the successive numbers, known as the factorial function (***n!***). Therefore, if we are interested in four objects, the result will be 4! = 4×3×2×1.

A further prominent notion is the ***permuted choices (combinations)*** – the number of distinct ways of picking ***k*** objects out of ***n*** objects regardless of the order of events. For example, imagine we want to select a team of two people out of four people (John, Mary, Sarah, Andy); how many teams can we form? We can see that there are the following six pairs:

(John, Marry), (John, Sarah), (John, Andy), (Marry, Sarah), (Marry, Andy), (Sarah, Andy)

The number of teams being formed can be calculated using a ***binomial coefficient*** as follows:

$$\binom{n}{k} = \frac{n!}{(n-k)!k!}$$

For example, say we have seven cars and watch to hold two. How many ways are there to pick two of them? $\frac{7!}{(7-2)!2!} = \frac{7\times6\times5\times4\times3\times2\times1}{5\times4\times3\times2\times1\times2\times1} = 21$

Probabilities can be more complicated than we have discussed so far. For instance, imagine rolling, tossing four coins, counting how many times the head is shown, and then tossing the coins that did not show the head the first time. Naturally, the probabilities of the second toss are not affected by the first toss. However, since we are only tossing the coins that did not show head in the first toss, the outcome of the second toss is no longer independent. However, we will not dive into the details of dependence, but we discuss how the probabilities are not always what they seem at first glance.

7.2.1.1 The Birthday Paradox

The birthday paradox asks somebody, "How likely is it that two people have the same birthday?" Here, we look for two events with the same result (***collision***). If we excluded leap years, the answer is 1/365. The first person's birthdate does not affect the second person's birthdate; the events are independent. Therefore, assuming the first person's birthdate is fixed, we calculate the probability of the second person's birthdate occurring on the same day (assuming a normal distribution and the birthday will be a random day).

That was fairly easy; now, let's see what happens when the question becomes, "What is the probability that at least two people out of three have the same birthday?" Since we are only concerned about two having the same birthday and not about an order, we have three different pairs to consider: P1-P2, P1-P3, and P2-P3. Any of these pairs may share the same birthday. At first glance, one may think we can add the probability of a collision three times or multiply it by three. But this does not scale well, as if we have 390 people. This would mean we have $\frac{390!}{(390-2)!2!} = 75,855$ different pairs, and therefore a $\frac{1}{365} \times 75,855 = 207.82\%$ probability, which is simply wrong, as the probability of an event should be equal or greater than 0 and less than or equal to 1.

This wrong answer results from adding a third person, which means adding two possible days to check, not one, because the 3rd person might match the 1st or 2nd person. Thus, adding the 2nd person notably expands the probability of a collision. Though the increment in probability is lessened each time we add another person. For instance, in a group of 363 persons and 364 persons, the difference is negligible between the probabilities of having a repeated birthday.

Let's look at the probability of no birthday collisions with ***n*** people and subtract the result from 1. In this example, we consider that the probability is completely random, and the person's birthday can be any day of the 365 days of the year, with each day having the same probability. Thus, having one person without collisions can happen any day and is guaranteed to have no collisions, which can be described as having ***n*** options from the ***n*** days with a probability of n/n. Adding a second person is slightly dependent on the first person, as to ensure no collision, the second person has ***n-1*** options to choose from ***n*** with a probability of ***(n-1)/n***. Similarly, adding a third person will result in a probability of ***(n-2)/n***. If we generalize this into ***k*** persons, then this would be $\frac{n-(k-1)}{n} = \frac{n-k+1}{n}$.

Now, when adding each person, and to ensure no collision happens, we need to calculate the probability for each person's birthday and multiply these probabilities, which results in the following:

$$Numerator = \frac{(n)(n-1)(n-2)\ldots(n-k+1)}{n^k}$$

This equation can be simplified into a usable form using some Calculus techniques to be

$$e^{-k(k-1)/(2n)}$$

It is easy to know that we have a 100% chance of a collision when we have ***k=n.*** But is it more useful to know the tipping point when the probability would be about half (0.5)? In this case, the probability of no repetition equals the probability of at least one repetition. Thus, we can set the probability of the previous equation to 0.5 and solve for ***k*** in terms of ***n***

$$\frac{1}{2} = e^{-k(k-1)/(2n)}$$

With some approximation and Calculus techniques, this will lead to

$$k \approx 1.774\sqrt{n}$$

This shows that if we have ***no possibilities, it would be sufficient to consider a constant time at*** the square root of the number of events to have a 50% chance of a collision. In the case of our birthday example, this means $k \approx 22.494$. This means that if we have a room with 23 people, we have a decent chance of having a repeated birthday. While this was discussed in the context of birthdays, it tells us that we can highlight the weaknesses of hashing algorithms with relatively little effort.

7.2.2 Number Theory

Many modern CRYPTO algorithms are based on number theory, especially divisibility and prime numbers [9]. Let's have a quick look at the classes of numbers, which are the **Integers** ($\mathbb{Z}$), **Rational Numbers** ($\Re$), and **Real numbers** ($\mathbb{Q}$). The integers are the numbers we use for counting, including the zero and the negative of these numbers: {…, –4, –3, –2, –1, 0, 1, 2, 3, 4, …}. The rational numbers are the ones that we can represent in the form of $n = \frac{\text{a}}{\text{b}}$ where both ***a*** and ***b*** are integers, for example, 2/3. The real numbers include the integers, the rational, and any other number that can be compared with integers and rational numbers. This includes the non-rational numbers that cannot be represented as $n = \frac{\text{a}}{\text{b}}$ and numbers that may have infinite digits to represent their exact value, such as $\sqrt{3}$ or π.

7.2.2.1 Prime Numbers

If we have an integer (a), we say that it is divisible by another integer (b) if (a) can be divided by (b) with a reminder of (0) and a result of another integer (c). Thus, $a = \text{b} \times \text{c}$. Consequently, if (b) is divisible by another number (d), it results in another integer (e). Then, (a) is divisible by (d), leading to $a = \text{c} \times \text{e} \times \text{d}$. An important concept regarding divisibility is the ***greatest common divisor*** **(GCD),** the largest positive integer that divides two integers. For example, gcd(24, 16) = 8. If the GCD of two integers is 1, then these two integers are called **relatively prime.** If a number shares no common divisors with any number less than it, then that number is defined as **prime**.

7.2.2.2 Congruences

As we use computers to build CRYPTO and cryptanalytic algorithms, we must understand the limitations of the computers' capabilities and their inability to process infinite numbers due to the limited resources. Therefore, we need to reduce the data set we can operate on; for example, instead of operating on all the integers, we need to take a subset of the integers and perform the operations on them. Fortunately, this can be done using the theory of congruences, which can be defined as if we have three integers ***a, b,*** and ***m,*** then we say that ***a*** is congruent to **b modulo m** if ***m*** divides (***a*** – ***b***), which is written as $\mathbf{a} \equiv \boldsymbol{b} (\text{mod } \boldsymbol{m})$. We refer to ***m*** as the **modulus**. Similarly, if $\mathbf{a} \equiv \boldsymbol{b} (\text{mod } \boldsymbol{m})$, Then, we know that ***m*** divides (***a*** – ***b***). Hence, we know that there is some integer ***k*** such that. $\mathbf{mk} \equiv \boldsymbol{a} - \boldsymbol{b}$.

Due to these features, congruent numbers with a certain modulus can be used interchangeably for many mathematical operations in that modulus. We often work with operations like addition, subtraction, and multiplication in mathematics. One operation that we use is modulo, which is denoted by the symbol %. For example, when we say 10% 12 = 2, 10 is congruent to 2 modulo 12. Another example is 12 + 12% 10, which gives us 4 modulo 10. Similarly, 2 + 2% 10 also equals 4 modulo 10. Subtraction and multiplication work similarly. Numbers equivalent to each other under a specific modulus are typically organized into a residue class. Moreover, if we have a complete set of residues (CSR), each integer will be equivalent to exactly one residue in the set. Continuing on the previous example of mod 10, the CSR can be {1, 2, 3, 4, 5, 6, 7, 8, 9, 10}. Another important set of residues to discuss that we often use to reduce the size of the CSR is the **reduced set of residues (RSR)**. In the RSR, we only consider the relatively prime to the modulus. To find the RSR for our example, we iterate over the residues and delete every number that is not relatively prime to 10. In our case, 2, 5, and 10 are deleted. Similarly, 4, 6, and 8 are deleted, resulting in the RSR:{1, 3, 7, 9}.

7.2.3 Algebra

Algebra can be defined as the study of objects and the operations that can be performed on those objects. These operations are examples of **functions** that take some input and generate an output for each possible input, where there can be only one output for each input. In other words, running a function any number of times using the same input will always generate the same result. As many CRYPTO algorithms are built on top of algebraic constructs such as elliptic curves, fields, and rings, we need some understanding to analyze and perform cryptanalytics against them.

7.2.3.1 Sets and Operators

Sets are groups of elements or objects usually denoted by a capital letter and enclosed in curly braces. For example, A={–1, 0, 1} is a set called A and contains the elements –1, 0, and 1. Any element in the set A can be denoted with the lowercase of the set name (a). Operators can be thought of as functions that take elements from different or the same set and generate an output that belongs to one of these sets or another time cap B goes to cap C, which is a multiplication operation that takes inputs from sets A and B and then generates an output that belongs to set C. Assuming A and B are sets of integers, the result will also be an integer.

In this case, the operator takes inputs from the same set and generates an output that belongs to the same set. For this to be useful, we need more properties to be satisfied; more precisely, we need an **identity** element, **inverse** element, and **associativity**. The identity element is an element that, when used with the operator and another element, will always result in the second element; we refer to the identity element as (e). For example, the addition operation has zero as the identity element. Adding zero to any element will result in the second element. The inverse element is an element that we need for each element in the set. The result will be the identity element when the operation is used on the element and its inverse. For the addition of integers, the negative number is the inverse of each number, and –3 is the inverse of 3, as adding both numbers will result in 0. Associativity satisfies the below equation:

$$a+(b+c)=(a+\mathrm{b})+c$$

This means that the order of applying two consecutive operations does not change the result. The addition and multiplication operations satisfy this property.

If we have a set that satisfies these properties for some operator, then they are called a **group**. A group is denoted as a pair of the set and the operator. For example, the integers satisfy these properties for the addition operation and are written as $(\mathbb{Z}, +)$. Additionally, if any two elements in this group satisfy the property such that $a+b=b+a$, the group is called an abelian or **commutative group**. As a reminder, the operation needs to be **well-defined**, which means applying the operation on two elements from the group should result in an output that belongs to the same group. For example, division is not a valid operation for integers such as 3/2 = 1.5, which is not an integer [10].

Besides the groups, another interesting structure is what we call a **ring**. The ring is when we have two operators on a set, such as $(\mathbb{Z}, +, \times)$. The first operator with the set should form an abelian group, wherein the second operator needs only to satisfy the associativity. This means that multiplication does not need an inverse or an identity. Suppose the second operator (multiplication in our example) has an identity element and inverse elements for each element in the group (except the identity of the first operator). In that case, this ring is a **field**. The multiplication does not satisfy these requirements under the integers set. However, if we used the real numbers instead of the integers, this would be a field $(\mathbb{Q}, +, \times)$. A very interesting field for cryptographers is a **finite field** with a finite number of elements.

An example of a finite field would be the integers 0 – 7, denoted as $\mathbb{Z}_7$, with the addition and multiplication operators $(\mathbb{Z}_7, +, \times)$. The regular addition and multiplication operations modulo 7 will function as anticipated; we only need to check if we have multiplicative inverses for each element except 0. The verification can be easily done as follows:

$$\begin{aligned}
&\mathbf{1}\times\mathbf{1}\equiv\mathbf{1}\ (\text{mod } \mathbf{7})\\
&\mathbf{2}\times\mathbf{4}\equiv\mathbf{1}\ (\text{mod } \mathbf{7})\\
&\mathbf{3}\times\mathbf{5}\equiv\mathbf{1}\ (\text{mod } \mathbf{7})\\
&\mathbf{6}\times\mathbf{6}\equiv\mathbf{1}\ (\text{mod } \mathbf{7})
\end{aligned}$$

All the elements, except the identity of the first operator (0), have multiplicative inverses. This is a finite field, which we refer to as the **Galois field**.

After this refresher on probability, number theory, and algebra, we can now dive into some CLSS techniques.

7.3 MODERN CLSS METHODS

After briefly refreshing the math skills needed for our study of CLSS, we dive into the cryptanalytic techniques. The cryptanalytic techniques are classified into General, Linear, and Differential cryptanalytic techniques.

7.3.1 General CLSS Techniques

The post-basic CLSS technique is to try all the possible keys, known as the **brute force attack**. This method does not require mathematics; we try all the possible keys.

This technique's main advantage is its ability always to find the key. However, finding the key can take a long if the search space is large. One technique that can speed up the process is dividing the search space into multiple sub-spaces and assigning each sub-space to a different processor. For example, an ENC algorithm like the DES, which uses a 56-bit key, has a search space of 2^{56}. Assuming each of our modern processors can perform 6 million AES ENCs per second, we can calculate $\mathbf{6 \times 10^6 \times 60 \times 60 \times 24 = 518{,}400{,}000{,}000 \approx 2^{39}}$. Thus, breaking such an algorithm with our processors is still impossible in a single day. There is a gap of $\mathbf{2^{17}}$. What do we need to cover to be able to try all the keys? This can be achieved by using more processors or by taking more time. On the other hand, simple ENC schemes that use ~40-bit keys are breakable in a day if your machine has a multicore processor and the task is parallelized.

7.3.1.1 Time-Space Trade-Off Attacks

In computer science, we can almost always improve the performance of a certain operation by using more space. Generally speaking, instead of calculating all the hashes to find a collision or solving a discrete logarithm problem faster, we can build large tables of hashes or powers of generators in various finite fields. The number of possibilities is infinite, but we can still apply this technique sometimes. For example, we encipher a chosen P.T. with various keys in the Hellman time-space trade-off attack. The process starts with a large number of keys (M) denoted as K_i and the chosen P.T. (P) to construct a list of C.T.s (C_i) by enciphering P with each key K_i as follows:

$$C_i^0 = Encrypt(P, K_i)$$

After that, we encipher P using the result of the previous ENC process. (C_i^0) to generate (C_i^1) and repeat the same process S several times. Note that if the length of the C.T. is larger than the key size, we use a simple function (R) to reduce the size of the C.T. when used for the ENC as follows:

$$C_i^1 = Encrypt\left(P,\ R\left(C_i^0\right)\right)$$

The complete process results in the following chains of C.T.s:

$$\begin{array}{cccc} C_0^0 \rightarrow & C_0^1 \rightarrow & C_0^2 \cdots & C_0^S \\ C_1^0 \rightarrow & C_1^1 \rightarrow & C_1^2 \cdots & C_1^S \\ \vdots & \vdots & \vdots & \vdots \\ C_M^0 \rightarrow & C_M^1 \rightarrow & C_M^2 \cdots & C_M^S \end{array}$$

For this attack, we only store the first and the last C.T., C sub i. to the 0 and C sub i. to the cap S, creating two lists of C.T.s. Assuming we intercept the C.T. (A) of the known P.T. that we used to generate these two lists, if A = C_i^S for any i, then we know that the used key is C_i^{S-1}. To boost the chances of finding the key, we not only compare A against the values of Ci. to S, but we also allow the same procedure we used to generate the chains of C.T.s. The process continues until we find that sub i. to the cap S that matches the key, or we give up after S times.

This method has two main drawbacks: false positives and convergence. The false positives are caused by the reduction function, which means we might find a match, but the matched key is not the key as the reduction function reduced it. Convergence can be split into two categories: self-convergence and convergence with another chain, which happens when two chains have the same key at some point and, therefore, will match each other for the rest of the chain. Convergence leads to waste storage and computation instead of improving the performance and the probability of finding the key. These drawbacks were addressed by **Rainbow tables**, which use a different reduction function to generate the next key for each iteration.

7.3.1.2 CLSS of Hash Functions

Hash functions generate a fixed length unique representation for a variable length input. The main goal of hash functions is being one-way, meaning that given a certain text hash, it should be impossible to obtain the original text. Additionally, if you have a P.T. and its hash, it should not be easy to produce another text that produces the same hash. However, due to the limited number of outputs and the infinite number of inputs, some texts may generate the same hash for different texts, which we call **collision**.

Our main concern in the CLSS of hash functions is to produce a collision or obtain information about the plain text. We will be discussing three main types of attacks on hash functions:

1. Getting two MSGs to generate the same hash without any link to any other item.
2. Given an MSG hash, we need to find a text that generates the same hash, called the **pre-image attack.**
3. Finding an MSG that generates the same hash as a given one, where a plausible alternative to some original item generates the given one. This is an extension of the pre-image attack.

The first attack is the simplest, a basic collision attack; we can keep selecting random texts, calculating the hash for these texts, and storing the pair in a table. Luckily, we do not have to try all the combinations; per the birthday paradox, we only need to calculate and store the $\sqrt{n}$ to have a decent chance of finding a collision. Unfortunately, this does not apply to the other types of collision attacks. Therefore, we need to calculate n hashes. Thus, any algorithm that requires less than the square an the squarean the $\sqrt{n}$ or n to find the collision is considered an improvement.

These attacks were used successfully against the MD5 and SHA-1 algorithms, which used to be the most commonly used hashing algorithms. Therefore, we are currently using the SHA-2 for extra security.

7.3.1.3 CLSS of Random Number Generators

The main reason we are interested in the CLSS of random number generators is their usage to produce a key for the typical ciphers. For example, the standard Java random number generator uses linear congruence seeded with the time in milliseconds. We can try to find the parameters of this generator by finding the values of ***a, c, and m*** by having three consecutively generated values (A, B, C). The linear congruential method works as follows:

$$X \leftarrow (a \times X + c) \ mod \ m$$

Using the three found values, we can solve the system of equations to extract the values of these parameters as follows:

$$C \equiv (a \times B + c) \ mod \ m$$

$$B \equiv (a \times A + c) \ mod \ m$$

If we subtract the second equation from the first equation, we get:

$$(C - B) \equiv (a \times (B - A)) \ mod \ m$$

If we know that m is a prime, then we can multiply (C – B) by the inverse of (B – A) (modulo m) to obtain a. Then, we can calculate c = B – a × A and verify that c = C – a × B.

7.3.2 Linear CLSS Techniques

Linear CLSS is a known P.T. attack, which means it uses a set of known P.T.s and their associated C.T.s enciphered with the same key, in which we aim to discover the key used for the ENC. The first thing we need to say is that this attack is a statistical attack that is not guaranteed to work but will work most of the time. The word "linear" in this attack stems from the mechanics of this attack, in which we build a system of **linear binary equations** and try to solve these equations to extract information about the key. The linear binary equations are represented as follows:

$$A_1 \oplus A_2 \oplus A_3 \oplus \cdots \oplus A_n = B$$

or as follows:

$$A_1 \oplus A_2 \oplus A_3 \oplus \cdots \oplus A_n \oplus B = 0$$

These equations associate bits from the input with bits from the output. Assuming we want to associate the 3rd and 5th bits from the input A with the 4th, 5th, and 6th bits of the output Y, the equation would be:

$$A_3 \oplus A_5 \oplus Y_4 \oplus Y_5 \oplus Y_6$$

This equation may be true sometimes, but not all the time. We aim to create numerous equations and use them to construct a linear approximation of the cipher. This estimation's final input and output bits will be based on the key, plaintext, and ciphertext. The more accurate this estimation, the less work we must do to find the key. It is worth noting that a seasoned cryptanalyst does not just assume random bits for the linear equations. Instead, we rely on the imperfect diffusion property of the cipher. Since a perfect diffusion will generate a 0 or 1 50% of the time, the imperfect diffusion will have some bits that do not have a probability of 0.5. Therefore, we aim to use more of these bits with the largest deviation from the probability of 0.5 to increase our chances of finding the key, which leads us to the next topic.

7.3.2.1 Matsui's Algorithms

Matsui proposed two algorithms for linear CLSS; one is very popular, and the other is not. Starting with the less popular algorithm, which assumes we have a linear expression of the following form:

$$P_{i1} \oplus P_{i2} \oplus \cdots \oplus C_{j1} \oplus C_{j2} \oplus \cdots \oplus = K_{k1} \oplus K_{k2} \oplus \cdots$$

where the P_{i1} represent the first bit from the plain text, the C_{j1} represents the first bit from the C.T., and the K_{k1} represents the first bit from the key. This algorithm is based on the probabilities of bits deviating from the supposed probability of ½, called **bias**. As we perform a known P.T. attack, we have several pairs of P.T.s and C.T.s; thus, we know several values of the P and C bits, and we will be looking for the K bits.

First, we must determine the probability P of this equation being true and then follow these steps:

1. Collect many pairs of P.T.-C.T. for a specific key (the number of pairs is determined by the probability *P* of the equation).
2. For each pair, we calculate the left side of the equation and count the number of times it equals zero; this number is referred to as T.
3. If T is greater than half of the pair and P is greater than ½, we assume the right side is zero.
4. If T is less than half of the pairs and P is less than ½, then we also assume the right side is zero.
5. Otherwise, we assume the right side is one.

The equation relies on the accuracy of the guessed probability of the equation P and does not provide much information about the key. This equation can retrieve the key if we have a large collection of P.T.-C.T. pairs and construct several similar equations with large biases. Due to the impracticality of this equation, good ciphers would usually have small biases. Therefore, Matsui issued a second algorithm that relies on a single number of linear expressions but many P.T.-C.T. pairs. The new algorithm uses the same equation as the one above, but instead of counting how many times the left side equals zero, we will try all the values of the K bits and count how many times the whole equation is true.

We must know the probability of this equation holding P for this algorithm to work.

$$P_{i1} \oplus P_{i2} \oplus \cdots \oplus C_{j1} \oplus C_{j2} \oplus \cdots \oplus = K_{k1} \oplus K_{k2} \oplus \cdots$$

Then we follow these steps:

1. Collect a large number of P.T.-C.T. pairs for a specific key.
2. For each candidate group of key bits, calculate the number of times the overall equation holds; we also refer to this number as T.
3. Identify the candidate keys furthest from 50% of the pairs. Calculate each candidate's T-(N/2), resulting in a set of key candidates maximizing |T-(N/2)|.

This algorithm attempts all combinations of key bits to identify the most probable candidate set. For instance, if we are working with a 64-bit key, and we create an expression that utilizes 32 key bits, this would necessitate 220 operations per key, then we would have O(220×232) = O(252) operations to derive 32 bits of the key. We could then brute force the remaining 32 bits in $O(2^{32})$, which would be equivalent to deriving the key in less than $O(2^{53})$ instead of $O(2^{64})$.

This type of analysis can be successfully used against complicated ciphers such as the AES engine's S-Boxes and the DES's Feistel structures. However, we will not dive into how to apply these techniques in such a context; we leave this for the curious reader to check the references.

7.3.3 Differential CLSS Techniques

This type of CLSS is very similar to the linear CLSS technique in probabilistics but differs in terms of the relationship it exploits to derive the ENC key. Differential CLSS is a chosen P.T. attack, which makes it more applicable than a linear CLSS attack. Despite this advantage, both techniques are structured similarly, using a simple model of separate cipher components and a predictive model of the entire cipher. We used linear techniques to analyze linear relationships between the collected pairs and the ENC key; in the differential techniques, we focus on finding relationships between changing some bits in the input and its impact on the output.

The XOR between any two values is called **differential**, which is denoted as Ω, and we use two differentials to form a **characteristic** written as: $\Omega_A \Rightarrow \Omega_B$.

This characteristic means that the differential Ω_A in an input indicates the differential Ω_B in the output. As this is a probabilistic analysis, the characteristic is not always true; it can be true sometimes and false at other times. Thus, we are usually concerned about the probability of the characteristic being true. For example, if we take the word "hello", which is represented as follows in ASCII:

$$68\ 65\ 6c\ 6c\ 6f$$

If we used an 8-bit cipher that uses "25" as an 8-bit key to XOR it with each byte of the MSG, then we get:

$$2f\ 22\ 2b\ 2b\ 28$$

Then, we can use a differential of all ones in the original P.T. and XOR the result with the key again to get:

$$d0\ dd\ d4\ d7$$

Finally, we can XOR both ciphers to obtain the differential:

$$ff\ ff\ ff\ ff$$

The result is the same differential we used with the P.T., which indicates the cipher is relatively weak.

In this example, we analyzed the input and output of a simple cipher. We follow similar steps to analyze the input and output of the S-Boxes to analyze certain cipher stages. As S-Boxes are popular in ciphers, we use this method as the first step to analyze the characteristics of inputs and outputs of these S-Boxes, which will then be stitched together to formulate characteristics of the overall cipher. For this purpose, we borrow an example from [4] that uses an EASY1 cipher. The EASY1 cipher is a 36-bit block cipher with an 18-bit key. EASY1 cipher splits the input into 6-bit segments, runs them through the S-Boxes, concatenates the results, permutates them, and then XOR the results with the key. This is illustrated in Figure 7.3.

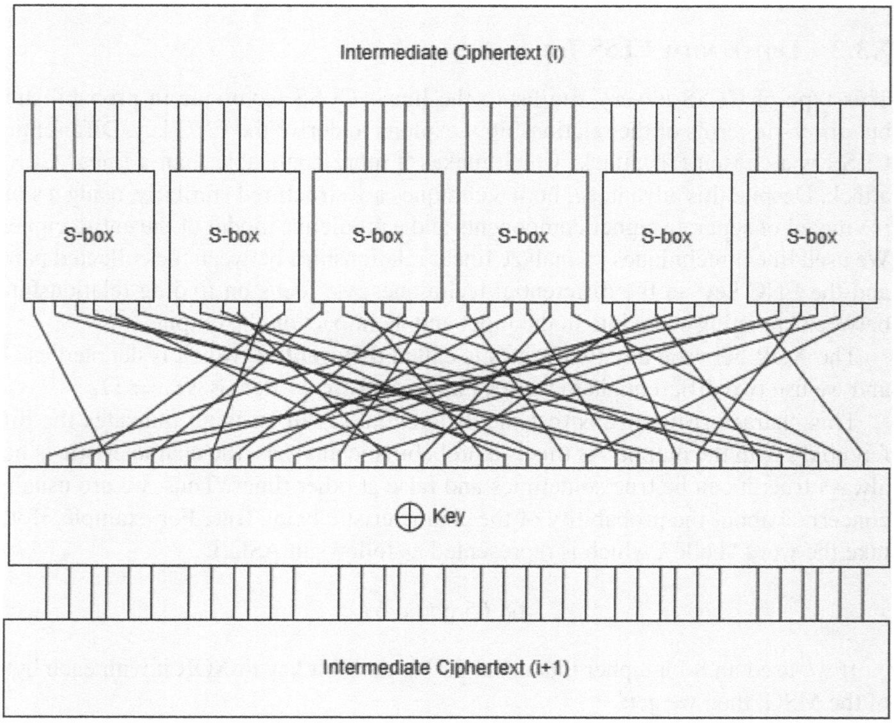

FIGURE 7.3 EASY1 cipher for a single round.

TABLE 7.2
Characteristics of EASY1 Cipher with Probability 6/64 and 8/64

	Probability 6/64		
000110⇒000110	000110⇒100001	000110⇒110000	000111⇒101001
001001⇒011000	001001⇒100010	001001⇒110010	001001⇒110111
001101110	001101⇒010100	001110⇒110001	010001⇒010100
010010⇒000001	010011⇒001000	011011⇒100101	011100⇒001100
011100⇒111111	011101⇒111001	011110⇒010101	011111⇒100110
100000⇒100111	100010⇒001101	100011⇒000110	100101⇒000001
101000⇒001100	101011⇒001100	101011⇒111100	101100⇒101011
101101⇒000011	110010⇒101101	110011⇒011111	110011⇒101111
111000⇒100000	111001⇒001001	111001⇒001101	111011⇒010100
111011⇒111110	111100⇒011100	111100⇒100000	111101⇒000100
	Probability 8/64		
001011⇒001010	010000⇒011001	011001⇒010110	110101⇒101001

To perform the differential analysis, assume we have the input and the output of one of the S-Boxes as X and Y, respectively. Assuming the input has two particular inputs, X_1 and X_2, and the output has two other outputs, Y_1 and Y_2, then we have the following differentials:

$$\Omega_x = X_1 \oplus X_2$$

$$\Omega_Y = Y_1 \oplus Y_2$$

To construct the differential relation between these inputs and outputs, we consider all the possible values of X_1 and X_2. We calculate and measure the resultant output Y1, Y2, and Ω_Y, and then record the results in a table. To save some space, we will not show the full table of these occurrences here, but we will show the two largest entries from the analysis of the EASY1 cipher S-Box. Table 7.2 shows the characteristics of the EASY1 cipher with probability 6/64 and 8/64.

One last thing we need to discuss in the characteristics of the S-Boxes is the key mixing stage that [11] takes place in the round keys after the bits are used in the S-Box. In our EASY1 cipher, we denote the input to the S-Box after key mixing as W, which is $W = X \oplus K$. Now, we need to repeat the analysis for Ω_W instead of Ω_x. With the same assumption, we will have $\Omega_W = W_1 \oplus W_2$, Which we substitute in the equation to get:

$$\Omega_W = W_1 \oplus W_2 = (X_1 \oplus K) \oplus (X_2 \oplus K) = X_1 \oplus X_2 = \Omega_X$$

The equation shows that mixing the key does not impact our analysis in this cipher, which is the case for most ciphers, except for ciphers such as the Blowfish, where the key determines the S-Boxes. After analyzing the S-boxes, we can now move to stitch the characteristics of these S-boxes to analyze the overall cipher [12].

7.3.3.1 Combining the S-Box Characteristics

Here, we can combine these characteristics by simply multiplying the probabilities to obtain the probability of both characteristics happening simultaneously. For example, the characteristics

$$001001 \Rightarrow 011000$$

$$010010 \Rightarrow 000001$$

Have probabilities of 6/64, and as we are expecting each characteristic to be independent of the other, the probability of both happening at the same time is:

$$\frac{6}{64} \times \frac{6}{64} \approx 0.008789$$

Now, we have built a characteristic for the overall cipher (three rounds), which has two input bits that affect one intermediate output bit sometimes. The same process can derive six bits of the [13].

7.4 CONCLUSIONS AND REMARKS

In conclusion, CLSS plays an essential role in Nsec by analyzing the complexity of CRYPTO systems and developing effective strategies. This chapter introduces CLSS, from traditional methods to cutting-edge quantum computing and machine learning techniques. In response to emerging threats, CRYPTO protocols require ongoing evaluation and adaptation. The future of cryptoanalysis will be influenced by trends such as quantum computing, machine learning, and post-quantum CRYPTO standards. Cryptanalysts should adjust to these changes, incessantly improving their approaches to defending Nsec concerns in a swiftly advancing world.

REFERENCES

1. Singh, Simon. *The code book: the science of secrecy from ancient Egypt to quantum CRYPTO.* Anchor, 2000.
2. Diffie, Whitfield, and Susan Landau. *Privacy on the line: The politics of wiretapping and ENC.* The MIT Press, 2010.
3. Cohen, Henri. *A course in computational algebraic number theory.* Vol. 138. Springer Science & Business Media, 2013.
4. Koblitz, Neal. *Algebraic aspects of CRYPTO.* Vol. 3. Springer Science & Business Media, 2012.
5. Swenson, Christopher. *Modern CLSS: techniques for advanced code breaking.* John Wiley & Sons, 2008.
6. Boyar, Joan. "Inferring sequences produced by pseudo-random number generators." *Journal of the ACM (JACM)* 36, no. 1 (1989): 129–141.
7. Reeds, James. "Cracking" a random number generator." *Cryptologia* 1, no. 1 (1977): 20–26.

8. Klima, Vlastimil. "Tunnels in hash functions: MD5 collisions within a minute." Cryptology ePrint Archive (2006).
9. Hellman, Martin. "A cryptanalytic time-memory trade-off." *IEEE Transactions on Information Theory* 26, no. 4 (1980): 401–406.
10. Oechslin, Philippe. "Making a faster cryptanalytic time-memory trade-off." In *Advances in Cryptology-CRYPTO 2003: 23rd Annual International Cryptology Conference, Santa Barbara, California, USA, August 17-21, 2003. Proceedings 23*, pp. 617–630. Springer Berlin Heidelberg, 2003.
11. Heys, Howard M. "A tutorial on linear and differential cryptanalysis." *Cryptologia* 26, no. 3 (2002): 189–221.
12. Matsui, Mitsuru. "Linear cryptanalysis method for DES cipher." In *Workshop on the Theory and Application of CRYPTO Techniques*, pp. 386–397. Springer Berlin Heidelberg, 1993.
13. Matsui, Mitsuru, and Atsuhiro Yamagishi. "A new method for known plaintext attack of FEAL cipher." In *Advances in Cryptology—EUROCRYPT'92: Workshop on the Theory and Application of CRYPTO Techniques Balatonfüred, Hungary, May 24–28, 1992 Proceedings 11*, pp. 81–91. Springer Berlin Heidelberg, 1993.

8 Drone Technology and Digital Forensics

Amal Saif and Qasem Abu Al-Haija

8.1 INTRODUCTION

The US Army defines drones as air vehicles, or as commonly called by the public, "the most disruptive technology in human history" because they are mainly used in wars. They are witnessing a very rapid increase in the market; by 2030, there will be 1 billion drones worldwide, making it a valuable source of digital evidence [1]. Drones were developed by amateurs, scientists, and commercial/defense sectors. The first digital proportional radio-control systems were commercially available in the 1970s [1]. These days, sales in Parrot, a French drone company, have increased by 300% per year (2012–2016) [2]. Drone sales will reach over $63.6 billion by 2026 [3]. Despite the drones' harmful use, they have significant benefits in many fields; 40 drone applications were mentioned in [4], such as disaster early detection, building firefighting, food delivery, tracking suspected criminals, and many others, as shown in Figure 8.1.

Other terms that refer to drones are Unmanned Aerial Vehicles (UAVs), Unmanned Aerial Systems (UASs), and Remotely Piloted Vehicles (RPVs). The main activities of drones can be concluded (see, sense, move, and transform); "see" means to monitor and collect data (providing visual data); sense means transforming the collected data into structured data; performing physical operations is the "move" concept, and "transform" is the concept that combines the three previous activities [5].

Some drone applications are discussed in the following subsections to learn the variety of data drones collect.

8.1.1 Drones in Agriculture

Drones have increased productivity and efficiency in agriculture by minimizing costs and increasing profits. Drones can contribute to disease detection [6], spraying operations [7], assessment of water stress [8], biomass estimation [9], enhancing precision agriculture [10], providing temporal and spatial sensing data [11], getting thermal images of water [12], and overall environmental monitoring [13]. However, those used in agriculture provide average image quality, have a limited power source, are compromised by collisions and cyberattacks, and have limited processing capability [14].

Bayer reports that a new multi-rotor drone powered by rechargeable batteries has been launched in China for crop protection applications in fields [15]. Since

DOI: 10.1201/9781003497868-8

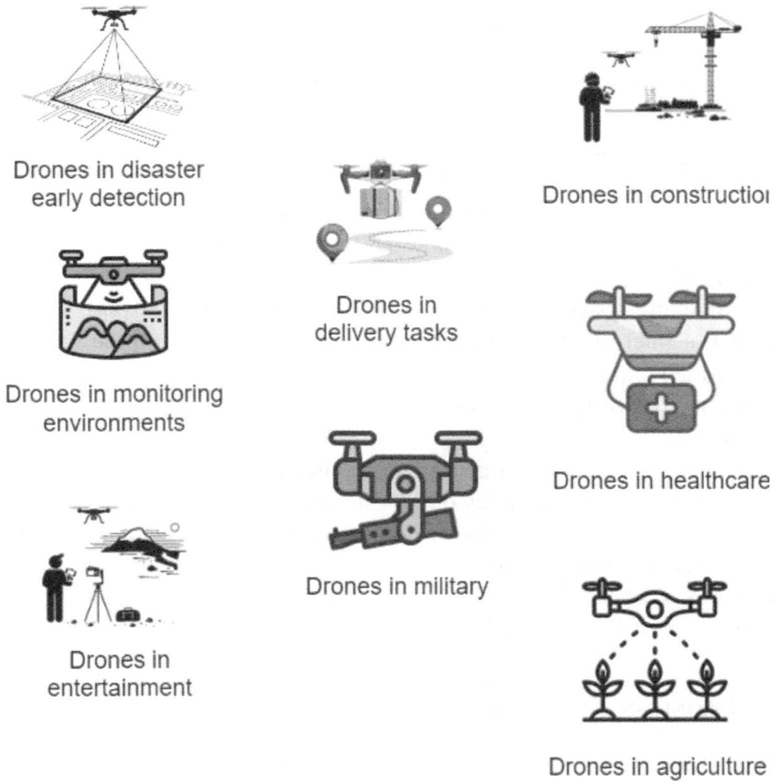

FIGURE 8.1 Drones' applications.

September 2016, Queensland (Australia) has allowed farmers to use drones to administer pesticides, following the footsteps of the United States, Switzerland, New Zealand, and China [16].

8.1.2 Drones in Education

Drones can be an educational tool for primary to high school levels and bachelor's and doctoral degrees; the students learn important skills to collect, analyze, and interpret data at the school level. For the higher education levels, researchers can learn how to construct drones, discuss security and legal issues with drones, analyze detailed components, and extract digital evidence from the drones [17].

Aerial drones can teach students mathematical modeling and simulation. Tello EDU Drones [18] and ROBOlink CoDrone [19] are used in teaching programming. Parrot MAMBO Educational Drone allows students to learn coding, commonly used in science, technology, engineering, and mathematics (STEM) education [17].

Another role of drones in education is the social drones in the classroom, where they can manage participation (like answering specific questions), enrich demonstrations, and monitor the classroom environment, such as ensuring everyone understands and hears the teacher and many other tasks. Still, drones have many challenges in this field, such as analyzing the students' behaviors by sensing more environmental features and enhancing their ability to interact with students [20].

8.1.3 Drones in Sports

The need for research has expanded as the sports sector has become more popular, and its audience has grown. This is now a billion-dollar industry, surpassing gaming and sports [21].

Video tracking systems play the main role in using drones in sports and tracking the Region of Interest (RoI), which is difficult. They outperform the fixed tracking cameras, which require localized at a specific height, which is impossible for many environments. Choosing the algorithm to analyze the collected data in real time is challenging [22].

Many athletes benefit from drones to monitor their performance, especially in sports that depend on the accuracy of movements or time. One of the most important benefits of using drones is that they can quickly track players and be present at hot spots to collect information, which is a challenge for coaches [21]. An interesting application was when the drone was used instead of the human boxer competitor. This application still has many limitations but is promising in the sports sector [23].

8.1.4 Drones in Healthcare

In emergency medicine, the time factor is essential, and drones improve response time as they can deliver medical supplies quickly. This is very useful for remote places and can direct medical specialists to those in need of care. However, there are ethical considerations and obstacles, such as concerns about privacy, people's safety, and compliance with laws, which are complex matters apart from technological limitations and general acceptance [24].

Drones help older adults by helping them with daily tasks, monitoring their health, and delivering medications. Drones with manipulator arms can help a lot. The Federal Aviation Administration (FAA) and the European Aviation Safety Agency (EASA) are developing a general framework that guarantees the safety of people and the security of their privacy in the medical field and other measurements [25].

8.1.5 Drones in Construction

Construction is one of the most critical industries in the world, with a volume exceeding \$8 trillion annually, but it often exceeds the specified budget by 80%, according to a McKinsey report [26]. Therefore, the presence of drones that can reach difficult places in large facilities provides important data and information that is used to increase safety, mapping, monitoring the progress of work, land surveying, etc. [26]

As in any other field, it is necessary to have a qualified person with permission to control the drones. There is a possibility of the drone falling and crashing due to malfunction or running out of power. Therefore, attention must be paid to the duration and location of the flight to preserve human safety. The collected data is affected by weather factors, which permanently limits its use. It is also possible for some aircraft to be affected if they are near magnetic field sources. The limitations of its use do not replace the need for practical and traditional inspection [27].

8.1.6 Drones in Wars and Military

There are currently multiple threats to the use of drones (the dark side of drones), as they can be used by malicious entities that can use them for illegal activities such as smuggling. Drones can be used in conflict areas for spying and delivering explosive materials. There is an urgent need to control the uses of drones, as their low cost is a reason for the ease of obtaining them. One of the ways to intercept drones is to use laser-based systems that thwart the drone mission. Drones have revolutionized warfare, providing high capabilities in surveillance, gathering intelligence, accelerating response to threats, and supporting ground operations. These drones may carry weapons and precise sensors that direct strikes at a specific target [28].

DARPA tested OFFSET in August 2019 to support military operations conducted with a swarm of uncrewed aerial vehicles and ground robots. DARPA analyzed two city blocks and showed how its robots could locate, surround, and secure a simulated city building [29].

Wars in recent times, like the 2020 Nagorno-Karabakh War, have highlighted how UAVs are causing revolutionary effects. As analysts have pointed out, drones have reshaped battlefields and geopolitics. The German Institute for Defense and Strategic Studies says armed adversaries like Azerbaijan would hardly have any chance against German forces. Soon, the unmanned flying of mighty drones will decide the fate of nations [30].

The most important roles of drones in the war between Ukraine and Russia have been to set the character of the conflict towards intelligence gathering and real-time reconnaissance to help the ground forces spot enemy positions. They enhance target acquisition, enhancing the accuracy of artillery strikes, and hasten engagement in combat. Indeed, both forces engage in offensive operations using drones, almost as consumable assets in disrupting opponents. This war underlines the economy of small, low-cost drones that can be deployed rapidly and scalable. Drones also give necessary situational awareness to ground troops and their innovative adaptations, such as when Ukrainians have turned commercial drones into military uses to fulfill the demands of modern warfare [31].

Based on US drone statistics, the drone market is expected to grow by 1.21% annually from 2023 to 2028. Agriculture, followed by construction, ranks first and second in the sectors using drones. By 2032, drones are expected to have a potential future worth of $127 billion across several industries. However, 4,250 injuries were recorded between 2015 and 2020 due to drone accidents [32].

8.2 UNDERSTANDING DIGITAL FORENSICS IN DRONES

"Digital forensics is the process by which information is extracted from digital systems or data storage media, rendered into a useable form, processed and interpreted to obtain intelligence for use in investigations, or evidence for use in criminal proceedings" [33].

In drones, data is collected from several sources, for example, from the flight control unit, memory, or logs, and they are analyzed, and the results are documented. Based on the uses of drones, the importance of the data retrieved from them lies. Digital forensics in drones aims to provide techniques and tools to determine everything related to drones, such as the type of drone, the activities that occurred, and the nature of the data. Upon analysis, parts of the drones are stopped to preserve the data without tampering, which is within legal caveats [34].

Challenges in digital forensics in drones are like any other digital forensics field; the anti-forensics techniques pose challenges such as data hiding, data tampering, obfuscation, altering the metadata, attacks on the forensics tools, and data wiping. Another challenge is limited storage in some drones, which leads to overwriting the data when the storage capacity runs out. This leads to data loss, so the memory should be checked regularly, and data can be extracted to a cloud or hard disk. In addition, there are drones that contain secure digital (SD) cards, which gives greater storage capacity [35].

The digital forensics process faces different stages of complexity, as it requires ensuring the chain of custody, creating a chain of evidence, and having models to be followed in extracting the digital evidence. Analyzing and processing memory and frequencies sometimes requires complex algorithms and produces big data [36]. In drone digital forensics, experts do not focus only on the drone itself but the whole drone system, including the data links, types of connections, and control station devices.

Due to a lack of well-established protocols or frameworks for investigating drones, the recent rise in drone usage and drone-related crimes presents a fundamental challenge to digital forensic investigations. Because of their multitude, quick development, and increased utility, crimes using technology have grown more challenging to evaluate. Investigators must operate on the presumption that the devices would save data similarly because most current drone investigation processes have been lifted from approaches created for handling forensic analysis of other technologies. Therefore, new protocols must be created whenever the target device's underlying technology changes to guarantee that the evidence is gathered and examined in a way that adheres to forensic best practices [37].

8.3 DRONE COMPONENTS AND DATA SOURCES

A drone system's hardware consists of the aircraft, the remote controller, and the payload, including cameras, sensors, the energy supply system, the local navigation assistance system, and the IT infrastructure. The software comprises the algorithms that manage the drone's payload and flight tasks and communicate with the controllers, navigation system, and IT systems. The support procedures encompass a variety of human-operated drone tasks, including manual piloting, setting up and maintaining the necessary infrastructure for automated or autonomous flight, and analyzing the data it has gathered [5].

Figure 8.2 delves more into the features of the drone, which are important in digital forensics because each type and component will have different techniques to get the information [38]. For example, fixed-wing drones can collect data over large areas due to their longer flight time than rotor drones [38]. In general, drones consist of a motor, receiver, transmitter, battery, camera that could be detachable, propellers, GPS module, and speed controller.

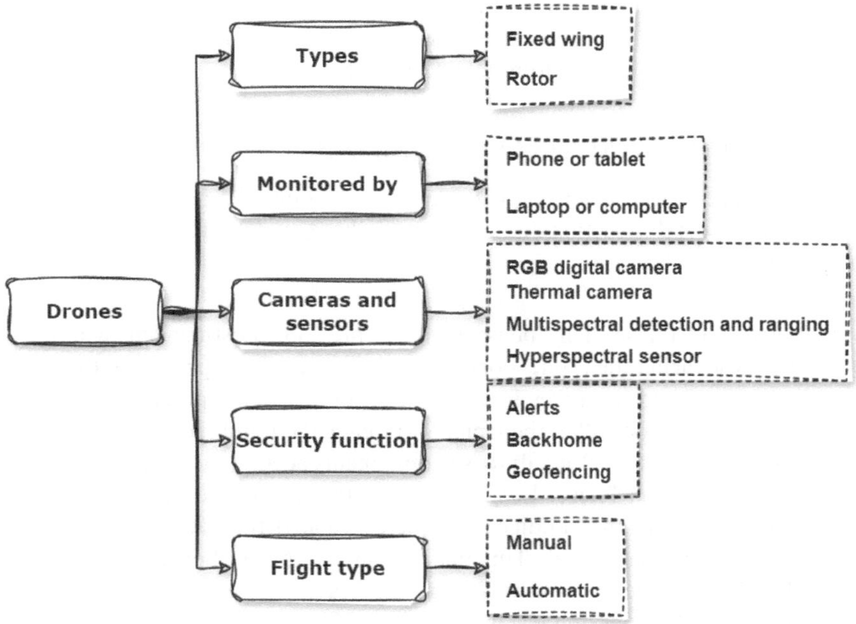

FIGURE 8.2 Feature diagram for drones.

The data in the drone systems can be classified into flight logs, media, sensors, and payload logs found in the internal and removal drone storage. This device controls the drone, the traffic data, and the data at rest, as shown in Figure 8.3 [39].

The drone's hardware composition would at least involve equipping the drone with a communication device, a control board, one or more actuators, and a power

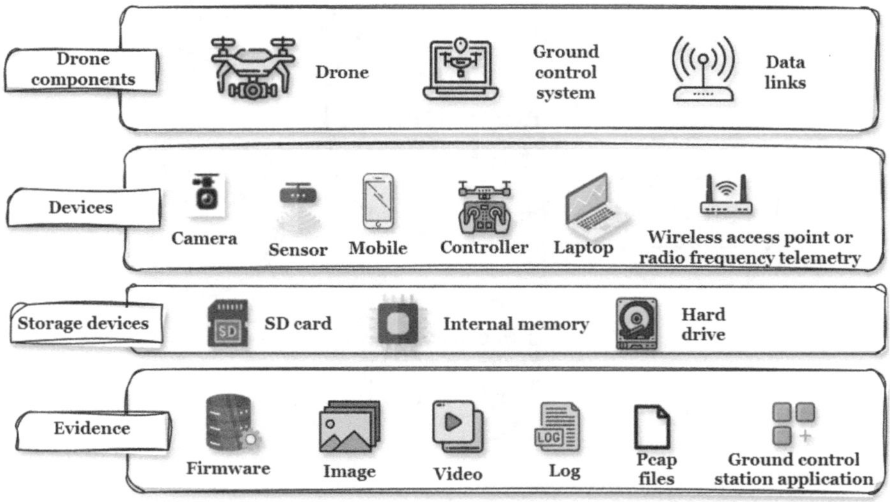

FIGURE 8.3 Evidence distribution.

source to perform simple 3D controlled motion actuation. These will interconnect electronically in order to set up and define the electronic system of the drone which is important in extracting the drone's fingerprint [3].

8.4 FORENSIC ANALYSIS OF DRONE DATA

Many researchers have been proposing models to unify the procedures of digital forensics methods; this section discusses one of these models. The model consists of three main steps [36]:

1. Preparation Phase: This phase includes pre- and post-incident activities such as securing the drone, documenting the scene, and preparing the necessary tools and resources for data acquisition. It is the process of seizing the drone, the controller, the laptop or mobile, the flight record, the battery, and the logs and labeling all these components accurately [40].
2. Data Acquisition Phase: In this phase, data integrity verification is conducted to ensure the validity of collected data. If the data is damaged, it needs to be re-acquired. Timeline reconstruction is then carried out to rebuild the sequence of events from the UAV. The acquisition phase has different techniques and levels, as shown in Figure 8.4 [39].
3. Data Analysis Phase: This phase involves the analysis of the diverse data sources from the UAV, including memory analysis, event reconstruction, and radiofrequency analysis.

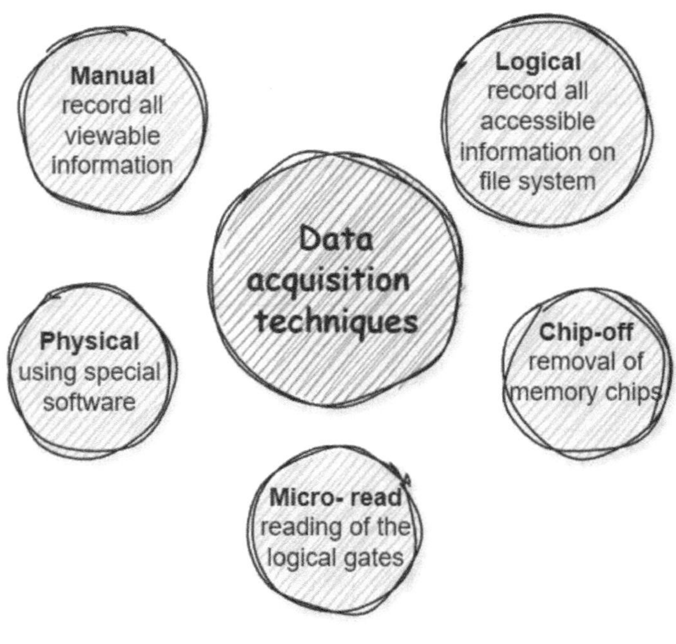

FIGURE 8.4 Data acquisition techniques.

Also, a vital step is documenting every single information and step related to the investigation processes. The data should be examined and verified for authenticity and explained.

Some tools that are used in the drone digital forensics [35]:

1. DJI Assistant 2 [41]: this software allows users to retrieve drone flight records. It can convert. DAT files, too. CSV so that they can be read using another tool called DatCon, which concerns motor, GPS, and aircraft condition information. To help with investigations into flight-related problems, DJI is the only entity capable of decoding the encrypted data found in black box devices.
2. DJI GO 4 App [42]: Using smartphones to operate drones requires this app. It offers less flight information than the internal memory. The app's cached data includes important information, but some are encoded and need additional investigation.
3. Cellebrite [43]: Drone data extraction is aided by Cellebrite's instruments, which need particular connectors and adapters. The UFED Physical Analyzer processes and decodes the extracted files, showing important evidence like battery and aircraft serial numbers. Although restricted to the most recent flight data, it generates flight timelines.
4. CsvView [44]: is used to extract information about the serial number, type, and connected devices.

Digital drone forensics takes into consideration voluntary and passive identifications. Methods of voluntary identifications are broadcasting encrypted IDs, which is basically ineffective in deterring malicious drone pilots from evasion, and cameras can ill function properly in many scenarios. Passive identifications involve cameras and computer vision; very much dependent on weather, lighting, and distance. As for the method of flight log identifications, it cannot be trusted because the devices can easily generate fakes or alterations. As for other passive measures, there is electromagnetic interference and acoustic emission; these, too, face considerable challenges across complex scenarios involving high noise levels or darkness [3].

Some standards can be followed in digital forensics processes in drones, such as International Organization for Standardization (ISO)/IEC 30121:2015, ISO/IEC 27042:2015, and ISO/IEC 27035 [45], released by the ISO. These standards are the guidelines for what information should not be disclosed, what appropriate tools and techniques can be used in each case, and how to design the investigation to get interpretable data. It is also a framework for all stages of digital forensics science [39].

8.5 LEGAL AND ETHICAL CONSIDERATIONS

Regarding drones, two main concerns emerge: the legal and ethical aspects. This section discusses them among the privacy issues, moral and legal considerations in drone-related investigations, the regulations frameworks in different countries, and other points of view. The main goal of these aspects is to minimize the harm of using drones.

8.5.1 Legal Considerations

Legislations among nations, regions, and locals guided the use of drones and defined a framework for the acquisition, investigation, processing, and publishing of the drones' imagery. Also, preserving the privacy and confidentiality of the drones' data is important, as it must be determined under a law that ensures it is not violated. Framing the safety of people and places and not violating national security within a unified law is a complex topic that is difficult to unify and ensure compliance with, as shown in Figure 8.5 [46]. Even within OECD countries, national legal frameworks for drone regulation vary significantly [47].

Drones often collect data over several jurisdictions, especially in cross-border conflicts or commercial operations. This results in complicated legal issues of jurisdiction and data sharing between countries; in other words, the definition of admissibility of digital evidence differs in each country. Investigating agencies navigate these differences as they collaborate on cases involving drone data.

The existence of laws governs that the person using drones must be qualified, the distances, heights, and places in which drones are allowed to be used, avoid crowded areas, and drones must carry licensed plates [48].

Liability and accountability: When a drone causes damage, whether through a physical accident or unauthorized data collection, determining who is liable can become legally complicated. Commercial drone operators take out liability insurance, but in the case of negligence or malicious use, legal liability may lie with the drone pilot, the manufacturing company, or even the organization that contracted with the drone to operate it. Accountability for police agencies may be compromised when drones are deployed without proper legal sanctions, like warrants, to surveil a target or collect evidence that may or may not be admissible in a court of law.

Judicial concerns also relate to using cloud storage to store information, making digital evidence difficult to prove and obtain. There are additional permissions

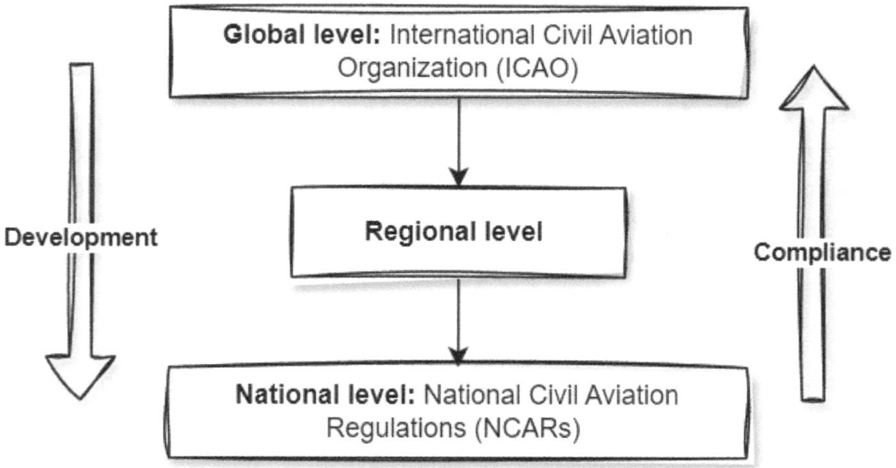

FIGURE 8.5 Civil aviation regulatory hierarchy.

and challenges associated with techniques of gathering and preserving evidence that determine whether it is accepted in one country but not in another. In contrast, many countries lack legislation governing this field, exacerbating legal issues, particularly when these countries allow drones without a license. The potential of contamination and tampered evidence complicates the challenge of defining evidence [49].

Admissibility of evidence: The admissibility of evidence within a legal case, where data coming from drones is presented as evidence, is strictly governed. Investigators have to be sure that the data has been collected legally and that it must be preserved in a manner such that its integrity is not tampered with. Chain of custody is an important aspect to avoid tampering or alteration of evidence. However, courts may reject drone data obtained without warrants or against certain privacy laws, such as the Fourth Amendment of the Constitution in the United States. More recently, this calls into question at what time and how drone data legally can be obtained and used in investigations.

8.5.2 Ethical Considerations

Some ethical considerations govern the use of drones, including respect for autonomy, which includes privacy in populated places, not harming people or the environment, the existence of a benefit from drones, and transparency in disclosing the reason for using drones. This governs the legality of the data collected by drones, whether it will be analyzed and used, and for what purposes [50]. The use of drones can be for mass surveillance and may be used by individuals or companies to monitor people without their consent. This creates conflict between the legitimate use of drones in law enforcement and emergency response and the rights of individuals not to be subjected to unjustified surveillance.

Apart from the presence of drones that have AI-powered capabilities that can make decisions without human intervention, this raises the question of who is responsible if the drone makes a mistake or violates ethical standards.

Concerns about social justice and equity include the possibility that drones could be used to monitor marginalized communities or groups that cannot afford to use drones, or to suppress dissent, limiting individual freedoms.

Ethical issues in digital forensics include data protection and establishing who can access drone information such as videos, images, and locations. Some of this data is extremely sensitive, including aircraft speed and altitude, and must be protected from unauthorized access. As a result, the investigation can be conducted remotely by eavesdropping in on the drone's data transmissions. This knowledge could also help trap the drones, steal them, and analyze their memory [51]. As previously stated, digital forensics depends on the entire drone system, not just the drone itself, which complicates privacy issues. Also, compliance with laws is another ethical challenge.

Regarding this issue, privacy and balancing the need to collect data for legal purposes with an individual's right to privacy is an unavoidable aspect of investigations and appropriate permissions must be obtained before accessing any sensitive data. It is also important to ensure that data is not misused in the possibility of biased interpretation or manipulation of the evidence collected. Hence, transparency in how data is collected and analyzed and not selectivity using data to support specific narratives emerges so that there are no significant social and legal consequences.

8.6 CONCLUSIONS AND REMARKS

In conclusion, the emergence of drones in diverse industries poses challenges and opportunities for digital forensics. This chapter has broadly explored the interaction between drone technology and digital forensics, concentrating on the distinctive forensic challenges presented by drones and the methods commissioned to address them.

By studying the applications of drone technology throughout sectors and highlighting concerns involving misuse, we have emphasized the need for vigorous forensic investigation protocols. The analysis has uncovered the complexities of obtaining and analyzing drone systems data, containing flight records, sensor data, and onboard storage devices.

Furthermore, investigating legal and ethical issues correlated with drone forensics, such as privacy associations and regulatory compliance, highlights the need for a holistic approach to research in this area. As drones progressively prevail, digital forensic specialists, law enforcement organizations, and academia must persist consistently with evolving methods and best practices.

ABBREVIATIONS

UAVs Unmanned Aerial Vehicles
ISO International Organization for Standardization

REFERENCES

1. S Watkins, J. Burry, A. Mohamed et al., “Ten questions concerning the use of drones in urban environments,” Building and Environment, vol. 167, Jan. 2020. https://doi.org/10.1016/j.buildenv.2019.106458.
2. S. E. Kreps, “Drones: What everyone needs to know – Sarah Elizabeth Kreps – Google books,” Oxford University Press. Accessed March 14, 2024. [Online]. Available: https://books.google.jo/books?hl=en&lr=&id=jT-BCwAAQBAJ&oi=fnd&pg=PP1&dq=what+are+drones&ots=ub-4FdsYaf&sig=rziCbcJpm9gWxnQG0Yri9TF5Stg&redir_esc=y#v=onepage&q&f=false
3. Z. Li, B. Chen, X. Chen, C. Xu, Y. Chen, F. Lin, C. Li, K. Dantu, K. Ren and W. Xu, “Reliable digital forensics in the air: Exploring an RF-based drone identification system,” Proceedings of the ACM on Interactive, Mobile, Wearable and Ubiquitous Technologies, vol. 6, no. 2, pp. 1–25, 2022.
4. B. Aydin, “Public acceptance of drones: Knowledge, attitudes, and practice,” Technology in Society, vol. 59, Nov. 2019. https://doi.org/10.1016/j.techsoc.2019.101180.
5. O. Maghazei and T. Netland, “Drones in manufacturing: Exploring opportunities for research and practice,” Journal of Manufacturing Technology Management, vol. 31, no. 6, pp. 1237–1259, 2020. https://doi.org/10.1108/JMTM-03-2019-0099.
6. A. Abbas, Z. Zhang, H. Zheng, M. M. Alami, A. F. Alrefaei, Q. Abbas, S. A. H. Naqvi, M. J. Rao, W. F. Mosa and Q. Abbas, et al., “Drones in plant disease assessment, efficient monitoring, and detection: A way forward to smart agriculture,” Agronomy, vol. 13, no. 6, p. 1524, 2023.

7. R. K. Sahni, S. P. Kumar, D. Thorat, Y. Rajwade, B. Jyoti, J. Ranjan and R. Anand, "Drone spraying system for efficient agrochemical application in precision agriculture," in Applications of computer vision and drone technology in agriculture 4.0, pp. 225–244, Springer, 2024.
8. A. Yacoob, S. Gokool, A. Clulow, M. Mahomed and T. Mabhaudhi, "Leveraging unmanned aerial vehicle technologies to facilitate precision water management in smallholder farms: A scoping review and bibliometric analysis," Drones, vol. 8, no. 9, p. 476, 2024.
9. A. Rayamajhi, H. Jahanifar and M. S. Mahmud, "Measuring ornamental tree canopy attributes for precision spraying using drone technology and self-supervised segmentation," Computers and Electronics in Agriculture, vol. 225, p. 109359, 2024.
10. I. Ioja, V. Nedeff, M. Agop, F. M. Nedeff and C. Tomozei, "Software Uses in Precision Agriculture Based on Drone Image Processing–A Review," in 2024 9th International Conference on Energy Efficiency and Agricultural Engineering (EE&AE), pp. 1–6, IEEE, 2024.
11. Y. Han, "Application of Unmanned Aerial Vehicle Remote Sensing for Agricultural Monitoring," in E3S Web of Conferences, vol. 553, p. 02022, EDP Sciences, 2024.
12. H. S. Ndlovu, J. Odindi, M. Sibanda and O. Mutanga, "A systematic review on the application of UAV-based thermal remote sensing for assessing and monitoring crop water status in crop farming systems," International Journal of Remote Sensing, vol. 45, no. 15, pp. 4923–4960, 2024.
13. A. Yablokova, D. Kovalev, I. Kovalev, V. Podoplelova and K. Astanakulov, "Environmental Safety Problems of Swarm Use of UAVs in Precision Agriculture," in E3S Web of Conferences, vol. 471, p. 04018, EDP Sciences, 2024.
14. A. Rejeb, A. Abdollahi, K. Rejeb and H. Treiblmaier, "Drones in agriculture: A review and bibliometric analysis," Computers and electronics in agriculture, vol. 198. Elsevier B.V., Jul. 01, 2022. https://doi.org/10.1016/j.compag.2022.107017.
15. Bayer. (2023, October 19). Drones revolutionize farmers' lives. Bayer Global. https://www.bayer.com/en/agriculture/article/drones-revolutionize-farmers-lives
16. H. Pathak, G. Kumar, S. D. Mohapatra, B. B. Gaikwad and J. Rane, "Use of Drones in Agriculture: Potentials, Problems, and Policy Needs," 2020.
17. O. Bai, H. Chu, H. Liu and G. Hui, "Drones in Education: A Critical Review," 2021. [Online]. Available: https://www.youtube.com/watch?v=zJ8LFzuoRQ
18. Ryze Tech. (n.d.). Tello EDU drone. Ryze Robotics. Retrieved September 13, 2024, from https://www.ryzerobotics.com/tello-edu
19. ROBOlink. (n.d.). CoDrone: The programmable drone for learning how to code. ROBOlink. Retrieved September 13, 2024, from https://www.robolink.com/codrone
20. W. Johal, D. Gatos, A. E. Yantac and M. Obaid, "Envisioning social drones in education," Front Robot AI, vol. 9, Aug. 2022. https://doi.org/10.3389/frobt.2022.666736.
21. N. P. Mali, "Modern technology and sports performance: An overview," ~ 212 ~ International Journal of Physiology, vol. 5, no. 1, pp. 212–216, 2020. [Online]. Available: www.journalofsports.com
22. T. G. Russomanno, P. Blauberger, O. Kolbinger, H. Lam, M. Schmid and M. Lames, "Drone-based position detection in sports—Validation and applications," Front Mater, vol. 13, Mar. 2022. https://doi.org/10.3389/fphys.2022.850512.
23. S. G. Zwaan and E. I. Barakova, "Boxing Against Drones: Drones in Sports Education," in Proceedings of IDC 2016 – The 15th International Conference on Interaction Design and Children, Association for Computing Machinery, Inc., Jun. 2016, pp. 607–612. https://doi.org/10.1145/2930674.2935991.
24. A. M. Johnson, C. J. Cunningham, E. Arnold, W. D. Rosamond and J. K. Zègre-Hemsey, "Impact of using drones in emergency medicine: What does the future hold?" Open access emergency medicine, vol. 13. Dove Medical Press Ltd., pp. 487–498, 2021. https://doi.org/10.2147/OAEM.S247020.

25. M. Balasingam, "Drones in medicine—The rise of the machines," International Journal of Clinical Practice, vol. 71, no. 9, Sep. 2017. https://doi.org/10.1111/ijcp.12989.
26. I. Zaychenko, A. Smirnova and A. Borremans, "Digital Transformation: The Case of the Application of Drones in Construction," in MATEC Web of Conferences, EDP Sciences, Aug. 2018. https://doi.org/10.1051/matecconf/201819305066.
27. E. Ciampa, L. De Vito and M. R. Pecce, "Practical Issues on the Use of Drones for Construction Inspections," in Journal of Physics: Conference Series, IOP Publishing Ltd., Jun. 2019. https://doi.org/10.1088/1742-6596/1249/1/012016.
28. A. Koubaa and A. T. Azar, "Unmanned Aerial Systems: Theoretical Foundations and Applications," 2021. [Online]. Available: https://www.elsevier.com/books/book-series/
29. M. Lehto and B. Hutchinson, "Mini-Drones Swarms and Their Potential in Conflict Situations," in The 15th International Conference on Cyber Warfare and Security, vol. 12, pp. 326–334, 2020.
30. A. Calcara, A. Gilli, M. Gilli, R. Marchetti and I. Zaccagnini, "Why drones have not revolutionized war: The enduring hider-finder competition in air warfare," International Security, vol. 46, no. 4, pp. 130–171, 2022.
31. D. Kunertova, "Drones have boots: Learning from Russia's war in Ukraine," Contemporary Security Policy, vol. 44, no. 4, pp. 576–591, 2023.
32. J. Leslie, "Drone Statistics [2024 Update]," Drone Survey Services. Accessed March 24, 2024. [Online]. Available: https://dronesurveyservices.com/drone-statistics/
33. G. Tully and T. Watson, "Title: Quality Standards for Digital Forensics: Learning from Experience in England & Wales Quality Standards for Digital Forensics: Learning from Experience in England & Wales."
34. F. Alotaibi, A. Al-Dhaqm and Y. D. Al-Otaibi, "A conceptual digital forensic investigation model applicable to the drone forensics field," Engineering, Technology and Applied Science Research, vol. 13, no. 5, pp. 11608–11615, 2023. https://doi.org/10.48084/etasr.6195.
35. S. Atkinson, G. Carr, C. Shaw and S. Zargari, "Drone Forensics: The Impact and Challenges." [Online]. Available: https://shura.shu.ac.uk/28441/
36. A. Al-Dhaqm, R. A. Ikuesan, V. R. Kebande, S. Razak and F. M. Ghabban, "Research challenges and opportunities in drone forensics models," Electronics (Switzerland), vol. 10, no. 13. MDPI AG, Jul. 01, 2021. https://doi.org/10.3390/electronics10131519.
37. K. Al-Room, F. Iqbal, T. Baker et al., "Drone forensics: A case study of digital forensic investigations conducted on common drone models," International Journal of Digital Crime and Forensics, vol. 13, no. 1, pp. 1–25, Jan. 2021. https://doi.org/10.4018/IJDCF.2021010101.
38. M. Ayamga, B. Tekinerdogan and A. Kassahun, "Exploring the challenges posed by regulations for the use of drones in agriculture in the African context," Land (Basel), vol. 10, no. 2, pp. 1–13, 2021. https://doi.org/10.3390/land10020164.
39. E. Mantas and C. Patsakis, "Who watches the new watchmen? The challenges for drone digital forensics investigations," Array, vol. 14. Elsevier B.V., Jul. 01, 2022. https://doi.org/10.1016/j.array.2022.100135.
40. A. A. Alhussan, A. Al-Dhaqm, W. M. S. Yafooz, S. B. A. Razak, A. H. M. Emara and D. S. Khafaga, "Towards development of a high abstract model for drone forensic domain," Electronics (Switzerland), vol. 11, no. 8, Apr. 2022. https://doi.org/10.3390/electronics11081168.
41. DJI. DJI Assistant. Accessed September 13, 2024. https://www.dji.com/support.
42. DJI. DJI GO 4. Accessed September 13, 2024. https://www.dji.com/global/downloads/djiapp/dji-go-4.
43. Cellebrite. Drone Data Collection. Accessed September 13, 2024. https://cellebrite.com/en/collect-and-review-data/drone-data-collection/.
44. Datfile. CSVView. Accessed September 13, 2024. https://datfile.net/.

45. International Organization for Standardization. ISO Standards. Accessed September 13, 2024. https://www.iso.org/standards.html.
46. M. Ayamga, B. Tekinerdogan, A. Kassahun and G. Rambaldi, "Developing a policy framework for adoption and management of drones for agriculture in Africa," Technology Analysis & Strategic Management, vol. 33, no. 8, pp. 970–987, 2021. https://doi.org/10.1080/09537325.2020.1858047.
47. O. Hall and I. Wahab, "The use of drones in the spatial, social sciences," Drones, vol. 5, no. 4, Dec. 2021. https://doi.org/10.3390/drones5040112.
48. U. Debangshi, "Drones-Applications in Agriculture," 2021. [Online]. Available: https://pphouse.org/cbm.php
49. A. Almusayli, T. Zia and E. U. H. Qazi, "drone forensics: An innovative approach to the forensic investigation of drone accidents based on digital twin technology," Technologies (Basel), vol. 12, no. 1, Jan. 2024. https://doi.org/10.3390/technologies12010011.
50. R. Hoek Spaans, B. Drumond, K. R. van Daalen et al., "Ethical considerations related to drone use for environment and health research: A scoping review protocol," PLoS ONE, vol. 19, no. 1, Jan. 01, 2024. https://doi.org/10.1371/journal.pone.0287270.
51. V. Sihag, G. Choudhary, P. Choudhary and N. Dragoni, "Cyber4Drone: A systematic review of cybersecurity and forensics in next-generation drones," Drones, vol. 7, no. 7. Multidisciplinary Digital Publishing Institute (MDPI), Jul. 01, 2023. https://doi.org/10.3390/drones7070430.

9 Cybersecurity and Forensics for Sustainable Energy Security

Mohammed I. Alghamdi

9.1 INTRODUCTION

Along with energy security, dealing with cyber risks is a very important concern and a vital aspect for strong economy and country as reported by the "World Energy Committee". There has been a rapid growth in cyberattacks over the past years in energy sector [1]. Cybersecurity is widely renowned as an insignificant agenda of board meetings until something goes wrong. A lot of large organizations have IT department having cybersecurity experts.

There is a lack of awareness and knowledge of cyber world at board level. Hence, their work is limited to the black box. Energy companies are often targeted by cybercriminals as they provide critical services and support. The utility and energy sector play a vital role in critical infrastructure of the country. Hence, it is a huge target for non-state and state performers when it comes to gain political and military leaders or leading to disruption. Being the component to disorder a national grid, it would have a ripple effect. It is very important to protect the grid from cyberattack in order to guarantee energy security.

In industrial and technological development of communication and energy resources, the steady growth is important to deal with latest security issues and threats. This matter has led to stimulating important customer data and profile as well as operations. In the energy sector, security is not limited to just four pillars of production or generation, it is beyond that. In a survey conducted in preparedness and maturity related to security in critical infrastructure, most businesses were not self-confident in their preparedness to improve security and face the existing intimidations in 2014. In addition, they were also not flexible enough to have proper risk analysis, alerts, and threat control [2]. Since power generation companies have both power and IT, their associations have gaps in terms of security. It is not possible to fully avoid current threats, but it is possible to minimize threats and their impacts.

9.2 DIGITAL FORENSICS AND ENERGY SECTOR

Digital forensics refers to the science of documenting, presenting, preserving, analyzing, and identifying data and evidence of from digital and electronic devices while

 DOI: 10.1201/9781003497868-9

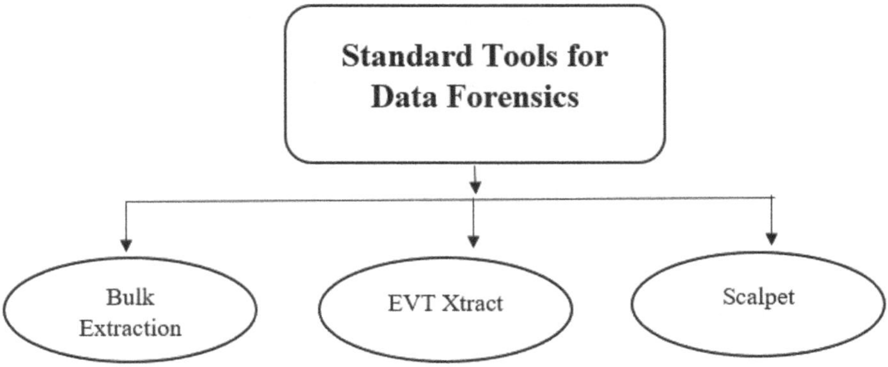

FIGURE 9.1 Tools for data forensics.

Source: Alherbawi *et al.* [5].

protecting user privacy [3]. In addition, it also uses scientific techniques to clarify and recreate sequence of events. Digital forensics are known to present invalid artifacts as evidence by recording, reviewing, and evaluating the sequences before the court of law. There are different domains of digital forensics for various kinds of analysis and processes. The following sections describe some of those application areas.

9.2.1 Data Forensics

Data forensics is based on digital data and how to use the same for investigation purposes and find the truth or actual evidence. The technique of "data carving" is the part of data forensic. Data carving refers to retrieval of data from raw fragments. Dezfouli and Dehghantanha [4] described the process of data carving and proposed an approach to manage the problem of fragmentation when assessing data. For data forensics, Figure 9.1 illustrates some of the tools in tree structure.

Figure 9.1 illustrates some of the widely used data for forensic tools like "EVTXtract, Bulk Extraction, and Scalpet". These tools are used for testing a file, disk image, or directory and relevant data is extracted without making any change to the structure of file system. Malicious tools, techniques and software are designed and implemented every day to affect private and public networks, while exploiting storage of data to extract vital data [6]. To deal with this rising threat in energy sector, digital forensics has gained a lot of attention to resolve cyber threats.

9.2.2 Cloud Forensics

Being the subpart of network forensics, cloud forensics focuses on vast networks and investigates the incident of cybercrime in energy sector. Cybercrimes are hard to detect, especially on the crowd as some of the basic and traditional digital forensic techniques don't work on the cloud [7]. Hence, there are some issues in cloud forensics. Physical access to cloud is not available to the investigation team in public

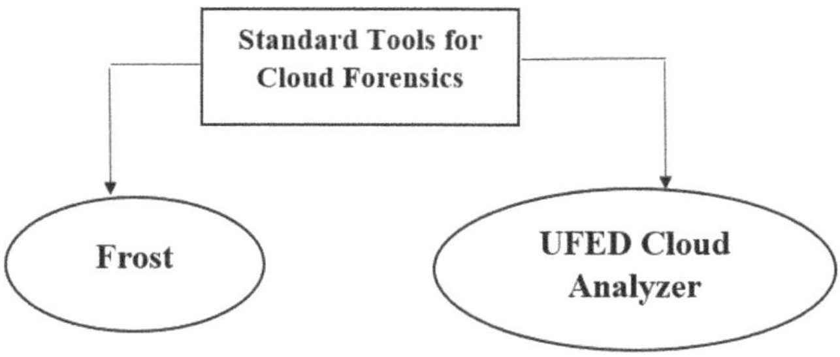

FIGURE 9.2 Standard cloud forensic tools for investigation.

cloud due to privacy issues [8]. It is very challenging for examiners as they are unable to assess the scene without accessibility. Figure 9.2 illustrates some of the standard cloud forensic tools that can be used at the time of investigation. Figure 9.2 shows some of the widely used tools for cloud forensics like Frost and UFED Cloud Analyzer. Both of these tools are effective for cloud investigation. They extract data from virtual disk, API logs, and firewall logs.

9.2.3 Mobile Forensics

This kind of forensics is growing significantly over the past decade with the rise in use of mobile phones. There has been a rise in crime rate and number of attacks in energy sector. Hence, mobile forensics is a very vital subdomain these days in digital forensics. All the ways are used in this kind of forensic techniques and inspected to find information or Metadata associated with the incident on the power company. Figure 9.3 illustrates some of the standard tools for mobile or android forensics.

Figure 9.3 illustrates some of the widely used tools for data forensics, including "Encase and Access Data FTK Imager". Both these tools are capable to record and locate digital evidence from mobile device to validate the same in energy sector. However, these tools can access only those data stored in the phone, not the SIM. It creates a gap between data access between the SIM and phone data as there is a huge scope and importance of research in mobile forensic.

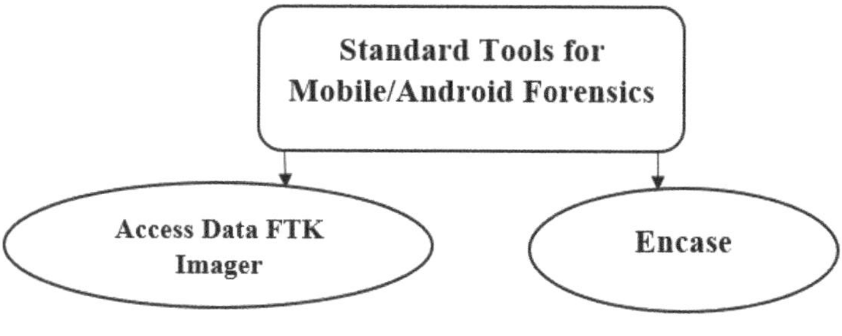

FIGURE 9.3 Standard tools used in mobile forensics.

Source: Walters and Petroni [9].

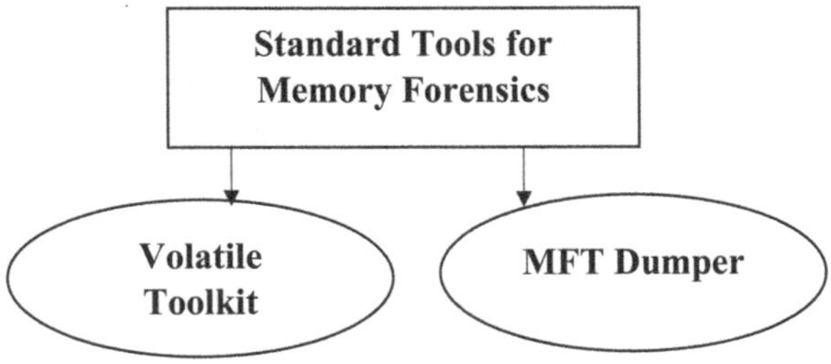

FIGURE 9.4 Some of the tools used in memory forensics.

Source: He *et al.* [12].

9.2.4 Memory Forensics

The investigator analyzes and investigates data that has been removed, altered, or deleted from the system, using various tools and techniques to locate potential metadata and uncover relevant evidence. When it comes to determine memory forensics, some of the vital tools used are MFT Dumper, Volatile Toolkit, etc. Memory forensics is a domain of digital forensics with several vital and key factors that can be important for energy sector. It adds a lot of prominence to this type of forensic as nothing can be hidden. There are different approaches to be anonymous and bypass the analysis stage too.

One of the common examples to bypass the same is the Onion Router (TOR) browser. It is almost impossible to trace any relevant data or evidence on the TOR network. The references and studies are available only for analyzing memory dump and tracking TOR traffic on the network [10]. Even this study is not much useful when it comes to prevent connection with the TOR and analyze the same. According to Chhabra and Singh [11] there is a huge research gap when it comes to analyze TOR dump memory to track potential attacks on the power company, so that an investigator can find relevant metadata and analyze the attacks on energy supply network. Figure 9.4 illustrates some of the standard data forensic tools.

Figure 9.4 illustrates some of the widely used tools for data forensics like MFT Dumper and Volatile Toolkit that are widely used for investigation. As a command-based toolkit, the Volatile Toolkit scans and analyzes volatile memory. Some examiners and investigators call it "Volatool" which can test time and data, open ports, running processes, and "process to port" mapping [13].

9.2.5 Network Forensics

Analysts gather and examine data from network layer and network in this domain of digital forensics. Cloud forensics is a part of this domain and it is a vast area. Network Miner, TCP Dump, and WireShark are some of the vital tools to assess network forensics. Klaer *et al.* [14] proposed a distributed framework for forensic analysis and discussed the value of distributed system. There are different issues related to network forensics like effective attack acknowledgment, storage space, etc.

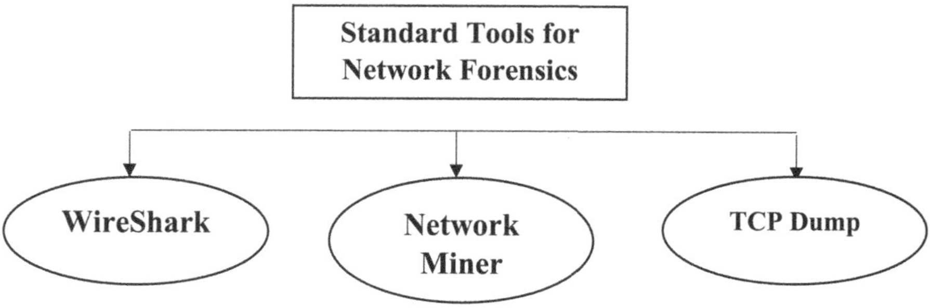

FIGURE 9.5 Some of the tools for network forensics.

Source: Wang *et al.* [15].

Hence, a distributed framework has been proposed with various levels of forensic investigations. Figure 9.5 illustrates some of the network forensics tools.

Figure 9.5 illustrates some of the widely used tools for data forensics like Network Miner, TCP Dump, and WireShark. These tools can analyze data packets, network traffic, and data transmission.

9.3 CYBERSECURITY IN POWER GRIDS – COMMUNICATION INFRASTRUCTURE

Power grids have come a long way from local grids to large-scale grids, spanning several countries or even continents [16]. Irrespective of its prominence in modern society, energy sector has been slow in adopting digital technology than other industries because of its demand and size of high availability. It is also observed by a legal perspective as power grids are considered as important infrastructure in different countries [17]. Due to the demand for higher efficiency, digital technologies have been highly large-scale and latest energy grid technology depends highly on high-frequency cycles of monitoring and adaptation to bottlenecks [18]. This trend has given rise to renewable and sustainable energy (i.e., from offshore wind farms to match power generated by traditional power plants to an individual household-based solar grid) [19]. This way, power generation has been highly distributed and less reliable, making it challenging to organize distribution and transmission of energy [20].

Previously, situation was highly under control when only a few large power production plants were needed. Though it is possible to rely on more renewable and traditional power plants to meet the increasing power demand, the grid should still support transmission of power generated. However, adding new lines to extend the grid is prohibitively costly and is also slowed down by protests of locals and regulations. Luckily, digitalization can help make the most of existing grid, resulting in high deployment of digital technologies to monitor, control, and maintain the distribution and transmission of power [21].

This rise in the use of digital technology needs a lot of networking potential and it connects components that have been once isolated by large-scale communication networks [22], resulting in a lot of dataflows [23]. Special protection is needed for critical infrastructure to lead to extreme security concerns due to rise in interconnected power grids [24]. Systems and protocols that were once developed for grids were not designed by considering security. Still, these systems are widely used along with latest technology and are widely exposed to external networks like internet. Similarly, the rising use of decentralized and digital technology offers a huge attack [18]. Various cyberattacks have targeted vital elements of power grid [25]. Large-scale outages and disruptions of electric supply have extensive financial and social effects [26].

Operators are often restricted with rapid changes in communication required and the way in which communication is needed with the rising digitalization of power grids. Hence, large scale communication is brought to power grids. Here, "grid" refers to "power grid" and "network" refers to "digital communication network". Serror *et al.* [27] proposed transmission of energy over distant cities and distribution of power for transmission on a small region or city. The "transmission system operators (TSO)" are responsible to monitor the transmission, while "distribution system operators (DSO)" are responsible for distribution of power.

To define the usual communication infrastructure in power grids, Lee *et al.* [28] illustrated a simple view of a TSO/DSO grid network (as shown in Figure 9.6). The separation between "process control network (PCN)" and office network is the network of grid operator. The office network is much like any other corporate network with data processing or email traffic capability. On the other hand, the PCN connects grid operation control room with field devices and substations, usually relying on "IEC 60870-5-104" protocol (rest of the world) and "DNP3" protocol (North America and some parts of Asia) [29].

The control messages are then construed by a "programmable logic controller (PLC)" and then transferred to the process layer. Usually, the control room has a "database (DB)" server or a "human-machine interface (HMI)" to manage grid data and a simulation server to compute the grid changes. The control room is then linked to various substations (each having an HMI, various PLCs, and a gateway) and can be combined with other "TSO/DSO SCADA" systems to ensure mutual control. Data

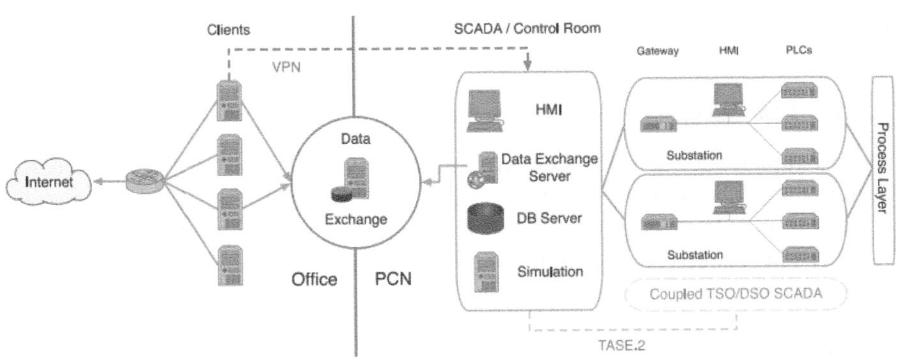

FIGURE 9.6 A basic illustration of a "TSO/DSO network".

Source: E-ISAC [31]

exchange between PCN and office network should be managed only with a specific server for data exchange, where every file is tracked for malware. There are several communication channels like VPNs for direct communication between the PCN and office network or remote maintenance lines for contractors or vendors [30]. The TSO/DSO network is split into office network (to perform data processing and other tasks over the internet) and process control network (for connecting control room with field devices and substations using SCADA traffic). A dedicated server is needed for data exchange. But these networks are usually connected together using VPNs (Figure 9.6)

9.4 CURRENT ISSUES AND CHALLENGES IN IMPLEMENTING CYBERSECURITY IN ENERGY SECTOR

Though digitalization of power grids is needed to deal with rising generation and power demands, it leads to major security issues, especially when power grids are critical infrastructure [32]. Here are some of the fundamental challenges in power grids affecting cybersecurity.

9.4.1 The CIA Triad

The "Confidentiality, Integrity, and Availability (CIA)" triad is a basic concept of data security that should be understood quite differently in power sector [33]. It is usually preferred to ensure integrity and confidentiality and some of the availability. Availability is the most significant measure of the triad in power grids as downtime may have severe consequences [34]. The longer the blackout lasts, the more the impact on the grid, and it will be more challenging to restore the grid [35]. The power grid in Germany had availability of 99.9995% to end-consumers in 2017 to beat the race for availability [36], in comparison to Google services that were highly available with 99.978% without scheduled maintenance [37]. The power grid has over 45-fold more availability when measuring in time. Since availability is the most significant measure, any measure for integrity and confidentiality in power grid must not affect availability of supply.

9.4.2 Managing Power Consumption and Generation

Electrical power grids need stable grid range of 50 to 60 Hz because of alternating current used. The frequency is stable only if power consumption and generation are at equilibrium. The frequency rises with more power generation and vice versa. The equilibrium between consumption and production is ensured by the operation at any time. The operation reserve is split into primary, secondary and minute reserve in Europe. The constant control of frequency load is the primary control where control is added as drop control split among various power plants. Hence, 3GW is the primary reserve of the operation, i.e., the power rating of nuclear power plants.

If frequency derivation holds, the minute and secondary reserves are activated. After five minutes of derivation of frequency, the secondary reserve should be activated and replaced by minute reserve after 15 minutes. These are both centrally activated by the operator where power deviation takes place in the grid area. Either some cities or consumers should be disconnected off the grid at deviations of 1 Hz (in lack of grid frequency) or power plants should be downregulated to prevent damage on generators [38]. The sensitive equilibrium among consumption and generation can be used by attackers as they just have to control small generation or consumption to use flowing effects in the grid to cause a blackout across the system [31] as power consumption and generation have time delays.

9.4.3 Decentralized Power Generation

The proliferation of green energy has encouraged a lot of organizations and people to join the energy sector [39]. For instance, households can easily feed their extra power to the grid. Naturally, the systems' security is not as tightly controlled as those of energy organizations. Hence, the use of software and hardware by people are not as secure as it must be to operate generation of power [40], possibly affecting distribution and transmission to the grid. Assuming the susceptibility in a lot of solar installations, attackers may control the power that is transmitted to the grid. On the other hand, an attacker can pose serious damage, although controlling a small amount of energy by using cascading effects [41]. By controlling power being fed, these cascading effects could be exploited in order to lead to a blackout across the system, affecting transmission and distribution [42].

9.4.4 Process Control Networks

A lot of devices in power grids like PLCs and protection devices are designed for using for multiple decades. They are neither replaced or patched. Some of the most common protocols are "IEC 60870- 5-104" and "DNP3" (Segall [30]; International Electrotechnical Commission, n.d.). These protocols are developed over two decades ago without any security concerns [43]. Irrespective of common use by TSOs and DSOs, neither protocol holds basic security systems like integrity protection or authentication, which have been taken lightly in various commercial sectors for years [44]. For instance, TSOs and DSOs are used in Europe and rest of the world, which use "IEC 60870- 5-104", and vulnerable to various attacks like "spoofing, man-in-the-middle, Denial of Service (DoS), replay, etc." (International Electrotechnical Commission, n.d.; [45]). Similar attacks have been reported on DNP3 protocol [46]. Despite offering additional cybersecurity measures, the standard IEC 62351 protocol is not majorly implemented (International Electrotechnical Commission, n.d.).

As grid operators usually rely on their own networks over specified cables, they could easily abandon further security previously, resulting in networks that may not use authentication, cryptography, integrity checks, or authentication. Previous attacks have proved that internet-connected office networks are usually not separated properly from the PCN, enabling lateral movement of attackers among the two [47]. Once an unsecured PCN is accessed by the attacker, simple communication tools in the protocol can be used to control devices required for grid operation.

9.4.5 Problem in "Physical Network Changes"

Field devices have planned lifetimes in power grids measured in years and decades [48]. Development cycles are a lot faster in IT, enabling development of attacks for devices that have been unused for several years. It is highly improbable that power companies can always follow existing best practices for security by just exchanging devices for latest models that help in modern protocols like IEC 61850 (International Electrotechnical Commission, n.d.). There is a need to implement modern security systems in program only and run on the hardware available or interface with the special devices that can be used by grid companies, without affecting power supply. A lot of devices that are being used may not be powerful enough to promote added functionality [49]. Although some devices are upgraded or exchanged with new software eventually, they are usually needed to help in legacy protocols to convey with older devices still depending on such protocols. On the other hand, transmission and distribution system operators face insecurity [50].

9.4.6 Problem of Weakest Link

In order to have disastrous effects, an attacker simply need to use cascading effects on the entire power grid as long as victim can control enough energy to alter the frequency of the grid, instead of targeting the whole grid. As smaller operators usually don't have ways to toughen systems as much as large-scale operators, those targets can be leveraged by attackers. An attacker controlling a lot of consumer goods like solar cells can still affect the grid frequency [51]. Hence, it is important to come up with solutions used by all relevant actors in interconnected grids and they cannot be deployed by large-scale operators.

9.4.7 Attack Scenarios and Vectors

In interconnected grids, practical cybersecurity is affected by different security issues. As a foundation to deal with those issues, attack scenarios and attack vectors are identified due to fundamental challenges. Attackers can use various attack vectors to attack the transmission network or distribution system to cause blackout or at least enough disruption in the power grid. An attacker can compromise PCN of targeted system to achieve this goal. The field devices or substations can be compromised by the attacker, potentially causing blackout. Table 9.1 lists some of the attack vectors exploited by an attacker to access PCN.

9.4.7.1 Lateral Movement

Attackers accessed the PCN with lateral movement in attacks on grid operators in Ukraine in 2015 from the office network [52] (Figure 9.6). Enabling communication between devices connected with the PCN and office network may be needed like to transfer some data, such as, environmental data among control room and office network. An attacker can affect the office network like by sending "spear phishing" emails to some employees or by exploiting system vulnerabilities as in office suites or web browsers [53]. After gaining access to a machine in office network, the attacker

TABLE 9.1
Attack Vectors in Energy Sector

Attack Vectors	Scope	Difficulty Level	Impact Level	References
Physical access	Local	Medium	Medium	Xie *et al.*, 2019; Vinson *et al.*, 2014; Parfomak, 2014
Lateral Movement	Single Operator	High	High	Lee *et al.*, 2017; Falliere *et al.*, 2011; Farwell & Rohozinski, 2011
Remote Maintenance Access	Multiple operators	High	High	Lee *et al.*, 2016
Insider Attack	Single	Low	High	Xie *et al.*, 2019; Brdiczka, 2014
Overcoming Air Gap	Local	High	Medium	Falliere *et al.*, 2011; Farwell and Rohozinski, 2011
Cascading Effects	Multiple	High	High	Amini *et al.*, 2016; Dabrowski *et al.*, 2017
Third-party exploit	Multiple	High	Medium	Lee *et al.*, 2017; Symantec Security Response, 2014

can search for VPN tunnel or listen to user data to access the PCN. Later movement is among the critical attack vectors from the office network for operators.

9.4.7.2 Physical Access

Energy providers usually rely on their own cable networks for communications. Though it provides added security layer, it doesn't have any protection once physical access is given to the attacker to a network device. For example, substations are mostly connected to the PCN and have remote access without any manual intervention. Hence, an attacker can physically access the network and break into substation and use the systems available manually or connect the same device [54]. Break-ins are very common in substations [55], even though mostly for stealing and selling copper cables [56]. Hence, this kind of theft can be a cover-up to trick grid operators to even search for traces of any kind of cyberattack. This type of attack can significantly affect grid operators. However, it is not scalable enough as it requires physical presence of attacker at various substations.

9.4.7.3 Third-Party Exploit

Attacks are not just limited to grid operator premises. Attack vectors often exploit subcontractors or suppliers. This type of attack is hard to control and dangerous. For instance, attackers used Dragonfly malware on energy supplies and affected 3 ICS equipment manufacturers and installed their malware on the manufacturers' portals [57]. Similarly, attackers compromised makers of field devices and tricked update installers on the public websites of manufacturers for attacking the power grid in 2016 in Ukraine [58]. Then, employees at the targeted DSO installed and applied such updates unknowingly and installed the malware from the attackers to give them access to devices connected through PCN.

Attackers can directly access "remote maintenance" of various grid operators once they compromise the control room software manufacturer. It is especially relevant in cloud resources [59]. In another case, a technician had accidently put an infected USB drive during maintenance in a turbine control room of a US-based power company and infected it with a virus [60]. This third-party exploit compromised the supply chain in manufacturing field devices. If attackers can tamper with devices before installing at grid operator, they can put a covert channel to gain remote access. This type of attack would be a huge impact and gain large access to the PCN. An individual exploit can control various grid operators.

9.4.7.4 Remote Access

There is a maintenance contract between manufacturers of hardware and software for control room with grid operators. These systems have some remote maintenance access to fix such systems on the go or to install software updates [61]. As per the security mechanisms and technology used, attackers can use this access of maintenance to access the PCN. Such access is usually challenged by cyberattacks. In case of vulnerability, an attack can possibly a significant impact on various operators and a lot of control over PCN. A security breach was reported by ICS-CERT at a public utility in 2014 where attackers used brute force to access a remote and password-protected access [62]. An incident from 2013 illustrated the risk of this attack vector where a vendor of a large Canada and US-based operator was compromised by attackers to exfiltrate credentials that can be used for remote access [63].

9.4.7.5 Air Gap

Even though PCN is disconnected from other networks physically, i.e., air-gapped, like office network to avoid lateral movements, it can still be attacked by placing USB devices smartly with malware across the facility to target. This way, helpful or curious employees may compromise those systems accidently by connecting them to company network devices. This attack would have a medium impact in local scope. Attackers could execute only those attacks that were pre-planned. There will be a lack of quick feedback on the success of an attack to an adversary due to this air gap. These attacks are very common on air-gapped systems in very secure areas like International Space Station and military bases [64].

9.4.7.6 Insider Attack

If an attacker compromises an employee or works already in the energy sector, they can directly access the field devices or control room and can control devices to put malware directly also to air-gapped devices. These attacks are not easy to predict and prevent. No further compromise is required in this attack as attacker has access to the operator. ICS-CERT [65] has reported several attacks by rogue employees who misused their position. For instance, a dissatisfied employee knocked out a Salt Lake City based substation and caused a blackout during Winter Olympics 2002 [66]. This attack could significantly affect the grid, especially when attacker has proper knowledge of how grids work and security measures to pick the target well.

9.4.7.7 Cascading Effects

Rather than compromising the network of various grid operators, the attacker just has to use cascading effects to lead to power outage in the grid. For instance, they can remotely control a lot of consumer goods like solar cells [67] and make the most of mechanics of reserve to impact the frequency [68]. Several organizations are there to manage various wind or solar plants centrally, such as, within the scope of power plant [69]. An attack on one of these providers may enable attackers to use same effects. With cascading effects, an attacker can be anywhere in the world making medium to high impact as per the amount of power under their control. But they have to compromise a lot of devices and control at the same time. These days, several botnets like WannaCry, Conficker, Hajime, etc. control thousands of millions of devices for those attacks [70]. The problem might escalate further with the growth of e-mobility like electric cars as well as charging stations [71]; electric vehicle charging infrastructure introduces unique cybersecurity challenges, particularly regarding communication protocols and physical access vulnerabilities [72].

They have different cyber threats as they consume a lot of energy.

9.5 RECOMMENDATION AND FUTURE WORKS FOR ENERGY SECURITY

This section focuses on existing challenges related to digital forensics in energy security and focused on some of the common tools used by professionals. This study enlightens the aspects that should be developed further in digital forensics to face the issues and exploits. It also explores techniques used in spoofing and manipulating forensic tools. In addition, policymakers should focus on making cybersecurity laws by considering the following areas:

- Mitigating the issue of big data in forensic tests
- Analyzing and proposing "International Standard for Digital Forensic"
- Providing impetus associated with "hardware system" to investigate cybercrime
- New cloud forensic process for examination

Considering the above arguments, here is the future scope in the field of digital forensics.

9.5.1 Artificial Intelligence (AI)

Big data plays a critical role in digital forensics for energy systems, requiring innovative approaches to manage volume and velocity [73]. With the significant rise in big data, there is a significant challenge for digital forensics when it comes to analyze large and complex volume of data that needs advanced computing and analysis. This way, AI has been a critical and well-known domain of computer science that can deal with computationally high and complex tasks in real-time [74]. Cybercrime has been more intricate and complex due to limited time and computational and human resources for organizations to address cybercrime. This way, digital forensic investigators find it hard to apply operations and get results in real-time.

It is possible to resolve this problem by combining digital forensic tools, methods, and techniques with the use of AI. Combining these domains have resulted in the increase of smart forensics, which can be an interdisciplinary approach that uses resources both efficiently and smartly, while also using technological advances to investigate [75]. Smart forensics uses different tools and techniques from computation modeling, social networking analysis, and AI to improve overall credibility and efficiency of investigations while significantly reducing the time needed to gather digital evidence. This interdisciplinary approach benefits from advances in computational intelligence and forensic applications, as discussed by Muda et al. [76]. The ability to perform digital forensics makes smart forensics stand out, both before and after the attack. Along with, smart forensics use AI and ML to help investigators to resolve generality and specificity issues as per the patterns of cybercrime.

Additionally, with the integration of AI in digital forensics, experts can be more reactive after cybercrime and proactively measure the outcome before the incident. Smart forensics have reactive capability for digital forensic investigation to gain detailed insight to the incident, which can be helpful for forensic officer when it comes to determine data sources for energy security [77]. This way, smart forensics uses different techniques like social network analysis and AI. It can be used proactively where modern techniques like deep learning and machine learning can predict potential threats as per previous trends.

It can be very helpful for investigators as they can predict digital resources to secure for evidence. With AI and computation intelligence, investigators can use various approaches of digital forensics while ensuring reliability and credibility of outcomes [78]. AI can also manage big datasets while gathering online evidence for forensics [79]. Recent advancements in wireless sensor networks have been instrumental in reducing data rates in IoT applications, aiding real-time forensic investigations in energy systems [80]. Hence, AI can dynamically transform the works of digital forensics while improving energy security and save time required to gather vital evidence.

9.5.2 Intrusion Detection Systems (IDS)

Due to rapidly growing attacks and development of digital systems, "IDS" have been very important for the field of digital forensics. IDS can detect intrusion that can either render a system unusable or unreliable, access critical evidence, or manipulate data [81]. Those systems are required for investigators in digital forensics as they reveal dubious behavior in the network. With efficient IDS, forensic analysts can find out whether computer system is attacked or data is being leaked [82]. This information matters a lot for investigators as experts can use this data to extract vital data that can be presented as evidence. If an attacker sabotages a private or public network, the incidence response (IR) will be triggered after identifying the attacker.

Combined with IR protocols, the investigation related to digital forensics would enable investigators to collect, preserve, and identify data [83]. Combined with IDS, digital forensic approaches will ensure that no changes would be made to the seized evidence and content. IDS can detect malicious and hostile activities for energy security, especially by blocking the attacks, analyzing acquired packets, and alerting the administrator to control the possible risks. These functionalities are important for investigation as attackers are always ready to remove digital footprint.

9.5.3 USB Forensics

USB or Universal Serial Bus is widely used device for data storage and it is also widely used for its capacity and flexibility. It usually relies on controller command to secure data. It is also used for cybercrimes because of easy availability. The USB contains the controller command to increase vulnerability in the process of user verification [84]. Luckily, since IP address is used by the USB, it can track bypassing. When it comes to energy security, USB can provide more data to digital forensics experts. Irrespective of its rising importance in the domain of digital forensics, it is unquestionable that USB poses a lot of threat to both sensitive data and systems. The small form factor, affordability, and easy availability make it ideal for removing digital footprint and committing crime [85].

Viruses and malicious program can be installed on individual systems or server with USB, either knowingly or accidently. Hence, attackers can completely camouflage or wipe up their activities. Hence, USB forensics is very important for investigations in energy sector so that experts can trace connections in link file folders, shortcuts, and prefetch [86]. These breadcrumbs can help investigators to detect several attacks for energy security like opening documents or copying pictures. It is an emerging area of research for analysts and it can help them identify digital evidence.

Digital evidence is mainly found in different media devices. Storage devices have internal or removable memory that consists of digital artifacts that can be found in the crime scene. These devices usually include laptops, cellphones, digital cameras, and media players that rely on optical, electrical, and magnetic media [87]. Metadata in USB device can help experts to identify digital data like geospatial data, copyright data, or even timestamps, which are important to examine evidence related to energy security.

9.6 CONCLUSION

Digital forensics has gained immense attention because of rise in cybercrimes. Irrespective of the growth of digitalization in different fields, several new ways have been observed for cybercrimes. Malicious techniques, software, and tools are widely implemented and designed in each passing day to threaten private and public networks and exploit data storage at the same time to exploit and extract vital data. These breaches and vulnerabilities have resulted in emergence of energy security to extract digital evidence from digital devices exploited by cybercriminals to present as legal evidence before the court of law.

This study has discussed potential threats, recent trends, and opportunities for digital forensics to gain a deeper insight to cybersecurity in energy security. Digital forensics need more research in industry and academic level. International standards and laws should be defined and established for digital forensics and cybersecurity as there is a lot of conflict among the jurisdiction and legal processes.

REFERENCES

1. World Energy Council (2016). New cyber resilience report : energy sector prime target for cyber-attacks. Retrieved from https://www.worldenergy.org/news-views/entry/new-cyber-resilience-report-energy-sector-prime-target-for-cyber-attacks.
2. Glenn, C., Sterbentz, D., & Wright, A. (2016). *Cyber threat and vulnerability analysis of the US electric sector* (No. INL/EXT-16-40692). Idaho National Lab.(INL), Idaho Falls, ID (United States).
3. Aminnezhad, A., & Dehghantanha, A. (2014). A survey on privacy issues in digital forensics. *International Journal of Cybersecurity and Digital Forensics (IJCSDF), 3*(4), 311–323.
4. Dezfouli, F., & Dehghantanha, A. (2014). Digital forensics trends and future. *International Journal of Cybersecurity and Digital Forensics (IJCSDF), 3*(4), 48–76.
5. Alherbawi, N., Shukur, Z., & Sulaiman, R. (2013). Systematic literature review on data carving in digital forensic. *Procedia Technology, 11*, 86–92.
6. Sonamjain, T. (2014). A review of cloud forensics issues & challenges. *International Journal of Advanced Research in Computer Science & Technology*, 55–57.
7. Burney, A., Asif, M., & Abbas, Z. (2016). Forensics issues in cloud computing. *Journal of Computer and Communications, 4*(10), 63–69.
8. Pandey, A. K., Tripathi, A. K., Kapil, G., Singh, V., Khan, M. W., Agrawal, A., & Khan, R. A. (2020). Current challenges of digital forensics in cybersecurity. *Critical Concepts, Standards, and Techniques in Cyber Forensics*, 31–46.
9. Walters, A., & Petroni, N. L. (2007). Volatools: Integrating volatile memory into the digital investigation process. *Black Hat DC, 2007*, 1–18.
10. Chhabra, G. S., & Singh, P. (2015). Distributed network forensics framework: A systematic review. *International Journal of Computer Applications, 119*(19), 31–35.
11. Krause, T., Ernst, R., Klaer, B., Hacker, I., & Henze, M. (2021). Cybersecurity in power grids: Challenges and opportunities. *Sensors, 21*(18), 6225.
12. He, X., Qiu, R. C., Ai, Q., Chu, L., Xu, X., & Ling, Z. (2016). Designing for situation awareness of future power grids: An indicator system based on linear eigenvalue statistics of large random matrices. *IEEE Access, 4*, 3557–3568.
13. Suciu, G., Sachian, M. A., Vulpe, A., Vochin, M., Farao, A., Koutroumpouchos, N., & Xenakis, C. (2021). Sealedgrid: Secure and interoperable platform for smart grid applications. *Sensors, 21*(16), 5448.
14. Klaer, B., Sen, Ö, van der Velde, D., Hacker, I., Andres, M., & Henze, M. (2020, September). Graph-based model of smart grid architectures. In *2020 international conference on smart energy systems and technologies (SEST)* (pp. 1–6). IEEE.
15. Wang, T., Long, Q., Gu, X., & Chai, W. (2020). Information flow modeling and performance evaluation of communication networks serving power grids. *IEEE Access, 8*, 13735–13747.
16. Javaid, N., Hafeez, G., Iqbal, S., Alrajeh, N., Alabed, M. S., & Guizani, M. (2018). Energy efficient integration of renewable energy sources in the smart grid for demand side management. *IEEE Access, 6*, 77077–77096.
17. Figueroa-Acevedo, A. L., Tsai, C. H., Gruchalla, K., Claes, Z., Foley, S., Bakke, J., & Prabhakar, A. J. (2020). Visualizing the impacts of renewable energy growth in the US midcontinent. *IEEE Open Access Journal of Power and Energy, 7*, 91–99.
18. Phuangpornpitak, N., & Tia, S. (2013). Opportunities and challenges of integrating renewable energy in smart grid system. *Energy Procedia, 34*, 282–290.
19. Ahmed, S. D., Al-Ismail, F. S., Shafiullah, M., Al-Sulaiman, F. A., & El-Amin, I. M. (2020). Grid integration challenges of wind energy: A review. *IEEE Access, 8*, 10857–10878.
20. Henze, M., Hiller, J., Hummen, R., Matzutt, R., Wehrle, K., & Ziegeldorf, J. H. (2017). Network security and privacy for cyber-physical systems. *Security and Privacy in Cyber-Physical Systems: Foundations, Principles and Applications*, 25–56.

21. Hiller, J., Komanns, K., Dahlmanns, M., & Wehrle, K. (2019, September). Regaining insight and control on SMGW-based secure communication in smart grids. In *2019 AEIT international annual conference (AEIT)* (pp. 1–6). IEEE.
22. Pennekamp, J., Henze, M., Schmidt, S., Niemietz, P., Fey, M., Trauth, D., & Wehrle, K. (2019, November). Dataflow challenges in an internet of production: a security & privacy perspective. In *Proceedings of the ACM Workshop on Cyber-Physical Systems Security & Privacy* (pp. 27–38).
23. Khurana, H., Hadley, M., Lu, N., & Frincke, D. A. (2010). Smart-grid security issues. *IEEE Security & Privacy*, *8*(1), 81–85.
24. van der Velde, D., Henze, M., Kathmann, P., Wassermann, E., Andres, M., Bracht, D., & Sethmann, R. (2020, September). Methods for actors in the electric power system to prevent, detect and react to ICT attacks and failures. In *2020 6th IEEE international energy conference (ENERGYCon)* (pp. 17–22). IEEE.
25. Zhang, H., Jin, X., Li, Y., Jiang, Z., Liang, Y., Jin, Z., & Wen, Q. (2019). A multi-step attack detection model based on alerts of smart grid monitoring system. *IEEE Access*, *8*, 1031–1047.
26. Karimipour, H., Dehghantanha, A., Parizi, R. M., Choo, K. K. R., & Leung, H. (2019). A deep and scalable unsupervised machine learning system for cyber-attack detection in large-scale smart grids. *IEEE Access*, *7*, 80778–80788.
27. Serror, M., Hack, S., Henze, M., Schuba, M., & Wehrle, K. (2020). Challenges and opportunities in securing the industrial internet of things. *IEEE Transactions on Industrial Informatics*, *17*(5), 2985–2996.
28. Lee, R. M., Assante, M. J., & Conway, T. (2017). *CRASHOVERRIDE: Analysis of the threat to electric grid operations*. Dragos Inc.
29. Petermann, T., Bradke, H., Lüllmann, A., Poetzsch, M., & Riehm, U. (2014). What happens during a blackout: Consequences of a prolonged and wide-ranging power outage.
30. Segall, A. (1983). Distributed network protocols. *IEEE Transactions on Information Theory*, *29*(1), 23–35.
31. E-ISAC (2016). Analysis of the cyber-attack on the Ukrainian power grid. *Electricity Information Sharing and Analysis Center (E-ISAC)*, *388*(1-29), 3.
32. Chapman, J. P., Ofner, S., & Pauksztelo, P. (2016, November). Key factors in industrial control system security. In *2016 IEEE 41st conference on local computer networks (lcn)* (pp. 551–554). IEEE.
33. Istiaque Ahmed, K., Tahir, M., Hadi Habaebi, M., Lun Lau, S., & Ahad, A. (2021). Machine learning for authentication and authorization in iot: Taxonomy, challenges and future research direction. *Sensors*, *21*(15), 5122.
34. Maynard, P., McLaughlin, K., & Haberler, B. (2014, September). Towards understanding man-in-the-middle attacks on iec 60870-5-104 scada networks. In *2nd International Symposium for ICS & SCADA Cybersecurity Research 2014 (ICS-CSR 2014)*. BCS Learning & Development.
35. Radoglou-Grammatikis, P., Sarigiannidis, P., Giannoulakis, I., Kafetzakis, E., & Panaousis, E. (2019, July). Attacking iec-60870-5-104 scada systems. In *2019 IEEE World Congress on Services (SERVICES)* (Vol. 2642, pp. 41–46). IEEE.
36. Robinson, M. (2013, September). The SCADA threat landscape. In *1st International Symposium for ICS & SCADA Cybersecurity Research 2013 (ICS-CSR 2013)*. BCS Learning & Development.
37. Darwish, I., Igbe, O., Celebi, O., Saadawi, T., & Soryal, J. (2015, November). Smart grid DNP3 vulnerability analysis and experimentation. In *2015 IEEE 2nd international conference on cybersecurity and cloud computing* (pp. 141–147). IEEE.
38. Xu, Y., Yang, Y., Li, T., Ju, J., & Wang, Q. (2017, November). Review on cyber vulnerabilities of communication protocols in industrial control systems. In *2017 IEEE conference on energy internet and energy system integration (EI2)* (pp. 1–6). IEEE.

39. Henze, M. (2020, June). The quest for secure and privacy-preserving cloud-based industrial cooperation. In *2020 IEEE conference on communications and network security (CNS)* (pp. 1–5). IEEE.
40. International Electrotechnical Commission. IEC 61850 Standard. Available online: https://webstore.iec.ch/publication/20082
41. Hummen, R., Hiller, J., Henze, M., & Wehrle, K. (2013a). Slimfit—A HIP DEX compression layer for the IP-based internet of things. In *2013 IEEE 9th international conference on wireless and Mobile computing, networking and communications (WiMob)* (pp. 259–266). IEEE.
42. Hummen, R., Hiller, J., Wirtz, H., Henze, M., Shafagh, H., & Wehrle, K. (2013b). 6LoWPAN fragmentation attacks and mitigation mechanisms. In *Proceedings of the sixth ACM conference on Security and privacy in wireless and mobile networks* (pp. 55–66).
43. Ackerman, P. (2017). *Industrial cybersecurity: Efficiently secure critical infrastructure systems*. Packt Publishing Ltd.
44. Parfomak, P. W. (2014). *Physical security of the US power grid: High-voltage transformer substations*. Congressional Research Service: Washington, DC, USA.
45. Vinson, C., Hallenstein, J., Fisher, R. L., & Perusquia, S. D. (2014). Review of physical security protection of utility substations and control centers. *State of Florida Public Service Commission Office of Auditing and Performance Analysis, Tech. Rep. [Online].* https://www.psc.state.fl.us/Files/PDF/Publications/Reports/General/Electricgas/PhysicalSecurity
46. Lee, R. M., Assante, M. J., & Conway, T. (2016). Analysis of the recent reports of attacks on US infrastructure by Iranian actors. *SANS Industrial Control Systems*, *4*, 9.
47. Xie, J., Stefanov, A., & Liu, C. C. (2019). Physical and cybersecurity in a smart grid environment. *Advances in Energy Systems: The Large-Scale Renewable Energy Integration Challenge*, 85–109.
48. Brdiczka, O. (2014). Insider Attacks Pose a Serious Threat to Critical U.S. Infrastructure. *Vectra.ai*. Available at https://www.vectra.ai/blog/insider-attacks-pose-a-serious-threat-to-critical-u-s-infrastructure.
49. Falliere, N., Murchu, L. O., & Chien, E. (2011). W32. Stuxnet dossier. *White Paper, Symantec Corp., Security Response*, *5*(6), 29.
50. Farwell, J. P., & Rohozinski, R. (2011). Stuxnet and the future of cyber war. *Survival*, *53*(1), 23–40.
51. Amini, S., Pasqualetti, F., & Mohsenian-Rad, H. (2016). Dynamic load altering attacks against power system stability: Attack models and protection schemes. *IEEE Transactions on Smart Grid*, *9*(4), 2862–2872.
52. Dabrowski, A., Ullrich, J., & Weippl, E. (2017). *Grid Shock: Coordinated Load-Change Attacks on Power Grids*. In Proceedings of the 33rd Annual Computer Security Applications Conference (ACSAC), Orlando, FL, USA.
53. Symantec Security Response (2014). Dragonfly: Cyberespionage attacks against energy suppliers. *Rapp. Tecn*, *7*.
54. Ligh, M., Adair, S., Hartstein, B., & Richard, M. (2010). *Malware analyst's cookbook and DVD: Tools and techniques for fighting malicious code*. Wiley Publishing.
55. Andress, J. (2014). *The basics of information security: Understanding the fundamentals of InfoSec in theory and practice*. Syngress.
56. Petermann, T., Bradke, H., Lüllmann, A., Poetzsch, M., & Riehm, U. (2014). *What happens during a blackout: Consequences of a prolonged and wide-ranging power outage*. BoD.
57. Knight, U. G. (2001). *Power systems in emergencies: From contingency planning to crisis management*. Wiley.
58. Bundesnetzagentur, n.d. Security of Supply. Available online: https://www.bundesnetzagentur.de/EN/Areas/Energy/Companies/SecurityOfSupply/QualityOfSupply/QualityOfSupply_node.html

59. Google (n.d.). Reliability. Available online: https://support.google.com/googlecloud/answer/6056635.
60. Wang, J., Wang, X., & Wu, Y. (2005). Operating reserve model in the power market. *IEEE Transactions on Power Systems*, *20*(1), 223–229.
61. ENTSO-E. Operation Handbook. Available online: https://www.ucte.org/resources/publications/ophandbook/.
62. Kenyon, R., Maguire, J., Present, E., Christensen, D., & Hodge, B. M. (2021). Bulk electric power system risks from coordinated edge devices. *IEEE Open Access Journal of Power and Energy*, *8*, 35–44.
63. Dahlmanns, M., Lohmöller, J., Fink, I. B., Pennekamp, J., Wehrle, K., & Henze, M. (2020, October). Easing the conscience with OPC UA: An internet-wide study on insecure deployments. In *Proceedings of the ACM Internet Measurement Conference* (pp. 101–110).
64. U.S. Department of Energy (2007). An Assessment of Copper Wire Thefts from Electric Utilities. Office of Electricity Delivery and Energy Reliability. Available at: https://www.oe.netl.doe.gov/docs/copper042707.pdf.
65. ICS-CERT (2012). Malware Infections in the Control Environment. ICS-CERT Monitor Newsletter ICS-MM201212. Available online: https://us-cert.cisa.gov/ics/monitors/ICS-MM201212
66. Henze, M., Matzutt, R., Hiller, J., Mühmer, E., Ziegeldorf, J. H., Van Der Giet, J., & Wehrle, K. (2017, April). Practical data compliance for cloud storage. In *2017 IEEE international conference on cloud engineering (IC2E)* (pp. 252–258). IEEE.
67. Henze, M., Matzutt, R., Hiller, J., Mühmer, E., Ziegeldorf, J. H., van der Giet, J., & Wehrle, K. (2020). Complying with data handling requirements in cloud storage systems. *IEEE Transactions on Cloud Computing*, *10*(3), 1661–1674.
68. Kruglov, K., & Goncharov, E. (2018). Threats posed by using RATs in ICS. Available https://securelist.com/threats-posed-by-using-rats-in-ics/88011/.
69. ICS-CERT (2014). Internet Accessible Control Systems at Risk. ICS-CERT Monitor Newsletter ICS-MM201404. Available online: https://us-cert.cisa.gov/ics/monitors/ICS-MM201404.
70. Lynn, W. F. III (2010). Defending a new domain-the Pentagon's cyberstrategy. *Foreign Aff*, *89*, 97.
71. Hannan, N. (2018). An assessment of supply-chain cyber resilience for the International Space Station. *The RUSI Journal*, *163*(2), 28–32.
72. Falk, R., & Fries, S. (2012). Electric vehicle charging infrastructure security considerations and approaches. *Proceeding of INTERNET 2012: The Fourth International Conference on Evolving Internet*, 58–64.
73. Adedayo, O. M. (2016, June). Big data and digital forensics. In *2016 IEEE international conference on cybercrime and computer forensic (ICCCF)* (pp. 1–7). IEEE.
74. Cardenas, D. J. S., Hahn, A., & Liu, C. C. (2020). Assessing cyber-physical risks of IoT-based energy devices in grid operations. *IEEE Access*, *8*, 61161–61173.
75. Pudjianto, D., Ramsay, C., & Strbac, G. (2007). Virtual power plant and system integration of distributed energy resources. *IET Renewable Power Generation*, *1*(1), 10–16.
76. Muda, A. K., Choo, Y. H., Abraham, A., & Srihari, S. N. (Eds.). ((2014). *Computational intelligence in digital Forensics: Forensic investigation and applications.* Springer International Publishing.
77. Rossow, C., Andriesse, D., Werner, T., Stone-Gross, B., Plohmann, D., Dietrich, C. J., & Bos, H. (2013, May). Sok: P2pwned-modeling and evaluating the resilience of peer-to-peer botnets. In *2013 IEEE symposium on security and privacy* (pp. 97–111). IEEE.
78. Asghari, H., Ciere, M., & Van Eeten, M. J. (2015). {Post-Mortem} of a Zombie: Conficker Cleanup After Six Years. In *24th USENIX Security Symposium (USENIX Security 15)* (pp. 1–16).

79. Herwig, S., Harvey, K., Hughey, G., Roberts, R., & Levin, D. (2019, February). Measurement and analysis of Hajime, a peer-to-peer IoT botnet. In *26th Annual Network and Distributed Systems Security (NDSS) Symposium* (pp. 24–27). San Diego, CA, USA: The Internet Society.
80. Yahya, O., Alrikabi, H., & Aljazaery, I. (2020). Reducing the data rate in internet of things applications by using wireless sensor network.
81. Irons, A., & Lallie, H. S. (2014). Digital forensics to intelligent forensics. *Future Internet*, *6*(3), 584–596.
82. Agrawal, S., & Agrawal, J. (2015). Survey on anomaly detection using data mining techniques. *Procedia Computer Science*, *60*, 708–713.
83. Ahmed, M., Mahmood, A. N., & Hu, J. (2016). A survey of network anomaly detection techniques. *Journal of Network and Computer Applications*, *60*, 19–31.
84. Al-Barazanchi, I., Abdulshaheed, H. R., & Sidek, M. (2019). Innovative technologies of wireless sensor network: The applications of WBAN system and environment. *Sustainable Engineering and Innovation*, *1*(2), 98–105.
85. Collie, J. (2013). The windows IconCache. DB: A resource for forensic artifacts from USB connectable devices. *Digital Investigation*, *9*(3-4), 200–210.
86. Roy, T., & Jain, A. (2012). Windows registry forensics: An imperative step in tracking data theft via USB devices. *International Journal of Computer Science and Information Technologies*, *3*(3), 4427–4433.
87. Vincze, E. A. (2016). Challenges in digital forensics. *Police Practice and Research*, *17*(2), 183–194.

10 Cybersecurity and Forensics in Transportation Security

Pawan Whig, Tabrej Ahamad, Ali Mehndi, Anumaan Whig, and Nikhitha Yathiraju

10.1 INTRODUCTION

In the modern era, transportation systems form the backbone of global connectivity, facilitating the movement of people, goods, and information across vast distances. From airplanes soaring through the skies to trains hurtling along tracks and ships navigating the oceans, the intricate network of transportation infrastructure shapes the dynamics of commerce, tourism, and societal interactions [1]. However, as these systems become increasingly reliant on digital technologies and interconnected networks, they also become more vulnerable to cyber threats and attacks. The convergence of transportation and cyberspace has given rise to a pressing need for robust cybersecurity measures and forensic techniques to safeguard critical transportation assets and ensure the continued reliability and safety of transportation systems [2].

10.1.1 The Intersection of Cybersecurity and Transportation Security

The integration of digital technologies in transportation infrastructure has revolutionized the efficiency and effectiveness of transportation systems [3]. Automated control systems manage traffic flow, optimize routes, and enhance safety, while interconnected networks enable real-time communication and coordination between various transportation components. However, this digital transformation also introduces new vulnerabilities and risks, as transportation systems become potential targets for cybercriminals, hacktivists, and state-sponsored actors [4]. Cyber threats facing transportation systems encompass a wide range of malicious activities, including hacking of control systems, unauthorized access to sensitive data, and disruption of critical services [5]. For example, a cyberattack targeting the control systems of a railway network could lead to train derailments or collisions, posing grave risks to passenger safety and infrastructure integrity. Similarly, a breach of airline databases could compromise passenger information, jeopardizing privacy and security [6]. In response to these evolving threats, cybersecurity has emerged as a critical component of transportation security, aiming to protect against cyber incidents and mitigate their impact on transportation operations [7]. By implementing robust

DOI: 10.1201/9781003497868-10

cybersecurity protocols, such as encryption, access controls, and intrusion detection systems (IDS), transportation stakeholders can fortify their defenses against cyber threats and enhance the resilience of transportation infrastructure [8–9].

10.1.2 The Role of Forensics in Transportation Security

In addition to proactive cybersecurity measures, forensic techniques play a crucial role in the aftermath of cyber incidents, enabling investigators to identify perpetrators, analyze attack vectors, and preserve digital evidence for legal proceedings. Digital forensics, the process of collecting, analyzing, and presenting digital evidence in a court of law, is essential for conducting thorough investigations into cyber incidents and holding perpetrators accountable for their actions [10]. In the context of transportation security, digital forensics is particularly valuable for reconstructing the sequence of events leading up to a cyber incident, identifying vulnerabilities in transportation systems, and implementing preventive measures to mitigate future risks [11–14]. For example, forensic analysis of a cyberattack on an air traffic control system could uncover vulnerabilities in software architecture or network configurations, prompting the implementation of patches or security updates to prevent similar incidents in the future. Digital forensics enables transportation authorities and law enforcement agencies to collaborate effectively in investigating cyber incidents and prosecuting perpetrators. By following established forensic procedures and adhering to chain of custody protocols, investigators can ensure the admissibility and integrity of digital evidence in legal proceedings, thereby facilitating the pursuit of justice and deterrence of cybercrime [15].

10.1.3 Challenges and Opportunities

Despite the growing recognition of the importance of cybersecurity and forensics in transportation security, significant challenges persist in addressing the dynamic nature of cyber threats and the complexity of transportation systems [16]. One of the primary challenges is the rapid pace of technological innovation, which often outpaces the development of cybersecurity solutions and forensic methodologies. As transportation systems become more interconnected and reliant on emerging technologies such as artificial intelligence (AI) and the Internet of Things (IoT), new vulnerabilities and attack vectors may emerge, necessitating continuous adaptation and innovation in cybersecurity and forensics [17]. The interconnected nature of transportation networks poses challenges for cross-sector collaboration and information sharing among stakeholders. Effective transportation security requires coordinated efforts between government agencies, transportation operators, technology vendors, and cybersecurity experts, yet achieving seamless collaboration and information exchange can be hindered by regulatory barriers, competitive interests, and resource constraints [18]. Despite these challenges, the intersection of cybersecurity and transportation security also presents opportunities for innovation and collaboration in developing resilient, adaptive, and secure transportation systems [19]. By leveraging advanced technologies such as blockchain, machine learning (ML), and quantum encryption, transportation stakeholders can enhance the integrity and confidentiality of data, bolstering the resilience of transportation infrastructure against cyber threats [20].

Cybersecurity and forensics play integral roles in ensuring the security, reliability, and resilience of transportation systems in an increasingly digitalized world [21]. By implementing proactive cybersecurity measures and leveraging forensic techniques to investigate and mitigate cyber incidents, transportation stakeholders can safeguard critical assets and uphold the trust and confidence of passengers and stakeholders [22–24]. Moving forward, continued collaboration and innovation in cybersecurity and forensics will be essential for addressing evolving cyber threats and maintaining the integrity of transportation infrastructure.

10.2 CYBER THREATS FACING TRANSPORTATION SYSTEMS

Transportation systems are increasingly reliant on digital technologies and interconnected networks, making them vulnerable to various cyber threats [25]. Understanding these threats is crucial for developing effective cybersecurity strategies to safeguard critical transportation assets. Here, we delve into three primary cyber threats facing transportation systems:

10.2.1 Hacking of Control Systems

Control systems are integral components of transportation infrastructure, governing the operation of vehicles, traffic lights, signaling systems, and other critical elements. Hackers may target these control systems to gain unauthorized access and manipulate their functions, leading to potentially catastrophic consequences. For instance, hackers could compromise the control systems of autonomous vehicles, causing them to deviate from their intended routes or collide with obstacles. Moreover, the hacking of control systems in aviation, maritime, and railway sectors poses significant safety risks. By infiltrating air traffic control systems, hackers could disrupt flight operations, leading to flight delays, diversions, or even collisions. Similarly, compromising maritime navigation systems could result in ship collisions, grounding, or unauthorized access to sensitive maritime areas. In the railway sector, hacking of signaling systems could lead to train derailments or collisions, endangering passenger safety and causing extensive damage to infrastructure.

10.2.2 Unauthorized Access to Sensitive Data

Transportation systems store vast amounts of sensitive data, including passenger information, cargo manifests, operational schedules, and maintenance records. Unauthorized access to this data can have serious implications for privacy, security, and operational integrity. Cybercriminals may target transportation databases and information systems to steal sensitive data for various malicious purposes, such as identity theft, financial fraud, or espionage. For example, a data breach in an airline's reservation system could expose passengers' personal and payment information, compromising their privacy and security. Similarly, unauthorized access to cargo manifests in the shipping industry could facilitate the theft of valuable goods or the smuggling of contraband. Moreover, hackers may target operational schedules and maintenance records to disrupt transportation operations or sabotage critical infrastructure.

10.2.3 Disruption of Critical Services

Cyberattacks targeting transportation systems often aim to disrupt critical services, causing widespread chaos, economic losses, and public inconvenience. These attacks may take various forms, including distributed denial-of-service (DDoS) attacks, ransomware attacks, or malware infections. By disrupting essential services such as ticketing systems, communication networks, or vehicle routing systems, cybercriminals can disrupt transportation operations and undermine public trust in the reliability and safety of transportation systems. For instance, a DDoS attack targeting an airline's reservation website could render it inaccessible to passengers, leading to flight cancellations, delays, and revenue losses. Similarly, a ransomware attack on a public transit agency's payment system could disrupt fare collection processes, causing financial losses and service disruptions. Moreover, malware infections targeting transportation control systems could impair their functionality, leading to operational disruptions or safety incidents.

In conclusion, cyber threats pose significant challenges to the security, reliability, and safety of transportation systems. By understanding the nature of these threats and implementing robust cybersecurity measures, transportation stakeholders can mitigate risks and ensure the resilience of critical transportation infrastructure. However, addressing these threats requires ongoing vigilance, collaboration, and innovation to stay ahead of evolving cyber threats in an increasingly digitalized transportation landscape.

10.3 PROACTIVE CYBERSECURITY MEASURES IN TRANSPORTATION SECURITY

Ensuring the security of transportation systems requires proactive measures to prevent cyber threats from exploiting vulnerabilities and disrupting critical operations. Implementing robust cybersecurity measures is essential to safeguarding transportation infrastructure against unauthorized access, data breaches, and malicious activities. Here, we explore in detail three proactive cybersecurity measures employed in transportation security:

10.3.1 Encryption

Encryption is a fundamental cybersecurity measure used to protect sensitive data from unauthorized access and interception. In transportation security, encryption is utilized to secure communication channels, data storage systems, and transmission protocols. By encoding data in a scrambled format that can only be deciphered with the appropriate decryption key, encryption helps prevent eavesdropping, data tampering, and unauthorized data access. In the context of transportation systems, encryption is applied to various components, including communication networks, onboard systems, and databases. For example, data transmitted between air traffic control centers and aircraft are encrypted to prevent interception by unauthorized parties. Similarly, encryption is used to secure passenger information stored in airline reservation systems, protecting it from unauthorized access and data breaches. Encryption plays a crucial role in securing wireless communication networks used in transportation, such as Wi-Fi networks on board aircraft or maritime vessels. By encrypting data transmitted over these networks, transportation operators can prevent unauthorized access and protect sensitive information from interception by cybercriminals or malicious actors.

10.3.2 Access Controls

Access controls are another essential cybersecurity measure employed in transportation security to manage and regulate access to critical systems, networks, and data. Access controls encompass a range of mechanisms, including authentication, authorization, and auditing, to ensure that only authorized users have the necessary permissions to access sensitive resources.

In transportation systems, access controls are implemented at various levels, including physical access controls, network access controls, and system access controls. For example, access to control rooms, data centers, and critical infrastructure facilities is restricted to authorized personnel through physical security measures such as biometric authentication, access badges, and surveillance systems. Network access controls are employed to regulate access to transportation networks and communication systems, preventing unauthorized devices from connecting to the network and compromising its security. Techniques such as firewall rules, network segmentation, and virtual private networks (VPNs) are used to enforce access policies and protect against unauthorized access attempts. System access controls are implemented to manage user privileges, restrict administrative access, and monitor user activities within transportation systems. By enforcing the principle of least privilege, transportation operators can minimize the risk of insider threats and unauthorized access to critical systems and data.

10.3.3 Intrusion Detection Systems

IDS are cybersecurity tools designed to detect and respond to unauthorized activities and security breaches within a network or system. IDS analyze network traffic, system logs, and other data sources to identify suspicious behavior, anomalies, and indicators of compromise indicative of a cyberattack. In transportation security, IDS play a crucial role in monitoring the integrity and security of critical infrastructure, such as control systems, communication networks, and operational systems. By continuously monitoring network traffic and system activities, IDS can detect and alert operators to potential security incidents, allowing them to respond promptly and mitigate the impact of cyber threats. There are two main types of IDS: network-based IDS (NIDS) and host-based IDS (HIDS). NIDS analyze network traffic in real-time to identify suspicious patterns or signatures associated with known cyber threats, while HIDS monitor activities and events on individual host systems, such as servers, workstations, and mobile devices. In transportation systems, IDS are deployed at key network ingress and egress points, as well as within critical infrastructure components, to provide comprehensive visibility into potential security threats and vulnerabilities. By correlating alerts from multiple sources and employing advanced analytics techniques, IDS help transportation operators identify and respond to cyber threats effectively, minimizing the risk of disruption to transportation operations and ensuring the integrity of critical systems and data. Proactive cybersecurity measures are essential for safeguarding transportation infrastructure against cyber threats and ensuring the reliability, safety, and resilience of transportation systems. By implementing robust encryption, access controls, and IDS, transportation stakeholders can mitigate risks, protect sensitive information, and maintain the trust and confidence of passengers and stakeholders in an increasingly digitalized transportation landscape.

10.4 DIGITAL FORENSICS IN INVESTIGATING CYBER INCIDENTS

Digital forensics plays a critical role in investigating cyber incidents within the realm of transportation security. It involves the collection, analysis, and preservation of digital evidence to identify the perpetrators, understand the attack vectors, and support legal proceedings and prosecution. Here, we delve into the three main components of digital forensics in investigating cyber incidents in transportation security:

10.4.1 Collection of Digital Evidence

The first step in digital forensics is the systematic collection of digital evidence from various sources, including computers, network devices, storage media, and communication channels. In the context of transportation security, digital evidence may include log files, system configurations, network traffic captures, and data stored on onboard systems, control systems, and communication networks. Digital forensic investigators use specialized tools and techniques to collect digital evidence while maintaining its integrity and chain of custody. They create forensic images of storage media, capture network traffic using packet sniffers, and extract data from volatile memory to preserve evidence for analysis and legal proceedings.

In transportation security, collecting digital evidence requires coordination among multiple stakeholders, including transportation operators, law enforcement agencies, cybersecurity experts, and forensic investigators. Timely and thorough collection of digital evidence is essential for reconstructing the sequence of events leading up to a cyber incident, identifying the scope and impact of the attack, and attributing responsibility to the perpetrators.

10.4.2 Analysis of Attack Vectors

Once digital evidence is collected, forensic analysts conduct a detailed analysis of attack vectors to determine how the cyber incident occurred, what vulnerabilities were exploited, and what methods were used by the attackers. This analysis involves examining system logs, network traffic patterns, malware artifacts, and other forensic artifacts to reconstruct the attack timeline and identify the techniques employed by the attackers. In transportation security, analysis of attack vectors may reveal vulnerabilities in control systems, communication protocols, or software applications used in transportation infrastructure. For example, forensic analysis of a cyberattack targeting an airline's reservation system may uncover vulnerabilities in web applications, authentication mechanisms, or third-party integrations exploited by the attackers.

Analysis of attack vectors helps transportation stakeholders understand the motives and objectives of the attackers, whether they are seeking financial gain, political motives, or sabotage. By identifying the tactics, techniques, and procedures (TTPs) used by the attackers, forensic analysts can develop countermeasures and preventive strategies to mitigate similar cyber threats in the future.

10.4.3 Legal Proceedings and Prosecution

Digital evidence collected and analyzed through forensic investigation plays a crucial role in supporting legal proceedings and prosecution of cybercriminals involved in transportation security incidents. Forensic analysts document their findings in detailed reports, which may include technical analysis, forensic artifacts, chain of custody documentation, and expert testimony to support legal proceedings. In transportation security, digital evidence is used to establish the facts of the case, prove the intent and culpability of the perpetrators, and support the prosecution's case in court. This may involve presenting evidence of unauthorized access, data theft, system tampering, or other illegal activities perpetrated by the attackers.

Forensic analysts collaborate with legal experts, law enforcement agencies, and prosecutors to ensure that digital evidence is admissible in court and meets the requirements of the legal system. This includes adhering to chain of custody procedures, preserving the integrity of digital evidence, and complying with legal standards for the admission of expert testimony. Digital forensics plays a crucial role in investigating cyber incidents in transportation security, enabling forensic analysts to collect, analyze, and preserve digital evidence to support legal proceedings and prosecution. By leveraging digital forensics techniques and methodologies, transportation stakeholders can enhance their ability to identify and respond to cyber threats effectively, ensuring the security, reliability, and resilience of transportation infrastructure in an increasingly digitalized world.

10.5 COLLABORATIVE EFFORTS IN TRANSPORTATION SECURITY

Collaboration is essential in addressing the complex and evolving challenges of transportation security. By fostering partnerships among stakeholders across different sectors, sharing information and best practices, and considering regulatory frameworks, transportation security can be strengthened. Here's a detailed exploration of collaborative efforts in transportation security:

10.5.1 Cross-Sector Collaboration

Transportation security is a multifaceted issue that involves various sectors, including government agencies, transportation operators, technology vendors, cybersecurity firms, and academia. Cross-sector collaboration brings together expertise, resources, and perspectives from different stakeholders to address common challenges and enhance the resilience of transportation infrastructure.

Government agencies play a central role in coordinating cross-sector collaboration efforts by facilitating information sharing, setting standards and regulations, and providing funding and support for transportation security initiatives. For example, agencies such as the Department of Homeland Security (DHS) in the United States and the European Union Agency for Railways (ERA) in Europe collaborate with transportation operators, industry associations, and other stakeholders to develop cybersecurity guidelines, conduct risk assessments, and coordinate incident response efforts. Transportation operators also play a crucial role in cross-sector collaboration by sharing insights, best practices, and threat intelligence with government agencies and industry partners. By participating in information-sharing forums, such as sector-specific Information Sharing and Analysis Centers (ISACs) or public-private partnerships, transportation operators can stay informed about emerging threats and vulnerabilities and collaborate on cybersecurity initiatives.

Technology vendors and cybersecurity firms contribute to cross-sector collaboration by developing innovative solutions, conducting research, and providing training and support to transportation stakeholders. By partnering with industry associations, academic institutions, and government agencies, technology vendors can align their products and services with the unique cybersecurity needs and challenges of the transportation sector.

10.5.2 Information Sharing Among Stakeholders

Information sharing is a cornerstone of effective transportation security, enabling stakeholders to identify and respond to emerging threats and vulnerabilities in real-time. By sharing threat intelligence, incident reports, and best practices, transportation stakeholders can enhance their collective situational awareness and develop proactive strategies to mitigate risks and protect critical infrastructure.

Information sharing among stakeholders occurs through various channels, including formal partnerships, industry working groups, sector-specific forums, and government-sponsored initiatives. For example, government agencies such as the Transportation Security Administration (TSA) in the United States and the International Civil Aviation Organization (ICAO) facilitate information sharing among aviation stakeholders through initiatives such as the Aviation Information Sharing and Analysis Center (A-ISAC).

Moreover, industry associations, such as the International Air Transport Association (IATA) and the International Association of Public Transport (UITP), play a vital role in promoting information sharing among transportation operators, technology vendors, and other stakeholders. These associations organize conferences, workshops, and training programs where stakeholders can exchange insights, discuss best practices, and collaborate on cybersecurity initiatives.

10.5.3 Regulatory Considerations

Regulatory frameworks play a crucial role in shaping collaborative efforts in transportation security by establishing standards, guidelines, and compliance requirements for cybersecurity. Government agencies enact regulations to ensure the safety, reliability, and resilience of transportation infrastructure, while also promoting innovation and competitiveness in the transportation sector. In the United States, regulatory frameworks such as the TSA regulations for aviation security and the Federal Transit Administration (FTA) regulations for public transit security establish cybersecurity requirements for transportation operators, technology vendors, and other stakeholders. These regulations mandate measures such as risk assessments, security training, incident reporting, and compliance audits to mitigate cyber threats and protect critical infrastructure.

Internationally, regulatory bodies such as the ICAO and the International Maritime Organization (IMO) develop global standards and guidelines for cybersecurity in transportation. These standards provide a common framework for addressing cybersecurity risks and promoting collaboration among countries, regions, and industry sectors. Moreover, regulatory compliance is often a driving force for cross-sector collaboration in transportation security, as stakeholders work together to meet regulatory requirements and demonstrate their commitment to cybersecurity. By aligning their efforts with regulatory frameworks, transportation stakeholders can enhance their resilience to cyber threats and maintain compliance with applicable laws and regulations. In conclusion, collaborative efforts in transportation security are essential for addressing the complex and evolving challenges of cybersecurity. By fostering cross-sector collaboration, sharing information among stakeholders, and considering regulatory frameworks, transportation stakeholders can enhance the security, reliability, and resilience of transportation infrastructure in an increasingly interconnected and digitalized world.

10.6 EMERGING TECHNOLOGIES IN TRANSPORTATION CYBERSECURITY

As transportation systems become increasingly digitalized and interconnected, the need for innovative cybersecurity solutions to protect critical infrastructure grows. Emerging technologies offer promising avenues for enhancing the security, resilience, and integrity of transportation systems against cyber threats. Here, we delve into three key emerging technologies in transportation cybersecurity:

10.6.1 Blockchain

Blockchain technology has gained traction as a powerful tool for enhancing the security and integrity of data in various industries, including transportation. Blockchain is a decentralized, distributed ledger technology that enables secure and transparent recording of transactions across a network of computers. By leveraging cryptographic techniques and consensus mechanisms, blockchain ensures the immutability and integrity of data, making it resistant to tampering and unauthorized access. In transportation cybersecurity, blockchain has several applications, including secure supply chain management, secure data sharing, and decentralized identity management. For example, blockchain can be used to track and authenticate the provenance of goods and materials in the transportation supply chain, reducing the risk of counterfeit products and supply chain disruptions.

Blockchain can facilitate secure and transparent data sharing among transportation stakeholders, such as government agencies, transportation operators, and logistics providers. By creating a tamper-proof audit trail of data transactions, blockchain enables trust and accountability in data exchange, enhancing collaboration and interoperability in the transportation ecosystem. Blockchain-based decentralized identity management systems can enhance the security and privacy of passenger information in transportation systems. By giving passengers control over their digital identities and credentials, blockchain enables secure and privacy-preserving authentication and authorization processes, reducing the risk of identity theft and fraud.

10.6.2 Machine Learning

ML is a branch of AI that enables computers to learn from data and make predictions or decisions without explicit programming. In transportation cybersecurity, ML algorithms can analyze large volumes of data, detect patterns and anomalies, and make intelligent decisions to identify and respond to cyber threats in real-time.

ML has several applications in transportation cybersecurity, including anomaly detection, predictive analytics, and threat intelligence. For example, ML algorithms can analyze network traffic patterns to detect anomalous behavior indicative of cyberattacks, such as denial-of-service (DoS) attacks or malware infections. ML can enhance predictive analytics capabilities in transportation security by identifying emerging threats and vulnerabilities based on historical data and trends. By analyzing data from past cyber incidents, ML algorithms can identify patterns and correlations that may indicate potential future attacks, enabling proactive risk mitigation measures. ML can augment threat intelligence capabilities in transportation cybersecurity by automating the analysis of threat intelligence feeds, malware samples, and security alerts. ML algorithms can classify and prioritize security threats, generate actionable insights, and recommend remediation actions to security analysts and incident response teams.

10.6.3 Quantum Encryption

Quantum encryption, also known as quantum cryptography, leverages the principles of quantum mechanics to secure communication channels against eavesdropping and interception. Unlike classical encryption algorithms, which rely on mathematical complexity to secure data, quantum encryption relies on the fundamental properties of quantum physics, such as the uncertainty principle and entanglement, to ensure the confidentiality and integrity of data. In transportation cybersecurity, quantum encryption offers a promising solution for securing communication networks, data transmission, and sensitive information. Quantum encryption protocols, such as quantum key distribution (QKD), enable the generation and exchange of cryptographic keys using quantum states, ensuring that any attempt to intercept or tamper with the keys is detectable. Quantum encryption provides forward secrecy and future-proof security against emerging threats, such as quantum computers, which could potentially break classical encryption algorithms.

By harnessing the inherent randomness and unpredictability of quantum phenomena, quantum encryption offers a robust defense against sophisticated cyberattacks in transportation systems.

Quantum encryption can enhance the security of emerging technologies in transportation, such as connected and autonomous vehicles (CAVs) and smart transportation systems. By securing communication channels and data exchanges between vehicles, infrastructure, and control centers, quantum encryption mitigates the risk of cyberattacks and ensures the trustworthiness and reliability of transportation systems. Emerging technologies offer promising opportunities for enhancing cybersecurity in transportation systems. By leveraging blockchain for secure data management, ML for threat detection and prediction, and quantum encryption for secure communication, transportation stakeholders can strengthen the resilience and integrity of critical infrastructure against cyber threats in an increasingly digitalized and interconnected transportation landscape.

10.7 CONCLUSION

In this chapter, we have explored the multifaceted landscape of cybersecurity in transportation systems, highlighting the challenges, strategies, and emerging technologies employed to safeguard critical infrastructure against cyber threats. From the hacking of control systems to unauthorized access to sensitive data and the disruption of critical services, transportation systems face a myriad of cybersecurity risks that necessitate proactive measures and collaborative efforts to mitigate. Proactive cybersecurity measures, such as encryption, access controls, and IDS, form the foundation of transportation security, providing essential defenses against cyber threats and vulnerabilities. By implementing robust cybersecurity protocols and leveraging advanced technologies, transportation stakeholders can fortify their defenses, protect sensitive information, and ensure the reliability and safety of transportation systems. Digital forensics plays a crucial role in investigating cyber incidents, enabling forensic analysts to collect, analyze, and preserve digital evidence to support legal proceedings and prosecution of cybercriminals. By employing forensic techniques and methodologies, transportation stakeholders can identify the perpetrators, understand the attack vectors, and strengthen their resilience to future cyber threats.

Collaborative efforts are essential in addressing the complex and evolving challenges of transportation security, fostering partnerships among stakeholders across different sectors, sharing information and best practices, and considering regulatory frameworks. By fostering cross-sector collaboration, sharing threat intelligence, and complying with regulatory requirements, transportation stakeholders can enhance their collective ability to identify and respond to cyber threats effectively. Emerging technologies offer promising opportunities for enhancing cybersecurity in transportation systems, including blockchain for secure data management, ML for threat detection and prediction, and quantum encryption for secure communication. By leveraging these technologies, transportation stakeholders can strengthen the resilience and integrity of critical infrastructure against cyber threats in an increasingly digitalized and interconnected transportation landscape. Cybersecurity is paramount in ensuring the reliability, safety, and resilience of transportation systems in an increasingly digitalized world. By implementing proactive cybersecurity measures, fostering collaborative efforts, and leveraging emerging technologies, transportation stakeholders can mitigate risks, protect critical infrastructure, and uphold the trust and confidence of passengers and stakeholders in transportation security.

10.8 FUTURE SCOPE

As the transportation industry continues to evolve and embrace digital technologies, the future of cybersecurity in transportation holds immense potential for innovation, collaboration, and resilience. Several areas present opportunities for future advancements and enhancements in transportation cybersecurity:

1. **Integration of AI and Automation:** The integration of AI and automation technologies offers promising avenues for enhancing cybersecurity in transportation. AI-powered threat detection systems, autonomous cybersecurity agents, and predictive analytics platforms can augment human capabilities and enable real-time response to cyber threats in transportation systems.
2. **Cyber-Physical Systems Security:** With the proliferation of IoT devices and cyber-physical systems (CPS) in transportation infrastructure, securing the interactions between physical and digital components becomes increasingly critical. Future research and development efforts should focus on developing robust security mechanisms and protocols for CPS in transportation, ensuring the integrity and reliability of critical infrastructure.
3. **Quantum-Safe Cryptography:** As the field of quantum computing advances, the threat landscape for classical encryption algorithms evolves. Future research in quantum-safe cryptography aims to develop encryption algorithms and protocols that are resistant to quantum attacks, ensuring the long-term security of communication channels and data exchanges in transportation systems.
4. **Cyber-Resilient Infrastructure:** Building cyber-resilient transportation infrastructure involves designing systems and networks that can withstand and recover from cyberattacks while maintaining essential functions and services. Future efforts should focus on incorporating resilience principles into the design, development, and operation of transportation systems, including redundancy, diversity, and adaptability.
5. **Supply Chain Security:** Securing the transportation supply chain is essential for ensuring the integrity and reliability of goods and materials transported across borders. Future initiatives should focus on enhancing supply chain visibility, authentication, and traceability using blockchain, IoT, and other emerging technologies, reducing the risk of counterfeit products, smuggling, and supply chain disruptions.
6. **Cybersecurity Education and Training:** Enhancing cybersecurity awareness and expertise among transportation professionals is crucial for building a resilient cybersecurity workforce. Future initiatives should focus on developing specialized training programs, certifications, and workforce

development initiatives tailored to the unique cybersecurity challenges and requirements of the transportation sector.

7. **International Collaboration and Standards:** Cyber threats in transportation are global in nature, requiring international collaboration and standardization efforts to address effectively. Future initiatives should focus on promoting information sharing, best practices exchange, and harmonization of cybersecurity standards and regulations across borders, ensuring a unified approach to transportation security worldwide.

The future of cybersecurity in transportation holds great promise for innovation, collaboration, and resilience. By embracing emerging technologies, enhancing collaboration among stakeholders, and investing in research and development initiatives, the transportation industry can strengthen its defenses against cyber threats and ensure the reliability, safety, and integrity of transportation systems in an increasingly digitalized and interconnected world.

REFERENCES

1. Sharma, P., & Gillanders, J. (2022). Cybersecurity and forensics in connected autonomous vehicles: A review of the state-of-the-art. *IEEE Access*, *10*, 108979–108996.
2. Akilal, A., & Kechadi, M. T. (2021). A forensic-ready intelligent transportation system. In *International summit smart City 360°* (pp. 617–630). Springer International Publishing.
3. Baig, Z. A., Szewczyk, P., Valli, C., Rabadia, P., Hannay, P., Chernyshev, M., & Peacock, M. (2017). Future challenges for smart cities: Cybersecurity and digital forensics. *Digital Investigation*, *22*, 3–13.
4. Alsulami, H. (2022). Implementation analysis of reliable unmanned aerial vehicles models for security against cyber-crimes: Attacks, tracebacks, forensics and solutions. *Computers and Electrical Engineering*, *100*, 107870.
5. Kelarestaghi, K. B., Foruhandeh, M., Heaslip, K., & Gerdes, R. (2018). Vehicle security: Risk assessment in transportation. *arXiv preprint arXiv:1804.07381.*
6. Pandey, A. K., Tripathi, A. K., Kapil, G., Singh, V., Khan, M. W., Agrawal, A., & Khan, R. A. (2020). Current challenges of digital forensics in cybersecurity. *Critical Concepts, Standards, and Techniques in Cyber Forensics*, 31–46.
7. Hussain, M. M., Alam, M. S., Beg, M. S., & Ali, R. (2019). Searching for IoT resources in intelligent transportation cyberspace (T-CPS)—Requirements, use-cases and security aspects. In *cybersecurity and privacy in cyber physical systems* (pp. 293–331). CRC Press.
8. Ghonge, M. M., Pramanik, S., Mangrulkar, R., & Le, D. N. (Eds.). (2022). *Cybersecurity and digital forensics: Challenges and future trends.* John Wiley & Sons.
9. Hyman, B. T., Alisha, Z., & Gordon, S. (2019). Secure controls for smart cities: Applications in intelligent transportation systems and smart buildings. *International Journal of Science and Engineering Applications*, *8*(6), 167–171.
10. Abedi, M., & Sedaghat, S. (2018). Crawler and Spiderin usage in cyber-physical systems forensics. *OIC-CERT Journal of Cybersecurity*, *1*(1), 53–61.
11. Choo, K. K. R., Fei, Y., Xiang, Y., & Yu, Y. (2016). Embedded device forensics and security. *ACM Transactions on Embedded Computing Systems (TECS*, *16*(2), 1–5.
12. Alharbe, M. A. (2020). Cybersecurity, forensics, and its impact on future challenges in Saudi Arabia smart cities. *International Journal*, *9*(2), 2464–2470.
13. Barbeau, S. J., Ligatti, J., Dennis, K., & Alibayev, M. (2019). Enhancing Cybersecurity in Public Transportation.

14. Strandberg, K., Nowdehi, N., & Olovsson, T. (2022). A systematic literature review on automotive digital forensics: Challenges, technical solutions and data collection. *IEEE Transactions on Intelligent Vehicles*, *8*(2), 1350–1367.
15. Glisson, W., & Choo, K. K. R. (2018). Introduction to the Minitrack on Cyber-of-Things: Cyber Crimes, Cybersecurity and Cyber Forensics. In *Proceedings of the 51st Hawaii International Conference on System Sciences (HICSS)* (pp. 1–8). Waikoloa, HI, USA. https://doi.org/10.24251/HICSS.2018.695
16. Khan, A. A., Shaikh, A. A., Laghari, A. A., Dootio, M. A., Rind, M. M., & Awan, S. A. (2022). Digital forensics and cyber forensics investigation: Security challenges, limitations, open issues, and future direction. *International Journal of Electronic Security and Digital Forensics*, *14*(2), 124–150.
17. Alexakos, C., Katsini, C., Votis, K., Lalas, A., Tzovaras, D., & Serpanos, D. (2021). Enabling digital forensics readiness for internet of vehicles. *Transportation Research Procedia*, *52*, 339–346.
18. Mohamed, N., Al-Jaroodi, J., & Jawhar, I. (2020, July). Cyber-physical systems forensics. In *2020 IEEE Systems Security Symposium (SSS)* (pp. 1–7). IEEE.
19. Pătraşcu, A., Simion, E., & NM, N. (2014). Cybersecurity evaluation of critical infrastructures systems. N., Bălan, L., Dănăilă, T. Neamţu (Eds.) *Autonomous vehicles. Nova Science Publishers, Inc.*, 185–205.
20. Kelarestaghi, K. B., Foruhandeh, M., Heaslip, K., & Gerdes, R. (2019). Intelligent transportation system security: Impact-oriented risk assessment of in-vehicle networks. *IEEE Intelligent Transportation Systems Magazine*, *13*(2), 91–104.
21. DeFranco, J. F., & Maley, B. (2022). *What every engineer should know about cybersecurity and digital forensics*. CRC Press.
22. Mughal, A. A. (2019). A comprehensive study of practical techniques and methodologies in incident-based approaches for cyber forensics. *Tensorgate Journal of Sustainable Technology and Infrastructure for Developing Countries*, *2*(1), 1–18.
23. Sun, X., Yu, F. R., & Zhang, P. (2021). A survey on cybersecurity of connected and autonomous vehicles (CAVs). *IEEE Transactions on Intelligent Transportation Systems*, *23*(7), 6240–6259.
24. Oriwoh, E., & Williams, G. (2015). Internet of Things: The argument for smart forensics. In *Handbook of research on digital crime, cyberspace security, and information assurance* (pp. 407–423). IGI Global.
25. Lacroix, J., El-Khatib, K., & Akalu, R. (2016, November). Vehicular digital forensics: What does my vehicle know about me? In *Proceedings of the 6th ACM Symposium on Development and Analysis of Intelligent Vehicular Networks and Applications* (pp. 59–66).

11 Cybersecurity and Forensics for Free and Fair Elections

Neeraj M. and Paul Joseph D.

11.1 INTRODUCTION

Free and fair elections are the fundamental principle of democracy, which guarantees that people can choose their representatives without being subjected to fraud, pressure, or intimidation. All eligible voters have equal opportunities to participate in such elections, and the electoral process is conducted transparently, with integrity and accountability. According to Robert Dahl, a free and fair election is one in which obligatory is relatively uncommon [1].

An election is deemed as "free" when individuals have the option to vote without constraint and can freely cast their vote for their preferred candidate or party without apprehension or coercion. Moreover, a "free'" election ensures that the identity of the chosen candidate remains confidential. Conversely, a fair election is characterized by equal voter registration opportunities, accurate vote tallying, and the announcement of results that truly reflect the actual votes [2]. To do this, elections must be accessible, inclusive, and trustworthy for voters and elected officials. Furthermore, there must be equal chances and legitimate political rivalry in the democratic process. International public law protects these core values via essential obligations, rights, and liberties.

For organizing free and fair elections in any country, the following eight standards must be met [3].

- One Person, One Vote – It is a frequently used phrase supporting free and fair elections. It denotes that all voters are entitled to cast one vote, ensuring that every vote has equal weight.
- Citizens can register to vote – Governments can limit who can register to vote. However, they cannot hinder eligible voters from doing so or make it harder for particular groups of individuals to register than for others [4].
- Availability of trustworthy information – Governments are prohibited from restricting media coverage of particular candidates or political parties and purposefully disseminating false information. Voters require access to dependable and impartial information to decide which candidate to endorse freely.

DOI: 10.1201/9781003497868-11

- Right to candidacy for citizens – Governments are barred from assaulting or intimidating individuals who choose to run for public office or from establishing prejudicial regulations concerning who is eligible to run. Voters cannot freely exercise their right to choose their leaders if certain political parties or candidates are unjustly prevented from running for office.
- Access to polling stations or alternative voting techniques – Individuals must be able to vote freely. Regardless of their identification or place of residence, voters need to be able to locate polling places, access them, and exercise their ballots. For instance, individuals facing disability, health issues, or transportation challenges should have access to alternative voting methods such as postal or email balloting. A digital voting platform can meet this standard.
- Voting without intimidation: It is essential that polling places are safe. Instances of violence, or the fear of violence, can induce fear in individuals, influencing their ability to vote for their preferred candidate or deterring them from voting altogether. The use of secret ballots can also serve as a deterrent against coercion or intimidation by preventing individuals from being targeted based on their voting choices.
- Prevention of voting fraud – It is crucial that every eligible voter only casts one vote, while ineligible voters are prevented from participating. When unfair ballots are included, the election fails to represent the voters' intentions.
- Accurate ballot counting and announcement of correct results – Once cast, ballots must not be tampered with or discarded, and all voter-issued ballots must be tallied. Ballots must be accurately counted for the election to genuinely mirror the voters' intentions.
- Respect for election results – Following the determination of the election outcome, it is vital that candidates honour the results of the vote. Peaceful transitions of power are fundamental to a democracy, and candidates who are unsuccessful in the election should not resort to violence or intimidation to seize power. Figure 11.1 shows a global map displaying the Free and Fair Election Index from 2002.

Figure 11.1 represents the election violence, government intimidation, fraud, significant irregularities, and vote buying on a scale of 0 to 1, 0 being fair and 1 being unfair elections.

11.2 DIGITAL VOTING OR ELECTRONIC VOTING

In contrast to the conventional ballot technique, incorporating a digital platform makes voting more accessible to everyone. Electronic voting employs electronic methods to assist or cater for the voting and tallying of ballots. Electronic voting technology is intended to speed up ballot counting, lower the expense of engaging people to tally votes and enhance physical accessibility for impaired voters. Furthermore, results may be reported and published faster, saving voters' time and resources by voting regardless of location. This may boost overall voter turnout.

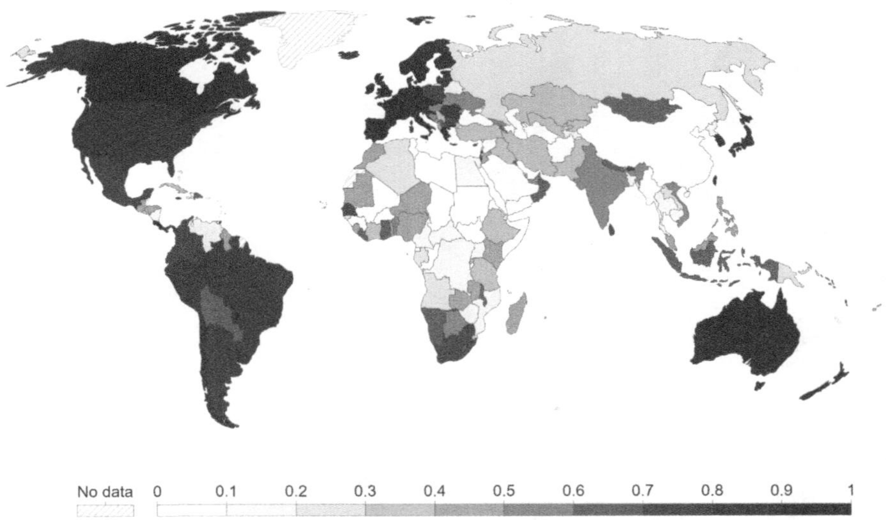

FIGURE 11.1 Free and fair election index in the year 2002.

Source: Coppedge *et al.* (2021) [5] – processed by our world in data

Citizens living overseas, in rural regions far from polling booths, and with disabilities benefit the most from electronic elections.

E-voting is generally observed in two distinct ways.

- E-voting, which is physically overseen by officials from government or independent election authorities, often involves the use of Electronic Voting Machines (EVMs). These EVMs are commonly found in local casting votes booths.
- Remote E-voting – Often known as i-voting, it is a method of submitting a vote electronically to election officials regardless of location.

11.3 ELECTRONIC VOTING MACHINES

E-voting in any country, especially India, is possible through EVM and a few hardware components. These EVMs are stand-alone devices and are not connected to the Internet or any other external networks during voting to ensure security and integrity. Figure 11.2 is a visual representation of the EVM process, showing voting and result tabulation.

Hardware components

- *Control Unit (CU)* – The CU is the main processing unit of an EVM, which typically contains a microcontroller or microprocessor, memory for storing data, a display unit, and input/output interfaces. This unit controls the overall functioning of the EVM, manages user interaction, and ensures the integrity of the voting process.

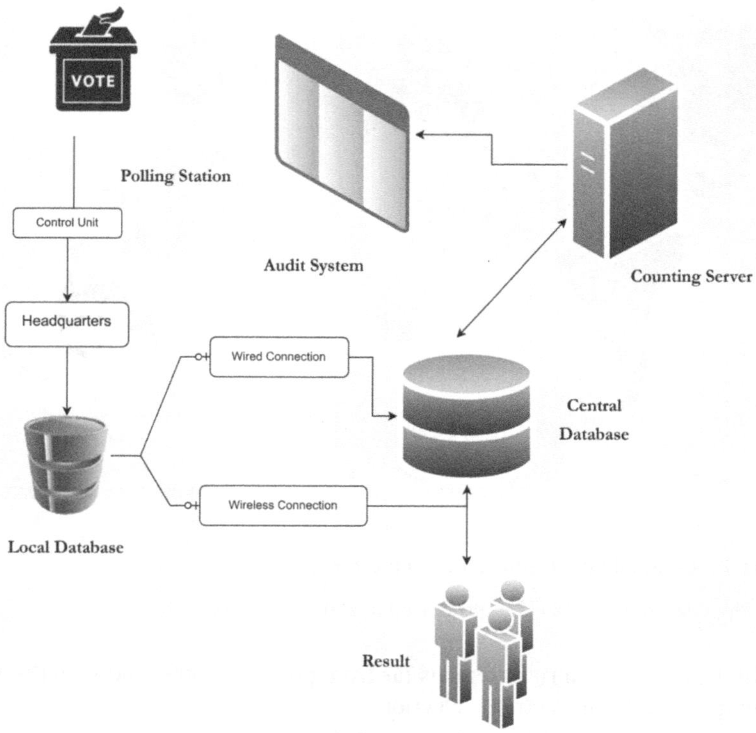

FIGURE 11.2 Representation of EVM process.

- *Ballot Unit (BU)* – The BU is where voters cast their votes. It consists of buttons, lamps, and candidate names or symbols, each corresponding to a specific candidate or option in the election. The BU records the votes cast by voters and communicates with the CU to transmit this data securely.
- *Voter-Verifiable Paper Audit Trail (VVPAT) unit* – This unit is optional in an EVM, which provides a paper trail of the votes cast by voters, including a printer, paper roll, and a viewing window. Once the voter casts their vote on the BU, the VVPAT prints a paper receipt displaying the chosen candidate's name or symbol, which the voter can verify through the viewing window. Finally, the paper receipt is stored securely within the EVM for later audit or recount purposes.

11.3.1 Software Components

- Firmware – An EVM's firmware is an embedded software that manages the microcontroller of the EVM and resides in volatile memory. This module is accountable for setting up the EVM, managing user input, logging votes, and interacting with other hardware (such the VVPAT unit).

- Security Protocols – Examples of security features in EVM includes encryption, which is used while exchanging data. The VVPAT unit, the CU and the BU communicate with each other through a secure communication channel using encryption/decryption protocols, which are implemented by EVM software to preserve the sanctity of the voting process. The following are the main goals of this security measure: Unauthorized access, unwanted data manipulation, restricted Software and hardware tampering.

An EVM's overall mechanism combines hardware and software components to provide a transparent, reliable, and efficient voting procedure while safeguarding the confidentiality and integrity of each vote cast.

11.3.2 Advantages of E-voting

- Accessibility – Digital voting systems can improve accessibility for voters with disabilities or mobility issues by providing features such as screen readers, magnification tools, and alternative input methods.
- Efficiency – Digital voting can streamline the voting process, reducing waiting times at polling stations and accelerating the announcement of election results
- Accuracy – Digital voting systems minimize the risk of errors in vote counting and recording, as votes are tallied electronically and are less susceptible to human error.
- Transparency – Digital voting systems can enhance transparency and accountability in the electoral process by providing audit trails, verifiable records, and real-time monitoring of voting activities.

11.3.3 Issues in Electronic Voting – Role of Cybersecurity

Even though E-voting benefits, many concerns still need to be addressed immediately. Any fraud, manipulation or rigging results in democracy corruption. Though few countries fear using E-voting, E-voting is still observed globally. While E-voting offers convenience and efficiency, addressing security, transparency, and technical challenges remains crucial for its widespread adoption [6, 7]. This section presents in-depth issues and challenges and offers solutions to overcome them.

11.3.3.1 Security Vulnerabilities

EVMs are vulnerable to various security threats, including hacking, malware, and cyberattacks. These vulnerabilities can compromise the integrity and confidentiality of elections [8]. Malicious actors could exploit security weaknesses to manipulate votes, undermine election results, or compromise voter privacy [9]. Such incidents can erode public trust in the electoral process and democratic institutions. Addressing security vulnerabilities in electronic voting systems is complex due to the evolving nature of cybersecurity threats and the need to balance security with accessibility and usability for voters.

Solution – Deploying effective cybersecurity methods, such as encryption, multi-factor identification, and systems for discovering intrusions, can help reduce security risks [10]. Regular security audits and penetration testing are essential for identifying and addressing vulnerabilities. Furthermore, collaboration between election officials, cybersecurity experts, and technology vendors is critical to safeguarding against security threats.

11.3.3.2 Lack of Transparency

Transparency in the electoral process ensures accountability, public trust, and confidence in election outcomes. However, many electronic voting systems lack transparency, making it difficult for voters and election officials to understand how votes are cast, transmitted, and counted [11]. Without transparency, voters may question the fairness and accuracy of election results. Lack of visibility into voting can also hinder efforts to detect and address irregularities or discrepancies. Achieving transparency in electronic voting systems requires striking a balance between providing access to information and protecting sensitive data and proprietary technology. Additionally, ensuring that the voting process is understandable and accessible to all stakeholders poses a challenge.

Solution – To enhance transparency, election authorities can provide access to source code, conduct public demonstrations of the voting process, and establish independent oversight mechanisms. Open-source voting software and stringent auditing practices further advance accountability and transparency. Election administrators may enhance transparency in electronic voting systems and assure election integrity by prioritizing openness and transparency.

11.3.3.3 Privacy Concerns

The preservation of democratic values and the assurance of being able to secure election integrity both require voter privacy and ballot secrecy. Lack of providing security for the voter privacy results in illegal access to personal information or information theft. The fear of privacy in each individual could negatively impact their participation in elections, and thus affecting democracy in the long run. There is a challenge in maintaining the balance between protecting voter personal information and verifying that one's vote was recorded correctly. Additionally, they are challenged in both securing efficient built-in security and compliance with privacy laws/spark regulations.

Solution – To mitigate the above challenges, election authorities would enforce strict data protection laws and encrypt voter information to maintain privacy. To improve the privacy protection of any individual, consent from each individual is considered in addition to the discussion of transparent data processing procedures. By focusing on privacy and the essential safeguards, election administrators can help to build trust and ensure timely voter turnout in elections conducted through electronic systems.

11.3.3.4 Reliability and Accuracy

Dependable election results should focus on three real-life aspects: reliability, security, and consistency of EVMs. There is a wide range of technical challenges, such as software bugs and hardware malfunctions, that could undermine not just accuracy and reliability but secure electronic voting as well. Deceptive or fraudulent election results can result in disputes, conflicts and reduced levels of trust in the democratic process. Balancing the reliability of an electronic voting system and allowing for accessibility and ease of use are a few challenging problems. This requires that these electronic voting systems function correctly and accurately, thus requiring substantial testing to validate their reliability in conjunction with necessary quality control measures and redundant controls.

Solution – To ensure the reliability of EVMs, comprehensive training for election officials and voters, in addition to implementing redundancy measures, can be an optimal solution. System performance and security holes must be addressed over time via regular maintenance, updates, etc. The best path forward is for the top priority to be not just accuracy but reliability too – which would leave many election administrators with an ability to protect democracy and assure confidence and reliability in free elections.

11.3.3.5 Cost and Maintenance

Significant financial resources are required to implement and operate electronic voting systems. To illustrate, money is needed to purchase technology infrastructure, personnel training, and ongoing support. However, the lack of funds or limited funds compromise the EVM's quality, maintenance and technical support. The exorbitant initial investment, maintenance costs over a prolonged period, and budgetary constraints are challenging that election authorities face while implementing or upgrading EVMs. The reliability of the elections is directly affected by insufficient funds, which results in obsolete technology, deficient training or diminished security. The critical challenge for any election administrator is maintaining the balance between enduring affordability, adaptability, and cost. Furthermore, planning and advocacy must be utilized to guarantee that resources are equitably allocated amongst urban, rural, and underserved communities, as well as to procure funding for operations and enhancements on an ongoing basis.

Solution – The potential savings and efficiencies of E-voting systems can be verified by cost-benefit analyses, which serve as a basis for making investment decisions. Exploring money from central government grants or private partnerships and trying alternative financing methods like joint public-private ventures or crowd-funding can reduce financial risk. Besides, investing in electoral officer training can increase the return rate of E-vote technology. To overcome various financial obstacles using strategic planning and resource management techniques, electoral administrators can finally relish the prospect of electronic voting.

11.3.3.6 Resistance to Change

The stakeholders' resistance to the EVMs is due mainly to uncertainty about unfamiliar technology, distrust of the electoral process and inclination towards paper ballots. However, some claim that modernization will encroach on their vested interests. Resistance to change can interfere with our efforts towards modernization and perpetuate inefficiency in election systems. Misconceptions or a lack of understanding about electronic voting may result in public outrage from voters, election officials or legislators. Overcoming resistance to change involves fixing fallacies and misunderstandings through more pervasive communication and education. Exhibiting the EVM benefits, such as enhanced accessibility, security, and efficiency, is pivotal for winning support and a voter's trust.

Solution – If stakeholders can participate in decision-making and provide themselves with feedback and the opportunity to participate and address those concerns and misconceptions openly and transparently, then resistance to change may be eased. Consistency and acceptance can also be increased by providing voters and election officials with adequate assistance, training, and public EVM displays. By addressing concerns and misconceptions and highlighting the benefits of electronic voting, election administrators can promote the acceptance and adoption of modern voting technologies.

11.3.3.7 Legal and Regulatory Compliance

Electronic voting systems must comply with legal and regulatory requirements to ensure elections' integrity, legality, and fairness. However, inadequate legal frameworks or regulatory oversight may leave electronic voting systems vulnerable to legal challenges or violations of voting rights. Inconsistencies or gaps in election laws, privacy regulations, or cybersecurity standards may create legal uncertainty or compliance risks for electronic voting systems. Failure to comply with legal requirements can undermine the legitimacy of elections and expose election authorities to legal liabilities. Navigating complex legal requirements and ensuring compliance with evolving regulations and standards pose challenges for election administrators. Coordinating efforts across multiple jurisdictions and stakeholders to address legal and regulatory issues requires effective communication, collaboration, and expertise.

Solution – Establishing clear legal frameworks, consulting legal experts, and conducting regular reviews of compliance practices can help ensure that electronic voting systems comply with applicable laws and regulations. Engaging with policymakers, advocacy groups, and other stakeholders to advocate for supportive legal frameworks and regulatory reforms can also facilitate compliance and enhance the legitimacy of electronic elections. By prioritizing compliance and staying informed about legal developments, election administrators can mitigate legal risks and maintain public trust in the electoral process.

11.3.3.8 Digital Divide

The digital divide refers to the fact that certain people are excluded from access to technology, internet connectivity and digital literacy, which widens existing gaps among unequal classes and contradicts democratic principles of fairness. Groups such as feature phone users, low-income households, rural communities, older citizens and disability sufferers who may not have access to technology or web connection are deleterious to electronic voting. As a result, some people's representation levels will be unfairly low compared to others, and they may be excluded from voting altogether, which serves to exaggerate social and political inequality. Bridging the digital divide means overcoming structural barriers like poor infrastructure, high access costs to this medium, and low levels of digital literacy. In such cases, policymakers, educators, and community leaders face the difficulty of assuring that people have fair access to technology, a comfortable connection with the Internet, and training programs.

Solution – Enterprises such as bringing technology infrastructure and broadband access to poor areas and offering low-cost devices and internet services are potential ways of narrowing the digital gap. Equipping people with digital literacy programs, training initiatives, and support services for under-served communities can also enable them to participate in electronic voting and engage in civil affairs. Suppose policymakers and community leaders have their digital divide-bridging activities as the utmost priority; in that case, they will ensure that all individuals are free to exercise their right to vote in a secure and comfortable manner, and thus, they contribute to the democratic election process.

11.3.3.9 Vendor Dependence

A greater part of the EVMs are based on retention software or hardware from specific vendors, which means that election technology has to rely on specific suppliers to operate normally. This increases vendor dependency and directly exposes it as a vulnerable reliance point. This raises questions essential to understanding how vendor lock-in may limit competition and growth in the electronic voting market. Not having transparency or control in proprietary technologies might push the public to doubt the fairness of elections, which would lead them away from electronic voting. Striking a balance between transparency, security, and independence while benefiting from vendor expertise is a struggle for election authorities. Planning and oversight are necessary to ensure accountability; invigorating competition and supporting multiple vendors while limiting the danger of vendor lock-in also demand close attention.

Solution – One can mitigate the dependency on vendors by promoting open standards, encouraging vendor diversity and cooperation between vendors and election authorities. Other ways to promote public trust in EVMs include training staff, establishing transparent procedures, competitive bidding, and signing user control-focused contracts at the top level. In taking action to mitigate excessive dependence on suppliers and encourage supplier diversity, administrators of elections may also enhance the credibility and security of electronic balloting.

11.3.3.10 Election Integrity

Election integrity is the possession of independent and unbiased controls on all processing within an electoral system, meaning those at final stage (voting) being free from fraud or manipulation. Election integrity must be maintained to guarantee that election outcomes serve as a true reflection of the will of voters, and therefore preserve public conviction in democracy. Any detected breach against election integrity, such as voter extortion or voter information mishandling or tampering, results in discord, riot, and threat. Lack of proper safeguards, transparency, or enforcement mechanisms can compromise elections and threaten the health of democracy. Election administrators, policymakers and law enforcement agencies face critical challenges in detecting and preventing threats to election integrity, which include cybersecurity breaches, fraud campaigns or foreign intervention. By securing electoral process infrastructure, developing or maintaining transparency in election campaigns and in finances, encouraging educated electorates helps in protecting the integrity in elections.

Solution – Adopting strong security features like encryption, multi-factor authentication and audit trails can reduce the risk of cyberattacks and preserve trust in E-voting system [6]. Ensuring transparency during the voter registration process and in election campaign investments can be effective methods against electoral integrity and support in elevating public trust. Government and non-profitable organizations can strengthen electoral systems to better underpin citizen rights and freedom in the face of advanced security threats by focusing on safeguarding election integrity and democratic principles.

11.3.3.11 Data Privacy Regulations (DPR)

DPR deals with how voter information and personal data are collected, used, and responsibly handled in electronic voting systems during the election process. Consent with jurisdictional regulations is critical in shielding voter's privacy, hampering illegal access, and ensuring secured data. Privacy measures or breaches of DPR may create the risk that voter information is no longer private, confidential, integral and secure. Public confidence in electronic voting systems can be diminished if unauthorized access to voter data or a leak of personal information from the system occurs. Election administrators and technology vendors face compliance challenges in understanding mega-trends around various data privacy laws globally. Robust privacy policies are also necessary to maintain transparency and data minimization in collecting voter data.

Solutions – Voter data can be well protected and in compliance with all relevant DPR by using one or more of several different kinds of privacy-enhancing technologies like encryption, anonymized actions for voter identities, and access control. Performing audits, privacy impact assessments, and cantilever monitoring of data handling practices also help reduce privacy risks and bring more transparency. By prioritizing compliance with privacy laws and adopting privacy-preserving measures, election administrators can uphold the confidentiality and integrity of voter information.

11.3.3.12 Digital Security of Voter Registration Systems

Voter registration systems store and manage voter registration data, including personal information, eligibility status, and voting history. Securing voter registration systems against cyber threats, data breaches, or unauthorized access is essential for protecting voter privacy and election integrity. Vulnerabilities in voter registration systems may expose voter data to unauthorized access, manipulation, or theft. Breaches of voter registration databases, identity theft, or fraud can compromise the accuracy, integrity, and security of electoral rolls and voter information. Ensuring the digital security of voter registration systems requires implementing robust access controls, encryption, and monitoring mechanisms. Addressing vulnerabilities, such as outdated software, weak passwords, or insider threats, poses technical, operational, and governance challenges for election administrators.

Solution – Adopting cybersecurity best practices, such as regular security updates, vulnerability assessments, and staff training, can help strengthen the digital security of voter registration systems. Implementing multi-factor authentication, audit trails, and encryption techniques can mitigate risks and enhance data protection. By prioritizing cybersecurity measures and investing in digital security infrastructure, election administrators can safeguard voter data and maintain the trust and confidence of voters.

11.3.3.13 Software Tampering

EVMs with the software can be tampered with by injecting malicious code that can alter the vote count or favour a candidate in any way. Since private companies manufacture these EVMs, neither the software is available to test the reliability nor allowed to public access [12].

11.3.3.14 Hardware Tampering

EVM needs a smart card to activate the machine and start voting. However, a fraudulent smart card could attempt to access voting multiple times, or even sometimes, a smart card can be pre-loaded with votes favouring a person.

11.3.3.15 Internet Attacks

Once the elections are complete, election data is transferred to the vote counting authority or CU over the Internet. During this transfer, there is a high chance for cyberattacks such as man-in-the-middle attacks, data theft, distributed denial of service, leak operations, etc. Table 11.1 depicts various threat vectors that affect the elections on a scale of 0 to 5, with 0 being less and five being highly influential [13].

Figure 11.3 demonstrates the possible cyberattacks on the voting machines, and the potential results are also shown. Since most of the attacks are cyber-based, digital forensics (DF) plays a vital role in identifying the source of attack, cause of attack, and eradication of the future attacks. The following section provides the importance of DF in E-voting.

TABLE 11.1
Various Threat Vectors Affecting Free and Fair Elections

Threat Vectors	Effect on Voters	Effect on Voting Officials	Effect on Voting Machines
Data theft	1	1	4
Unauthorized access	3	1	5
Cyber threats	0	0	5
Denial of service attacks	5	2	5
Hacking and leaking operations	5	1	5
Network intrusion	5	0	5
Destruction of data	0	0	5
Insider threat	1	0	5
State-sponsored cyber threats	0	0	5
Infrastructure attacks	0	0	5

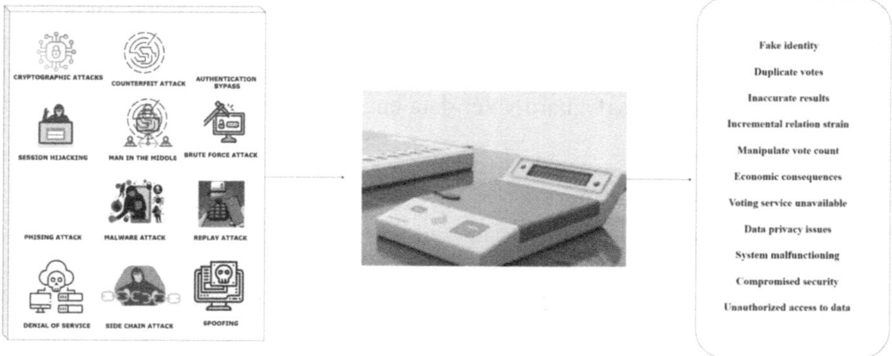

FIGURE 11.3 Possible attacks on the EVMs and the outcomes.

11.4 ROLE OF DIGITAL FORENSICS IN ELECTIONS

DF is a branch of forensic science that focuses on recovering and investigating material found in digital devices involved in cybercrimes either directly or indirectly [14, 15].

DF consists of seven phases broadly but is categorized into five phases [16].

- Identification
- Collection and preservation
- Analysis
- Documentation
- Preservation

DF is crucial for investigating tampering with EVMs and ensuring election processes' integrity, security, accountability, and credibility. This section presents the role of DF in EVMs in the case of any cyberattack. Furthermore, we highlight the problems, challenges, and possible solutions for each phase of DF.

11.4.1 Identification

The role of DF investigators is to identify the EVM which is suspected to be tampered with. Identifying the source of tampering when an EVM is suspected will be challenging, especially if it involves sophisticated manipulation which changes the internal components or software within the EVM. These results can be used in evidence to show that the device was tampered with and, further, leverage this data for DF analysis, which could encounter challenges such as obtaining access to a tampered EVM, ensuring the integrity of collected evidence or analysing complex digital footprints so as to reconstruct events temporally after the EVM tampering. Due to the investigator's safe, fair and unbiased contribution, the election's integrity is endorsed.

11.4.2 Evidence Collection

Digital forensic experts are responsible for collecting and preserving digital evidence related to tampered EVMs in a forensically sound manner. This involves documenting the state of the EVM, capturing volatile data, and securing physical components for analysis. The major challenge in this phase lies in maintaining the integrity and authenticity of digital evidence while ensuring no data is lost or altered during the process. Challenges may include volatile data loss, data contamination, and the need to adhere to strict legal and procedural requirements. One possible solution to this phase is using sophisticated DF tools and techniques to collect and preserve the evidence so that forensic experts can establish the credibility and reliability of their findings in court.

11.4.3 Analysis

Digital forensic experts analyse digital artefacts from tampered EVMs or digital devices to identify signs of tampering, manipulation, or unauthorized access. This involves examining system logs, configuration settings, and other digital traces left behind by the tampering activity. However, the challenge in analysing digital artefacts is distinguishing between legitimate system activities and malicious tampering, especially if the tampering was carefully concealed or designed to evade detection. Furthermore, interpreting complex data structures, reconstructing the timeline of events, and correlating digital evidence to establish a coherent narrative of the tampering incident is quite challenging to the investigators. By meticulously examining digital evidence, forensic experts can piece together the sequence of events leading to the tampering and provide valuable insights into the nature and scope of the incident.

11.4.4 Reporting

DF experts may be called upon to provide expert testimony and prepare detailed reports on their findings regarding tampered EVMs. Their testimony explains technical aspects of the investigation to non-technical stakeholders, such as judges, juries, or election oversight bodies. The major challenge during this phase is to provide expert testimony by effectively communicating complex technical concepts and forensic findings clearly and understandably. It also includes challenges such as presenting evidence in legal proceedings, responding to cross-examination, and ensuring that the court or relevant authorities fully comprehend the significance of forensic findings. Finally, this phase includes preparing comprehensive reports documenting the methodologies, key findings, and conclusions in a format accessible to non-technical audiences.

11.4.5 Chain of Custody Management

Apart from the above phases, the following sub-sections also demonstrate the role of DF in elections.

DF experts are responsible for maintaining the chain of custody for all evidence collected during the investigation of tampered EVMs. This involves documenting evidence's handling, storage, and transfer to ensure its integrity and admissibility in legal proceedings. Since many individuals are involved independently, ensuring they adhere to strict protocols and procedures to prevent tampering, loss, or contamination is a great challenge. Furthermore, tracking multiple pieces of evidence, coordinating with various stakeholders, and maintaining accurate records of evidence movements and transfers is arduous. To overcome a few problems in this area, experts establish a robust chain of custody procedures, including tamper-evident packaging, secure storage facilities, and documented sign-in/sign-out logs by training responsible persons. By implementing rigorous protocols and procedures, forensic experts ensure that evidence remains secure and untainted throughout the investigation.

11.4.6 Collaboration with Law Enforcement

DF experts collaborate with law enforcement agencies to provide technical assistance and participate in joint investigative efforts. However, coordinating efforts across different agencies and jurisdictions, each with its own investigative priorities and legal frameworks is a significant challenge. One possible solution is establishing formal communication channels and cooperation with law enforcement agencies to align objectives, share resources, and coordinate investigative activities. By working together effectively, DF experts and law enforcement agencies can enhance the chances of identifying and holding perpetrators accountable for their actions.

11.4.7 Public Awareness and Education

DF experts play a role in raising public awareness and educating stakeholders about the importance of DF in safeguarding the integrity of electoral processes. Their role involves communicating the value of forensic investigations in detecting and deterring tampering with EVMs. However, reaching diverse audiences, including voters, election officials, and policymakers, with targeted messages about the role and significance of DF in ensuring electoral integrity. Public awareness and education are essential for fostering trust and confidence in the electoral process. By engaging with stakeholders and communicating the value of DF in detecting and deterring tampering with EVMs, forensic experts help build resilience against threats to electoral integrity.

11.4.8 International Collaboration

DF experts may engage in international collaboration to address tampering with EVMs that have cross-border implications. Their role involves working with counterparts in other countries to share intelligence, expertise, and resources to investigate and combat electoral fraud. Overcoming legal, cultural, and logistical barriers to information sharing and cooperation between countries with varying legal frameworks is a significant challenge for the DF domain. Further challenges also include diplomatic sensitivities, reconciling differences in investigative procedures and standards, and establishing trust and rapport with foreign counterparts. To overcome such problems, DF experts can leverage existing international networks, such as Interpol, Europol, and regional law enforcement alliances participate in joint investigations, intelligence-sharing initiatives, and capacity-building efforts to strengthen cross-border cooperation.

11.5 CONCLUSION

This chapter presents in-depth information on digital voting, EVM, and its components. Apart from the general information, this chapter mainly contributes to in-depth issues and the challenges that digital voting mediums or EVMs face. Furthermore, we also present the optimal solutions to overcome the root issues found in digital voting. Additionally, this chapter identifies and presents various possible cyberattacks on digital voting machines and EVMs and depicts the outcomes of the attacks. When any such attack happens on the voting machines, DF plays a vital role in judicially identifying, acquiring, analysing, and presenting the report. For this, we discussed the role of DF and cybersecurity elaborately so that, by incorporating the solutions offered in this chapter, cyberattacks can be prevented soon. Together, cybersecurity and DF contribute to free and fair elections, reinforcing the democratic foundation and upholding citizens' rights by safeguarding the integrity of elections. Their continuous improvement is essential to maintain the integrity of our electoral systems.

REFERENCES

1. Dahl, Robert A., and Margaret Levi. "A conversation with Robert A. Dahl." Annual Review of Political Science 12, no. 1 (2009): 1–9.
2. Finkelman, Paul, ed. Encyclopedia of American Civil Liberties. Routledge, 2013.
3. Bader, Max. "OSCE electoral assistance and the role of election commissions." Security and Human Rights 23, no. 1 (2012): 19–29.
4. Garnett, Holly Ann, and Toby S. James. "Cyber elections in the digital age: threats and opportunities of technology for electoral integrity." Election Law Journal: Rules, Politics, and Policy 19, no. 2 (2020): 111–126.
5. Coppedge, Michael, John Gerring, Carl Henrik Knutsen, Staffan I. Lindberg, Jan Teorell, Lisa Gastaldi, Ana Good God, and Sandra Grahn. "V-Dem Country Coding Units v14." V-Dem Working Paper Forthcoming (2024).
6. Agate, Vincenzo, Alessandra De Paola, Pierluca Ferraro, Giuseppe Lo Re, and Marco Morana. "SecureBallot: A secure open source e-voting system." Journal of Network and Computer Applications 191 (2021): 103165.
7. Butler, Alan. "Election Cybersecurity Amid a Global Pandemic." Human Rights 45, no. 3 (2020): 9–11.
8. Muller, S. Raschid, Darrell Norman Burrell, Calvin Nobles, Horace C. Mingo, and Andreas Vassilakos. "Exploring cybersecurity, misinformation, and interference in voting and elections through cyberspace." In Effective Cybersecurity Operations for Enterprise-Wide Systems, pp. 221–241. IGI Global, 2023.
9. Pope, Amy E. "Cybersecuring our elections." Journal of Cyber Policy 3, no. 1 (2018): 24–38.
10. Marwala, Tshilidzi. "Cybersecurity in politics." In Artificial Intelligence, Game Theory and Mechanism Design in Politics, pp. 135–155. Singapore: Springer Nature Singapore, 2023.

11. Farooq, Muhammad Shoaib, Usman Iftikhar, and Adel Khelifi. "A framework to make voting system transparent using blockchain technology." IEEE Access 10 (2022): 59959–59969.
12. Feldman, Ariel J., J. Alex Halderman, and Edward W. Felten. "Security analysis of the Diebold AccuVote-TS voting machine." In Proceedings of the USENIX Workshop on Accurate Electronic Voting Technology (EVT'07). USENIX Association, USA (2007).
13. Google Cloud Blog. "Google Cloud Blog," n.d. https://cloud.google.com/blog/topics/threat-intelligence/understand_action%20intelligence-information-operations.
14. Beebe, Nicole. "Digital forensic research: The good, the bad and the unaddressed." In Advances in Digital Forensics V: Fifth IFIP WG 11.9 International Conference on Digital Forensics, Orlando, Florida, USA, January 26–28, 2009, Revised Selected Papers 5, pp. 17–36. Springer Berlin Heidelberg, 2009.
15. Garfinkel, Simson L. "Digital forensics research: The next 10 years." Digital Investigation 7 (2010): S64–S73.
16. Paul Joseph, D., and Jasmine Norman. "An analysis of digital forensics in cybersecurity." In First International Conference on Artificial Intelligence and Cognitive Computing: AICC 2018, pp. 701–708. Springer Singapore, 2019.

12 Cybersecurity and Forensics for Migration and Citizenship Issues

Gopichand Vemulapalli, Saydulu Kolasani, Anumaan Whig, and Pawan Whig

12.1 INTRODUCTION

In the present interconnect, development and citizenship processes are crucial pieces of overall elements and societies [1]. As individuals search for better entryways, they cross limits and relationship to regulate complex movement and citizenship frameworks. Regardless, amidst these cycles lie different troubles. In this way, the blend of organization security and lawful sciences emerges as need might arise to protect these techniques and keep up with the genuineness of movement and citizenship structures [2].

12.1.1 Migration and Citizenship Processes

Movement and citizenship processes include an expansive range of exercises, going from visa applications and boundary control to naturalization and citizenship services. These cycles are administered by public and worldwide regulations which fluctuate fundamentally across locales. Headways in innovation have altered these cycles and data trade between partners. Understanding the complexities of relocation and citizenship techniques is fundamental for grasping the weaknesses that digital dangers posture to these frameworks [3].

12.1.2 Cybersecurity and Forensics

The significance of online protection and legal sciences in movement and citizenship processes couldn't possibly be more significant. As these cycles progressively depend on computerized foundations, they become vulnerable to different digital dangers. Unapproved admittance to delicate data can think twice about classification accessibility of information and surprisingly, public safety gambles. Also, the ramifications of safety breaks reach out past people to influence legislatures featuring the direness of carrying out strong network protection measures and criminological strategies to alleviate gambles and guarantee trust in movement and citizenship frameworks [4–7].

DOI: 10.1201/9781003497868-12

12.1.3 Scope of the Chapter

This part expects to dive into the crossing point of network safety and citizenship, investigating the difficulties, methodologies, and arrangements relevant to defending these cycles in the computerized age. It will look at the advancing scene of movement and citizenship, dissecting the job of innovation in forming these elements. It will explain the weaknesses intrinsic in movement and citizenship frameworks, clarifying the digital dangers and measurable difficulties looked by partners. The section proposes best practices to upgrade network protection strength in this way guaranteeing the honesty of movement and citizenship processes [8, 9]. The literate review with research gap is shown in Table 12.1.

12.2 CHALLENGES

As movement and citizenship processes become progressively digitized, they experience a heap of network protection challenges that undermine the respectability of these frameworks. Understanding and addressing these difficulties are basic to defending delicate data, keeping up with administrative consistency in public trust. This segment investigates three noticeable network protection challenges experienced in movement and citizenship frameworks:

12.2.1 Identity Theft and Fraudulent Activities

Personality fake exercises present critical dangers to relocation and citizenship frameworks. Vindictive entertainers might take advantage of weaknesses in advanced stages to take individual data for illegal purposes. Such exercises not just trade off the character and protection of people yet additionally sabotage the honesty of the whole framework. Fraud can lead to financial losses and damage to reputation for the two people and associations engaged with movement and citizenship processes [10].

12.2.2 Data Breaches and Privacy Concerns

Information breaks address a grave danger to movement and citizenship frameworks, presenting delicate data to unapproved access. Whether its very own information submitted during visa applications, biometric records put away in migration data sets connected with citizenship procedures, the openness of such data can have extensive results. Past monetary ramifications of information breaks dissolve public trust and may bring about legitimate punishments for resistance [11].

12.2.3 Threats to Border Security and Immigration Controls

Digital dangers additionally reach out to the domain of line security and migration controls, where malignant entertainers might take advantage of weaknesses in advanced foundation to evade line checks. Such breaks sabotage public safety as well as risk public security by empowering unapproved people to enter or leave a nation undetected. Besides digital assaults focusing on movement controls can upset

TABLE 12.1
Literature Review in Tabular Form with Research Gap

Reference	Main Points	Research Gap
[2]	Provides essentials for cybersecurity, emphasizing protection against cyber threats.	The specific challenges and solutions for cybersecurity in different organizational contexts are not deeply explored.
[3]	Focuses on digital evidence and computer crime, delving into forensic techniques and their application in legal contexts.	There is a lack of recent updates on emerging digital crime trends and corresponding forensic methodologies.
[4]	Examines the EU's Digital Agenda with a focus on cybersecurity and fundamental rights in telecommunications law.	The effectiveness of existing EU cybersecurity policies and their alignment with evolving technological advancements needs further investigation.
[7]	Reviews the evolution and current state of digital forensics, highlighting its importance in cybersecurity.	Future directions for advancing digital forensic techniques to keep pace with rapidly evolving cyber threats are not thoroughly explored.
[9]	Explores vulnerabilities, threats, and attacks in the Internet of Things (IoT) landscape, emphasizing cybersecurity challenges.	Strategies for mitigating IoT-related cyber threats and ensuring the security of interconnected devices require further investigation.
[10]	Discusses digital forensics and cybercrime, presenting research papers from an international conference, offering insights into recent advancements.	The gap between academic research presented at conferences and its practical implementation in cybercrime investigations needs to be bridged.
[13]	Introduces the Framework for Improving Critical Infrastructure Cybersecurity, providing guidelines for enhancing cybersecurity resilience.	The implementation challenges and real-world effectiveness of the NIST framework across different sectors and organizations require examination.
[17]	Addresses various aspects of cybercrime, including definitions, types, and global responses, highlighting the need for international cooperation.	Strategies for enhancing international collaboration and standardizing legal frameworks to combat cybercrime need further exploration.
[19]	Explores principles of cybercrime, offering insights into the legal and technical aspects of cybercriminal activities and investigations.	The evolving nature of cybercrime and its implications for law enforcement agencies and legal systems require ongoing analysis and adaptation.
[22]	Focuses on migration and development, emphasizing the socio-economic impacts of migration and the need for sustainable development strategies.	The role of cybersecurity in protecting migrant data and ensuring the security of migration-related systems and infrastructure warrants investigation.

fundamental administrations strain assets, in this manner blocking the powerful administration of relocation streams and line tasks. Tending to these network safety challenges requires an all-encompassing methodology that consolidates mechanical developments. By moderating the dangers related with fraud to line partners can upgrade the versatility and adequacy of movement and citizenship frameworks in an undeniably interconnected world [12–15].

12.3 DIGITAL FORENSICS TECHNIQUES

In the domain of cybersecurity, digital forensics plays a crucial role in investigating cyber incidents. This part investigates three basic advanced legal sciences strategies utilized in examining digital occurrences.

12.3.1 Digital Evidence Collection and Preservation

The most vital phase in advanced legal sciences is the precise assortment and safeguarding of computerized proof. This interaction includes recognizing and getting likely wellsprings of proof, for example, PCs [16]. Computerized proof should be gathered in a forensically sound way to guarantee its honesty and suitability in legal procedures. Strategies, for example, making criminological pictures of capacity gadgets, recording the chain of guardianship, and utilizing compose hindering devices to forestall information altering are fundamental for protecting the evidentiary worth of computerized antiques. Appropriate documentation and metadata investigation are basic for laying out the specific circumstance and validness of computerized proof during measurable assessment [17].

12.3.2 Data Recovery and Analysis

When computerized proof is gathered and safeguarded, legal examiners continue with information recuperation and investigation to separate important data connected with the digital occurrence. This includes utilizing specific devices and methods to recuperate erased files activities paving the way to and following the episode [18, 19]. Record cutting are normal strategies used to distinguish dubious relics. Criminological examination might include analyzing network traffic, memory dumps, and filesystem metadata to reveal hints of interruption, information exfiltration, or malware spread. Through extensive information examination, measurable specialists can recreate the arrangement of occasions, decide the extent of the digital occurrence, and trait pernicious exercises to explicit entertainers or danger entertainers [20].

12.3.3 Attribution and Incident Response

Attribution is a basic part of digital occurrence reaction, as it includes distinguishing the people, gatherings, or elements liable for executing the digital assault. Computerized criminology procedures assume a critical part in attribution by examining computerized proof, recognizing marks of give and take Indicators of Compromise (IOCs), and following the beginning of noxious exercises back to their source [21–23]. This might include relating scientific discoveries with danger knowledge, directing malware examination, and teaming up with policing or network safety specialists to recognize and capture cybercriminals. Incident response groups leverage forensic insights to contain the impact of the digital incident, remediate security vulnerabilities, and implement measures to prevent future attacks. By coordinating advanced criminology into occurrence reaction techniques can improve their capacity to distinguish episodes actually [24].

Computerized criminology procedures are irreplaceable for researching digital episode and crediting malignant exercises to their culprits. By utilizing progressed measurable apparatuses and methodologies can upgrade their digital flexibility and reinforce their capacity to battle developing digital dangers in the present advanced scene [25].

12.4 CASE STUDIES IN CYBERSECURITY AND FORENSICS FOR MIGRATION AND CITIZENSHIP

The crossing point of network protection and criminology with movement and citizenship processes presents a novel arrangement of difficulties. This part looks at three convincing contextual analyses that represent the basic job of network protection and computerized legal sciences in defending movement:

12.4.1 Identity Theft in Citizenship Applications

In a nation encountering a flood in citizenship applications, specialists saw a disturbing pattern of data fraud influencing the honesty of the naturalization cycle. Thought people were submitting deceitful reports and individual data to acquire citizenship unlawfully in the computerized application framework.

Computerized criminology specialists were called upon to research the episodes of wholesale fraud and decide the degree of the break. Through measurable examination of utilization data sets, specialists distinguished shared characteristics among false applications and followed them back to a modern cybercriminal network working internationally. By teaming up with policing and executing improved validation measures, specialists had the option to alleviate the gamble of data fraud and fortify the security of the citizenship application process.

The examination prompted the anxiety and arraignment of people engaged with the data fraud conspire, in this way protecting the honesty of the citizenship framework and reestablishing public confidence in the naturalization cycle.

12.4.2 Cyberattacks on Immigration Databases

A progression of digital assaults designated the data sets of a public movement organization, bringing about unapproved admittance to delicate data, including visa records. The assaults disturbed migration tasks, endangering line security and causing public worry over the well-being and protection of individual information.

Computerized criminology groups were assembled to research the digital assaults, distinguish the weaknesses took advantage of by danger entertainers, and evaluate the degree of information split the difference. Measurable investigation uncovered proof of complex malware diseases, insider dangers, and double-dealing of obsolete programming frameworks. By conducting memory forensics, network bundle examination, and malware picking apart investigators gained insights into the tactics, techniques, and procedures (TTPs) used by the attackers.

The criminological examination empowered the movement organization to carry out remediation measures, upgrade online protection guards, and further develop episode reaction abilities. Cooperation with network safety specialists and danger knowledge suppliers helped characteristic the digital assaults to a country state entertainer, provoking strategic reactions and conciliatory endeavors to address the hidden international pressures.

12.4.3 Digital Forensics Investigations in Immigration Fraud Cases

An expansion in movement misrepresentation cases provoked migration specialists to use advanced criminology strategies to explore false exercises, including report fabrication, visa extortion, and illegal exploitation. Thought people were taking advantage of weaknesses in the migration framework to sidestep security checks and gain unlawful passage into the country.

Computerized criminology examinations were led to break down electronic proof, for example, produced archives, correspondence logs, and monetary exchanges, connected to movement extortion plans. Scientific analysts used legal imaging examination to recreate advanced trails, reveal stowed away resources, and distinguish culprits associated with coordinated criminal organizations.

The scientific discoveries gave significant proof to policing to arraign individuals engaged in immigration fraud and illicit migration channels. The experiences acquired from computerized criminology examinations informed arrangement changes, line security improvements, and global collaboration endeavors to battle transnational coordinated wrongdoing and illegal exploitation.

These contextual analyses feature the diverse idea of network safety and advanced criminology in tending to the complicated difficulties presented by relocation and citizenship processes.

12.5 LEGAL AND ETHICAL CONSIDERATIONS

The convergence of network safety, computerized criminology, relocation, and citizenship delivers a bunch of legitimate and moral contemplations. In exploring this, it is essential for partners to stick to worldwide legitimate framework strike a fragile harmony between security objectives and protection freedoms. This part looks at three critical elements of legitimate and moral contemplations:

12.5.1 International Legal Frameworks and Regulations

Movement and citizenship processes are represented by a complicated trap of global settlements, shows, and arrangements that lay out lawful standards and norms for the insurance of common freedoms, protection, and information security. Global associations like the Assembled Countries (UN), the Worldwide Association for

Movement (IOM), and the Global Common Flight Association (ICAO) assume a huge part in molding these legitimate structures.

12.5.2 Moral Issues in Digital Examinations

The lead of digital examinations with regard to movement and citizenship raises a host of ethical considerations, including the need to avoid undue harm and uphold professional integrity. Forensic professionals must adhere to ethical codes established by organizations such as the International Association of Computer Investigative Specialists (IACIS), the International Society of Forensic Computer Examiners (ISFCE), and the American Academy of Forensic Sciences (AAFS).

12.5.3 Adjusting Security and Protection Privileges

Accomplishing a harmony between security goals and protection freedoms is maybe the most squeezing challenge in the domain of network safety and movement. While strong network safety measures are fundamental for shielding movement and citizenship frameworks from vindictive entertainers, they should be carried out in a way that regards people's more right than wrong to security and information security. Tending to lawful and moral contemplations is fundamental for guaranteeing the honesty, network safety, and criminology rehearses in movement and citizenship frameworks. By sticking to global lawful structures, maintaining moral guidelines, and cultivating a culture of responsibility, partners can explore the mind-boggling difficulties innate in this space while shielding the freedoms and nobility of people impacted by movement processes.

12.6 COLLABORATION AND INFORMATION SHARING

Strong joint exertion and information sharing are the central help focuses for keeping an eye on the assorted troubles in network security. This part explores three basic pieces of facilitated exertion and information sharing:

12.6.1 Interagency Cooperation and Associations

Concerning migration and citizenship, interagency support and affiliations expect a crucial part in developing coordination among various government workplaces, policing, and worldwide affiliations drew in with supervising development streams and ensuring line security. By sharing information, resources, and authority, associations can redesign their abilities for perceiving, preventing, and noting computerized risks, character distortion, and other unlawful activities. Interagency groups, joint undertakings spots, and information sharing stages work with continuous correspondence engaging accomplices to address emerging challenges effectively.

12.6.2 Worldwide Joint Exertion on Organization Well-being Drives

Computerized risks transcend public lines, requiring worldwide joint exertion. In the space of organization assurance, worldwide drives proportional and multilateral game plans work with information exchange, joint assessments, and normal assistance with noting advanced episodes with crossline ideas. By using overall associations and using shared resources, countries can invigorate their flexibility against computerized risks and ease threats to migration and citizenship structures on an overall scale.

12.6.3 Recommended Systems Sharing and Cutoff Building

Sharing recommended methods and breaking point building are basic pieces of agreeable undertakings to redesign network security flexibility and logical capacities in development and citizenship systems. Drives, for instance, getting ready studios, data sharing social occasions, and joint exercises work with the exchanging of capacity, delineations learned, and innovative plans among subject matter experts. Furthermore, public-private affiliations engage the secret region to contribute development, resources, and pieces of information to help government attempts in protecting fundamental system, getting progressed organizes, and fighting cybercrime. By placing assets into diligent learning accomplices can build major areas of strength for a power outfitted with the data and capacities expected to address creating computerized risks, as a matter of fact.

Joint exertion is fundamental for keeping an eye on the multifaceted hardships at the intersection point of organization insurance. By developing interagency investment, overall composed exertion, and data exchange, accomplices can support their total response to advanced risks and keep up with the opportunities and pride of individuals influenced by development processes.

12.7 FUTURE TRENDS AND CHALLENGES

As innovation proceeds to progress and worldwide relocation designs develop, the crossing point of online protection will confront a bunch of future patterns and difficulties. This segment looks at three vital elements of future patterns and difficulties.

12.7.1 Arising Advances and Developments

The quick speed of mechanical advancement will drive huge changes in relocation and citizenship frameworks, introducing the two valuable open doors and difficulties. Arising innovations will upset character check, line the executives, and migration processes. Simulated intelligence fueled chatbots will improve client support and smooth out visa applications, while blockchain-based personality, the board frameworks will give secure and sealed advanced certifications.

12.7.2 Advancing Danger Scene

The advancing danger scene presents critical difficulties to the security and uprightness of relocation and citizenship frameworks. Cybercriminals, state-supported entertainers, and coordinated criminal organizations will keep on taking advantage of weaknesses in advanced foundations, focusing on delicate data. Advanced

TABLE 12.2
Quantitative Results

Key Findings	Percentage of Respondents (%)
Awareness and Importance	
- Acknowledgment of cybersecurity and digital forensics	87
- Perception of cybersecurity risks in migration processes	72
- Recognition of the role of digital forensics	68
Challenges and Vulnerabilities	
- Identity theft and fraudulent activities	64
- Data breaches and privacy concerns	58
- Concerns about cyberattacks on immigration databases	76
Collaboration and Capacity Building	
- Importance of interagency cooperation and partnerships	82
- Emphasis on international collaboration	68
- Need for sharing best practices and capacity building	76
Policy Implications	
- Call for prioritizing data protection laws and standards	79
- Recommendation for investing in cybersecurity education	72
- Urging policymakers to balance security with privacy rights	68

Persistent Threats (APTs) will pose significant risks to immigration databases, border control systems, and identity verification platforms.

12.7.3 Approach Suggestions and Proposals

The powerful idea of relocation and citizenship processes expects policymakers to expect future patterns and difficulties and adjust administrative structures in like manner. Strategy suggestions incorporate fortifying information insurance regulations, upgrading network safety norms, and elevating global participation to address transnational digital dangers. Suggestions for policymakers remember financial planning for online protection schooling and preparing programs, cultivating public-private organizations, and advancing data dividing and best practices spread between partners.

Tending to future patterns and difficulties in the convergence of network protection requires proactive measures, cooperative endeavors, and groundbreaking strategies. Quantitative results are mentioned in Table 12.2.

12.8 CONCLUSION

The crossing point of online protection gives an intricate and dynamic scene diverse difficulties and open doors. The reconciliation of innovation into relocation processes has upset how people get across borders, yet it has likewise uncovered weaknesses that vindictive entertainers exploit for detestable purposes. Digital dangers, for example, fraud, information breaks, and digital assaults on movement data sets present huge dangers to the uprightness, security, and reliability of relocation and citizenship frameworks.

Proactive measures and strategies can mitigate these risks and improve the strength of relocation and citizenship frameworks. By advancing interagency participations can fortify their aggregate reaction to digital dangers and encourage a culture of network safety mindfulness and readiness.

REFERENCES

1. Böcker, A., Vitoroulis, I., & Wissink, H. (2019). The Migration Crisis, EU Solidarity and the Rule of Law: Is There Still a Common European Asylum Policy? In The Rule of Law in the European Union (pp. 193–214). Springer.
2. Buchta, J. (2021). Cybersecurity Essentials: Protect your Organization from Cyber Threats. Packt Publishing Ltd.
3. Casey, E. (2011). Digital Evidence and Computer Crime: Forensic Science, Computers, and the Internet. Academic Press.
4. Dörr, S. (2016). The European Union's Digital Agenda: Cybersecurity and Fundamental Rights Protection in Telecommunications Law. Journal of Intellectual Property, Information Technology and Electronic Commerce Law, 7(3), 232–243.
5. European Union Agency for Cybersecurity (ENISA). (2020). Good Practices for Protecting the Digital Identity of Citizens. https://digital-strategy.ec.europa.eu/en/library/eidas-compliant-eid-solutions-report-enisa?utm_source=chatgpt.com
6. Federal Bureau of Investigation (FBI). (2020, September 16). FBI strategy addresses evolving cyber threat. https://www.fbi.gov/news/stories/wray-announces-fbi-cyberstrategy-at-cisa-summit-091620.
7. Goode, E. (2020). The Future of Digital Forensics: A Review of Its Evolution, Current State, and Requirements for Cybersecurity. Digital Investigation, 34, 101902.
8. Kajzer, M., & Piotrowski, P. (2018). Digital Forensics for Cybersecurity and Privacy: 12th International Workshop, D-For 2018, Regensburg, Germany, July 3–6, 2018, Revised Selected Papers. Springer.
9. Kierkegaard, S. (2017). Cybersecurity and the Internet of Things: Vulnerabilities, Threats, Intruders, and Attacks. CRC Press.
10. Lee, S. M. (2020). Digital Forensics and Cyber Crime: Seventh International Conference, ICDF2C 2015, Seoul, South Korea, October 6–8, 2015, Revised Selected Papers. Springer.
11. Lewis, J. A. (2018, February 21). Economic Impact of Cybercrime – No Slowing Down. Center for Strategic and International Studies & McAfee. https://www.csis.org/analysis/economic-impact-cybercrime
12. Batalova, J. (2021). Frequently Requested Statistics on Immigrants and Immigration in the United States. Migration Policy Institute. https://www.migrationpolicy.org/article/frequently-requested-statistics-immigrants-and-immigration-united-states-2021
13. Barrett, M. P. (2018, April 16). Framework for Improving Critical Infrastructure Cybersecurity (Version 1.1). National Institute of Standards and Technology. https://doi.org/10.6028/NIST.CSWP.04162018.
14. Framework for Improving Critical Infrastructure Cybersecurity, Version 1.1 (PDF)
15. Rouse, M. (2020). *Identity theft*. TechTarget. https://www.techtarget.com/searchsecurity/definition/identity-theft
16. Savage, S. J., & Schwartz, P. M. (2021). The Future of Forensic DNA Testing: Predictions of the Research and Development Working Group.
17. United Nations Office on Drugs and Crime (UNODC). (2019). Global Programme on Cybercrime: Progress Report 2013–2019. Vienna: United Nations. Retrieved from https://www.unodc.org/documents/organized-crime/cybercrime/CYBERCRIME_REPORT_2013-2019.pdf

18. United States Department of Homeland Security (DHS). (2021, April 7). *CISA* 2020 Year in Review. Cybersecurity and Infrastructure Security Agency. https://www.cisa.gov/resources-tools/resources/cisa-2020-year-review
19. Van der Merwe, A., & O'Connor, K. (2016). Principles of Cybercrime. Cambridge University Press.
20. Wang, D., & Liu, P. (2017). Digital Forensics and Cyber Crime: 13th International Conference, ICDF2C 2018, New Orleans, LA, USA, September 10–12, 2018, Revised Selected Papers. Springer.
21. Bowen, P., Hash, J., & Wilson, M. (2006). Information Security Handbook: A Guide for Managers (NIST Special Publication 800-100). National Institute of Standards and Technology. https://csrc.nist.gov/pubs/sp/800/100/upd1/final
22. World Bank. (2021, November). Migration and Development Brief 35. Migration and Remittances Unit. https://www.worldbank.org/en/topic/socialprotectionandjobs/publication/migration-and-development-brief-35
23. Xiong, K., Yang, B., & Zhong, Y. (2021). Cybersecurity and Privacy in Cyber-Physical Systems: Foundations, Principles, and Applications. CRC Press.
24. Yoo, J., & Kim, H. (2018). Digital Forensics and Cybersecurity for Modeling and Simulation. IEEE Access, 6, 61897–61906.
25. Zeadally, S., Badra, M., & Shabut, A. M. (2021). Cybersecurity and Privacy in the Cloud. CRC Press.

13 Cybersecurity and Forensics for Multimedia Investigation

Surbhi Mathur and Anubhav Singh

13.1 INTRODUCTION TO CYBER AND MULTIMEDIA FORENSICS

The internet stands among the biggest innovations of the 21st century, deeply influencing our daily routine. It has broken down barriers and transformed how we communicate, play games, work, shop, make friends, listen to music, watch movies, order food, pay bills, and celebrate birthdays or anniversaries. Whatever we need, there's now an app for it. By making tasks easier, the internet has brought comfort and convenience. The days of waiting in long lines to purchase groceries or to pay electricity bills are over. Now, with just a click, we purchase anything and can make payments from the comfort of our home or office. With advancing technology, internet access is not limited to a computer. With internet-enabled smartphones, palmtops, and other devices, we can stay connected to friends, family, and work 24/7. The internet has not only made life more convenient but also made many things more affordable and accessible.

It has revolutionized communication, allowing us to connect with our relatives and friends through video conferencing using Skype, WhatsApp, Webex, Zoom, and Google Meet, all at very low costs. Televisions are no longer just for watching shows and movies; they can also be used for video calls and chatting with friends. Mobile phones have evolved beyond making calls to enable us to watch the latest movies. We can stay connected with others, regardless of our location. Working parents can monitor their children at home and assist with homework, while business owners can keep an eye on their staff, office, and stores with just a click. The internet has significantly improved our lives in various ways.

While there are many advantages of the internet in today's world, there are also several issues and difficulties that may impact individuals or society. The increasing presence of personal data on the internet has created numerous threats and challenges, such as data breaches, privacy breaches, circulation of fake information, online harassment, cyberbullying identity theft, and phishing attacks that can impact the overall well-being, security, and privacy of the individuals [1]. Therefore, the rise in cybercrimes has made it evident that suitable methods and techniques are required to properly investigate and counter these threats.

Both cyber forensics and multimedia forensics are significant branches of digital forensics that concentrate on distinct facets of gathering, evaluating, and preserving

DOI: 10.1201/9781003497868-13

evidence in the context of cybercrime investigations. *Cyber forensics* plays a crucial role in preventing and investigating hacking, malware attacks, network disruptions, network logs, and data breaches. It is particularly effective in situations where threat actors and cybercriminals exploit security vulnerabilities and attempt to hide their actions [2].

The techniques used in cyber forensics involve tracing the origin of an attack, understanding the attackers' methods, and identifying their malicious intentions. Professionals in this field are well-versed in cybersecurity laws and regulations, networking infrastructure, and the latest tactics employed by cybercriminals.

Analyzing digital information, available in the form of images, videos, and audio, is the main goal of *Multimedia forensics*. To solve cybercrimes, spot digital fraud, and confirm the legitimacy of multimedia information, this field is essential. The term "multimedia" is derived from the combination of "multi," which means "many," and "media" which means "communication." It includes the display of text, pictures, sound, and video as well as tools and links that let people navigate, engage, create, and communicate on a computer [3]. Multimedia is essentially the computer-assisted fusion of text, drawings, graphics, audio, animation, still and moving images (videos), and any other type of media that allows for the digital expression, storage, processing, and communication of information.

13.1.1 Need for Securing Digital Multimedia Assets

Security is increasingly becoming a pressing concern in a world that is increasingly defined by multimedia. The digital age has resulted in a significant increase in multimedia availability in the form of photographs, movies, audio recordings, and digital documents. The recent rise of multimedia applications, including mobile TV, video messaging, telemedicine, telebanking, teleshopping, etc. has heightened the influence of multimedia and its security on our daily lives [4].

As these capabilities evolve, they provide huge prospects for creativity, communication, and commerce nevertheless, this imaginative application also creates a logical breeding environment for cybercriminal activity. The rapid distribution of multimedia on the internet has become a significant tool for aiding harmful actions such as spreading rumors and phishing attacks (phishing); therefore, cybersecurity measures should be combined with techniques unique to any forensic analysis [5].

An incident was reported in the year 2020, where a bug in Google Photos gave unauthorized access to fraudsters to use the personal images of others without their consent. This security flaw sparked conversations about data privacy and user control over multimedia material by raising serious concerns about how shared albums were managed.

In the same year, one more incident came into existence involving a privacy breach on the data available on the Zoom platform. Even though Zoom is the best-known platform for video conferencing, it had several security problems, such as the Zoom bombing, which allowed private video footage to be shared during meetings without authorization, sparking questions concerning the management of multimedia data in online meetings [5].

Another popular incident reported in the year 2014 famously known as "The Fappening" case, involved a massive attack on the private iCloud accounts of numerous celebrities, causing their private images and videos to be leaked on sites like Reddit and 4chan. The incident sparked immense public outrage when these private audiovisual files were posted. The event brought to light cloud storage service's security flaws as well as how simple it is to steal and disseminate multimedia information without the owner's permission [6].

According to an IBM report in 2024, the average data breach cost in India has hit a record high of ₹19.5 crore in the current year. This marks a 39% increase since 2020 and a 9% rise compared to the previous year. In today's tech-driven world, as multimedia-based attacks have grown in scale and sophistication, there is a strong requirement to secure these digital assets, where large volumes of data and content are constantly created, shared, and stored online [6].

13.1.2 Multimedia Evidence in Crime Investigation

Modern crimes have emerged with the influence of technology, as the forms and trends in crimes have changed. Crime has escalated to a non-traditional nature due to technology, and criminals have become much more sophisticated and non-physical in their methods. It requires a new approach to solving crimes because these criminals plan their moves according to new techniques and strategies. Today, around 60% of evidence consists of digital data (CCTV footage, audio recordings, image and metadata, etc.), and all of these need to undergo examination and analysis as well. This necessitates skills that are more specialized and expertise in modern, unconventional technologies.

To adapt to the changing behavior of criminals and the evolution of crime, the future of forensic investigation is to modernize solutions to combat these "new age" crimes. A field within forensic science, multimedia forensics, is the scientific examination, authentication, and evaluation of multimedia evidence, such as audio, video, and images.

Multimedia forensics is one of those subfields within forensics that has a very close relation with computer forensics. Computer forensics extracts evidence from digital sources in a way that can be used in court through the use of investigative techniques, while multimedia forensics analyses the extracted evidence in the form of audio, video, images, or digital documents. This is the process of analyzing digital evidence, which is important to establish digital evidence integrity, source, and authenticity [7].

With heavy use of various technological devices ranging from the ubiquitous phone to the laptop means that it is very hard to go through a day without using such devices. Described as "medicine" for changemaker argonaut's minds, it offers both crime preemption and crime detection.

Multimedia forensics involves analyzing the digital fingerprints left on evidence to prevent and detect crime through the various software used in the processes to authenticate and scientifically examine digital materials. One alarming fact is that digital evidence, including images, audio, or video recordings, may not necessarily be authentic criminals tamper with this type of content to divert investigations [7]. Thus, validating evidence before being used is a vital part of the investigative process.

Many criminals utilize multimedia files such as to spread misinformation, carry out scams, and facilitate other illegal acts including but not limited to deepfake media content creation, cyberbullying, harassment, scam operations, intellectual property theft, sexual exploitation/traffic, terrorism, radicalization, etc.

However, there are many challenges a multimedia forensic expert may face when analyzing digital evidence. In many cases, the audio and video samples are corrupted and extremely low quality, making any extraction of information nearly impossible. These samples are of such quality that they represent a major hurdle for the experts. In addition, experts can be responsible for performing an analysis on thousands of samples, where they must screen each sample, and determine the areas of interest that can yield data and study areas—this is a long process that takes time and patience [7]. Sometimes, only a few words were recorded in the audio given to the experts to identify the source.

For a sheer number of crime scenes, another big challenge for multimedia experts is the improvement of low-quality pictures and videos we can get at the locality to recognize suspects. However, the images submitted for analysis are often of very low resolution and CCTV tracking footage taken from distant cameras does not allow proper understanding of the events. Additionally, it is no secret that camera placement is key in surveillance, and in many instances, the wrong placement of CCTV cameras prevents professionals from identifying culprits seen in footage presented in court [8].

For example, when investigating the 2011 serial bomb blasts in Mumbai, India, multimedia forensic specialists encountered several difficulties. CCTV footage from outside the car used in the attack, which authorities believe carried the explosives, was submitted to the court. Public CCTV footage of the vehicle was made available in case experts could find a way to identify the license plate. However, the experts were unable to enhance the number plate because the quality of the footage was quite low and the camera was badly positioned. However, the multimedia savants analyzed and covered various other concreted characteristics of said ships-in-suspection [9].

The growing concern over the integrity of the evidence presented in court has made this process even more crucial. To ensure that digital evidence is authentic and reliable, multimedia forensic experts provide authentication certificates, confirming the legal admissibility of such evidence in court.

13.2 EMERGING CYBER THREATS TARGETING DIGITAL CONTENTS

In today's digital age, cyber threats are becoming more frequent and complex. Cyberattacks are getting more sophisticated and affecting multimedia material more rapidly. These dangers aim to compromise the confidentiality, accessibility, and integrity of multimedia information, including documents, audio, video, and images [10]. These cyber threats are detrimental in several ways and may result in data breaches, which could cause data loss or modification. Some emerging cyber threats to multimedia content include the following:

a. ***Ransomware attacks***: Ransomware usually locks users out of their systems or personal files, blocking access until a ransom is paid to the attacker. If the ransom is not met, data may be permanently lost or, in some cases, publicly exposed. In recent years, the number of ransomware incidents has surged exponentially. Attackers have refined their methods, making their attacks more sophisticated and targeted [10].

   Although ransomware has dominated the headlines for the past five years, the concept of taking user files or computers hostage by encrypting files, restricting system access, or employing other methods has a long history.

   In the late 1980s, criminals were already encrypting files and demanding cash payments sent through the postal service. One of the earliest documented ransomware attacks was the AIDS Trojan (PC Cyborg Virus), which was distributed via floppy disk in 1989. Victims were instructed to send $189 to a P.O. Box in Panama to regain access to their systems, even though the virus itself was relatively simple and used symmetric cryptography.

   Targets of these attacks can be either generalized or specific, focusing on individuals, organizations, or countries that speak a particular language. Typically, the ransom is requested in the form of cryptocurrency. The NCC Group's Global Threat Intelligence team reported a historic high of 502 ransomware attacks in July 2023, marking a 16% increase from the 434 attacks recorded in June 2023 and more than double the number of attacks seen in July 2022. Additionally, Malwarebytes' "2023 State of Ransomware" report revealed that there was a total of 1,900 ransomware attacks across four countries the United States, France, Germany, and the United Kingdom within a single year, with the US accounting for nearly half of these incidents.

   Ransomware attacks are among the most damaging cyber threats that now target multimedia content. These assaults use malicious software to encrypt items, including digital media, audio, video, and photographs, rendering the owners unable to access them unless a ransom is paid. With an increasing number of businesses and individuals storing crucial multimedia content ranging from personal images and videos to essential business documents, ransomware has developed into a profitable form of cybercrime that poses a significant threat to the integrity and accessibility of multimedia assets. Unlike text-based material, large multimedia is typically not backed that frequently, making them more susceptible to ransomware attacks.

   Ransomware is characterized by four types: [10]

   - *Scareware* is the type of malware that presents a pop-up message indicating that a malware infection has been detected, requiring a payment to remove it. If the user does not comply, they will be continuously bombarded with pop-ups, but no harm is inflicted on their files.

- *Screen lockers*, also referred to as non-encrypting ransomware, these attacks display a full-size window featuring a logo from a government agency upon system startup, claiming that illegal activity has been detected on the device and demanding payment. The user is unable to perform any tasks as the screen is locked or the device is overwhelmed with pop-ups.
- *Encrypting ransomware*, also known as crypto-ransomware, this type encrypts files and removes them from the system. A payment is required to decrypt and restore access to the files.
- *Mobile ransomware* which affects mobile devices through malicious apps or drive-by downloads. A message appears stating that due to illegal activity, the device is locked, and a penalty must be paid to unlock it. However, because of automated cloud data backup options, the encryption of data is less beneficial to attackers.

Ransomware frequently enters systems via hacked downloads, malicious links, or phishing emails. Due to their widespread use, multimedia files are frequently targeted because they may be found on almost any system or device. After infecting a system, ransomware uses sophisticated algorithms to find and encrypt multimedia files. It might target particular file formats, such as .jpeg, .mp4, .wav, and others, that are frequently connected to multimedia. Following encryption, the ransomware shows a notification requesting money, frequently in cryptocurrency, to unlock the contents. Anonymous payment methods are commonly used by attackers, making money recovery and traceability challenging.

Several ransomware strains, such as Ryuk, Sodinokibi (REvil), and Maze, are well known for attacking multimedia files. These ransomware attacks target businesses that rely heavily on multimedia, such as media outlets, entertainment enterprises, and healthcare services, where multimedia content is vital and widely available.

b. ***Malicious code embedded in multimedia files***: Cybersecurity experts are becoming increasingly concerned about malicious code that is embedded in multimedia files. With the proliferation of digital media across multiple platforms, hackers are increasingly using multimedia assets, including audio, video, and photos, to spread malware. Both consumers and companies are in danger from this technique since it can result in data theft, unauthorized access, or even a complete system breach [11].

The term "malicious code" describes any software intended to interfere with, harm, or obtain unauthorized access to networks or systems. This code may appear in a variety of formats when included in multimedia files, including:

- *Scripts*: Upon opening or playing a multimedia file, certain scripts (like JavaScript) may be included. Such destructive operations like downloading more malware or taking advantage of system vulnerabilities can be carried out by these programs [11].
- *Exploits*: Multimedia files can be designed to take advantage of well-known flaws in the programs that manage them. A well-crafted video

file, for instance, could cause media player vulnerability, giving the attacker the ability to run code on the victim's computer [11].

- *Payloads*: After the multimedia file is run, it can contain a payload, which is the portion of the virus that carries out the desired destructive operation, including data exfiltration, system modification, or additional malware installation [11].

Attackers spread multimedia files with malicious malware using a variety of techniques including phishing campaigns that aim to attach malicious multimedia files to phishing emails, tempting recipients to download and open them. Using social engineering, attackers may utilize hacked websites or malicious domains to host infected multimedia files and deceive users into downloading them.

It can also be observed that by taking advantage of user's trust, attackers can spread malware by posting compromised multimedia files on social networking or file-sharing websites. Malicious multimedia files on physical media, like USB drives, can be distributed in public areas to infect devices when users connect the drives [11]. Sometimes an attacker might modify the metadata of a multimedia file to include a malicious payload that executes when the file is processed by certain applications.

c. ***Phishing attacks using multimedia links***: It is a type of cyber-attack in which the attacker poses as a trustworthy organization in an attempt to fool victims into divulging private information, including credit card numbers, passwords, and personal information. This kind of assault can be carried out via email, social media, SMS, and instant messaging. Cybersecurity experts are quite concerned about the fact that attackers have changed their strategies to incorporate multimedia links to make their phishing attempts more effective [12]. These attacks exploit multimedia resources, including images, movies, and audio files, to deceive victims into divulging personal information or downloading harmful software.

The most prevalent type is when hackers disguise the virus as multimedia files, such as music or video files, and send it over email or chat apps. When users download and open these files, the virus they contain can infect their computers and steal private information [12]. Another method is for an attacker to offer a link to a seemingly harmless movie that directs consumers to a phishing page designed to collect login information.

They may also produce fictitious visuals or films that depict critical situations such as account verification, where the victims may feel pressured to click on links in these multimedia communications that take them to phishing websites [13]. Cybercriminals frequently use logos and recognizable multimedia content to mimic well-known brands. When visitors click on embedded links on these phoney websites, they are tricked into divulging personal information. Currently, new challenges have emerged known as "smishing attacks" and "vishing assaults" that can use text messages and voice notes, respectively, to deliver phishing attempts. Text notes or voicemails left by attackers may push victims to click on links to address pressing problems. According to a new report by Truecaller, 26% of Americans lost money after being scammed through phones in 2022. That statistic suggests that these kinds of attacks are becoming increasingly common and that many folks are not well informed about them. In a bold phishing attack, fraudsters mimicked the *Reserve Bank of India* (RBI) by sending fake emails, as if, to RBI. In these phishing emails, the recipients were promised Rs. 10 lakhs as a prize in 48 hours and were provided with a website that looked exactly like the official RBI website, even having a similar web address and logo. Victims were subsequently lured into entry of their personal information, including password, i-pin number, and details of their savings account. Consequently, the RBI released an alert against this phishing mail on its official portal.

d. ***Deepfakes and synthetic media manipulations***: Deepfakes are tools of deception and mistrust in the digital age, posing a significant risk to our sense of digital integrity by erasing the line between reality and illusion and, in the process, making it harder for us to find truth in an age of increasingly advanced forms of deception. Artificial intelligence (AI) has imbibed the machinery the ability to think, learn, and make decisions like a human in a cognitive way which has resulted in improved efficiency and performance. The basic building blocks of AI machine learning (ML) natural language processing and deep learning are the technologies that will dominate future technologies, automating intricacies, and complexity and doing it with nearly human-like proficiency and skill [13].

Deepfakes have existed since the 1990s, when CGI was being employed by researchers to generate images of human beings. Nonetheless, the technology received a boost during the 2010s with access to large sets of data, new machine-learning techniques, and high-speed computing devices, resulting in rapid advances in the field. Deepfakes began gaining traction in 2014, a widening path, the first breakthrough in deep learning in this decade made by Ian Goodfellow along with his team. It was a seminal work that signaled the introduction of Generative Adversarial Networks (GANs), which would eventually enable the next generation of sophisticated image, video, and audio deepfakes [14]. A per GAN is composed of a generator and a discriminator neural network. While the synthetic media is created by the generator, the discriminator assesses whether or not the media is real. It allows for training both networks together, so when the discriminator gets better at distinguishing true from fake content, the generator can get better at generating realistic results.

In 2017, videos of public figures such as Barack Obama and Mark Zuckerberg made headlines regarding deepfakes on social media websites. Some of these videos were for fun and others caused panic and confusion in the general public and dropped the stock market. Reddit user of the same name the year he created the term "Deepfake" was coin in the late 2017. So, this user created a space on the online news and aggregation platform to host porn videos employing open-source face swap technology. The term has since been expanded to include "synthetic media applications" that preceded the Reddit page, along with innovations such as StyleGAN, a method for generating "realistic-looking images of non-existent people".

So deepfakes have pretty much become ubiquitous in society and have developed into a big threat in that they proliferate misinformation and spread distrust and ambiguity among people. Especially in the case of the computer-generated images and videos which are synthesized by deep learning with the use of AI that seem very much like reality to the naked eye and only a dedicated effort is enough to furnish them from actual media [15]. Given the groundbreaking capabilities of deepfake technology, it has become a favored tool for criminals seeking to manipulate and exploit it. The increasing use of deepfakes for deceptive purposes has serious implications for society, as they are commonly employed to disseminate fake news, influence elections and political affairs, generate non-consensual pornographic material, and fabricate convincingly false evidence.

Over 75% Indians who are active online, came across deepfake content in the past one year, 2023 as per a survey conducted by one of the key players in cybersecurity: McAfee. Same goes for the survey which also reported none over 38% of respondents ended up being victim of a deepfake scam over the just as long time period. The Asia-Pacific region came a close second to North America in the world for deepfake incidents from 2022 to 2023, with the number of incidents fully jumping sky high. The number of deepfake fraud cases in the region rose 25.3% in Vietnam, the largest increase, and 23.4% in Japan. Examples of deepfake can include visage scrambling (such as could be left out of a video or an image of one face and passed by another) or manufacture of counterfeit voices (imitating similar appearance, one of making their voice by clicking the ear related to the switch).

The effectiveness of the deepfake content is dependent on the size of datasets of data that feed the learning of the system. Forensics becomes much harder for experts to get if certain advanced AI models are used to have the deepfake content made. The modes for making deepfakes are growing more complex as tech evolves, which means that previously effective detection methods based on visual or scientific inconsistencies are starting to fail [16].

Earlier also this technology was misused by criminals for scamming and hoaxes using impersonation of the famous personalities. In India, victims of these abuses are especially great victims in the absence of specific laws regulating deepfake technology. The existing laws on copyright infringement, defamation, and also cybercrimes can be leveraged to counter the misuse. Moreover, deepfake technology complicates the efforts of experts to establish and verify the authenticity of the original source of media. The integrity of such evidence is often questionable, impacting its admissibility in court. Forensic experts must conduct extensive research to analyze such evidence, as contemporary tools and literature on this topic remain limited [17]. The underlying technology behind deepfake generation is advancing rapidly, creating a significant gap between available scientific techniques and effective detection methods.

e. ***Exploitation of Internet of Things (IoT) and surveillance multimedia feeds***: An "IoT" network is a collection of physical objects that have been equipped with sensors, software, and other technologies to enable data sharing and communication with other devices over the internet. This includes surveillance systems, wearable technologies, smart appliances, and industrial sensors. The IoT, which enables the seamless automation and connectivity of many objects, has fundamentally changed the way we engage with technology. However, this connectedness also comes with significant cybersecurity risks, particularly in relation to the misuse of IoT devices and the multimedia streams they offer [18]. The increasing usage of security cameras, smart home appliances, and other connected technologies has made it easier for hackers to exploit vulnerabilities, steal personal information, and launch malicious attacks. In order to create surveillance multimedia feeds that can be used for data analysis, security, and monitoring, IoT-enabled cameras and microphones can record audio and video data. Due to their frequent real-time transmission, these feeds are attractive targets for exploitation, which can result in invasions of privacy and illegal monitoring. Cybercriminals can also secretly change multimedia feeds by using man-in-the-middle (M2M) attacks to intercept data sent between IoT devices and their control systems, or by using targeted networks as components of a botnet to overload them with data and disrupt services using Distributed Denial of Service (DDoS) attacks [19]. Many IoT devices are designed for the convenience of use rather than security. Often, this results in outdated firmware, weak default passwords, and inadequate encryption, all of which make them more susceptible to hackers. Many IoT devices communicate via insecure networks, are not updated frequently, or are configured improperly, allowing hackers to intercept data transfers and gain unauthorized access to equipment [20]. As a result, users must comprehend the potential threats and put strong security measures in place to safeguard their data integrity and privacy in a world that is becoming more interconnected by the day.

f. ***Use of AI and automated tools for hacking multimedia content***: Multimedia information can now be exploited in new and powerful ways because of the growing integration of automation and AI in hacking tools. These advanced techniques present unique challenges since they can increase and simplify attacks, often in ways that are difficult to detect or defend [21].
   - *AI-driven malware*: Such AI systems could autonomously learn to develop new variants of malware that ensure their code signatures are different enough to elude detection by anti-virus solutions. They can hide in multimedia files that exploit security holes when these files are opened and then insert themselves in music, video, or image files to infect systems [21].
   - *Automated phishing campaigns with multimedia*: AI-based tools can create tailor-made phishing messages, and include pictures and videos to make them even more professional. This includes generating fake emails using AI and then using manipulated images and videos. Automation could also increase the probability of successful spear-phishing attacks by customizing multimedia to the interests or professional contacts of the target [22].

- *Analyzing and reconnaissance of metadata*: Photos and videos contain metadata, such as timestamps, device information, and location information. AI systems have the ability to automatically scrape this metadata from many different files, allowing them to create profiles of prospective targets. An insight into an individual's personal or professional background helps attackers to plan their attacks better or take advantage of the private information to coerce someone else [22].
- *Automated profiling*: When various multimedia data are fed into AI systems, they can generate detailed profiles of individuals or organizations—including an individual's social connections, an organization's daily activities, regularly visited places, and more. Such profiles can then be exploited by attackers to plan and carry out social engineering or targeted attacks [23].
- *Automated surveillance analysis*: Image-recognition software that employs AI can detect patterns or behavior in video, such as faces in surveillance footage. If hackers get local IoT cameras or surveillance equipment, then AI techniques may be exploited to track movements, identify individuals, and even to determine security weaknesses in real-time! Such automated processing might put individuals or businesses at risk from a variety of privacy and security threats [23].
- *Content extraction and manipulation*: AI can edit and enhance images and videos and it may disturb the physical evidence of the crime scene. Real-time or post-surveillance data hacking can manipulate visual data, while raising security and/or legal issues as a result [23].
- *AI avatars and bots*: These create non-realistic but sublimely convincing synthetic personalities via artificially simulated human interaction in movies, or in real-time that suggests and suggests quasi-plausible believable human-y types. They can be applied in businesses to manipulate people to provide their private details or do social engineering attacks [24].
- *Automated chatbots*: These have been added to phishing or social engineering attacks. These bots can circulate photographs, imitate video conversations, or stream pre-recorded audio to give the satisfaction of a genuine experience to the phishing endeavor. With the help of multimedia, attackers can reach and exploit a larger variety of targets with more success [24].
- *AI for decryption and pattern recognition*: The AI systems that does this finds patterns or weaknesses in the encryption methods by examining the decrypted multimedia data which cannot be decrypted through cryptography. Through analyzing encrypted and decrypted content pairs, ML algorithms can occasionally predict or estimate encryption keys, enabling hackers to gain access to private images or videos [24].
- *Use of AI for removal of digital watermarks*: AI tools can discover and strip watermark and other digital rights management (DRM) techniques embedded in many multimedia files by pixel manipulation. This poses a

serious threat to proprietary content, as AI provides a means for quickly disabling protections that were previously difficult to bypass [24].

- *Malicious code hides behind multimedia files*: Hackers are specifically using AI where they apply steganography (hiding data inside another file) to insert a code in multimedia files (photos or videos). Although these files appear like normal image or video files, when they are visited, they execute malware which makes detection very difficult. The use of AI-based techniques can also automate and enhance the embedding process, making the task of identifying hidden malware even more difficult [24].
- *Automated extraction and execution*: AI technologies may also be used to automatically extract and execute dangerous code hidden in multimedia files. This represents a significant threat after all, automated tools can execute these actions on infected systems, quickly propagating malware across networks.

13.3 ACQUISITION AND PRESERVATION OF MULTIMEDIA DATA

Digital storage can hold vast amounts of information in a compact physical form. Its presence in cases is increasing due to the widespread use of cell phones, social media, and various digital assistants, commonly known as the IoT.

The preservation of multimedia files stored as digital evidence brings unique challenges that differ from those in traditional evidence preservation, as the digital data can be easily altered. Digital evidence includes any information in binary form that could be useful in criminal investigations or other legal proceedings. Digital evidence is stored on physical media, but it is typically the content and associated information, rather than the media itself, that holds the most significance [25]. Thus, it is a top priority for the digital forensic examiner to acquire and safeguard this valuable information to prevent any loss.

13.3.1 Source of Multimedia Evidences

Physical media encompasses hard drives within computers and mobile devices, along with external storage options like USB drives, CDs, and DVDs. There are various forms of physical media [26].

- Digital images and files are created when digital evidence is transferred from physical media or other systems. These may be sourced from remote (cloud-based) systems, from devices that remain in the field, or from those seized and added to an evidence management system.
- Other digital entities include a broad array of digital materials that are not strictly images or files, such as online accounts.
- Law enforcement-produced digital evidence is also significant, particularly from body-worn camera (BWC) programs, in-car video systems, and other electronic records, comprising both physical devices and digital data.

13.3.2 Acquisition of the Multimedia Data/File from the Digital Devices

Preparing for the acquisition of digital evidence necessitates effective communication between the examiner and the investigative team. This communication should cover the nature and scope of the potential evidence to be collected and any unique constraints that could affect the acquisition process. The legal guidance can also be taken by the examiner, in case of any questions regarding legal authority of the evidence to be collected.

Examiners should determine the most suitable methods for acquiring data from identified sources and also recognize the limitations associated with each acquisition method, in order to plan strategies to address these limitations when applicable. The forensic examiner must comprehend the potential impact of their selected acquisition technique on the source item and strive to minimize any adverse effects as much as possible. If it is not feasible to completely prevent changes to the source item, examiners must document the acquisition process in sufficient detail to account for any artifacts resulting from that process [27]. Whenever possible, the procedures followed during the acquisition should be designed to be auditable and repeatable.

In a standard procedure, physical devices or media are collected and transported to a digital forensics laboratory, where they are logged into an evidence management system. The laboratory then utilizes various tools to create a digital image of the data on the device or media. FTK Imager or Falcon is the most common tool used for preparing such digital copies. This image is stored in a case management system or another computer system, typically separate from the Evidence Unit. In some cases, data is acquired directly in the field using forensic tools rather than in the laboratory [28]. Often, data is extracted from a device or media without physically seizing the item, as is common with multi-user servers, cloud-based storage, or other systems that are impractical to bring to the laboratory or take offline.

Digital images can also be obtained from third-party organizations through formal requests, copied without forensic tools, or provided by government or private surveillance systems, as well as by public witnesses to a potential crime, often in the form of cell phone videos.

Acquisition procedure of the digital evidence requires following points to be considered [28]:

a. Hardware or software write blockers should be used when possible to prevent writing to the original evidence.
b. Forensic image(s) should be acquired using hardware or software that is capable of capturing a complete bit stream image of the original media, supporting both proprietary and open format of the data to be acquired.
c. Detailed records of the original source of an image or file should be kept, along with information on how it was created or transferred to law enforcement.
d. Hash value of all the digital images and other digital objects should be calculated using NIST (National Institute of Standards and Technology) and SWEDGE approved hashing algorithm (usually MD5 or SHA-1), with the resulting hashes stored securely and separately from the image or file.

e. Verify that the acquisition completed successfully and that the initial hash value for the evidence matches the acquisition hash value for the forensic image.
f. The imaged evidence files should be stored on a system that is offline and highly secure, featuring individual authentication, access controls, and activity logging. For organizations using a cloud-based system, robust security measures like proper encryption are essential.
g. Digital images and files are typically stored either on local media or in remote (cloud-based) systems, depending on their size or storage requirements. Given the potentially large volume of digital evidence, organizations may benefit from selecting various storage strategies based on factors like the required preservation duration for case evidence, storage costs, and, for cloud storage, the likelihood of needing to retrieve the data.
h. Examiners should record the acquisition of digital evidence according to organizational policy. The proper photography and videography is ensured throughout the process of collection and preservation of digital/multimedia evidences.
i. The records should include specific identifiers (e.g., make, model, serial number, and asset tag), source location of the digital evidence when initially found, investigation identifiers (e.g., case name and case number), acquisition specifics (e.g., acquisition method, imaging tool, and version used), name and title of the individual acquiring the evidence, date of acquisition, any issues or errors encountered during acquisition, and any other information required for maintaining proper chain of custody.

13.3.3 The Important Considerations while Acquiring and Preserving the Digital Data

a. Acquisitions should take place in a secure, controlled environment to ensure the integrity and authenticity of the digital evidence. These acquisitions may occur either onsite or offsite. During onsite acquisitions, examiners should take additional precautions and assess any environmental factors that may be beyond their control, such as power stability. If external factors pose a risk of disruption, examiners should prioritize acquiring the most critical data first to ensure essential information is captured before any potential interruptions occur [29].
b. In case of encryptions in the data, the examiners should have a thorough understanding of encryption at the device, volume, container, and file levels. Various methods can be used to access decrypted data. For instance, examiners might perform a live memory capture before imaging the disk to retrieve any encryption keys in volatile memory. They may also opt for a live acquisition of the source media to create logical images of unencrypted data.

   Some encryption technologies enable saving recovery keys on local or removable media, in the cloud with third-party providers, or through enterprise management systems. The examiners can also explore non-technical approaches to access encryption keys or unencrypted data, such as requesting keys from holders, finding them in written records, or using legal processes to compel third parties to provide access [29]. Additionally, unencrypted versions of target data may be available from third-party providers through legal channels.

c. Examiners may need to review the contents of potential data sources before acquisition to limit the amount of data collected, avoid irrelevant information, or adhere to search authority restrictions. This triage process typically involves examining the attributes and contents of potential data sources through automated or manual methods to assess their relevance to the investigation. Depending on the complexity of the case, this process may involve multiple iterations [29].

   Examiners should utilize forensically sound methods for triage whenever feasible and document the triage process in detail to ensure it can be repeated and to account for any artifacts generated during the process.

d. When there is no statute or retention policy from the relevant jurisdiction, best practice suggests retaining digital evidence for a timeframe set by the organization to ensure consistency (e.g., five years, and six months) following the conclusion of the case. This period should account for any criminal or civil proceedings, including the appeals process [29].

13.4 EXAMINATION AND ANALYSIS OF MULTIMEDIA EVIDENCE

Multimedia forensics is a science that blends forensic procedures and investigations with the analysis of various digital media content, including audio, video, and photos. Finding, separating, and analyzing important components in multimedia files in order to gain knowledge or confirm authenticity is part of this process [30]. Experts in forensics use a variety of instruments and methods to improve, verify, and examine multimedia evidence while ensuring its integrity. The accuracy and dependability of the evidence can have a big influence on how an investigation turns out, which makes this step important in criminal, civil, and cybersecurity matters [31].

13.4.1 Analysis of Audio Evidences

The main facets of audio forensics include verifying the authenticity of audio evidence, enhancing audio recordings to make speech more understandable and low-level sounds more audible, analyzing and recording acoustic evidence, including speaker identification, dialogue transcription, and the reconstruction of crime scenes and establishing the timelines [32].

13.4.1.1 Identification of the Speaker

Speaker recognition encompasses various activities aimed at linking a speech sample to its speaker by analyzing its acoustic or perceptual properties. The information within a spoken utterance includes speaker characteristics, the phrase spoken, emotions, background noise, and transformations due to different channels.

The human voice is a unique personal trait, as matching voices would require two individuals to have identical vocal mechanisms and perfect synchronization of their articulators, which is highly unlikely. However, even samples from the same speaker show some variation, as it is nearly impossible for a person to reproduce an utterance identically each time [33].

Speaker recognition is broadly categorized into two applications: speaker identification and speaker verification. Speaker identification involves recognizing the speaker of a given utterance from a set of known speakers. In this process, the unknown speaker is identified as the one whose voice model most closely matches the input sample.

Speaker verification, on the other hand, is a more focused approach aimed at either confirming or rejecting a speaker's claimed identity. Essentially, this process determines if the speaker is indeed who they say they are, presenting it as a true-or-false binary decision task. Today, verification forms the foundation of most speaker recognition applications and is the most commercially viable aspect of the field [33].

A person's voice can serve as an effective biometric feature, as it is user-friendly and can be recorded easily with low-cost microphones or other simple hardware. Voice recognition provides an alternative, more secure method of granting access without the need for remembering passwords, lock combinations, or using physical keys, magnetic cards, or other devices prone to theft.

However, while a person's voice cannot be directly stolen, it can be recorded and replayed using simple devices. This makes it essential for voice-based security systems to have safeguards against such vulnerabilities. Another concern is voice disguise, where an imposter might mimic the genuine speaker to gain unauthorized access. Additionally, legitimate users may be denied access due to temporary changes in their voice caused by illness, emotional stress, or physical strain [33].

With the widespread use of telephones, mobile devices, and recording equipment, these technologies are often misused in crimes like kidnapping, extortion, blackmail, obscene calls, anonymous or harassing calls, ransom demands, terrorist threats, and match fixing. Criminals frequently rely on these communication methods, assuming that they can remain anonymous and untraceable. However, this assumption is increasingly unfounded, as a person's voice can be accurately identified, linking them to their crimes.

In the year 1932, in Charles Lindbergh's baby kidnapping and murder case, investigators narrowed potential candidates by analyzing the voice traits from the several ransom call made by the perpetrator. Even though there were no contemporary methods for identifying voices at the time, the case is seen as a forerunner of the use of vocal evidence in criminal investigations.

For identification purposes, various widely accepted standard techniques will be employed to ensure the validity of the work, with the choice of method tailored to meet specific requirements:

a. *Listener's method/auditory analysis*: This approach relies on recognizing a voice by its familiarity, a skill humans possess with remarkable precision and adaptability. In this method, experts listen to samples repeatedly, assessing similarities and differences between two speech events by analyzing linguistic, phonetic, and acoustic features. Various utterances are separated by speaker through repeated listening, allowing experts to identify unique linguistic elements and phonetic characteristics, such as speech quality, articulation rate, speech flow, voice impairments, prosodic features, vowel and consonant formation, timing, and pauses. These vocal cues are distinctive, enabling the identification of familiar voices. Specific words are then selected from both the questioned and reference samples for instrumental analysis.

Human listeners are highly resilient in recognizing speakers, even when dealing with degraded speech. Listener performance remains effective despite factors like signal-to-noise ratio, speech bandwidth, limited speech material, and distortions in speech signals from coding or transmission systems [34].

b. *Spectrographic analysis*: A sound spectrograph is a device that provides a permanent record of the changing energy-frequency distribution over the duration of a speech wave. Spectrograms, or visual representations of amplitude relative to both frequency and time, capture information not only about the spoken message but also about the speaker's identity. Commonly referred to as a voiceprint analyzer, a term coined by L. Kersta in 1962, the spectrograph transforms voice patterns into visual graphs, which move through the instrument at a steady speed, marking patterns on paper as it progresses. By analyzing these charts, one can compare an individual's typical speech pattern with recordings of that person in a questioned scenario, such as concerning a crime. These voiceprints serve as valuable tools for law enforcement in identifying suspects, using the unique features within the spectrographic impressions of individuals' voices—similar to the distinctiveness of fingerprints.

In this approach, a trained examiner can provide an assessment of the similarity between two samples based on characteristics such as fundamental frequency, formant frequency, pitch, energy contours, loudness, bandwidth distribution, transitional characteristics, spectral correlation, tones, and noises [35].

Most of the information regarding the use of spectrographic voice identification evidence in court originates from various jurisdictions in the United States. This is largely because the technique was developed and is most commonly applied there, as well as the presence of leading scientists and significant studies on the subject within the country. Spectrographic evidence was first deemed admissible in the 1966 case of *People v. Straehle*, where expert witness Kersta testified using his own voiceprinting method. This marked the beginning of an ongoing debate over the admissibility of spectrographic evidence, a discussion that continues to this day.

c. *Automatic approach*: This method represents a significant departure from traditional identification techniques, as it is both universal and automatic. It is termed universal because it does not concentrate on specific acoustic features but instead treats speech as a continuously varying complex wave or signal. Its automatic aspect minimizes subjective assessments of speech material. Currently, most automatic identification systems utilize techniques such as deep learning, neural networks, hidden Markov models, and Gaussian mixture models.

13.4.1.2 Authentication of Audio Files

Generally, the authentication of audio recordings is of paramount importance in forensic science and for crime detection. Authentication of digital audio recordings measures whether the recorded events were captured with fidelity and detects attempts at manipulation. These days, with the quality of digital audio editing tools, making edits is not only simpler than days gone by, hiding edits has become a sort of an art form. Audio forgery can be of several types like copy-move, deletions, insertions, substitutions, and splicing. Audio recordings are important files for solving criminal cases, and they can be used as evidence in court [36]. But, non-authentic/un-genuine or fabricated media can create a huge impact in delivering a verdict in the courts of law. In addition, evidence of audio recording loses its value unless there is evidence to prove it is authentic and free from editing or manipulation.

In 2010–2011, a contentious audio recording cropped up in the hearing of a case against famous Indian lawyer and former Union Minister Shanti Bhushan and others, which was ultimately proved to have been doctored in many parts. The recording allegedly involved some parties engaged in corrupt practices and others who were discussing certain privileged and legally protected matters. The case gained notoriety for higher issues of authenticity and privateness in recorded contacts, but in addition as a key part of the audio proof in court cases.

Shanti Bhushan and his associates disputed the validity of the recording, claiming it had been edited or taken out of context to misrepresent the conversations and motives of the parties involved. To resolve authenticity conflicts, the forensic audio experts regularly examined the recording with waveform analysis, content frequency, and any indicators of editing or manipulation.

It is here where it raised the significance of audio evidence and the factors to be established for the admissibility of such evidence in a court of law. This case also highlighted the issues of audio authentication in the courtroom and the requirement of high-end NLP forensic methods to validate audio material. It also cited concerns about privacy, possible abuse of recorded conversations, and ethics of recording conversations into court documents.

Detecting alterations in audio recordings presents a formidable challenge for forensic scientists, necessitating careful attention in this area [37].

a. *Critical listening*: It is a review of the submitted recording, conducted without any processing, can provide valuable insights for directing further analyses. Besides offering an initial assessment, it is important to observe voices, changes in background noise, unusual sounds that might suggest equipment issues, as well as potential recording and editing events, and any other relevant areas. To thoroughly examine each of these aspects, multiple playbacks will be necessary. Additionally, it may be essential to repeatedly review both the unprocessed and processed versions of the recording during the examination.
b. *Waveform analysis*: It shows how time and amplitude relate to the recorded acoustic data, making it possible to analyze the temporal and amplitude properties of a digital file, be it a single sample or the full recording. The waveform can be used to graphically depict problems found during critical listening,

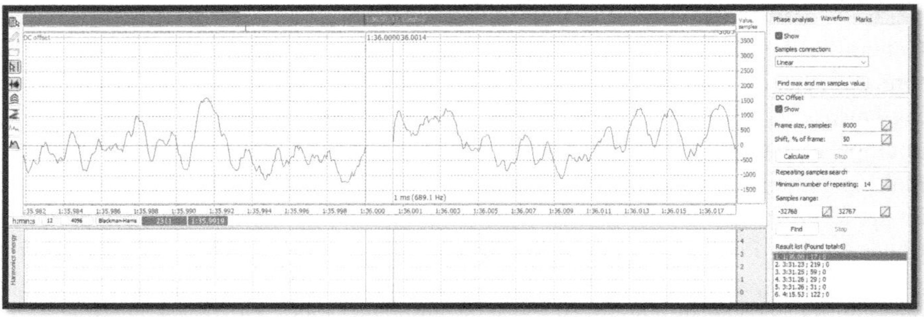

FIGURE 13.1 Waveform indicating similar patterns in case the same audio clip is pasted multiple times to repeat in the sample.

such as dropouts, clipping, and repeated words. Figure 13.1: A waveform graph showing repeated patterns indicative of audio clip duplication.

c. *Signal power*: The power of an audio signal can be calculated over short time intervals and represented as a trajectory that spans the entire signal. This analysis can help uncover potential loss of information in the acoustic signal caused by mechanical failures, compression artifacts, or the addition of silent segments. Signal power is based on observations and measurements, and the accuracy of these measurements is influenced by distortion (such as clipping) and the length of the analysis window.
d. *Identification of the date of creation (DOC), the date of modification (DOM), and hash value*: The creation date and modification date are crucial in authenticating audio files. If the media file is original and located in its original place, both the DOC and the DOM will remain unchanged.

   When a file is copied to a different destination or media, a new file is created while the original file remains unchanged in its original location. As a result, the newly created file will display a new DOC, but since the original file has not been edited or modified, its DOM will remain the same.

   When a file is moved from its original location to another place, both the original DOC and the DOM remain unchanged, as the file has neither been created nor modified. However, if the file is edited and then saved, both the DOC and the DOM will be updated.

   Additionally, the hash value of a file is determined by its contents rather than its name, meaning that moving, copying, or renaming the file in any media or location does not alter its hash value. It gets changed if there is some modification in the contents.
e. *File format analysis*: This involves a type of observational analysis where an examiner utilizes applications that can reveal metadata and HEX values from multimedia files along with their corresponding values. This metadata may encompass details such as the make and model of the recorder, its serial number, the settings used during the recording, the date and time it was recorded, the duration of the recording, and user-specific information like the investigator's name or case number.

When a recording is opened in a software application that can make edits, it frequently leaves a trace in the HEX data of the recording, indicating which software is utilized. By comparing the evidence and reference file, the forensic expert can analyze the metadata and HEX information of both files. Any discrepancies in the data may indicate potential tampering.

f. *File structure analysis*: The file structure, which encompasses header metadata, recorded content, metadata combined with the recorded content, and any footer data of the submitted recording, should undergo observational analysis and be compared with exemplar recordings taken from the submitted devices or other test recordings. If the actual original recording device is unavailable or cannot be used, a device of the same make and model should be utilized instead. Document these structures, including both hexadecimal and American Standard Code for Information Interchange (ASCII) fields along with their respective byte offsets.

g. *Quantization level/bit depth analysis*: This approach enables the examination of a signal's native bit depth to identify consistencies with the technical specifications of the claimed recorder, potential transcoding or signal processing, the bit depth trajectory of a signal, and to uncover signs of local interpolation. Quantization level analyses can be either observational or measurement-based, with measurement uncertainty in quantization level analysis being influenced by bit depth and quantization error.

h. *Direct current (DC) offset analysis*: It refers to the average direct current that arises when components within a recording system—such as microphones, microphone preamplifiers, interconnections, or recording circuitry—introduce DC voltages to an audio signal. This results in a waveform that is not aligned with the midline or x-axis. Since DC offset originates from the recording chain of the device, measuring the DC signal of a recording can help identify signs of editing. In some cases, DC analysis can also be used to verify the authenticity of a claimed recorder, provided the same recording chain and environment are used. Figure 13.2: A DC offset break visualization indicating signal jumps in manipulated audio. To achieve more accurate results, tests should be conducted with the evidence recorder under identical settings, environment, and similar transmission channel characteristics (e.g., microphone). Longer recordings of both evidence and exemplar will yield more comprehensive data for analysis.

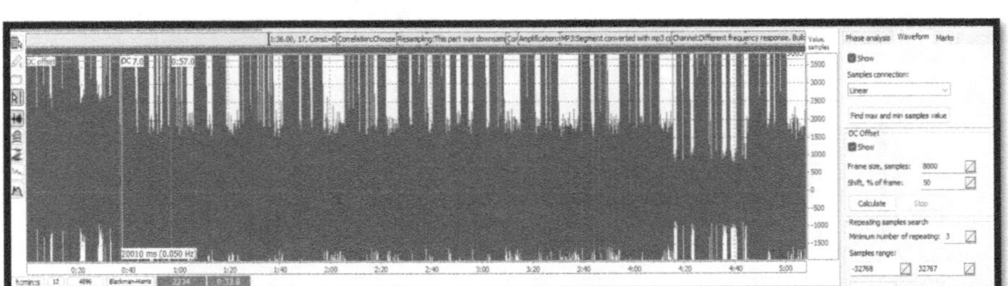

FIGURE 13.2 DC offset breaks highlighting signal jump.

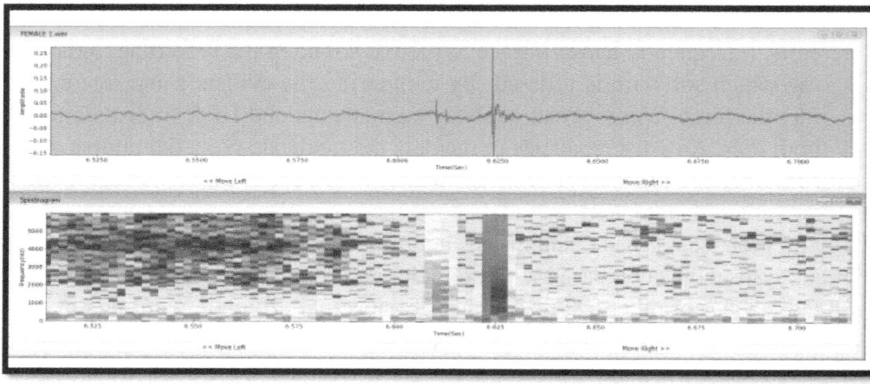

FIGURE 13.3 Vertical line showing spectral discontinuity in the spectrograph.

i. *Spectral analysis*: This technique is based on measurements, and their uncertainty in measurement is influenced by factors such as sampling frequency, bit depth, windowing function, and the order of the fast Fourier transform (FFT).

   The long-term average spectrum (LTAS) of a signal represents its power in decibels (dB) plotted against frequency, averaged over predefined FFT time windows. It is inherently related to the sample rate of the digital recorder but may also be affected by the encoding algorithm used in Figure 13.3: A spectrogram with vertical discontinuities suggesting audio editing. Figure 13.4: A side-by-side spectrogram comparison highlighting copy-paste operations in an audio file and Figure 13.5: A waveform diagram illustrating pause detection in an audio sample. Consequently, the characteristics of the LTAS can be examined to verify the settings and origin of the recorder.

j. *Compression level analysis (CLA)*: It is a technique utilized for authenticating audio files by examining the effects of digital compression. An analysis

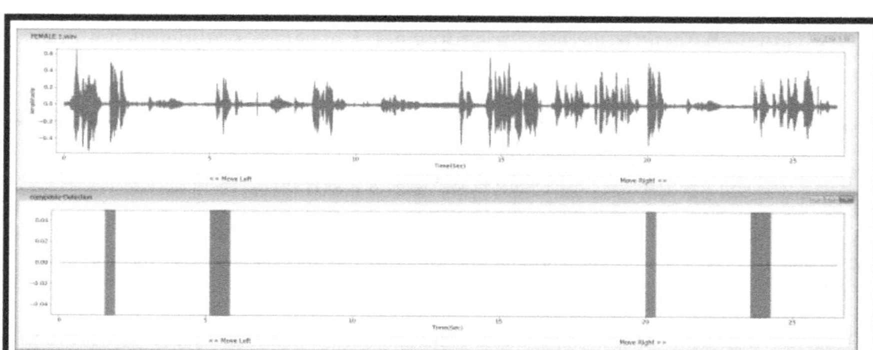

FIGURE 13.4 Detecting copy paste operations in spectrogram.

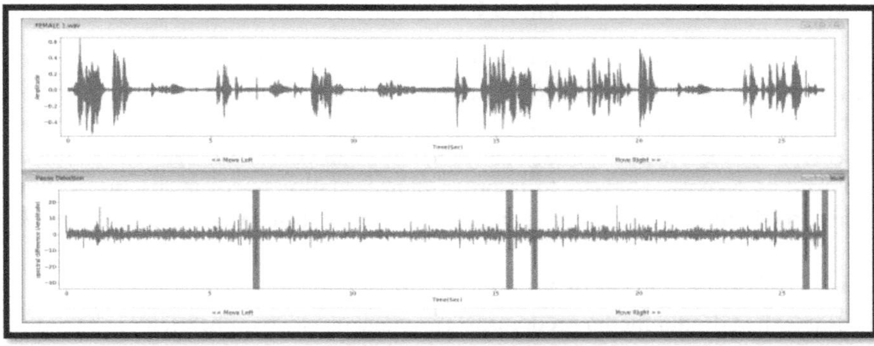

FIGURE 13.5 Pause detection in spectrogram.

of the compression level of an audio file is important to ascertain its origin, particularly to determine whether it aligns with an original audio file or if it has undergone recompression (as seen in Figure 13.6: A levelogram displaying amplified, compressed, or merged audio sections).

k. *Electric network frequency (ENF)*: ENF value from a power grid can be present in certain recordings, leaving a trace signal which is beneficial in specific situations. Digital recording devices, whether powered by mains or batteries, can capture the ENF, which becomes an additional frequency component within the recorded audio file. By applying band-pass filtering to the audio signal, the ENF can be isolated, allowing for the extraction of its unique pattern. Assuming that the ENF fluctuations are random, this effectively timestamps the audio recording since the ENF pattern is distinct for the specific time when the recording was made.
l. *Spectrographic analysis*: It represents the audio content by plotting frequency against time, allowing for a general assessment of the recording as well as a closer examination of specific events. Observable phenomena in spectrograms may include signs of digital aliasing, sample band-pass filtering, questioned signals, background noises, convolution and transmission characteristics, and power line frequency components.

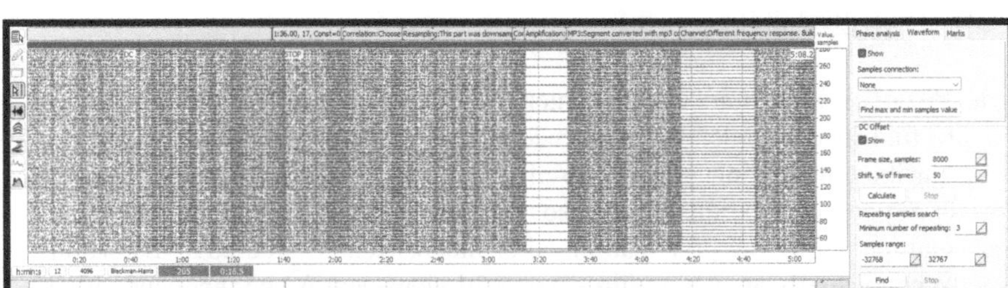

FIGURE 13.6 Levelogram depicting amplified, compressed, or merged audio samples.

13.4.2 Analysis of Image/Video Evidences

Analysis of images and videos is essential to forensic investigations since it provides important information about illegal activity and aids in the legal process. In this field, visual media are examined to extract information that can be used to construct timelines, identify suspects, and produce evidence in court. A range of methods are employed by forensic analysts to improve image quality, uncover obscure features, identify the individuals or objects, and confirm the legitimacy of digital content [38].

13.4.2.1 Authentication of Video and Image File

In a time when digital media predominates, image or video authenticity is becoming a major worry. Forensic video and image authentication is more important than ever due to the proliferation of video/photo editing software and modification methods.

Image and video spoofing significantly impacts cybersecurity, as scammers have long used fake visuals to deceive people into giving away money. They may send a picture of a sad child they claim needs help and financial assistance, an image of a celebrity endorsing suspicious schemes, or even an AI-generated video of victim's family member, persuading them to comply with the scammers' demands [38].

Since a picture is worth a thousand words these days, the veracity of photos can affect how people see things, how decisions are made, and even how legal actions are handled. However, a major problem is the simplicity with which photographs can be altered. The ability to manipulate images has led to questions over the accuracy of visual information, from judicial evidence to social media hoaxes.

Recently in May 2024, an FIR was filed under Section 354 (molestation) of the Indian Penal Code and other provisions of the IT Act after the school principal filed a complaint against a 15-year-old in Class 9 at a private school, reportedly creating morphed images of his classmates and a teacher into an offensive video and sharing it within his groups.

In another case reported in 2024, a case of defamation has been reported where two men made pornographic videos of Italian PM Giorgia Meloni by superimposing her face on another person's body.

Forensic video and image authentication is a multidisciplinary field utilizing scientific techniques to verify the authenticity of digital videos/images. This process involves detailed examination of metadata, pixel-level characteristics, and other factors to determine evidence integrity. It is essential in legal contexts, such as criminal investigations and courtroom cases, where confirming the authenticity of visual evidence is critical [38].

a. *Visual examination*: Visual elements are closely scrutinized in this process to find inconsistencies or evidence of manipulation. By identifying irregularities in lighting, shadows, reflections, and object dimensions, experts can spot modifications. They also analyze details that could indicate digital manipulation, like pixelization, color inconsistencies and edge distortions. When visually analyzing films, you will view each frame independently to check for similarity (duplicate frames), audio-video sync, compression artifacts, face movement as well as unnatural transition among others.

b. *File structure and format analysis*: JPEG, PNG, MP4, or AVI for image or video are all examples of file format and each of these has a defined internal structure and includes metadata (the headers, the content data, and, optionally, the footers). Through this structure, forensics may find abnormalities which can be a sign of evil. By scouring a file's metadata, experts gain context information about the camera model, settings, creation date, and change history. In order to make sure that the original material is unchanged and hasn't undergone changes or re-encoding, they additionally confirm for consistency in details concerning the framework of a data consisting of signs such as headers and also byte series. If the file type, format, or anything else is different, that could indicate tampering.
c. *Hex analysis*: In hex string of each kind of media file format, there have portions that play the role of a header and footer which are typically recognized as unique identifiers. By comparing these baselines with accepted and approved measures, researchers can determine if a file has been modified, re-encoded, or even corrupted. We can also analyze hex to identify abnormal data injections that might indicate tampering—such as traces of editing tools, signs of compression artifacts, etc.
d. *EXIF analysis*: Such metadata includes information such as the make and model of the camera, the date and time the photo was taken, the GPS location where it was taken, as well as particulars about the camera settings such as exposure and resolution; digital cameras and cell phones tend to automatically store these. Manipulations can be indicated by differences in the timestamps, GPS locations, and information about camera models and such. Also, if the EXIF data contains a strangely structured data pattern, or traces of editing software, it may indicate that the file was changed after first version was captured.
e. *Brightness dispersion and frozen points detection in video*: Original files usually exhibit a natural brightness variance that reflects actual lighting, item placement, and environmental influences. Anomalies in brightness dispersion, including sudden shifts or irregularities in light levels throughout a picture or video frame, could be signs of manipulation, like adding or removing objects.

   Frozen points analysis looks at individual frames in a video to identify aspects that should be changing but stay the same throughout time. Dynamic settings naturally show subtle, continuous pixel changes between frames in a real recording. Splicing, frame repetition, and video looping are examples of manipulation that can be shown by frozen points, which are areas where specific pixels stay abnormally consistent.
f. *Discrete cosine transform (DCT) plot analysis*: It is frequently used in compression methods (like JPEG and some video codecs) for both photos and films to convert spatial data into frequency data, which helps minimize file size without sacrificing visual quality.

   DCT plots typically show a natural distribution of low- and high-frequency components that match real textures and edges in real-world photos or films. However, these frequency distributions may become erratic

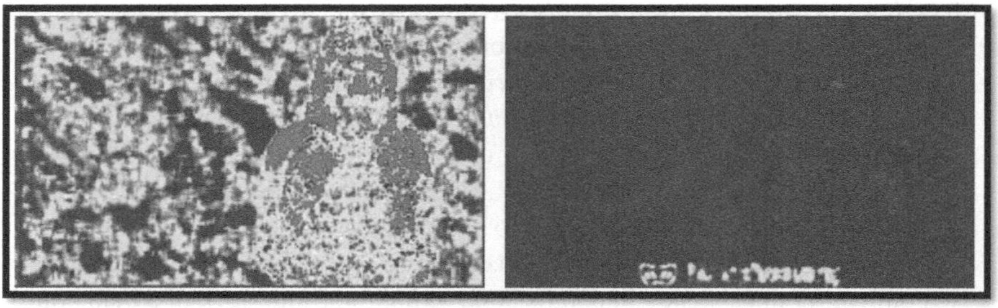

FIGURE 13.7 Ghost artifacts observed in modified/compressed image *(right)*.

and exhibit odd spikes or artifacts when an image or video is altered, for example, by editing, adding objects, or recompressing. Finding splicing, compression artifacts, or other minute changes that might not be noticeable with only eye inspection can be made easier with the help of this technique.

g. *JPEG ghost for images*: Because each compression cycle leaves behind unique "ghosts" or artifacts that could reveal whether a file has been modified or recompressed, this method is particularly helpful for JPEG images.

   The original, undamaged parts of a photo or video frame often have distinct compression artifacts than the altered parts. By re-compressing the image at various quality settings and examining the "ghost" artifacts that emerge, forensic analysts can spot inconsistencies. Figure 13.7: A forensic analysis showing ghost artifacts in a compressed or altered image.

h. *Histogram analysis*: The histogram, which shows the distribution of pixel intensities (dark to light), helps forensic experts recognize patterns and anomalies that suggest manipulation. The histogram of a standard realistic photograph or video shows a well-balanced collection of pixel values reflecting the scene's luminance. On the other hand, if the image has been manipulated, that means histogram will be corrupted and we will see some changes like gaps in the histogram, a displaced histogram, or multiple peaks in the histogram. It's also useful for spotting compression artifacts and for general dynamic range of the image. Then forensic investigators will compare the histograms of the suspected altered images with those of verified legal photos and examine the differences, which should highlight evidence of editing or signal a modification.

i. *Color gradient analysis*: In real-world photographs and videos, color gradients typically display smooth transitions and organic changes that represent the textures and lighting of the environment. However, color gradients may show abrupt shifts, odd transitions, or uneven color distributions when a picture or video is edited, for as through compositing or digital editing. Figure 13.8: A side-by-side comparison of color gradient differences between an original and tampered image. These anomalies could indicate that the data has been mixed or altered from other sources. Forensic experts can spot issues like cut-and-paste editing—the act of integrating elements from multiple photos without correctly blending them—by using color

FIGURE 13.8 Color gradient variations in (i) original and (ii) tampered images.

gradient analysis, which leaves visible lines or uneven edges. Additionally, this study can help identify whether the media has been intentionally enhanced with filters.

j. *Photo response non-uniformity (PRNU) identification*: This forensic technique verifies the authenticity of images and videos by examining the unique noise patterns produced by digital cameras during the picture-taking process. Numerous factors, including the imaging environment, intrinsic electrical noise, and manufacturing variances of the sensor, can influence the distinct noise characteristics of each camera sensor. By comparing the recovered noise pattern of the questioned image or video with the reference fingerprints, forensic experts can determine whether the material was most likely taken by the same device.

k. *Error level analysis (ELA)*: This technique reveals anomalies that might point to alteration by examining the variations in error levels across an image or video after it has been compressed and stored. In this process, a compressed version of the original image or video is made using the same compression algorithm, in order to determine the error levels—basically, the variations between the two versions. Then the discrepancies in these two images are mapped. In a normal ELA result, regions with uniform and consistent error levels are probably original content, whereas areas with noticeably greater or lower error levels might be signs of possible modifications, including adding, removing, or changing image parts. This is due to the fact that when an image is altered and then saved again, the edited portions error level frequently varies from the unaltered portions. Figure 13.9: An error level analysis (ELA) image revealing compression inconsistencies in an edited picture. By using ELA to videos frame by frame, forensic investigators can spot discrepancies and possible alterations throughout the whole video sequence. This approach is very helpful for identifying splicing, deepfakes, and other forms of video manipulation.

l. *Noise mapping*: Noise, or the random variation in brightness or color information, is present in all digital images and videos to some extent. The camera sensor, illumination, and image processing techniques are some of the variables that can affect this noise. Noise map analysis is the process of

FIGURE 13.9 ELA algorithm showing variations in compression rate in (ii) edited image, in comparison to the (i) original.

visualizing the noise levels throughout an image or video frame for use in forensic investigations. Figure 13.10: A noise pattern comparison demonstrating differences between an original image and a tampered image. This is achieved by examining the noise patterns and contrasting them with the noise properties that are anticipated for a particular camera or sensor.

13.4.2.2 Enhancement of Image and Video

In forensic investigations, image and video enhancement is essential since it greatly facilitates the analysis and interpretation of visual evidence. This procedure entails applying a number of strategies to enhance the visibility, clarity, and general quality of pictures and videos that might be low resolution or distorted by motion blur, bad lighting, or other issues [38, 39]. A lot of forensic investigations depend on visual evidence that was taken under challenging circumstances. By bringing to light crucial elements that might not be immediately apparent, like license plate numbers, face features, or particular objects in a scene, enhancement techniques can increase the evidence's value for identification and analysis and can aid in crime scene reconstruction, suspect identification, and witness testimony. Enhancement techniques can encompass various methods, including sharpening, motion deblurring, hue and saturation adjustments, color modifications, brightness or contrast adjustments, spotlight

FIGURE 13.10 Variations in the noise patterns seen in (i) original and (ii) tampered images.

detection, and frame averaging, among others. Visual evidence that is distinct and easy to understand is more convincing and has the power to greatly affect the jury's verdict [40]. The comprehensiveness of the investigation can also be shown through effective enhancement.

13.4.2.3 Person Identification from Image and Video

Forensic investigations and security applications depend heavily on the ability to identify individuals from photos and videos. In order to determine the identification of people captured in visual media, this method mostly uses biometric techniques, especially facial recognition technology [41]. Facial recognition systems analyze a person's face's distinctive characteristics, such as the distance between their eyes, the curve of their nose, the shape of their orbits, the shape and size of their zygomatic arc, and their jawline, to produce a digital representation that can be compared to databases of recognized faces. This technology helps identify suspects or missing people by rapidly matching a captured image or video frame with the identities kept in surveillance or law enforcement databases. Facial recognition and other biometric authentication methods improve cybersecurity by limiting unwanted access to key systems and data. Even if credentials are compromised, these systems provide an extra layer of security, preventing unauthorized access. They are particularly crucial in protecting mobile devices and high-security environments [42]. Apart from facial recognition, additional biometric indicators, such as gait analysis which looks at a person's movement—or the recognition of unique apparel and accessories can also be used to identify a person. Gesture recognition, gait recognition, and other new multimedia security technologies are used alongside existing biometric technologies for human-computer interaction. It uses video data that is automatically analyzed by technology to identify persons based on their specific habits or movement patterns. When it comes to cybersecurity, methods like these could be used in high-security locations such as military installations gait recognition is already being used by the United States Defense Forces for secondary biometric authentication to ensure that only authorized personnel enter or exit premises; for situations where bio-input options are both risky and impractical, gesture recognition-based touchless authenticators can add an extra layer of security [43]. Photogrammetrical tools can also be used to determine the height of the person about the reference points at the crime site. These methods have been further refined by ML algorithms, which enable more precise and effective person identification from vast amounts of video.

13.4.2.4 Video-Based Surveillance and Monitoring

Physical security is an important part of cybersecurity because it relies heavily on multimedia technology, specifically CCTV cameras and other forms of video monitoring. These systems help to keep track of who has access to secure areas such as data centers and server rooms. These gadgets can give digital security measures that help to deter unwanted physical entry by utilizing high-definition video. In addition, network monitoring systems constantly use multimedia data to track communication activities on a network in real time. These systems will highlight unexpected patterns in user behavior or data flow that could suggest a security risk [44]. They can also be used to monitor irregularities in user behavior, system activity/inaction, and site logins.

13.5 EMERGING CYBERSECURITY PROTOCOLS FOR PROTECTING MULTIMEDIA CONTENT

The field of cybersecurity is always changing, and securing sensitive data and averting cyberattacks requires staying on top of developments. Since new technologies are always being developed, staying up to date with the newest trends and advancements can be difficult. Cyber risks are increasingly targeting multimedia assets, such as audio, video, and photos, due to the quick development of digital media technology. As the use of multimedia in communications, social media, and commercial processes continues to expand, there is a strong need for advanced cybersecurity measures to protect the validity and integrity of these digital assets [45]. By implementing the newest cybersecurity solutions, companies can improve their security posture and reduce possible threats. In a nutshell, staying up-to-date with the knowledge of the most recent cybersecurity technology is now essential to protecting sensitive data and maintaining the integrity of procedures adopted [46].

13.5.1 Content Integrity Verification Systems

The primary function of content integrity verification systems is to detect and prevent unwanted alterations in multimedia files. The concept is that these systems scan multimedia content, seeking changes and cross-validating them against credible copies. A digital signature is generated for a piece of multimedia using cryptographic hashing and check-summing techniques to compare it to later versions derived from it [47]. This method can be used to ensure that media content transferred in various ways across an approved network has not been illegally or fraudulently altered. This is especially essential in situations where audiovisual materials are exchanged on social media, file-sharing websites, and cloud storage systems. Such systems can be integrated with version control approaches to let users trace changes in multimedia over time. This, however, boosts the credibility of digital evidence in court by establishing (or fabricating) a chain of custody [48].

13.5.2 Deepfake Detection and Digital Content Verification

Every few weeks, a new wave of deepfakes surfaces AI-generated manipulated images or videos that alter visual and audio elements in media. These deepfakes can threaten personal, commercial, or national security, often in scenarios where phishing is a concern. To address these risks, detection algorithms have been developed, utilizing multimodal analysis to spot irregularities in digital footage, such as unnatural facial movements, mismatched lighting, or inconsistent speech. These algorithms help cybersecurity systems verify the authenticity of multimedia content, preventing the spread of misleading or harmful information in crucial discussions [49].

13.5.3 Blockchain Technology for Multimedia Authentication

Blockchain technology could help to overcome the problem of multimedia data manipulation. By keeping permanent records of the times and dates multimedia files were generated, transferred, or modified, investigators may work back down a chain to their roots using blockchain, guaranteeing they remain untouched/unchanged during distribution. This unique signature is created by assigning a hash to each multimedia file and then saving it in an immutable record of the blockchain ledger, allowing any adjustments done outside its capacity to be identified when the records are compared to their current state [50]. For example, a blockchain-based system may keep track of critical facts about the video clip itself, such as where it came from, when and how it was shot (whether or not it was edited), etc. In terms of national security, this would be useful for validating surveillance recordings and ensuring that adversaries cannot manipulate the evidence.

13.5.4 Advanced Encryption Techniques

While encryption is frequently used to safeguard multimedia material, improved solutions to encrypt your data are becoming increasingly important to stay ahead of the latest online threats. End-to-end encryption, for example, works to ensure that multimedia content cannot be viewed by anyone who does not have authorization during a vital period of its lifespan, from production to transportation and finally at rest. Audiovisual content is now being exposed to predicted threats posed by quantum computing, which can prepare cryptographic systems for a failsafe mode without breaking traditional encryption in advance, and more advanced encryption approaches such as post-quantum/quantum-resistant cryptography is currently being researched [51]. Furthermore, homomorphic encryption protects privacy and allows for digital forensics while maintaining multimedia data secrecy by directly processing encrypted content. This approach is remarkable for covert investigations into businesses where privacy issues are critical, which may contain considerable personal identifying information.

13.5.5 Watermarking and Digital Fingerprinting

Digital watermarking serves as a last-resort solution to prevent users from unlawfully utilizing or altering multimedia. By including watermarks, the owner can insert visible or invisible signatures in multimedia files The watermarks include author, license, and change-related information. Binary-level invisible watermarks from a forensic perspective are found efficient for both images and sounds. This is especially useful in a world in which digital ownership must often be proven, for instance, against prosecution for copyright infringement. An analogy would be digital fingerprinting, which generates unique labels for media fingerprint files. In forensic applications, digital fingerprints can help identify where online piracy or breaches originated and track multimedia assets while they are in transit [52].

13.5.6 AI-Based Threat Detection Systems

AI or ML techniques have gained significant momentum in other domains and are now being used for cyber threat detection and prevention in multimedia forensics. With the advent of purely AI-based systems that have the capability to automatically detect suspicious content—based on pixel pattern shifts, illumination variations, or other digital signals not apparent to human observation—content verification and digital forensic analysis have become significantly more accurate and efficient. Moreover, advanced social engineering ploys and media-realistic phishing assaults (based on audio samples, videos, or photos) can be detected and blocked by cyber defenses powered by AI algorithms [53]. AI can also identify signs of altered content, such as deepfake videos and edited audio clips, and alert computers that a piece of material should not be allowed to spread or be repurposed. In deepfake detection, AI searches a video for subtle facial movements, or minor pitch changes voice and claims the origin has been altered by AI. Through early precautions, we can extremely reduce the spread of deepfake media contents that spread lies or ruin reputations on social media [53, 54].

13.5.7 Steganography Detection

Steganography is a method of hiding information in multimedia assets like audio, video, or photos and is widely used by hackers to communicate secretly or transfer files without notice. So, for example, an innocent looking image file can have a payload or a code hidden in it. Steganalysis is a multimedia forensics technology that discovers and investigates steganographic content. It is one of the most prominent variations of binary steganography, important for anyone researching cybercriminals and stopping nefarious waves as it allows peeking into the waveforms of a sound file or pixel structure of an image to unveil data that hackers traditionally bury their data within [55].

13.5.8 Anomaly Detection Systems

Anomaly detection is a critical detection strategy that aids in identifying unexpected or suspicious activities in multimedia data. To do this, apply ML in anomaly detection systems to establish normal behavior for multimedia access, which can be extremely beneficial from within the network organization. Once this baseline has been established, the system monitors for deviations that could indicate a security breach or cyberattack [56]. For example, if all multimedia files are viewed or shared on a large scale by one unusual user, an anomaly detection system should be able to detect this pattern and alert it for further inspection; this is a preventive measure to recognize inward risks, unauthorized access in the organization, or exporting important multimedia content, particularly from organizations that manage patent information with their secret assets.

13.5.9 Zero-Trust Architecture

Meanwhile, the zero-trust security model is a more sophisticated preventative measure. It ensures that media content accessed from the public domain or private cloud installations (i.e., not from within the network boundary) is verified and authenticated before proceeding. Running with the notion that no program, user, or device should be inherently trusted under any circumstances is not a novel concept; nonetheless, it does represent a significant advancement in IT security and risk management. Access to multimedia assets, on the other hand, requires constant validation. A zero-trust architecture will protect essential multimedia forensics tools and assets, preventing even authorized consumers from consuming content that they are only permitted to see, alter, or share [57]. This lowers the likelihood of data breaches, insider threats, and illegal access to multimedia. In addition, zero-trust systems commonly validate user identification and device security, as well as multi-factor authentication (MFA) configurations for multimedia data protection.

13.5.10 Secure Cloud Storage Solutions

As the cloud becomes a repository for an increasing number of multimedia files, it is vital to protect these storage solutions. A secure cloud storage solution comprises access control measures, encrypted transfer and storage, and regular vulnerability checks to ensure that multimedia content is protected from unwanted access or data breaches [58]. In response to rising demand, many popular cloud service providers are increasingly offering forensic-ready cloud environments with built-in logging and audit trails (to follow behavior) rather than simply supplying data to clients. These capabilities enable cybersecurity specialists and forensic investigators to detect illicit activity and determine the source of security breaches, allowing them to preserve evidence for future investigations [59].

13.5.11 Multimedia in Threat Intelligence

Another advantage of threat intelligence is the multimedia data it employs to help identify emerging threats—we're talking about images, video files, and audio recordings from any source available, such as social media forums, dark web forums, and communication channels. For example, the metadata in an image or movie published online may reveal vital information such as location and device information, which can be used to detect hackers. Threat intelligence platforms are looking for discussions about hacks, credentials that have been made public, or those that are about to be utilized in unlawful activities [60]. When paired with established vectors of concern, multimedia analysis can provide a more comprehensive understanding of spotting potential cyber threats.

13.6 LEGAL CONSIDERATIONS IN MULTIMEDIA FORENSICS

However, multimedia use in legal situations must consider the reliability and legitimacy of digital evidence. The chain of custody must be maintained to ensure that multimedia files have not been altered or tampered with during their transition from evidence to presentation in court. A break in the chain of custody may indicate that evidence is inadmissible and, depending on the finding of an appropriate court or tribunal, may result in its rejection. Similarly, courts must adhere to exceedingly strict criteria of admissibility for multimedia evidence [61]. Specifically, authenticity and authentication of multimedia files. This is when forensic experts guarantee that the multimedia evidence's integrity and authenticity are maintained by a series of processes such as digital signatures, hashing techniques, metadata analysis, and so on. These approaches enable the creation of forensic evidence that proves beyond a reasonable doubt whether any changes have been made to obtain multimedia data.

Privacy and ethical considerations are equally important in multimedia forensics. Investigators must strike a balance between collecting evidence and respecting the privacy of everyone whose multimedia data may be used in an investigation. It matters when it comes to sensitive information handling (e.g., private photos or videos) for privacy and a more profound research point of view. Having those sync passes open in some way allows for a better investigation into the companies' practices on how they protect our data without breaching their trust agreement with us developers who pay them money each month through safe business conduct [61].

13.7 RECOMMENDATIONS FOR CYBERSECURITY OF MULTIMEDIA ASSETS

13.7.1 Incident Response and Recovery Planning

Even with the greatest precautions in place, multimedia cybersecurity events can occur. It is difficult to detect, isolate, and remediate a compromise unless an incident response strategy is in place. The plan specifies how hacked multimedia assets can be recognized, and kept as evidence, and complex investigations conducted alongside cybersecurity professionals to prevent further damage. Planning for recuperation is equally important. If multimedia content is lost, modified, or even taken and maybe destroyed from its source, backup copies (access to media) enable the recovery of data without destroying fundamental evidence [62]. Furthermore, post-incident reviews help firms improve their cybersecurity posture by assessing how a breach occurred and changing the desired security policies.

13.7.2 International Collaboration and Standards

Furthermore, the avoidance of cyber threats in multimedia forensics requires an enforcement framework that includes international cybersecurity standards and encourages global cooperation. Because these cyber threats are typically hybrid operations involving international actors that leverage the borderless feature of multimedia interchange (the 0/1 rule), collaboration between governments and existing assets in law enforcement or cybersecurity know-how organizations is critical. Common international standards, such as the ISO/IEC 27037 guidelines, govern how digital evidence should be collected and handled, while forensic tool interoperability ensures consistency in multimedia forensics procedures worldwide, ensuring a level of uniformity, reliability, and legal admissibility across jurisdictions. Furthermore, international cooperation enables global combat of multimedia cybercrime, as well as the monitoring and capture of cybercriminals who cross national borders [63].

13.7.3 Supporting Cybersecurity and National Security

Advancements in multimedia tools used for cybersecurity and national security frameworks have dramatically altered how risks are discovered, managed, and examined.

Both forensic detection technologies and biometric analysis give actionable intelligence and act as a force multiplier in the prevention of illegal conduct. The ability to integrate digital forensic evidence with intelligence and physical data, such as surveillance footage or gait analysis, helps law enforcement agencies respond far more comprehensively when dealing with cybercrime—or anything related to national security [64]. They also use multimedia responses to improve cybersecurity and give solid guarantees for protecting vital infrastructure (private-sector information systems and state-owned information resources) from hostile influence and attack. As our lives become more digitized, the use of multimedia technologies becomes increasingly important in protecting data from unauthorized access or alteration by anything to be monitored in real time, such as cloud-based event monitors and biometric controls for accessing digital devices after an event.

13.7.4 Regulatory Framework for the Protection of Privacy of Multimedia Contents

The necessity for a robust regulatory framework to safeguard individual privacy and guarantee consent in the distribution of multimedia files has been brought to light by the quick development of digital technology, particularly in the areas of multimedia creation and sharing. A structure like this is required for several reasons [65]:

a. *Protection of privacy*: Individuals have the right to control the distribution and use of their identity, in forms such as a photograph, video clip, or audio recording. If there aren't sufficient rules, multimedia content might be distributed without authorization. This could lead to a breach of privacy and misuse such as identity fraud, cyberbullying, or risk to reputation.
b. *Informed consent*: To share multimedia files, consent is required, both ethical and legal. People must have complete knowledge of who is granted access to their digital content, how it will be utilized, and the potential ramifications of making it visible. A legislative framework would prevent misuse of individual private multimedia corpus by ensuring that appropriate consent processes are established.
c. *Handling deepfakes and manipulation*: With deepfakes and tampering of multimedia content, fears over fraud and disinformation have grown. This can provide a legal framework that sets standards for content authentication and penalizes individuals who spread manipulated or misleading media.
d. *Cybersecurity and data protection*: Metadata embedded in multimedia data may also contain private information (e.g., device or location information). Regulations should say that encryption and other security measures should be needed to stop illegal access or unlawful loss or misuse of personal data, and there should also be safe handling and sharing procedures.
e. *Legal Accountability*: It can make platforms and people legally liable for violations by putting down clear rules for you to share with the public. It would also provide victims of privacy violations with the ability to seek damages.

13.7.5 Public Awareness and Education

As multimedia files such as pictures, videos, and audio recordings are increasingly becoming our most vulnerable data in the digital era, the public must become conscious of how secure or insecure are such multimedia files. Countless users are at risk of data breaches as they store private multimedia files unwittingly on unsecured publications or devices. Individuals can become familiar with stronger security protocols like encryption and secure storage methods that preserve their multimedia data by gaining awareness about cybersecurity practices [66]. Users have no idea what the various threats are to their multimedia files, be it ransomware, malware, or social engineering scams, how to identify this atypical behavior, or how to share their information securely. In this regard, awareness campaigns can reduce the chances of being victimized by cyberattacks for them [66]. Such insight can also promote ethical conduct in cyberspace and help people understand the legal consequences of their actions.

REFERENCES

1. Saxena, A., Shrivastava, G., & Sharma, K. (2012). Forensic investigation in cloud computing environment. *The International Journal of Forensic Computer Science*, *2*, 64–74.
2. Snodgrass, R. T., Yao, S. S., & Collberg, C. (2004, August). Tamper detection in audit logs. In Proceedings of the thirtieth international conference on very large data bases (Vol. 30, pp. 504–515). Morgan Kaufmann Publishers.
3. Shrivastava, G., Gupta, D., & Sharma, K. (Eds.). (2021). *Cyber crime and forensic computing: Modern principles, practices, and algorithms*. De Gruyter.
4. Pavlou, K. E., & Snodgrass, R. T. (2008). Forensic analysis of database tampering. *ACM Transactions on Database Systems (TODS)*, *33*(4), 1–47.
5. Shrivastava, G., Peng, S. L., Bansal, H., Sharma, K., & Sharma, M. (2020). *New age analytics: Transforming the internet through machine learning, IoT, and trust modeling*. Apple Academic Press.
6. Kaur, S., & Kushwaha, A. K. S. (2018, December). A comparative study of various video tampering detection methods. In *2018 First international conference on secure cyber computing and communication (ICSCCC)* (pp. 418–423). IEEE.
7. Mall, V., Roy, A. K., & Mitra, S. K. (2013, December). Digital image tampering detection and localization using singular value decomposition technique. In *2013 Fourth national conference on computer vision, pattern recognition, image processing and graphics (NCVPRIPG)* (pp. 1–4). IEEE.
8. Rogers, M. K. (2008). Cyber forensics. In G. Voeller (Ed.), *Wiley handbook of science and technology for homeland security* (pp. 1–14). John Wiley & Sons, Inc.
9. Lian, S., Kanellopoulos, D., & Ruffo, G. (2009). Recent advances in multimedia information system security. *Informatica*, *33*, 1.
10. Boll, S., Aizawa, K., Briasouli, A., Gurrin, C., Jalali, L., & Meyer, J. (2016, October). Multimedia for personal health and health care. In Proceedings of the 24th ACM international conference on multimedia (pp. 1491–1492). Association for Computing Machinery. https://doi.org/10.1145/2964284.2980536
11. Skoudis, E. (2001). *Counter hack: A step-by-step guide to computer attacks and effective defenses*. Prentice Hall PTR.
12. Johnson, A., Jani, G., Pandey, A., & Patel, N. (2019). Digital tooth reconstruction: An innovative approach in forensic odontology. *Journal of Forensic Odonto-Stomatology*, *37*, 3.

13. Hou, S., Yiu, S. M., Uehara, T., & Sasaki, R. (2013). A privacy-preserving approach for collecting evidence in forensic investigation. *International Journal of Cybersecurity and Digital Forensics (IJCSDF)*, *2*(1), 70–78.
14. Hou, S., Uehara, T., Yiu, S. M., Hui, L. C., & Chow, K. P. (2011, October). Privacy preserving confidential forensic investigation for shared or remote servers. In *2011 Seventh international conference on intelligent information hiding and multimedia signal processing* (pp. 378–383). IEEE.
15. Hou, S., Uehara, T., Yiu, S. M., Hui, L. C., & Chow, K. P. (2011, November). Privacy preserving multiple keyword search for confidential investigation of remote forensics. In *2011 Third international conference on multimedia information networking and security* (pp. 595–599). IEEE.
16. Shinder, D. L., & Cross, M. (2008). *Scene of the cybercrime*. Elsevier.
17. Shrivastava, G. (2017). Approaches of network forensic model for investigation. *International Journal of Forensic Engineering*, *3*(3), 195–215.
18. Bianchi, T., De Rosa, A., & Piva, A. (2011). Improved DCT coefficient analysis for forgery localization in jpeg images. In *2011 IEEE international conference on acoustics, speech and signal processing (ICASSP)* (pp. 2444–2447). IEEE.
19. Bourlai, T. (Ed.). (2016). *Face recognition across the imaging spectrum*. Springer.
20. Chen, X., Li, F., Yang, J., & Yu, J. (2012). A theoretical analysis of camera response functions in image deblurring. In *European conference on computer vision* (pp. 333–346). Springer.
21. Chen, C., McCloskey, S., & Yu, J. (2019). Analyzing modern camera response functions. In *IEEE winter conference on applications of computer vision*, WACV 2019, Waikoloa Village, HI, USA, January 7–11, 2019 (pp. 1961–1969). IEEE.
22. Dirik, A. E., & Memon, N. (2009). Image tamper detection based on demosaicing artifacts. In 2009 16th IEEE international conference on image processing (ICIP) (pp. 1497–1500). IEEE.
23. Hsu, Y.-F., & Chang, S.-F. (2010). Camera response functions for image forensics: An automatic algorithm for splicing detection. *IEEE Transactions on Information Forensics and Security*, *5*(4), 816–825.
24. Jia, Y., Shelhamer, E., Donahue, J., Karayev, S., Long, J., Girshick, R., Guadarrama, S., & Darrell, T. (2014). Caffe: convolutional architecture for fast feature embedding. arXiv:1408.5093
25. LeCun, Y., Bottou, L., Bengio, Y., & Haffner, P. (1998). Gradient-based learning applied to document recognition. *Proceedings of the IEEE*, *86*(11), 2278–2324.
26. Liu, C., Freeman, W. T., Szeliski, R., & Kang, S. B. (2006). Noise estimation from a single image. In *2006 IEEE computer society conference on computer vision and pattern recognition* (Vol. 1, pp. 901–908). IEEE.
27. Mahdian, B., & Saic, S. (2009). Using noise inconsistencies for blind image forensics. *Image and Vision Computing*, *27*(10), 1497–1503.
28. Maji, S., Berg, A. C., & Malik, J. (2008). Classification using intersection kernel support vector machines is efficient. In *IEEE conference on computer vision and pattern recognition, 2008*. CVPR 2008 (pp. 1–8). IEEE.
29. Ng, R. (2006). Digital light field photography. PhD thesis, Stanford, CA, USA. AAI3219345.
30. Ng, T.-T., Chang, S.-F., & Tsui, M.-P. (2007). Using geometry invariants for camera response function estimation. In *2007 IEEE conference on computer vision and pattern recognition*. (pp. 1–8). IEEE.
31. Pentland, A. P. (1987). A new sense for depth of field. *IEEE Transactions on Pattern Analysis and Machine Intelligence PAMI*, *9*(4), 523–531. https://dl.acm.org/doi/10.1109/TPAMI.1987.4767940
32. Ronneberger, O., Fischer, P., & Brox, T. (2015). U-net: Convolutional networks for biomedical image segmentation. In *Medical image computing and computer-assisted intervention (MICCAI)* (Vol. 9351, pp. 234–241). LNCS. Springer. arXiv:1505.04597 [cs.CV]

33. Mathur, S., Choudhary, S. K., & Vyas, J. M. (2013). Speaker recognition system and its forensic implications. *Open Access Scientific Reports*, *2*(4), 723.
34. Mathur, S., Choudhary, S. K., & Vyas, J. M. (2016). Effect of disguise on fundamental frequency of voice. *Journal of Forensic Research*, *7*(327), 2.
35. Simonyan, K., & Zisserman, A. (2014). Very deep convolutional networks for large-scale image recognition. arXiv:1409.1556
36. Tai, Y.-W., Chen, X., Kim, S., Joo Kim, S., Li, F., Yang, J., Yu, J., Matsushita, Y., & Brown, M. S. (2013). Nonlinear camera response functions and image deblurring: Theoretical analysis and practice. *IEEE Transactions on Pattern Analysis and Machine Intelligence*, *35*(10), 2498–2512.
37. Tsin, Y., Ramesh, V., & Kanade, T. (2001). Statistical calibration of CCD imaging process. In *Eighth IEEE international conference on computer vision, 2001. ICCV 2001. Proceedings* (Vol. 1, pp. 480–487). IEEE.
38. Singh, N., & Joshi, S. (2015). Digital image forensics: Progress and challenges. Paper presented at the 31st National Convention of Electronics and Telecommunication Engineers, Jaipur, India.
39. Wronski, B., Garcia-Dorado, I., Ernst, M., Kelly, D., Krainin, M., Liang, C.-K., Levoy, M., & Milanfar, P. (2019). Handheld multi-frame super-resolution. *ACM Transactions on Graphics*, *38*(4).
40. Böhme, R., Freiling, F. C., Gloe, T., & Kirchner, M. (2009, August). Multimedia forensics is not computer forensics. In *International workshop on computational forensics* (pp. 90–103). Springer.
41. Hsu, C. Y., Kang, L. W., & Liao, H. Y. M. (2013, July). Cross-camera vehicle tracking via affine invariant object matching for video forensics applications. In *2013 IEEE international conference on multimedia and expo (ICME)* (pp. 1–6). IEEE.
42. Schultz, E., & Shumway, R. (2001). Incident response: A strategic guide to handling system and network security breaches, Sams, Carmel, Indiana.
43. Aneja, P., Sharma, P., Sood, K., Solanki, K., Choudhary, S. K., & Mathur, S. (2024). Artificial intelligence in multimedia forensics. In *Artificial intelligence in forensic science* (pp. 43–64). CRC Press.
44. Palmer, G. (2001, August). A road map for digital forensic research. First digital forensic research workshop, Utica, New York (pp. 27–30).
45. Parveen, S. S., & Palanikkumar, D. (2015). A novel approach for inter frame copy move forgery detection. *International Journal of Applied Information Communications Engineer*, *1*, 60–62.
46. Zhang, L., Zhang, D., & Wang, L. (2010, October). Live digital forensics in a virtual machine. In *2010 International conference on computer application and system modeling (ICCASM 2010)* (Vol. 4, pp. V4–328). IEEE.
47. Mathur, S., & Vyas, J. (2016). Acoustic analysis for comparison and identification of normal and disguised speech of individuals. *Journal of Forensic Science and Criminology*, *4*(4), 403.
48. Hoelz, B., Ralha, C., & Mesquita, F. (2011, January). Case-based reasoning in live forensics. In *IFIP international conference on digital forensics* (pp. 77–88). Springer.
49. Shrivastava, G., Sharma, K., Khari, M., & Zohora, S. E. (2018). Role of cybersecurity and cyber forensics in India. In *Handbook of research on network forensics and analysis techniques* (pp. 143–161). IGI Global.
50. Sharma, K., Makino, M., Shrivastava, G., & Agarwal, B. (Eds.). (2019). *Forensic investigations and risk management in mobile and wireless communications.* IGI Global.
51. Shrivastava, G., & Gupta, B. B. (2014, October). An encapsulated approach of forensic model for digital investigation. In *2014 IEEE 3rd global conference on consumer electronics (GCCE)* (pp. 280–284). IEEE.

52. Singh, A., Joshi, A., Sankhla, M. S., Saini, K., & Choudhary, S. K. (2024). AI in data recovery and data analysis. In *Artificial intelligence in forensic science* (pp. 142–164). CRC Press.
53. Al-Athamneh, M., Kurugollu, F., Crookes, D., & Farid, M. (2016). Digital video source identification based on green-channel photo response non-uniformity (G-PRNU). In Proceedings of the Sixth International Conference on Computer Science, Engineering & Applications (ICCSEA 2016) (pp. 51–60). AIRCC Publishing Corporation. https://doi.org/10.5121/csit.2016.61105
54. Kallitsis, M., Stoev, S. A., Bhattacharya, S., & Michailidis, G. (2016). AMON: An open source architecture for online monitoring, statistical analysis, and forensics of multi-gigabit streams. *IEEE Journal on Selected Areas in Communications*, *34*(6), 1834–1848.
55. Wolfe, H. B. (2002, June). Encountering encrypted evidence (potential). In Proceedings of the 4th conference on information technology curriculum (pp. 1–4). ACM.
56. Li, S., Dhami, M. K., & Ho, A. T. (2015). Standards and best practices in digital and multimedia forensics. In *Handbook of digital forensics of multimedia data and devices* (pp. 38–93). Wiley Online Library.
57. Baker, D. W., Brothers, S. I., Geradts, Z. J., Lacey, D. S., Nance, K. L., Ryan, D. J., Sammons, J. E., & Stephenson, P. (1988). Digital evolution: History, challenges and future directions for the digital and multimedia sciences section. In D. H. Ubelaker (Ed.), *Forensic science: Current issues, future directions* (pp. 252–291). Wiley-Blackwell.
58. Ng, T. T., Chang, S. F., Lin, C. Y., & Sun, Q. (2006). Passive-blind image forensics. In *Multimedia security technologies for digital rights management* (pp. 383–412). Academic Press.
59. Shrivastava, G., Kumar, P., Gupta, B. B., Bala, S., & Dey, N. (Eds.). (2018). *Handbook of research on network forensics and analysis techniques*. IGI Global.
60. Franke, K., & Srihari, S. N. (2007, August). Computational forensics: Towards hybrid-intelligent crime investigation. In Third international symposium on information assurance and security (pp. 383–386). IEEE.
61. Khari, M., Shrivastava, G., Gupta, S., & Gupta, R. (2017). Role of cybersecurity in today's scenario. In *Detecting and mitigating robotic cybersecurity risks* (pp. 177–191). IGI Global.
62. Kruchten, P. (2010). A survey on digital forensics trends. *IEEE Software*, *27*(3), 92–94. https://doi.org/10.1109/MS.2010.70
63. Mikkilineni, A. K., Chiang, P.-J., Ali, G. N., Chiu, G. T. C., Allebach, J. P., & Delp III, E. J. (2005). Printer identification based on graylevel co-occurrence features for security and forensic applications. Security, steganography, and watermarking of multimedia contents VII, *5681*(0219893), 430. https://doi.org/10.1117/12.593796
64. Xidonas, P., Kountzakis, C. E., Hassapis, C., & Staikouras, C. (2016). A use of Black-Scholes model in market risk. *International Journal of Financial Engineering Risk Management*, *2*(3), 200. https://doi.org/10.1504/ijferm.2016.082983
65. Zakariah, M., Khan, M. K., & Malik, H. (2018). Digital multimedia audio forensics: Past, present and future. *Multimedia Tools Application*, *77*(1), 1009–1040. https://doi.org/10.1007/s11042-016-4277-2
66. Battiato, S., Emmanuel, S., Ulges, A., & Worring, M. (2012). Multimedia in forensics, security, and intelligence. *IEEE Multimedia*, *19*(1), 17–19. https://doi.org/10.1109/MMUL.2012.10

14 Global Security Agencies and Cyberwar Forces

Roopali Pahwa and Vinayak Gupta

14.1 INTRODUCTION

Security is the state of being protected against any potential threat of criminal activity to harm any person, institution, organisation, state, or nation. All these beneficiaries are interrelated. If one of the beneficiaries is abused, it will have some impact on the other. Of these, the most crucial is the nation's security, as all other factors depend on national security. The nation's government must protect the country against any internal or external invasions by utilising its military forces and with the help of some government or private security agencies. The organisation and the government frame the international laws and policies to regulate the attacks and ensure national or global security in a highly webbed world [1]. As a result, there has been a shift in perception regarding national security strategies, the organisation of national security, the structures to preserve it, and the skills needed in this respect, including civil-military cooperation [2].

Weapons such as axes, swords, and crossbows were initially used in warfare. The introduction of gunpowder led to the development of cannons and guns, which became increasingly precise and sophisticated over time. Finally, the creation of nuclear weapons, extremely potent and capable of causing massive destruction, occurred [3]. Additionally, recognition of the connection between internal and external security is growing worldwide. In order to address a problem at its source, relevant actors have begun collaborating on various projects. These projects include military and civilian operations conducted in the framework of the Common Security and Defence Policy (CSDP) [3]. With more technical advancements, Cyberattacks can be employed in combat and have become an imminent threat to national security. Globally, cybercrime has evolved and increased tremendously in the past few years and has become more severe and complex to tackle [1].

As cybercrime is done illegally over interconnected networks or devices worldwide, it may spread rapidly over the Internet. It may affect several devices, harming the nation's crucial data as there are no cyber borders [4]. To handle the cyberattacks on the organisational or state level, the government is utilising intelligence agencies, and at the military level, different units of cyberwar forces are introduced that are trained to defend against cyberwarfare and also work as an emergency cyber response team. The cyberwar forces have become the fourth military domain. The air, coast, terrain, space, and cyberspace are the five spheres of military operations within NATO. Cybersecurity may help the other domains in the long term as it is fast

DOI: 10.1201/9781003497868-14

and easily reachable, whereas other domains may fail to reach as it has no borders or social or cultural barriers [5, 6].

The cyber force still needs some advancement in defence technologies as crime is more heinous with time, and criminals may use new offensive tricks to hack and steal data. Thus, the personnel must also be trained and equipped accordingly [7]. The cases of cyberwarfare are increasing nowadays as it is easier and cheaper than the conventional methods where more manpower, weapons, and resources are required and bring the same results. Cybersecurity personnel must be highly skilled in computer technologies and good at decision-making. Also, they must follow the trends in digitalisation, cyberattacks, and defence technologies [6].

14.2 GLOBAL SECURITY AGENCIES

A country's intelligence agency or global security agency is responsible for providing the government and any organisation in power with reliable, accurate, and credible information that could help them strengthen their security. These agencies work nationally and internationally to protect the country from foreign invaders and espionage [8]. Furthermore, intelligence serves more than just the basis for state policy. It has always played a crucial role in guiding and performing actions that might be against national or global legislation and may not always be accepted. In addition to their relatively passive role of gathering intelligence on international affairs, intelligence services attempt to subtly affect events through clandestine means [9]. These agencies support the other security frameworks of the country, such as the law department, military security, and public security, and help maintain international relations [8]. Security agencies at the state level have the potential to save lives. However, on the international stage, they can either promote peace or be used to justify conflict, leading to loss of life [10].

This intelligence is often clandestine, consisting of information that an adversary seeks to hide and withhold. While it is generally acknowledged that the topic of intelligence studies is under-theorised, some areas have gotten more attention than others. Since this field has had the most thorough conceptualisation, policymakers must take precautions against unexpected attacks, which is one of the most important needs for intelligence. Furthermore, intelligence services have long argued that stability is enhanced by their capacity to provide general transparency to the global system. Countries are trying to strengthen their security infrastructure by upgrading their weapons and military [11]. The government has security agencies that employ highly skilled personnel, but sometimes, they get help from **Private Intelligence Agencies (PIAs)**. The work of intelligence agencies often needs to be kept secret to be effective. In the past, intelligence has been controlled by a small group of people, but it is essential to remember that intelligence is too crucial to be left solely to spies [9].

In the 21st century, there is no universally accepted definition of intelligence [12]. According to Mark Lowenthal (2002), there are three alternative interpretations of the term "intelligence". Firstly, it is seen as gathering, analysing, and providing information to consumers such as policymakers and operational commanders. Secondly, this process is commonly called the "intellectual cycle", although its essence is currently widely debated. Thirdly, it is evident that states rely on both external and internal security for their well-being. However, external intelligence has focused most on managing international relations. The possibility of organising intelligence in a transnational manner is also being considered [9]. The security agencies of some prominent countries are listed as follows.

14.2.1 US Intelligence Agencies

The United States has a large intelligence fraternity consisting of 18 independent entities, each operating under its veil of secrecy (Figure 14.1). The Department of Defense or Congress typically oversees these institutions, leaving the common public unaware of how they operate. Quantifying how much the United States spends on these clandestine operations each year is impossible, given that they are funded chiefly by classified budgets. However, one 2012 estimate puts the cost at $75 billion [13].

After revisions were made to the National Security Act (1947), the Intelligence Reform and Terrorism Prevention (IRTP) Act, 2004 was passed. This act designated the officer in charge of **National Intelligence (NI)** as the executive officer of the United States Intelligence fraternity, supervising and guiding the National

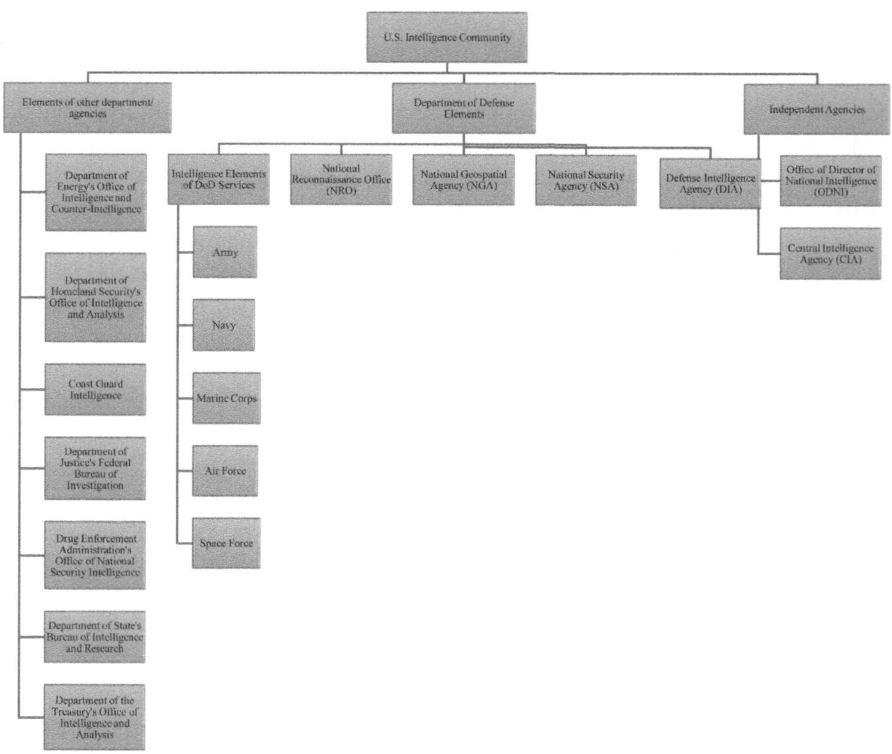

FIGURE 14.1 Different departments of the US Intelligence Fraternity.

Intelligence Program's deployment and acting as the principal consultant on national security intelligence matters to the US president, the Homeland and National Security Councils. Figure 14.1: A structured chart displaying the different departments of the US Intelligence Community. The President appoints the director of NI with the senate's advice and approval [13].

The **Central Intelligence Agency (CIA)** was formed on September 18, 1947. It comprises interdisciplinary mission centres integrating all analytic, operational, support, technological, and digital capabilities. To safeguard US national security interests, in response to directives from the head of the nation, it conducts clandestine operations, obtains foreign intelligence, and offers independent evaluation. To address high-priority issues like the prohibition on proliferation, the fight against terrorism, intelligence countermeasures, organised crime, drug trafficking, and weapons control, they oversee specialised mission centres. Develop partnerships among intelligence collection disciplines, conduct all-source analysis, and contribute to community-wide efforts. Manage standard services such as imagery analysis and open-source collection and collaborate on technical research and development [14].

On July 26, 1908, Bonaparte instructed Department of Justice attorneys to inform 34 agents to the Chief Examiner and select one agent to handle most of the investigating matters. This led to the formal establishment of the **Federal Bureau of Investigation (FBI)**, with the mission of conducting investigations on behalf of the Department of Justice [15]. The primary goals of the FBI are to defend civil rights, combat worldwide criminal enterprises, combat grave acts of violence, fight serious cybercrime, safeguard the United States from terrorist acts of terrorism, and combat foreign intelligence, intelligence gathering, and cyber operations [16].

14.2.2 British Intelligence Agencies

The United Kingdom is home to multiple intelligence and security services. The military's many branches have historically been in charge of procuring intelligence. However, distinct intelligence services have taken on more significant roles since 1909, functioning in tandem with and apart from the military. **Security Service (MI5)** is the Secret Service Bureau's domestic branch, which was established in 1909. It is in charge of defending the nation against dangers to state security, including espionage, the spread of Weapons of Mass Destruction (WMDs) and terrorism. Although MI5 is not a division of the Home Office, it functions under the authority of the Home Secretary.

Overseas intelligence gathering is the responsibility of the **Secret Intelligence Service (MI6)**, which was set up around 1909 as the Secret Service Bureau's Foreign Section. It operates as a body for the Foreign and Commonwealth Office. In 1919, it was known as the Government Code and Cypher School (GCCS) before becoming the Government Communications Headquarters (GCHQ). It is responsible for preventing and detecting major crime and supplying signal information to the government. The Foreign Secretary is the minister in charge of GCHQ [16].

The **National Cybersecurity Centre (NCSC)** employs industry and academic expertise to foster the United Kingdom's cybersecurity capability. It comprehends cybersecurity and simplifies this information into widely accessible practical advice.

It handles cybersecurity issues in a way that minimises the harm they do to businesses and the United Kingdom. With its head office located in London, NCSC was founded in October 2016. It combines the knowledge of the GCHQ information assurance division, CESG, CERT-UK, and the Centre for Protection of National Infrastructure, renamed the National Protective Security Authority (NPSA) in March 2023 [17].

Other than these intelligence agencies, the United Kingdom has British Army Intelligence, Naval Intelligence, Air Ministry Intelligence, Defence Intelligence (DI), Joint Intelligence Organisation (JIO), Special Operations Executive (SOE), Joint Services School of Intelligence (JSSI), National Technical Assistance Centre (NTAC), National Crime Agency (NCA), Serious Fraud Office (SFO), Financial Conduct Authority (FCA), Her Majesty's Revenue and Customs (HMRC), UK Border Force, and Metropolitan Police Counter Terrorism Command (CTC) [17].

14.2.3 Security Agencies of India

India's external intelligence organisation, the **Research and Analysis Wing (RAW)**, has long been criticised for meddling in the affairs of its neighbours. Initially established in 1968 as an antagonist to China's influence, it has gradually turned its attention to Pakistan. The organisation has been acknowledged for having substantially raised India's influence overseas over the previous 40 years and broadened its scope. When RAW was established, its top aims were to further develop its capacity for gathering intelligence on China and Pakistan as well as to execute covert operations in East Pakistan (now Bangladesh). Observing the political and military events in neighbouring nations, which directly affect India's national security and foreign policy formulation, is one of the broader goals that RAW has expanded to incorporate over time, seeking to regulate and restrict the flow of military gear, mainly from China, the United States, and Europe, to Pakistan.

Serving as India's internal security agency and in charge of reducing internal threats, the **Intelligence Bureau (IB)** is regarded as the oldest intelligence body still operational in the world. The IB works under the supervision of the Ministry of Home Affairs. The director of IB may respond directly to the prime minister and is a member of the Joint Intelligence Committee (JIC) of the National Security Council and the Strategic Policy Group. The Major tasks performed by the IB of India involve counterterrorism, counterintelligence, border intelligence collection, and VIP security.

Through the National Investigation Agency (NIA) Act of 2008, the **NIA** came into being. NIA is India's counterterrorist organisation. The agency can address terror-related crimes across states without requiring additional consent from those jurisdictions [18]. Figure 14.2: An infographic showcasing India's major security agencies.

14.2.4 Pakistani Intelligence Community

The Federal Investigation Agency (FIA), Intelligence Bureau (IB), Military Intelligence (MI), and Inter-Services Intelligence (ISI) are Pakistan's top security agencies, handling both foreign and domestic matters. Pakistan's most significant

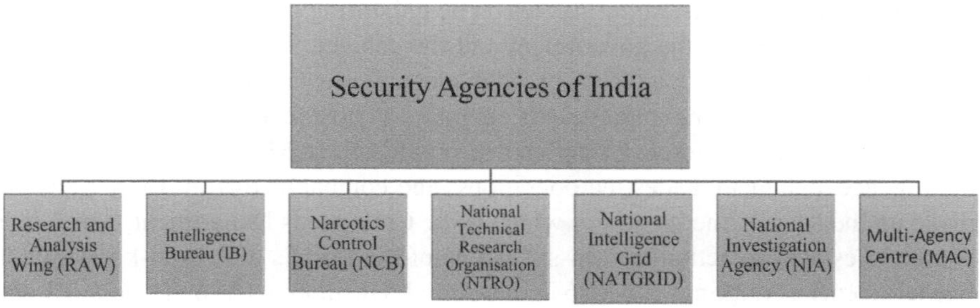

FIGURE 14.2 Different security agencies of India.

domestic intelligence and reconnaissance organisation is the **IB**. The IB keeps tabs on suspected terrorists, foreign intelligence agents, politicians, and political activists. It is responsible for pressuring internal opposition groups and for keeping an eye on political operatives from countries that it deems hostile to Pakistan's interests. According to credible allegations, the authorities often use wiretapping and occasionally intercept and open mail [19].

The **Inter-Service Intelligence (ISI)** was established in 1948 to improve intelligence cooperation between the air, naval, and military forces soon after the first conflict with India. Major General R. Cawthorne led it initially. His leadership of ISI persisted until 1956. Following that, it remained decapitated for nearly three years as Pakistan experienced constitutional unrest that ultimately resulted in Ayub Khan's first martial law takeover. JIX, or Joint Intelligence Headquarters, was the name given to the ISI headquarters; JIN, or Joint Intelligence North, could represent the location of field deployments. Additionally, there were sections labelled JCIB (Joint Counter Intelligence Bureau), JIM (Joint Intelligence Muslim/Middle East), and JIB (Tech) [20].

The Pakistan Army's chief intelligence branch, **Military Intelligence (MI)**, has its headquarters at the Army General Headquarters in Rawalpindi, Pakistan. MI's primary goal is to control military capabilities and other intelligence about adversarial nation's armed forces. The Pakistan Navy's Naval Intelligence (NI) and the Pakistan Air Force's Air Intelligence (AI) chiefs collaborate with the MI. They submit all of their work reports to the MI Director-General. Every officer and person who has been commissioned is an Army veteran. The Pakistan Army officers are closely monitored by the MI as well. In addition, MI's responsibilities include gathering offensive counterinsurgency intelligence, locating and eliminating foreign agent sleeping cells, and carrying out other anti-state activities in Pakistan [21].

14.2.5 Intelligence Agency of Israel

Following the October 7 attack on the State of Israel, which Hamas spearheaded, the international community has paid more attention to the Israeli Intelligence Community. This piece will not address Israel's October 7 intelligence failure. **Aman** is the Israel Defence Forces (IDF)'s military intelligence branch. Its main objective is to give the IDF and the government intelligence alerts. Consequently, Aman drafts daily intelligence reports, target studies on neighbouring Arab nations, and national intelligence reports for the government and the cabinet. To do this, Aman collects intelligence from military attachés based in embassies overseas, surveillance flights, and reconnaissance commando squads operating in hostile areas.

Mossad is Israel's foreign intelligence organisation. Mossad personnel gather intelligence, conduct clandestine operations, and combat terrorism. Eight divisions make up the agency, the biggest of which is the Collections Department, which is in charge of espionage activities. Mossad is one of the world's most well-known intelligence agencies, ranking with MI6 in the United Kingdom, CIA in the United States of America, and the Russian Federal Security Service. Like the FBI in the United States, **Shin Bet** is Israel's domestic counterintelligence and counterterrorism organisation. The Israeli Prime Minister, other government figures, the defence industry, key economic sites, Israeli posts overseas, and El Al, the country's flag carrier, are all under the protection of Shin Bet [21].

14.2.6 Russian Intelligence Agency

The **Federal Security Service** or **Federal'naya Sluzhba Bezopasnosti (FSB)** is a Russian internal security and counterintelligence agency established in 1994 to replace the Soviet-era KGB. It is in charge of countering espionage, anti-terrorist operations, and military inspections. The FSB operates from the former KGB headquarters in Downtown Moscow. During the late 1980s, when the Soviet government and economy collapsed, the KGB fared superior to the majority of state agencies, with significantly less staff and budget layoffs. The agency was abolished, however, following an attempted coup over Mikhail Gorbachev, the Soviet President, in August 1991, in which several KGB units were involved. The KGB's internal security operations were rebuilt in early 1992, initially as the Department of Security and then as the Russian Federal Counterintelligence Service (FSK) only two years afterwards, which eventually came under presidential authority. In 1995, Russian President Boris Yeltsin reorganised FSB's services. He expanded its capabilities, allowing it to enter private residences and conduct intelligence operations in Russia and abroad in collaboration with the Russian Foreign Intelligence Service (SVR) [22].

14.2.7 German Intelligence Agency

The **Bundesnachrichtendienst** is the Federal Republic of Germany's foreign intelligence body that acquires military, financial, and political data. The federal government has assigned it a higher level of authority. The Bundesnachrichtendienst's diverse responsibilities set it apart. A plethora of experts in numerous sectors ensures that it stays current, whether about changes in politics in the East, hacking groups, or the latest advances in weapons technology [23]. Their task entails gathering information outside what is generally known about both facts and beliefs. This allows them to investigate what goes on, cast light on the situation, and provide an unbiased perspective – always in the interests of Germany's security and the legal structure. It frequently operates in the shadows, and their accomplishments are rarely visible. There are six divisions of the BundesÂnachrichtendienst, that include research and training, cutting-edge technologies, evaluation, intelligence capabilities, centralised assistance jobs, intelligence gathering, and IT support [24].

14.3 CYBERSPACE AND CYBERWARFARE

Cyberspace is a crucial area for special operations like warfare and cyberwarfare. It was underlined how special wars function as a form of "soft power". Since there are an infinite number of possible adversaries for the nation in the event of cyberwar, elements of cyber-civilian infrastructure, basically military readiness including the mobilisation of soldiers via the civilian sector, are also likely targets and are in grave danger [6]. To accomplish goals in or via cyberspace, activities in cyberspace use cyberspace capabilities. Managing and protecting the global information grid are examples of such operations, as are computer network operations [25].

Hybrid warfare is a particular kind of cyberwar or warfare. Military theories identify cyberspace as the fifth battlespace. This fifth fighting area, which has no boundaries and disregards social, cultural, or physical restrictions, is rapidly growing. This area intrudes into every person's privacy, and using sophisticated algorithms and analytical tools, it "learns" all of the user's habits.

"Hybrid warfare" does not refer to traditional military combat with weapons. The unorthodox methods used in hybrid warfare mainly apply information technology in the "new space" produced when we characterise it as cybernetic. To identify potential threats originating from this region and carrying out specific psychological operations following the established objectives, which may include protecting a state, a community, a population, critical infrastructure, or even significant individuals, has grown increasingly significant in the field of security services [6].

Cyberwarfare describes the employment of cyberattacks by a state or organisation to compromise information stored on computer systems, computer networks, and computer infrastructures of another state or organisation in warfare. Since cyberwarfare is a subset of traditional warfare and a distinct field of endeavour, the justification for these goals is comparable to other forms of warfare [26]. Cyberwarfare refers to measures a country's government takes to cause harm or disruption by breaking into the IT infrastructure or systems belonging to another country. According to this view, cyberwarfare only occurs between national governments to further national agendas like informational supremacy [27]. Cyberwarfare includes state-sponsored activities and non-governmental organisations entities, including corporations or hacker groups, whose objective is independent of a country's goal [28].

Trojan horses, viruses, and worms are only a few weapons used in cyberwarfare's digital battles. Such weapons render systems inoperable, resulting in data loss or malfunctions. Critical Information Infrastructure (CII) overloading is also done using different applications to abuse or cause interruption. Networks or systems monitoring computer literacy (CI) and the programs the government and significant organisations deploy are known as CIIs [29].

Cyberterrorism refers to actions that use computer technology to threaten the public, sway government policies, or affect government behaviour through coercion [28]. While the objectives, tactics, and methods of carrying out cyberterrorism and cyberwarfare are identical, the subjects of their strategies and attackers are different. While states frequently fund cyberwarfare, cyberterrorism is considered not state-sponsored. When a cyberattack that targets servers or networks produces sufficient collateral damage to incite dread akin to a real-life act of terrorism, it represents cyberterrorism [29].

14.4 CYBERWARFARE INCIDENTS AND WEAPONS USED IN CYBERWAR

Cybercrime, according to Chandra and Snowe (2020), is any criminal conduct that makes use of computer technology. "Cyber-dependent" and "cyber-enabled" crimes are the subdivisions of cybercrime. Prior to the advent of technological advances in computers, cyber-enabled crimes were more difficult to prosecute. Examples include identity theft, drug trafficking, stalking, and white-collar crime. At the same time, cyber-dependent offences rely on computer technology to occur. Malware is used in such instances to commit crimes.

Iran's nuclear power plants were compromised by the Stuxnet malware. Since Iran's nuclear facilities, state's critical infrastructure was the attack's primary target, it qualifies as cyberwarfare. The fact that the nuclear centrifuges were destroyed suggests a cyberwarfare occurrence, as these events usually attempt to damage or destroy computer infrastructure.

APT Moonlight Maze targeted multiple US CIs. The online assault was thought to have been launched by another state, namely Russia, and it was directed at a state's cyber infrastructure. The assailants exacerbated political problems by stealing confidential data.

Distributed Denial of Service (DDoS) assaults were made against AMMAR, a Tunisian government-owned ISP, as well as the state. Due to the fact that a state-owned enterprise and Internet properties of the Tunisian government were the targets of DDoS assaults, this incident can be classified as cyberwarfare. The attacks were motivated by politics and resulted in significant disruptions. A non-governmental entity was the assailant [30].

Fatal ransomware assault NotPetya, which at first looked like ransomware, mostly affected Ukrainian enterprises but also affected institutions across the globe. But it swiftly expanded throughout the world, impacting businesses across a range of industries. Both major disruption and monetary losses were brought about by it. The attack's origin is still unknown; however, it is generally accepted to have been a state-sponsored operation with the intention of causing financial harm.

There was yet another episode in Ukraine, in December 2015, a Trojan horse named BlackEnergy compromised the Ukrainian power distribution infrastructure. The energy supply to about 225,000 people was cut off by this attack. Moreover, it was revealed that BlackEnergy was supposed to be used to erase picture and video files that could sway the outcome of the Ukrainian election around the time of the election [31].

These instances show how cyberattacks can seriously affect a country's security by compromising critical systems, resulting in financial losses, disclosing confidential data, and occasionally even worsening tensions between nations.

14.5 CYBERWARFARE FORCES

Though relatively new, it has only been around for a few years. Many nations and organisations have indeed started towards formal cyberwarfare troops. In many instances, substantial organisations have appeared seemingly out of nowhere despite their incomplete operational readiness to tackle a significant battle. Since plenty of these departments and organisations have yet to be tested in real-world situations, it is even unclear precisely what qualifies as operational [25].

14.5.1 Cyber and Information Domain Command, Germany

The new organisational unit is responsible for defending Germany's digital assets and cyberspace, mirroring the roles of the army, air, space, and sea. For everyone, digitalisation holds a wealth of options and possibilities. Almost everyone uses these new technologies in their personal or professional lives. Nevertheless, digitalisation has come with a lot of issues. The Internet has long since stopped being a fictional threat. This trend also affects the Bundeswehr. As an adversary, the Bundeswehr is a valuable target because of its advanced weaponry and information technology. The Cyber and Information Domain Service's responsibilities include guarding, safeguarding, and mitigating attacks on information systems and networks used by the Bundeswehr.

Furthermore, the Cyber and Information Domain Service is responsible for espionage and influence on foreign systems. The Bundeswehr has pooled its IT expertise in the Cybersecurity and Information Domain Service to ensure optimal readiness for upcoming advancements. The goal is to use the benefits of technological advancement while reducing the risks that come with it. Cyber and Information Domain command was found in 2017. Its headquarters is in Bonn. The chief is in charge of staff, supplies, and purchases, in addition to overseeing the operations and training of service members. It is responsible for the Bundeswehr Geoinformation Centre, the Strategic Reconnaissance Command, the Bundeswehr Communication and Information Systems Command, and its affiliated agencies [32].

14.5.2 People's Liberation Army, China

The People's Liberation Army (PLA) has created an officially recognised cyberwarfare paradigm. It organises suitable training for its officers and carries out military drills and cyberwarfare scenarios within the confines of a unified national strategy. To assist the objectives of the government, Beijing's intelligence services keep gathering data on science and technology, and the Chinese economy prioritises goods manufactured locally to suit its technological demands. Although the PLA and its Russian counterpart have close links, there is a strong indication that Beijing is trying to create a distinct model for conducting cyberwarfare. The Chinese military started investigating cyberattacks as an unconventional way to fight a more technologically advanced opponent online and offline. The PLA has generated a cyberwarfare ideology, given its officers rudimentary training, and carried out cyberwarfare drills with the assistance of an organised national plan. China asserts that it is creating a novel approach to cyberattacks. However, upon closer inspection, much of what is supposedly novel resembles studies conducted by US specialists in cyberwarfare.

China has one of the world's greatest conventional forces but lacks digital C4I capabilities. The Chinese military has made significant investments in modernising its C4I networks. Efforts have highlighted the fragility of widely available technology, leading to increased spending on computer network defence, particularly against viruses. The Chinese military conducts regular training on information technology breakthroughs for its officers. Chinese training incorporating cyberattacks into regular circumstances has improved their understanding of information operations dynamics. PLA is recruiting technical expertise to strengthen its cyberwarfare capabilities. Despite this, the PLA is aware of its limited efficacy because it cannot project force and engage in a full-scale conventional conflict with the United States. In March 2002, the DoD calculated that China's publicly disclosed military budget amounted to $20 billion. However, much of PLA spending, including R&D and acquisitions of foreign weapons, has not been disclosed. Estimates for the PLA budget range from $65 billion to $77 billion [33].

14.5.3 Indian Defence Cyber Agency

In 2018, the Government of India and the Ministry of Defence agreed to improve the cyber posture of defence forces. The Defence Cyber Agency (DCA) and the Cyber Groups of Army, Navy, and Air Force were established to protect and defend the technological and informational assets of defence forces and deter adversary's endeavours in cyberwarfare. The following operations have notably contributed to improving the Defence Force's Cybersecurity procedure: (i) Greater cooperation among cyber groups and national cyber authorities; (ii) enhanced data protection measures, including strengthened technology, efficient oversight, safe procedures, raised user awareness, harmonised processes, and audit controls, and (iii) improved readiness for cyberwarfare, including an organised reaction to incidents using centralised threat databases, libraries, and event recordings [32].

The Government of India laid the foundation of DCA in 2019 to handle the escalating dangers in cyberspace. Strong cybersecurity measures are now essential due to the quick digitalisation of many industries, including defence. DCA was established to strengthen India's cyber capabilities, safeguard vital defence infrastructure, and fend off hostile cyberattacks [34].

In 1998, the Indian Army publicly proclaimed a change of ideology to include information operations and electronic warfare. This new ideology, often known as the IT Roadmap, lists ambitious goals through 2008. These initiatives aim to "enhance the IT quotient" per soldier by addressing hardware, software, and human resource development. The goal of the Roadmap is to establish a strong information technology infrastructure to act as a force multiplier through the implementation of a completely computerised and networked operational and executive information system, supplemented by fully information-skilled manpower [35].

14.5.4 Cyber Defence Command and Islamic Revolutionary Guards Corps Cybersecurity Command, Iran

Iran is quickly establishing itself as an influential force in the constantly evolving environment of global cyberwarfare, illustrating complex cyberattacks that pose an enormous challenge to its adversaries. The expansion of Iran's cyber arsenal indicates its strategically important expenditure on cyberwarfare as a means of national defence and strength projection [36]. Cyber Defence Command is the Iranian military's Cyber Headquarters, which coordinates offensive cyber assaults with the Basij Cyber Council. The organisation could be a spin-off from the United States Cyber Command [37].

The Islamic Revolutionary Guard Corps is a division of the Iranian Armed Forces that supervises offensive cyber actions [37]. This team specialises in adversarial cyber activities, including sabotaging vital systems and espionage. It is noted for its mobility and the use of advanced cyber tools. The United States recognised the Islamic Revolutionary Guard Corps as a foreign terrorist group in 2019. APT33, aka "Elfin" aka "Holmium" (Shamoon), APT34 (OilRig), and APT35 (Charming Kitten) are the key operational units to carry out cyber offensive operations [36].

14.5.5 13th Signal Regiment UK

13th Signal Regiment, the Army's newest and sole Cyber Unit, is accountable for safeguarding the Army's information technology assets from opponent cyber threats both at the Pentagon and abroad. It was created in June 2020 and specialises in Defensive Cyber Operations. The signal squadron mentioned below operates in conjunction with the 13th signal regiment.

224 (Cyber Protection Team) Signal Squadron is Army's tactical Defensive Cyber Operations specialist. The Squadron houses Cyber Protection Teams, which are made up of Cyber Engineers, Cyber Threat Analysts, and their particular devices. Cybersecurity Units respond to deployments and drills worldwide to defend networks against real-world cyber hazards. They monitor and harden friendly networks using various technologies and their technical expertise while also hunting for and analysing criminal activity on these networks.

The Army Cyber Information Security Operating Centre (ACyISOC) is located at 233 Signal Squadron. It offers 24 × 7 support to the Army's primary network of wide-area networks and data infrastructure for communication. Its staff serve as subject matter experts in various fields, offering worldwide assistance for army operations. The ACyISOC offers dedicated cyber defence to the army's essential data systems.

The 259th Signal Squadron (Global Information Systems) provides defence-wide, specialist assistance regarding tactical communication networks and how they smoothly communicate, sharing information with other systems, within as well as their connections and globally. The squadron's technical competence also assists actual CIS during both training exercises and actual operations. The squadrons, which bring united military personnel, mariners, and airmen from 17 different cap badges, play an important role in equipping units that will use these systems and integrate them with those of all of our worldwide allies. The CIS Trials Development Unit (TDU) plays an important role since technology on the front lines constantly changes. Their work is done in close collaboration with commerce to test and assess the most cutting-edge communication systems for use in the military [38].

14.5.6 North Atlantic Treaty Organization

North Atlantic Treaty Organization (NATO) is a military and political alliance that includes nations from Europe and North America. Its participants are dedicated to safeguarding one another from any attack. To resolve concerns, develop trust, and eventually prevent conflict, NATO promotes democratic norms and allows members to discuss and collaborate on defence and security issues. It is geared towards addressing conflicts amicably. It has the military capability to take emergency action if diplomatic efforts fail. The activities are conducted either independently or in collaboration with other countries and organisations worldwide. This is done in compliance with a United Nations directive or under the cooperative defence clause of the fifth article of the Washington Agreement, which was NATO's founding document. Member nations confer and make judgements on security matters daily across many domains and at all levels. Since all decisions are made by collaboration, a "NATO decision" represents the combined will of the 32 member nations. Together with national delegations and the staff at NATO's main office, hundreds of government officials, as well as public and armed forces personnel, visit NATO Headquarters every day to discuss ideas, exchange information, and assist in decision-making when necessary [39].

14.6 INTELLIGENCE GATHERING METHODS

The intelligence-gathering process is essential to modern warfare since it tells us about potential adversary actions as well as their future plans. To mention a few, intelligence may cover things like adversary weaponry, unit numbers, troop mobility, and future operations schedules. There are various methods for intelligence gathering, like using human informants, utilising satellites to capture specific region images. Intelligence information, regardless of how it is obtained, is utilised to decide how to proceed with offensive and defensive combat operations inside the impacted battlefield [40]. The major intelligence gathering methods are discussed as follows.

14.6.1 Human Intelligence

Human intelligence (HUMINT) obtains data to gather important information and insights, intelligence professionals may employ debriefings, informants, interviews, and espionage.

14.6.2 Signals Intelligence

Signals intelligence (SIGINT) involves the analysis and interception of electronic signals, such as those sent by radio, phone, and the Internet. It facilitates keeping an eye on and comprehending the actions of people, groups, and countries.

14.6.3 Imagery Intelligence

Imagery intelligence (IMINT) utilises imagery captured by drones, satellites, or surveillance planes. It provides visual data valuable for following movements, analysing infrastructure, and monitoring military actions.

14.6.4 Measurement and Signature Intelligence

Measurement and signature intelligence (MASINT) gathers information about targets' technical and physical characteristics, including their chemical makeup, radiation exposure, and radar signatures. It helps to recognise and define particular threats.

14.6.5 Cyber Intelligence

Cyber intelligence (CYBINT) is concerned with keeping an eye on and evaluating dangers and digital activity in cyberspace. This entails monitoring hacker group's activities, vulnerabilities, and cyberattacks.

14.6.6 Financial Intelligence

In order to identify illicit or questionable operations, such as money laundering, financing of terrorism, and economic espionage, financial intelligence (FININT) entails monitoring and evaluating financial transactions.

14.6.7 Geospatial Intelligence

Geospatial intelligence (GEOINT) creates geospatial information by fusing data from multiple sources. It facilitates the mapping and comprehension of topography, geographic features, and how they affect operations.

14.6.8 Social Media Intelligence

Social media intelligence (SOCMINT) monitors and examines social media sites to learn about trends, public opinion, and possible dangers. It is useful for gauging public sentiment and newly emerging issues.

14.6.9 Chemical, Biological, Radiological, and Nuclear Intelligence

The chemical, biological, radiological, and nuclear (CBRN) intelligence is concerned with identifying and evaluating risks related to chemicals, biological, radiological, and nuclear sources, including WMDs. Governments, law enforcement agencies, and intelligence organisations rely on a variety of information collection methods to stay informed, make sound decisions, and protect national security [5].

14.7 CONCLUSION

The organisation and the government frame the international laws and policies to regulate the attacks and ensure national or global security in a highly webbed world.

As a result, there has been a shift in perception regarding national security strategies. The data presented in the six preceding nation studies demonstrates that foreign armies and authorities pursue cyberwarfare technologies for various reasons and purposes. The reasons why different nations try to intrude or penetrate other's systems vary. These include integrity of data breaches, software vandalism, surveillance collection, and perception maintenance. To further contextualise the nation evaluations in the aforementioned report, this chapter compiles a number of aspects of the cyberwarfare environment. With the advancement and evolution of cyberwarfare programs, intellectual complexity rises. However, as a general rule, we discriminate between exploiting Internet connectivity (as a carrier) to attack critical facilities and exploiting networks (the target). Consequently, it is critical to distinguish between targets that are spatially localisable and those that are global or even national in scale, such as the community transport network's communications infrastructure or the systems of federal and state government organisations. This chapter summarises a number of aspects of cyberwarfare units, international security agencies, and intelligence collection techniques. With the advancement and evolution of cyberwarfare programs, intellectual complexities rise. A nation-state can carry out an attack by spoofing or hiding the source of the digital hops in cyberspace, in addition to employing or funding cyberwarfare agents. There are multiple methods to conceal origins, all thanks to modern technologies. By disguising the source of the attack, such laundering methods have the tendency to erode traditional discouragement, which is based on the prospect of a prompt and precise counterattack.

REFERENCES

1. Malik, F., & Bengio, Y. (2024). The role of international law in governing cyber attacks and national security. *ResearchGate* (Vol. 23, No. 1, pp. 296–304). Springer. https://doi.org/10.13140/RG.2.2.12178.67527
2. Drent, M., Dinnissen, R., Van Ginkel, B., Hogeboom, H., Homan, K., Sandee, D., & Meijnders, M. (2022). *Relationship between external and internal security.* Clingendael Institute.
3. DeVries, K. R., DeVries, K., & Smith, R. D. (2012). *Medieval military technology.* University of Toronto Press.
4. Chang, W., Chung, W., Chen, H., & Chou, S. (2003). An international perspective on fighting cybercrime. In *Intelligence and security informatics: First NSF/NIJ symposium, ISI 2003*, Tucson, AZ, USA, June 2–3, 2003 Proceedings 1 (pp. 379–384). Springer.
5. Mattila, J. K. (2024). Arranging the defence of the cyber environment as a part of military affairs: Tactical, operational and strategic approach in retrospect of the Russian-Ukrainian war 2022. In *Proceedings of the 23rd European conference on cyber warfare and security (ECCWS 2024*. Academic Conferences International. https://doi.org/10.34190/eccws.23.1.2353
6. Trifunović, D., & Bjelica, S. (2020). Cyber war: Trends and technologies. *National Security & Future*, *21*(3).
7. Kalberg, J., Beitlman, M. V., Mitusoka, M. V., Officer, C. W., Pittman, J., Boyce, M. W., & Arnold, L. C. T. W. (2022). The tactical considerations of augmented and mixed reality implementation. *Military Review*, *662*, 105.
8. BYJU'S. (2022, July 4). V-I graph of which material shows the straight line. Byjus.com; BYJU'S. https://byjus.com/free-ias-prep/intelligence-agencies-of-different-countries/v

9. Kupcikas, K. (2013, November). The importance of intelligence to international security. *E-International Relations Students*. https://www.e-ir.info/2013/11/08/importance-of-intelligence-to-international-security/
10. Gill, P., & Phythian, M. (2013). *Intelligence in an insecure world*. John Wiley & Sons.
11. Aldrich, R. J. (2010). Intelligence and international security. In *Oxford research encyclopedia of international studies*. Oxford Research Encyclopedia.
12. Andrew, C., Aldrich, R. J., & Wark, W. K. (2009). *Secret intelligence: A reader*. Routledge.
13. Office of the Director of National Intelligence. (n.d.). What we do. https://www.dni.gov/index.php/what-we-do
14. *Central Intelligence Agency*. (n.d.). www.cia.gov. https://www.cia.gov
15. Federal Bureau of Investigation (FBI). (n.d.). Mission & priorities. https://www.fbi.gov/about/mission
16. Intelligence Studies: Types of Intelligence Collection. (2024, May 20). U.S. Naval War College. Retrieved September 25, 2024, from https://usnwc.libguides.com/c.php?g=494120&p=3381426
17. EU Intelligence. (2023, September 24). 15 powerful British intelligence agencies. https://euintelligence.com/intelligence/british-intelligence-agencies/. About the NCSC. ncsc.gov.uk. https://www.ncsc.gov.uk/section/about-ncsc/what-we-do
18. *Updated Value Addition Material 2024*. (n.d.). Retrieved December 17, 2024, from https://cdn.visionias.in/value_added_material/5edaf-challenges-to-internal-security-through-communication-networks.pdf
19. Pike, J. (n.d.). Intelligence Bureau – Pakistan intelligence agencies. Retrieved [September 17, 2024], from https://www.globalsecurity.org/intell/world/pakistan/ib.htm
20. Banerji, R. (2011). Pakistan: Inter-services intelligence directorate (ISI) – an analytical overview. *Journal of Defence Studies*, *5*(4), 19.
21. Calderon, J. An overview of the Israeli intelligence community. ONC. https://www.ournationalconversation.org/post/an-overview-of-the-israeli-intelligence-community. Last accessed: July 29, 2025.
22. Pringle, R. W., & Ransom, H. H. (n.d.). Intelligence | Definition, history, agencies, examples, & facts. Encyclopedia Britannica. https://www.britannica.com/topic/intelligence-international-relations
23. *About BND*. (n.d.). BND. https://www.bnd.bund.de/EN/About-BND/the_bnd_node.html
24. *Bundesnachrichtendienst (BND)*. (n.d.). Homepage. https://www.bnd.bund.de/EN/Home/home_node.html
25. Andress, J., & Winterfeld, S. (2013). *Cyber warfare: Techniques, tactics, and tools for security practitioners*. Elsevier.
26. Asbaş, C., & Tuslukaya, Ş. E. (2023). Cyberwarfare: War activities in cyberspace. In *Handbook of research on war policies, strategies, and cyber wars* (pp. 128–145). IGI Global.
27. Clarke, R. A., & Knake, R. K. (2010). *Cyber war: The next threat to national security and what to do about it*. HarperCollins.
28. Robinson, M., Jones, K., & Janicke, H. (2015). Cyber warfare: Issues and challenges. *Computers & Security*, *49*, 70–94.
29. Vilić, V. M. (2017). Dark web, cyber terrorism and cyber warfare: Dark side of the cyberspace. *Balkan Social Science Review*, *10*(10), 7–25.
30. Bhaiyat, H., & Sithungu, S. (2022, March). Cyberwarfare and its effects on critical infrastructure. *International Conference on Cyber Warfare and Security*, *17*(1), 536–543.
31. Digmelashvili, T. (2023). The impact of cyberwarfare on national security. *Future Human Image*, *19*, 12–19.
32. *Cyber Warfare*. (2021, December 3). https://www.pib.gov.in/PressReleasePage.aspx?PRID=1777609

33. Billo, C., & Chang, W. (2004). Cyber warfare. *An analysis of the means and motivations of selected nation states.* Dartmouth, ISTS.
34. *Defence Cyber Agency (DCA) - GKToday.* (n.d.). www.gktoday.in. https://www.gktoday.in/defence-cyber-agency-dca/
35. Pandit, R. (2002, September 30). Army logs on to e-highway to beat enemy in IT race. *The Times of India.*
36. Ferrante, M. D. (n.d.). Iran's cyber warfare: Strategies and global defense. *CITANEX.* https://citanex.com/resources/irans-cyber-offensive-capabilities-structure-strategy-countermeasures/
37. Theohary, C. A. (2020). Iranian offensive cyberattack capabilities, Congressional Research Service.
38. The Royal Corps of Signals 13 Signal Regiment. (n.d.). Army be the best. https://www.army.mod.uk/who-we-are/corps-regiments-and-units/royal-corps-of-signals/13-signal-regiment/
39. North Atlantic Treaty Organization (NATO). (n.d.). What is NATO? https://www.nato.int/nato-welcome/index.html
40. Pearson, S., & Watson, R. (2010). New age of warfare: How digital forensics is reshaping today's military. In *Processing the digital crime scene; digital triage forensics* (pp. 1–11), Syngress.

15 Security Testing
Cyber Incident and Vulnerability, Mitigations and Forensics

Khadija Slimani, Vinay Aseri, Aayush Gupta, and Arnav Dua

15.1 INTRODUCTION TO SECURITY TESTING

15.1.1 Defining Security Testing

Security testing is a subdivision of software testing, which is primarily dedicated to demonstrating that applications, systems, or networks cannot be compromised or abused by outside threats. However, functional testing investigates whether the states of a system are performing their intended features while security testing is geared toward discovering weaknesses of the system that may be institutionalized by hackers or anybody else. This will therefore include checking possible breaking, unauthorized access, data leakages, and conformity with the internal and external security policies and standards.

Functional testing verifies the "what" of a system to ensure that the features behave as expected. Security testing analyzes the "how" and defines how hard the system can withstand real attacks. Functional testing cares more about user experience and operational success. In contrast, security testing cares about resilience and trust [1].

Key types of security testing include:

1. **Vulnerability Scanning:** Identifying known vulnerabilities in the system.
2. **Penetration Testing:** Simulating real-world attacks to exploit vulnerabilities.
3. **Security Audits:** Reviewing code, configurations, and policies for compliance.
4. **Risk Assessment:** Evaluating the likelihood and impact of potential threats.
5. **Ethical Hacking:** Conducting authorized hacking activities to discover vulnerabilities.
6. **Posture Assessment:** Assessing the overall security readiness of an organization.

These methods collectively aim to fortify the systems, safeguard user data, and ensure business continuity against security threats caused by bad actors.

DOI: 10.1201/9781003497868-15

15.1.2 The Importance of Security Testing in Modern Software Development: A Non-Negotiable Imperative

Today, software applications are an essential support for interconnected critical infrastructure, financial systems, healthcare, and international communication. The reliance on software has thus increased the security stakes immensely. Nowadays, cyber threats and data thefts are the very core of the risk, so security testing is an indisputable necessity. Instead of an optional activity, security testing is now a central element of the software development life cycle (SDLC), which all should consider for their businesses, users, and vital systems.

15.1.2.1 Rising Security Threats in the Age of Digital Transformation: An Expanding Attack Surface

Although it brings enormous advantages, digital transformation has also been responsible for greatly expanding the attack surface for malicious operators. The adoption of cloud computing, Internet of Things (IoT) devices, artificial intelligence (AI), and remote work practices has made new vulnerabilities and provided more opportunities to exploit them.

- **Risks to Cloud Security:** While cloud environments provide a remarkable scale and flexibility, they introduce some unique security problems. Example misconfiguration and insecure Application Programming Interfaces (APIs), as well as vulnerabilities in cloud-native applications that cybercriminals can leverage when exploiting their interest.
- **IoT Vulnerabilities:** The rise of IoT devices creates a very wide network of access points for the attacker with little to no security features in them. Insecure firmware, weak default credentials and lack of encryption make IoT devices open to compromise.
- **AI-Powered Attacks:** As AI technologies mature, attackers increasingly use them to automate their attacks, defeat security perimeters, and carry out more targeted and effective malicious campaigns.
- **Remote Work Security Gaps:** With the new work-from-home regularization, the boundary of organizations has extended, thus directing the spotlight onto new security issues concerning endpoint security, access control, and data protection.
- **Vulnerabilities in Supply Chains:** Software supply-chain attacks, such as the SolarWinds incident, can wreak havoc among organizations because they have one vendor that can be compromised. By increasing their reliance on third-party components and software, organizations have put themselves at an even greater risk of supply-chain risks than before.
- **Ransomware Attack:** Organizations all over the world face challenges with data stolen, encrypted, and held at ransom by malware. The impact on an organization can cripple several functional areas, and in many cases, it leads to significant losses in revenue.
- **Sophisticated Phishing Campaigns:** Modern phishing attacks are so sophisticated that they almost exclusively target selected individuals or

organizations as their direct victims, using highly personalized and convincing bait. These lures manage to bypass either internal security practices of email clients and compromise user credentials.

The increasing sophistication and frequency of these threats underscore the critical need for robust security testing throughout the SDLC.

15.1.2.2 Impact of Vulnerabilities on Businesses and Users: Far-Reaching Consequences

The consequences of inadequate security testing extend far beyond financial losses. Breaches can have devastating impacts on businesses and users alike.

Impact on Businesses

- **Monetary Losses:** Data breaches cost a great deal in terms of remediating damages, legal advice and fines by government regulatory agencies, in addition to loss in revenue.
- **Degradation of Reputation:** A breach is a potential source of a very heavy blow to reputation, pouring lost trust from clients into its negative influence in brand loyalty.
- **Regulatory Penalties:** Among other types of penalties, an organization might pay heavy fines for lack of compliance with relevant data security and privacy regulations like GDPR, CCPA, and HIPAA.
- **Operational Changes:** In the event of cyberattacks, businesses can be disrupted resulting in downtime, loss of productivity, and interruptions of services.
- **Intellectual Property Theft:** Cyber criminals might plunder valuable intellectual property, such as trade secrets, and research data, causing a competitor to suffer a considerable disadvantage when that value becomes non-competitive.

Impact on Users

- **Identity Theft:** When personal data is breached then identity theft takes place. This can lead to identity theft activities that create fraudulent activities and financial losses.
- **Financial Fraud:** Stolen financial records are the new tool that used to unauthorized transactions, which drain down the bank accounts and incur debts.
- **Privacy Violation:** A breach of data can expose sensitive personal information that violates privacy and emotional turmoil.
- **Loss of trust:** Users could lose faith in organizations that fail to demonstrate that their data are better protected and thus become less involved with the brand, a situation termed as churn.

15.1.2.3 Proactive Security Testing: A Shift-Left Approach

In the modern process of developing software, security testing is not an after-the-fact process but rather proactive throughout and early. This is where it falls beautifully into line with DevSecOps. It is the shift-left testing approach to software engineering practices, which emphasizes taking care of design and code security at the beginning of the development lifecycle.

- **Reduced Costs:** Early identification and treatment of development process vulnerabilities may save a lot of money as compared to their later correction after deployment.
- **Faster Time-to-Market:** Faster time-to market is made achievable by the integration of security testing into the development process thereby enabling efficient engineering of the most secure software.
- **Improved Security Posture:** Proactive security testing enables organizations to discover and mitigate vulnerabilities before they may be exploited and thus greatly enhances their overall security posture.
- **Enhanced Collaboration:** Shift-left security enables collaboration between developers, testers, and security personnel as regards security efforts.
- **Continuous Improvement:** Regular security testing and continuous monitoring allow organizations to adopt and adapt to the threat landscape and improve security practices continuously.

Organizations can improve their cyberattack prevention, secure really important assets, and maintain customers' and stakeholders' trust by becoming proactive about security testing and seamlessly build it into their SDLC. The long-term success of the security and resilience program may also require continuous improvement in security from new emerging threats and changes to the system as conditions change over time.

15.1.3 Evolution of Security Testing

15.1.3.1 Historical Context: From Manual to Automated Tools

Security testing dates back to the days of computing when security checks were manual and limited. Early testers adopted ad-hoc methods, usually concentrating on password strength and access control. As systems became complex, the necessity for systematic methodologies for security testing grew.

The advent of the automated tool in the late 1990s turned the stage. Tools such as Nessus and Metasploit converted vulnerability scanning and penetration testing into straightforward and repeatable methodologies for testers. These very tools lay the foundation for modern security testing practice, which now easily integrates into CI/CD pipelines.

The emergence of SAST and DAST was reaching toward holistic applications security solutions in the 2000s. Thus, developers could find more vulnerabilities while coding and runtime, respectively. Recently, IAST and RASP have attracted a lot of attention as they use real-time surveillance with advanced analytics for threat detection and mitigation.

15.1.3.2 Emerging Trends in Security Testing

The developments in security testing have not been static but changed as new threats emerged and technologies progressed. The following are some key trends shaping the future of security testing:

1. **Shift-Left Security:** It refers to the early testing that helps identify application vulnerabilities during development rather than later during the remedial stage, thus reducing costs.
2. **AI and Machine Learning (ML):** The use of AI to discover and predict irregularities and threats, as well as automate repetitive steps, creates faster and more precise testing.
3. **Cloud Security Testing:** Testing for risks that are cloud originating, such as misconfiguration or API vulnerabilities, that have their specific issues.
4. **Zero-Trust Architecture (ZTA):** These require intensive security testing, strict identity verification, and least privileged access.
5. **IoT Security Testing:** This is being done to ensure the security of connected devices and the entire mobility ecosystem spanning networks from being exploited by malicious elements.
6. **Compliance-Driven Testing:** Testing that aligns with compliance frameworks, such as GDPR, HIPAA, and PCI DSS, focuses on data protection and legality.

Finally, making security testing a seamless part of DevSecOps workflows has become a best practice and is now considered adding security in every life cycle stage of the SDLC. Developers can use such tools as GitHub Advanced Security and OWASP ZAP to address vulnerabilities without having to disrupt their work [2].

15.1.3.3 The Role of Continuous Monitoring

Modern security testing doesn't end with deployment. Continuous monitoring ensures that applications remain resilient against evolving threats. Techniques like security orchestration, automation, and response (SOAR) enable real-time detection and mitigation of incidents, minimizing downtime and impact.

15.2 TYPES OF SECURITY TESTING

15.2.1 Vulnerability Scanning

15.2.1.1 Purpose and Methodology

Vulnerability scanning is a central and baseline component of security testing, which is known to identify known flaws in the systems, applications, and networks. The whole idea is pretty much to make a complete report for an organization about the condition of its security posture by determining weaknesses that can be exploited by potential intruders. Helps organizations to remain compliant with the rules and regulations of the industries with requirements such as PCI-DSS, HIPAA, and GDPR.

The methodology involves the use of automated tools to:

1. **Network Scanning:** Enumerate open ports, discover running services, extract system configurations, and identify operating systems.
2. **Check for Known Vulnerabilities:** To check within the Common Vulnerabilities and Exposures or National Vulnerability Database.
3. **Generate Reports:** Includes the vulnerability description, risk levels, and mitigation strategy recommendation detail.

Vulnerability scanning can be conducted in two main ways:

- **Internal Scanning:** Performing scans from within the organization's network is to discover the kinds of vulnerabilities that a hacker might exploit using insider knowledge or compromised systems.
- **External Scanning:** Performing security scans from outside the network; it is for testing perimeter defenses such as firewalls and external-facing servers.

Popular Tools

1. **Nessus:** Used for scanning from an overall standpoint of network, application, and operating system purposes. Anticipating plugins for extending function and upgrading vulnerability databases in real-time, Nessus is compatible with each plugin in order to extend these features [3].
2. **OpenVAS:** Open-Source Alternative, Excellent for Network Vulnerability Scanning, With Abundant Reporting Features, and Highly Customizable for Scan Configuration [4].
3. **Qualys Vulnerability Management:** Cloud-based platform vulnerability detection solutions that work in real-time in hybrid environments. Qualys incorporates patch management solutions for easier remediation.
4. **Rapid7 InsightVM:** Risk-based vulnerability prioritization, with actionable insights and dynamic dashboards for easy visualization [5].

15.2.2 Penetration Testing

15.2.2.1 Goals and Approaches

Penetration testing, or pentesting, assesses by simulating an actual attack against the security measures. While vulnerability scanning involves discovering the existing and known problems, penetration testing breaches these barriers and determines how the weaknesses can actually be exploited and the extent of damage possible. Penetration testing is actually one of the significant validation processes that can be undertaken to ensure the vulnerability is really capable of being exploited and dangerous.

Approaches to penetration testing include:

1. **Black-box Testing:** The tester has no prior knowledge of the system, mimicking an external attacker. This approach is useful for assessing the organization's external attack surface.
2. **White-box Testing:** The tester has full access to the system, including source code, architecture, and design documents, to uncover deep-seated vulnerabilities. This method is particularly effective for identifying logical errors and complex vulnerabilities.
3. **Grey-box Testing:** Combines elements of black-box and white-box testing, where the tester has partial knowledge of the system. This approach balances efficiency and coverage.

Real-World Examples

- **Threat Simulation:** Colonial Pipeline Attack Following the 2021 ransomware attack, simulated pen tests revealed weaknesses in operational

technology networks, underscoring the critical need for striking the right security posture to protect critical national infrastructure at large.
- **Banking Systems:** Keeping a regular pentest practice shows discovered vulnerabilities in ATMs and online banking platforms significantly reducing the risks of unauthorized transactions or even data breaches.
- **IoT Devices:** Pentesting smart cameras, industrial sensors, and a number of other IoT devices has uncovered default configurations, legacy firmware, and weak security protocols in the device communications [6].

Popular Tools

- **The Metasploit Framework:** A potent simulator of attacks and validator of vulnerabilities. Built to allow scripting and enriching assessments by integrating other security tools.
- **Burp Suite:** This primarily works for web application penetration testing and it allows one to proxy, spider and vulnerability scan their applications.
- **Kali Linux:** A Linux distribution specifically made for penetration testers and comes with a high number of pre-installed tools such as Wireshark, Hydra, and Aircrack-ng.

15.2.3 Risk Assessment Testing

Risk assessment testing focuses on identifying, analyzing, and prioritizing potential risks to an organization's systems and data. Unlike vulnerability scanning, which identifies technical flaws, risk assessment evaluates the likelihood and impact of various threat scenarios, helping organizations develop strategic responses.

Key Steps

1. **Risk Identification:** Catalog potential threats such as malware attacks, insider threats, accidental or intentional changes in system configurations, and supply-chain vulnerabilities.
2. **Risk Analysis:** Determine the probability and extent of damage for each threat scenario using qualitative or quantitative techniques; risk scores are calculated according to asset value or vulnerability severity multiplied by likelihood of a threat.
3. **Risk Prioritization:** Build up a hierarchical risk inventory in terms of severity and business impact. Risk-based priority action measures risks that will cause maximum damages.
4. **Mitigation Planning:** Formulate and execute measures to reduce risks, such as policy application and upgrade of systems and additional control measures.

15.2.3.1 Outputs

A risk assessment return is a risk matrix that classifies risks by their likelihood and impact. Such a matrix helps decision-makers in the allocation of resources toward risk management efforts.

15.2.4 Static and Dynamic Application Security Testing (SAST and DAST)

15.2.4.1 Comparing SAST and DAST Tools

- **SAST (Static Application Security Testing):**
  - Examines source code for vulnerabilities without executing the application.
  - Ideal for identifying coding errors, hardcoded credentials, and insecure APIs.
  - Popular tools: SonarQube, Checkmarx, Fortify.
  - Advantages: Provides early detection of vulnerabilities during the development phase, reducing remediation costs.
  - Limitations: Limited in identifying runtime vulnerabilities.
- **DAST (Dynamic Application Security Testing):**
  - Evaluates running applications by simulating real-world attacks.
  - Focuses on runtime vulnerabilities like SQL injection, cross-site scripting (XSS), and authentication issues.
  - Popular tools: OWASP ZAP, Burp Suite, Acunetix.
  - Advantages: Identifies vulnerabilities in real-time and validates the effectiveness of security controls.
  - Limitations: Requires a running application and cannot pinpoint the exact source of the vulnerability in the code.

15.2.4.2 Integration into CI/CD Pipelines

To ensure continuous security, SAST and DAST tools are integrated into CI/CD pipelines. For example:

- **Pre-commit Checks:** Developers use SAST tools to catch vulnerabilities before committing code.
- **Runtime Analysis:** DAST tools scan staging environments for runtime vulnerabilities.
- **Automation:** Tools like GitHub Advanced Security, Jenkins plugins, and GitLab CI/CD pipelines streamline integration, reducing manual effort.
- **Shift-Left Approach:** Incorporating security testing early in the development lifecycle ensures vulnerabilities are addressed promptly.

15.2.5 Security Regression Testing

Security regression testing ensures that newly deployed updates, patching work, or additions do not introduce vulnerabilities into the application. This becomes very important during the stage of agile development because changes are frequent [7].

Key Practices

1. Automated Testing: Automated test suites can check whether the security controls are intact after modifications. Selenium and Cypress can be used for security test automation.

2. Baseline comparisons: Compare the new build to old baselines for drift. Known vulnerabilities are re-tested also.
3. Continuous Monitoring: Continuous monitoring detects the introduction of new vulnerabilities after deployment. Integrated with tools such as Splunk and ELK Stack, it supports real-time monitoring of application logs and security events.

15.2.6 Fuzz Testing

15.2.6.1 Purpose

Fuzz testing—otherwise called fuzzing—is a method by which random or malformed unexpected data is inputted to applications to discover aberrant behavior or vulnerabilities. It attempts to improve the robustness of edge cases by forcing such behaviors due to crashes or memory leaks or other security issues. Fuzz testing would supplement the test methods by finding out why they fail rather than covering those found using traditional descriptions.

15.2.6.2 Methodology

1. **Input Generation:** Random or malformed inputs are to be generated using fuzzing tools. Nowadays fuzzers are coverage guided to have an improved input generation.
2. **Application Execution:** The inputs are fed into the application, and behaviors are monitored, often in terms of memory usage, response times, and error messages.
3. **Crash Analysis:** Identifying the sources of crashes or strange behaviors. Diagnosing such memory issues is possible using tools such as AddressSanitizer and Valgrind.

15.2.6.3 Popular Tools

- **AFL (American Fuzzy Lop):** Efficiently fuzzes applications and identifies vulnerabilities. AFL's guided fuzzing approach ensures high code coverage.
- **LibFuzzer:** Integrates with LLVM to provide coverage-guided fuzzing. It's particularly effective for libraries and APIs.
- **OWASP DefectDojo:** A platform that integrates fuzzing with other security testing tools, providing centralized reporting and management.
- **Peach Fuzzer:** Focused on fuzzing protocols, file formats, and APIs, making it suitable for a wide range of applications.

15.2.6.4 Case Studies

- **Heartbleed Vulnerability:** Fuzz testing revealed the infamous Heartbleed bug in OpenSSL, which exposed sensitive data from servers.
- **IoT Device Security:** Fuzzing firmware for IoT devices has identified vulnerabilities in communication protocols, such as Zigbee and MQTT.

15.3 COMMON VULNERABILITIES AND TESTING APPROACHES

15.3.1 Overview of OWASP Top Ten Vulnerabilities

The OWASP Top Ten is a universal benchmark in web application security, presenting a ranked collection of the most crucial security risks that organizations face today. This year's OWASP Top Ten has also included emerging threats related to cloud-native applications as well as APIs and AI systems. So, by 2024, it still signals the evolution of threats in cyberspace. This chapter is a must-have for any developer, security expert, or organization intent on seeking protection against attacks with their software.

1. **Attacks With Injection:** Injection vulnerabilities such as SQL injection and LDAP injection are still hazards in attack vectors. To exploit such types of flaws in a system, an attacker injects malicious data into input fields designed for different purposes to manipulate various backend systems. For instance, an important financial platform encountered a breach because unvalidated input from a user enabled access to some sensitive databases. The biggest defenses against this are, among others, parameterized queries and input validation frameworks.
2. **Fraudulent Authentication:** The authentication vulnerabilities have been diversified as attackers have started employing the usage of credential stuffing and multifactor fatigue attacks. This needs to be considered as access to the portal for most employees has been by remote access, and this offers a platform that can easily be manipulated. Phishing attacks targeting login portals are increasingly common and emphasize the need for strong multifactor authentication and good session management practices. Weak authentication issues leading to data breaches in the healthcare and e-commerce space were highlighted in case studies from 2022 to 2023.
3. **XSS:** The injection of malicious scripts by an attacker in the web application so that it gets executed in a user's browser. With the advent of client-side frameworks such as React and Angular, the momentum has shifted toward mitigating DOM-level XSS attacks. However, the wave of storage attack and reflected attack is still in force and very much a threat. 15% of the web vulnerabilities reported in 2023 were XSS-related attacks.
4. **Security Misconfigurations:** Misconfigurations have often been a potential cause for breaches such as exposed cloud storage buckets, unpatched applications, and unnecessary enabled features. Among recent incidents include some that involved attacking publicly available databases on cloud platforms leading to millions of records being leaked. Automated tools like Kubernetes security scanners are now increasingly being used to search for these kinds of misconfigurations and fix them.
5. **Insecure Design:** It's a new class here mentioned in the 2021 OWASP update. Unsecure processes or processes not designed keeping in mind security practices at the beginning can prove to be the points of no return. Design flaws cannot be corrected after deployment, like inadequate threat modeling. Research in 2024 stated that embedding secure design principles within the development lifecycle reduces vulnerabilities by 40%.

6. **Insecure APIs:** Modern applications tend to be based on APIs and at the same time, API remains one of the most major attack vectors. Insufficient Authentication, Rate-limiting Issues, and Data Exposure are some common vulnerabilities in APIs. There are other examples that include 2023 T-Mobile API attack among others, which have specified the need to have very secure API measures.
7. **Sensitive Data Exposure:** They still can access sensitive unprotected data with increasingly improved encryption technologies, such as attaching plain text passwords in logs or exposing personal data from improperly configured cloud environments. Having end-to-end encryption and being compliant with standards such as GDPR remains critical.
8. **Vulnerable and Outdated components:** Dependency on third-party libraries and frameworks increases the risk if they are not updated and patched. The echoes of a supply-chain attack on one of the most widely used JavaScript libraries solemnly remind us of the importance of dependency management processes in 2023.
9. **Identification and Authentication Failures:** This category focuses on authentication mechanisms, which emphasizes on the risks like default credentials and poor password policies. With the rise of biometric authentication there are new challenges which have emerged, including spoofing and deepfake-related attacks.
10. **Inadequate Asset Handling:** As an organization digitally scales; it becomes hardly possible to keep an inventory of all assets. Untracked and unmanaged assets, such as forgotten sub domains or legacy systems, are the primary targets for an attacker. Modern asset management tools take AI to detect and secure such vulnerabilities.

The OWASP Top Ten serves as the basic foundation for security tests, helping organizations prioritize and overcome the most critical vulnerabilities for the ever-changing threat landscape. Security professionals need to regularly upgrade their practices and tools so as to always counter an attacker.

15.3.2 Testing for Input Validation and Injection Attacks

15.3.2.1 Understanding Input Validation Vulnerabilities

Furthermore, one of the most severe security issues in modern applications remains input validation vulnerabilities. Applications do not validate, filter, or cleanse the user input correctly, resulting in malicious code or command being executed by the attacker. The impact of such vulnerabilities has evolved from the advent of increasingly complex applications and new technologies developed for use in web environments.

15.3.2.2 Common Injection Attack Vectors

15.3.2.2.1 SQL Injection Testing

SQL injection, as one of the most popular attacks, is still mentioned in OWASP Top Ten. It has evolved further when compared to just using simple concatenation attacks. Modern methods for SQL injection attacks include quite high innovations.

The advanced attacker now employs time-based blind SQL injection techniques when direct output is not possible. Database time delays are effective means of inferring objectives and data from those systems. More common, especially for complex applications, is the second-order SQL injection, where input from a user has been stored in the database and is executed at a later point in time.

Testing methodology should include:

1. Manual testing using both classic and modern payload sets
2. Examination of both synchronous and asynchronous responses
3. Testing for blind vulnerabilities using Boolean-based and time-based techniques
4. Verification of stored procedures and ORM implementations

15.3.2.2.2 NoSQL Injection Testing

With the widespread adoption of NoSQL databases such as MongoDB and Redis, NoSQL injection has become a critical testing requirement. These attacks often exploit JavaScript-based query languages which can bypass traditional SQL injection protection mechanisms.

15.3.2.2.3 GraphQL Injection

As GraphQL adoption has grown, new injection vectors have emerged. Attackers can exploit nested queries and fragments to perform resource exhaustion attacks or bypass access controls. Testing should include:

- Introspection query manipulation
- Nested query depth analysis
- Fragment spread validation
- Directive manipulation checks

15.3.2.2.4 Command Injection Testing

Command injection vulnerabilities have become more sophisticated with the integration of cloud services and containerized environments. Modern testing approaches must consider:

Remote Code Execution (RCE) through template injection has become increasingly common, especially in applications using template engines like Jinja2 or Handlebars. Testers should examine both direct command execution and indirect injection by the means of system functions.

15.3.2.3 Advanced Testing Methodologies

15.3.2.3.1 Automated Testing Tools

Modern testing relies heavily on sophisticated tools that can identify complex injection patterns:

1. DAST tools with ML capabilities can identify context-aware injection points.
2. Interactive Application Security Testing (IAST) tools provide runtime analysis to detect injection vulnerabilities during normal application usage.

3. Custom fuzzing frameworks that can generate context-aware payloads based on application behavior.

15.3.2.3.2 Manual Testing Techniques

Although automated tools are more valuable than manual testing. Manual testing serves as an important component used for identifying complex injection vulnerabilities:

1. Context-aware payload crafting based on application architecture
2. Business logic bypass attempts through injection
3. Multi-step injection chains that combine multiple vulnerability types

15.3.2.4 Modern Mitigation Strategies

15.3.2.4.1 Input Validation Frameworks

Modern applications should implement multiple layers of input validation:

1. Client-side validation for user experience
2. API gateway validation for initial filtering
3. Application-level validation using context-aware validation rules
4. Database-level controls including prepared statements and stored procedures

15.3.2.4.2 Runtime Protection

Modern protection mechanisms include:

1. RASP programs which are designed to detect and prevent threats in real-time can effectively combat attempts at injection attacks.
2. ML-backed context-aware web application firewalls help in identifying more advanced patterns of attacks.
3. API security gateways provide custom isolation to modern applications built on API-based technologies.

15.3.2.4.3 Secure Development Practices

Prevention of injection vulnerabilities begins with secure development:

1. Usage of modern frameworks that come with built-in defenses from common types of injection attacks.
2. The implementation of Content Security Policy (CSP) headers that prevent script injections for the customers.
3. Regular security training for development teams, keeping them updated with emerging threats.

15.3.2.5 Emerging Trends and Future Considerations

15.3.2.5.1 Cloud-Native Application Security

With the shift to cloud-native applications, new injection vectors have emerged:

1. Container escape through command injection
2. Cloud service template injection
3. Serverless function injection

15.3.2.5.2 AI/ML System Vulnerabilities

As applications increasingly incorporate AI/ML components, new types of injection attacks have emerged:

1. Model poisoning through crafted inputs
2. Training data injection
3. Prompt injection in AI-powered systems

15.3.2.5.3 IoT Device Testing

IoT devices present unique injection testing challenges:

1. Limited processing power affecting traditional protection mechanisms
2. Proprietary protocols requiring specialized testing approaches
3. Firmware-level injection vulnerabilities

15.3.2.6 Best Practices for Continuous Security Testing

Organizations must implement continuous security testing processes:

1. Regular automated scanning integrated into CI/CD pipelines.
2. Occasional manual penetration tests targeting injection vulnerabilities.
3. Bug bounty programs to reap the expertise of the community.

Frequent update of the methodologies of testing with the newly emerging threats.

Injection testing remains a very important element of application security testing and demands a wide-ranging automated, manual, and modern protection mechanism to be in place. The growing complexity of applications and the emergence of advanced technologies demand the continuous evolution of testing methodologies when inside the system so as to accommodate emerging attack vectors and types of vulnerabilities.

15.3.3 Authentication and Session Management Testing

Authentication and session management are critical components of web application security. Misconfigured mechanisms can lead to unauthorized access and session hijacking.

15.3.3.1 Testing Weak Authentication Mechanisms

- Check for predictable or default passwords.
- Test multi-factor authentication implementations to ensure robustness.
- Conduct brute-force attacks using tools like Hydra to identify weak credentials.

15.3.3.2 Session Management Testing

- Ensure session IDs are randomized and expire after inactivity.
- Test for session fixation vulnerabilities by analyzing cookie behavior.
- Validate secure transmission of session tokens through HTTPS.

Real-world breaches, like the Facebook data exposure incident, emphasize the importance of secure authentication and session handling.

15.3.4 Web Application Security: Cross-Site Scripting (XSS) and Cross-Site Request Forgery (CSRF)

15.3.4.1 Cross-Site Scripting (XSS)

XSS remains one of the most prevalent web application security vulnerabilities, ranking consistently in the OWASP Top Ten. In recent years, the landscape of XSS attacks has evolved significantly with the increasing complexity of modern web applications and the widespread adoption of JavaScript frameworks.

15.3.4.2 Understanding XSS Types

15.3.4.2.1 Stored (Persistent) XSS

Stored-in XSS attacks occur when malicious scripts are stored permanently in targeted web servers, typically in databases, message boards, visitor logs or comment fields. They automatically invoke the script for other users when viewing the affected page. Modern web applications have APIs which are vulnerable to stored XSS because they accept and retain JSON, which can later be rendered onto the DOM.

15.3.4.2.2 Reflected (Non-Persistent) XSS

Reflected XSS is defined as a malicious script that immediately reflects off the web server, for example, in a search result or error message. The payload usually arrives as part of the victim's request, often via the URL parameters, and, although modern browsers tend to be well equipped with XSS protection mechanisms, highly sophisticated attacks can still use methods such as polyglot payloads and encoding variations to get around this protection.

15.3.4.2.3 DOM-Based XSS

DOM-based XSS has become more common due to single-page applications (SPAs) and client-side rendering frameworks. This is the type of XSS that occurs whenever unsafe forms of writing client-side data into the DOM via unsafe jQuery operations or template literals. DOM-based XSS is already quite mitigated by using modern frameworks such as React and Vue, but developers often undermine that protection through dangerous patterns like using dangerouslySetInnerHTML or v-html directives.

15.3.4.2.4 Modern Testing Approaches

Security testing for XSS is no longer confined to mere payload injections. Current strategies are as follows within the domain:

1. **Dynamic Analysis:** Tools such as OWASP ZAP and Burp Suite now incorporate dynamic ML for automatic scanning to discover subtle XSS and ensure reduced false positives. With these capabilities, dynamic analysis tools can discover context-sensitive XSS opportunities that may not be available with traditional pattern matching.

2. **IAST:** New breed for tests that superimposes dynamic testing and instrumenting the running application to provide an accurate detection of XSS vulnerabilities as it understands the complete context of data flow.

15.3.4.2.5 Advanced Prevention Techniques

Modern XSS prevention extends beyond traditional input validation and output encoding.

CSP has matured significantly, with Level 3 specifications introducing features like strict-dynamic and unsafe-hashed-attributes. Properly configured CSP headers can effectively mitigate most XSS attacks, though implementation challenges remain in legacy applications.

15.3.4.3 Cross-Site Request Forgery (CSRF)

CSRF attacks continue to evolve, particularly as web applications become more complex and integrate multiple third-party services.

15.3.4.3.1 Modern CSRF Attack Vectors

Recent CSRF attacks have become more sophisticated, exploiting:

- Same-site cookie vulnerabilities
- Cross-origin resource sharing (CORS) misconfigurations
- WebSocket connections
- API endpoints that accept JSON data

15.3.4.3.2 Advanced Testing Methodologies

Modern CSRF testing has evolved beyond simple HTML forms:

1. Automated Testing: Tools like OWASP ZAP and Burp Suite now include sophisticated CSRF detection capabilities, including the ability to detect token-based protections and their implementation flaws.
2. API Testing: With the rise of REST APIs, CSRF testing now includes scenarios involving different content types and authentication mechanisms, particularly focusing on session handling in modern web frameworks.

15.3.4.4 Contemporary Prevention Strategies

CSRF prevention has evolved significantly.

According to the recent strategies associated with prevention of CSRF attacks, it is well known that their techniques have evolved tremendously. Token-Based Protection is mostly sought in application because most modern frameworks will automatically generate and verify CSRF tokens and also integrate with front-end frameworks to create a seamless implementation. Another form of protection is Same-Site Cookies, emphasizing the SameSite cookie attribute, with full support across all browsers. By default, the "Lax" setting mitigates the majority of CSRF scenarios by preventing cookies from being sent across different domains during requests. In addition, Custom Headers in AJAX requests form another front of defense as browsers do not permit cross-origin requests to set custom headers without the presence of explicit

CORS policies. Combinations of these factors form a very strong security defense against CSRF attacks on modern web applications.

15.3.4.5 Integration with Modern Architectures

Modern web applications (like token-based authentication—JWT and stateless architectures) offer an innate protection against CSRF when chaired correctly. Advancement implies new challenges related to authentic token storage, which is often done in HttpOnly cookies or local storage, and careful attention needs to be paid to XSS and CSRF risks involved with them. Besides RESTful APIs, CORS protocol has to be supplied and validated according to its Origin of requests, especially concerning data-modifying endpoints. During this period in 2023 and stretching to early 2024, a growing concern has been found in incorporating security headers with all the modern CDN services and in automating security testing in CI/CD pipelines, along with adopting RASP runtime application self-protection solutions and the zero-trust security model for web applications. As they evolve, both developers and even the security professionals will have to keep pace with the changing security measures and knowledge of how to implement correctly within modern frameworks.

15.3.5 Testing for Insecure APIs

APIs serve as the vital point of access between various software systems, thereby enabling seamless communication and information flow to them. APIs thus make possible enhancements in effective functioning through internalization and better user access. But APIs also come with a large proportion of risk in terms of security, as they become the wide attack surface through which the miscreants could penetrate systems. An insecure API becomes the source of information leakage, unauthorized access to privileged systems, and interruption in organizational operations. Problems like lack of or improper authentication, absence of encryption, or even inadequate access control all culminate into a maximum impact breach. Hence, the critical requirement of API security testing is to discover and mitigate risks before they can be exploited. With the extensive reliance on APIs in contemporary applications, it thus becomes more of a proactive approach in safeguarding them in today's interconnected digital world. As evident from the most recent high-profile breaches that have occurred mostly because of leveraging vulnerable APIs to divulge sensitive data, the importance of effective API protection and its regular vigilance from threats keeps growing. Flowcharts illustrating vulnerability life cycles, DevSecOps security integration, method layouts, and security best practices are shown in Figures 15.1–15.4.

15.3.5.1 Case Studies of API Breaches

Several recent incidents highlight the severe consequences of insecure APIs:

- **Facebook (2018, continuing):** One of the most cited API-based security challenges at Facebook has been the "View As" vulnerability discovered in 2018; data-leak and privacy violation occurrences, furthermore, continue to validate the difficulty in securing a complex API ecosystem.

- **T-Mobile (2021, 2022, 2023):** In the past few years, T-Mobile has faced several data breaches with almost all of these due to an API vulnerability. The incidents involved customer data, including personal identifiers, creating a recurrent proof of API security breaches and calls for continuous observation.
- **Okta (2022):** The case of Okta was even worse in that it revealed the use of insecure APIs within the supply chain as the threat actor, Lapsus$, used a third-party vendor to penetrate Okta's internal systems. Therefore, it has made it imperative to secure APIs not only for one's company but also those of partners and vendors.
- **Twilio (2022):** Several Twilio employees fell victims of an innovative phishing campaign that led to unauthorized access to customer data, rather than by directly hacking the API. It however illustrates some of the ways in which compromised credentials can be used to exploit APIs. Hence more emphasis needs to be put on strong authentication and access control measures, such as multi-factor authentication.
- **LastPass (2022, announced 2023):** The machine of a developer got compromised that led to the stealing of source codes and technical information. However, the stolen information could identify API vulnerabilities and exploit them tremendously, although the initial breach wasn't directly related to their API, indicating that such breaches in security would affect API security.
- **Peloton (2023):** A security researcher found an API vulnerability that enabled unauthorized access to user profile data, including private workout data. This further indicates the requirement for a comprehensive API security testing schedule, which will help identify and fix such flaws.

15.3.5.2 Testing Techniques

Effective API security testing requires a multifaceted approach that combines various techniques:

- **Authentication and Authorization Testing:** Make sure there are appropriate mechanisms for user authentication in place. This includes tests for weak or missing API keys, weaknesses in their OAuth implementation, and ensures that the endpoints are only available to authorized users. Check for broken object-level authorization (BOLA), where users can access resources that should not be permitted to them.
- **Input Validation and Fuzz Testing Injection:** It involves completing all injection attacks, such as SQL injection subtypes, XSS, and command injection by a fuzzy input validation. Random or malformed inputs are also sent to the API in fuzz testing. It helps in checking the unforeseen behavior and identifying possible weaknesses in handling edge cases.
- **Parameter Tampering and Manipulation:** It will check how the API will behave when parameters are altered or manipulated. Check insecure direct object reference (IDOR) and server-side request forgery (SSRF). Manipulating parameter values regarding object identifiers, URL path, or file path provides the required tests.

- **Business Logic Testing:** Business logic of the API implements should be tested more closely. Test logic weakness that would allow unauthorized access, data manipulation, or unintended actions. This usually requires a complete understanding of the functionality that is intended to be provided and testing the functionality bypass or abuse.
- **Testing for Rate Limiting and Denial of Service (DoS):** Challenges the API with its resistance to DoS attacks through testing of the rate limiting mechanisms as well as handling of these big or frequent requests. It also includes slow HTTP attacks and other forms of overwhelming the API.
- **Security Misconfiguration Testing:** Test properly configures the API as well as its underneath infrastructure. That includes testing for default credentials, unnecessary services and insecure server settings, proper security headers including but not limited to CSP, HTTP strict transport security (HSTS) as well.
- **Sensitive data leakage:** Analyzes API Request and Response Headers, as well as Response Body: You may also include such sensitive data as API keys, database credentials, internal IP addresses, and user data. Mask the data, and ensure that such information is never transmitted unless legitimately necessary.
- **API Documentation Review:** Review of Incomplete or Inaccurate Documentation APIs can mislead people and lead them into security risks. Ensure, also, that documentation covers security best practices and how to use the API accurately.

15.3.5.3 Tools for API Security Testing (Updated to 2024)

- **Postman:** Being a famous tool for manual API testing and exploration with features for requests creation and managing collections are valuable, as for functional testing so for security testing.
- **Burp Suite Professional:** A web security testing platform for almost all-in-one available for API vulnerability scanning, automated testing, and manual exploitation.
- **OWASP ZAP (Zed Attack Proxy):** Free and open-source web security scanner that users can also use for API security testing. Automated scanning, manual testing tools, and rich feature sets for vulnerability identification are available.
- **SoapUI:** A dedicated API testing tool, specifically designed to test SOAP and REST APIs. With a simple user interface, it creates test cases, manages test suites, and automates API tests.
- **REST-Assured:** Java library simplifies the testing of REST APIs, providing a domain-specific language to write expressive and readable tests.
- **pytest:** The most popular framework for Python testing: Very extensible, flexible, and powerful for automated testing with unique libraries such as requests for API testing.
- **OWASP Amass:** Still a valuable tool for using API enumeration and analysis to discover hidden or undocumented APIs.

- **Nuclei:** Fast and customizable vulnerability scanner, for scanning servers and APIs for a variety of known vulnerabilities. Its template-based approach makes custom checks easy to create and share.
- **Gauntlt:** The framework for defining security tests and executing them. With this suite, one can have an automated pipeline for security testing. It integrates with various security tools.

15.3.5.4 API Security Best Practices

Beyond testing, implementing security best practices is crucial for minimizing API risks:

- Authentication and Authorization: Create good strong authentication mechanisms such as OAuth 2.0 and OpenID Connect (OIDC). Implement fine-grained authorization controls on the principle of least privilege.

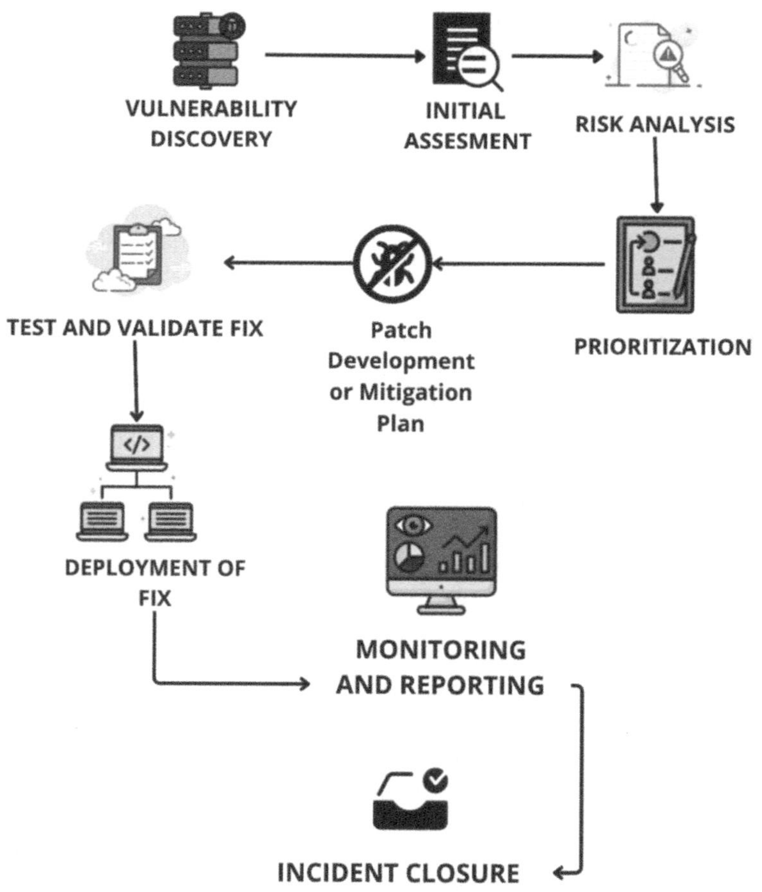

FIGURE 15.1 Flowchart depicting the life cycle of a vulnerability, from discovery to mitigation.

- Input Validation and Leasing: Prodigiously validate all user inputs because injection attacks can be prevented. Sanitize data for it to conform to the expected form and to prevent execution of malicious code.
- Output Encoding: Encode all output so that no XSS vulnerabilities would be there. Context-dependent encoding is important to ensure proper encoding depending on the output context (e.g., HTML, JavaScript, JSON).
- Rate Limiting and Throttling: Set up rate limiting for denying a DoS attack and also, protecting resources of API from abuse.
- Security Logging and Monitoring: All API requests and response together with timestamps, user agents, and IPs will be logged. The log files will then be monitored for probably suspicious activities and security incidents.
- Regular Security Assessment: Regular activities of an API regarding its security assessment is penetration testing and scans for vulnerability as proactive operational security weakness identification and addressing.
- Documentation and Training of API: API should be well-documented and kept updated. Developers should train on secure development and testing techniques for APIs.

15.4 TOOLS AND TECHNIQUES FOR SECURITY TESTING

Security testing is a critical process for identifying vulnerabilities in software, systems, and networks. It involves using various tools and techniques to simulate real-world attacks and assess the effectiveness of security controls. A comprehensive approach requires both automated and manual testing, leveraging the strengths of each to provide a thorough security evaluation. Furthermore, the integration of security testing into the software development lifecycle (SDLC), especially within DevSecOps practices, is crucial for building secure systems from the ground up.

15.4.1 Automated Security Testing Tools

Automated security testing tools play a vital role in identifying common vulnerabilities quickly and efficiently. These tools can scan large codebases, networks, and web applications, automating tasks that would be time-consuming and prone to human error if performed manually.

- **Burp Suite:** Burp Suite is a much-utilized web security testing platform with functions to intercept, manipulate HTTP requests, vulnerability scanning, and automated attacks. Its different features are web applications crawler, web vulnerability scanner, an intruder tool with which custom attacks can be performed, and a repeater to analyze specific requests and responses.
- **Metasploit Framework:** Metasploit is an open-source penetration testing framework packed with all the possible exploit, payload, and auxiliary modules that best match each testing conducted on different systems and applications. It helps simulate real-world attacks and assess vulnerability impacts. Additionally, it can serve in automating vulnerability scanning, exploiting, and post-exploitation.

- **OWASP ZAP (Zed Attack Proxy):** ZAP will study new approaches and applications based on the theory of automatic web application security scanning. It could also be automated, as well as manual testing. Automated scanning, spidering, active scanning, fuzzing, just to name a few of the mechanisms that ZAP uses, help in detecting a wide range of web vulnerabilities.
- **Nessus Essentials:** Vulnerability scanner that analyzes different systems to evaluate whether they have been affected by known weaknesses in security. The scanner has a huge vulnerability database, and it can evaluate different operating systems, network devices, and applications.
- **Qualys VMDR:** A cloud-hosted architecture providing a continuous process of vulnerability management and detection. Automated scanning and priority of discovered vulnerabilities as well as asset discovery are among the functions.
- **Snyk:** A developer-oriented security tool that integrates into the development workflows in order to detect and correct vulnerabilities in the code, open-source dependencies, and containers.
- **Checkmarx Suite:** This is an SAST tool that analyzes the source code for security vulnerabilities without running the code. The tool supports different programming languages and frameworks.

15.4.2 Manual Testing Techniques

Automated tools are important to find the fault quickly; however, manual testing techniques remain an important part of finding those vulnerabilities that are most complex in nature, such as logical flaws that cannot be easily identified through automated approaches. Humans are invaluable as they can bring intuition and understanding into play regarding the context of a specific application or system whereby they can then create more specific testing.

- **Penetration Testing:** The definition of penetration testing is an open test between a simulated cyberattack toward a target with more or less accessible applications, systems, and networks targeted to discover the weak points in these security mechanisms. Some of these techniques include vulnerability scanning, exploitation, and social engineering, all of which inform the penetration testers of the security posture of the target.
- **Code Review:** This is essentially manual source code scrutinizing to discover security vulnerabilities and errors in coding. Peer code review can be done or security specialists can conduct the review. It is one of the best techniques to discover vulnerability early in the development cycle.
- **Threat Modeling:** Identifying threatened and vulnerable sites in a system or application. Threat modeling has to do with system architecture analysis, possible attack vector discovery, and mitigation strategy development.
- **Security Audits:** Periodic planned evaluations for security controls and practices to comply with security policies and standards. Internal and external auditors can conduct a security audit.

- **Exploit Development:** Develop custom exploits to test the effect of vulnerabilities by using this advanced but well thought out technique that requires a deep understanding of systems and software internals.

15.4.3 Emerging Tools Leveraging AI and ML

AI and ML are increasingly used in every part of security testing tools and techniques. Such technologies can speed up the performance of complex tasks, improve accuracy, and reduce the time required for security testing.

- **Vulnerability Scanners Powered by AI:** These scanners are equipped with ML algorithms that scan and point out vulnerabilities more efficiently than the traditional scanners. In fact, it learns from past vulnerability reports and changes itself to new acts of attack. A few examples include the vendors like Synopsys and Veracode who have incorporated AI into their SAST/DAST offerings.
- **AI-Powered Penetration Testing Platforms:** The main areas automated by a penetration testing platform are vulnerability discovery, exploitation, and report generation. These platforms are customizable and offer tailored simulation according to the environment under test. Such tools include Pentera for automated penetration testing.
- **ML-Based Malware Detection:** ML algorithms analyze the characteristics and behavior of a file to filter them as malware. It helps to uncover the new and optimum forms of malware, which might slip out of the traditional signature-based detection mechanism. CrowdStrike and SentinelOne are a few companies using ML for endpoint security solutions.
- **AI Security Automation and Orchestration:** Security automation manages standard security tasks with the help of AI, like incident response and vulnerability remediation, which frees human capital to concentrate on a more strategic approach. Increasingly, AI is being integrated into Security Information and Event Management (SIEM) platforms for threat detection and response.

15.4.4 Integrating Security Testing into DevSecOps

The DevSecOps practice integrates security into the entire application development life cycle. It automates the activity of securing test automation into the continuous integration and continuous delivery (CI/CD) pipeline.

- Shift-Left Security: Security testing is moved earlier in the development process such that vulnerabilities are found and fixed before production.
- Automated Security Testing in CI/CD: Because security testing is not appended or an afterthought but part of the CI/CD pipeline, security testing tools are integrated into the CI/CD environment for automated security checks throughout all the phases of development.
- Security as Code (SaC): Security resources and rules represented as code are managed in the same way that IT infrastructure is treated as code. This

paves the way toward automation, versioning, and the integration required for DevSecOps workflows. Both Ansible and Terraform can be used in providing the SaC.

- Continuous Security Monitoring: This involves keeping a watch over systems and applications to detect threats and vulnerabilities in real time. This can include the use of IDS or SIEM, where IDS means Intrusion Detection System and SIEM stands for Security Information and Event Management.

Integrating the security testing in DevSecOps brings the organizations to build software that is secure, fast, and efficiently. It makes security a consideration in every stage of the development lifecycle toward more resilient and robust systems. By automating tools and manual techniques in shaping their work plan by strategically

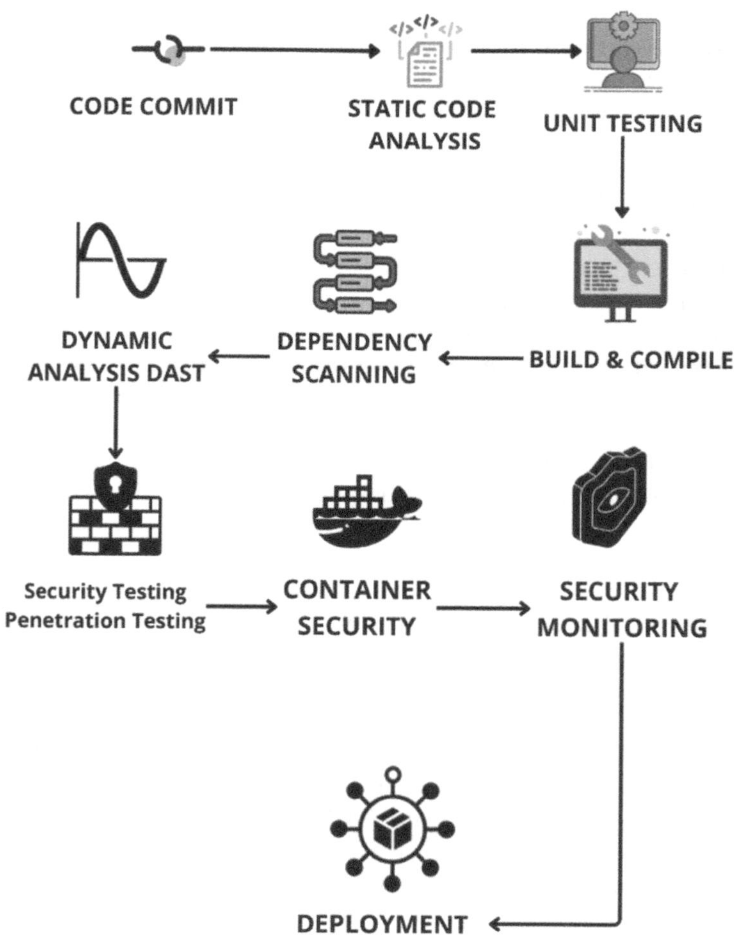

FIGURE 15.2 Pipeline showcasing where security tests can be integrated into DevSecOps.

applying AI/ML to their operation efforts, organizations can effectively face the continuous evolving threats to a strong security posture [8].

15.5 STRATEGIES FOR MITIGATING VULNERABILITIES

The mitigation of vulnerabilities is a seamless and continuous process that necessitates incorporation of a multi layered approach. The proactive measures are—secure coding practices followed by regular security testing to ensure that the identified vulnerabilities are not introduced in the first place. However, as these systems can never be completely invulnerable to attacks, robust incident response plans thus become critical to minimize the damage which a successful breach can cause. Regular patching and updating along with the training of users are the essential key components of a well-rounded vulnerability mitigation strategy.

15.5.1 Proactive Approaches

Anticipate vulnerabilities before exploitation as most effective strategies for securing systems and applications. The proactive measure that embedded security in an SDLC life cycle and culture within organizations to recognize by security awareness.

- **Secure Coding Practices:** With the best possible secure coding guidelines and standards, a developer may write code which reduces the chances of having vulnerable code. Enabling input validation, output encoding, error handling, and proper authentication and authorization mechanisms may be included as secure coding practices for organizations. Such organizations can also use tools like SAST, for example, to help find coding errors. The OWASP Secure Coding Practices and CERT Secure Coding Standards are just a few examples of secure coding standards.
- **Regular Code Reviews and Audits:** Manual code reviews with periodic automated security audits are required to find those vulnerabilities missing its automated tools. This exercise opens up opportunities for peers or security specialists to inspect the code for potential faults in security. However, automated static analysis tools can also be used to scan the code for common vulnerabilities [9].
- **Threat Modeling:** Threat model is analysis of possible threats and vulnerabilities in a system or application. Identification attack vectors and design appropriate mitigation strategies are possible through threat modeling. The well-known methodologies are STRIDE, PASTA, and DREAD.
- **Software Composition Analysis (SCA):** Finding and monitoring open-source components and their vulnerabilities in a software project. SCA tools include tracking dependencies, known vulnerabilities, updates, etc.
- **Vulnerability Scanning:** Scanning systems and applications for known vulnerabilities at regular intervals using automated tools. It allows identifying weaknesses prior to interference by the attackers. DAST tools can crawl and interrogate a live application to discover weaknesses. IAST techniques combine SAST and DAST to have a more profound analysis.

15.5.2 Incident Response Plans

Despite anticipatory efforts, there are occasions when security breaches do occur for which a well-furnished incident response plan contributes to limiting such breaches' damage.

- **Preparation:** An incident response team should be set up with specific roles and responsibilities as well as procedures related to handling security incidences. It should be tested and updated regularly.
- **Identification:** Security incidents must be detected and identified, and such activity should involve closely monitoring critical systems for signs of suspicious activity and reporting it through established pathways. This may be disconnecting systems from the network, disabling compromised accounts, etc.
- **Eradication:** Cause of incident needs to be removed. This might be malware or compromised accounts. Some involved tasks are patching systems, reinstalling software, and/or resetting passwords.
- **Recovery:** It involves the restoration of affected systems and data to its pre-incident state, including backup restoration, reconfiguration of systems, and integrity verification. Learning from an incident entails getting a post-incident report of incident review and looking for opportunities to improve the incident response plan and security posture of the organization [10].

15.5.3 Patching and Updating

Patch and update software and systems consistently to reduce known vulnerabilities.

- **Automated Patching:** Set up automated patching systems for the timely updates and reduced scope for manual errors. Greatly important in the case of a large environment, as manual patching can be slow and inaccurate.
- **Building a Vulnerability Management Program:** Develop a vulnerability management program for knowing known vulnerabilities, thereby facilitating the efforts put into patching activities. It involves using the vulnerability scanning tools to know the vulnerability and prioritizing them according to their severity or potential impact.
- **Policies for Software Update:** Have well-laid out policies for software updates, including the testing of updates prior to deployment and scheduling of updates for off-peak hours.

15.5.4 User Awareness and Training

Security awareness training is essential to reduce social engineering attacks and other threats.

- **Awareness Training Security:** Regular awareness training sessions for employees on issues like phishing, password security, and social engineering. Make such training sessions interesting and worthwhile for employees.

- **Simulated Phishing Scams:** Execute repeated simulated phishing attacks to evaluate how well the workforce has learned to respond to phishing assaults and reinforce the lessons taught.
- **Security Policies and Procedures:** These should be clear, unambiguous security policies and procedures regarding system and data use and communication to employees, keeping in mind the confidentiality of the policies and compliance with them.

15.5.5 Case Study: The LastPass Breach (2022, Disclosed 2023)

The example of the LastPass breach illustrates how a single vulnerability can create a domino effect and also shows the value of a holistic and comprehensive security approach. As the initial compromise stemmed from a compromised developer account, sensitive customer data ultimately fell into the hands of the perpetrators.

- **Initial Compromise:** An attacked third-party media software vulnerability enabled intrusion into a developer's home computer, giving remote attackers access to internal corporate resources.
- **Lateral Movement:** The attacker exploited the compromised developer account to access other internal systems, sensitive data such as source code, technical information, and customer vault data.
- **Impact:** Though it was stealing vault data of customers, it raised concerns about possible future decryptions because the data was stolen while encrypted.

Mitigation Steps Undertaken by LastPass

- **Containment and Inquiry:** They contained the incident and carried out forensic investigations with external cybersecurity experts.
- **Additional Security Procedures:** They added supplemental security which strengthened endpoint detection and response capabilities and multifactor authentication.
- **Communication and Openness:** LastPass communicated the breach to clients and later put updates about the investigation and remedial actions.

Key Lessons

- **Defense in Depth:** This incident brings to mind a necessity of multiple layers of security since a fail point would have devastating consequences.
- **Best Secure Development Practice:** Even more so emphasizes the need for secure coding practices, code review, and vulnerability scanning for identifying faults within software and systems.
- **Incident Response Planning:** An effective and efficient incident response plan is very high on the priority list with regard to minimizing the damage and devastation incurred by security breaches.
- **Supply-Chain Security:** The software supply chain has to be secure. Due to the presence of third-party software, it becomes more exploitable by the external world for compromise and secret access to systems.

Organizations should introduce a proactive approach, develop a stringent incident response plan, and promote a culture of security awareness to minimize the chances of security breaches and successfully mitigate their impacts. Continuous improvement is invariably essential, as threats change constantly, thus affecting and maintaining a good posture for security operations.

15.6 EMERGING TRENDS IN SECURITY TESTING

The landscape of security testing is continuously evolving in order to keep pace with the changing threat landscape along with the introduction of new technologies. Such trends which are already emerging include shift-left security, cloud security testing, IoT security, and ZTA—these new trends require new techniques and tools needed to cope with complete security coverage.

15.6.1 Shift-Left Security: Integrating Security Early in the SDLC

Shift-left security shifts thinking regarding software development—from reinforcing security early on within the entire life cycle of an application to helping it. Traditionally, security was examined mostly at the end of the development cycle. Many times later, one could detect a security problem—an expensive fix that took a lot of time. Shift-left security believes that it should always be necessary to address security concerns; reduce vulnerabilities and thus improve software quality; and create culture around security within software development.

15.6.1.1 Early Vulnerability Detection

Shift-left security, at its core, refers to the practice of discovering vulnerabilities as early as possible. This can be done by bringing in various security testing techniques into the actual component development and testing parts of the SDLC.

- **SAST:** SAST tools enable the use of static analysis of source code without executing it to identify potential vulnerabilities from SQL injection, XSS, and buffer overflows. SAST integrated within the IDE provides instant development feedback on security issues during code writing.
- **SCA:** Modern application kits often use a significant number of open-source components, making SCA necessary. SCA tools scan these components for known vulnerabilities and license compliance issues, ensuring that the application does not inherit the associated security risks from those components.
- **Threat Modeling:** Threat modeling consists of identifying possible threats on the application and building countermeasures against practically estimated threats. While conducting the design phase of an application, threats can be identified relating architectural weaknesses and risks to security.
- **Architecture Analysis:** Reviewing the application architecture for security flaws and weaknesses. This can include the use of tools and techniques to assess the design security and find possible vulnerabilities.

15.6.1.2 Developer-Focused Security

The shift-left security allows the developer to drive the ownership process for implementing the security control mechanism in applications. It involves equipping the developers with the required tools, training, and support they need.

- **Secure Coding Training:** It primarily concerns training developers about secure coding practices and teaching them to avoid commonly known vulnerabilities. It has to be a permanent measure specific to the technologies and frameworks used by the development team. Integrated Security Tools: Integrates security testing tools directly into the developers' integrated development environment (IDE) to get real-time feedback on security issues that should be fixed right away.
- **Security Champions:** Identifying and training security champions from development teams would help induce the best practices and assist the other developers.
- **Gamification and Incentives:** Using some gamification elements coupled with incentives may inspire developers to implement secure coding practices and positively alter the security posture of applications.

15.6.1.3 Automated Security Testing in CI/CD

The role of automation is crucial in the shift-left approach toward security. In fact, it makes security checks automated in every phase of development by incorporating security testing in CI/CD pipeline.

- **Automated SAST and SCA:** The incorporation of SAST and SCA tools in CI/CD pipeline provides automated scanning of code for vulnerabilities before deployment.
- **Automated Security Unit Tests:** Writing security-focused unit tests, developers can verify how secure individual components of application are.
- **DAST in Staging:** DAST tools analyze running applications to identify vulnerabilities. It integrates DAST into the staging environment for production-simulated testing.
- **Policy Enforcement:** Imposing policies within CI/CD pipelines for security requirements such as certain levels of code coverage for security tests or preventing code with known vulnerabilities from being deployed.

15.6.1.4 DevSecOps Integration

Shift-left security is the most critical concept of DevSecOps, which is building security into DevOps as culture and practices.

- **Breaking Down Silos:** DevSecOps shatters the colonial masks of development, security, and operations and allows those people to work well with the other to take equal responsibility for security.
- **Collaboration and Communication:** As for the first step in this aspect of making the move to shift-left security, open communication and collaboration between these teams is necessary.

- **Common Security Metrics:** Common security metrics and related KPIs are supposed to provide teams with clarity in aligning their works and convey the progress made toward the achievement of security objectives [11].
- **Continuous Monitoring and Feedback:** It is built up through the concept of continuous monitoring and feedback loop that security issues can be anticipated and handled in a timely manner.

Organizations applying such strategies would incorporate shift-left security so that a process of development will be secure and applications will be more probed and productive. This will ensure that the scale of vulnerabilities is lower and the cost of remediation is decreased while fostering a security culture across the whole organization.

15.6.2 Cloud Security Testing: Navigating the Evolving Cloud Landscape

Cloud computing alters the very perceptions of how an organization can build, deploy, and manage applications and infrastructure. It also creates an aspect of dynamicity and distribution in the environments; hence, presenting some unique security challenges which need to be adequately addressed by specialized testing approaches. This means that the historical approaches to security testing have not been sufficient when it comes to dealing with the intricacies of cloud deployments; hence, the need for cloud security-related testing methodologies.

15.6.2.1 Multi-Cloud Environments

Many organizations nowadays prefer multi-cloud service providers such as incorporation of AWS, Azure, GCP, etc., or use hybrid cloud infrastructure that combines on-premises with cloud resources. This combination adds complexity when it comes to security testing.

- **Technology-Specific Security Controls:** Diverse security controls and different security configurations are offered by different cloud providers. Security testing must address this kind of variation in order to realize collective security among the various platforms. This includes understanding the nuances concerning the Identity and Access Management (IAM), network security groups, etc., along with specific provider features.
- **Interoperability and Data Portability:** It also requires testing the secure transfer and management of data across different cloud environments. To this end, it includes checking the security of data migration processes and compliance with relevant data privacy regulations.
- **Centralized Security Requirements:** Centralized security management through policies and tools across cloud service providers ensures a consistent security posture and reduces the complexity of their security monitoring and incident response.

15.6.2.2 Cloud-Native Applications

Cloud-native applications built on microservices, based on containers, and serverless functions pose brand-new security challenges.

- **Microservices Security:** This testing concerns the security of individual microservices and their interactions. This will involve verifying authentication and authorization between services, securing API communication, and ensuring data integrity.
- **Container Security:** It involves scanning container images to detect vulnerabilities and misconfigurations. Vulnerability scanning tools like Clair and Anchor may be used to analyze container images for security issues at the early stages.
- **Serverless Security:** Security issues related to serverless functions, including access control, dependency management, and data protection. Configuration of functions, access to cloud resources, and function code integrity should all be secured.

15.6.2.3 Infrastructure as Code (IaC) Security

IaC has automated the provision and management of cloud infrastructure. But a misconfiguration in the IaC templates can even leave behind a security vulnerability.

- **IaC Scanning:** Scanning IaC templates for security misconfigurations and vulnerabilities before they are deployed. Checkov, Terrascan, Cloudknox: Static analysis tools for identifying security risks in IaC code.
- **Policy as Code:** Security policy definition and enforcement in the form of code. So policy checks become automated and uniform across the cloud environments. Examples include the Open Policy Agent (OPA) as policy as code entities.
- **Version Control and Change Management:** Manage IaC templates using version control systems and implement change management processes to track changes and to ensure that security best practices are followed.

15.6.2.4 Cloud Security Posture Management (CSPM)

Cloud Security Posture Management (CSPM) tools continuously monitor cloud environments, spotting security misconfigurations, and achieving compliance with industry policies. Instant Access to Monitoring gives an almost immediate view into the few metrics which really concern cloud security posture—an organization being able to assess and act on security concerns quickly. Compliance Monitoring enforces important security regulations that the cloud environments should follow, such as PCI DSS, HIPAA, SOC 2, to ensure that organizations meet regulatory compliance. Some CSPM solutions even offer Automated Remediation options that enable one to automatically correct security misconfigurations without the need for manual interventions. This forward-looking blend of intelligent monitoring and regulatory compliance automation can bring your organization closer to running a secure and compliant cloud infrastructure while minimizing risks and increasing operational efficiency.

15.6.2.5 Cloud Workload Protection Platforms (CWPP)

Cloud Workload Protection Platforms (CWPPs) give essential security controls for protecting the workloads-in-the-cloud. Some features are Vulnerability Management, which identifies and mitigates vulnerabilities in cloud workloads; Intrusion Detection and Prevention systems that detect and block malicious activities targeting these workloads; Malware Protection, which keeps workloads safe from malware and other sorts of cyberattacks; and Microsegmentation, which isolates workloads and their impacts from any security breaches. An end-to-end cloud security test strategy addressing the very specific challenges imposed by multi-cloud environments, cloud-native applications, and IaC. This involves making use of the right tools and techniques that identify vulnerabilities early. Real-time adaptation to the shifting security landscape in the cloud and continuous monitoring is essential to achieve a strong resilient security posture in more dynamic cloud environments.

15.6.3 IoT and Embedded Systems Security: Addressing the Unique Challenges of a Connected World

The increase in the IoT and embedded devices has formed a highly networked constellation of physical devices around the world. However, the tremendous interconnectedness has brought with it a great deal of security challenges. Often, IoT devices lack proper and robust security measures that are foreseen in traditional computers, thereby being easily susceptible to different threats. Devices like these need a specialized security testing approach which considers their peculiarity and constraints [12].

15.6.3.1 Device-Specific Vulnerabilities

Constrained with limited processing power and memory, such IoT devices have inherent device-specific vulnerabilities, such as insecure firmware that some of them continue to run without any update or patch, constituting a viable entry point for attackers (thus, firmware analysis and fuzzing becomes necessary for discovery of weaknesses). Another common weakness is default credentials that are weak, which security testing should ensure prompt a user to change default passwords during installation to prevent access. Not encryption on data sent between IoT devices and backend systems, it makes the data interception prone and, therefore, emphasizes the necessity for well-enforced mechanisms that will encrypt the data in transit and at rest. And there are other hardware vulnerabilities such as booting insecurely and exposing a debug interface, which open the doors to making these hardware devices vulnerable, hence the need for employing Hardware Security Modules (HSM) that will keep cryptographic keys and sensitive data. But of course, without thorough testing, all these might render an IoT deployment unsafe and vulnerable.

15.6.3.2 Connectivity and Network Security

IoT devices use different network protocols and mostly use wireless technologies to communicate and transfer data. Secured communication channels are required to avoid any type of unauthorized access or tampering. All protocol vulnerabilities must be subject to thorough testing, such as by evaluating communication protocols like MQTT, CoAP, and Zigbee, for weaknesses at both network and protocol implementation levels so that attackers can exploit them.

Network segmentation is another important security measure, which ensures that IoT networks are isolated from critical systems and that, if any breach occurs, it affects only a limited area. This could be done with the help of firewalls and other security control measures, therefore ensuring that secure separation of IoT devices from main networks happens, making it harder, if not impossible, for attackers to move laterally through the system. Wireless Security should come highly prioritized on the use of very resilient encryption protocols such as WPA3 and ensuring very tight access controls against inappropriate access into the network. This is because, under most circumstances, IoT devices rely on wireless communications [13].

Besides those two, there must also be API Security in IoT security. APIs that control and communicate with the devices need to be secured from vulnerabilities like authentication bypass, authorization flaws, and injection attacks. Access and control of IoT systems must be protected by ensuring that security mechanisms will not allow attackers to change or control any access into the systems via these weak interfaces.

By addressing these vulnerabilities, organizations will have gone a long way toward enhancing the IoT device and communication network security significantly.

15.6.3.3 Data Security and Privacy

Due to the extremely sensitive nature of the data handled by the various IoT devices available, data security and data privacy are essential parameters in deployment and use. An example of this would be the encryption of data both during transport and at rest, and also on the device. This would protect data from interceptions and unauthorized access. This includes encrypted data on-device as well as secured data transferred over the network. Data Minimization practices are also imperative to limit the number of sensitive data collected and therefore the exposure risk by reducing what is actually kept on the device. The access control mechanism plays an essential role in noise proofing the sensitive information by controlling the entry in case it relates to the role played by the user in gaining authorization for it to be viewed. The only people who will thus interact with sensitive data files will be those who are authorized. Strong authentication and authorization protocols are therefore very important in enforcing the access control. Data Integrity must also be protected through techniques like checksums and hashing, such that no unauthorized modification or deletion of data occurs on the data collected by the IoT devices, ensuring that such data is reliable and accurate.

By addressing these environments, organizations continue to improve security and confidentiality for IoT ecosystems in order to protect sensitive data from breaches or misuse.

15.6.3.4 Physical Security

Timely physical access to these IoT devices can pose very serious security threats, as attackers may readily manipulate the device, as well as obtain confidential information without detection. For the most part, there exist physical security measures which can be deemed important in mitigating the risks brought about by such threats. Tamper-Proof Enclosures should prevent unauthorized access and tampering with internal components of IoT devices. Proper Holistic Storage to Secure IoT devices becomes increasingly relevant when dealing within unethical high-risk surroundings to prevent loss of equipment or access. Harsh conditions or disaster can further present a real threat to devices, where Physical IDS detect and generate alerts while they can warn whenever unauthorized physical access has been attempted on these devices.

Securing Internet of Things (IoT) deployments requires a holistic approach, as device security, network security, and data protection must be treated as integral components of a unified security model. Such a holistic approach assures that IoT ecosystems do not just suffer from digital threats but also from potential physical compromise. Most often, extra attention to the continuous monitoring and frequent security testing has to be done to ensure that the environment remains safe, well-integrity, well-secured, and private with minimal risks from new threats.

15.6.4 Zero-Trust Architectures: Security Testing in a Trustless World

The zero-trust security model challenges the previous paradigm of security which is limited to perimeter defenses. Previously, the organization would assume that anyone who is inside the perimeter is trustworthy. Now, every access request is to be verified before being granted whether the request is from a user at home, an employee in a branch, or a product supplier. This principle "never trust, always verify" has become one of the most preferred philosophies in environments that are geographically distributed or interconnected. Security risks, formerly confined to a single, inaccessible network boundary, have become a major risk. Under the zero-trust model, security testing is advanced correspondence to the continuous verification and assessment in real-time concerning user identity, device health, and contextual access. Microsegmentation is another factor. Networks are divided into smaller portions, isolated from each other so that a probable incident impacts just a small part of the overall network. Testing typically involves rigorous analysis of access control policies, data encryption, multi-factor authentication, and intersegment communication. Security controls are enforced all over the infrastructure so that security is applied uniformly across the entire infrastructure with high tight control, hence reducing unauthorized access.

15.6.4.1 Continuous Authentication and Authorization

In a zero-trust environment, authentication and authorization are continuous processes that always need to be independently validated for effectiveness. Security testing must evaluate multifactor authentications rigorously to ensure that services are not bypassable through other routes. Functional tests not only include authentication by such factors and demonstrate how they act differently for push notifications, one-time passwords, and biometric authentication, but also demonstrate their resistance against phishing and other social engineering attacks. In addition, relevant access control policies also need to be contextualized, including the factors of user runtime, device posture, and application sensitivity. Security testing must also ensure that access decisions can be scaled to the relevant contexts and denial of unauthorized access depending on that. Finally, session management security must be thoroughly tested to verify that it implements proper session terminations and is protected from hijacking. It also tests session timeout-related issues, session fixation, and other possible weaknesses in the session management mechanisms. This exhaustive testing would ensure that access and attacks always remain unauthorized and dynamic.

15.6.4.2 Microsegmentation

Microsegmentation improves network security as it partitions the network into smaller portions to contain any successful security breaches. One of the aspects of security testing is to help ascertain the integrity of the segments as security conferring strength. Access control enforcement testing between the microsegments has also been done keeping in mind that only authorized users and applications should be allowed for communicating across microsegments, whereas unauthorized access is blocked. The access should even be ensured by intersegment communication being not exceptional for scrutiny with such considerations in returns so that the transaction traffic is properly inspected and filtered and the sensitive data is protected during transit. Additionally, consistent policy application should be measured among microsegments to ensure that the security policies are associated within a standard context. Any differences in such a policy within all segments in a microsegment are subjected to being checked using the automated tools without fail to prove that these countermeasures agree with the consistency over the whole network. Comprehensive testing helps to ascertain the segmentation of networks that are less vulnerable and those that cannot be exploited by attackers for lateral movement.

15.6.4.3 Data Security and Access Control

Within a zero-trust structure, the protection of data is a must. Its guarantee ensures the redressal of cases under which incorrect data is not properly encrypted or only available to users and applications with authorization. It validates the status of data encryption both during rest and during transit, incorporates strong algorithms, and assesses the encryption key management process under which secure storage and handling of keys takes place. Further, testing DLP mechanisms to ensure that DLP policies prevent unauthorized data exfiltration, together with testing its functionality, will also be meaningful. Access control policies will also have to undergo scrutiny to ensure that they are in line with the least privilege principle and that users are granted access only to the minimum extent necessary to perform their job function. Security testing should indicate revoking access promptly if it is no longer necessary, ensuring dynamic and secure permission management through user life cycles.

15.6.4.4 Identity and Access Management (IAM)

IAM systems are needed to enforce the zero-trust principles, which revolve managing user identity and restricting access to resources. The security tests in this atmosphere entails looking across the identity lifecycle, provisioning and deprovisioning users to password management and access revocation; there is supervision, ensuring that accounts are managed well while access is immediately revoked when appropriate; and it checks Private Access Management (PAM) solutions to show privileged

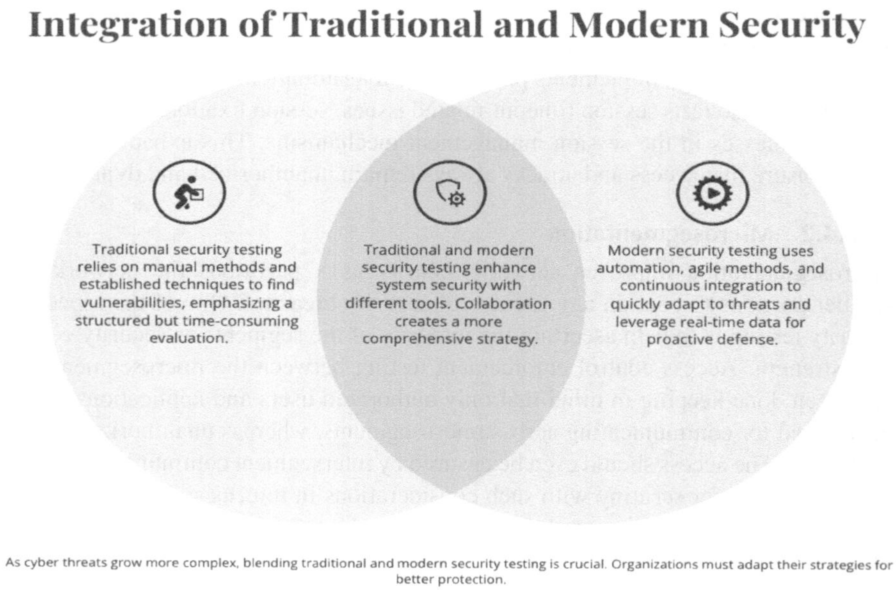

FIGURE 15.3 Method integration layout.

account protection, and heavy restricted access control to its most sensitive systems. Identify and address PAM system vulnerabilities, and demonstrate that privileged access is granted usually on a need-to-know basis. This should extend to authentication and authorization systems such as identity provider and any SSO solution in order to show weaknesses such as authentication bypass and flaws in authorization processes so that robust access control can be ensured across the organization.

The zero-trust framework is a necessity for all types, wide and continuous strategies of security testing. Organizations will have a solid foundation of zero-trust posture to mitigate various risks from modern-day cyber threats when coupled with continuous validation, microsegmentation, data security, and best practices in IAM. Conduct regular security assessments and penetration tests, as this form of feedback proves the efficacy of zero-trust controls and uncovers weaknesses in them. Likewise, for adaptation of testing methodologies toward the emerging security scenarios related to zero-trust and automation, the environment should be highly robust in today's contemporary world.

15.7 CHALLENGES AND BEST PRACTICES IN SECURITY TESTING

Though the significance of security testing is understood worldwide, framing practical security testing procedures is difficult. Organizations often experience budgetary, staffing, and tool hostages, which management must clear. Practitioners should adopt business best practices to achieve these nonfunctional requirements: security-minded toward people, seamlessly collaborative across development and testing, and comprehensive test case coverage.

15.7.1 Challenges in Implementing Security Testing

Several factors can hinder the effective implementation of security testing.

15.7.1.1 Budget Constraints

Security testing involves a lot of money, which include acquisition of specialized tools, training and personnel costs. Organizations may incur huge expenses in securing advanced security tools and even recruiting highly trained personnel who are paid high salaries. Such expenses mostly strain the budgets of organizations. Further, inviting thorough testing takes time, which is time cost paid off in labor. Because such budgets are small, organizations may be forced to limit their testing coverage, so critical systems might be only ones tested while less visible or less important applications would still be left susceptible. Such debts hamper an organization's security and can be exploited by an attacker. For example, a small startup may not have the cash for expensive commercial penetration testing and rely solely on less extensive vulnerability scanning, which creates gaps in security that could easily be exploited.

15.7.1.2 Lack of Expertise

The art of security testing is a highly specialized one that has deep technical knowledge and experience; hence, it becomes really difficult to find and retain qualified professionals in this domain. This demand is increasingly challenging, given the strong job market for talents in cybersecurity. Also, without adequate expertise, security testing is on the verge of failure since the inexperience of the testers often results in missed major vulnerabilities or misinterpretation of the results leading to a state of false security. Let us take the case of hiring an IT generalist in a company to perform the security tests. This person may not have the requisite knowledge and skills to perform penetration testing and thus miss out reporting on some of the key risks to security. Hence, it is really important that the security tests are done by well-qualified persons, as this is the only way one could identify and treat vulnerabilities correctly.

15.7.1.3 Tool Limitations

Security testing tools are vital to discovering vulnerabilities, but they are not perfect; they can yield false positives—finding important threats as benign issues—or false negatives—having real ill effects escape detection. Most rely on specialized knowledge to operate, though, so false positives cost valuable time and resources by investigating nonissues, while false negatives leave key vulnerabilities untouched. Another point to mention is that complex tools, used by those who are not trained in them, may lead to inaccurate results. For example, a vulnerability scanner would state that a sanitized code snippet is vulnerable for SQL injection for unnecessary investigation and resource allocation. Such problems are important but can certainly be addressed with proper training and selection of tools.

15.7.1.4 Integrating Security Testing into Agile and DevOps

Speed and frequent releases are the primary characteristics of Agile and DevOps, key methodologies often at odds with traditional security testing, which is generally manual and slow. Adding security tests will create bottlenecks, postponing releases and causing friction between development and security teams. For instance, arranging a long penetration test just before a release will delay the process while adding pressure to shortcut security. For effective security testing to be done, it should be streamlined and automated, allowing it to be seamlessly integrated into the continuous delivery pipeline without affecting velocity.

15.7.1.5 Testing Complex Environments

To keep pace with the complexity of present-day IT environments cloud infrastructures, microservices, IoT devices, and mobile applications—it would surely spell very special security challenges. Traditional pentesting paradigms probably allow very little room for dealing with the complexities different environments set up. Therefore, the right tools and the right experts are required for handling each technology's very specific security concerns. For instance, testing a cloud-native application's security entails understanding the access controls and configurations of the cloud provider, as well as container security complexities. Considering the pace at which these environments are evolving, security-testing measures will also need to follow suit to cover all infrastructure layers comprehensively.

15.7.1.6 Keeping Up with Evolving Threats

The whole landscape of cybersecurity is perpetually changing, with novel vulnerabilities and attack techniques continuously coming into the scenery, and this aspect will always make things difficult to keep in touch with. The security testing programs will need to be flexible enough so that they will be able to ebb and flow with the speedy moving new threats. This entails being in a continual education mode, keeping tools and techniques current, and regularly having access to the latest in security research findings. For example, patching and updating the security testing procedures would be necessary where a new zero-day vulnerability on a well-known web server was discovered to be patched immediately to identify and prevent the exploiting of machines. The ever-changing threat landscape will always have to be adapted continually regarding the security strategy the organization has committed to ensure holistic protection.

15.7.1.7 Data Security and Privacy Regulations

The compliance with regulations such as GDPR, CCPA, and HIPAA makes security testing much tougher due to stringent data protection and privacy requirements; security testing programs are devised with such regulatory requirements in mind and, most often, require additional tests and documentation to confirm compliance. Thus, systems will ensure that they effectively handle sensitive information with minimized risks of repercussions from legal actions or fines. For example, if a company provides the system for handling medical data, it should comply with HIPAA's particular requirement for security testing regarding data encryption and access control since these regulate the extent of protection against unauthorized access. While following these regulations complicates the testing process, such adherence is essential in order to secure data privacy as well as in compliance with regulations.

15.7.1.8 Resistance to Change

Effective security testing usually requires changes within existing development processes and across the organization. Unfortunately, any such modifications incur resistance from developers, testers, or management. This resistance sometimes poses challenges against the adoption of the changes in security testing practices or tools. As a result, the security posture of the entire organization may be weakened. By way of example, some developers may be reluctant to adopt secure coding practices because it is perceived as delaying development or making unnecessary complexity. Hence the gaps in security increase, shortening timeframes for identifying vulnerabilities and making it difficult to keep robust security measures in place throughout the software lifecycle.

The first step toward maturing and effectively building a security testing program is understanding these challenges and potential impacts. Addressing such challenges must also be strategic. This includes sufficient budgeting and investment in training and expertise, appropriate tooling, integration into the SDLC, and creating an awareness culture across the organization.

15.7.2 Best Practices for Effective Security Testing: A Proactive and Comprehensive Approach

Effective security testing requires more than just running a few tools. It demands a proactive, comprehensive approach integrated throughout the SDLC. Implementing these best practices helps organizations build robust security testing programs that minimize risks and protect valuable assets.

15.7.2.1 Building a Security-First Mindset

A project must be built on security and enshrined in the basic consciousness, not an afterthought. This would call for a cultural shift-pushing for a security-first mindset in all teams within the SDLC. Security would be embedded throughout every step in the SDLC—from threat modeling during design—to secure coding practices in development—to rigorous security testing for all. In adopting a shared-responsibility model, developers, testers, project managers, and operations teams would direct clear communication and well-defined security goals toward aligning collaboration on security objectives. Security awareness programs, together with embedding security requirements in project documentation, complete the approach to holistic vulnerability mitigation systems against crime as it changes.

15.7.2.2 Creating Comprehensive Test Plans

Effective security testing must be thoroughly planned and strategized, and the plans should cover specific applications or systems. It should begin with a comprehensive threat modeling exercise that will surely uncover available attack vectors, vulnerabilities, and threat actors, hence laying the groundwork for narrowed-down tests. Specific measurable test cases must be designed to cover their effects thoroughly. The chosen tools and techniques for threat evaluation such as SAST, DAST, IAST, and penetration tested or need to occur in line with the application's architecture and threat landscape. For example, a web application test plan must include test scenarios for vulnerabilities such as SQL injection, XSS, and broken authentication so that a strong security posture is achieved.

15.7.2.3 Prioritizing Vulnerabilities

Prioritize and rank the vulnerabilities because they do not all represent the same levels of risk in the effective security management of an organization. Organizations must put their energy into remediating the most important risks to the affected organizations. One way to achieve that is to apply well-established risk assessment techniques or tools, such as Common Vulnerability Scoring System (CVSS) severity score-assignment into vulnerabilities. The scores consider the impact on such factors as exploitability, expected business effect, and mitigation availability to form a solid normative structure for threats.

In addition to CVSS, another integral element is a comprehensive business impact analysis. The vulnerability would also assess how different operational impacts could be aggravated by introducing the risk of data breaches and possible reputational damage. For example, a vulnerability with a high CVSS score enabling RCE should take precedence over a lower scoring vulnerability with very few consequences such as low information leakage [14].

15.7.2.4 Automating Security Testing

Security testing entry automation is absolutely an aiding factor in the dynamic development space for continuous, uninterrupted, yet assuring productivity. Security checks integrated into CI/CD continuously include automated security tools that lead to regular and continuous security checks according to every stage of the development process. This ensures, if possible, that identified threats have a much earlier remediation cost and quality code. All-round efficiency and effectiveness in testing are offered with the use of methodologies such as SAST, DAST, and SCA. A CI/CD pipeline will be configured to issue SAST scans at each code commit and also DAST scans at each build, ensuring proactive and continuous security throughout the development lifecycle in which these kinds of practices are fit and will enable the security testing readiness toward scaling agility in teams while maintaining stringent security standards in dynamic development environments.

15.7.2.5 Leveraging Different Testing Techniques

Even though every single approach targets certain aspects of application vulnerability, a full-blown comprehensive strategy for security testing cannot stand alone as multiple methodologies will provide its efficacy. SAST is based solely on source code and does not run the application. It recognizes coding mistakes at early life cycle stages, like unsafe handling of input. DAST tests the application in a running state with dynamic data and identifies run-time vulnerabilities, including injection flaws and authentication bypasses. IAST provides a link between SAST and DAST through the instrumentation of the application at runtime. The result is a more accurate view of static and dynamic vulnerabilities, along with their affected code sections. Last, penetration tests add the complete picture, simulating actual attacks, thus giving a more realistic score of vulnerability ratings and impact.

For example, a well-rounded test workflow could commence with SAST to identify areas in the code that potentially result in SQL injection, then use DAST on the application running to validate the exploitability of such vulnerabilities before concluding with penetration testing to gauge the actual severity of the threats coming from exploitation of such vulnerabilities.

15.7.2.6 Regular Security Assessments

Security evaluations are mandatory at intervals to secure an independent assessment of the security posture of an organization. An external penetration test simulates a "real-world" attack and helps to identify those vulnerabilities that might not be found by anyone else through internal testing. A regular automated vulnerability scanning identifies risks already known, while at intervals conducting audits ensures compliance with security policies and standards. For example, conducting annual penetration tests on critical systems and applications gives a very thorough assessment of security defenses and what needs to be improved.

15.7.2.7 Continuous Monitoring and Improvement

Security testing is something that is done continuously and requires continuous monitoring and updating. SIEM solutions are the ones that keep security logs in real-time, and analyze them in order to detect threats immediately. Intrusion Detection and Prevention Systems permeate even deeper into the network to detect and also block any malicious activity. Regular updates to security testing tools and processes help stay ahead of risks about which you are yet to hear. This may include things like monitoring security logs for suspicious activity or keeping vulnerability scanning tools updated with current definitions frequently for system-protection against new risks.

15.7.2.8 Collaboration and Communication

Testing the effectiveness of security measures strongly depends on the working together of development teams, security teams, and operations teams for such tests. This means that communication lines should be clearly set out so that people can share details about the identified vulnerabilities, the remediation strategies considered for specific vulnerabilities, and other security practices to be rolled out along various actors in the organization. Code reviews, security test case reviews, and security configuration reviews possess the possibility of gathering all this information at a higher level in turn allowing better exposure to more extensive risk management. As, for instance, a meeting schedule with entries happening at certain intervals between the development team and the security team to discuss security findings and remediation plans, it all combines to develop a more effective security-driven culture and hearty enhancement of security posture in general [15].

15.7.2.9 Training and Education

Investing in training and education is really important for developing security knowledge to keep teams updated with the latest threats and best practices. Such secure coding has to be taught to developers so that they learn how to avoid most of the vulnerabilities that often occur. Static analysis training should be done for testers on the various techniques of security testing and the effective use of testing tools. Introducing general awareness training for all employees in an organization creates the grounds for letting them know what security threats are and what best practices are. For example, arranging regular workshops on secure coding practices specifically associated with languages used by the development team as a workforce would enhance their ability to write secured codes and potential risk identification skills.

Through the adoption of the various best practices, organizations can make up to quite a mature and effective security testing program that enhances the overall security posture and guards the organization against an evolving threat landscape. Besides, continuous improvement and an ability to adapt all stages in the SDLC hold an impressive promise of long-term success in security testing.

15.7.3 Collaboration Between Developers and Testers: Bridging the Gap for Enhanced Security

Effective security testing remains part of a common activity between developers and testers; not just one of the responsibilities concerning the dedicated security team. It ought to build a common understanding of what security risks are and how the respective teams can coordinate and constantly take action in identifying and remedying vulnerabilities. Breaking down silos has been made possible and can be strengthened with better communication, which leads eventually to secure software.

15.7.3.1 Shared Responsibility for Security

Security should go with the shared responsibility of all departments and not just the security department. Developers have to write secure code by adopting secure coding practices, rectifying identified vulnerabilities, and considering security implications at design and development stages. Testers are responsible for ascertaining whether security controls deploy as intended, discovering security vulnerabilities that developers have missed, and advising developers on security issues. For instance, developers can receive training on secure coding while the testers can carry out penetration testing exercises for improved capabilities in detecting and mitigating such security risks.

15.7.3.2 Early Involvement of Security Testers

Integrated Security Testing Early into the SDLC, Shifting Left tends to be possible where potential vulnerabilities can be identified and remediated even before developing the code. Thus, reducing the costs related to development risks overall. Such security testers come along during the design phases and add value by understanding and exposing potential threats, providing possible countermeasures, and confirming that security is incorporated right from the start. Those actions would, in turn, bring the need for costly end fixes into the cycle. Consistent developer and security tester collaboration during the course of development would also play a critical role by pinpointing issues early on and allow for real-time team referencing if any questions or concerns arise. For instance, security testers could go through design documents or take part in sprint planning meetings for that complete security inclusion during the development process. Threat Dragon can be used to collaboratively model threats and risks through the design phase, literally creating collaboration efforts, reducing the vulnerabilities left within the final product.

15.7.3.3 Joint Security Reviews

Joint security reviews of code and test cases allow sharing of knowledge and so ensure that security is incorporated from both points of view: the developer's and the tester's. Security testers can participate in code review sessions, carrying out reviews with a slant toward identifying potential vulnerabilities and offering proper feedback on secure coding practices, while developers are also able to evaluate test cases created by security testers based on relevancy in ensuring coverage of important security scenarios. This means that both developer and testing teams have a common understanding of the risks posed by security as well as remediation approaches. For example, joint coding review sessions in which the developer and security tester discuss vulnerabilities go a long way in identifying the early onset of issues and arriving at appropriate solutions. Further, such reviews create a shared responsibility for security with built-in mechanisms for continuous improvement and proactive reduction of risks along with development.

15.7.3.4 Open Communication and Feedback

Establish clear channels of communication between developers and testers that enable effective collaboration. Their real-time feedback allows developers to solve security issues in their very early stages of development. This can be facilitated either by integrating security testing tools into the IDE or by setting dedicated communication channels that help articulate security issues. Feedback must also be constructive, focused and actionable on specific vulnerabilities with tangible guidance for remediation instead of attributing the security issues within the organization to the developers. As an example, by using a bug tracking system, an organization can log vulnerabilities, track their resolutions, and ensure transparency. Regular meetings between developers and testers can help promote other channels to enable them to share their findings on security issues and best practices alongside conventional ways to ensure security—concern for the entire development lifecycle. Thus, one could create a culture of security in constructively proactive communication and effect early detection of vulnerabilities before they mature into issues of critical concern.

15.7.3.5 Knowledge Sharing

Knowledge sharing between developers and testers increases security awareness and skills. Introducing "security champions" in development teams makes space for secure coding practices and sharing of security knowledge. Security "lunch and learn" sessions can also keep the two groups up to date on new threats and vulnerabilities. Besides cross-training, opportunities are given to developers and testers to understand each other's work, thereby promoting collaboration. It creates a common joint repository for both development and QA teams regarding security materials such as secure coding guidelines, security testing tools, and vulnerability databases. An edited example would be that such a shared wiki might contain secure coding guidelines, relevant to various programming languages, and some blog articles with respect to recent vulnerabilities could be posted there to support the continuous learning process. Workshops on security testing techniques may also supplement the same value of elevating awareness of security, as well as possibly improve the skills of both teams to tackle security issues through collaboration.

15.7.3.6 Collaboration Tools and Technologies

Tools and technologies that have transformed collaboration between developers and testers for better security concerns include platforms like Slack and Microsoft Teams, in addition to dedicated project management applications like issue tracking systems like Jira and Bugzilla. They allow the tracking and management of security vulnerabilities and remediation activities from any part of the organization. Automated testing of security in CI/CD pipelines can give instant feedback to developers to keep all development under consistent safety checks. Advanced DevSecOps tools like GitLab and Azure DevOps embed security testing within the Development pipeline that improves collaboration among development and operations teams with security. In all, these tools help to flow information effortlessly, identify vulnerabilities rapidly, and make the process of remediation more efficient, which leads to making the software development environment more secure.

Fostering a culture of shared responsibility, open communication, and investment in knowledge sharing is the way forward for organizations to bridge the gap between developers and testers and create a more secure development environment. Such an approach will thus ensure more secure software, reduction in the cost of remediation, and increased overall security posture of the organization. Remaining constantly on the lookout for new tools, techniques, and best practices is necessary for continuous improvement and adaptation to the ever-changing threat landscape.

FIGURE 15.4 Checklist for implementing security best practices.

15.8 REAL-WORLD APPLICATIONS AND CASE STUDIES

15.8.1 Case Studies on Security Testing in Action

With security testing, organizations from the finance, healthcare, e-commerce, and other industries have become aware of the great risks they face. These organizations have suffered a lot from security threats because these attacks usually touch sensitive data and valuables stored in the systems and processes behind such industries. They have engaged security testing in a complex way to curb such risks and maintain customer trust.

A great example here is **JPMorgan Chase** in the finance sector, which was attacked in 2023. It was a cyber breach that affected millions of records, and in that incident, the company discovered areas with gaps in security with its APIs causing it to adopt a tougher protocol for testing its premises. It combined DAST with penetration testing to assess and strengthen its systems. Furthermore, the bank has installed AI threat simulation tools, which allow it to empathically identify vulnerabilities that reduce response time to incidents by about 40%.

The growing reliance on electronic health records has accentuated the importance of security measures in the healthcare sector. In 2022, the ransomware attack on a hospital in the United States highlighted how patient data could be exposed if security testing is not given its due importance. The hospital, having conducted SAST alongside fuzz testing in its overhauled defenses, ensured compliance with HIPAA regulations and the prohibition of similar breaches in 2023 onward.

In 2023, an online retailer had a session management vulnerability that resulted in account takeovers. This forced the company to adopt zero-trust principles and step up their security testing by using automated vulnerability scanning tools like Nessus. This way, they identified and patched the vulnerabilities before they were reported by attackers and restored user confidence, especially in protecting financial transactions.

15.8.2 Lessons Learned from Past Breaches: A Foundation for Proactive Security

Investigating historical security incidents would offer essential findings for an organization that seeks to improve its security defenses. Such incidents are reminders of the evolving weaponry and the serious need for proactive and adaptive security measures. Understanding past breaches helps organizations to know the vulnerabilities present in their security posture and redress them with effective mitigation strategies.

15.8.2.1 The SolarWinds Supply-Chain Attack (2020 and Beyond)

The SolarWinds attack, which involved supply-chain compromise and carefully constructed techniques, brought many impacts, including the immediate effect on several organizations, including government and Fortune 500 companies. Attackers inserted malicious codes into the Orion platform, which is a leading IT management software and distributes it to customers of SolarWinds through software updates.

- **Learning Points:** The attack revealed a destructive hole in the software supply chain and the potential of damages from one point in a chain. Many lessons on the need for a well-structured third-party risk management practice and increased scrutiny of software updates were also learned [16].

- **Impact on Security Testing:** Organizations recently adopted comprehensive policies for vendor risk management that now require vendors to demonstrate security practices and undergo regular security assessments. Software bill of materials (SBOM), which allows organizations to understand the components of software and identify potential vulnerabilities from third parties, has gained acceptance. Thus, security testing now includes supply-chain analysis, dependency scanning, and vulnerability assessments of the third-party components [17].

15.8.2.2 The Marriott Data Breach (2014–2018, Disclosed 2018)

The Marriott breach is as long as it has stretched through the years, and it has revealed a secret of personal identification, with hundreds of million guests having their privacy exposed. This incident exposed PII on the customers for a series of years and traces its origin to a pervaded Starwood Hotels system that was not completely assimilated into Marriott for security after the acquisition [18].

- **Lessons Learned:** It was majorly observed that asset management coverage must be heavy during mergers and acquisitions. Not to forget that legacy systems carry risks and also the importance of visibility to IT assets in its entirety [19].
- **Impact on Security Testing:** Asset discovery and management are now included in every organization's overall security test initiatives. Automated asset discovery has been adopted to identify all devices and systems connected to the organization's network, thus including legacy systems usually overlooked. Security assessments of organizations have now become all-inclusive in covering identified assets and not the most flagrant [20].

15.8.2.3 The Colonial Pipeline Ransomware Attack (2021 and Its Continuing Impact)

The sound of the Colonial Pipeline ransomware attack, roaring with its mighty trumpet blast, eventually proved disruptive from the southernmost to eastern edges of the United States. Critical infrastructure vulnerability to cyberattack showed as-the-phishing-found in this case. The company's network was accessed using a compromised password.

- **Lesson Learned:** This incident assisted very well in some major strong needs for event incident response strategy development and recurrent plan tests into action. Critical infrastructure interconnectedness and chances it could leave a single attack cascading on others were also visualized.
- **Impacts on Security Testing:** For example, organizations today are embarking on more realistic incidents tests as part of their overall security program, especially those in critical infrastructures. Activities organized under red teams and tabletop simulations have been employed to test an

organization's ability to detect, respond, and recover from ransomware and other cyberattacks. More emphasis is directed toward endpoint security, password management, and network segmentation to prevent initial access and limit scope of the impact of dedicated attacks.

15.8.2.4 The Log4j Vulnerability (2021 and Ongoing Mitigation)

Log4j brought the importance of open-source components in a system to the forefront when it opened another can of worms in severe vulnerabilities in software. Such a form of exploitation lets a remote attacker conduct code execution, often giving them the same access to the systems as that of physical insiders.

- **Learnings Learned:** Identify and learn from the lessons that the incident of Log4j focused on SCA and the need for continuous monitoring of open-source dependency vulnerabilities. The challenges in patching widely deployed software components have been acknowledged, revealing the possibility of long-tail risks.
- **Impacts on Security Testing:** SCA is being integrated into the developmental pipeline and the security testing programs of organizations to discover and manage any vulnerabilities in open-source components. Automated tools are used to scan the codebases for vulnerable dependencies and consequently prioritize patching efforts. The monitoring processes for vulnerability management are enhanced and robust patching strategies developed.

15.8.2.5 The Okta Breach (2022)

The incident involving Okta's breach clearly emphasized the critical requirement of supply-chain security and the threat that the breach would bring to privileged access management (PAM) by an attacker having an inside hand with an internal system of Okta through a third-party vendor.

- **Lesson Learned:** The incident only underscored the need for very strong vendor risk management programs, thorough assessments of the security of these suppliers as part of the access control policies enforced, and overuse privileges issues and their mitigation through the least-privilege principle.
- **Impacts on Security Testing:** Organizations are currently on a stricter lookout for the security practices adopted by their third-party vendors as they demand proof regarding adherence to the prescribed security standards, besides their regular security assessments. This puts more emphasis on PAM, enforced through strong lashing authentication and authorization controls directed at privileged accounts while limiting access to highly sensitive systems and information.

The above case studies reiterate that learning from the experience of past security breaches should enable organizations to improve their security practices to avoid facing such incidents in the future. It should advocate that organizations take on a proactive approach to security by learning from these and other incidents and incorporating them into the security testing programs, incident response plan, and overall security strategy. Continuous monitor, adaptation, and improvement would be key for keeping up with the rapidly evolving threat landscape to maintain a robust security posture.

15.8.3 Success Stories of Vulnerability Management: Proactive Security in Action

Although security breaches frequently steal headlines, many organizations are successfully implementing proactive security testing and continuous improvement to effectively manage security vulnerabilities. Those success stories represent the potential value of thorough security management and offer a promising example for other organizations to pursue.

15.8.3.1 Microsoft's Evolving Bug Bounty Program

Microsoft has pioneered the development of vulnerability identification through the use of bug bounty programs. They have employed this across their entire range of products and services, such as Azure, Office 365, Windows, and Edge.

- **Continual Improvement:** Microsoft always nurtures its bug bounty program by extending the lines on which one can report bugs. They recently also included specialist bug bounty programs that focus on specific domains such as cloud security and election security.
- **Collaboration with Security Ecosystem:** Microsoft actively interacts with the security research community toward having a hybrid approach to vulnerability disclosure-internal and external. For example, Microsoft already incentivized a lot of researchers who reported security flaws to them.
- **Effect:** The bugs and loopholes are usually identified in thousands; thus, the company could secure itself from the potential threats posed by malicious threats exploiting such vulnerabilities. This proactive measure secures the products and services and rubs millions of users across the world. It continued to refine its developments in 2024 along with researcher feedback and development in emerging technologies.

15.8.3.2 Netflix's Chaos Engineering for Enhanced Resilience

Innovative security testing is what Netflix is known for, and applies the principles of chaos engineering for the resilience of the systems.

- **Chaos Monkey and Its Evolution:** The identification of weakness and improvement of fault tolerance in the system architecture are carried out by a tool called Chaos Monkey—which randomly shuts down virtual machines once in a while from the production environment. Netflix then went on broadening its portfolio of chaos engineering tools to include Latency Monkey, Conformity Monkey, and Security Monkey that primarily test failovers by introducing various models of disruption for each tool.

- **API Security Testing Integration:** Acknowledge the rising prominence of APIs; hence, the APIs are included in the chaos engineering practice of Netflix for security testing on being more prepared on unforeseen failures and malicious attacks. Automated API security test tools and techniques will also be used to find out vulnerabilities and ensure streaming service reliability.
- **Impacts:** Chaos engineering has impacted the resilience imparted into cloud infrastructure and streaming services for Netflix. While the systems are tested constantly under real-world stresses, Netflix found and fixed flaws proactively before they can cause impact outages or security incidents. This in turn keeps high availability of service so that millions of subscribers worldwide get less interruption to their streaming experience.

15.8.3.3 Capital One's Transformation to Cloud-Native Security

After the significant breach in data in the year 2019, the security strategy of capital one was transformed from due diligence and compliance to cloud-native security principles that fully integrate investments in automated security testing.

- **Automated Testing into CI/CD:** Automated security testing tools are well integrated in the CI/CD pipeline of Capital One. Here, the tools provide the capability to fast vulnerability identification and remediation. A shift-left approach is applied in ensuring that security checks are done as early and often in the development life cycle as required.
- **Cloud-Native Security Tooling:** They set aside funding for cloud-native security testing tools built to take on cloud environments and their particular challenges. Tools for CSPM, CWPPs, and IaC security scanning fall under this category.
- **Impacts:** Capital One's plans of automated testing and cloud-native security are indeed looking like a best case as far as risk exposure is concerned. Their early discovery and resolution of vulnerabilities in system development have limited the consequences of breaches while at the same time strengthening the overall security posture of their cloud environment. It serves as an outstanding and research-worthy use case for other organizations gearing to cloud.

15.8.3.4 United States Department of Defense (DoD) "Hack the Pentagon" Program

The Department of Defense's "Hack the Pentagon" initiative is a giant leap in the field of government cybersecurity-cum-bug bounty program inviting vetted security researchers for the purpose of identifying vulnerabilities in the DoD systems.

- **Crowdsourced Security:** The program leverages the expertise of the cybersecurity community to identify those vulnerabilities that would have been missed by traditional security testing methods.
- **Continuous Expansion:** The "Hack the Pentagon" has already made a name for itself and has since been expanded to other government agencies.

- **Impacts:** Besides allowing them to be patched and secured before malicious actors could exploit them, it has also discovered several vulnerabilities within DoD systems. Cost-effective by design, this crowdsourced methodology has proven to be the efficient means of enhancement toward government cybersecurity.

The most striking of the success stories is the evidence in favor of proactive security testing, continuous improvement, and collaboration with the security community. Organizations would be wise to adopt and customize such practices to augment their security posture, minimize security breach risks, and protect their valuable assets. It is important for organizations to regularly take stock of novel tools, techniques, and emerging threats in order to remain successful in managing a vulnerability.

15.8.4 Industry-Specific Challenges and Innovations in Security Testing

Every industry faces unique threats and has different security testing approaches. Connected cars metaphorize automotive industries, remote learning platforms picture education, and every critical infrastructure that government agencies must have all exemplify how security testing should adapt to risk and vulnerabilities. Security testing is all about adapting to new innovations as well as staying in touch with a world that's moving much faster and creating more technologically advanced threats.

15.8.4.1 Automotive: Securing the Connected Car Ecosystem

The evolution of the automotive industry is changing rapidly with the advent of connected and self-driving cars, which are dependent on complex software systems and external communication networks relative to the new attacks they pose for the cybercriminals [21].

- **Creation of Specialized Testing Frameworks:** They needed the long-winded special testing frameworks because automotive software and hardware have different qualities, with the special communications protocols and embedded systems as well real-time operating systems, which the vehicle uses [22].
- **Simulation of Real-World Scenarios:** It also needs to simulate attacks in the real-life context. This includes remote exploitation of vulnerabilities in the connected car system or accessing and manipulating driving features autonomously. Advanced AI and ML systems are currently employed to design such simulations for attack [23].
- **Example:** The security testing programs from Tesla use AI to simulate various forms of attack scenarios and apply these against their autonomous driving systems to identify issue areas or possible vulnerabilities. Other automotive manufacturers have worked together on an industry-wide safety standard and a testing framework, for example, the EVITA project (E-safety Vehicle Intrusion proTected Applications) [24].

15.8.4.2 Education: Protecting Remote Learning Platforms and Sensitive Student Data

Recently, the education sector has witnessed a high increase toward online learning and digital resources. Thus, bringing new security issues to educational institutions, sensitive data of students have to be secured along with the integrity of their online learning environment.

- **SAST/DAST for Learning Management Systems (LMS):** Many educational institutions now deploy SAST or DAST tools to locate vulnerabilities in the LMS or web applications. These will help mitigate attacks that need student data, destroy learning, or damage the reputation of their institutions.
- **Collaboration and Shared Frameworks:** To counter sector-specific risks, consortium universities and educational organizations are designing common security testing frameworks and best practices. It brings institutions together in pooling resources and expertise toward bettering the security posture in the education sector.
- **Example:** A security testing requirement shared framework is formed by a consortium of universities in which this framework consists of secure coding guidelines, penetration testing for LMS as well as incident response procedures designed specifically for educational institutions in 2024 [25].

15.8.4.3 Government: Defending Critical Infrastructure and Sensitive Data from Advanced Threats

Government agencies are targets of sophisticated cyberattacks, mostly from nation-state actors. Thus, there is an urgent requirement for advanced security testing methodologies to protect regulatory critical infrastructure, sensitive data, and national security interests.

- **AI-Driven Penetration Testing:** Government agencies are beginning to implement AI penetration test tools to automate and enhance security testing without the associated inefficiencies. Such tools find vulnerabilities more conveniently and simulate more complex attack scenarios than the old penetration testing approach [26].
- **Red Teaming and Advanced Persistent Threat (APT) Simulation:** Performing red teaming exercises, which provide members with an actual near-real-world attack scenario from a very high-skilled opponent, grows in relevance for most government agencies. In addition, this will help determine the weak links that need to be addressed and enhance the capability of the organization in detecting and responding to complex attacks involving APTs.
- **Adoption of Zero-Trust Security Model:** Government agencies are moving toward zero-trust security architectures, which assume no implicit trust, no need for verification of access requests for each entry. Zero-trust environments provide a basis for security testing which helps in validating

the effectiveness of access controls, microsegmentation, and continuous authentication and authorization mechanisms [27].

- **Example:** The US Department of Defense keeps the expanded "Hack the Pentagon" bug bounty going and invests in new AI-powered penetration testing tools to proactively identify shortcomings in the critical systems. Other government agencies are starting similar initiatives, considering crowd-sourced security and innovative testing methodologies as part of the future.

15.8.4.4 Healthcare: Protecting Patient Data and Ensuring the Safety of Medical Devices

Healthcare security challenges are inherently specific and increasingly faced with modernity in data-linked medical equipment.

- **Testing Security of Medical Devices:** There are several specialized security testing frameworks and tools for assessing the security of medical devices including implanted devices, wearables, health trackers, and connected medical instruments. Testing on such devices includes searching for vulnerabilities in the firmware and wireless communication protocols, as well as testing for security in data encryption mechanisms [28].
- They include other regulations like HIPAA regulations requiring security testing to be conducted in compliance with such regulations. HIPAA regulation stipulates strict adherence to the security and privacy requirements of protected health information (PHI) [29].
- For example, medical device manufacturers are applying stricter protocols with regard to security testing such as penetration testing and vulnerability scanning to discover and take action against vulnerabilities before devices are released to the market, while healthcare also imposes stringent access controls and monitoring of security levels for patient data in the broader view of meeting HIPAA compliance [30].

15.8.4.5 Critical Infrastructure: Enhancing Resilience against Cyber-Physical Attacks

Cyber assaults, including increasing threats, to critical infrastructure sectors such as energy, transportation, and water supply could have physical impacts which can impact the lives of individuals living in that area or supposedly country devastatingly [31].

- **Cyber-Physical Security Testing:** Specialized security testing methodologies need to be developed for assessing the risks associated with cyber-physical attacks, which could essentially involve assessing the sum of the total interdependence between the cyber and physical systems. Such simulations include attacks against industrial control systems (ICS) and other components of critical infrastructure [32].
- **Example:** Energy companies conduct red teaming exercises regarding power grid attacks with some indicative vulnerabilities on the way power could be cut off. Water treatment plants carry out security testing against attacks that lead to water contamination [33].

Understanding security challenges particular to an industry and employing the best-practice innovative testing approaches would mean better understanding of how these organizations can protect their systems, data, and operations from changes in the evolving threat landscape. Continuous monitoring and committed improvement through collaboration are some of the ways to have sustained robustness of security while covering the entire ecosystem today. Such innovation in security testing will remain a top driving feature across all industries in enhanced cybersecurity from now on, as outdated technologies are always being put forward to counter cyberattacks in more sophisticated ways.

15.8.5 Emerging Trends in Security Testing Applications: Adapting to the Evolving Threat Landscape

Security testing has a route to reformation that it among other things applies in part to the dynamic nature of the cyber threats as well as the increasing complexities that modern systems possess. Emerging trends, brought about by updated AI, methodologies of development, and new security architecture implementations, are all weighing as factors finally to change the future of security testing.

15.8.5.1 AI and Machine Learning for Enhanced Threat Detection

Security testing is becoming more accurate in prediction and efficiency with the help of AI and ML.

- **Automatic Vulnerability Detection:** AI engines can inspect through massive code, network traffic, and security logs searching for patterns or discrepancies that signal vulnerabilities. This automates finding vulnerabilities and greatly minimizes the manual efforts in improving efficiency [34].
- **Predictive Security Analytics:** Using historical security data commonly stored by many organizations, ML is trained to predict future threats and attacks. The organization now has a chance to fix such vulnerabilities before the damage can be done [35].
- **Behavior Analysis and Anomaly Detection:** The AI-powered set of testing sees beyond normal pattern identification to behavior. It looks out for behavior from the baseline established by the organization. When it differs, then aberration notices that such employment are malicious. Extremely effective for the identification of zero-day attacks and other sophisticated methods that employ signature technology as detection attempts [36].
- **Example:** Some examples of such companies that have utilized AI as well as ML include DeepInstinct, Darktrace, and CrowdStrike, which offer security testing services. Automating vulnerability scanning, detecting malware, identifying malicious network activity, and providing better threat intelligence are some of the processes that are now being automated via such tools. AI-powered code analysis tools are emerging again to help developers in real-time identification and correction of security vulnerabilities [37].

15.8.5.2 Shift-Left Security and DevSecOps Integration

In essence, shift-left security refers to bringing the security test as early as possible in the SDLC. This is the proactive principle of DevSecOps, which means that security is imbued in every aspect of development [38].

- **SAST and Threat Modeling in Design:** Conducting SAST and threat modeling during design will let security find and fix security holes before they get embedded into the code. This will significantly lower the cost and effort of remediation late in the development cycle [39].
- **Design Phase:** SAST and Threat Modeling: Performing SAST and threat modeling in the design phase enables discovery and addressing of security risks even before the risks become entrenched inside the code. Such a course of action significantly reduces the cost and effort needed for subsequent remediation in later development phases.
- **Built-In Automated Security Testing within CI/CD Pipelines:** With the introduction of automated security testing tools into CI/CD pipelines, all security checks come as a regular and automatic accompaniment in the different development stages, enabling consistent security testing without halting the course of development.
- **Infrastructure as Security (AaC):** Infrastructure and security policies can be managed as source code thus providing automation and version control with much easier integration into DevSecOps workflows.
- **Examples:** This includes how organizations evolve toward DevSecOps by moving toward already available integrated platforms such as GitLab and Azure DevOps that contain security tools and workflows. Then they would start integrating SAST into their IDEs. These would ultimately provide real-time feedback to developers while writing code.

15.8.5.3 Zero-Trust Architectures and Continuous Verification

With the evolving adoption of zero-trust architectures, security testing methodologies will use security testing strategies, where zero-trust does not assume implicit trust and requires everyone requesting access to be authenticated, irrespective of location or network [40].

- **Continuous Authentication and Authorization:** Security testing in zero-trust environments focuses not only on penetration testing but also on evaluating the effectiveness of continuous authentication and authorization mechanisms, such as MFA and contextual access control [41].
- **Microsegmentation Testing:** Security Testing Microsegmented Networks: This testing involves checks on the implementation of access control in communication segmentation and security in that communication.
- **Data Security and Access Control Validation:** Security tests must ensure that data gets encrypted and access granted only to authorized users and applications based on least privilege [42].

- **Example:** Organizations are implementing zero-trust security solutions and conducting tests for penetration and red teaming to validate the effectiveness of zero-trust controls. Specific security testing tools are being constructed for a zero-trust environment and concern IAM, microsegmentation, and data security [43].

15.8.5.4 API Security Testing: Protecting the Interconnected Web

APIs can be said to comprise the structural skeletons of contemporary applications. On this premise, they present communication and allow for data exchange between different systems. API security testing is better becoming a topic of concern as APIs expose some very sensitive functionalities and also very sensitive data [44].

- **Automated API Security Testing Tools:** Automatic tools are to scan APIs for various vulnerabilities such as those that occur, for instance, when an authentication break has been caused, in authorizing bypass, or even injection vulnerability [45].
- **API Fuzzing:** For example, some API fuzz-testing techniques send invalid inputs to analyze APIs' behaviors or monitor API conditions when application calls encounter unexpected inputs [46].
- **Example:** Organizations have started integrating API security tools such as Postman, SoapUI, and OWASP ZAP as part of automated efforts for API security testing. They even integrate API security testing in their CI/CD pipelines to continuously test APIs throughout their development process [47].

15.8.5.5 Blockchain Security Testing: Ensuring the Integrity of Distributed Ledger Technologies

The decentralized and immutable features of Blockchain technology have a lot of promises regarding security. But they too are not exempted from vulnerabilities.

- **Smart Contracts Security Testing:** Smart contracts are self-executing contracts on the blockchain that may be programmed with vulnerabilities that can be exploited by attackers. Security testing tools and techniques have been developed for smart contract security analysis in terms of security flaws [48].
- **Consensus Mechanism Testing:** Testing the resilience of blockchain consensus mechanisms to attacks as, for instance, a 51% attack is essential for the assurance of integrity and availability of these systems [49].
- **Example:** Specialized security testing tools and techniques being used by organizations developing blockchain applications identify vulnerabilities in smart contracts while ensuring the security of their blockchain implementations [50].

Incorporating these new trends and changing their security testing methods, an organization will be well protected against evolution in the threat landscape. An organization will keep up a healthy security posture in this interconnected world via continuous learning, collaborating with the security community, and committing to perpetual improvement. Innovation in security testing will repeat its roaring in all industries as an important factor for continuous improvement in advanced cyber defense. As exciting new technologies develop and very sophisticated cyber threats are encountered, innovation in security testing will remain a continuously growing force in enhanced security across all industries.

15.9 CONCLUSION AND FUTURE DIRECTIONS: NAVIGATING THE EVOLVING CYBERSECURITY LANDSCAPE

Security testing is critical for the software systems to prevent them from falling victim to a more intricate threat landscape. This chapter emphasizes its importance—from integrating security testing in the SDLC to adopt vulnerability scanning, penetration testing, static and dynamic analyses, and API security testing tools and techniques. Next, the study has thus presented emerging trends such as AI-powered tools, zero-trust security, and blockchain security testing which offers new strategies and techniques in securing the overall security landscape.

The futuristic dimension appears to be transformed by AI and ML into the domain of security testing through intelligent vulnerability identification, automated penetration testing, and predictive security analysis. These modern techniques are enhanced in accuracy, reduced in the incidence of false-positive signals, and will be expected to result in a major offensive capability of organizations against predictive vulnerabilities. The shift-left approach is thus expected to gain further momentum and embed the security consideration very early in the SDLC, empowering developers to build secure software right from the design phase.

As the usage of Cloud becomes more pervasive, the requirements for cloud-native security tests would become absolutely critical not only serverless and containers but also IaC scanning. The same trend goes with the increasing number of IoT devices and embedded systems propagating the need for specialized testing techniques like firmware analysis, fuzzing, and IoT penetration testing. Similarly are the requirements for applications built in blockchain technology or smart contracts which are to be thoroughly tested, applying formal verification processes to remove any fallibilities.

It is anticipated that human expertise will still be indispensable, such that testers will continue to work alongside AI tools and adversary simulation exercises like red teaming. Security testing will instead change from being an isolated event to a continuous and adaptive process, integrated across the entire SDLC and responsive to emerging threats. With open arms to such changes and by encouraging innovative cultures, organizations can take a stand about a threat to maintain its posture in future spaces of cyber risk.

REFERENCES

1. M. Felderer, M. Büchler, M. Johns, A. D. Brucker, R. Breu and A. Pretschner, "Security Testing," in *Advances in computers*, vol. 101, Elsevier, 2016, pp. 1–51. doi: 10.1016/bs.adcom.2015.11.003.

2. A. H. A. Kamal, C. C. Y. Yen, G. J. Hui and P. S. Ling, and Fatima-Tuz-Zahra, "Risk Assessment, Threat Modeling and Security Testing in SDLC," 2020, *arXiv*. doi: 10.48550/ARXIV.2012.07226.
3. B. H. Thacker, D. S. Riha, S. H. K. Fitch, L. J. Huyse and J. B. Pleming, "Probabilistic engineering analysis using the NESSUS software," *Struct. Saf.*, vol. 28, no. 1–2, pp. 83–107, 2006. doi: 10.1016/j.strusafe.2004.11.003.
4. M. Sharma, D. Desai, A. R. Arun and N. Rajagopalan, "OpenVAS vs the Rest: Unveiling the Competitive Edge in Vulnerability Scanners," in *2024 3rd International Conference for Innovation in Technology (INOCON)*, Bangalore, India, IEEE, March 2024, pp. 1–6. doi: 10.1109/INOCON60754.2024.10511864.
5. D. Erhardt and J. Zhan, "A Proactive Approach to Detecting and Reducing Information Security Threats in Billing Systems," in *2010 5th International Conference on Future Information Technology*, Busan, Korea (South): IEEE, 2010, pp. 1–6. doi: 10.1109/FUTURETECH.2010.5482636.
6. K. A. Cochran, *Cybersecurity essentials: Practical tools for today's digital defenders*. Berkeley, CA: Apress, 2024. doi: 10.1007/979-8-8688-0432-8.
7. M. Zaydi, Y. Khourdifi, B. Nassereddine and J. Zhang, *Agile security in the digital era: Challenges and cybersecurity trends*, 1st ed. Boca Raton: CRC Press, 2024. doi: 10.1201/9781003478676.
8. C. Feio, N. Santos, N. Escravana and B. Pacheco, "An Empirical Study of DevSecOps Focused on Continuous Security Testing," in *2024 IEEE European Symposium on Security and Privacy Workshops (EuroS&PW)*, Vienna, Austria: IEEE, July 2024, pp. 610–617. doi: 10.1109/EuroSPW61312.2024.00074.
9. A. S. Ami, K. Moran, D. Poshyvanyk and A. Nadkarni, "'False negative - that one is going to kill you': Understanding Industry Perspectives of Static Analysis based Security Testing," in *2024 IEEE Symposium on Security and Privacy (SP)*, San Francisco, CA, USA: IEEE, May 2024, pp. 3979–3997. doi: 10.1109/SP54263.2024.00019.
10. J. Edwards Dr., *Critical security controls for effective cyber defense: A comprehensive guide to CIS 18 controls*. Berkeley, CA: Apress, 2024. doi: 10.1007/979-8-8688-0506-6.
11. M. S. Merkow, *Practical security for agile and DevOps*, 1st ed. Boca Raton: Auerbach Publications, 2021. doi: 10.1201/9781003265566.
12. T. Bakhshi, B. Ghita and I. Kuzminykh, "A review of IoT firmware vulnerabilities and auditing techniques," *Sensors*, vol. 24, no. 2, p. 708, 2024. doi: 10.3390/s24020708.
13. A. Fatima *et al.*, "Impact and Research Challenges of Penetrating Testing and Vulnerability Assessment on Network Threat," in *2023 International Conference on Business Analytics for Technology and Security (ICBATS)*, Dubai, United Arab Emirates: IEEE, March 2023, pp. 1–8. doi: 10.1109/ICBATS57792.2023.10111168.
14. A. Aghazadeh Ardebili, M. Lezzi and M. Pourmadadkar, "Risk assessment for cyber resilience of critical infrastructures: Methods, governance, and standards," *Appl. Sci*, vol. 14, no. 24, p. 11807, 2024. doi: 10.3390/app142411807.
15. R. N. Rajapakse, M. Zahedi and M. A. Babar, "Collaborative Application Security Testing for DevSecOps: An Empirical Analysis of Challenges, Best Practices and Tool Support," 2022, *arXiv*. doi: 10.48550/ARXIV.2211.06953.
16. R. Alkhadra, J. Abuzaid, M. AlShammari and N. Mohammad, "Solar Winds Hack: In-Depth Analysis and Countermeasures," in *2021 12th International Conference on Computing Communication and Networking Technologies (ICCCNT)*, Kharagpur, India: IEEE, July 2021, pp. 1–7. doi: 10.1109/ICCCNT51525.2021.9579611.
17. J. Huddleston, P. Ji, S. Bhunia and J. Cogan, "How VMware Exploits Contributed to SolarWinds Supply-Chain Attack," in *2021 International Conference on Computational Science and Computational Intelligence (CSCI)*, Las Vegas, NV, USA: IEEE, December 2021, pp. 760–765. doi: 10.1109/CSCI54926.2021.00190.

18. S. C. Wingreen and A. Samandari, Eds., *Information technology security and risk management: Inductive cases for information security*, 1st ed. Boca Raton; London: CRC Press, Taylor & Francis Group, 2024.
19. M. U. Tariq, "Data breach incidents and prevention in the hospitality industry," in *Advances in hospitality, tourism, and the services industry*, P. Thealla, V. Nadda, S. Dadwal, L. Oztosun, and G. Cantafio, Eds., IGI Global, 2024, pp. 181–199. doi: 10.4018/979-8-3693-2715-9.ch010.
20. Z. Aivazpour, R. Valecha and R. Chakraborty, "Data breaches: An empirical study of the effect of monitoring services," *ACM SIGMIS Database: Database Adv. Inf. Syst*, vol. 53, no. 4, pp. 65–82, 2022. doi: 10.1145/3571823.3571829.
21. S. Ray, W. Chen, J. Bhadra and M. A. Al Faruque, "Extensibility in Automotive Security: Current Practice and Challenges: Invited," in *Proceedings of the 54th Annual Design Automation Conference 2017*, Austin TX USA: ACM, June 2017, pp. 1–6. doi: 10.1145/3061639.3072952.
22. A. Dorri, M. Steger, S. S. Kanhere and R. Jurdak, "BlockChain: A distributed solution to automotive security and privacy," *IEEE Commun. Mag*, vol. 55, no. 12, pp. 119–125, 2017. doi: 10.1109/MCOM.2017.1700879.
23. F. Sommer, J. Dürrwang and R. Kriesten, "Survey and classification of automotive security attacks," *Information*, vol. 10, no. 4, p. 148, 2019. doi: 10.3390/info10040148.
24. D. K. Oka, *Building secure cars: Assuring the software development lifecycle*, 1st ed. Wiley, 2021. doi: 10.1002/9781119710783.
25. V. Icheku, "Challenges of protecting personal data and privacy during online teaching and learning," *Acad. Lett*, 2021. doi: 10.20935/AL3083.
26. Simmons-Edler, R., Badman, R., Longpre, S., & Rajan, K. (2024). AI-powered autonomous weapons risk geopolitical instability and threaten AI research. arXiv preprint arXiv: 2405.01859.
27. S. Rose, O. Borchert, S. Mitchell and S. Connelly, "*Zero trust architecture*," National Institute of Standards and Technology, August 2020. doi: 10.6028/NIST.SP.800-207.
28. S. Nifakos *et al.*, "Influence of human factors on cybersecurity within healthcare organisations: A systematic review," *Sensors*, vol. 21, no. 15, p. 5119, Jul. 2021, doi: 10.3390/s21155119.
29. F. Özdemir Sönmez, C. Hankin and P. Malacaria, "Decision support for healthcare cybersecurity," *Comput. Secur*, vol. 122, p. 102865, 2022. doi: 10.1016/j.cose.2022.102865.
30. A. T. Alanazi, "Clinicians' perspectives on healthcare cybersecurity and cyber threats," *Cureus*, 2023. doi: 10.7759/cureus.47026.
31. B. Ojo, J. Chilenovu Ogborigbo and M. Oluchukwuamaka Okafor, "Innovative solutions for critical infrastructure resilience against cyber-physical attacks," *World J. Adv. Res. Rev*, vol. 22, no. 3, pp. 1651–1674, 2024. doi: 10.30574/wjarr.2024.22.3.1921.
32. L. Che, X. Liu, Z. Li and Y. Wen, "False data injection attacks induced sequential outages in power systems," *IEEE Trans. Power Syst*, vol. 34, no. 2, pp. 1513–1523, 2019. doi: 10.1109/TPWRS.2018.2871345.
33. B. W. Tuinema, J. L. Rueda Torres, A. I. Stefanov, F. M. Gonzalez-Longatt and M. A. M. M. Van Der Meijden, "Cyber-physical system modeling for assessment and enhancement of power grid cybersecurity, resilience, and reliability," in *Probabilistic reliability analysis of power systems*, Cham: Springer International Publishing, 2020, pp. 237–270. doi: 10.1007/978-3-030-43498-4_8.
34. M. Satheesh Kumar, J. Ben-Othman, K. G. Srinivasagan and P. Umarani, "Machine learning methods for enhanced cybersecurity intrusion detection system," in *Advances in computing, informatics, networking and cybersecurity*, P. Nicopolitidis, S. Misra, L. T. Yang, B. Zeigler, and Z. Ning, Eds., in *Lecture notes in networks and systems*, vol. 289, Cham: Springer International Publishing, 2022, pp. 733–754. doi: 10.1007/978-3-030-87049-2_27.

35. "Revolutionizing Cybersecurity: Unleashing the Power of Artificial Intelligence and Machine Learning for Next-Generation Threat Detection," *Int. Res. J. Mod. Eng. Technol. Sci.*, Mar. 2024, doi: 10.56726/IRJMETS32644.
36. A. S. Shaik and A. Shaik, "AI enhanced cybersecurity methods for anomaly detection," in *Machine intelligence, tools, and applications*, S. Dehuri, S. B. Cho, V. P. Padhy, P. Shanmugam, and A. Ghosh, Eds., in *Learning and analytics in intelligent systems*, vol. 40, Cham: Springer Nature Switzerland, 2024, pp. 348–359. doi: 10.1007/978-3-031-65392-6_30.
37. A. Srivastava, D. Thakkar, S. Valiveti, P. Shah and G. Raval, "Anticipated Network Surveillance – An extrapolated study to predict cyber-attacks using Machine Learning and Data Analytics," 2023, *arXiv*. doi: 10.48550/ARXIV.2312.17270.
38. N. Islavath, "Shifting security left: Integrating DevOps with secure development practices," *J. Artif. Intell. Mach. Learn. Data Sci.*, vol. 1, no. 1, pp. 1368–1371, October 2022, doi: 10.51219/JAIMLD/nagaraju-islavath/311.
39. A. H. Jerónimo, P. M. Moreno, J. A. V. Camacho and G. C. Vega, "Techniques of SAST Tools in the Early Stages of Secure Software Development: A Systematic Literature Review," in *2024 IEEE International Conference on Engineering Veracruz (ICEV)*, Boca del Rio, Veracruz, Mexico: IEEE, October 2024, pp. 1–8. doi: 10.1109/ICEV63254.2024.10766004.
40. I. Matiushin and V. Korkhov, "Continuous authentication methods for zero-trust cybersecurity architecture," in *Computational science and its applications – ICCSA 2023 workshops*, O. Gervasi, B. Murgante, A. M. A. C. Rocha, C. Garau, F. Scorza, Y. Karaca, and C. M. Torre, Eds., in *Lecture notes in computer science*, vol. 14109, Cham: Springer Nature Switzerland, 2023, pp. 334–351. doi: 10.1007/978-3-031-37120-2_22.
41. Y. He, D. Huang, L. Chen, Y. Ni and X. Ma, "A survey on zero trust architecture: Challenges and future trends," *Wirel. Commun. Mob. Comput*, vol. 2022, pp. 1–13, 2022. doi: 10.1155/2022/6476274.
42. P. Phiayura and S. Teerakanok, "A comprehensive framework for migrating to zero trust architecture," *IEEE Access*, vol. 11, pp. 19487–19511, 2023. doi: 10.1109/ACCESS.2023.3248622.
43. uburn University at Montgomery, Department of Information Systems Alabama, United States et al., "Zero trust architecture: Trend and impact on information security," *Int. J. Emerg. Technol. Adv. Eng*, vol. 12, no. 7, pp. 140–147, 2022. doi: 10.46338/ijetae0722_15.
44. E. M. Pasca, R. Erdei, D. Delinschi and O. Matei, "Enhancing API Security Testing Against BOLA and Authentication Vulnerabilities Through an LLM-Enhanced Framework," in *The 19th International Conference on Soft Computing Models in Industrial and Environmental Applications SOCO 2024*, H. Quintián, E. Corchado, A. Troncoso Lora, H. Pérez García, E. Jove, J. L. Calvo Rolle, F. J. Martínez De Pisón, P. García Bringas, F. Martínez Álvarez, Á. Herrero Cosío, and P. Fosci, Eds., in *Lecture notes in networks and systems*, vol. 889, Cham: Springer Nature Switzerland, 2025, pp. 231–240. doi: 10.1007/978-3-031-75010-6_23.
45. A. S. Isha and M. Revathi, "Automated API Testing," in *2018 3rd International Conference on Inventive Computation Technologies (ICICT)*, Coimbatore, India: IEEE, Nov. 2018, pp. 788–791. doi: 10.1109/ICICT43934.2018.9034254.
46. Y. Deng, C. Yang, A. Wei and L. Zhang, "Fuzzing Deep-Learning Libraries via Automated Relational API Inference," in *Proceedings of the 30th ACM Joint European Software Engineering Conference and Symposium on the Foundations of Software Engineering*, Singapore: ACM, November 2022, pp. 44–56. doi: 10.1145/3540250.3549085.
47. P. X. Mai, F. Pastore, A. Goknil and L. Briand, "Metamorphic Security Testing for Web Systems," 2019, *arXiv*. doi: 10.48550/ARXIV.1912.05278.

48. R. M. Parizi, A. Dehghantanha, K. K. R. Choo and A. Singh, "Empirical Vulnerability Analysis of Automated Smart Contracts Security Testing on Blockchains," 2018, doi: 10.48550/ARXIV.1809.02702.
49. C. Lal and D. Marijan, "Blockchain Testing: Challenges, Techniques, and Research Directions," 2021, *arXiv*. doi: 10.48550/ARXIV.2103.10074.
50. R. Koul, "Blockchain Oriented Software Testing - Challenges and Approaches," in *2018 3rd International Conference for Convergence in Technology (I2CT)*, Pune: IEEE, April 2018, pp. 1–6. doi: 10.1109/I2CT.2018.8529728.

16 Major Global Digital Policy Frameworks

Abdul Salam Shah, Muhammad Adnan Kaim Khani, Haidawati Nasir, Adidah Lajis, Asadullah Shah, and Asif Ali Laghari

16.1 INTRODUCTION

The combination of standards, rules, and regulations, is recognized as pillars of the digital policy frameworks that monitor the usage, and administration of digital technologies and the internet. These standards address characteristics of the digital ecosystem including digital rights to cybersecurity, internet governance, and data protection, as regulations help to maintain the high standards of data protection globally for better development of digital economies [1, 2]. These frameworks also protect critical infrastructure from cyberattacks, as the protection is necessary for the economic stability and overall maintenance of national cybersecurity [3]. It provides proper guidelines to develop and maintain cybersecurity practices, ultimately reducing the rate of cyber incidents and data breaches. Safe digital cyberspace facilitates cross-border trade by maintaining cybersecurity standards and reducing barriers as the majority of the payments are being made using digital payment methods. The clear and concise regulations and implementations of cybersecurity frameworks encourage investment and bring innovations in digital technologies [4]. The policies secure and guarantee access to digital technologies and the internet to every person as they promote digital presence and bridge the digital divide by upholding digital rights, covering the freedom of expression in better democratic societies [5]. Each country has its regulations hence creates problems while doing international business as it requires the unrestricted flow of information and digital services. Separate policies create challenges for organizations seeking to operate globally, as policies between two countries may conflict and impose different regulatory requirements [6]. The solution to these problems can be a design of global policy in coordination with different countries to help in sharing threat intelligence and best practices. Global cooperation is essential for developing joint defense mechanisms and conducting international cyber exercises. Harmonized digital policies can reduce trade barriers, making it easier for industries to operate internationally and access new markets. Coordinated policies promote economic integration and cooperation, benefiting global economic growth [7].

Establishing universal standards for digital rights ensures that fundamental human rights are protected in the digital realm across all countries. Coordinated

DOI: 10.1201/9781003497868-16

efforts can help bridge the digital divide, confirming that advancements in digital technologies benefit all segments of society [8]. Developing international cybersecurity norms and standards to protect global digital infrastructure. Hence, frameworks for digital trade agreements and e-commerce regulations are needed to support global economic growth. The World Economic Forum (WEF) and International Telecommunication Union (ITU) play significant roles in fostering international cooperation and developing global digital policies [9]. Initiatives like the EU-US Privacy Shield and various bilateral digital trade agreements aim to harmonize digital policies between regions and countries [10]. Events like the internet governance forum (IGF) provide platforms for stakeholders from everywhere in the world to deliberate and coordinate digital policy issues.

16.2 HISTORICAL CONTEXT

During the initial phase of the internet (1960s–1980s) the Advanced Research Projects Agency Network (ARPANET) placed the groundwork for future digital communications and policies [11]. Later on, guidelines were issued for the data flow between borders of countries during the 1980s by the Organization for Economic Cooperation and Development (OECD) on the safety of privacy, influencing global data protection policies [12]. Most of the standards at that time were developed by the Internet Engineering Task Force (IETF) and governance of the internet was focused on ensuring interoperability by introducing standards and protocols [13]. Initial users of the internet were limited hence the governance was handled by the government agencies and academic institutions as it does not require any regulatory frameworks, but with the announcement of WWW digital commerce has emerged the need for frameworks for secure transactions [14, 15].

The Internet Corporation for Assigned Names and Numbers (ICANN) introduced the Domain Name System (DNS) in the 1990s, for the unique identifiers in the services of the internet [16]. The advancements in the internet have caused security and privacy issues, hence intellectual property rights management has become mandatory through the regulatory approaches [17]. The United States has imposed Communications Decency Act (1996) for maintaining online obscenity and decency which has become the source of protecting online platforms [18].

16.3 MILESTONES IN THE DEVELOPMENT OF GLOBAL DIGITAL POLICIES

The EU Data Protection Directive (1995) focused on data privacy and security providing a legislative act in Europe and serving as a stepping stone for data protection laws like GDPR [2, 19]. World Summit on the Information Society (WSIS-2003-2005) was an initiative intended to bridge the global digital divide and foster an inclusive information society and it has later served handy platform for the Geneva Plan of Action for the information society [20, 21]. The GDPR in 2018 was adopted worldwide for data privacy and protection with an impression

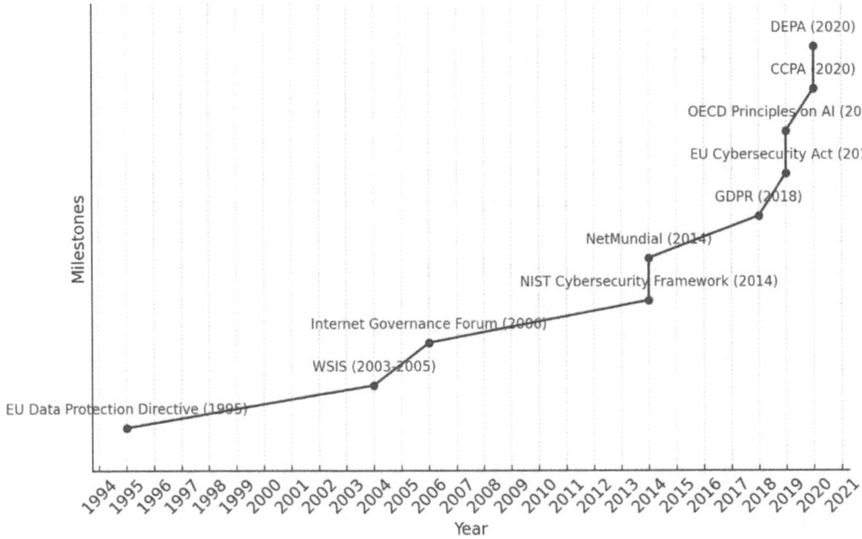

FIGURE 16.1 Milestones in developing global digital policies.

of strict regulations on data handling, user consent, and the rights of individuals. The California Consumer Privacy Act (CCPA-2020) provides greater privacy rights and consumer protection [22]. The major milestones in the expansion of global digital policies are summarized in Figures 16.1–16.4: Frameworks for global digital policies, including NIST Cybersecurity Framework, China's cybersecurity laws, and Japan's regulations.

The industry standards were developed as a Cybersecurity Framework by the National Institute of Standards and Technology (NIST) in 2014 for companies to handle different cybersecurity risks [23]. EU has always remained ahead and introduced the Cybersecurity Act (2019) for the certification framework for the improvement of the security of digital products and services of local industry [24]. The UN platform for the multistakeholder dialogue for public policy issues is the IGF which handles internet governance [25]. Another platform is the NetMundial (2014) meeting for the future of internet governance, highlighting principles such as directness, security, and human rights [26].

The World Trade Organization established a moratorium on customs duties for electronic transmissions, fostering the expansion of the global digital economy [9]. Digital Economy Partnership Agreement (DEPA, 2020) was a pioneering agreement between Chile, Singapore, and New Zealand, aimed at establishing rules and best practices for digital trade and data flows [27]. Various frameworks and guidelines have emerged, such as the OECD Principles on Artificial Intelligence (AI), addressing the ethical use and regulation of AI technologies [28]. In the modern world, countries and organizations are developing regulations to address the challenges and openings accessible by blockchain technology and digital currencies.

16.4 KEY GLOBAL DIGITAL POLICY FRAMEWORKS

16.4.1 General Data Protection Regulation (GDPR)

GDPR is a data protection law to complement the laws of data privacy across the EU, to protect data privacy and transform how governments handle it [29]. The regulation aims to grant individuals greater control over data including the rights to access, correct, remove, and port data, and to object to and controlled processing [30]. Certain administrations are obligated to hire a DPO to supervise agreements with GDPR, monitor data protection strategies, and ensure data security practices [31]. The regulation has led to increased scrutiny and enforcement actions across the EU. The GDPR imposes strict regulations to transfer data outside the EU to confirm high standards of data protection are upheld [32].

16.4.2 Digital Services Act (DSA) and Digital Markets Act (DMA)

European Commission has proposed legislative initiatives like DSA and DMA. Their goals are to ensure a safer digital environment, and users' fundamental rights and to generate a fair and competitive landscape for businesses [33]. DSA focuses on regulating digital services to create a safer online environment by addressing illegal content, ensuring transparency, and protecting users' rights. The online platforms are the target of DMA as they recommend fair competition and identify the gatekeepers for setting obligations and prohibitions for smooth operations [34]. It is important to handle illegal content, protect the data of users, enhance transparency in the advertisement, and handle user complaints [35]. Compliance with new requirements and adjustment of operations are needed for the implementation of content moderation, for increased transparency for user rights protection. The DMA defines the set of instructions for gatekeepers covering data usage restrictions, bans on self-preferencing, and requirements to permit interoperability with third-party services, the DMA aims to substitute a modest digital market, for businesses to compete efficiently [36].

16.4.3 Federal Communications Commission (FCC) Regulations

US-based organization FCC focused on net neutrality in the early 2000s, with the most important governing milestones occurring in 2015 and 2017 like the classification of broadband internet as Title II telecommunication service [37]. It has enforced the rules to ban ISPs from blocking, throttling, or prioritizing certain traffic, later on, the rules were repealed in 2015 considering them as blocking the innovation and investment [38]. The repeal of net neutrality has sparked ongoing legal and political conflicts, with numerous states enacting their net neutrality laws [39].

The impact on consumers and businesses continues to be a contentious issue. Spectrum management refers to the regulation and allocation of radio frequencies to guarantee efficient and interference-free use of radio spectrum. FCC oversees spectrum management in the United States, balancing the needs of various stakeholders, including government agencies, commercial enterprises, and public services [40]. The FCC allocates spectrum bands for different uses, such as broadcasting, mobile communication, and satellite services, through licensing and auctions. The FCC promotes innovation by making spectrum available for new technologies, such as 5G, and facilitating research and development in wireless communication [41]. The FCC ensures that adequate spectrum is reserved for public safety communications and national security operations.

16.5 CYBERSECURITY POLICIES AND FRAMEWORKS

The NIST is a voluntary set of standards, guidelines, and best practices meant to help organizations manage and reduce cybersecurity risks. It has been widely adopted across various industries in the United States. Framework was formed to improve cybersecurity of critical infrastructure including enhancing the resilience of organizations, protecting sensitive information, and promoting risk management [42]. Understanding the context, resources, and risk management strategy. Safeguarding critical infrastructure services through appropriate measures. Identifying the occurrence of cybersecurity events [43]. Taking action regarding a detected cybersecurity incident. Restoring services and capabilities affected by a cybersecurity incident. The overview of the NIST is provided in Figure 16.2.

Profiles align the framework's standards, guidelines; it practices to the organization's requirements, risk tolerances, and resources. The NIST has been extensively accepted by both public and private sector organizations, helping them strengthen their cybersecurity posture and improve their resilience to cyber threats [44].

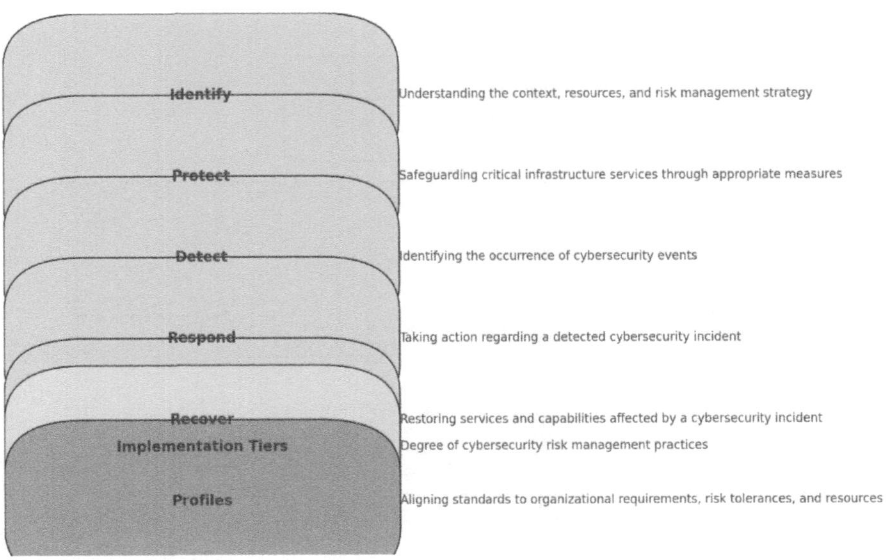

FIGURE 16.2 NIST cybersecurity framework.

16.5.1 China's Cybersecurity Law

China's Cybersecurity Law took effect on June 1, 2017, is a comprehensive regulation aimed at securing cyberspace and protecting national security [45]. The law imposes stringent requirements on companies operating in China regarding data protection, network security, and content regulation. The law dictates that individual information and significant data composed or produced by critical information infrastructure (CII) operatives within China necessity be stored domestically [46]. Transfers of such data overseas require security assessments and regulatory approval. Companies are required to undergo security assessments for their network products and services, especially those used in critical sectors like finance, healthcare, and telecommunications [47]. The law outlines stringent requirements for the assembly, storage, and dispensation of personal data, including obtaining user agreement and ensuring data accuracy and security. Internet service providers must monitor and report illegal content, cooperate with public security authorities, and implement real-name registration systems. The China Cybersecurity Law is presented in Figure 16.3.

Non-compliance through the law can effect in significant penalties, suspension of business operations, and revocation of business licenses [48]. The enforcement is overseen by various governmental bodies, including the Cyberspace Administration of China (CAC). China's Cybersecurity Law has significant implications for global businesses operating in or interacting with the Chinese market [49]. Companies must invest in local data centers and implement robust cybersecurity measures to comply with data localization and security assessment requirements. The broad and sometimes ambiguous provisions of the law increase regulatory risk and uncertainty, requiring businesses to continuously monitor and adapt to evolving regulatory interpretations and enforcement practices [50]. The law imposes substantial compliance costs, including investments in technology, legal consultation, and restructuring of

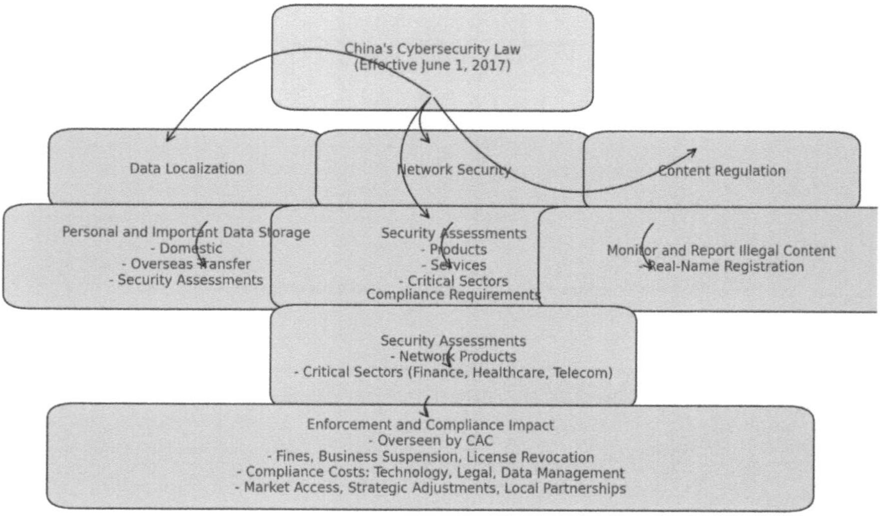

FIGURE 16.3 China's Cybersecurity Law.

data management practices. Businesses must navigate the complex regulatory landscape to maintain market access and competitive advantage in China, often necessitating strategic adjustments and partnerships with local entities.

16.5.2 Japan's Basic Act on Cybersecurity

Japan's Basic Act on Cybersecurity, enacted in 2014 and revised in 2018, establishes the framework for national cybersecurity policy and coordination [51]. The Act aims to enhance Japan's cybersecurity capabilities, protect critical infrastructure, and promote international collaboration. The details are accessible in Figure 16.4.

The act mandates the growth and periodic review of cybersecurity strategy to address emerging threats and technological advancements. The formation of the Cybersecurity Strategic Headquarters and the Cybersecurity Council to oversee and coordinate national cybersecurity efforts, involving government agencies, the private sector, and academia [52]. Act emphasizes securing infrastructure sectors like finance, energy, telecommunication, and transportation through risk assessments, information sharing, and implementation of best practices. It encourages collaboration between the government and private sector to enhance cybersecurity measures, share threat intelligence, and develop innovative solutions. It promotes international partnerships and cooperation to address global cybersecurity challenges, including participation in multilateral frameworks and bilateral agreements. Japan's Basic Act on Cybersecurity has an essential role in the development of regional cybersecurity

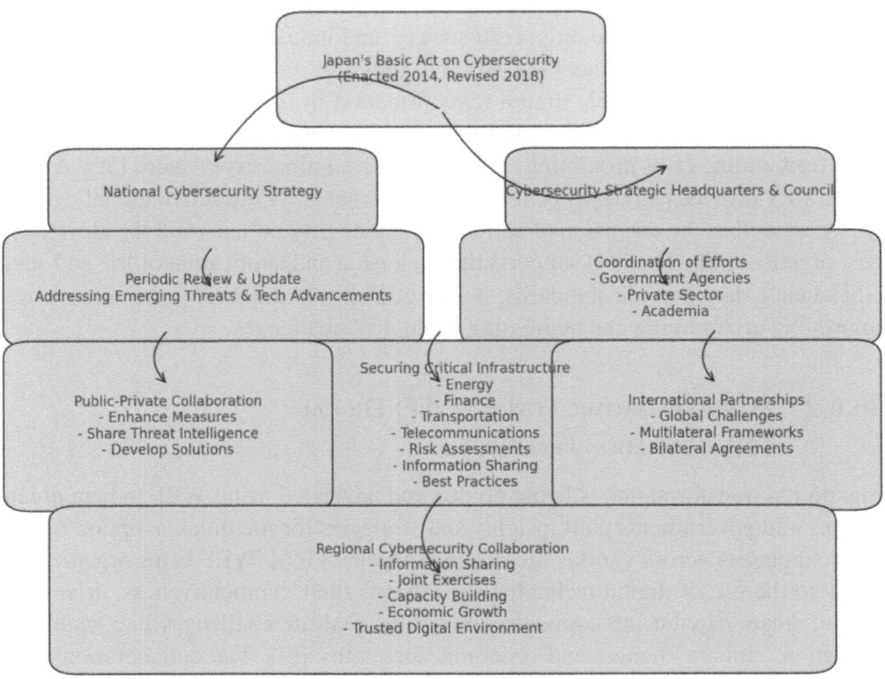

FIGURE 16.4 Japan's Basic Act on Cybersecurity.

collaboration and the country is considered a regional leader, encouraging strong cybersecurity standards, practices, and policies within international forums and organizations [53]. The country has participated in joint cybersecurity events to enhance cybersecurity measures and information sharing and capacity-building initiatives with adjacent countries [54]. Hence Japan has contributed to regional stability, secure cyberspace, economic growth, and a trusted digital environment through public-private collaboration and development of cybersecurity technologies and solutions.

16.6 INTERNATIONAL ORGANIZATIONS

16.6.1 International Telecommunication Union (ITU)

The ICT-related issues are being handled by the ITU for the UN for better global digital governance and the ITU develops international standards to advance the efficiency and global of telecommunication networks and services and ensures interoperability and reliability [55]. Global communication has been improved due to the implementation of standards and it helps in the continuous integration of new technologies, avoiding interference and guaranteeing the efficient utilization of resources [56]. The Government and Private Institutions utilize ITU for the development of policies and regulations that encourage the development and reasonable access to ICTs and address cybersecurity, internet governance, and digital inclusion. The ITU helps developing nations manage and deploy ICT infrastructure and services and supports capacity-building initiatives for the enhancement of skills and capabilities and fostering international cooperation and dialogue among stakeholders, like governments, academia, civil society, and industry to discourse global ICT challenges and opportunities [57]. An ITU initiative aims to accomplish universal connectivity and sustainable digital transformation by 2030 focusing on expanding broadband access, promoting digital literacy, fostering innovation, protecting children from online risks promoting safe and positive online experiences [58]. An ITU framework provides strategic goals and endorsements for attractive global cybersecurity, as well as the extension of national cybersecurity policies and the elevation of best practices [59]. The ITU supports the expansion and application of IoT and smart cities hence they provide standards, policy guidelines, and pilot projects, aiming at improving urban living and addressing ecological challenges.

16.6.2 World Economic Forum (WEF) Digital Transformation Framework

The digital transformation is being guided and navigated using WEF to help organizations and governments gain insights and strategies for the quick adoption of digital technologies across various sectors and industries [60]. WEF helps organizations promote the use of digital technologies, enhance their competitiveness, drive innovation, create new business models, and handle real-life challenges like healthcare, education, climate change, and economic inequality [61]. The collaboration of the private and public sectors has been increased due to WEF as it helps to foster partnerships for digital transformation and highlight the standing of engaging customers at the center of digital transformation efforts. It helps to understand customer needs, improve customer experiences, and deliver personalized services. WEF encourages organizational agility and a culture of constant innovation, iterative development, adoption of agile methodologies, and research to quickly respond to varying market circumstances and technological progressions [62]. There is a need to focus on maintaining data quality, data analytics, and data insights for smart decision-making and optimization of business processes. It pressures the need to build and participate in digital ecosystems, internal and external collaboration, suppliers, customers, and other stakeholders can create synergies, foster innovation, and enable new value propositions. WEF emphasizes strong leadership for digital initiatives, and organizations should invest in training and upskilling their workforce [63]. It activists for robust cybersecurity measures and data privacy practices hence organizations must protect their digital assets, confirm compliance with regulations, and build trust with customers and partners. Finally, the framework encourages the integration of sustainability and inclusivity into digital transformation strategies [64]. Organizations should leverage digital technologies to drive environmental sustainability and guarantee that the assistance of digital transformation is available to all segments of society.

16.7 COMPARATIVE ANALYSIS OF GLOBAL DIGITAL POLICIES

In recent years, numerous global digital policies have been implemented, primarily focusing on privacy, data protection, cybersecurity, and digital trade. Given the importance of data privacy, several key policies have been introduced to address these areas [65]. The GDPR sets high standards for data protection, has shaped regulations globally, and grants individuals rights such as access to data, rectification, restriction of processing, data portability, and the ability to object to data processing. CCPA is applicable to businesses that gather private data of California people and meet certain criteria related to revenue or data processing volumes [65]. Businesses must inform consumers about data collection practices and purposes. Civil penalties for non-compliance and private right of action for data breaches hence it is state-level data privacy laws in the United States, influencing other states and federal privacy legislation discussions [66]. Personal Information Protection and Electronic Documents Act (PIPEDA) – Canada spread on to businesses in the private sector that gather, utilize, or reveal personal data while conducting business to provide the consent requirements, access and correction rights, and accountability for data protection [67]. Promotes fair information practices and aligns with international data protection standards. The LGPD (Lei Geral de Proteção de Dados) in Brazil applies to the processing of personal data within the country. It establishes requirements for consent, data subject rights, data protection officers, and data breach notifications [68]. The law strengthens data protection in Brazil and enhances mechanisms for international data transfers.

16.8 DIVERSE APPROACHES TO CYBERSECURITY REGULATION AND ENFORCEMENT

In the United States the sector-specific regulations and voluntary frameworks like the NIST Cybersecurity Framework [69]. Federal agencies such as the DHS, FBI, and sector-specific regulators enforce cybersecurity requirements. In the United States, voluntary standards like the NIST Cybersecurity Framework and sector-specific laws like the HIPAA for healthcare and the GLBA for financial services. The Cybersecurity Act strengthens the mandate of the European Union Agency for Cybersecurity (ENISA) to establish a cybersecurity certification framework. Member states' authorities enforce regulations, with coordination and support from ENISA [70]. In China, the Cybersecurity Law mandates strict data localization, security assessments, and monitoring requirements. In Japan, the Basic Act on Cybersecurity provides a framework for national cybersecurity strategy and coordination [71]. The Security of Critical Infrastructure Act and the Cybersecurity Strategy emphasize protecting critical infrastructure and enhancing national resilience.

16.9 POLICIES PROMOTING DIGITAL TRADE AND E-COMMERCE

Prohibiting data localization requirements and facilitating cross-border data flows are two features of trade agreements like the United States-Mexico-Canada Agreement (USMCA) and the Comprehensive and Progressive Agreement for Trans-Pacific Partnership (CPTPP) [72]. It promotes digital trade by reducing barriers to data transfer and enhancing legal certainty for businesses. Regulations ensure consumer rights in online transactions, including dispute resolution mechanisms and transparency in digital marketplaces. Policies address the taxation of digital goods and services and regulatory support for better innovation to ensure fair competition and revenue generation. The 5G drives economic development and enables new business models intended to stretch relegated societies' reasonable access to digital technology and advance their digital literacy [73]. The skills of the digital economy can be enhanced by training and education programs that equip workers and promote employment and economic growth while participation in global standard-setting bodies confirms interoperability and reliability in digital policies by dropping trade blockades and endorsing collaboration, bilateral trade agreements for the evolution of the digital economy [74].

16.10 CHALLENGES AND OPPORTUNITIES

Regulatory fragmentation refers to the difficulties that arise when different regions implement fluctuating and often conflicting regulations leading to implications for global businesses, policymakers, and consumers. International businesses must navigate a complex web of regulations, and laws, often demanding diverse compliance actions for each jurisdiction increasing operational costs and administrative burdens [75]. The unreliable policies can create problems for businesses to start, especially SMEs, resulting in limiting the ability to expand globally and resulting in market fragmentation [76]. The variations in regulations increase legal uncertainties and risks, as businesses may scuffle to understand and comply with conflicting laws, possibly leading to legal disputes and penalties. It also makes cross-border data transfers difficult due to numerous data protection regulations, like the CCPA in California and GDPR in Europe; hence businesses need to put in place complex mechanisms to guarantee compliance with various data protection rules [22].

Different regulatory methods can smother innovation by creating an uneven playing field hence companies may be discouraged from developing new technologies or entering new markets due to regulatory reservations and costs. Emerging technologies like AI are changing the digital landscape and warning the need for adaptive policies as they bring up issues with accountability, transparency, and bias. The policymakers have developed frameworks to ensure ethical AI development and deployment, including guidelines on fairness, transparency, and accountability [77]. Governments provide regulations to handle the use of AI in finance, healthcare, and autonomous vehicles. There are still some challenges like Blockchain's decentralized nature has conflicts with traditional regulatory frameworks hence policymakers need to address the privacy, data security, and the legal status of blockchain transactions [78]. The growth of cryptocurrencies increased risks hence there is a need for regulations for the prevention of fraud, money laundering, and ensuring financial stability.

The Internet of Things (IoT) devices generate and gather huge volumes of data at regular intervals, raising security and privacy concerns hence rules are being formed for IoT devices' data security and guarantee compatibility between IoT systems [79]. For the improvement of communication and integration of IoT devices, policymakers are drafting uniform standards although for the legislators, keeping the balance of protection and innovation of customers is a crucial task. The policies must be adaptable to technological developments without restricting new ideas which can be achieved with regulatory sandboxes [80]. Governments can incentivize modernization by providing grants, and support for research and development in emerging technologies but the policies must ensure the safety of consumers' rights, like security, data privacy, and right to informed consent. On the other hand, the regulations must address misleading advertising, data breaches, and unfair business practices and ensure safety standards for new technologies with minimal risks to users for AI safety, IoT device security, and blockchain transaction integrity. The engagement of stakeholders, consumer advocates, industry experts, and academics, ensures that policies are well-informed and balanced; public consultation and transparent policy-making help build trust and ensure that regulations reflect societal values and expectations [81]. Finally, international cooperation can reduce regulatory fragmentation hence involvement of ITU, WEF, and OECD plays a crucial role in facilitating global dialogue and cooperation.

16.11 CASE STUDIES

16.11.1 Case Study 1: GDPR Implementation and Impact

The GDPR aims to protect EU citizen's data, which was introduced on May 25, 2018, it has substantial implications, further, it enhances the awareness of data protection among global businesses, consumers, and organizations, ensuring better data handling and transparency [2]. The law has recognized a global benchmark for data protection, inspiring laws akin to Brazil's LGPD and CCPA [82]. A proportion of variations are needed by businesses, like designating Data Protection Officers (DPOs), carrying out data protection impact assessments (DPIAs), and guaranteeing data subject rights [83]. The SMEs the costs of accomplishing and maintaining compliance with GDPR can be significant as it requires struggle and resources like staff training, regular audits, and robust data management practices. Differences in interpretation and enforcement among EU member states create uncertainties. Companies often face challenges in understanding and implementing GDPR requirements uniformly. The requirement to report data breaches within 72 hours has been challenging for many organizations, necessitating the need for efficient incident response mechanisms [84]. GDPR enforces severe rules on transferring data outside the EU, creating challenges for multinational companies in managing international data flows. Ensuring compliance while fostering innovation and using data for business growth remains a delicate balance.

16.11.2 Case Study 2: US Net Neutrality Debate

The idea behind "net neutrality" is that ISPs should handle all data in an equal manner, without charging or treating users, websites, or applications differently. The debate over net neutrality in the United States has seen significant policy shifts. In 2015 the FCC, under the Obama administration, adopted the Open Internet Order, classifying broadband as a Title II service under the Communications Act, thereby enforcing strict net neutrality rules [38]. Under the Trump administration in 2017, the FCC repealed the 2015 rules, reclassifying broadband as a Title I service, which significantly reduced the regulatory oversight on ISPs. Concerns arose that without net neutrality, ISPs could prioritize certain content or services, leading to slower access or higher costs for consumers [85]. The repeal could exacerbate the digital divide, as ISPs might prioritize high-paying customers or services, affecting equal access to information. Startups SMEs and smaller companies could face disadvantages if ISPs charge for prioritized access, limiting their ability to compete with larger, established firms. By putting up obstacles to entry for new services and applications, potential prioritization and throttling could impede innovation [86]. Several states enacted their net neutrality laws, leading to a fragmented regulatory environment and ongoing legal battles. The net neutrality debate remains politically charged, with potential for future policy reversals depending on the administration and FCC leadership.

16.11.3 Case Study 3: China's Great Firewall

The Great Firewall of China (GFoC) is a comprehensive internet censorship and surveillance system that controls and restricts access to information online within China. The GfoC is one of the best examples describing the mechanism adopted by governments to control the information flow and implement restrictions on global content, although it raises concerns about freedom of speech [87]. China's internet policies have remained a topic of debate due to a clash with international principles and norms of open internet. These policies have created challenges for the IGFs to handle the data flow and even lead to tensions and diplomatic challenges for the governments. It supports technological sovereignty, for the maintenance of strict regulators over digital structure and data, influencing other countries to adopt policies for national security and political stability. These restrictions affect Chinese citizens' approachability to global websites and online services hence limiting exposure to the useful information available on digital platforms [88]. The Great Firewall monitors online activities, privacy violations, and the suppression of dissent encouraging other authorities to adopt similar measures for the controlled global internet. The laws create problems as international businesses have to be bound to follow the local rules remain under censorship and often require substantial adjustments. The Great Firewall limits foreign competition but encourages domestic tech giants like Baidu, Alibaba, and Tencent [89]. China has adopted the approach to balance economic growth and information control.

16.12 TRENDS IN DIGITAL POLICY DEVELOPMENT, EMERGING POLICY AREAS, AND POTENTIAL FUTURE FRAMEWORKS

As technology continues to evolve rapidly, new and emerging policy areas are coming to the forefront. Policies are being developed to ensure AI systems are used ethically, with frameworks for accountability, transparency, and fairness [90]. New privacy laws inspired by GDPR are emerging globally, emphasizing user consent, data portability, and stringent breach notifications. Countries are increasingly focusing on data localization requirements and control over data generated within their borders and strengthening regulations to protect critical infrastructure from cyber threats, including energy, transportation, and healthcare sectors [91]. The progress is ongoing to enhance policies for mandatory cybersecurity incident reporting and coordinated response mechanisms and develop frameworks for secure, universally accepted digital identities to facilitate online transactions and access to services. There is a requirement to balance the need for digital identity verification with robust privacy and security measures and create security standards and certification processes for IoT devices to prevent vulnerabilities and implement consumer data protection. Organizations should encourage laws that guarantee compatibility between various IoT devices and systems. Countries are developing clear regulations for the use and trade of cryptocurrencies and blockchain technology to prevent fraud and ensure market stability, addressing the regulatory challenges posed by DeFi platforms and ensuring consumer protection [92]. Comprehensive frameworks are being developed to address ethical considerations in technology development and deployment, including AI, robotics, and biotechnology. Policies promoting sustainable practices in ICT development and usage, including energy-efficient data centers and e-waste management, safeguarding reasonable access to digital technologies, and bridging the digital divide through targeted policies and investment in digital literacy programs [93]. Regulatory frameworks for smart city initiatives, addressing issues related to data governance, privacy, and public-private partnerships.

16.13 EFFORTS TO HARMONIZE DIGITAL POLICIES AND PROMOTE GLOBAL COOPERATION

Global collaboration and harmonization of digital policies are critical to addressing the multinational landscape of digital technologies and ensuring a cohesive approach to digital governance. The organizations are addressing the multinational nature of digital technologies and guaranteeing a coherent approach to digital governance requires international cooperation and harmonization of digital policies [94]. The ISO creates international standards for information security management, data protection, and other digital policies and brings all EU members' digital policies into line to establish a single market for digital goods and services. The United States-Mexico-Canada Agreement (USMCA) has rules about cybersecurity, data protection, and digital trade to promote cross-border trade [95]. Different data transfer and establishing agreements, like the EU-US privacy shield facilitate compliant cross-border data transfers [96]. The cybersecurity pacts, forming international alliances and agreements to enhance collective cybersecurity measures and share threat intelligence. The G20 digital economy task force addresses global digital economy issues and promotes international cooperation on digital policy development. The OECD has been developing guidelines and recommendations for digital policy, including AI ethics and data governance [97].

The countries have been collaborating on research projects in emergent technologies, like AI, quantum computing, and 5G, and establishing international innovation hubs and incubators to foster collaboration between startups, industry, and academia. The are different international organizations offering training programs and workshops to build digital policy expertise among policymakers and regulators. These platforms help in sharing best practices and successful policy frameworks to help countries develop effective digital regulations [98]. Now the governments started working with technology companies to co-develop policies and standards that promote innovation while ensuring regulatory compliance by involving civil society, industry stakeholders, and academia in the policymaking procedure to ensure diverse perspectives and balanced outcomes.

16.14 SUMMARY

In conclusion, the chapter explores pivotal global digital policy frameworks: the EU's stringent data protection regulation, influencing global standards with its robust data subject rights, consent requirements, and severe penalties for non-compliance; California's influential CCPA, empowering residents with rights to access, delete, and control data, setting a precedent for US state and federal laws; China's rigorous cybersecurity framework, emphasizing data localization and government oversight, posing challenges for international businesses and shaping global data governance debates; the fluctuating landscape of US net neutrality from its enforcement to repeal, fueling ongoing discussions on internet equality and prompting diverse state-level responses; international efforts by the ITU to standardize telecommunications and ICT, promoting interoperability and cybersecurity; the WEF's guidance on ethical digital transformation for sustainable development; and NIST's voluntary cybersecurity framework, adopted globally to enhance resilience across sectors through its comprehensive approach from identification to recovery. These frameworks highlight the diverse regulatory approaches and ongoing efforts to navigate the complexities of digital governance while striving for harmonization and global cooperation in a rapidly evolving digital landscape.

REFERENCES

1. M. J. Sule, M. Zennaro and G. Thomas, "Cybersecurity through the lens of digital identity and data protection: Issues and trends," *Technology in Society*, vol. 67, p. 101734, 2021.
2. C. J. Hoofnagle, B. Van Der Sloot and F. Z. Borgesius, "The European Union general data protection regulation: What it is and what it means," *Information & Communications Technology Law*, vol. 28, no. 1, pp. 65–98, 2019.
3. P. Lis and J. Mendel, "Cyberattacks on critical infrastructure: An economic perspective," *Economics and Business Review*, vol. 5, no. 2, pp. 24–47, 2019.
4. Y.-C. Chin and J. Zhao, "Governing cross-border data flows: International trade agreements and their limits," *Laws*, vol. 11, no. 4, p. 63, 2022.
5. J. M. Balkin, "Digital speech and democratic culture: A theory of freedom of expression for the information society," in *Law and society approaches to cyberspace*, Routledge, 2017, pp. 325–382.
6. K. W. Abbott and D. Snidal, "The governance triangle: Regulatory standards institutions and the shadow of the state," in *The spectrum of international institutions*, Routledge, 2021, pp. 52–91.
7. J. P. Meltzer, "Maximizing the opportunities of the internet for international trade," *ICTSD and World Economic Forum, (2016)*, 2016. WEF_Digital_Trade_report_2015_1401.pdf
8. P. K. Yu, "Bridging the digital divide: Equality in the information age," *Cardozo Arts and Entertainment Law Journal*, vol. 20, p. 1, 2002.
9. M. Larionova and A. Shelepov, "Emerging regulation for the digital economy: Challenges and opportunities for multilateral global governance," *International Organisations Research Journal*, vol. 16, no. 1, pp. 29–63, 2021.
10. R. F. Fefer, S. I. Akhtar and W. M. Morrison, "Digital trade and US trade policy," Current Politics and Economics of the United States, *Canada and Mexico*, vol. 19, no. 1, pp. 1–52, 2017.
11. S. Furst, "The Advanced Research Projects Agency Network (ARPANET)," 1977.
12. C. Kuner, "Regulation of transborder data flows under data protection and privacy law: past, present, and future," *TILT Law & Technology Working Paper,* no. 016, 2010.
13. C. Cath and L. Floridi, "The design of the internet's architecture by the internet engineering task force (IETF) and human rights," *Science and Engineering Ethics*, vol. 23, pp. 449–468, 2017.
14. C. T. Marsden, *Internet co-regulation: European law, regulatory governance and legitimacy in cyberspace*, Cambridge University Press, 2011.
15. G. O'Regan and G. O'Regan, "The internet and world wide web," *World of Computing: A Primer Companion for the Digital Age*, pp. 239–256, 2018.
16. H. Klein, "ICANN and internet governance: Leveraging technical coordination to realize global public policy," *The Information Society*, vol. 18, no. 3, pp. 193–207, 2002.
17. P. Samuelson, "Privacy as intellectual property," *Stanford Law Review*, vol. 52, p. 1125, 1999.
18. P. Ehrlich, "Communications decency act sec. 230," *Berkeley Technology Law Journal*, vol. 17, p. 401, 2002.
19. O. Lynskey, *The foundations of EU data protection law*, Oxford University Press, 2015.
20. J. W. Berry, "The World Summit on the Information Society (WSIS): A global challenge in the new Millennium," 2006.
21. A. Bryne, "Promoting the global information commons: A commentary on the library and information implications of the WSIS Declaration of Principles" Building the information society: a global challenge in the new millennium"(Document WSIS/PC-3/DT/6)," 2005.
22. G. Park, "The changing wind of data privacy law: A comparative study of the European Union's general data protection regulation and the 2018 California Consumer Privacy Act," *UC Irvine Law Review,* vol. 10, p. 1455, 2019.

23. S. J. Shackelford, A. A. Proia, B. Martell and A. N. Craig, "Toward a global cybersecurity standard of care: Exploring the implications of the 2014 NIST cybersecurity framework on shaping reasonable national and international cybersecurity practices," *Texas International Law Journal*, vol. 50, p. 305, 2015.
24. A. Khurshid, R. Alsaaidi, M. Aslam and S. Raza, "EU cybersecurity act and IoT certification: Landscape, perspective and a proposed template scheme," *IEEE Access*, vol. 10, pp. 129932–129948, 2022.
25. J. Hofmann, "Multi-stakeholderism in internet governance: Putting a fiction into practice," *Journal of Cyber Policy*, vol. 1, no. 1, pp. 29–49, 2016.
26. M. Fraundorfer, "Brazil's organization of the NETmundial meeting: Moving forward in global internet governance," *Global Governance*, vol. 23, pp. 503–523, 2017.
27. E. Jones, B. Kira and R. Tavengerwei, "Norm entrepreneurship in digital trade: The Singapore-led wave of digital trade agreements," *World Trade Review*, vol. 23, no. 2, pp. 208–241, 2024.
28. L. Vesnic-Alujevic, S. Nascimento and A. Polvora, "Societal and ethical impacts of artificial intelligence: Critical notes on European policy frameworks," *Telecommunications Policy*, vol. 44, no. 6, p. 101961, 2020.
29. J. M. Fromholz, "The European Union data privacy directive," *Berkeley Technology Law Journal*, vol. 15, p. 461, 2000.
30. P. Voigt and A. Von dem Bussche, "The EU General Data Protection Regulation (GDPR)," *A practical guide*, 1st ed., Springer International Publishing, vol. 10, no. 3152676, pp. 10–5555, 2017.
31. A. Šidlauskas, "Opportunities for DPO (Data Protection Officer) occupational training and improvement," in *INTED2019 Proceedings*, 2019: IATED, pp. 808–814.
32. L. Moerel, *Binding Corporate rules: Corporate self-regulation of global data transfers*, Oxford University Press, 2012.
33. M. L. Chiarella, "Digital markets act (DMA) and digital services act (DSA): New rules for the EU digital environment," *Athens Journal of Law*, vol. 9, p. 33, 2023.
34. L. Cabral, J. Haucap, G. Parker, G. Petropoulos, T. M. Valletti and M. W. Van Alstyne, "The EU digital markets act: A report from a panel of economic experts," *The EU Digital Markets Act, Publications Office of the European Union, Luxembourg*, 2021.
35. C. Cauffman and C. Goanta, "A new order: The digital services act and consumer protection," *European Journal of Risk Regulation*, vol. 12, no. 4, pp. 758–774, 2021.
36. C. Koenig, "Obligations for gatekeepers," in *Steinrötter, Heinze, Denga (eds), EU Platform Regulation, Beck Nomos Hart, Forthcoming*, 2024.
37. A. Powell and A. Cooper, "Net neutrality discourses: Comparing advocacy and regulatory arguments in the United States and the United Kingdom," *The Information Society*, vol. 27, no. 5, pp. 311–325, 2011.
38. A. A. Gilroy, *Net neutrality debate: Access to broadband networks*, Congressional Research Service, 2017.
39. A. Ritz, "The Network Neutrality Debate in the US: The FCC's Regulatory Transformation in Broadband Policy," Available at SSRN 2663095, 2015.
40. R. Galvin and J. R. Schlesinger, *Spectrum management for the 21st century: A report of the CSIS commission on spectrum management*, CSIS, 2003.
41. S. Asif, *5g mobile communications: Concepts and technologies*, CRC Press, 2018.
42. E. A. Fischer, E. C. Liu, J. Rollins and C. A. Theohary, *The 2013 cybersecurity executive order: Overview and considerations for congress*, Congressional Research Service Washington, 2013.
43. C. W. Ten, G. Manimaran and C.-C. Liu, "Cybersecurity for critical infrastructures: Attack and defense modeling," *IEEE Transactions on Systems, Man, and Cybernetics-Part A: Systems and Humans*, vol. 40, no. 4, pp. 853–865, 2010.

44. C. I. Cybersecurity, "Framework for improving critical infrastructure cybersecurity," *Framework*, vol. 1, no. 11, 2014.
45. A. Qi, G. Shao and W. Zheng, "Assessing China's cybersecurity law," *Computer Law & Security Review*, vol. 34, no. 6, pp. 1342–1354, 2018.
46. G. Greenleaf, "China's completed personal information protection law: Rights plus cybersecurity," 2021.
47. T. Pereira, L. Barreto and A. Amaral, "Network and information security challenges within industry 4.0 paradigm," *Procedia Manufacturing*, vol. 13, pp. 1253–1260, 2017.
48. D. Song, "Internet real-name system and cybercrime prevention in China: A critical perspective," *Jura: A Pecsi Tudomanyegyetem Allam-es Jogtudomanyi Karanak Tudomanyos Lapja*, p. 470, 2019.
49. M. Parasol, "The impact of China's 2016 cybersecurity law on foreign technology firms, and on China's big data and Smart City dreams," *Computer Law & Security Review*, vol. 34, no. 1, pp. 67–98, 2018.
50. K. A. Bamberger, "Technologies of compliance: Risk and regulation in a digital age," *Texas Law Review*, vol. 88, p. 669, 2009.
51. R. Carapeto, "The Japanese basic act on cybersecurity and the historical development of the Japanese legal framework for cybersecurity," *International Cybersecurity Law Review*, vol. 2, no. 1, pp. 65–76, 2021.
52. K. P. Newmeyer, "Elements of national cybersecurity strategy for developing nations," *National Cybersecurity Institute Journal*, vol. 1, no. 3, pp. 9–19, 2015.
53. W. Vosse, "EU–Japan cooperation in combatting cybercrime: From the strategic partnership agreement to global partnerships," in *Europe and Japan cooperation in the fight against cross-border crime*, Routledge, 2022, pp. 147–164.
54. B. Bartlett, "Why do states engage in cybersecurity capacity-building assistance? Evidence from Japan," *The Pacific Review*, vol. 37, no. 3, pp. 475–503, 2024.
55. I. Citaristi, "International Telecommunication Union—ITU," in *The Europa directory of international organizations 2022*, Routledge, 2022, pp. 365–369.
56. A. L. Allison, *The ITU and managing satellite orbital and spectrum resources in the 21st century*, Springer Science & Business, 2014.
57. U. ESCAP, "Good practices in information and communication technology policies in Asia and the Pacific: Promotion of enabling policies and regulatory frameworks for information and communication technology development in the Asia-Pacific region," 2004.
58. S. Livingstone, "Regulating the internet in the interests of children: Emerging European and international approaches," *The Handbook of Global media and Communication Policy*, pp. 505–524, 2011.
59. S. AlDaajeh, H. Saleous, S. Alrabaee, E. Barka, F. Breitinger and K. K. R. Choo, "The role of national cybersecurity strategies on the improvement of cybersecurity education," *Computers & Security*, vol. 119, p. 102754, 2022.
60. R. D. O. Andrade and R. Gonçalo, "Digital transformation by enabling strategic capabilities in the context of 'BRICS'," *Revista de Gestão*, vol. 28, no. 4, pp. 297–315, 2021.
61. C. R. Reddy, "The challenges and opportunities of using technology to promote social development," *Journal of Survey in Fisheries Sciences*, pp. 183–187, 2021.
62. S. Kolasani, "Innovations in digital, enterprise, cloud, data transformation, and organizational change management using agile, lean, and data-driven methodologies," *International Journal of Machine Learning and Artificial Intelligence*, vol. 4, no. 4, pp. 1–18, 2023.
63. A. Putnam and A. Sanchez, "Digital skills for the 21st-century workforce," *Federal Reserve Bank of Philadelphia*, pp. 1–11, 2019.
64. A. Kwilinski, O. Lyulyov and T. Pimonenko, "Unlocking sustainable value through digital transformation: An examination of ESG performance," *Information*, vol. 14, no. 8, p. 444, 2023.

65. D. L. Baumer, J. B. Earp and J. Poindexter, "Internet privacy law: A comparison between the United States and the European Union," *Computers & Security*, vol. 23, no. 5, pp. 400–412, 2004.
66. M. Bloom, "Protecting personal data: A model data security and breach notification statute," *John's Law Review*, vol. 92, p. 977, 2018.
67. C. J. Bennett, "The accountability approach to privacy and data protection: Assumptions and caveats," in *Managing privacy through accountability*, Springer, 2012, pp. 33–48.
68. P. P. Pinheiro, "Privacy and Data Protection Law in Brazil," 2023.
69. M. F. A. El Rob, "A narrative review of advantageous cybersecurity frameworks and regulations in the United States healthcare system," *Issues in Information Systems*, vol. 24, no. 4, 2023.
70. M. Dunn Cavelty and M. Smeets, "Regulatory cybersecurity governance in the making: The formation of ENISA and its struggle for epistemic authority," *Journal of European Public Policy, Vol*, vol. 30, no. 7, pp. 1330–1352, 2023.
71. N. Shafqat and A. Masood, "Comparative analysis of various national cybersecurity strategies," *International Journal of Computer Science and Information Security*, vol. 14, no. 1, pp. 129–136, 2016.
72. X. Quan, "The governance of cross-border data flows in trade agreements: Is the CPTPP framework an ideal way out?" *Frontiers Law China*, vol. 15, p. 253, 2020.
73. W. Lehr, "5G and the future of broadband," in *The future of the internet*, 2019, Nomos Verlagsgesellschaft mbH & Co. KG, pp. 109–150.
74. L. DeNardis, "E-Governance policies for interoperability and open standards," *Policy & Internet*, vol. 2, no. 3, pp. 129–164, 2010.
75. H. Deresky, *International management: Managing across borders and cultures*, Pearson Education India, 2000.
76. G. Cardoza, G. Fornes, P. Li, N. Xu and S. Xu, "China goes global: Public policies' influence on small-and medium-sized enterprises' international expansion," *Asia Pacific Business Review*, vol. 21, no. 2, pp. 188–210, 2015.
77. S. K. Katyal, "Private accountability in the age of artificial intelligence," *UCLA Law Review*, vol. 66, p. 54, 2019.
78. P. Yeoh, "Regulatory issues in blockchain technology," *Journal of Financial Regulation and Compliance*, vol. 25, no. 2, pp. 196–208, 2017.
79. R. Neisse, G. Steri and G. Baldini, "Enforcement of Security Policy Rules for the Internet of Things," in *2014 IEEE 10th International Conference on Wireless and Mobile Computing, Networking and Communications (WiMob)*, 2014, IEEE, pp. 165–172.
80. H. J. Allen, "Regulatory sandboxes," *The George Washington Law Review*, vol. 87, p. 579, 2019.
81. C. Anastasi, *Strategic stakeholder engagement*, Routledge, 2018.
82. M. A. de Magalhães, "Data protection regulation: A comparative law approach: Proteção de dados: Estudo comparado de normas nacionais," *International Journal of Digital Law*, vol. 2, no. 2, pp. 33–53, 2021.
83. P. Donos, "New data protection regulation impact on European Institutions," *European Journal of Privacy Law & Technologies*, p. 124, 2020.
84. R. Knight and J. R. Nurse, "A framework for effective corporate communication after cybersecurity incidents," *Computers & Security*, vol. 99, p. 102036, 2020.
85. M. P. Carey and K. A. Francis, *The Trump administration and the unified agenda of federal regulatory and deregulatory actions*, Congressional Research Service, 2017.
86. C. C. Markides and P. A. Geroski, *Fast second: How smart companies bypass radical innovation to enter and dominate new markets*, John Wiley & Sons, 2004.
87. K. M. Reed, "From the great firewall of China to the Berlin firewall: The cost of content regulation on internet commerce," *The Transnational Lawyer*, vol. 13, p. 451, 2000.

88. J. DeLisle, A. Goldstein and G. Yang, *The internet, social media, and a changing China*, University of Pennsylvania Press, 2016.
89. C. Su and T. Flew, "The rise of Baidu, Alibaba and Tencent (BAT) and their role in China's belt and road initiative (BRI)," *Global Media and Communication*, vol. 17, no. 1, pp. 67–86, 2021.
90. O. Akinrinola, C. C. Okoye, O. C. Ofodile and C. E. Ugochukwu, "Navigating and reviewing ethical dilemmas in AI development: Strategies for transparency, fairness, and accountability," *GSC Advanced Research and Reviews*, vol. 18, no. 3, pp. 050–058, 2024.
91. D. Markopoulou and V. Papakonstantinou, "The regulatory framework for the protection of critical infrastructures against cyberthreats: Identifying shortcomings and addressing future challenges: The case of the health sector in particular," *Computer Law & Security Review*, vol. 41, p. 105502, 2021.
92. E. Igbinenikaro and A. O. Adewusi, "Financial law: Policy frameworks for regulating fintech innovations: Ensuring consumer protection while fostering innovation," *Finance & Accounting Research Journal*, vol. 6, no. 4, pp. 515–530, 2024.
93. W. G. Voss, "Cross-border data flows, the GDPR, and data governance," *Washington International Law Journal*, vol. 29, p. 485, 2019.
94. S. J. Shackelford and A. N. Craig, "Beyond the new digital divide: Analyzing the evolving role of national governments in internet governance and enhancing cybersecurity," *Stanford Journal of International Law*, vol. 50, p. 119, 2014.
95. J. P. Meltzer, "The United States-Mexico-Canada agreement: Developing trade policy for digital trade," *Trade Law & Development*, vol. 11, p. 239, 2019.
96. E. Linn, "A look into the data privacy crystal ball: A survey of possible outcomes for the EU-US privacy shield agreement," *Vanderbilt Journal of Transnational Law*, vol. 50, p. 1311, 2017.
97. M. Dempsey, K. McBride, M. Haataja and J. Bryson, "Transnational digital governance and its impact on artificial intelligence," in *The Oxford handbook of AI governance*, Oxford University Press, 2022.
98. C. Bonina, K. Koskinen, B. Eaton and A. Gawer, "Digital platforms for development: Foundations and research agenda," *Information Systems Journal*, vol. 31, no. 6, pp. 869–902, 2021.

17 Enhancing Log File Analysis in Digital Forensics and Incident Response through Machine Learning

Arul Kumar Natarajan, Mohammad Gouse Galety, Nilamadhab Mishra, Prabu M., Manimaran A., and Gobi Ramasamy

17.1 INTRODUCTION

Log file analysis is an important step in investigating and responding to digital security incidents creates records for every activity on that particular system or network, which plays a crucial role in identifying what went wrong. In the wider scope of digital forensics and incident response sub-discipline, analyzing log files is key to following malicious behavior, recognizing changes or anomalies that have happened, and rebuilding events leading to security incidents. The increased complexity and sheer volume of log data make traditional approaches to analysis inadequate to handle new datasets, requiring more sophisticated sets of methods for log analysis. This chapter discusses the essential nature of log file analysis and its obstacles. This chapter discusses the importance and hurdles of analyzing log files. It introduces a new (Python) machine learning approach to make our errors-and-omissions correction process faster while also discussing many trade-offs or restrictions on why traditional methods fail.

Research on system log clustering finds applications in improving cybersecurity by effectively analyzing a large amount of log data and identifying anomalies. The log files generated by computer systems capture large amounts of unstructured, varied data and add complexity to the analysis automation. To tackle such challenges, the summarization is enhanced by leveraging several clustering techniques to condense log data, making it ready for further analysis. One of the most extensive surveys categorizing existing approaches according to their techniques, ability to be used, and objectives, which have filtering, signature extraction and anomaly detection (Landauer et al., 2020).

Based on the initial methodology review, this chapter presents the first preprocessing and feature extraction approach with several machine learning models. These were

 DOI: 10.1201/9781003497868-17

compared with other models (RandomForestClassifier, GradientBoostingClassifier, SVM, and MLPClassifier). The accuracy is 0.9198 from XGBoost. Finally, the chapter discusses challenges, limitations, and future research directions and visualizes key findings for better comprehension. The chapter contains background research, methodology overview, model evaluation, dataset discussion, and future work and limitations.

17.1.1 Importance of Log Files in Digital Forensics

Log files are important in digital forensics for complete per-recorded documents of all activities and events on systems and networks. These records can help forensic investigators chase attacks, identify breach points, and reconstruct incident timelines. It analyzes logs to discover evidence, assess the severity of incidents, and assist in recovery and mitigation efforts.

This is a big leap in the world of data threats as fileless malware. It is effective in stealth, as it does not use the file system and can bypass traditional detection systems (Sudhakar & Kumar, 2020). This malware type uses legitimate system tools to perform its activities, thus evading the standard anti-virus security solutions. This work provides insight into fileless malware detection techniques and forensic methodologies proposed in the literature, suggests a process model to address these attacks, and provides our perspective on major research deficiencies and challenges. At the same time, as software systems become more and more complex, the amount of log data is huge (Heldens et al., 2022), and manual analysis of logs further enhances the work in reliability engineering. This research surveys automated log analysis techniques for automating logging statement generation, log compression, and log parsing into structured formats and their applications in anomaly detection and failure prediction (He et al., 2021). In addition, the authors discussed the open-source tools and datasets and proposed a prospective direction to improve the real-world applicability of log analysis.

The surge of data scavenging assaults in IoT is down for far more advanced forensic tactics. Shakeel et al. (2021) introduced a BSAF model based on a logistic regression model with the help of cross-validation to enhance attack detection using access log analysis. In this work, the authors investigated how the BSAF framework improves the accuracy of data analysis and efficiency in virtualized resources, with special attention devoted to the contribution of BSAF to IoT forensic data analysis challenges.

In digital forensics, log files are some of the most important resources as they contain a long and recording network and system operations record. They log important information, including timestamps, IP addresses, user actions, and results. For instance, let us take the following log records as an example:

- 2024-08-09 14:32:12 INFO 192.168.1.1 - [USER: john_doe] - [ACTION: Login] - [STATUS: Success]
- 2024-08-09 14:33:45 WARN 192.168.1.2 - [USER: admin] - [ACTION: File Upload] - [STATUS: Failure] - [REASON: Invalid File Type]
- 2024-08-09 14:35:22 ERROR 192.168.1.3 - [USER: jane_smith] - [ACTION: Data Deletion] - [STATUS: Failure] - [REASON: Insufficient Permissions]

These are critical log entries for forensic investigations, including user actions and how the system responds. In this case, the log entry where john_doe logged in successfully proves that he accessed the system legitimately. Simultaneously, it may also indicate that admins are trying to introduce unauthorized files by failing the file type on upload. If we repeat the same exercise as before with jane_smith deleted from the data successfully, this failed deletion attempt appears that unauthorized parties are attempting to change or delete sensitive information (which is a risk). The page view from the guest looks like normal usage.

These records allow investigators to scan the events before and after a security incident. These log files help identify attack vectors, recreate the incident timeline, and assess security breaches. They reveal malicious behavior patterns, providing insight into how security threats live and attack the processes, surpassing counters to these threats' shortcomings. They are the first attempts of digital forensics, which tell a lot and help to investigate and clarify many security holes. Given their detailed and well-structured nature, they can enable the perfect reconstruction of events, allowing for effective incident management—thereby improving cybersecurity practice.

17.1.2 Challenges in Log File Analysis

Analyzing log files is fundamentally a difficult task, as the large amount of data logged by modern systems becomes just numbers with lines processed by parsers. Landauer et al. (2024) studied how various log datasets are unsuitable for benchmarking sequence-based anomaly detection techniques because many anomalies in these datasets do not align with pairwise dependencies and can be easily caught by existing rule-based methods. Pan et al. (2024) present a new method named RAGLog that uses the Retrieval Augmented Generation model for log anomaly Detection and shows improved performance in identifying different anomalies in log data with the help of a Question-and-Answer configuration pipeline.

The following challenges are particularly noteworthy:

- **Data Volume and Variety:** Modern systems generate large amounts of log data from various events, activities, and statuses. Processing large volumes of disparate information demands heavy computing resources and sophisticated analytical methods.
- **Real-Time Analysis:** Log data is generated when an activity initiates, so it is generated continuously and in real-time, which requires quick processing to detect security incidents. The main problem is the need to process log entries rapidly enough to see new attack patterns, and precautions must be taken as soon as possible to minimize issues related to security violations.
- **Noise Filtering and Anomaly Detection:** The capability to distinguish between noise from log files and performance data must be filtered out before identifying any useful insights from the performance of a security operation. Sophisticated techniques for removing background noise and identifying true anomalies that, if left unidentified, could result in a cyber breach or other significant problems. High-level algorithms and methods are to be applied to decode the data accurately.

TABLE 17.1
Key Challenges in Log File Analysis

Challenge	Description
Volume of Data	Large amounts of log data need significant resources to process.
Real-Time Analysis	Logs are generated continuously, requiring quick analysis to respond to security incidents.
Noise and Anomalies	Identifying meaningful information and detecting anomalies can be difficult.
Non-Standard Formats	Different systems use various log formats, making combining and analyzing data hard.

- **Lack of Standardized Formats:** Different forms for capturing within the systems and applications: Not all systems/applications will generate logs in a similar form. This is because they do not have a standard means of writing that forces the use of libraries or systems, which complicates combining and analyzing data from multiple sources. Therefore, processing, standardizing, and consolidating logs from various systems require advanced tools and techniques.

Table 17.1 recaps these challenges in log file investigation.

17.2 MOTIVATION FOR USING PYTHON AND MACHINE LEARNING

17.2.1 Need for Advanced Analytical Tools

This has fueled a resurgence in the utilization of traditional log analysis techniques. These methods require manual inspection and basic pattern matching, usually outside modern demands. These conventional methods could be more resourceful for managing big data, advanced and altered attack signatures, and determining between benign and malevolent behaviors. This poor effectiveness hurts the efficiency of incident response actions and allows other security incidents to remain undiscovered.

This need arises from the modern world of cyber threats, in which log file analysis needs a better analytical tool that can function faster and more effectively. It is also important that these tools can handle ever-increasing amounts of data and are ready to change and respond quickly enough to the shifting threat landscape (Thomas et al., 2020).

17.2.2 Python's Role in Enhancing Analysis

Python: Another strong choice, Python is a high-level language with clean syntax and loads of great libraries, making it an ideal tool for creating more complex log file analysis tools (think anomaly detection patterns or predictive analytics). Since Scikit-learn will standardize the integration level of libraries or frameworks by keeping a deeper and more stable relationship, there would be less pressure to maintain it in machine learning-based analytics continuously. It continually changes its face to suit the new demands of cybersecurity professionals as a community. Additionally, Python automation and the ability to simplify complex workflows make it a good choice to use for log file analysis. Python has a very big impact in this fast decision environment, especially if we deal with log file analysis—conclusion (Chunyue et al., 2006; Dhruv et al., 2021; Heldens et al., 2022; Siebert et al., 2021).

The following Python packages were used for comparison and prediction tasks in the research work.

17.2.2.1 Pandas

For data manipulation and preprocessing, such as reading in datasets and encoding of categorical features.

- Import: import pandas as pd

17.2.2.2 Scikit-Learn

- For machine learning model training and evaluation (Hackeling, 2017; Hao & Ho, 2019).
- Modules
  - train_test_split for splitting data.
  - RandomForestClassifier, GradientBoostingClassifier, SVC, and MLPClassifier for classification models.
  - accuracy_score for evaluating model performance.
  - LabelEncoder for encoding target labels (Jackson & Agrawal, 2019).

17.2.2.3 Import

- They are used to import the libraries (e.g., RandomForestClassifier)

17.2.2.4 XGboost

- For the XGBoost classifier (Zhang et al., 2022)
- *Import: import xgboost as xgb*

Data preprocessing, model training, and performance evaluation are the essential parts used as packages in this research.

17.2.3 Existing Work in Machine Learning in Log File Analysis

Machine learning has modernized log file analysis using automated, data-driven techniques. The models can learn from supervised, unsupervised, and deep learning methods. ML algorithms can identify complex patterns and detect types of attacks better than traditional detection. It was a milestone in digital forensics and incident response that improved our ability to contain and respond to security breaches.

Sarker (2023) emphasized that the key to official cybersecurity is autonomous data analysis and machine learning tools. This line of work provides further insights from cybersecurity data that can be used for more intelligent defenses. The chapter aims to provide an in-depth overview of how the science and business of machine

TABLE 17.2
Traditional vs. Machine Learning Methods

Aspect	Traditional Methods	Machine Learning Models
Adaptability	Requires manual updates	Adapts automatically from data
Threat Detection	Limited to predefined patterns	Detects new and sophisticated threats
Learning Approach	Not applicable	Utilizes supervised and unsupervised learning
Data Analysis	Manual processing	Automates data analysis
Scalability	Difficult to scale	Easily scalable for large datasets
Continuous Improvement	Static performance	Continuously improves with new data

learning can develop next-generation security technologies by examining current methods, their shortcomings, and possible future ventures.

Table 17.2 represents the basic characteristics of traditional methods and machine learning models in log file analysis.

17.3 PROPOSED WORK

The methodology uses Python and machine learning to enhance log file analysis by automating data processing, feature extraction, and model training. Figure 17.1 is a

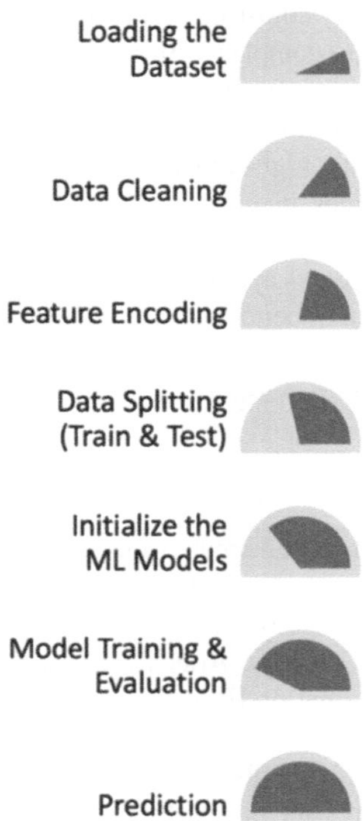

FIGURE 17.1 Workflow for log file analysis using machine learning.

TABLE 17.3
Key Features of the Machine Learning Algorithms

Algorithm	Main Feature	Strength	Use Case
Random Forest Classifier	Multiple decision trees	Reduces overfitting	Classification
Gradient Boosting Classifier	Builds models in sequence	High accuracy	Complex tasks
Support Vector Machine (SVM)	Finds the best boundary	Handles complex data	Classification
XGBoost	Fast gradient boosting	Very accurate	Classification, regression
Multi-Layer Perceptron (MLP)	Neural network with layers	Learns complex patterns	Classification, regression

workflow diagram illustrating log file analysis using machine learning, showing the steps from data collection to model training and anomaly detection.

17.3.1 Description of the Machine Learning Algorithms

RandomForestClassifier is an ensemble learning method that uses multiple decision trees to prevent overfitting and uncertainty; hence, it is suitable for mocking high-dimensional or complex data (Palimkar et al., 2022). Similarly, GradientBoostingClassifier is a machine learning paradigm that seeks to enhance prediction power by iteratively adjusting predictions from a previous model and performs well with missions too complex with refined data (Chakrabarty et al., 2019). The SVM can accurately identify optimal hyperplanes even in high dimensions (Ding et al., 2017), and its advance has opened the way for predicting non-linear relations. XGBoost can handle high-dimensional low-sample data due to its regularization, and compute resources are employed, which will make accurate predictions faster (Obiora et al., 2021). Finally, Multi-Layer Perceptron (MLP) architecture that involves fully connected layers is applied. It provides backpropagation to learn non-linear patterns, making them fit better with log file data containing complex relations between events of different types (Esmaily et al., 2015). As shown in Table 17.3, the data indicate a clear trend of increasing efficiency.

17.4 DESCRIBING THE DATASET

The UNSW-NB15 dataset has been created specifically for this purpose. It is a comprehensive dataset containing network attacks publicly free to researchers in cybersecurity, ML, and Data Mining. Some key attributes were chosen for our research inside the dataset: Attack Category, Attack Subcategory Protocol (TCP or UDP), Source IP, Source Port, Destination IP, and Destination Port. The initial dataset had 174,349 records, which were preprocessed and cleaned by removing inconsistencies or irrelevant ones. Figure 17.2 is a tabular representation of the UNSW-NB15 dataset attributes, listing key features such as protocol type, source and destination IP, and traffic characteristics.

```
  Attack category   Attack subcategory Protocol      Source IP  Source Port  \
0  Reconnaissance                 HTTP      tcp  175.45.176.0      13284.0
1        Exploits     Unix 'r' Service      udp  175.45.176.3      21223.0
2        Exploits              Browser      tcp  175.45.176.2      23357.0
3        Exploits  Miscellaneous Batch      tcp  175.45.176.2      13792.0
4        Exploits            Cisco IOS      tcp  175.45.176.2      26939.0

   Destination IP  Destination Port
0  149.171.126.16              80.0
1  149.171.126.18           32780.0
2  149.171.126.16              80.0
3  149.171.126.16            5555.0
4  149.171.126.10              80.0

Number of records: 174349
```

FIGURE 17.2 UNSW-NB15 dataset attributes and record statistics.

Next, we summarize the UNSW-NB15 dataset (Figure 17.2 shows its features). It also gives an idea of the size of the original record set, 174,349 records, and what looks like a step in data preprocessing.

17.4.1 Dataset Source

This work uses the UNSW-NB15 dataset, which consists of extensive network traffic data. We have cleaned the dataset by eliminating inconsistencies and irrelevant records. The dataset after dropping duplicate Rows Initially, there were 174,349 rows in my dataset. Now, after preprocessing, the dataset includes 85,619 records. Figure 17.3 is a bar chart summarizing records in the dataset, highlighting the

```
  Attack category   Attack subcategory Protocol      Source IP  Source Port
0  Reconnaissance                 HTTP      tcp  175.45.176.0      13284.0
1        Exploits     Unix 'r' Service      udp  175.45.176.3      21223.0
2        Exploits              Browser      tcp  175.45.176.2      23357.0
3        Exploits  Miscellaneous Batch      tcp  175.45.176.2      13792.0
4        Exploits            Cisco IOS      tcp  175.45.176.2      26939.0

   Destination IP  Destination Port
0  149.171.126.16              80.0
1  149.171.126.18           32780.0
2  149.171.126.16              80.0
3  149.171.126.16            5555.0
4  149.171.126.10              80.0

Number of records after cleaning: 85619

Cleaned data saved to /content/NUSW-NB15_GT_Cleaned.csv
```

FIGURE 17.3 Records summary (sample).

distribution of different types of network activity logs, and shows a sample of the UNSW-NB15 dataset, with the main attributes after data cleaning (85,619).

17.5 BASIC ANALYSIS

Descriptive statistics provide us with the essential features of the data, some of which are mean, median, and standard deviation. Primary statistics like mean, median, and standard deviation give researchers a global (or overall) view of the diversity within data. These statistics are essential to understanding the data characteristics

```
Unique value counts for each categorical column:
Attack category            13
Attack subcategory        163
Protocol                  129
Source IP                   4
Source Port             40374
Destination IP             10
Destination Port         3142
dtype: int64

Value counts for 'Attack category':
Attack category
Exploits              35296
 Fuzzers              16379
 Reconnaissance       11060
DoS                    9625
Generic                4652
 Fuzzers               3725
Reconnaissance         1740
 Shellcode             1288
Analysis               1282
Shellcode               223
Backdoors               180
Worms                   167
Fuzzers                   2
Name: count, dtype: int64
```

FIGURE 17.4 Descriptive statistics.

and any disturbances in the data that might disturb its evaluation later. An analysis of unique values across categorical columns, value distribution in 'Attack Category' and 's Protocol' attributes, and most frequent attack type and protocols Hash Sets. Description statistics were generated for the cleaned UNSW-NB15 dataset. Figure 17.4 is a statistical table displaying descriptive metrics such as mean, median, and standard deviation for network traffic features.

17.6 DATA VISUALIZATION

Seeing these incidents' distribution, frequency, and characteristics through different attack methods makes them more pervasive. We can represent these patterns of information graphically to identify with perspective the trends or anomalies that might concern us. This section presents two primary visualizations that provide insights into the network traffic data, special protocols, and port usage.

17.6.1 Protocol Analysis

A more focused analysis was carried out on the top ten most common protocols to determine the distribution of network protocols within the dataset. This analysis helps illuminate the more dominant protocols on the network and aids in understanding how protocol communications influence a possible attack window. Figure 17.5 shows the distribution of the top ten protocols across the dataset, showing many TCP and UDP protocols. The two most common protocols are TCP, with 55,333 rows, and UDP, with 12,745 rows.

17.6.2 Port Usage Analysis

Analyzing the source and destination ports in network traffic can reveal key information about the types of services and applications that are exploited or accessed.

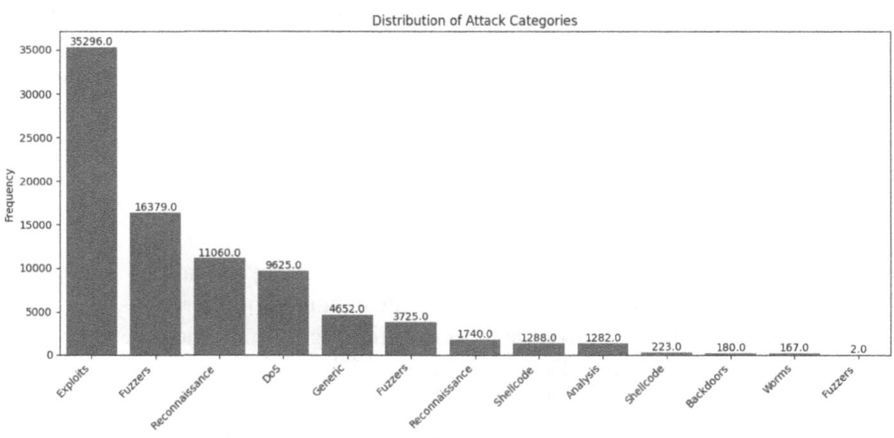

FIGURE 17.5 Distribution of top ten protocols.

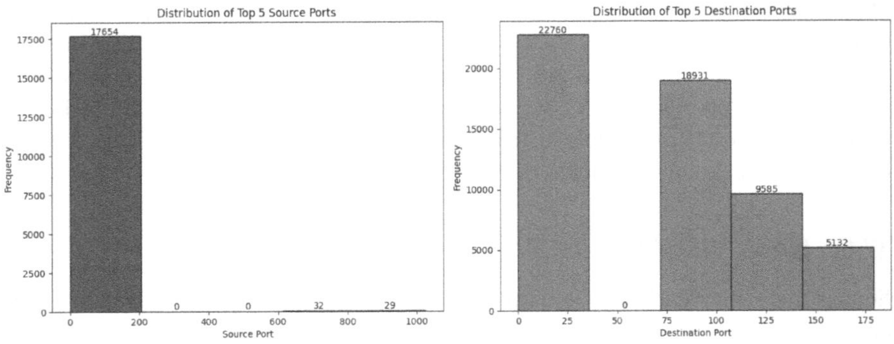

FIGURE 17.6 Distribution of top five source and destination ports.

The visualizations below illustrate the distribution of the five most frequent source and destination ports, manifesting port usage trends in this dataset. This distribution is shown in Figure 17.6 (revealing the most accessed ports): The analysis shows the traffic concentrated through ports 0 to 200 source and 0 to 40 destination tone ports, and appears with more counts for each: 17,654. Their results are paramount for pinpointing vulnerabilities, translating to more secure networks. Figure 17.5 is a bar graph representing the distribution of the top ten network protocols observed in the dataset, with TCP, UDP, and ICMP as common protocols.

17.7 ASSESSING THE PERFORMANCE OF DIFFERENT MACHINE LEARNING TECHNIQUES

Here, we show a detailed method to evaluate different machine learning models from classification based on a log file dataset. The idea is to answer how well models can classify the log data, thus leading to better digital forensics and response efforts. Accompanied by a full code framework for model training and experiments in Python, as demonstrated in Figure 17.1. For the model, we used RandomForestClassifier, GradientBoostingClassifier, Support Vector Classifier (SVC), XGBoostClassifier, and MLPCLassifier. These algorithms have been published for research and also help in high accuracy speed when analyzing log files. Figure 17.6 is a heatmap visualizing the most frequently used source and destination ports in network communications, identifying hotspots of cyber activity.

The outcome of the algorithm is as follows:

- This research systematically compares the efficiency of various machine learning algorithms for classifying log file data in digital forensics.
- The study aims to identify the most effective algorithm for log file analysis by analyzing each model's performance.
- The results indicate that the XGBoostClassifier demonstrates superior performance, particularly in handling dataset complexities, achieving higher accuracy than other models.

- XGBoostClassifier is identified as the most suitable model for this business application due to its accuracy and efficiency.
- The structured analysis illustrates the practical applicability of these models, highlighting their potential to enhance the precision and efficiency of log file interpretation in digital forensics.

In the following sections we analyze the result for this implementation and thoroughly compare the models against one another. Figure 17.7 shows an algorithm to assess machine learning models for log file classification. Figure 17.7 is a decision tree flowchart showcasing the algorithm used for classifying log file data into different security event categories using machine learning.

Algorithm 1 Evaluation of Machine Learning Models for Log File Classification

```
Input: Dataset file path /content/NUSW-NB15_GT_Cleaned.csv
Output: Accuracy of different machine learning models
Step 1: Load the dataset
    Read the dataset using pandas.read_csv(file_path)
Step 2: Clean the target column
    Remove leading/trailing whitespace from Attack category column
Step 3: Encode categorical features
    Apply one-hot encoding to Attack subcategory, Protocol, Source IP,
    and Destination IP
Step 4: Encode target labels
    Transform Attack category using LabelEncoder
Step 5: Split the dataset
    Separate features X and target y
    Split data into training set (80%) and testing set (20%) using
    train_test_split
Step 6: Initialize machine learning models
    RandomForestClassifier with n_estimators=100
    GradientBoostingClassifier with n_estimators=100
    SVC (Support Vector Classifier)
    XGBClassifier with eval_metric='mlogloss'
    MLPClassifier with max_iter=500
Step 7: Train and evaluate models
for each model in models do
    Train the model using fit(X_train, y_train)
    Predict using predict(X_test)
    Calculate accuracy using accuracy_score(y_test, y_pred)
    Print model name and accuracy
end for
```

FIGURE 17.7 Algorithm used for log file classification (machine learning).

17.7.1 Key Steps in the Algorithm

The key steps in the algorithm are as follows:

- Import Libraries
- Load the Dataset
  - The dataset is loaded from a CSV file using pandas.read_csv().
  - File path:/content/NUSW-NB15_GT_Cleaned.csv.
- Data Cleaning
  - The Attack category column is cleaned by removing any leading or trailing whitespace characters.
- Feature Encoding
  - Categorical features (such as Attack subcategory, Protocol, Source IP, and Destination IP) are converted into Numerical features using one-hot encoding.
  - The target variable, Attack category, is encoded into integers using LabelEncoder.
- Feature and Target Separation
  - Thus, X—Features (independent variables) and y-Target (dependent variable). Similarly, the column 'Attack category' will be removed from features or should not be used in model training.
- Data Splitting
  - The dataset is partitioned into training and testing sets using the train_test_split() function, with 80% of the data allocated for training and 20% reserved for testing.
- Model Initialization: Five machine learning models are initialized.
  - RandomForestClassifier
  - GradientBoostingClassifier
  - SVC (Support Vector Classifier)
  - XGBoostClassifier
  - MLPClassifier (MLP)
- Model Training and Evaluation
  - Each model is trained using the training dataset.
  - Predictions are generated for the testing dataset.
  - The accuracy of each model is computed and displayed using accuracy_score.

17.7.2 Output Analysis

The following section analyzes the performance of several machine learning models and presents their classification results on the log file dataset: Results for different machine learning models RandomForestClassifier, GradientBoostingClassifier, SVM, XGBoost, MLPClassifier. Performance for each model was assessed based on accuracy, with the highest accuracy of 0.9198 attained by XGBoost. Figure 17.8 displays these results, showing the accuracy of each model. Figure 17.8 is a result table displaying performance metrics such as accuracy, precision, recall, and F1-score for different classification models after implementation.

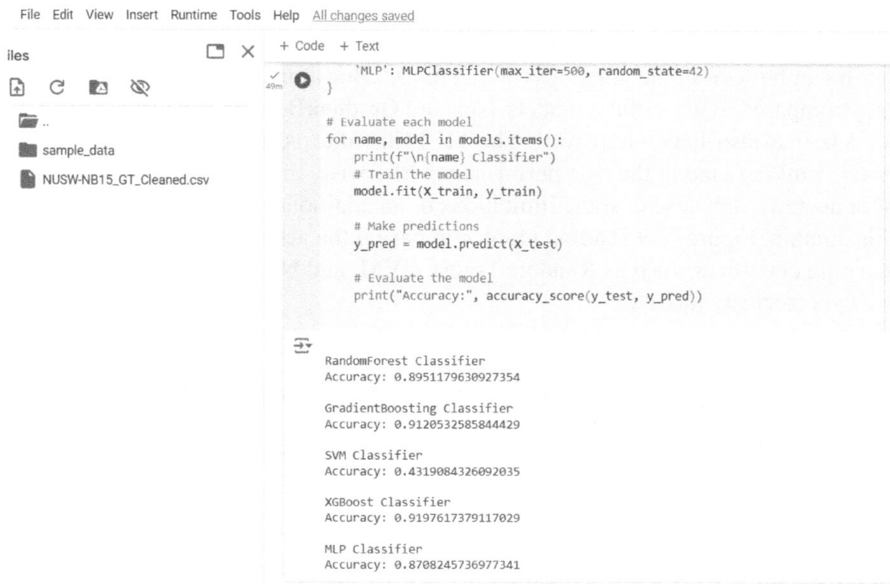

FIGURE 17.8 Results obtained after implementation.

17.7.3 Visualizing the Results

The graph in Figure 17.9 compares the accuracy of different machine learning models, including XGBoost, Gradient Boosting RF (Random Forest), MLP, and SVM.

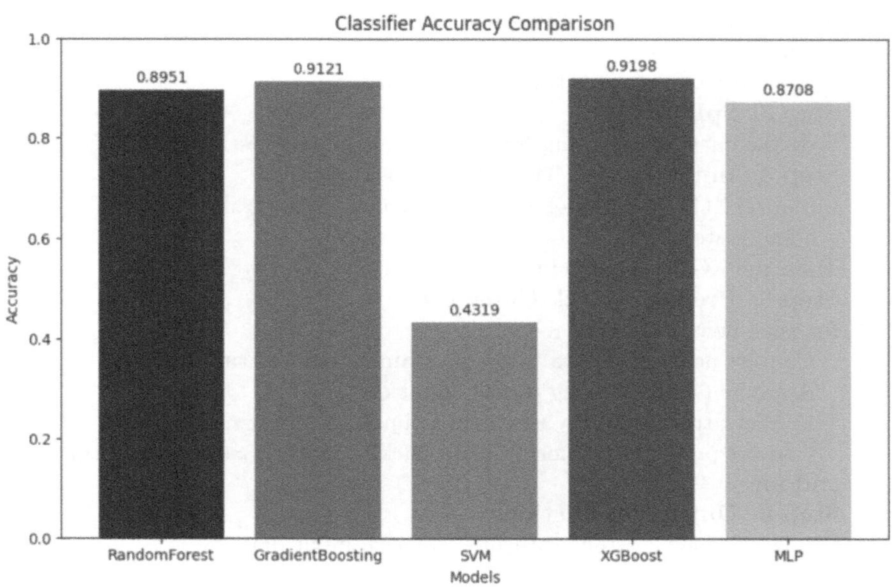

FIGURE 17.9 Classifier accuracy comparison.

One advantage of this graphical representation is that it maps the model performance and shows where each algorithm excels and fails to do so when working on the dataset. It can be seen in the graph above that the XGBoost model provided better accuracy compared to most of the models. Next are GradientBoosting and RandomForest models that also have fared well. The MLPClassifier is more efficient but with a wrong ranking among the best performers. Otherwise, the SVM model might show poor accuracy because of some limitations or an additional need for optimization in this domain. Figure 17.9 is a line graph comparing the accuracy of various machine learning classifiers, such as Random Forest, SVM, and Neural Networks, in detecting cybersecurity threats.

17.8 ALGORITHM EXPLANATION AND OUTPUT ANALYSIS

The algorithm shown in Figure 17.10 illustrates the application of a trained XGBoost model to predict attack categories from log file data.

Algorithm 2 Predicting Attack Categories Using XGBoost

Input: Dataset with log file records, new input data for prediction
Output: Predicted attack categories for new input data
Step 1: Load and Preprocess Data
Load the dataset from CSV file
Remove leading and trailing whitespaces from the 'Attack category' column
Apply one-hot encoding to categorical features ('Attack subcategory', 'Protocol', 'Source IP', 'Destination IP')
Encode 'Attack category' labels into numerical values
Step 2: Feature and Target Selection
Define features X by dropping the 'Attack category' column
Define target y as the 'Attack category' column
Step 3: Split Data
Split the data into training set (X_{train}, y_{train}) and testing set (X_{test}, y_{test})
Step 4: Initialize and Train XGBoost Model
Initialize XGBoost model with parameters (e.g., eval_metric='mlogloss', random_state=42)
Train the XGBoost model using X_{train} and y_{train}
Step 5: Predict Attack Categories
for each new input data record **do**
    Convert new input data to match training data feature format
    Apply one-hot encoding to new input data
    Predict attack category using the trained XGBoost model
    Convert predicted numerical label back to original categorical form
end for
Step 6: Output Predictions
Display predicted attack categories for new input data

FIGURE 17.10 Predicting attack categories using XGBoost.

17.8.1 Input Data

The XGBoost model is used to test the input. Each test cases are prepared using input data to evaluate the XGBoost model for log entries. For each test case, the following properties are used:

- Attack Subcategory
- Protocol
- Source IP
- Source Port
- Destination IP
- Destination Port

17.8.2 Test Cases and Its Attributes

Each test case has been carefully formatted to include the relevant attributes, ensuring compatibility with the trained XGBoost model for accurate predictions. Some samples are given below.

17.8.2.1 Test Case 1

- Attack Subcategory: HTTP
- Protocol: TCP
- Source IP: 175.45.176.0
- Source Port: 13284
- Destination IP: 149.171.126.16
- Destination Port: 80

17.8.2.2 Test Case 2

- Attack Subcategory: Unix 'r' Service
- Protocol: UDP
- Source IP: 175.45.176.3
- Source Port: 21223
- Destination IP: 149.171.126.18
- Destination Port: 32780

17.8.2.3 Test Case 3

- Attack Subcategory: Browser
- Protocol: TCP
- Source IP: 175.45.176.2
- Source Port: 23357
- Destination IP: 149.171.126.16
- Destination Port: 80

17.8.3 Output Analysis

Figure 17.11 illustrates this output analysis of the test cases by visualizing the classification outcomes for the given test cases.

```
    # Make a prediction
    prediction = xgb_model.predict(input_encoded)
    predicted_label = label_encoder.inverse_transform(prediction)
    return predicted_label[0]

# Test cases
test_cases = [
    {'Attack subcategory': 'HTTP', 'Protocol': 'tcp', 'Source IP': '175.45.176.0', 'Sourc
    {'Attack subcategory': 'Unix \'r\' Service', 'Protocol': 'udp', 'Source IP': '175.45.
    {'Attack subcategory': 'Browser', 'Protocol': 'tcp', 'Source IP': '175.45.176.2', 'Sc
    {'Attack subcategory': 'SCADA', 'Protocol': 'tcp', 'Source IP': '175.45.176.3', 'Sour
    {'Attack subcategory': 'SIP', 'Protocol': 'udp', 'Source IP': '175.45.176.3', 'Source
]

# Make predictions for each test case
for i, case in enumerate(test_cases, start=1):
    predicted_category = predict_attack_category(pd.DataFrame([case]))
    print(f"Test Case {i}: Predicted Attack Category: {predicted_category}")
```

```
Test Case 1: Predicted Attack Category: Reconnaissance
Test Case 2: Predicted Attack Category: Shellcode
Test Case 3: Predicted Attack Category: DoS
Test Case 4: Predicted Attack Category: Exploits
Test Case 5: Predicted Attack Category: Generic
```

FIGURE 17.11 The outcome of the given test cases.

The following is a detailed analysis of some of the sample test cases used in the analysis.

17.8.3.1 Test Case 1

- Input: HTTP protocol, TCP, with specific source and destination IPs and ports.
- Output: Predicted as Reconnaissance. This suggests that the model identified the log entry as a reconnaissance attack.

17.8.3.2 Test Case 2

- Input: Unix 'r' Service, UDP, with specified IPs and ports.
- Output: Predicted as Shellcode. The model classified this entry as a shellcode attack, which indicates that the log entry might involve exploiting vulnerabilities.

17.8.3.3 Test Case 3

- Input: Browser, TCP, with given source and destination details.
- Output: Predicted as DoS. This implies that the model recognized the log entry as a Denial-of-Service attack.

17.9 FUTURE WORK

Future research directions should concentrate more on the model accuracy. Like hyperparameter tuning to enhance model performance, feature selection for selecting the most important data attributes and using external data sources to separately aggregate relevant information on supplementary training. This will be crucial if we want to eventually look for the best hyperparameter configurations and more advanced techniques to improve our models' predictions. Such developments may provide more precise and accurate results, suggesting improved log file analysis/digital forensics development.

17.10 CONCLUSION

This chapter provides readers with a detailed insight into log file analysis in digital forensics and incident response, considering log files as vital artifacts during security investigations. This research represents a significant leap over traditional by linking Python programming and sophisticated machine learning algorithms together for analysis. Incident detection and response accuracy and efficiency have been significantly improved in recent years using automated data processing and more advanced analytical techniques. The results of the four models were evaluated, and noticed that the XGBoostClassifier had exceptional classification accuracy. This shows its excellent ability to deal with the intricacies of log file data. The proposed approach is far more improved in many factors, nevertheless, there exist some restrictions. The chapter discusses practical challenges and limitations such as integration with existing forensic tools, dealing with diverse log formats, and efficient performance of sizable data processed.

These limitations can be addressed by tuning model parameters, considering more log types, and integrating this system with real-time incident response tools. These advancements are needed to strengthen existing digital forensic and incident response strategies. The research findings also highlight the potential for new approaches to help address the growing challenge of only being able to collect a small volume of log and other security-related data.

REFERENCES

Chakrabarty, N., Kundu, T., Dandapat, S., Sarkar, A., & Kole, D. K. (2019). Flight arrival delay prediction using gradient boosting classifier. In Emerging Technologies in Data Mining and Information Security: Proceedings of IEMIS 2018, Volume 2 (pp. 651–659). Springer Singapore.

Chunyue, Z., Yun, L., & Hongke, Z. (2006, December). A pattern matching based network intrusion detection system. In 2006 9th International Conference on Control, Automation, Robotics and Vision (pp. 1–4). IEEE.

Dhruv, A. J., Patel, R., & Doshi, N. (2021). Python: the most advanced programming language for computer science applications. Science and Technology Publications, Lda, 292–299.

Ding, S., Zhu, Z., & Zhang, X. (2017). An overview on semi-supervised support vector machine. Neural Computing and Applications, 28, 969–978.

Esmaily, J., Moradinezhad, R., & Ghasemi, J. (2015, May). Intrusion detection system based on multi-layer perceptron neural networks and decision tree. In 2015 7th Conference on Information and Knowledge Technology (IKT) (pp. 1–5). IEEE.

Hackeling, G. (2017). Mastering Machine Learning with scikit-learn. Packt Publishing Ltd.

Hao, J., & Ho, T. K. (2019). Machine learning made easy: a review of scikit-learn package in python programming language. Journal of Educational and Behavioral Statistics, 44(3), 348–361.

He, S., He, P., Chen, Z., Yang, T., Su, Y., & Lyu, M. R. (2021). A survey on automated log analysis for reliability engineering. ACM computing surveys (CSUR), 54(6), 1–37.

Heldens, S., Sclocco, A., Dreuning, H., van Werkhoven, B., Hijma, P., Maassen, J., & van Nieuwpoort, R. V. (2022). litstudy: A Python package for literature reviews. SoftwareX, 20, 101207.

Jackson, E., & Agrawal, R. (2019). Performance evaluation of different feature encoding schemes on cybersecurity logs (pp. 1–9). IEEE.

Landauer, M., Skopik, F., & Wurzenberger, M. (2024). A critical review of common log data sets used for evaluation of sequence-based anomaly detection techniques. Proceedings of the ACM on Software Engineering, 1(FSE), 1354–1375.

Landauer, M., Skopik, F., Wurzenberger, M., & Rauber, A. (2020). System log clustering approaches for cybersecurity applications: A survey. Computers & Security, 92, 101739.

Obiora, C. N., Ali, A., & Hasan, A. N. (2021, August). Implementing extreme gradient boosting (xgboost) algorithm in predicting solar irradiance. In 2021 IEEE PES/IAS PowerAfrica (pp. 1–5). IEEE.

Palimkar, P., Shaw, R. N., & Ghosh, A. (2022) Machine learning technique to prognosis diabetes disease: Random forest classifier approach. In M. Bianchini, V. Piuri, S. Das, & R. N. Shaw (Eds.), *Advanced computing and intelligent technologies* (Vol. 218, pp. 235–243). Lecture Notes in Networks and Systems. Springer, Singapore. https://doi.org/10.1007/978-981-16-2164-2_19

Pan, J., Liang, W. S., & Yidi, Y. (2024, May). RAGLog: Log Anomaly Detection using Retrieval Augmented Generation. In 2024 IEEE World Forum on Public Safety Technology (WFPST) (pp. 169–174). IEEE.

Sarker, I. H. (2023). Machine learning for intelligent data analysis and automation in cybersecurity: current and future prospects. Annals of Data Science, 10(6), 1473–1498.

Shakeel, P. M., Baskar, S., Fouad, H., Manogaran, G., Saravanan, V., & Montenegro-Marin, C. E. (2021). Internet of things forensic data analysis using machine learning to identify roots of data scavenging. Future Generation Computer Systems, 115, 756–768.

Siebert, J., Groß, J., & Schroth, C. (2021). A systematic review of python packages for time series analysis. arXiv preprint arXiv:2104.07406.

Sudhakar, & Kumar, S. (2020). An emerging threat Fileless malware: a survey and research challenges. Cybersecurity, 3(1), 1.

Thomas, T., Vijayaraghavan, A. P., & Emmanuel, S. (2020). Machine learning approaches in cybersecurity analytics (pp. 37–200). Springer.

UNSW. (n.d.). UNSW-NB15 dataset. UNSW Research. https://research.unsw.edu.au/projects/unsw-nb15-dataset. Accessed April 11, 2024.

Zhang, P., Jia, Y., & Shang, Y. (2022). Research and application of XGBoost in imbalanced data. International Journal of Distributed Sensor Networks, 18(6), 15501329221106935.

18 Ethics and Professional Standards of Cybersecurity, Digital Forensics, and National Security

Shantanu Bindewari and Mansi Trivedi

18.1 OVERVIEW OF CYBERSECURITY, DIGITAL FORENSICS, AND NATIONALSECURITY

- Cybersecurity, information security, and digital forensics security play a massive role the internet world; various entities play a crucial role in this area are majorly protecting digital assets, national security, banking systems, and also national security interest. It refers to computer systems, data, information, devices, unauthorized access, identity revealing, confidentiality breaches, financial and banking transactions, and organizational and government database breaches [1].
- Digital forensics refers to evidence, analysis, collection of raw materials and proof, assembly of data, detection and monitoring of databases and devices, monitoring of fraud and criminal activity, and digital and criminal footprints at crime scenes. It is also required to understand the terminology [2] concerning the circumstances of the crime.
- National security plays the most important role in today's internet, government agency [3] confidentiality, national information systems, intelligence agencies, protection from cybercriminals, and cyber terrorism. There are required digital forensics experts [4], cyber warriors, and government and non-government agencies for the national security interest. Figure 18.1 shows a structured framework diagram illustrating ethical and professional standards in cybersecurity, detailing compliance, governance, and best practices for digital ethics.
- Ethics is the fundamental duty in cybersecurity, digital forensics, and national security, and it is impactful for the considered various personal privacy [5], data confidentiality, national and global stability, diplomacy at the international level, investigation of crimes [6], and involves various national and global agencies and their higher level of security.

DOI: 10.1201/9781003497868-18

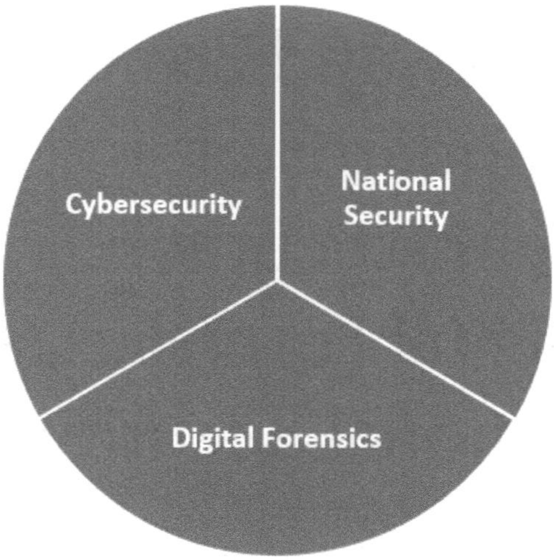

FIGURE 18.1 Framework for ethics and professional standards.

- Balanced the system with protection with user privacy [7, 8] and confidentiality also requires ethical rules must be adopt. The level of complexity to breach privacy and confidentiality and unprofessional and unethical practices must be preventive in a professional environment it could benefitted by your competitor or another country.
- All the ethical operations regulate to ensure competency with the ethical framework of the law and enforcement directorate all such cybercriminal activities.

18.2 FOUNDATIONAL ETHICAL PRINCIPLES IN CYBERSECURITY

- **Integrity:** Integrity is the most valuable entity in cybersecurity which ensures two parties maintain secrecy and confidentiality between them; it should show trustworthiness and commitment to safeguarding data, information, systems, and networks from harm. Integrity [9, 10] is satisfied the verified transaction between two parties also confirms information shared by the legitimate party. Figure 18.2 presents a conceptual chart that outlines foundational ethical principles in cybersecurity, including integrity, confidentiality, accountability, and professional responsibility [11, 12].

For example, there are two parties A and B communicating [13]. A sends the message *m* to B and B receives the message; B has ensure received message is the original one such that integrity of the two party communication secure and there is no intruder between them.

- **Confidentiality:** Confidentiality is a cybersecurity principal; it's being used everywhere to ensure secrecy of the message or information, and

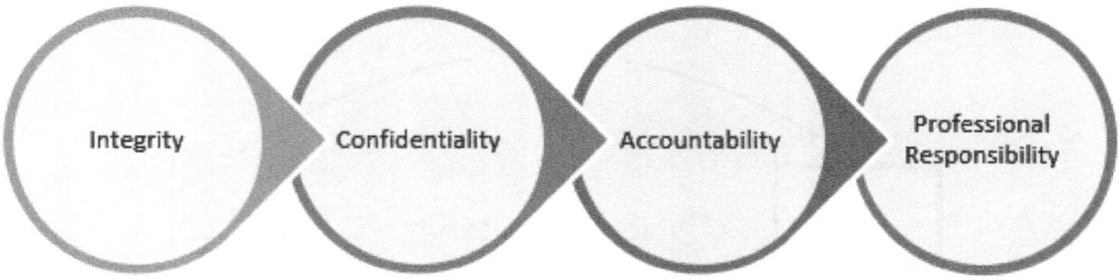

FIGURE 18.2 Foundational ethical principles in cybersecurity.

confidentiality is the most common factor in the analysis of the message it intersects with a third party or not whether A sends the high confidential information to B and its message eavesdrop someone and confidential information [13–16] reveal publicly or hacker and attacker can influence the people with negative intent. Therefore, government and non-government organizational data information contains highly confidential data so it has to be ensured confidentiality, data theft, information revealing, gaining knowledge, and impact to the society and any organization. Figure 18.3 shows a visual representation of a passive attack scenario, where a hacker is eavesdropping on a Integrity between two communicating parties without altering the message.

- **Accountability:** In cyberspace [17], multiple factors are involved, including computers, desktops, laptops, mobiles, data, files, drives, servers, and information. Nowadays, organizational infrastructures are increasingly interconnected, with rapid growth in information sharing and gathering. Therefore, data accountability plays a vital role. However, the growing complexity of managing all this data and its exchange significantly impacts any organization's system infrastructure and necessitates efficient management and organization for accountability.
- **Professionally responsibility:** Organizational environment adopting the ethical framework, legal compliance, regularization, authority, rules, and

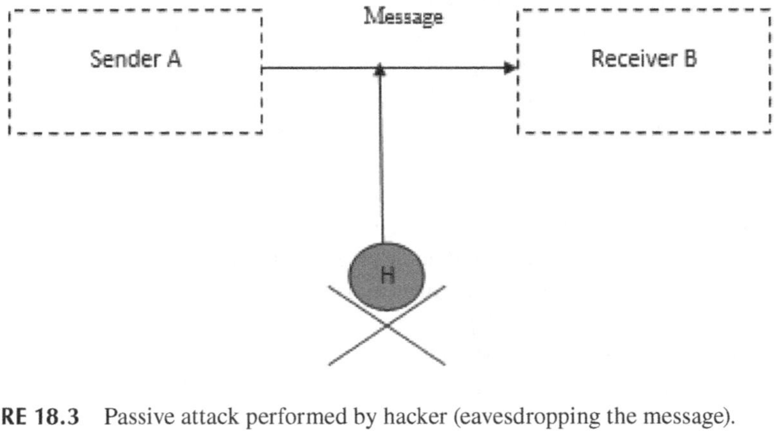

FIGURE 18.3 Passive attack performed by hacker (eavesdropping the message).

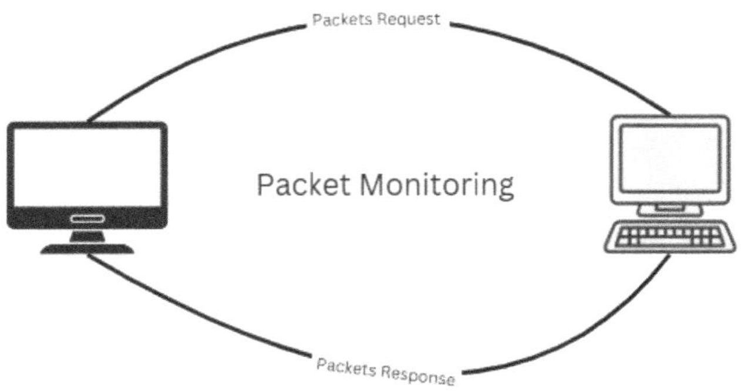

FIGURE 18.4 Packet monitoring.

infrastructural responsibility adopting best practices, avoiding malpractices with respect to the governing bodies and organizational sustainability strengthen the system, they must be aware that social well-being and ethically follow the compliance and resist with the unprofessional malpractices to the less vulnerable environment, therefore it can be resistance with the system access, file, and data theft information leak and such kind of accessibility avoidance. And make sure the organizational digital infrastructure must be accountable and secure. Figure 18.4 shows a schematic diagram illustrating packet monitoring in cybersecurity, depicting how network packets are captured and analyzed for security compliance and threat detection.

18.2.1 Ethical Frameworks in Cybersecurity

Ethical framework sanitizes the unethical and malpractices toward the organizational and social responsibility; it can provide resistance from the violation of ethics there must abide certain rules, policies, legitimate access, authentication, and authorization as per the user's level; there are certain policies, regulation and also based on the ethical framework on ethical code of conduct for the better way to [18, 19] organize the medium to big scale of infrastructure some of the ethical frameworks to avail the decision-making capability to break the malfunctioning the system. Figure 18.5 shows an illustration of a cybersecurity, expert actively monitoring malicious activity on servers, desktops, and network infrastructure, identifying potential threats.

1. **Deontological ethics (duty-based):** Deontological ethics based on Immanuel Kant's theory and idea is given for the action taken against the consequences in the organizational infrastructure for safeguarding the system, information, legitimate access, and ensure the environmental protection to provide a sustainable ecosystem for resisting the violation of cybersecurity rules and regulations and must make the legal, rules, policies,

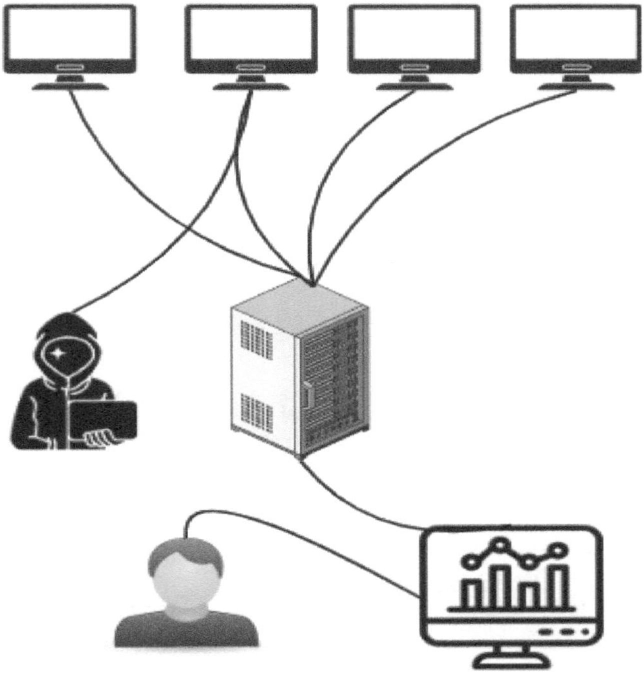

FIGURE 18.5 Cybersecurity expert monitoring the malicious activity.

and regulation for safeguarding the system for the violation of cybersecurity rules and regulations and must safeguarding the system and avoidance of break security and information violation and everyone ensure their duty toward the companies policies, USP, and their secret and confidential information must be secure and not violated by anyone. Figure 18.6 shows a comparative infographic displaying various ethical frameworks in cybersecurity, highlighting key regulatory standards and ethical considerations essential for preventing cyber violations.

2. **Utilitarian ethics (consequence-based):** Utilitarian ethics, a theory proposed by Jeremy Bentham and John Stuart Mill, is a consequence-oriented ethical framework that guides the assessment of organizational security vulnerabilities and risk management aimed at safeguarding the company. A security compliance manager plays a crucial role in maximizing the protection of the system while minimizing information security breaches and losses.

   Various security measures are applied to analyze system loopholes and vulnerabilities, including penetration testing to proactively identify weaknesses in the infrastructure. Detecting such vulnerabilities is critical, as they could lead to dangerous information leaks and breaches of confidentiality. Ultimately, the broader objective is to ensure the organization's overall security and protect its highly sensitive data.

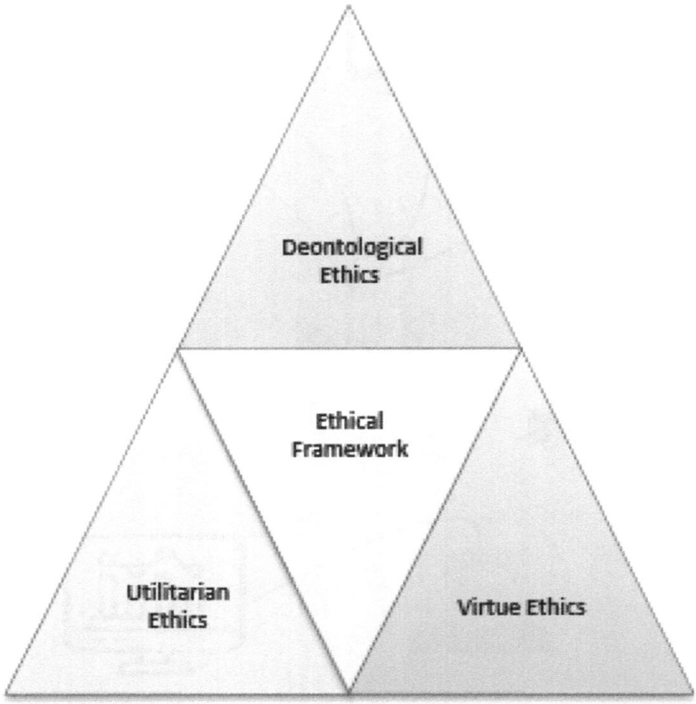

FIGURE 18.6 Ethical frameworks in cybersecurity.

3. **Virtue ethics (character-based):** Virtue-oriented ethics, as proposed by Aristotle, emphasize moral character and personal qualities grounded in the assessment and adherence to cyber laws, rules, and regulations. Individuals must embody values such as honesty, integrity, courage, willingness, wisdom, and responsibility. This ethical framework focuses on human characteristics that align with rules and regulations, ensuring actions are ethically and morally correct while complying with established standards.

   Accordingly, ethical considerations involve safeguarding organizational information security and privacy by never disclosing confidential information. Failure to respect the privacy and confidentiality of employees can lead to serious consequences.
4. **Ethical decision-making models in cybersecurity:** Ethical decision-making framework followed by certain rules and regulations for compliance with the safeguard of the system step by step. One frequent model is the identify-analyze-act approach:
   - Recognize ethical dilemmas and challenges by identifying the involved parties, relevant information, and potential risks. Utilize ethical frameworks such as utilitarianism, virtue ethics, and deontology to evaluate the situation. This step aids in weighing responsibilities, outcomes, and character-based considerations.

- Action: Make a decision, implement it, and review the outcome to gain insights for future actions.
- PAPA, an acronym for Privacy, Accuracy, Property, and Accessibility, is a popular cybersecurity framework that focuses on these four key ethical dimensions.
  - Privacy: Are personal information rights respected?
  - Accuracy: Ensuring the accuracy of data and holding individuals accountable for any mistakes.
  - Property: Determining data ownership and ensuring the rights of data owners are upheld.
  - Accessibility: Deciding who has access to the data and ensuring that access is granted fairly and equitably.

There are numerous issues facing to adopt ethical and professional considerations to imply the security standards and to balance the legitimacy and confidentiality among the professionals.

- Both frameworks provide the standard for cybersecurity procedures, and their experts create extensive security systems that can change threats and also support the organizations and industry to follow the best practices for compliance and legislation.

18.3 COMPLIANCE AND LEGAL REQUIREMENTS

Compliance and regulatory bodies must be required to ensure cybersecurity regulation toward the data protection, privacy, security, and legislation of government and non-government bodies, and a variety of laws and regulations to intact with the integrity of data and systems, Cybersecurity experts must be reachable with these frameworks to stay compliant.

Key compliance frameworks include the following:

- The General Data Protection Regulation (GDPR) is mandatory to extensive data protection and privacy requirements in the European Union organizations and must store and acknowledge the breaches within three days.
- Health Insurance Portability and accountability require healthcare organizations in the United States to secure sensitive health records from the hackers. There is a huge amount of health information record data. Payment Card Industry Data Security Standard (PCI DSS) enables security standards for organizations' credit card information, includes encrypted system, to access limits and monitoring.

18.3.1 Cybersecurity Professionals Must Understand the Ethics and Law

Cybersecurity professionals should understand and abide by the rules and promote the regulations to ensure the data is secure and avoid the legal penal charges for non-compliance. That is, ensuring that organizations not only to secure the data but also to comply with laws and rules.

18.4 ROLE OF CERTIFICATIONS (CISSP, CISM, AND CEH)

Certification is the most powerful asset to the industry standard, and the organization's ethical framework testifies to the rules and regulations and meets the compliance requirement of security standards:

- **Certified Information Systems Security Professional (CISSP):** Offered by **(ISC)^2**, CISSP is one of the most well-recognized cybersecurity certifications. It supports industry user management, access control, privileges [20] control and manage security regulations, and privacy management.
- **Certified Information Security Manager (CISM):** ISACA's CISM promotes the management and governance of security standards. Intent for the organization those who execute the plans, and information security programs, aligned with the security strategies for their business milestones.
- **Certified Ethical Hacker (CEH):** The EC-Council's CEH [20] certification is intended to identify the vulnerability and assessment tools having loopholes in the system and how can secure and prevent cybersecurity attacks and manage the policies as per security patches and up-to-date the system meet the current requirements.

These cybersecurity credentials play a massive role in the government and organization to handle and organize the digital system, prevent cybersecurity attacks, prevent the violation of the security standards, and meet compliance requirements.

18.5 PRIVACY AND ETHICAL CHALLENGES IN CYBERSECURITY

1. **Data protection:** It is of utmost importance to ensure that sensitive and personalized information is protected from unauthorized sources and misuse. The data must be limited for access to users which includes encryption of data and having [21, 22] control over the same to keep the data safe. There must be the presence of an accurate and complete date. This can be done through validation by checking whether the data received is proper or not. Only those people who can be relied upon must have access to the data and the system. There must be availability of backup and disaster recovery systems so that the data can be minimized or rather be completely ruled out.
2. **Ethical consequences:** This requires the privacy of an individual to be secured keeping in mind that the data must not be leaked in any condition. The explicit consent of the individual must be taken before gathering any kind of data. The individual must know for what purpose the data is used and to what extent this data will be used. There must be transparency in the use of data of an individual which must be communicated to the individual. The informed prior permission must be obtained. The data collection and information must be required and not the full information.

Data minimization can help in reducing the risk of breach. Instead of excessive data collection, only the important data can be obtained. These data retention procedures should adhere to legal and ethical frameworks. The individual has the right to delete their personal information. The organization must respect the privacy of an individual and not have any backup or residue of data that the individual does not want to retain. The individual has control over their information.

18.6 CHALLENGES IN AI AND MACHINE LEARNING IN CYBERSECURITY ABOUT MORALITY

1. **Biasness:** The recent advancements in artificial intelligence (AI) and machine learning can create biases weakening the fairness and efficiency of security control [23]. AI can be biased according to the data received by it leading to malpractice as well. For example, targeting a specific group on certain aspects can be biased toward the group posing a threat to individuals. Some AI models lack accountability or inaccuracy, due to which they should be transparent, accountable, and fair for the output.
2. **Privacy unease:** Sometimes, access to big data sets is required which contain personal information, which can be a privacy concern on using the data and scrutiny. Training for AI models is necessary for the compliance of privacy rules. The data collected must be secured and go through proper scrutiny. Data anonymization is one hundred percent effective, thereby leaving some chances of privacy breaches of data. The practitioners must be aware and specialized in the proper identification of hazards and the reliability of techniques.

18.7 SOCIAL ENGINEERING AND INSIDER THREATS

1. **Social engineering:** The theory of social engineering is that people can be more sensitive toward each other. This sensitivity tricks an individual into revealing the information, jeopardizing [24] the security of people. The use of misleading tactics to access unauthorized information raises concerns about the manipulation and autonomy of an individual. There need to be boundaries set to acceptable deceit. Ethical considerations include such kind of acquisition of data which needs transparency whenever possible. Such threats can damage the trust between the organization and individuals. Credibility is the key content of social engineering.
2. **Insider threats:** These threats are nothing but those individuals having access to information in an organization. They are insider threats. Insider threats need continuous monitoring so that any malevolent intentions can be avoided. Employee privacy rights must ensure the use of techniques is fair and proportionate. A culture of trust and responsibility is the key to avoiding unethical practices in an organization. Proper training can ensure the reduction of the danger of insider threats while upholding ethical standards.

In cybersecurity, a careful bridge can be created wherein the use of technology with care and caution must be the agenda followed by individuals. Effective strategies can lead to responsible ethical standards and data protection and security from insider threats. In the cybersecurity industry, fairness and respect for privacy are crucial to sustaining confidence and integrity.

18.8 EMERGING ETHICAL ISSUES IN CYBERSECURITY AND NATIONAL SECURITY: CYBERWARFARE

1. **Just war theory and cyberwarfare:** The just war theory is a doctrine of military ethics that aims at ensuring that a war is justiciable and ethical. The application of this theory in national security is a defensive step for a country. Cyberattacks should have a justifiable ground for attacking or being a threat to national security. Cyberwarfare is one of its kind which involves determining the ethical issues [25] of executing any cyberattack. The attack should not be with the purpose of financial gain or an aggressive mode of operation but an appropriation of threat. The threat must differentiate between the civilians and the military. The cyberattack on non-combatants is an unethical move and should not be practiced in any circumstances.
2. **Credibility and liability:** Cyberwarfare is very critical while understanding ethical issues. There are challenges with respect to the credibility and responsibility of the state. Cyberwarfare gives rise to retaliations, and this retaliation must be backed by some proof without which the morals cannot exist. The international standards and laws relating to warfare should be responsive to the unethical behaviors holding both state actors and no state actors credible to cyberwarfare.

18.9 THE ETHICS OF ENCRYPTION BACKDOORS

1. **Privacy vs. security:** The encryption backdoor entry questions the contradictions between privacy and security. Strong encryption protects the security of data, but the backdoor entry for these encryptions can jeopardize the privacy of an individual and permit unauthorized access to data. The investigators and government advocate for backdoor entry to support national security operations. This is an ethical dilemma to balance privacy and encroaching privacy through back door entry. There is a potential hazard to individuals.
2. **Risks of backdoors:** Another point to add to backdoor entry is exploitation of backdoors can be created. The malicious actors can exploit this encryption, thereby having a risk to the privacy. It increases the risk of unauthorized access to data. Technology cannot be trusted always. If violation of trust, the users may difficult to believe the system blindly., thereby being reluctant to share the information required for the data. The trust in the security system might be lost in totality.

18.10 ROLE OF CYBERSECURITY IN SAFEGUARDING CRITICAL INFRASTRUCTURE

1. **Ethical responsibility of cybersecurity professionals:** The experts have a moral responsibility to safeguard the vital infrastructure. It is the responsibility of professionals to save the infrastructure from cyber threats in finances, healthcare, power grids, etc. The well-being and public safety must be the priority of the professional. Operational needs should be seen in a way not to curtail public privacy or lessen security measures.
2. **Impact on public safety:** The different measures taken by the professionals have a major impact on the individuals. People are more concerned about their safety than the operational measures. It becomes more vital for the safety of the infrastructure as a concern for people. The threat detection must be quick action with strategical responses. Risk management works based on preventing disturbances that are at high risk of causing harm. Effective communication of potential dangers and mitigation actions is critical for gaining the trust of the public and regulating safety measures.

18.11 ETHICAL DILEMMAS IN HIGH-PROFILE CYBERSECURITY BREACHES

1. **Equifax data breach (2017):** Equifax data breach [26] of 2017 is one of the leading credit reporting agencies. It suffered a great breach of data as the personal information of millions of individuals was exposed. There was found to be a vulnerability in the Apache Struts web application which caused the breach. The hack was not revealed earlier, for which Equifax was criticized for not doing so. It was not notified or communicated to the public, raising transparency issues. The vulnerability could not be resolved timely, and the failure of prompt decisions brought forth the non-adherence to accountability toward cybersecurity ethics and professional standards.
2. **Yahoo data breach (2013–2014):** The famous case of the Yahoo data breach, in 2016, yahoo reported two significant data breaches affecting [27] around 500 million people. The breach was detected years later when the act to be found done by the state actors. Yahoo delayed taking any action regarding the same and failed to take ethical responsibility against the breach toward the stakeholders and users. The delay put the people at potential risk of data exploitation.
3. **Aadhaar data breach (2018):** Aadhaar is a biometric identification system that stores the data of an individual channeling public services. The data was made available online in 2018 causing the data breach of the entire nation due to the lack of a system. The data leak worries individuals for their privacy, security, and ethical standing of personal information. The national security was at risk at this point [28]. The government and third-party agencies were responsible for securing the data of citizens. The data breach led to a strict legal system in the country and protective data handling of information was the need of the hour. The case resulted in

the regulation data protection bill and the recent bill of 2021 which has increased the penalties of data breach.

4. **Zomato Data Leak (2017):** The biggest data leak of the millennia, the Zomato leak of 2017, the personal information of users was hacked and released in the dark web. The hack was acknowledged by the corporation and reassured the [29] customers that no financial information of the users was compromised. The issue of transparency occurred questioning whether Zomato is truthful in stating that no financial information was released. The corporation had to revise the ethical standards to recreate the trust of people. This contributes to increased user trust in Indian technological enterprises.

18.12 FAMOUS CASES OF WHISTLEBLOWING IN CYBERSECURITY

1. **Edward Snowden (2013):** Edward Snowden, a contractor in NSA, had exposed the surveillance program which was run globally by US intelligence. This program represented the agencies where the communication was made between people, without their knowledge. It contained classified information about the metadata. There was an ethical issue raised in this case with respect to the privacy and security of people.
2. **Chelsea Manning (2010):** Highly classified military activities, including videos of air strikes, were revealed by Chelsea Manning, and given to WikiLeaks. This disclosure raised the questions of ethical and national security of the United States. It endangered [30] the intelligence secret assets and information, which was a serious matter of accountability and professional standards. Though this leak was only to project immoral behavior during conflict, the issue gave way to ethical morality and a national security breach of the nation.
3. **Christopher Wylie and Cambridge Analytica (2018):** The case of Christopher Wylie, a former Cambridge Analytica employee, revealed that the company had gathered data from Facebook users without their consent so that it could influence the presidential elections [31] in 2016. He uncovered the truth of ethical dangers of using the personal data of people to manipulate them. This case has raised data breach concerns in a digital age where elections and public opinion can be manipulated. Such manipulation has given way to strict regulations and ethical framework to secure data. Whistleblowing is a critical way to reveal unethical practices which can incur serious legal consequences. There must be legislative safeguards for protection from such cyberattacks.

18.13 DEVELOPING ETHICAL LEADERSHIP IN CYBERSECURITY AND NATIONAL SECURITY

1. **Ethical leadership:** It is a guiding principle for an organization to give more weightage to decision-making, integrity, and transparency and have a

balance between security and public accountability. The leaders must have insights to deal with the complications of privacy abuse and data breaches. It promotes integrity and trust for national security and cybersecurity. The stakeholders and public benefited from such balance have a feeling of security in the nation. It is the responsibility of the leaders to set such professional standards that can resolve the issues of cyberattacks and reduce the risk to national security. The ethical leaders take the decisions going beyond the ambit of the law. It follows moral values even though the law might be ambiguous or may not apply directly to cybersecurity. There needs to be parity between privacy and security by ethical leaders, only then there can be professional standards for national security and cybersecurity. For instance, using the surveillance tool for data collection must be verified so that such kind of information does not violate the code of conduct. There can be a safe environment for all the people involved in the team so that they can be free to report any kind of fraudulent acts or unethical norms.

18.14 BUILDING ETHICAL CULTURES WITHIN CYBERSECURITY TEAMS AND ORGANIZATIONS

1. **Forming ethical framework:** Establishment of a good framework that has acceptable conduct regarding data protection, privacy, and cybersecurity. A formal validity is the need to edifice the ethical culture in an organization. This includes rules and regulations that govern the use of technology in the cyber world and the security of data along with maintaining sensitive data protection and confidentiality. There can be often data breaches and cyberattacks, wherein the team of Ethical Incident Management must undertake strict mechanisms and decision-making standards very cautiously and seriously.
2. **Encouraging ethical workplace culture:** Good leadership is creating an environment for individuals on the team to be credible for professional behavior. To cater to this culture, a leader must have positive conduct toward others so that the employees can sustain and appreciate the ethical norms. It leads to good decision-making and contributes to the proper operations of individuals responsible for minimizing cybersecurity. There can be seen as an ethical grid which has an important role to play in an organization.

18.15 TRAINING AND EDUCATION FOR CYBERSECURITY AND FORENSICS PROFESSIONALS

1. **The need for ethics training in cybersecurity:** The growing development and advancement of technology and the rapidness of complex issues are crucial for professionals for their training to deal with the ethical problems arising from cybersecurity and digital forensics.
2. **Ethics training in digital forensics:** Digital forensics can make all the digital footprints consolidation and make the ethics for the consideration

of ethical framework to resist the violation of privacy and secrecy of information and data. Such data plays a vital role in catching the evidence. To avert data tampering and misrepresentation in courts of law, there must be various guidelines to maintain the integrity of digital evidence in the court through proper professional standards. It is the expertise of forensic professionals to investigate the crime scene properly while keeping in mind the rights of privacy of an individual. There shall be restrictions on the disclosure of data of an individual. In certain cases, there must be trained leaders to address the issues related to privacy and ethical investigation.

3. **Constant professional ethical enhancement:** The ambit of digital forensics and cybersecurity has broadened with time. The experts must have quality training with new evolving problems regarding ethics and emerging technologies. This continued training must be aligned with the new advancements in machine learning, AI blockchain, etc. The increasing scope of AI has been integrated into cybersecurity. This integration can bring violations of privacy if used without meticulous professionalism [5]. There must be ethics focusing on the utilization of cybersecurity [8] and digital forensics in a manner to not disrupt the encryption standards and open new frontiers for cybersecurity. The states must be prepared for any kind of concerns raised while there is a use of cybersecurity operations. It is vital to have secured interconnections to protect national security [16]. There must exist a developed system for securing the integrity and transparency of the nation. The experts need to be well prepared to have a good ethical standard to deal with the issues in the digital era and set an example for others which can lead to better frameworks in society. Ethical guidance always remains a strong pillar of credibility and confidentiality which protects privacy [32] and security of the nation.

18.16 CONCLUSION

Looking at the bright future of digital forensics, cybersecurity, and national security, it becomes even more necessary to create a balance between advanced technologies and maintaining professional standards. The increasing innovations in technology are constantly reshaping the methodologies and tools that can be applied to maintain the privacy and security of people. The changing era poses difficulties for ethical leadership responsibility toward professional standards, being the foremost requirement of cybersecurity, national security, and digital forensics. Government agencies will have to foresee the future with the ethical establishment with the growing difficulties of dangers arising from the cyber world and extreme reliance on technology across the nation. The administration [6] of the country can have advanced cybersecurity systems and forensic experts to manage ethical difficulties regarding data privacy, transparency, and surveillance. The adaptability of the ethical framework including AI and computing must be taken care of to maintain professional standards [3] of integrity, public interest [11], and accountability. Forensic experts strike the balance between justice and the protection of privacy. The new reforms and enactments are necessary to be brought forth to have a pecuniary technique that can be more sophisticated and is not invasive. National security brings a sense of interconnectedness between countries [21], which needs careful evaluation and a balance to curb terrorism [18] in its entirety.

The digital system available globally is expanding at a greater rate which is bringing the entire world under one bracket. There can be seen individuals, different organizations, and governments have come together for the growth of digitalization. The interconnection between the countries will eliminate the problems of cyberattacks, international privacy standards, data protection, cross-border data sharing, etc. There shall be expertise required for these purposes which can bring ethical examination into question, which can be broadened to the national borders countries. The new inventions of software and the advent of AI are raising ethical concerns which are weakening the encryption standards and widespread identification threats. The nations must develop standards and guidance so that a moral decision that can protect individuals' confidence can be established. Cyberwarfare [15] and cyberattacks can be seen used frequently against other countries posing a threat to national security. This requires urgent attention to develop professional standards [24]. There is also need for trained professionals with experience in combating cybersecurity.

The future of cybersecurity, digital forensics, and national security lies in the hands of effective ethical frameworks to necessitate the human rights of individuals. As there is immense development in digitalization, a strong progressive technological discipline in this regard needs to do for the benefit of society and its security.

REFERENCES

1. Cybersecurity and Digital Forensics. (2024). In lecture notes in networks and systems. https://doi.org/10.1007/978-981-99-9811-1
2. Apau, R., & Koranteng, F. N. (2020). An overview of the digital forensic investigation infrastructure of Ghana. Forensic Science International Synergy, 2, 299–309. https://doi.org/10.1016/j.fsisyn.2020.10.002
3. Jacobs, N., Brewer, S., Craigon, P. J., Frey, J., Gutierrez, A., Kanza, S., Manning, L., Munday, S., Pearson, S., & Sacks, J. (2021). Considering the ethical implications of digital collaboration in the food sector. Patterns, 2(11), 100335. https://doi.org/10.1016/j.patter.2021.100335
4. Burr, C., Taddeo, M., & Floridi, L. (2020). The ethics of digital well-being: A thematic review. Science and Engineering Ethics, 26(4), 2313–2343. https://doi.org/10.1007/s11948-020-00175-8
5. Van Hooren, R. H., Van Den Borne, B. W., Curfs, L. M. G., & Widdershoven, G. A. M. (2007). Ethics of prevention: An interactive computer-tailored program. Scandinavian Journal of Public Health, 35(5), 503–509.
6. Vallor, S. (2010). Social networking technology and the virtues. Ethics and Information Technology, 12(2), 157–170.
7. Shahriari, K., & Shahriari, M. (2017). IEEE standard review — Ethically aligned design: A vision for prioritizing human wellbeing with artificial intelligence and autonomous systems. In Presented at the 2017 IEEE Canada international humanitarian technology conference (IHTC) (pp. 197–201). https://ieeexplore.ieee.org/document/8058187
8. Mahoney, D. F., Purtilo, R. B., Webbe, F. M., Alwan, M., Bharucha, A. J., Adlam, T. D., et al. (2007). In-home monitoring of persons with dementia: Ethical guidelines for technology research and development. Alzheimer's & Dementia, 3(3), 217–226.

9. Formosa, P., Wilson, M., & Richards, D. (2021). A principlist framework for cybersecurity ethics. Computers & Security, 109, 102382. https://doi.org/10.1016/j.cose.2021.102382
10. Fenech, J., Richards, D., & Formosa, P. (2024). Ethical principles shaping values-based cybersecurity decision-making. Computers & Security, 140, 103795. https://doi.org/10.1016/j.cose.2024.103795
11. Cremer, F., Sheehan, B., Fortmann, M., Kia, A. N., Mullins, M., Murphy, F., & Materne, S. (2022). Cyber risk and cybersecurity: A systematic review of data availability. The Geneva Papers on Risk and Insurance. Issues and Practice, 47(3), 698–736. https://doi.org/10.1057/s41288-022-00266-6
12. Macnish, K., & Van Der Ham, J. (2020). Ethics in cybersecurity research and practice. Technology in Society, 63, 101382. https://doi.org/10.1016/j.techsoc.2020.101382
13. Macnish, K. (2020). Privacy in research ethics. In Iphofen, R. (Ed.), Handbook of research ethics and scientific integrity. Springer, Cham. https://doi.org/10.1007/978-3-030-16759-2_9
14. Agre, P. E. (1998). Introduction. In: Agre, P. E & Rotenberg, M. (Eds.), Technology and privacy: The new landscape (pp. 1–28). The MIT Press, Cambridge, MA/London, at 7.
15. Boyce, M. W., Duma, K. M., & Hettinger, L. J. (2011). Human performance in cybersecurity: A research agenda. Proceedings of the Human Factors and Ergonomics Society Annual Meeting, 55(1),1115–1119. https://doi.org/10.1177/1071181311551233
16. Loi, M., & Christen, M. (2020). Ethical frameworks for cybersecurity. In The international library of ethics, law and technology (pp. 73–95). https://doi.org/10.1007/978-3-030-29053-5_4
17. Landwehr, C., Boneh, D., Mitchell, J. C., Bellovin, S. M., Landau, S., & Lesk, M. E. (2012). Privacy and cybersecurity: The next 100 years. Proceedings of the IEEE, 100(Special Centennial Issue), 1659–1673. https://doi.org/10.1109/jproc.2012.2189794
18. Resnik, D. B., & Finn, P. R. (2017). Ethics and phishing experiments. Science and Engineering Ethics, 24(4), 1241–1252. https://doi.org/10.1007/s11948-017-9952-9
19. Berkel, H., Estmann, C., & Rand, J. (2022). Local governance quality and law compliance: The case of Mozambican firms. World Development, 157, 105942. https://doi.org/10.1016/j.worlddev.2022.105942
20. ByteHide. (2024, April 30). CISM vs CISSP: The Ultimate Comparison 2024. DEV Community. https://dev.to/bytehide/cism-vs-cissp-the-ultimate-comparison-2024-5b4c
21. The role of cybersecurity in securing critical infrastructure – Intelligent CIO Europe. (2024, April 22). Intelligent CIO Europe. https://www.intelligentcio.com/eu/2024/04/22/the-role-of-cybersecurity-in-securing-critical-infrastructure/
22. Protecting the cybersecurity of critical infrastructures and their supply chains. (2024). In ICC Working Paper. https://docs-library.unoda.org/Open-Ended_Working_Group_on_Information_and_Communication_Technologies_-_%282021%29/ICC-2024_Protecting-the-cybersecurity-of-critical-infrastructures-and-their-supply-chains.pdf
23. Ethical Issues Related to Data Privacy and Security: Why We Must Balance Ethical and Legal Requirements in the Connected World – IEEE Digital Privacy. (n.d.). https://digitalprivacy.ieee.org/publications/topics/ethical-issues-related-to-data-privacy-and-security-why-we-must-balance-ethical-and-legal-requirements-in-the-connected-world
24. Social Engineering and Insider Threats. (2017, October 1). IEEE Conference Publication | IEEE Xplore. https://ieeexplore.ieee.org/document/8250331/
25. Sethi, N., Thakur, A., & Lok Sabha Secretariat. (2017). CYBER WARFARE AND NATIONAL SECURITY CHALLENGES. In MEMBERS' REFERENCE SERVICE [Report LARRDIS]. https://www.studocu.com/in/document/university-of-allahabad/bachelor-of-law/cyber-warfare-and-national-security-challenges-rn-refjuly2017/122953649
26. Equifax Data Breach Settlement. (2024, July 24). Federal Trade Commission. https://www.ftc.gov/enforcement/refunds/equifax-data-breach-settlement

27. Daswani, N., & Elbayadi, M. (2021). The Yahoo breaches of 2013 and 2014. In Big breaches. Apress, Berkeley, CA. https://doi.org/10.1007/978-1-4842-6655-7_7
28. ETtech. (2023, October 31). Aadhaar data leak | Personal data of 81.5 crore Indians on sale on dark web: Report. *The Economic Times*. https://economictimes.indiatimes.com/tech/technology/aadhar-data-leak-personal-data-of-81-5-crore-indians-on-sale-on-dark-web-report/articleshow/104856898.cms?from=mdr
29. Zomato Acknowledges Breach Affecting 17 Million. (n.d.). https://www.bankinfosecurity.asia/zomato-acknowledges-breach-affecting-17-million-a-9934
30. The Chelsea Manning Case: A Timeline | ACLU. (2023, February 27). American Civil Liberties Union. https://www.aclu.org/news/free-speech/chelsea-manning-case-timeline
31. Hern, A. (2018, May 7). Cambridge Analytica: How did it turn clicks into votes? *The Guardian*. https://www.theguardian.com/news/2018/may/06/cambridge-analytica-how-turn-clicks-into-votes-christopher-wylie
32. Choi, J. P., & Fershtman, C. (2005, October). Internet Security, Vulnerability Disclosure and Software Provision. CEPR Discussion Paper No. 5269, Available at SSRN: https://ssrn.com/abstract=843709

19 Evidence Presentation, Real-World Case Studies, and Courtroom Testimony in Cybersecurity Cases

Vijaya Kittu Manda and Renuka Lenka

19.1 INTRODUCTION TO EVIDENCE PRESENTATION

19.1.1 Definition and Importance of Evidence Presentation in Cybercrime

Cybercrime is often associated with phrases such as "computer-related crimes," "cybercrime," and "high-tech crime." It denotes various offenses committed through or against computer systems and communications networks (Ciobanu, 2020; Babanina et al., 2021). Academic researchers classified cybercrimes into the following topologies: cyber-trespass, cyber-deception/theft, cyber-pornography and obscenity, and cyber violence (Barnor & Patterson, 2022). While controlling cybercrime is one challenge, investigating and bringing cybercriminals to justice is another. Evidence management and presentation are crucial to cybercrime investigations (forensic analysis) and prosecutions (legal adjudication). It plays a vital role in establishing guilt or innocence and ensuring the fair administration of justice (Harshwardhan et al., 2022). Digital evidence forms the backbone of cybercrime investigations. It comes with unique challenges regarding its collection, preservation, analysis, and presentation.

The definition of "evidence" varies across jurisdictions. However, it generally refers to information or objects that tend to prove or disprove a fact. Evidence is required in handling cybercrime cases for the reconstruction of events and the identification of perpetrators. The evidence can be electronic records, digital devices, network logs, and other forms of data. Building trust in forensic science is important because a sense of distrust exists because of four factors (Table 19.1) (Kapageorgiadou, 2024).

19.1.2 Background and Context

The background and context of evidence presentation are rooted in the principles of logic, rhetoric, and epistemology. They have evolved over centuries of legal practice. The origins of evidence presentation can be traced back to ancient Greece and Rome.

 DOI: 10.1201/9781003497868-19

TABLE 19.1
Reasons for Distrust of Forensic Science

Factor	Description
Perception	Public trust gets impacted due to negative presentation or misinterpretation by the media. Sometimes, this is a consequence of cybersecurity professionals not paying attention to explaining science in an easy-to-understand manner, especially to the court (Furnell, 2020).
Process	The public does not easily understand the forensics processes because of the opaque process. Inconsistent practices complicate further (G. Sarkar et al., 2023).
Miscarriage of Justice	Lack of technical knowledge and human effort by frontline officers can lead to improper evidence handling, eventually leading to a miscarriage of justice (Nelufule et al., 2024).
Resources	Insufficient and inconsistent funding and the unavailability of a skilled workforce can lead to limited resources and disallows active policing (Haque et al., 2023).

During those days, legal proceedings were governed by strict evidence and argumentation rules, though "fairness" was given more importance, and the courts sometimes took exceptions (Harris, 2013). Over time, these principles were refined and codified in various legal systems, which gave rise to modern evidentiary standards and practices. Over time, the importance shifted slightly from rules to reasons and more of an interdisciplinary approach (Roberts, 2023), questioning the sustainability of traditional evidence law (Wang, 2020). The present era is the digital age, with the legal system moving toward digitization using Information and Communication Technologies (ICT) such as electronic case processing. Research reports that doing so reduces court burden and enhances justice, especially for adjudication and enforcement (Castelliano et al., 2023). Cybercrimes themselves are constantly evolving (Babanina et al., 2021). Evidence presentation has taken on new dimensions.

The presentation of digital evidence in cybercrime investigations has become increasingly complex. It requires an understanding of the legal, technical, and procedural frameworks. A thorough understanding and subject expertise are necessary at different investigation levels – collection, analysis, and presentation. Recently, there has been an apparent increase in cyberattacks, data breaches, and other cyber-enabled criminal activity – a proportionate increase in experts for effective evidence presentation in legal proceedings is also naturally required. The digital nature of these crimes poses significant challenges for investigators because complexities will come when handling digital forensics, network protocols, and data storage systems. Further, law researchers established that oral expert evidence and cross-examination are inevitable in cases involving foreign law owing to its complexity and novelty (Ward & Plenderleith Ferguson, 2024).

The legal system and processes surrounding digital evidence are evolving rapidly due to technological changes. Courts are dealing with issues that were earlier considered difficult or even impossible. Some examples include the admissibility of digital evidence, the reliability of digital forensic tools, and the burden of proof in cybercrime cases. Considering these new developments, investigators, lawyers, and judges must stay up-to-date with the latest developments in digital evidence presentation.

Over time, they will probably use advanced analytics, machine learning (ML), and artificial intelligence (AI) to analyze and present complex digital evidence.

19.1.3 Challenges of Presenting Technical Evidence

Several challenges arise when investigators, lawyers, legal counsel, judges, and juries present technical evidence in cybersecurity. These challenges must be addressed because the case outcome will depend on them. The gap between technical expertise and legal understanding must be bridged (Kaur, 2014). Technical evidence requires a high level of specialized knowledge. Converting or translating technical terms is generally tricky, especially for non-technical stakeholders. A deep understanding of the technology and the legal context in which the evidence will be presented is required. So, the person dealing with and presenting the evidence would typically come from a multi-disciplinary background.

Evidence presentation from cloud-based systems (Khachatryan, 2022), IoT devices (Chougule et al., 2022), or encrypted communications demands specialized expertise and tools. These are often beyond the basic levels of computer knowledge and know-how. New technologies and software are continually being developed to deal with pre- and post-attack. The increasing cybersecurity threats and their complexity make it more challenging. Further, this is a dynamic and rapidly evolving field. Newer techniques are emerging at a faster pace than before. Sometimes, even experts find it challenging to stay current with the pace of technological developments, let alone the courts. Proving the authenticity and reliability of technical evidence can also be a challenge. Hence, collecting, preserving, and presenting evidence in a way that maintains integrity is crucial (Miha & Pekmezi, 2024). Only then can the evidence become admissible and weighted in court.

Another risk is that there can be misinterpretation or miscommunication of technical evidence. Technical experts often use jargon or technical terms. It is a part of their regular vocabulary. Research shows that readability has decreased, and jargon usage has increased over the years. However, these terms will be unfamiliar and challenging for non-technical individuals to understand and comprehend. Hence, the evidence is prone to misunderstandings or misinterpretations. Further, the presentation of technical evidence must be clear, concise, and logically organized. By doing so, its relevance and significance can be effectively conveyed.

The expertise of investigators or lawyers and the tools and technologies they use will influence the presentation of technical evidence (Nelufule et al., 2024). It also potentially impacts the credibility and reliability of the evidence. It is typical human nature to build biases over time. Technical experts are no different. They may have their own biases and assumptions. The legal proceedings are generally adversarial, meaning that an opposing or confronting approach between parties is involved. This approach would further increase the bias of the experts. They may feel pressure to present their evidence in a way that supports their client's position.

Cybercrimes are global and happen broadly. Attackers mask their physical location and operate from a different geographical location where law enforcement forces do not have jurisdiction (Chen et al., 2023). No wonder researchers began mapping the global geography of cybercrime with the World Cybercrime Index (Bruce et al., 2024). From an investigation and judicial point of view, the global nature of crimes brings jurisdictional complexities into play. Cybercrimes are significantly underreported, adding to the difficulties of gathering evidence and following the investigation procedures and processes (Baror et al., 2020). It requires following varying legal standards and admissibility criteria across different regions. The quantum (volume) of information (and data) generated daily is enormous, bringing logistical hurdles. Effective data reduction and visualization techniques are required to extract relevant evidence from such datasets. Visual aids can help by summarizing data in an easy-to-understand pictorial format. Diagrams and flowcharts can help facilitate the presentation of technical evidence. However, misinterpreting is always possible if they are not correctly understood.

On the other hand, oversimplification of terms might undermine the severe nature of the evidence. So, there is a need to balance technical accuracy with legal and procedural requirements. Effective communication strategies are essential at this juncture. Investigators, lawyers, and judges who regularly deal with cybersecurity cases should receive periodic specialized training programs to learn and catch up with developments in the cybersecurity world.

19.2 FOUNDATIONS OF EVIDENCE PRESENTATION

19.2.1 Types of Evidence in Cybercrime Cases

Modern criminal law gives importance to evidence-based sentencing (EBS). The quality of the scientific evidence on which EBS is based and the available data on the extent to which it achieves (or does not) its intended goals are of interest to legal researchers (Martínez-Garay, 2023). Evidence presentation is essential in establishing the facts of a cybercrime case. These are necessary to prove the guilt or innocence of the accused. Dealing with evidence in cybercrimes is a complex process. Cybercrime investigations and prosecutions often use a combination of two types of evidence to establish the elements of the crime and identify the perpetrator (Shanker, 2024):

1. Digital evidence, which includes all forms of electronic records
2. Documentary evidence

Digital evidence is information stored or transmitted in an electronic format that is used in an investigation. It is often volatile and easily modifiable, so collecting and preserving it forensically sound is crucial to ensure its integrity and admissibility in court. Examples of digital evidence are presented in Figure 19.1.

Documentary evidence refers to written or printed materials that can be used to prove a fact in an issue. Documentary evidence can provide context and support for the digital evidence, helping to establish the timeline of events, identify the perpetrator, and prove the defendant's intent. Examples of Documentary evidence are presented in Figure 19.2.

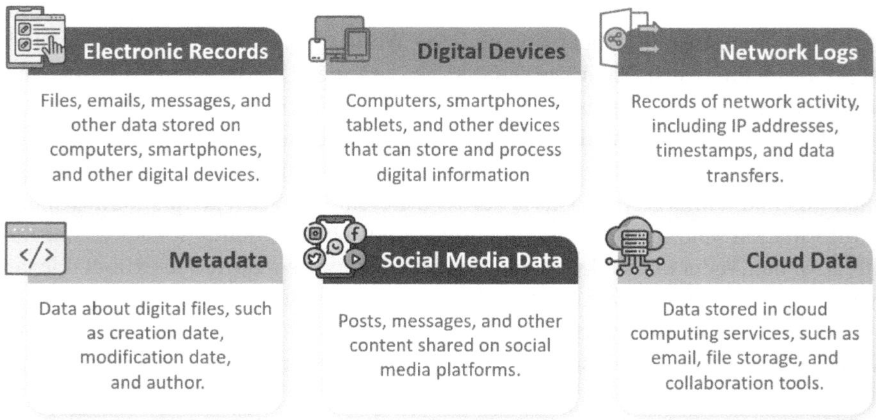

FIGURE 19.1 Examples of digital evidence.

There are two popular broad types of evidence – digital and documentary evidence. Both these types play a vital role in cybercrime investigations and prosecutions. Besides the above two, other forms of evidence are relevant to cybercrime cases. Various types of digital evidence collected in cybercrime cases are shown in Figure 19.3.

Apart from these, expert testimony from forensic experts, cybersecurity professionals, and other experts may be necessary to interpret and analyze the evidence. The presentation of evidence in cybercrime cases calls for comprehensive expertise in the technical and legal aspects of the case. Further, the presenter must communicate complex technical information effectively to a non-technical audience. Law enforcement and prosecutors should focus on increasing the likelihood of a successful outcome and ensuring justice. This is possible by effectively collecting, preserving, and presenting these types of evidence.

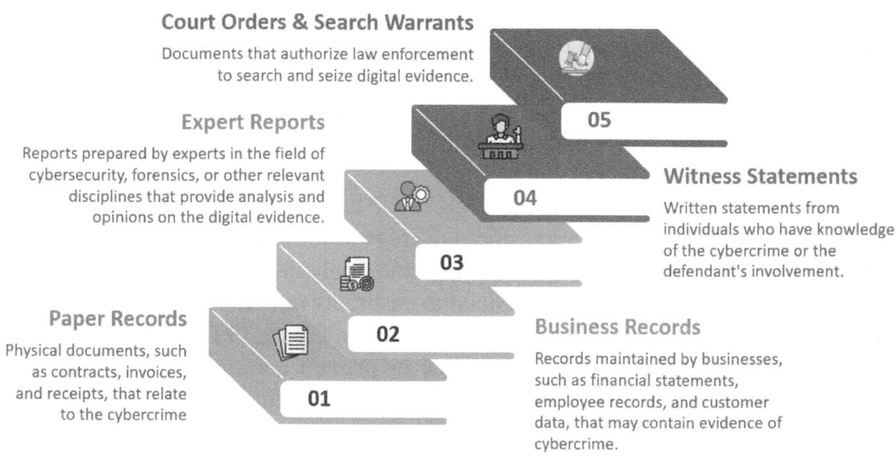

FIGURE 19.2 Examples of documentary evidence.

FIGURE 19.3 Various types of digital evidence collected in cybercrimes.

19.2.2 Legal Frameworks for Admissibility of Digital Evidence

A complex set of legal frameworks controls the acceptability of digital evidence in courts. Of course, these frameworks are still evolving. Further, they vary across jurisdictions. There are three fundamental aspects of the admissibility of evidence – authentication, reliability, and relevance. accuracy, trustworthiness, and verifiability further explain the reliability of evidence. These are shown in Figure 19.4.

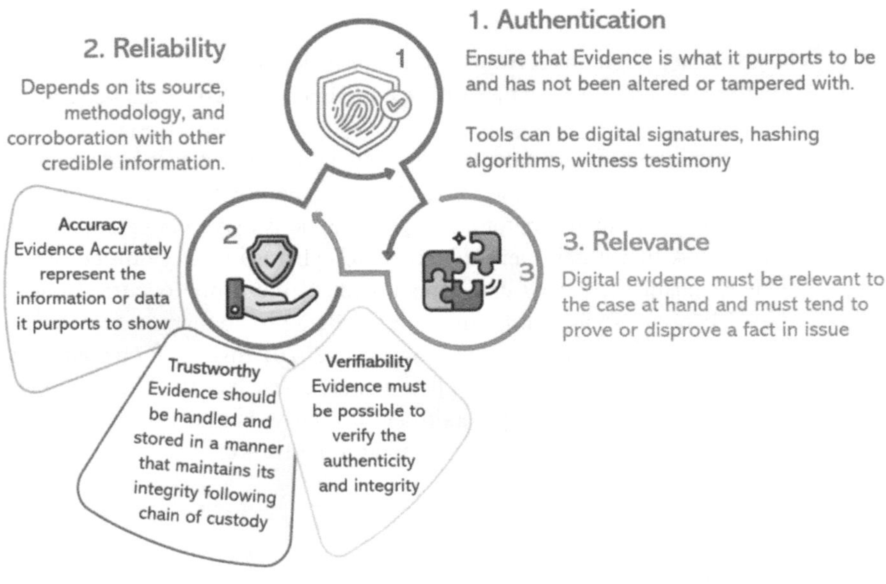

FIGURE 19.4 Fundamental aspects of admissibility of evidence.

Cybercriminals are subjected to domestic (country-specific) or international laws (B. Sarkar et al., 2023). In the United States, the Federal Rules of Evidence (FRE) govern the admissibility of digital evidence in federal courts. Rule 901 of FRE deals with authentication and identification requirements of evidence. Evidence can be claimed through direct testimony, circumstantial evidence, or other means. Along with the FRE, the Electronic Communications Privacy Act (ECPA) and the Computer Fraud and Abuse Act (CFAA) also play essential roles in shaping the legal framework for digital evidence. The ECPA regulates the interception and disclosure of electronic communications. The CFAA criminalizes unauthorized access to computer systems. The Daubert standard and Frye test assess digital forensic methodologies' reliability and scientific validity.

The UK's digital evidence handling and admissibility guidelines are through the Police and Criminal Evidence Act 1984 (PACE) and the Criminal Justice Act 2003. Some critical legislations in India regarding this are Bharatiya Sakshya Adhiniyam (earlier The Indian Evidence Act), the Information Technology Act, 2000, The Information Technology (Reasonable Security Practices and Procedures and Sensitive Personal Data or Information) Rules, 2011, Information Technology (Preservation and Retention of Information by Intermediaries Providers) Rules, 2021, The Information Technology (Intermediary Guidelines and Digital Media Ethics Code) Rules, 2021, and Cybercrime Prevention Amendment Rules, 2018. Similarly, Indonesia's Electronic and Transactions Law (EIT Law) is a noteworthy mention (Mahrina et al., 2023).

19.2.2.1 Understanding Jurisdiction

Cybercrime often goes beyond national borders. It requires understanding the jurisdictional issues involved in collecting and using digital evidence. Jurisdictional issues can also arise in digital evidence in two main circumstances:

1. When evidence is obtained from multiple jurisdictions or
2. When the accused is located in a different jurisdiction from the crime scene.

In such cases, courts must consider the laws and regulations of each jurisdiction to determine which laws apply (Moussa, 2021). Courts generally have jurisdiction over crimes that occur within their territory, though exceptions exist. For example, some countries have laws that allow them to prosecute cybercrimes committed against their citizens or businesses. This can happen even if the crime occurred outside their borders. There are some conflicting areas in data protection and law enforcement regarding Digital Law in EU and US (Shurson, 2020). Investigation complexity arises when countries move out of a jurisdictional area – such as the UK moving out of the EU (Shurson, 2020). Investigators today use cross-border criminal forensic measures (Zhang & Gong, 2024). Some techniques in this are:

1. Public extraction
2. Remote electronic data inspection
3. Real-time monitoring

Of course, there is always a lingering question about potential data sovereignty and judicial violations in such measures. Jurisdictional complexities arise when digital evidence spans multiple geographic locations or involves cloud-based data. The Budapest Convention on Cybercrime provides a framework for international cooperation in cybercrime investigations. It promotes cross-border evidence collection and preservation. However, there are conflicting data protection regulations as well. For example, the EU's General Data Protection Regulation (GDPR) and the US CLOUD Act can impede transnational digital evidence acquisition. Jurisdiction and Legislation conflicts might become glaringly visible during joint operations or international law enforcement cooperation (Billow, 2023).

19.2.2.2 Chain of Custody and Documentation

The prosecution must explain that the evidence is handled correctly so that they can support the conduction of the inquiry (Horsman, 2022). The evidence might have to be subjected to reliable tests to ensure this. The chain of custody is the sequence of events that documents the handling and storage of evidence from when it is collected until it is presented in court (Geldenhuys Kotie, 2024). This includes the identification of all individuals who have handled the evidence and the storage and transportation of the evidence. Maintaining a proper chain of custody for digital evidence ensures its integrity and admissibility in court. The chain of custody documents the movement of the evidence from the point of collection to the point of presentation in court. It should include the following information:

1. Who collected the evidence?
2. When and where was the evidence collected?
3. How was the evidence stored and transported?
4. Who had access to the evidence?
5. Any changes made to the evidence?

Comprehensive logging of all interactions with digital objects is necessary – from seizure to analysis and presentation. This documentation will include:

1. Timestamps
2. Personnel involved (login id)
3. Actions performed
4. Environmental conditions during evidence handling.

Digital signatures and cryptographic hashing techniques are employed to verify the authenticity and immutability of evidence throughout the forensic process. The principle of "forensic soundness" speaks about the admissibility of digital evidence (Casey, 2010). Forensic processes should not alter the original data. Write-blockers and hardware-based imaging solutions can be used to create forensically sound duplicates of storage media. The concept of "best evidence" in digital forensics often refers to the closest available copy of the original data, as direct examination of original devices may compromise evidence integrity.

Challenges in digital evidence admissibility include the dynamic nature of electronic data, the potential for remote alteration or deletion, and the complexity of cloud-based services. Courts have grappled with issues such as the admissibility of social media content, blockchain-based evidence, and data recovered from encrypted devices. The legal landscape is getting complicated because of the ongoing debate surrounding decryption and Fifth Amendment protections against self-incrimination.

In order to establish the reliability of digital evidence, forensic tool validation and error rate assessment are done. As a part of this, the standards set by organizations are to be used. Doing so increases the credibility of forensic methodologies. Some organizations involved in this are the Scientific Working Group on Digital Evidence (SWGDE) and the International Organization on Computer Evidence (IOCE). Expert witnesses must demonstrate the scientific validity of their techniques and articulate potential limitations or sources of error. Unfortunately, there is no proper standardization for sample collection. This led to inconsistent and arbitrary practices, mainly chemical, biological, radiological, nuclear, and explosive (CBRNE). Significant efforts are to be put into Digital Custody Management (DCM) to ensure the process at the custody transfer points (CTPs). A suitable Digital Chain of Custody (dCoC) process should address challenges related to metadata standardization. It should promptly trigger alert messages to stakeholders to monitor the custodianship of the evidence items (Pestana & Sofou, 2024). In (Interpol, 2020)'s *Guide for Criminal Justice Statistics on Cybercrime and Electronic Evidence*, the capability of criminal justice authorities to understand better, measure, and address cybercrime through statistical data is discussed.

The principle of proportionality in digital evidence collection balances the need for comprehensive data acquisition against privacy concerns and resource constraints. Courts increasingly scrutinize the scope and methods of digital searches, requiring investigators to justify broad seizures and subsequent analysis of electronic data. Filing proper documentation and reports is also crucial in digital forensic examination to support the chain of custody (Horsman, 2021). This documentation should include:

1. Photographs of the crime scene and evidence
2. Notes and reports from law enforcement officers and forensic examiners
3. Laboratory reports and other analytical results

By following the legal frameworks and best practices, law enforcement and prosecutors can increase the likelihood that digital evidence will be admissible in court and used to prosecute cybercrimes successfully.

19.2.3 Preparing and Presentation for Effective Evidence Presentation

Preparing to present digital evidence in a courtroom requires an understanding of the legal audience and the specific requirements of the case. The presentation should be well-structured. It can significantly impact the weight and relevance of the evidence. To ensure effective presentation, cybersecurity professionals should (Budde et al., 2023):

1. Presenting the evidence logically and coherently is essential. So, a clear and concise narrative is to be developed. The narrative should explain the significance of the digital evidence and its relevance to the case.
2. Utilizing visual aids, such as timeline reconstructions, network diagrams, charts, graphs, data flow charts, and other diagrams, can help illustrate complex technical concepts and facilitate understanding for non-technical audiences.
3. Work and efforts are to anticipate potential objections and build cross-examination strategies. The specific focus is on the admissibility of the evidence and preparing counterarguments. This background work will pro-actively help address counterarguments. It strengthens the credibility and persuasiveness of expert testimony.
4. Prepare to answer questions from the judge, jury, and opposing counsel as clearly and concisely as possible. It is important to rehearse the presentation to be smooth and lead to a confident delivery.

Demonstrative exhibits such as sanitized log files and packet capture analyses can be used. Such things can significantly enhance comprehension of cyber incidents. Moreover, developing a lexicon that bridges technical jargon with legal terminology is essential. It facilitates clear communication between expert witnesses and legal professionals.

19.2.3.1 Understanding the Legal Audience

Knowing the audience and their expectations is vital for cybersecurity professionals when presenting digital evidence. The legal audience typically comprises individuals with varying levels of technical expertise. They can be judges, attorneys, jurors, and opposing counsel. Evidence presentation should be customized based on the audience can help. A few points on how cybersecurity professionals effectively communicate with the court audience are shown in Figure 19.5.

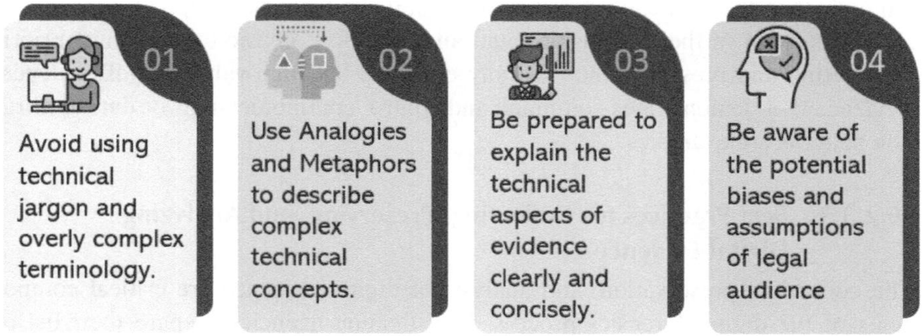

FIGURE 19.5 Cybersecurity professional communication in court.

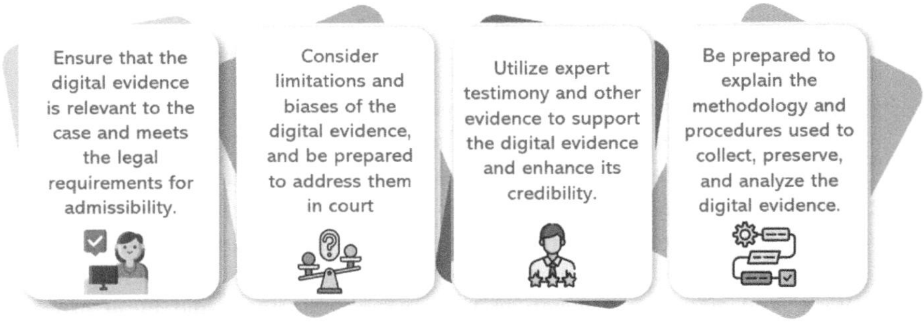

FIGURE 19.6 Evidentiary weight and relevance considerations for cybersecurity professionals.

The communication should be simplified so that complex technical terms can be understood. However, it should not be oversimplified that the meaning changes. Further, it should maintain scientific rigor and ensure accessibility. The cognitive load theory already says that information retention is optimized when presented in manageable segments. So, expert witnesses should structure their testimony in a modular format. This allows for incremental assimilation of technical concepts.

19.2.3.2 Evidentiary Weight and Relevance

Whether digital evidence is admissible depends on its weight and relevance. These factors also impact the outcome of the case. Four critical considerations regarding evidentiary weight and relevance for cybersecurity professionals are shown in Figure 19.6.

Almost all legal communities emphasize the scientific validity of forensic methods and the role of forensic testimony in bringing about justice (Albright et al., 2023). Courts worldwide are increasingly applying the Daubert standard to evaluate the scientific validity of digital forensic methodologies. Expert witnesses must articulate their analytical techniques' empirical foundations and error rates.

The principle of proportionality in e-discovery is note worth mentioning. It requires that the evidentiary value of digital artifacts be weighed against the resources spent in their acquisition and analysis. So, forensic experts must prioritize getting and presenting not just any evidence but high-value digital evidence. Evidence that demonstrates command and control communications or data exfiltration patterns are examples.

19.2.3.3 Best Practices for Collecting, Preserving, and Analyzing Digital Evidence

The collection, preservation, and analysis of digital evidence are critical components of the digital forensics process. Investigation agencies prepare their list of best practices so that the staff follows them in ways that make the evidence easily acceptable to courts. Cybersecurity professionals play a role in this. They are in great demand, considering that all large organizations are trying to have their in-house cybersecurity teams because of a shortage of skilled workforce (Furnell, 2021). Cybersecurity professionals should (Budde et al., 2023):

1. Follow established protocols and guidelines for collecting and preserving digital evidence, such as the guidelines, standards, and best practices for using digital evidence in criminal proceedings (UNODC, 2019).
2. Employ specialized tools and techniques to collect and analyze digital evidence, such as digital forensics software and network protocol analysis. For example, write-blocking technologies can be implemented during data acquisition. They help preserve original evidence. Similarly, cryptographic hashing algorithms can be used to verify data integrity throughout the forensic process. Live memory analysis techniques are increasingly used in cybersecurity investigations. Cases involving sophisticated malware or insider threats can benefit from these. Some examples of these techniques are specialized tools for volatile data capture. Early forensic software is proprietary, while modern ones are available from both private and government. Furthermore, there is an increased use of AI and Machine Learning (ML) algorithms can be used for data triage and anomaly detection (Preeti & Sharma, 2024).
3. Ensure the digital evidence is properly preserved and stored to prevent contamination or tampering.
4. Document all aspects of the digital forensics process, including collecting, preserving, and analyzing the digital evidence.

19.3 REAL-WORLD CASE STUDIES

19.3.1 Case Study 1: Cyber Espionage and Intrusion Detection

Tulsa, Okla-based software major SolarWinds is famous for its system management tools used in network and infrastructure monitoring. Its software, Orion Platform, was at the center of an undetected sophisticated attack for months, only to surface in December 2020 (Oladimeji & Kerner, 2023).

The threat actors got illegal access to the SolarWinds network in September 2019. They tested the initial code injection into Orion in October 2019. On February 20, 2020, a malicious code called Sunburst was injected into Orion. SolarWinds unknowingly began sending out Orion software updates with hacked code on March 26, 2020. The attack was termed "the largest and most sophisticated attack the world has ever seen" by Microsoft President Brad Smith in February 2021.

The attackers indulged in a supply chain attack, inserting malicious code into the Orion software updates. These updates were distributed to SolarWinds customers worldwide, including several Fortune 500 companies. Because the software is an IT monitoring software, it has privileged access to logs and system performance data. Hackers use this feature to create a backdoor through which they can access and impersonate users and accounts of victim organizations. The wide deployment of the software and the previously available access facilitated the hack. The supply chain attack in 2020–2021 has become an essential case for discussion, spanning various subject areas. The case allows learning about incident response, evidence collection, digital forensics analysis, and presentation.

19.3.1.1 Incident Response and Evidence Collection

SolarWinds and its customers quickly launched an incident response investigation. A large-scale investigation was called for, and an incident response team was formed. The team had members from FireEye, SolarWinds, and multiple US government agencies.

The team used the MITRE ATT&CK framework to categorize and track attacker Tactics, Techniques, and Procedures (TTPs) (G. Sarkar et al., 2023). The incident response process started isolating compromised systems. Security certificates potentially exposed during the breach are revoked. Simultaneously, efforts to collect evidence have started. The NIST SP 800-86 guidelines are adhered to for integrating forensic techniques into incident responses. The team collected and analyzed logs, network traffic, and other data to determine the scope of the breach and identify attackers.

Forensic images of affected systems were acquired. Magnet ACQUIRE and Belkasoft X are used to preserve volatile data. Memory dumps were collected using Volatility 3, capturing critical runtime artifacts. Network traffic was captured and analyzed using Zeek (formerly Bro) and Suricata, focusing on identifying command and control (C2) communications (0xMan1sh, 2024).

The team collected and preserved various log sources, including:

1. Windows Event Logs
2. SolarWinds Orion application logs
3. Firewall and intrusion detection system (IDS) logs
4. Active Directory logs
5. DNS server logs
6. Web server access logs

These logs were centralized and normalized using Splunk Enterprise Security, facilitating correlation analysis and timeline reconstruction.

19.3.1.2 Digital Forensics Analysis and Evidence Presentation

The digital forensics analysis phase employed a multi-dimensional approach to uncover the full extent of the breach. The digital forensics analysis is necessary to capture irrefutable evidence of the breach. It helped in the identification of the attackers. This evidence was presented in court as part of the criminal prosecution of the individuals responsible for the attack. Disk forensics was conducted using X-Ways Forensics and BlackBag BlackLight. The presence of the SUNBURST malware was revealed. Malware is the weaponized software update that is the initial infection vector (Lee & Soh, 2020).

Malware analysis was performed using static and dynamic techniques. Tools such as IDA Pro, Ghidra, and Joe Sandbox were used. The tools explained the sophisticated nature of the SUNBURST backdoor (McDade, 2024). The analysis revealed its ability to blend in with legitimate SolarWinds traffic, evade detection, and establish persistence through novel techniques. Memory forensics using Volatility 3 and Rekall uncovered evidence of post-exploitation activities, including credential dumping using Mimikatz and Cobalt Strike beacons for lateral movement. Timeline analysis, conducted with log2timeline/Plaso and visualized using TimeSketch, provided a comprehensive view of the attacker's activities over an extended period.

Network forensics, leveraging tools such as NetworkMiner and Wireshark, identified the exfiltration of sensitive data to attacker-controlled infrastructure. The team employed JA3 fingerprinting to detect and cluster malicious TLS communications, revealing previously unknown command and control servers.

The forensics team prepared a comprehensive report detailing their findings, including:

1. Initial access vector: Compromised SolarWinds build system
2. Persistence mechanism: SUNBURST backdoor embedded in legitimate software updates
3. Lateral movement: Use of TEARDROP malware and Cobalt Strike beacons
4. Data exfiltration: Encrypted transfers to multiple C2 servers
5. Impact: Unauthorized access to numerous government agencies and private sector organizations

The team leveraged advanced visualization techniques for courtroom presentation to convey the complex technical findings to a non-technical audience. They employed Cellebrite Inspector to create interactive timelines and network graphs, illustrating the attacker's progression through the compromised environments.

The presentation of digital evidence is required to strictly comply with the Federal Rules of Evidence, with particular attention to Rule 902(14) regarding the self-authentication of electronic evidence. The team implemented a proper chain of custody process. Each step of the evidence-handling procedure is documented using Magnet AXIOM Cyber's case management features. Expert witnesses from the forensics team provided detailed testimony on the technical aspects of the investigation. They utilized analogies and visual aids to explain complex concepts, such as the nature of supply chain attacks and the significance of the SUNBURST malware's evasion techniques (SophosLabs Threat Research, 2020).

The integrity and authenticity of the evidence can be maintained by using Blockchain technology. Guardtime KSI Blockchain helped create immutable timestamps for all collected artifacts (Guardtime, 2024). This innovative approach provided an additional layer of verification, ensuring the evidence remained tamperproof throughout the investigation and legal proceedings.

The SolarWinds case study exemplifies the evolving complexity of cyber threats and the sophisticated forensic methodologies required to investigate and attribute such incidents. It underscores the critical importance of comprehensive incident response, advanced digital forensics techniques, and compelling evidence presentation in addressing modern cybersecurity challenges.

19.3.2 Case Study 2: Financial Fraud Investigation

The Wirecard scandal is described primarily as a case of financial fraud (accounting fraud) because of a corporate governance failure and misconduct (Baur, 2021;

Jo et al., 2021) and audit failure that led to the eventual filing of bankruptcy of the company (Baranidharan et al., 2023). However, cybersecurity can be classified as a complex Identity Theft and Financial Fraud case with significant cybersecurity implications. While not a traditional cybersecurity attack like hacking or malware, the Wirecard case demonstrates how financial fraud in the digital age intersects significantly with cybersecurity concerns. The case highlights three aspects:

1. Need for strong cybersecurity measures in financial systems
2. Importance of digital forensics in fraud investigations
3. Challenges of maintaining data integrity in complex financial ecosystems.

The scandal involves a leading German payment processing company named Wirecard AG. The issue was discovered in June 2020 because of investigative reports by the *Financial Times* and other media outlets. Media reports revealed that Wirecard's financial statements were inaccurate and that the company had been hiding its financial situation. It involved a massive accounting fraud involving Wirecard's management and auditors. Three early issues identified are:

1. Falsifying financial statements
2. Hiding the company's financial situation
3. Manipulating accounting data.

The investigation found that Wirecard's management had been using a complex web of shell companies and fake transactions to hide the company's financial losses and create the illusion of profitability. Wirecard's CEO, Markus Braun, and several other top executives were forced to resign. Braun was later arrested for false accounting and market manipulation (Chen, 2022). Auditors E&Y were criticized for their role in the scandal and blamed for failing to detect the fraud despite being responsible for auditing the financial statements. The "German Enron" scandal significantly declined Wirecard's stock price, erasing investor wealth. The company eventually filed for insolvency in August 2020.

19.3.2.1 Evidence Collection

The Wirecard scandal can be considered the most complex and far-reaching financial fraud in history. As a result, the evidence-collection process was also highly complex and challenging. Investigators had to collect evidence from a wide range of sources, including records from:

1. Parent company
2. Shell companies
3. Banks and other financial institutions
4. Auditors E&Y
5. Regulator
6. Customers and partners

The investigators interview a large number of parties and witnesses (Baranidharan et al., 2023), including:

1. Wirecard executives
2. Wirecard employees
3. EY auditors
4. Wirecard customers and partners
5. Law enforcement officials

The deliberate destruction of evidence by top executives made the evidence-collection process complicated. For example, the executives shredded documents and deleted electronic files. Despite these challenges, investigators have collected much evidence to prove Wirecard's fraud, including:

1. Documents that showed that the parent company is using shell companies to inflate its sales and profits
2. Emails and other communications that showed that the executives were aware of the fraud
3. Bank records showed that the company was moving money through shell companies to create the appearance of legitimate transactions.

19.3.2.2 Court Trial

The Wirecard court trial was one of the most closely watched recent trials. The trial lasted for several months and featured testimony from a wide range of witnesses.

The prosecution presented a considerable quantity of evidence that proved Wirecard's fraud. The defense argued that Wirecard's executives were unaware of the fraud. However, the prosecution's evidence showed that the executives were directly involved in the scheme. Researchers and media also examined the failure of regulators (Jakubeit, 2021). Ultimately, the jury found Wirecard's former CEO, Markus Braun, guilty of fraud and other charges. Braun was sentenced to eight years in prison. The Wirecard trial was a landmark case conveying that financial fraud would not be tolerated. The trial also showed that even the most complex and sophisticated fraud schemes can be uncovered and prosecuted.

19.4 COURTROOM TESTIMONY FOR CYBERCRIME CASES

19.4.1 The Role of the Digital Forensic Expert Witness

Digital Forensic expert witnesses play a crucial role in cybercrime investigations and trials. Experts testify in a court in a direct examination or a cross-examination, and most experts struggle to convey essential points (Lubet & Boals, 2020). They provide specialized knowledge, insights, and expertise to assist the court. They help present and interpret digital evidence in court. They help in understanding the technical aspects of cybercrime investigations and prosecutions. The extent to which recent developments displace the traditional role of the expert and enhance that of the advocate is debated in research circles, especially in the context of Foreign Law (Ward & Plenderleith Ferguson, 2024).

Digital Forensic expert witnesses are typically individuals who have extensive experience. Their expertise will generally be in cybersecurity, computer science, or a related discipline. Their primary responsibility is to assist the court in understanding complex technical evidence and to provide expert opinions on matters related to the case. This may involve analyzing digital evidence, reconstructing cyberattacks, or explaining technical concepts to non-technical jurors.

The digital forensic expert witness is a crucial intermediary in the investigation and provides opinion evidence (Horsman & Shavers, 2022). They help challenge or corroborate digital evidence presented by opposing parties. Their skills will help simplify the technical complexities of digital forensics and the legal frameworks (standards) within which cyber-related cases are adjudicated. Their primary function is simplifying complex technical concepts, methodologies, and findings. The simplification should be in a manner that is understandable to court and legal professionals who may lack specialized knowledge in cybersecurity and digital forensics.

Expert witnesses will be frequently called upon to provide testimony on a diverse array of topics. The list of topics includes but is not limited to (Pal, 2022):

1. Network intrusion detection
2. Malware analysis
3. Data exfiltration techniques
4. Digital evidence acquisition and preservation
5. Interpretation of log files and metadata.

Their role extends beyond mere factual exposition. They are often required to offer professional opinions on the following:

1. Implications of Digital Evidence
2. Likelihood of specific cyber events
3. Technical feasibility of alleged cybercriminal activities.

They must be prepared to articulate the scientific basis for their conclusions. They must defend their methodologies under cross-examination and address potential alternative interpretations of the digital evidence. They are expected to state with a "reasonable degree of certainty" within their profession or field of study (Lubet & Boals, 2020). Expert witnesses are generally called upon to:

1. Explain the methods used to collect and analyze digital evidence
2. Interpret the results of forensic examinations
3. Offer opinions on the significance of the evidence
4. Assist in developing and presenting exhibits and demonstrative evidence

19.4.1.1 Qualifications and Expertise

Digital forensic expert witnesses should possess specific educational qualifications, training, and experience in digital forensics. The qualifications and expertise required are multifaceted and reflect cybercrime's complex and rapidly evolving nature. These are generally a combination of academic and professional qualifications. The dynamic nature of cybersecurity necessitates ongoing education and professional development to remain current with emerging technologies and threat vectors. These requirements include:

1. A graduate degree at undergraduate or postgraduate level is necessary. The specialization can be in computer science, information assurance, information security, cybersecurity, digital forensics, or a related field, which is preferred (Accenture, 2024).
2. Certification from a recognized forensic organization/industry helps establish the expert's credibility. Some famous certifications in this area are:
   a. Certified Information Systems Security Professional (CISSP) (ISC2, 2024)
   b. Certified Ethical Hacker (CEH) (EC Council, 2024)
   c. EnCase Certified Examiner (EnCE) (Opentext, 2024)
   d. GIAC Certified Forensic Analyst (GCFA) (GIAC, 2024)

   These certifications serve as benchmarks of technical proficiency. These certifications often require periodic renewal. The idea is that the expert's knowledge remains current and up-to-date.
3. Extensive practical experience in the field of conducting digital forensic investigations is necessary. The experience can be field work in any form – as a cybersecurity professional, law enforcement agent, or digital forensic analyst. Courts and legal professionals generally give considerable weightage to an expert's track record of hands-on experience. Aspects related to investigating cyber incidents, conducting digital forensic analyses, and implementing cybersecurity measures are observed. This experience can be in corporate, government, and law enforcement contexts. The expert must demonstrate flexibility and need a strong understanding of diverse cybersecurity challenges. Employment applicants with cybercrime records can have a faint positive signal of getting an IT job for having the skills practical for employment compared to a criminal record for a property crime, which will be treated as a negative characteristic (Peelen et al., 2023).
4. Familiarity and knowledge of the legal framework and procedures governing the admissibility of digital evidence can help. They should also thoroughly understand the rules of evidence and the legal standards governing expert testimony in their jurisdiction.
5. Publication in peer-reviewed journals and presentations at reputable conferences helps. Such activities show the contribution of the expert to the field/body of knowledge. It also indicates the ability to articulate complex technical concepts to diverse audiences. These are considered crucial skills in courtroom settings.

19.4.1.2 Ethical Considerations and Objectivity

Cybercrime investigation professionals can be expert witnesses for a court. They are bound by a code of ethics and maintain objectivity and impartiality. Some of the considerations and objectivity expected from the expert witnesses are (Steinberg, 2024):

1. They must avoid bias and conflicts of interest and are duty-bound to disclose them.
2. They must present their findings and opinions fairly and unbiasedly so that the lay audience can understand (Moldovan, 2022).

3. Should maintain independence from the parties involved in the case.
4. Should refrain from expressing opinions and speculation and offer opinions that can be supported by evidence.
5. Be aware of the potential risks and consequences of their testimony.
6. Should understand the possibility of being cross-examined or challenged by opposing counsel.
7. To maintain objectivity, expert witnesses often follow a rigorous methodology when analyzing evidence, including establishing protocols and procedures for digital forensic analysis.
8. Should testify truthfully and accurately, thereby helping the court reach its verdict.

19.4.2 Preparing and Delivering Effective Courtroom Testimony

Convincing courtroom testimony requires careful preparation and strategic delivery. Expert witnesses should display their expertise and credibility to the court. Hence, they should prepare for the case thoroughly. They should review relevant case materials such as digital evidence, forensic reports, and legal documents. They should spend time familiarizing themselves with the court's procedures and protocols. They should also anticipate potential lines of questioning from both prosecution and defense. They need preparation in advance to give clear and concise responses. The responses should not compromise accuracy. Hence, care and caution should be taken to maintain the balance. The scientific basis for their conclusions must be prepared to be said by them. They should delineate the analytical processes employed. The expert witness is not an advocate for either party. However, they are an objective source of information for the court.

19.4.2.1 Clear Communication and Technical Jargon

Clear and effective communication in the courtroom makes a substantial difference (Bali et al., 2020). This is more so when presenting complex technical information to non-technical jurors in an easy-to-understand language (Moldovan, 2022). Technical terms are to be defined when necessary. Digital forensic expert witnesses must be able to simplify complex technical information into clear and concise language. Of course, technical terms, to some extent, may be unavoidable. It helps establishment of a shared vocabulary and conceptual framework. It facilitates deeper exploration of technical evidence as the testimony progresses. The expert must remain cautious for signs of confusion or misunderstanding among the audience. They need to be prepared to rephrase or elaborate on concepts as necessary.

This requires high emotional intelligence and the ability to read non-verbal cues from judges and jurors (Nobles, 2022). They should remain calm and respectful under pressure. They must remain composed under cross-examination, responding to challenging questions with equanimity and professional detachment. When confronted with questions that reveal misunderstandings, the expert should address these misconceptions directly and patiently, ensuring a solid foundation of understanding before proceeding to more advanced topics.

Non-verbal communication also is vital in the effective delivery of expert testimony. Some ways of significantly enhancing the credibility and persuasiveness of testimony are:

1. Maintaining eye contact
2. Employing measured gestures
3. Projecting confidence through posture and vocal modulation

19.4.2.2 Using Visual Aids and Demonstrations

Visual aids and demonstrations can be valuable tools for Digital forensic expert witnesses (Johnson, 2022). They improve comprehensibility and make them more accessible to non-technical jurors. This way, they impact expert testimony in cybercrime cases. These pedagogical devices can simplify complex technical processes. They help in illustrating the sequence of events in a cyber incident. They can help visualize abstract concepts in network architecture and data flow.

Digital forensic expert witnesses can use diagrams, flowcharts, and screenshots (Wilding & Stowell, 2016). Visual aids can simplify complex information without oversimplification, present clear hierarchies when using color and contrast, and when the judicious application of text and labels is required. Each of the tools has a different purpose. Diagrams are used to illustrate the network architecture of a compromised system. Flowcharts are used to illustrate the sequence of events in a cyberattack. Screenshots are used to illustrate the appearance of malware or other malicious software. Demonstrations can be used to explain how a particular technical concept works. Topics such as encryption or decryption can be explained in this way. Infographics, flowcharts, and network diagrams can be particularly effective in illustrating the interconnected nature of cybersecurity systems and cyberattack propagation.

Dynamic visualizations are also used. Similarly, demonstrations are used to illustrate technical concepts. For example, they can explain how a particular malware works or how a cyberattack was carried out. These tools help in step-by-step reconstructions of data exfiltration processes can be used. Such activities can provide compelling illustrations of complex technical concepts. However, such animations must be carefully adjusted to avoid overwhelming the audience. Sometimes, this can lead to inadvertently introducing bias through dramatic presentation.

Physical demonstrations, when feasible, can provide valuable insights into digital processes. For instance, demonstrating the principles of hash functions using physical objects can elucidate the concept of data integrity verification. Similarly, using hardware components to illustrate the physical manifestation of digital evidence can bridge the conceptual gap between abstract data and concrete evidence.

In some cases, real-time demonstrations can be integrated. This can be in the form of a live forensic analysis or malware behavior simulation. However, such demonstrations must be meticulously planned and rehearsed. This is necessary to mitigate the risk of technical failures or unexpected outcomes that could undermine the expert's credibility. Experts must be prepared to explain the methodology and assumptions underlying any visual aids or demonstrations presented. This includes articulating the software tools used to generate visualizations, the data sources informing simulations, and any simplifications or abstractions employed in creating demonstrative exhibits.

Visual aids and demonstrations must strictly follow the legal and procedural requirements governing the presentation of evidence. Unlike in the past, courts are now open to accepting newer forms of evidence – digital photographs, 3D visualizations, or a 3D-printed model (Errickson et al., 2020). Experts should work closely with legal counsel to ensure that all visual materials comply with the rules of evidence and are appropriately authenticated and disclosed to opposing parties as required by law. Interactive presentations, where permissible, can enhance engagement and comprehension. Techniques such as zooming into specific areas of a network diagram or toggling between different views of a data structure can give jurors a sense of agency in exploring the evidence, potentially increasing retention and understanding of key technical concepts.

The expert must guide the audience through visual materials, explicitly connecting graphical elements to crucial points in the testimony and ensuring that visual aids clarify rather than complicate the case narrative. Using visual aids and demonstrations effectively, digital forensic expert witnesses can help make complex technical information more accessible to non-technical jurors (Errickson et al., 2020). They increase the impact of their testimony and make it both informative and persuasive in the courtroom.

19.4.3 Responding to Cross-Examination

Cross-examination is an essential part of the adversarial process. In cybersecurity cases, cross-examination often challenges the expert's methodology, tools, and interpretations. Digital forensic expert witnesses will be subjected to rigorous cross-examination by opposing counsel. Hence, they should be prepared to respond effectively. A key strategy is to anticipate and prepare for potential lines of questioning. This involves:

1. Reviewing the opposing counsel's discovery requests
2. Reviewing the case file
3. Identifying potential areas of weakness in the evidence.

Experts can anticipate challenges and develop targeted responses. This way, they can avoid being caught off guard. To maintain credibility, experts must:

1. Anticipate and prepare for questions regarding the chain of custody, particularly in digital evidence cases. Meticulous documentation of evidence-handling procedures is crucial.
2. Be prepared to explain complex technical concepts in understandable terms without oversimplifying. They can develop analogies and use visual aids that accurately represent digital forensic processes.
3. Address potential biases in forensic tools or analysis methods. Acknowledge limitations and uncertainties in the field, demonstrating a commitment to scientific objectivity.
4. Differentiate between factual observations and expert opinions. When offering interpretations, clearly state the basis for conclusions, citing relevant research and industry standards.

5. Resist attempts to elicit speculative responses. Maintain professional boundaries by declining to comment on hypothetical scenarios outside the scope of the examined evidence.

19.4.3.1 Anticipating Challenges and Maintaining Composure

Compelling testimony requires not only technical expertise but also emotional intelligence and strategic foresight:

1. Conduct thorough pre-trial preparation, including mock cross-examinations that simulate hostile questioning. This helps identify potential vulnerabilities in testimony and builds resilience.
2. Develop strategies for managing cognitive load during intense questioning. Techniques such as controlled breathing and mental rehearsal can help maintain focus and composure.
3. Anticipate attempts to undermine credibility based on past cases, publications, or statements. Prepare concise, factual responses that contextualize previous work and demonstrate consistency in methodology.
4. Be prepared for challenges and questions related to the reliability of digital evidence. Arguments about potential tampering or alternative explanations for digital artifacts can arise. Develop robust responses that highlight the safeguards and verification processes employed.
5. Maintain a neutral, professional appearance and conduct even when faced with aggressive or misleading questioning. Emotional reactions can be exploited to undermine credibility.

Maintaining composure during cross-examination is essential for digital forensic expert witnesses. This can be done in three ways:

1. Staying focused on the case
2. Avoiding distractions by not entering into arguments.
3. Managing their emotions by remaining calm and respectful even under pressure
4. Avoiding emotional outbursts
5. They can take breaks if needed to collect their thoughts and regain composure.

Experts must be prepared to address potential areas of contention and maintain their composure under pressure to anticipate and handle the challenges.

19.4.3.2 Effective Rebuttal Strategies

Contradiction and refutation strategies allow digital forensic expert witnesses to respond to challenges during cross-examination and strengthen their testimony (Daniel, 2022). This involves:

1. Identifying weaknesses in the testimony and preparing counterarguments
2. Using prior statements made by the opposing expert or witness contradicting their testimony.

3. Presenting new evidence supports the expert's testimony
4. Impeaching the opposing expert's qualifications, experience, or credibility.
5. Answering questions directly and concisely without volunteering unnecessary information.
6. Objecting to improper, irrelevant, speculative, or otherwise improper questions.
7. Referring to peer-reviewed literature and industry standards and reports
8. Using visual aids to explain complex technical concepts or data relationships and help avoid misrepresenting during cross-examination.
9. Address any apparent inconsistencies to provide additional context or clarify misunderstandings.
10. Conducting additional analysis or simulations to address the challenges raised during cross-examination.
11. Articulate the limitations of alternative explanations or theories presented by opposing experts.
12. Address questions about the current state-of-the-art technologies and their implications for earlier analyses.

19.5 FUTURE DIRECTIONS

19.5.1 Future Directions for Research and Practice

Cybercrime is a relatively new topic in criminology but has increased interest in the scholarly community. Further, cybercrime is often an international topic and is interdisciplinary (Payne & Hadzhidimova, 2020; Roberts, 2023). Considering the rapid pace of technological advancements, the fields of cybersecurity, forensics, and national security are constantly evolving. This makes the presentation of evidence in courtroom testimony changing, too. Future research and practical directions in this area can broadly be summarized as:

1. New technologies for collecting and analyzing digital evidence, such as for conducting virtual trials (Bandes & Feigenson, 2020) and dealing with newer forms of menace, such as deepfakes and impersonation (Klasén et al., 2024), crimes in the metaverse (Marshall & Tompsett, 2024) amongst others.
2. New methods for collecting and analyzing digital evidence admissible in court are evolving and require researcher evaluation (Ingram, 2021). Modern evidence forms include scientific evidence, electronic evidence, and process-based evidence (Wang, 2020).
3. Exploring the use of data analytics to identify patterns and trends in cybercrime
4. Integration of AI and ML in the courtroom across various processes (Campbell, 2023)
5. Use of virtual and augmented reality (VR and AR) to enhance the presentation of digital evidence in court (Nordin & Zekan, 2021)
6. Explore the potential of Blockchain technology to build a Digital Evidence Management System (DEMS) that can ensure the integrity and authenticity of digital evidence (Chougule et al., 2022).
7. Investigating the ethical and legal implications of using digital evidence in court (Vecellio Segate, 2021)

8. Inter-departmental and international cooperation in digital evidence management is to be promoted. The Swedish Collaborative Network on Digital Forensics is a modern success story (Klasén et al., 2024). Similarly, standardization or standardized protocols are to be promoted for collecting, analyzing, and presenting digital evidence.
9. Investigating the impact of cognitive biases on jurors' perceptions of digital evidence

19.5.2 Implications for Policy and Practice

The increasing use of digital evidence in courtroom testimony has significant implications for policy and practice, including:

1. Specialized training programs must be developed for law enforcement and legal professionals (judges, lawyers, and jurors) (Kaur, 2014). They must be trained on digital evidence's unique challenges and opportunities and be equipped to handle complex cybercrime cases. Reporting digital evidence is soon turning into a fundamental skill (Horsman, 2022). Hence, the task of conducting training programs is paramount. It can be taken up by institutions like the School of Magistrate that focus on continuing the training of magistrates (Miha & Pekmezi, 2024).
2. The establishment of dedicated cybercrime courts to handle the unique challenges of these cases
3. The need for policymakers to prioritize the development of robust cybersecurity measures to prevent cybercrime
4. Governments and organizations must develop policies and procedures for collecting, analyzing, and presenting Digital evidence in court.

19.5.3 Importance of Skilled Evidence Presentation

The importance of skilled evidence presentation in cybersecurity, forensics, and national security cannot be overstated. A skilled evidence presenter can effectively communicate complex technical information to a non-technical audience. Furthermore, he can ensure that the evidence is admissible and presented fairly and impartially. Effective evidence presentation in criminal trials is paramount because it can (Moussa, 2021):

1. Enhance the credibility and admissibility of digital evidence.
2. Improve the understanding of complex technical concepts
3. Increase the likelihood of a successful prosecution

19.5.4 The Future of Cybercrime Evidence and Courtroom Practices

The future of cybercrime evidence and courtroom practices is likely to be shaped by several factors, including (Horan & Saiedian, 2021):

1. The continued evolution of technology
2. The use of technologies, such as AI and Ml

3. The extent of international cooperation
4. The standardization of procedures.

As the field evolves, researchers, practitioners, and policymakers must work together to ensure that the courtroom remains a fair and effective venue for resolving disputes and upholding justice. Further, to stay ahead of the curve, there is an increased need to develop innovative methods for presenting evidence clearly and concisely.

19.6 CONCLUSION

Increasing cybercrimes require cybersecurity professionals, law enforcement, and the judiciary to stay updated with the technology to counter digital crimes. Special training programs are needed to handle digital evidence, convince the courts about how the crime happened, and get the wrongdoers punished. While the legal systems are not that standard globally, several legal frameworks are available to deal with the evidence and chain of custody to some extent. Two case studies – SolarWinds for Cyber Espionage and Wirecard for financial fraud scandal- are examined. Digital forensic expert witnesses bring value to court proceedings. They must be efficient, prepared, and deliver while dealing with technical jargon. The use of visual aids, demonstrative presentations, and rebuttal strategies helps. The chapter ends with a discussion on future directions for research and practice.

REFERENCES

0xMan1sh. (2024, July 2). *Network Traffic Analysis with Zeek*. https://medium.com/@manish0x/network-traffic-analysis-with-zeek-967156879dc2

Accenture. (2024). *Cybersecurity Graduate Programme*. https://www.accenture.com/gb-en/careers/local/cyber-security-graduate-programme

Albright, T. D., Baltimore, D., Mazza, A.-M., Mnookin, J. L., & Tatel, D. S. (2023). Science, evidence, law, and justice. *Proceedings of the National Academy of Sciences*, *120*(41), e2312529120. https://doi.org/10.1073/pnas.2312529120

Babanina, V., Tkachenko, I., Matiushenko, O., & Krutevych, M. (2021). Cybercrime: History of formation, current state and ways of counteraction. *Revista Amazonia Investiga*, *10*(38), 113–122. https://doi.org/10.34069/AI/2021.38.02.10

Bali, A. S., Edmond, G., Ballantyne, K. N., Kemp, R. I., & Martire, K. A. (2020). Communicating forensic science opinion: An examination of expert reporting practices. *Science & Justice*, *60*(3), 216–224. https://doi.org/10.1016/j.scijus.2019.12.005

Bandes, S. A., & Feigenson, N. (2020). Virtual trials: Necessity, invention, and the evolution of the courtroom. *Buffalo Law Review*, *68*(5), pp. 1275–1352. https://dx.doi.org/10.2139/ssrn.3683408

Baranidharan, S., Ajekwe, C. C. M., & Nakitende, M. G. (2023). Accounting fraud and bankruptcy: The case of Wirecard AG. In A. Rafay (Ed.), *Advances in Finance, Accounting, and Economics* (pp. 222–244). IGI Global. https://doi.org/10.4018/979-8-3693-1190-5.ch012

Barnor, J. N., & Patterson, A. A. (2022). Cybercrime research: A review of research themes, frameworks, methods, and future research directions. In I. R. Management Association (Ed.), *Research Anthology on Combating Cyber-Aggression and Online Negativity* (pp. 1560–1582). IGI Global. https://doi.org/10.4018/978-1-6684-5594-4.ch079

Baror, S. O., Ikuesan, R. A., & Venter, H. S. (2020, March). *A Defined Digital Forensic Criteria for Cybercrime Reporting*. International Conference on Cyber Warfare and Security; Reading. DOI:10.34190/ICCWS.20.056

Baur, D. (2021). *The Wirecard Scandal 2020. Wirecard and related Corporate Governance Issues* (1. Auflage). GRIN Verlag.

Billow, J. (2023). No country is an island: Embracing international law enforcement cooperation to reduce the impact of cybercrime. *Journal of Cyber Policy*, *9*(2), pp. 1–10. https://doi.org/10.1080/23738871.2023.2245417

Bruce, M., Lusthaus, J., Kashyap, R., Phair, N., & Varese, F. (2024). Mapping the global geography of cybercrime with the World Cybercrime Index. *PLOS ONE*, *19*(4), e0297312. https://doi.org/10.1371/journal.pone.0297312

Budde, C. E., Karinsalo, A., Vidor, S., Salonen, J., & Massacci, F. (2023). CSEC framework assessment dataset: Expert evaluations of cybersecurity skills for job profiles in Europe. *Data in Brief*, *48*, 109285. https://doi.org/10.1016/j.dib.2023.109285

Campbell, R. W. (2023). Artificial Intelligence in the Courtroom: The Delivery of Justice in the Age of Machine Learning. *Revista Forumul Judecatorilor*, *15*.

Casey, E. (2010). Introduction. In *Handbook of Digital Forensics and Investigation* (pp. 1–17). Elsevier. https://doi.org/10.1016/B978-0-12-374267-4.00001-X

Castelliano, C., Grajzl, P., & Watanabe, E. (2023). Does electronic case-processing enhance court efficacy? New quantitative evidence. *Government Information Quarterly*, *40*(4), 101861. https://doi.org/10.1016/j.giq.2023.101861

Chen, J. J. (2022). Wirecard. In *International Cases of Corporate Governance* (pp. 67–82). Springer Nature Singapore. https://doi.org/10.1007/978-981-19-3238-0_5

Chen, S., Hao, M., Ding, F., Jiang, D., Dong, J., Zhang, S., Guo, Q., & Gao, C. (2023). Exploring the global geography of cybercrime and its driving forces. *Humanities and Social Sciences Communications*, *10*(1), 71. https://doi.org/10.1057/s41599-023-01560-x

Chougule, H., Dhadiwal, S., Lokhande, M., Naikade, R., & Patil, R. (2022). Digital evidence management system for cybercrime investigation using proxy re-encryption and blockchain. *Procedia Computer Science*, *215*, 71–77. https://doi.org/10.1016/j.procs.2022.12.008

Ciobanu, P. (2020). Forensic investigation of cybercrime. *Perspectives of Law and Public Administration*, *9*(2), 205–208.

Daniel, L. (2022, April 1). *Expert Testimony: The "How-To's" Securing the Right Digital Forensics Expert Witness Testimony*. https://www.invistaforensics.com/knowledge-center/insights/articles/expert-testimony-the-how-to-s-securing-the-right-digital-forensics-expert-witness-testimony/

EC Council. (2024). *Become a Certified Ethical Hacker*. https://www.eccouncil.org/train-certify/certified-ethical-hacker-ceh/

Errickson, D., Fawcett, H., Thompson, T. J. U., & Campbell, A. (2020). The effect of different imaging techniques for the visualisation of evidence in court on jury comprehension. *International Journal of Legal Medicine*, *134*(4), 1451–1455. https://doi.org/10.1007/s00414-019-02221-y

Furnell, S. (2020). Technology use, abuse, and public perceptions of cybercrime. In T. J. Holt & A. M. Bossler (Eds.), *The Palgrave Handbook of International Cybercrime and Cyberdeviance* (pp. 45–66). Springer International Publishing. https://doi.org/10.1007/978-3-319-78440-3_9

Furnell, S. (2021). The cybersecurity workforce and skills. *Computers & Security*, *100*, 102080. https://doi.org/10.1016/j.cose.2020.102080

Geldenhuys Kotie. (2024). The Importance of the chain of custody. *Servamus Community-Based Safety and Security Magazine*, *117*(7), 44–45. https://doi.org/10.10520/ejc-servamus_v117_n7_a11

GIAC. (2024). *GIAC Certified Forensic Analyst (GCFA)*. https://www.giac.org/certifications/certified-forensic-analyst-gcfa/

Guardtime. (2024). *KSI Blockchain Timestamping*. https://guardtime.com/timestamping

Haque, E. U., Abbasi, W., Murugesan, S., Anwar, M. S., Khan, F., & Lee, Y. (2023). Cyber forensic investigation infrastructure of Pakistan: An analysis of the cyber threat landscape and readiness. *IEEE Access*, *11*, 40049–40063. https://doi.org/10.1109/ACCESS.2023.3268529

Harris, E. (2013). How strictly did the Athenian courts apply the law? The role of Epieikeia. *Bulletin of the Institute of Classical Studies*, *56*(1), 27–48. https://doi.org/10.1111/j.2041-5370.2013.00049.x

Harshwardhan, C., Sunny, D., Mehul, L., Rohit, N., & Patil, R. (2022). Management of digital evidence for cybercrime investigation—A review. In V. S. Reddy, V. K. Prasad, J. Wang, & K. T. V. Reddy (Eds.), *Soft Computing and Signal Processing* (Vol. 1413, pp. 133–143). Springer Nature Singapore. https://doi.org/10.1007/978-981-16-7088-6_11

Horan, C., & Saiedian, H. (2021). Cyber crime investigation: Landscape, challenges, and future research directions. *Journal of Cybersecurity and Privacy*, *1*(4), 580–596. https://doi.org/10.3390/jcp1040029

Horsman, G. (2021). The different types of reports produced in digital forensic investigations. *Science & Justice*, *61*(5), 627–634. https://doi.org/10.1016/j.scijus.2021.06.009

Horsman, G. (2022). Technical reporting in digital forensics. *Journal of Forensic Sciences*, *67*(6), 2458–2468. https://doi.org/10.1111/1556-4029.15108

Horsman, G., & Shavers, B. (2022). Who is the digital forensic expert and what is their expertise? *WIREs Forensic Science*, *4*(5), e1453. https://doi.org/10.1002/wfs2.1453

Ingram, J. L. (2021). *Criminal Evidence* (14th ed.). Routledge. https://doi.org/10.4324/9781003092360

Interpol. (2020, October). *Guide for Criminal Justice Statistics on Cybercrime and Electronic Evidence*. Council of Europe Directorate General Human Rights and Rule of Law.

ISC2. (2024). *CISSP – Certified Information Systems Security Professional*. https://www.isc2.org/Certifications/CISSP

Jakubeit, R. (2021). *The Wirecard scandal and the role of BaFin: A case for unifying capital markets supervision in the European Union* (Working Paper No. 5/2021). https://leap.luiss.it/wp-content/uploads/2022/09/WP5.21-The-Wirecard-scandal-and-the-role-of-Bafin.pdf

Jo, H., Hsu, A., Llanos-Popolizio, R., & Vergara-Vega, J. (2021). Corporate governance and financial fraud of Wirecard. *European Journal of Business and Management Research*, *6*(2), 96–106. https://doi.org/10.24018/ejbmr.2021.6.2.708

Johnson, M. (2022). Technology for Courtroom Displays and Demonstrative Presentations. In *Handbook of Forensic Photography* (1st ed., p. 8).

Kapageorgiadou, V. (2024). *Trust in Forensic Science Evidence*. https://doi.org/10.17605/OSF.IO/UHJ5C

Kaur, J. (2014). Development in law and use of technology: Relevance for judge's research. *Nirma University Law Journal*, *4*(1), 23–26.

Khachatryan, G. (2022). Analysis of cybercrime investigation problems in the cloud environment. *International Journal of Computer Science and Network Security*, *22*(7), 315–319. https://doi.org/10.22937/IJCSNS.2022.22.7.38

Klasén, L., Fock, N., & Forchheimer, R. (2024). The invisible evidence: digital forensics as key to solving crimes in the digital age. *Forensic Science International*, 112133. https://doi.org/10.1016/j.forsciint.2024.112133

Lee, J.-U., & Soh, W.-Y. (2020). Comparative analysis on integrated digital forensic tools for digital forensic investigation. *IOP Conference Series: Materials Science and Engineering*, *834*(1), 012034. https://doi.org/10.1088/1757-899X/834/1/012034

Lubet, S., & Boals, E. I. (2020). *Expert testimony: A guide for expert witnesses and the lawyers who examine them* (Fourth edition). National Institute for Trial Advocacy.

Mahrina, M., Sasmito, J., & Zonyfar, C. (2023). The electronic and transactions law (EIT Law) as the first cybercrime law in Indonesia: An introduction and its implementation. *Pena Justisia: Media Komunikasi Dan Kajian Hukum*, *21*(2). https://doi.org/10.31941/pj.v21i2.2680

Marshall, A. M., & Tompsett, B. C. (2024). The metaverse—Not a new frontier for crime. *WIREs Forensic Science*, *6*(1), e1505. https://doi.org/10.1002/wfs2.1505

Martínez-Garay, L. (2023). Evidence-based sentencing and scientific evidence. *Frontiers in Psychology*, *14*, 1309141. https://doi.org/10.3389/fpsyg.2023.1309141

McDade, M. (2024, July 4). *The Top 10 Malware Analysis Tools*. Expert Insights. https://expertinsights.com/insights/the-top-malware-analysis-tools/

Miha, E., & Pekmezi, I. (2024). Electronic evidence in the criminal process. *Academic Journal of Business, Administration, Law and Social Sciences*, *10*(2), 1–11. https://doi.org/10.2478/ajbals-2024-0010

Moldovan, A. (2022). Technical language as evidence of expertise. *Languages*, *7*(1), 41. https://doi.org/10.3390/languages7010041

Moussa, A. F. (2021). Electronic evidence and its authenticity in forensic evidence. *Egyptian Journal of Forensic Sciences*, *11*(1), 20. https://doi.org/10.1186/s41935-021-00234-6

Nelufule, N., Masango, M., & Singano, T. (2024). The future of digital forensic investigations: Keeping the pace with technological advancements. *2024 47th MIPRO ICT and Electronics Convention (MIPRO)*, 1843–1848. https://ieeexplore.ieee.org/document/10569461; https://doi.org/10.1109/MIPRO60963.2024.10569461

Nobles, C. (2022). Stress, burnout, and security fatigue in cybersecurity: A human factors problem. *HOLISTICA – Journal of Business and Public Administration*, *13*(1), 49–72. https://doi.org/10.2478/hjbpa-2022-0003

Nordin, C., & Zekan, A. (2021). *Taking Virtual Reality into the Courtroom: An exploratory study of how to implement Virtual Reality within Swedish court* [Master's Thesis/MSc in Industrial Design Engineering (MPDES), Chamlers University of Technology]. https://hdl.handle.net/20.500.12380/303979

Oladimeji, S., & Kerner, S. M. (2023, November 3). *SolarWinds hack explained: Everything you need to know*. https://www.techtarget.com/whatis/feature/SolarWinds-hack-explained-Everything-you-need-to-know

Opentext. (2024). *EnCase Training and Certifications*. https://www.opentext.com/learning-services/learning-paths-encase-certifications

Pal, D. (2022, March 31). *How to: Detect and prevent common data exfiltration attacks*. APNIC. https://blog.apnic.net/2022/03/31/how-to-detect-and-prevent-common-data-exfiltration-attacks/

Payne, B. K., & Hadzhidimova, L. (2020). *Disciplinary and Interdisciplinary Trends in Cybercrime Research: An Examination*. https://doi.org/10.5281/ZENODO.3741131

Peelen, A. A. E., Van De Weijer, S. G. A., Van Den Berg, C. J. W., & Leukfeldt, E. R. (2023). Employment opportunities for applicants with cybercrime records: A field experiment. *Social Science Computer Review*, *41*(5), 1562–1580. https://doi.org/10.1177/08944393221085706

Pestana, G., & Sofou, S. (2024). Digital chain of custody innovation management roadmap. *The European Physical Journal Plus*, *139*(7), 633. https://doi.org/10.1140/epjp/s13360-024-05420-8

Preeti, Kumar, M., & Sharma, H. K. (2024). A guide to digital forensic: Theoretical to software based investigations. In A. Bhardwaj & K. Kaushik (Eds.), *Cyber Forensics and Investigation on Smart Devices* (pp. 20–48). Bentham Science Publishers. https://doi.org/10.2174/9789815179576124010005

Roberts, P. (2023). Theorising evidence law. *Oxford Journal of Legal Studies*, *43*(3), 629–649. https://doi.org/10.1093/ojls/gqad007

Sarkar, B., Mitra, A., & Chatterjee, S. (2023). Cybercrime and cybersecurity laws in current and future contexts with evolving crimes across national boundaries: In N. Mateus-Coelho & M. Cruz-Cunha (Eds.), *Advances in Digital Crime, Forensics, and Cyber Terrorism* (pp. 268–281). IGI Global. https://doi.org/10.4018/978-1-6684-8422-7.ch014

Sarkar, G., Singh, H., Kumar, S., & Shukla, S. K. (2023). Tactics, techniques and procedures of cybercrime: A methodology and tool for cybercrime investigation process. *Proceedings of the 18th International Conference on Availability, Reliability and Security*, 1–10. https://doi.org/10.1145/3600160.3605013

Shanker, N. R. (2024). The role of digital evidence in legal proceedings: The Indian perspective. *International Journal of Research Publication and Reviews*, *5*(5), 7889–7893. https://doi.org/10.55248/gengpi.5.0524.1321

Shurson, J. (2020). Data protection and law enforcement access to digital evidence: Resolving the reciprocal conflicts between EU and US law. *International Journal of Law and Information Technology*, *28*(2), 167–184. https://doi.org/10.1093/ijlit/eaaa011

SophosLabs Threat Research. (2020, December 21). *How SunBurst malware does defense evasion*. https://news.sophos.com/en-us/2020/12/21/how-sunburst-malware-does-defense-evasion/

Steinberg, J. (2024, January 18). *Choosing an Expert Witness in Cybersecurity: Key Considerations for Hiring*. https://theamberpost.com/post/choosing-an-expert-witness-in-cybersecurity-key-considerations-for-hiring

UNODC. (2019, March). *Standards and best practices for digital forensics*. https://www.unodc.org/e4j/en/cybercrime/module-4/key-issues/standards-and-best-practices-for-digital-forensics.html

Vecellio Segate, R. (2021). Cognitive bias, privacy rights, and digital evidence in international criminal proceedings: Demystifying the double-edged AI revolution. *International Criminal Law Review*, *21*(2), 242–279. https://doi.org/10.1163/15718123-bja10048

Wang, Z. (2020). The fate of evidence law: Two paths of development. *The International Journal of Evidence & Proof*, *24*(3), 329–348. https://doi.org/10.1177/1365712720930797

Ward, T., & Plenderleith Ferguson, A. (2024). Proof of foreign law: A reduced role for expert evidence? *Journal of Private International Law*, *20*(1), 95–116. https://doi.org/10.1080/17441048.2024.2347720

Wilding, E., & Stowell, A. (2016). Using digital forensics. In *Fraud: The counter fraud practitioner's handbook* (p. 29). Routledge.

Zhang, H., & Gong, X. (2024). The research on an electronic evidence forensic system for cross-border cybercrime. *The International Journal of Evidence & Proof*, *28*(1), 21–44. https://doi.org/10.1177/13657127231187059

20 Efficient Data Visualization for Cybersecurity Using Multi-Objective Genetic Optimized Adaptive XGBoost

Shashi Kant Gupta, V. Suresh Kumar, Mohammad Israr, Justyna Żywiołek, and Amena Mahmoud

20.1 INTRODUCTION

Technology security has become a major concern, costing businesses at least $15 million. Cybercrime may be costly if risks are not detected and handled in a timely manner. Visualizing cybersecurity is one technique to obtain a better grasp of it. Data visualization may help users have a better knowledge of cybersecurity. It focuses on displaying how web browser antimalware tools decide if a download is safe for the user employs a program to grab online traffic and store it in a database, which is then displayed by utilizing tables on location data based on the IP address's geolocation (Nadeem and Huang, 2018).

During the COVID-19 pandemic, we were needed to give a data visualization solution to a group of epidemiologists and modeling scientists in order to suit their demands. Due to the urgency, a plan for progressive development, a timeline for rapid deployment, and mechanisms for effective and efficient operation were necessary (Khan et al., 2022). Immersive environments with stereoscopic output are garnering more and more interest in the realm of visualization and interaction as more cheap commercial equipment become available. The stereoscopic display of scientific data offers a lot of promise due to the natural match between the spatial properties of the dataset and the three-dimensional (3D) visual output space, as well as the possible integration of input devices other than the usual mouse. The benefits of stereoscopic viewpoints were also highlighted in a later research for jobs requiring the processing of scientific data with volume or isosurface representation, both of which are inherently spatial (Wang et al., 2022). Users must have the ability to intuitively receive sensor data, comprehend robot status, and provide directions while

DOI: 10.1201/9781003497868-20

dealing with robots. Through a two-dimensional (2D), screen-based visual interface, the well-known software tool RViz1 provides these features for the creation of robotics applications based on the Robot Operating System (ROS) framework. However, it is unavoidably difficult to provide user-intuitive visuals and interfaces for a 3D environment on a 2D screen (particularly when it comes to spatial awareness). Users must often shift their attention away from the physical robot and its surroundings in order to observe the visualization, obtain information, or manage the robot through a screen-based interface. Reduced levels of efficiency and safety are the outcome of this attention shifting while using or interacting with robots (Hoang et al., 2022).

They may not always provide data summaries and graphics in a way that makes it straightforward to contrast several watershed simulations of alternative management techniques and evaluate "what-if" scenarios. Models start to become more approachable and user-friendly thanks to web-based user interfaces. Managers must be aware of the main factors affecting the visual system as well as how sensitive they are to the movement of attacks in network. This will assist them in developing an action plan and ensuring the use of suitable and efficient management techniques. Process-based models may generate a large amount of simulated output. This is particularly true when the model is used to analyze alternative management choices over time in different land types within a watershed. Watershed managers, for example, would need significant competence in geospatial analysis and modeling to execute the findings (Deval et al., 2022).

20.2 PROBLEM STATEMENT

We now live in a time of digital and information societies, but there is a new issue that has to be addressed: every day, data volumes increase dramatically and sometimes without effective supervision, and this lack of control may have negative effects on an organization's finances and reputation. The occurrence of data leaks or businesses that have been the target of cyber incidents and that the personal data of their customers or employees was unreasonably exposed is becoming more frequent in the news. This situation has an impact on the image and reputation of organizations because it can change the trust that customers have in businesses that offer services and/or products. The main challenge is defining the similarity between two visuals in order to accomplish effective retrieval of comparable images. Studies already conducted generally concentrate on calculating the degree of similarity between representations based on data or perceptual similarity. The present approaches based on data similarity concentrate on the properties of the data, such as data distribution, while frequently ignoring the visual appeal of visualizations. The use of visualization retrieval methods based on data similarity is highly constrained because the original data is not always accessible with the representations. We suggested multi-objective genetic optimized adaptive XGBoost (MGOAX) to get over this problem.

20.3 PROPOSED WORK

Cybersecurity attack assessment and defensive verification research and experiments are steadily growing. On the other hand, the visualization approach to cybersecurity

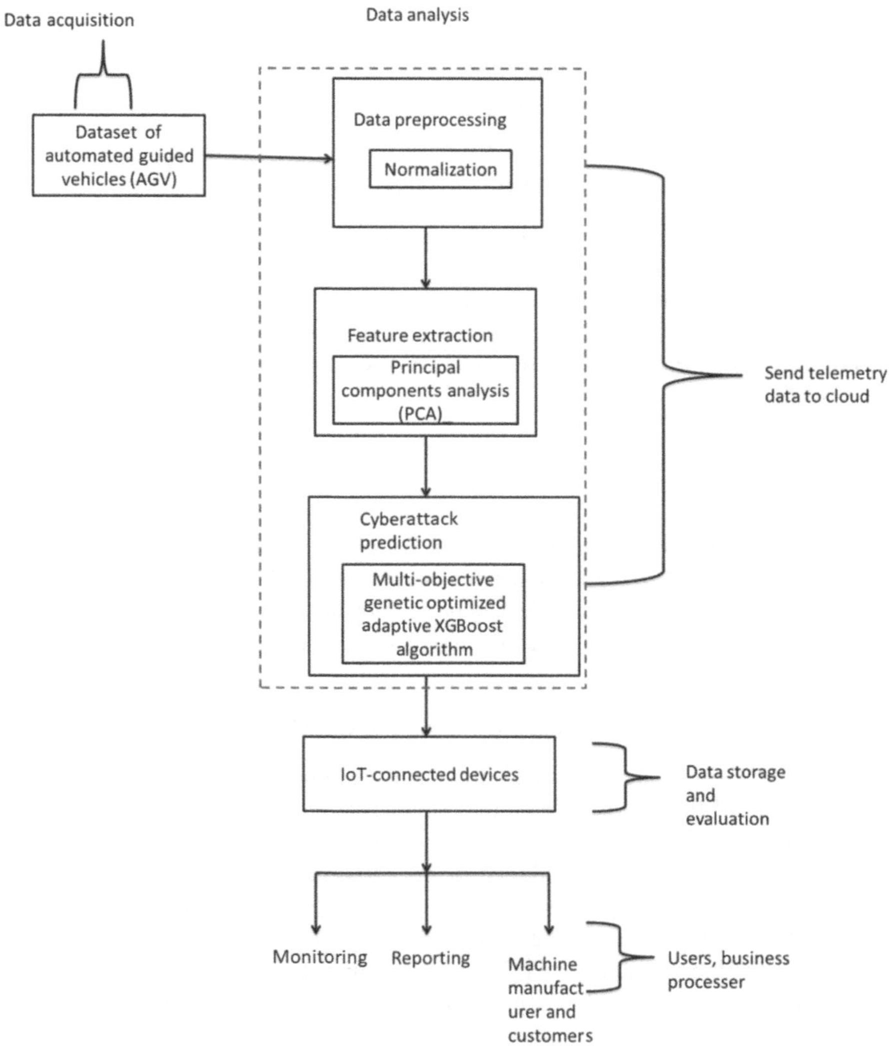

FIGURE 20.1 Representation of our proposed methodology.

attack and defense has received comparatively little investigation. In specifically, visualization is a theory, approach, and technology that turn data into visuals or images for presentation on the screen and then interactive processing utilizing computer graphics and image processing tools. Figure 20.1 represents a proposed methodology.

20.3.1 Dataset of Automated Guided Vehicles

The rotation speed and velocity of the data were obtained from an actual automated guided vehicle (AGV) and assigned the number 0. Randomly distributed functions over the AGV signal range provided the fake data that represented the cyberattack. To create one dataset, both the genuine data and the false data were joined. A total of 3563 samples were gathered for the dataset, of which 713 samples were used for testing and 2850 samples were used for training (Elsisi and Tran 2021).

20.3.2 Data Preprocessing Using Normalization

Several methods, including "min-max" normalizing, "z-score" normalizing, "decimal scaling", standardized moment, etc., may be used to normalize datasets. Z-score normalization and min-max normalization are the two widely used and popular normalizing methods. Our work used the min-max method.

For min-max normalization, equation (20.1) is used to normalize features with a range of [0, 1].

$$v' = \frac{v - min_E}{max_E - min_E} \tag{20.1}$$

The minimum and maximum values of feature E are shown here by min_E and max_E, respectively. The attributes' original and normalized values are represented by the values v and v', respectively. As can be seen from equation (20.1), the maximum and minimum feature values are converted to 1 and 0, respectively.

20.3.3 Feature Extraction Using Principal Component Analysis

Principal component is a statistical approach for condensing information from a big collection of linked variables into a small number of variables (referred to as "principal components") without ignoring the data set's intrinsic variability. The variables in the data set are combined linearly to create the principle components, with weights selected to make the principal components uncorrelated with one another. The arrangement of the components ensures that the initial few account for the majority of the variability and that each component additionally provides fresh data about the set. Assume that population U is a random vector in equation (20.2):

$$U = (u1, u2, \ldots um)^S \tag{20.2}$$

And that population's mean is represented by equation (20.3),

$$\mu_u = F(U) \tag{20.3}$$

The same data set's covariance matrix is expressed in equation (20.4):

$$U = B(U - \mu_u) \tag{20.4}$$

By definition, the covariance matrix is always symmetric.

We may create an orthogonal basis by calculating the eigenvalues and eigenvectors of such a symmetric covariance matrix. An ordered orthogonal basis may be produced by arranging the eigenvectors in decreasing order of eigenvalues, with the first eigenvector designating the direction with the biggest variation in the data. This makes it possible for us to pinpoint the directions with the highest energy concentrations in the data set.

Let B be a matrix with the row vectors being the eigenvectors of the covariance matrix. We obtain the following by transforming (equation (20.5)) the data vector U:

$$U = B^S Z + \mu_u \tag{20.5}$$

This is a coordinate in the eigenvector-defined orthogonal system. The coordinates in the orthogonal basis may be thought of as components of Z. From Z, we may reassemble the initial data vector U in equation (20.6):

$$Z = B_L \left(U - \mu_u\right) \tag{20.6}$$

As a result, the orthogonal basis' coordinate axes were projected onto the original vector U. The orthogonal basis vectors were then linearly combined to recreate the original vector.

We may opt to represent the information using just a few orthogonal basis vectors rather than all of the covariance matrix's eigenvectors. Similar transformations may be made if the matrix with the "L" initial eigenvectors is denoted as rows by B_L in equations (20.7) and (20.8).

$$U = B_L^S Z + \mu_u \tag{20.7}$$

$$D_u = F\left\{\left(U - \mu_u\right)\left(U - \mu_u\right)^S\right\} \tag{20.8}$$

We initially projects the actual data vector onto the coordinate axes with size "L" and then combine the basis vectors in a linear way to reverse the vector transformation. By employing a certain number of eigenvectors, this reduces the mean square error between the information and the representation. The representation is made simpler and the data may be compressed without losing much information if it is kept in a linear sub-space. To lose the least amount of mean-square data, we choose the eigenvectors with the greatest eigenvalues. By choosing a predetermined number of eigenvectors and matching eigenvalues, the data may be consistently represented or abstracted. This keeps different amounts of the original data. As an alternative, we may choose about the same energy along with variable numbers of eigenvectors and eigenvalues. As a result, at the price of changing representations with respect to the sub-dimension, spaces this would provide a somewhat constant quantity of information. Here, we have conflicting objectives to pursue: Reducing the size of the representation is one method for making the problem simpler. However, we make every effort to keep as much of the information's original substance as we can. Principal component analysis (PCA) provides a practical way to address the trade-off between knowledge loss and making the present issue simpler. This is plausible given that the bulk of the eigenvalues are comparably very tiny and have no impact on the oscillations in the data, while only a small percentage will be considerably greater. As a result, only the directions with the greatest variations are retained. In signal processing applications, PCA is performed on a sequence of time samples rather than a data set of variables. The analysis often uses samples taken from the same segment point throughout the course of various intervals of the signal when a signal is recurring in nature, such as the electrocardiogram (ECG) signal. Almost all ECG analysis systems used today include signal processing, which has shown to be essential for improving network attack detection. Signal processing is used in analysis to solve issues such as data compression, beat detection and classification, noise reduction, signal separation, and feature extraction. PCA was originally created to store and retrieve ECGs efficiently, but it has now evolved into a crucial technique for overcoming many of these issues.

20.3.4 Multi-Objective Genetic Optimized Adaptive XGBoost Algorithm

A machine learning package called adaptive XGBoost specializes on gradient boosting methods. In essence, "adaptive XGBoost" is the merging of many classification and regression trees ("CARTs"). The CART is a tree-based kind that can be used to both classification and regression issues. Adaptive XGBoost is an ensemble learning approach that is improved based on the Gradient Boosting Decision Tree (GBDT) but does not include feature extract. After iteration, the residual tree of several rounds is superimposed by the conventional GBDT objective function to forecast the target classes. Adaptive XGBoost concurrently adds a regular term based on the original function to the traditional GBDT target function, reducing the possibility of overfitting and accelerating convergence. In order to filter features, adaptive XGBoost can automatically determine which characteristics are important. We used the adaptive XGBoost method to determine the most relevant traits during the first feature selection.

In equation (20.9), $K\left(z_j,\hat{z}_i\right)$ is the square deviation's loss as a function of the true value z_j and predictive value $\hat{z}_i$ and $\Omega\left(a_j\right)$ is a phrase for regularization. In equations (20.9) and (20.10), γ is the **tree complexity (or regularization) coefficient**, used to **control the complexity** of the tree (not "divided" for regulating), S is the number of leaf nodes, while $k2$ represents the regularity factor.

$$Obj(d)=\sum_{j=1}^{m}K\left(z_j,\hat{z}_j\right)+\sum_{j=1}^{d}\Omega\left(a_j\right) \tag{20.9}$$

$$\Omega\left(a_d\right)=\gamma^{\mathrm{D}}+\frac{1}{2}\lambda\sum_{j=1}^{\mathrm{D}}\omega_i^2 \tag{20.10}$$

The anticipated value may be expressed as in equation (20.11):

$$\hat{z}_j^{(d)}=\hat{z}_j^{(d-1)}+a_d\left(u_j\right) \tag{20.11}$$

The goal function may then be changed in equation (20.12):

$$Obj(d) = \sum_{j=1}^{m} K\left[\left(z_j, \hat{z}^{(d-1)}\right) + a_d\left(u_j\right)\right] + \Omega\left(a_d\right) \tag{20.12}$$

XGBoost is different from GBDT. In order to generate a new objective function with a greater accuracy and quicker convergence rate than the original GBDT, it could increase the loss function based on Taylor's formula's second derivative. As demonstrated in equations (20.13), (20.14), and (20.15), the ultimate goal function is expressed.

$$Obj(d) \cong \sum_{j=1}^{m} K\left[\left(z_j, \hat{z}^{(d-1)}\right) + C_i a_d\left(u_j\right) + \frac{1}{2} r_j a_d^2\left(u_j\right)\right] \Omega\left(a_d\right) \tag{20.13}$$

$$C_i = \frac{\partial\left(K\left(z_i, \hat{z}^{(d-1)}\right)\right)}{\partial \hat{z}^{(d-1)}} \tag{20.14}$$

$$r_j = \frac{\partial\left(K\left(z_i, \hat{z}^{(d-1)}\right)\right)}{\partial \hat{z}^{(d-1)}} \tag{20.15}$$

Here, g_i and h_i are the loss function's L (φ) first and second derivatives.

The GA is a technique for naturally adaptive optimization that models the issue at hand as a process of attacks in network. Duplication, crossover, and mutation are used to create new solutions, while solutions with poor fitness function values are eventually eliminated. The GA may concurrently utilize the search data from many search points. The local optimum solution may be avoided by using probabilistic search technology instead of iterative information points. The GA can quickly provide the global optimum solution and has considerable search versatility. In many challenging optimization issues, it has been extensively used. An intricate and difficult-to-solve optimization problem is the adaptive XGBoost problem with multi-objective optimization. The use of genetic algorithms to tackle multi-objective optimization problems is one of the many different solution strategies that researchers have created as a result, and it is quite successful. Solving the optimization conundrum of several objective functions while adhering to a set of restrictions is the aim of the multi-objective optimization problem. This problem is formally described as follows.

Let $O = (U, Z, E)$ be an initial dataset of choice, When Z is the class set, U is the sample set, and $E = \{e_1, e_2, \ldots, e_n\}$ is a feature set. Conflicts between several goals are common in multi-objective optimization problems, and an optimum solution set often includes the solution, which is not unique. Consequently, we must identify a collection of traits $T = \{e_1, e_2, \ldots, e_l\} \in E(l \leq n)$ from the optimal solution set. Additionally, the chosen feature subset's feature count should be as low as feasible.

20.4 RESULT AND DISCUSSION

The MGOAX model was created utilizing the given training and testing datasets, which included 150 epochs, to predict the state of the AGV. The supplied values were used to construct four hidden layers with a default batch size of 32. In order to reduce the overfitting issue and enhance the functionality of the suggested MGOAX model, early termination criteria and dropout methods were also included into the training model. In order to compare the model fairly against other machine learning models, the remaining hyperparameters were left at their default settings. Figure 20.2 shows the effectiveness of the suggested MGOAX for the AGV's cyberattack detection.

It demonstrates that within 20 epochs, both the training and testing procedures may easily achieve accuracy levels greater than 95%. After 110 epochs, the deep neural network (DNN) model produced exceptional accuracy with a training accuracy of about 97.25% and a testing accuracy of around 96.77%. At the steady point, the testing loss value was only a little bit greater than the training loss value. It showed that the model had a decent fit without being overfit. The training loss and testing loss are shown in Figure 20.3 and both of their values were progressively reduced.

Furthermore, the created MGOAX's performance was evaluated by comparing it to other models, such as the "DNN", "support vector machine" (SVM) model, and "logistic regression" (LR). Figure 20.4 depicts the detection of accuracy with the existing methods.

For a comparison, we trained each model with the default hyperparameters using the identical training dataset and testing datasets. They demonstrate that the suggested MGOAX method performed better than the other models; in particular, the false AGV tracking could be identified with an accuracy of 91.72%, while the true

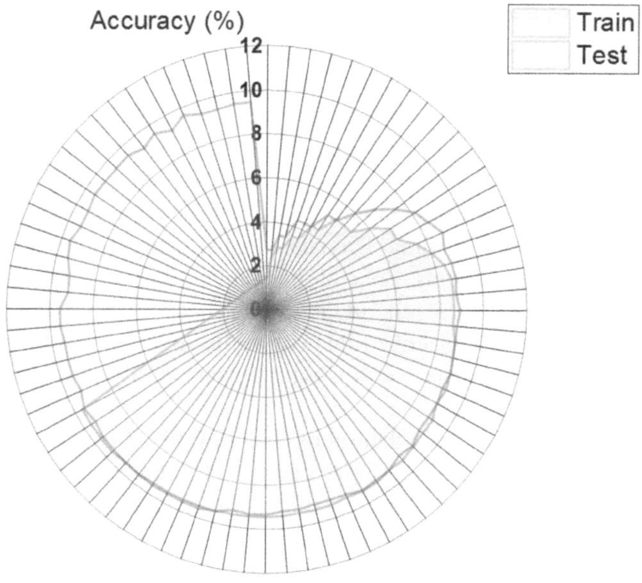

FIGURE 20.2 Accuracy of the proposed MGOAX for AGV cyberattack detection.

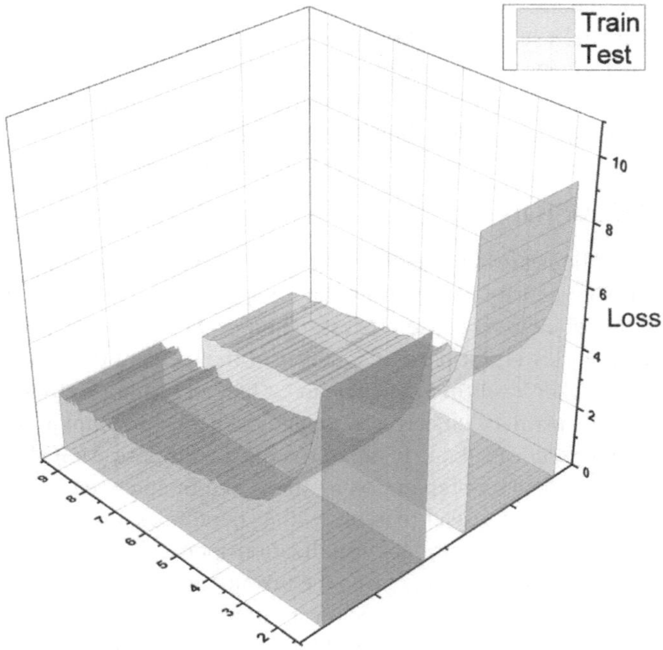

FIGURE 20.3 Representation of loss function.

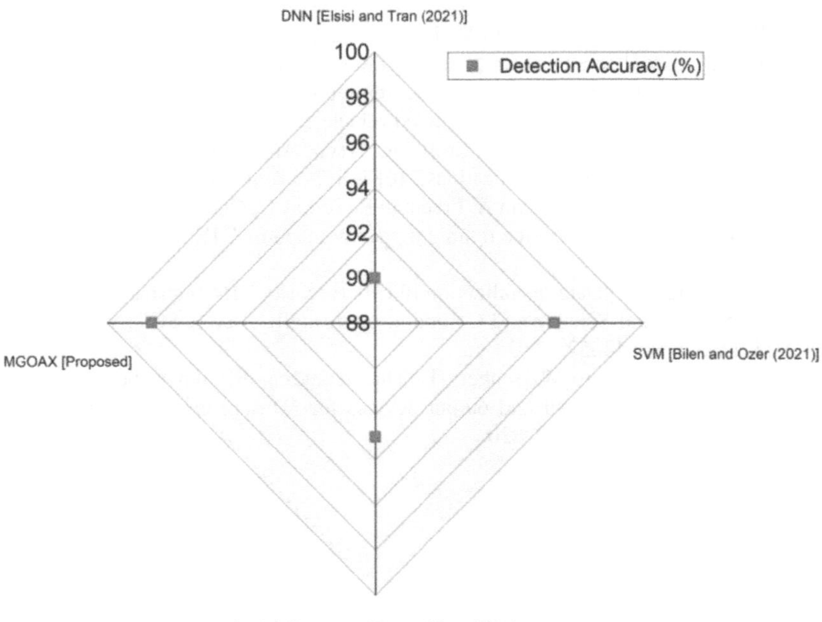

FIGURE 20.4 Representation of detection of accuracy.

tracking could be detected with an accuracy of 98.92%. This occurred as a result of the MGOAX model's superior ability to recognize intricate elements included in the fictitious data. The various models provide the categorization accuracy. The results of the experiments showed that the suggested MGOAX model performed best, followed by the "SVM" model, which had an accuracy of 94%.

20.5 CONCLUSION

Visualization methods are very helpful for deciphering and in certain circumstances describing specific security occurrences. These approaches also fit in with the regular phases of the incident response process. There is, however, certain visualization approaches that work well for particular stages of the incident response process and this may lead to higher levels of efficiency and effectiveness in spotting specific dangers. This project's primary objective is to analyze hacking techniques and provide the available cybersecurity data. In this project, we propose MGOAX method to detect and improve the data preparation methods and interactive visualizations that might help us find a better answer to issues with cyberattacks. Future research on this subject will examine the various data visualization approaches and determine which ones are most appropriate for usage given the taxonomic and particular classification of security events. Future studies may show a sample of business leaders the visualizations presented in this study and record their comments about the significance of the patterns for their organization.

REFERENCES

Deval C, Brooks ES, Dobre M et al. "Pi-VAT: A web-based visualization tool for decision support using spatially complex water quality model outputs." J Hydrol. 2022; 607:127529.

Elsisi M, Tran MQ. "Development of an IoT architecture based on a deep neural network against cyber-attacks for automated guided vehicles." Sensors (Basel). 2021; 21(24):8467.

Hoang KC, Chan WP, Lay S, Cosgun A, Croft EA. "Arviz: An augmented reality-enabled visualization platform for ROS applications." IEEE Robot Automat Mag. 2022; 29(1):58–67.

Khan S, Nguyen PH, Abdul-Rahman A, Freeman E, Turkay C, Chen M. "Rapid development of a data visualization service in an emergency response." IEEE Trans Serv Comput. 2022; 15(3):1251–1264.

Nadeem SF, Huang CY. "Data visualization in cybersecurity". In: International Conference on Computational Science and Computational Intelligence (CSCI); vol 2018. IEEE; 2018, December: 48–52.

Wang X, Besançon L, Ammi M, Isenberg T. "Understanding differences between combinations of 2D and 3D input and output devices for 3D data visualization." Int J Hum Comput Stud. 2022; 163:102820.